twelfth canadian edition

macroeconomics

Campbell R. McConnell
University of Nebraska – Emeritus

Stanley L. Brue
Pacific Lutheran University

Sean M. Flynn
Scripps College

Thomas P. Barbiero
Ryerson University

McGraw-Hill Ryerson
Connect. Learn. Succeed.

Macroeconomics
Twelfth Canadian Edition

Copyright © 2010, 2007, 2005, 2002, 1999, 1996, 1993, 1990, 1987, 1984, 1981, 1978 by McGraw-Hill Ryerson Limited, a Subsidiary of The McGraw-Hill Companies. Copyright © 2009, 2008, 2005, 2002, 1999, 1996, 1993, 1990, 1987, 1984, 1981, 1978, 1975, 1972, 1969, 1966, 1963, 1960 by The McGraw-Hill Companies, Inc. All rights reserved. No part of this publication may be reproduced or transmitted in any form or by any means, or stored in a data base or retrieval system, without the prior written permission of McGraw-Hill Ryerson Limited, or in the case of photocopying or other reprographic copying, a license from The Canadian Copyright Licensing Agency (Access Copyright). For an Access Copyright licence, visit www.accesscopyright.ca or call toll free to 1-800-893-5777.

Statistics Canada information is used with the permission of Statistics Canada. Users are forbidden to copy this material and/or redisseminate the data, in an original or modified form, for commercial purposes, without the expressed permission of Statistics Canada. Information on the availability of the wide range of data from Statistics Canada can be obtained from Statistics Canada's Regional Offices, its World Wide Web site at http://www.statcan.gc.ca and its toll-free access number 1-800-263-1136.

ISBN-13: 978-0-07-096953-7
ISBN-10: 0-07-096953-1

1 2 3 4 5 6 7 8 9 10   WCD   1 9 8 7 6 5 4 3 2 1 0

Printed and bound in the United States of America.

Care has been taken to trace ownership of copyright material contained in this text; however, the publisher will welcome any information that enables it to rectify any reference or credit for subsequent editions.

VICE PRESIDENT AND EDITOR-IN-CHIEF: Joanna Cotton
SPONSORING EDITORS: James Booty, Bruce McIntosh
EXECUTIVE MARKETING MANAGER: Joy Armitage Taylor
DEVELOPMENTAL EDITORS: Daphne Scriabin, Andria Fogarty
EDITORIAL ASSOCIATE: Stephanie Hess
PERMISSIONS/PHOTO RESEARCHER: Lynn McIntyre
SENIOR SUPERVISING EDITOR: Joanne Limebeer
COPY EDITOR: Kelli Howey
PROOFREADER: Judy Sturrup
TEAM LEAD, PRODUCTION: Paula Brown
COVER DESIGN: Sarah Orr/ArtPlus Limited
COVER IMAGE: Lloyd Sutton/Alamy
INTERIOR DESIGN: Sarah Orr/ArtPlus Limited
PAGE LAYOUT: Heather Brunton, Lesley Lavender/ArtPlus Limited
PRINTER: Worldcolor

Library and Archives Canada Cataloguing in Publication Data

Macroeconomics / Campbell R. McConnell ... [et al.]. — 12th Canadian ed.
  Includes index.

Previous eds. by Campbell R. McConnell, Stanley L. Brue, and Thomas P. Barbiero.

ISBN 978-0-07-096953-7

  1. Macroeconomics—Textbooks.   I. McConnell, Campbell R.

HB172.5.M3345 2009   339   C2009-905341-1

Dedication

To Elsa, Marta, Emilia, Robert, and past instructors.

About the Authors

Campbell R. McConnell earned his Ph.D. from the University of Iowa after receiving degrees from Cornell College and the University of Illinois. He taught at the University of Nebraska-Lincoln from 1953 until his retirement in 1990. He is also coauthor of *Contemporary Labor Economics*, seventh edition, and *Essentials of Economics*, first edition (both The McGraw-Hill Companies), and has edited readers for the principles and labour economics courses. He is a recipient of both the University of Nebraska Distinguished Teaching Award and the James A. Lake Academic Freedom Award, and is past-president of the Midwest Economics Association. Professor McConnell was awarded an honorary Doctor of Laws degree from Cornell College in 1973 and received its Distinguished Achievement Award in 1994. His primary areas of interest are labour economics and economic education. He has an extensive collection of jazz recordings and enjoys reading jazz history.

Stanley L. Brue did his undergraduate work at Augustana College (South Dakota) and received its Distinguished Achievement Award in 1991. He received his Ph.D. from the University of Nebraska–Lincoln. He is a professor at Pacific Lutheran University, where he has been honored as a recipient of the Burlington Northern Faculty Achievement Award. Professor Brue has also received the national Leavey Award for excellence in economic education. He has served as national president and chair of the Board of Trustees of Omicron Delta Epsilon International Economics Honorary. He is coauthor of *Economic Scenes*, fifth edition (Prentice-Hall), *Contemporary Labor Economics*, seventh edition, *Essentials of Economics*, first edition (both The McGraw-Hill Companies), and *The Evolution of Economic Thought*, seventh edition (South-Western). For relaxation, he enjoys international travel, attending sporting events, and skiing with family and friends.

Sean M. Flynn did his undergraduate work at the University of Southern California before completing his Ph.D. at U.C. Berkeley, where he served as the head graduate student instructor for the Department of Economics after receiving the Outstanding Graduate Student Instructor Award. He teaches at Scripps College in Claremont, California, and is also the author of *Essentials of Economics*, second edition (The McGraw-Hill Companies). His research interests include finance and behavioural economics. An accomplished martial artist, he has represented the United States in international aikido tournaments and is the author of *Understanding Shodokan Aikido* (Shodokan Press). Other hobbies include running, travel, and ethnic food.

Thomas P. Barbiero received his Ph.D. from the University of Toronto after completing undergraduate studies at the same university. He is a professor at Ryerson University in Toronto. Professor Barbiero teaches an economic history course to Ryerson students in Rome during the spring semester. His research interests include the economic history of modern Italy and international institutions. He spends his summers in Fontanarosa, a small town in his native region of Campania in southern Italy.

Brief Contents

Contents

**WEB SITE BONUS CHAPTERS (FOUND AT
WWW.MCGRAWHILLCONNECT.CA)**

CHAPTER 15W: Current Issues in Macro Theory
and Policy

CHAPTER 17W: The Economics of Developing
Countries

Preface

Welcome to the Twelfth Canadian Edition of *Macroeconomics*. Thousands of Canadian students have studied economics from the Canadian editions of *Macroeconomics* and *Microeconomics*. An estimated 14 million students worldwide have now used a version of the McConnell textbooks, making them the world's best-selling economic principles textbooks.

A Note about the Cover and the New U.S. Co-author

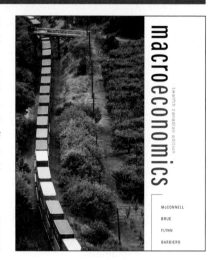

We chose the cover to reference the additional material included in the Twelfth Canadian Edition on economic growth, and supply and demand.

Our new co-author, Sean M. Flynn, has helped to modernize the content of the book from cover to cover. Sean did his undergraduate at the University of Southern California, received his Ph.D. from U.C. Berkley (in 2002), teaches principles at Scripps College, and is the author of *Essentials of Economics*, second edition. We are greatly pleased to have Sean working on the text because he shares our commitment to present economics in a way that is understandable to all.

Fundamental Objectives

We have three main goals for *Macroeconomics*, which are to:

- Help the beginning student master the principles essential for understanding economic problems, specific economic issues, and the policy alternatives.

- Help the student understand and apply the economic perspective, and reason accurately and objectively about economic matters.

- Promote a lasting student interest in economics and the economy.

What's New and Improved?

This is the most significant revision of *Macroeconomics* since the eighth edition. It has greatly benefitted from the addition of our new co-author. One of the benefits of writing a successful text is the opportunity to revise—to delete the outdated and install the new, to rewrite misleading or ambiguous statements, to introduce more relevant illustrations, to improve the organizational structure, and to enhance the learning aids. The more significant changes include the following:

Fully Updated, Totally Contemporary Macroeconomics

We recast the entire macro analysis in terms of the modern, dominant paradigm of macroeconomics, using economic growth as the central backdrop and viewing business fluctuations as significant and costly variations in the rate of growth. In this paradigm, business cycles result from demand shocks (or, less often, supply shocks) in conjunction with inflexible short-run product prices and wages. The degree of price and wage stickiness decreases with time. In our models, the *immediate short run* is a period in which the price level and wages are not only sticky, but stuck; the *short-run* is a period in which product prices are flexible and wages are not; the *long-run* is a period in which both prices and wages are fully flexible. Each of these three periods—and thus each of the models based on them—is relevant to understanding the actual macro economy and its occasional difficulties.

New Chapter 4 introduces the macro framework in a lively, intuitive way, using the example of a hypothetical single-firm economy. It also makes a clear, critical distinction between the broader concept of financial investment and the narrower subset of investment called economic investment in a way that allows us to use both ideas. A chapter on the measurement of nominal and real GDP follows. With real GDP clearly defined and measured, we present a chapter on economic growth. This early placement of the growth chapter allows students to understand the importance of economic growth and the factors that drive it. This growth chapter is followed by a chapter that introduces business fluctuations along the economy's growth path and the problems of unemployment and inflation that may result.

Following this set of core beginning chapters, we immediately begin to build models of the economy for the immediate short run and the short run. Students are therefore quickly introduced to models in which recessions and inflation can occur. This approach allows us to use the short-run AD-AS model to address fiscal policy and monetary policy relatively earlier in the text. Students are made fully aware from the start that the rate of economic growth is fundamentally important for standards of living. Yet, the quick introduction of sticky price models enables students to understand demand shocks, recession, stimulatory fiscal policy, Bank of Canada monetary policy actions, and other topics that dominate the news about the macro economy. After eventually developing the long-run AD-AS model, we directly link this long-run analysis back to our earlier discussions of growth. We finish *Macroeconomics* with two chapters that provide further analysis of international trade, balance of payments, exchange rates, and trade imbalances. The book ends with a bonus Web chapter on the requisites for, and impediments to, economic growth in developing nations.

Although the framework in which this textbook is built has been extensively revised, the revisions were made to preserve the main elements of the chapters in the previous edition. We simply have wrapped the macroeconomics analysis into a modern package of growth, expectations, shocks, price stickiness, time horizons, and international linkages.

Our macro content is also fully modern in terms of its coverage of contemporary problems and policies. For example, we cover the global financial crisis that started with the mortgage loan crisis in the U.S., the economic slowdown that followed the financial crisis, the Bank of Canada's reductions of the overnight lending rate, the fiscal stimulus tax package of the federal and provincial governments, and more.

Two New Chapters

Two chapters are new to the print version of *Macroeconomics*. Our common purpose for both chapters is to incorporate contemporary analytical themes and address current economic issues.

CHAPTER 4 INTRODUCTION TO MACROECONOMICS

As previously noted, this new chapter introduces the revised macroeconomic content in an interesting, concise way. It motivates the study of macroeconomics and establishes the analytical framework to the subject that we use in the book.

CHAPTER 14 FINANCIAL ECONOMICS

This new chapter examines ideas such as compound interest, present value, arbitrage, risk, diversification, and the risk-return relationship. Students need a better grounding in such ideas to truly understand the modern economy. In view of the problems in the financial markets over the recent past, we think that integrating financial economics more directly in the macro principles course makes good sense. For many students, this course will be their only (classroom!) opportunity to learn that promises of high, unguaranteed returns reflect high, uninsured risk. Even if instructors cannot find time to assign and cover the entire chapter, they may want to discuss the beginning portion, which addresses the time value of money and provides easy-to-understand real-world examples of present value.

To make room for our two new chapters, we had to make certain accommodations. Specifically, we have moved the lengthy historical discussions of the gold standard and the Bretton Woods system from the chapter on exchange rates to the supplemental material for the chapter at our website. Other, lesser deletions or abridgements have occurred throughout the book.

New Appendix

An additional chapter appendix is available for optional assignment in this edition, and is supported by the supplementary materials. The concise new appendix is:

CHAPTER 3: ADDITIONAL EXAMPLES OF SUPPLY AND DEMAND

At the end of Chapter 3 we provide several additional examples of supply and demand, including concrete examples of simultaneous shifts in supply and demand curves. Products covered include lettuce, corn and ethanol, pink salmon, gasoline, and sushi. We also use the Olympic Games to illustrate examples of pre-set prices, shortages, and surpluses.

New (or Relocated) "Consider This" and "Last Word" Boxes

Our **Consider This** boxes are used to provide analogies, examples, or stories that help drive home central economic ideas in a student-oriented, real-world manner. For instance "Market Failure and the Need for Government" demonstrates that while markets are generally efficient, they sometimes fail and government intervention is needed. These brief vignettes, each accompanied by a photo, illustrate key points in a lively, colourful, and easy-to-remember way.

New or relocated Consider This boxes include such disparate topics as an economic comparison of the two Koreas (Chapter 2), patent reform in India (Chapter 6), negative growth rates in Canada during the global financial crisis (Chapter 7), a rise in the Canadian unemployment rate during the recession of 2008–09 (Chapter 7), the transmission of the global financial crisis through international trade (Chapter 9), the decrease of aggregate demand during the global financial crisis (Chapter 10), how the financial crisis in the U.S. spilled into Canada (Chapter 11), the impact on government finance from severe economic downturn (Chapter 11), the action of the Bank of Canada during the global financial crisis (Chapter 13), stock market performance during the global financial crisis (Chapter 14), the relative returns on standard versus ethical investing (Chapter 14), deep recession and policy intervention (Chapter 15), the global financial crisis and the plunge of international trade (Chapter 16), and global recession and the deterioration of Canada's current account (Chapter 17).

Our **Last Word** pieces are lengthier applications and case studies located toward the end of chapters. New or relocated Last Words include those on the role of inventory management in reducing recessions (Chapter 4), the U.S. banking crisis during the Great Depression and the similarities with the current global financial crisis (Chapter 12), the U.S. Federal Reserve's response to the mortgage loan crisis (Chapter 13), the relative performance of index funds versus actively managed funds (Chapter 14), and fair trade products (Chapter 16).

Contemporary Discussions and Examples

The twelfth Canadian edition refers to and discusses many current topics. Examples include the additions of countries to the European Union and to the euro zone, normal trade relations status, China's rapid growth rate, the business downturn of late 2008 and early 2009, the stimulus package to counter the slowdown that followed the global financial crisis, the federal budget deficits, the mortgage loan crisis in the U.S., recent Bank of Canada monetary policy, the Taylor rule, the decline of world trade during the financial crisis, and many more.

Integrated Text and Web Site

We continue to integrate the book and our Web site by including icons in the text margin that direct readers to additional content. **Worked Problems** are now available at the McConnell Web site and provide students with a step-by-step illustration of how to solve a problem. These pieces consist of side-by-side computational questions and the computational procedures used to derive the answers. In essence, they extend the textbook's explanations involving computations—for example, of real GDP, real GDP per capita, the unemployment rate, the inflation rate, per-unit production costs, and more. At relevant points in the text, the Worked Problem icon directs the student to the Web site for this additional support.

For those students who want to explore the mathematical details of the theoretical concepts covered in the text, **Math** icons direct the students to the McConnell Web site.

Also on the Web site are **Origin** articles. These brief histories examine the origins of 70 major ideas identified in the book. Students will find it interesting to learn about economists who first developed such ideas as opportunity cost, equilibrium price, the multiplier, and comparative advantage and elasticity. The Origin icon directs students to the McConnell Web site for this extension material.

For selected Key Graphs, **interactive graphs** are available on the McConnell Web site (**www. mcgrawhillconnect.ca**). Developed under the supervision of Norris Peterson of Pacific Lutheran University, this interactive feature depicts major graphs and instructs students to shift the curves, observe the outcomes, and derive relevant generalizations.

Web Chapter

Bonus Web chapters available in PDF format for easy download at **www.mcgrawhillconnect.ca**. They are: 15W, "Current Issues in Macro Theory and Policy," and 17W, "The Economics of Developing Countries."

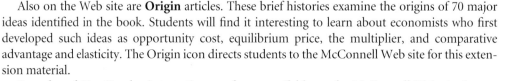

Distinguishing Features

- *Comprehensive Explanations at an Appropriate Level* *Macroeconomics* is comprehensive, analytical, and challenging, yet fully accessible to a wide range of students. Its thoroughness and accessibility enable instructors to select topics for special classroom emphasis with confidence that students can independently read and comprehend other assigned material in the book. Where needed, an extra sentence of explanation is provided. Brevity at the expense of clarity is false economy.

- *Fundamentals of the Market System* Many economies throughout the world are making difficult transitions from planning systems to market systems. Our detailed description of the institutions and operation of the market system in Chapter 2 is even more relevant than before. We pay particular attention to property rights, entrepreneurship, freedom of enterprise and choice, competition, and the role of profits because these concepts are often misunderstood by beginning students.

- *Step-by-Step, Two-Path Macro* As in the previous edition, our text continues to be distinguished by a systematic step-by-step approach in developing ideas and building models. Explicit assumptions about price and wage stickiness are posited and then systematically peeled away, yielding new models and extensions, all in the broader context of growth, expectations, shocks, and degrees of price and wage stickiness over time.

  In crafting this step-by-step macro approach, we took care to preserve the "two-path macro" that many instructors appreciated. Instructors who so choose can bypass the immediate short-run model (Chapter 9) and can proceed without loss of continuity directly to the short-run AD-AS model (Chapter 10), fiscal policy, money and banking, monetary policy, and the long-run analysis.

- *Emphasis on Technological Change and Economic Growth*   This edition continues to emphasize economic growth. Chapter 1 uses the production possibilities curve to show the basic ingredients of growth. Chapter 6 discusses the causes of growth, looks at productivity growth, and addresses some controversies surrounding economic growth. The Last Word in that chapter examines the rapid economic growth in China. Chapter 17W focuses on developing countries and the growth obstacles they confront.

- *Integrated Text and Web Site*   *Macroeconomics* and its Web site are highly integrated through in-text Web icons, bonus Web chapters, Web newspaper articles, Web math notes, and other features. Our Web site is part and parcel of our student learning package, customized to the book.

Organizational Alternatives

Although instructors generally agree as to the content of principles of economics courses, they sometimes differ as to how to arrange the material. *Macroeconomics* includes six parts, and that provides considerable organizational flexibility. For example, the two-path macro enables covering the full aggregate expenditures model or advancing directly from the basic macro relationships chapter to the AD-AS model. Also, the section of Chapter 15 that discusses the intricacies of the relationship between short-run and long-run aggregate supply can easily be appended to Chapter 9 on AD and AS.

Pedagogical Aids

Macroeconomics has always been student oriented. Economics is concerned with efficiency—accomplishing goals using the best methods. Therefore, we offer the student some brief introductory comments on how to improve their efficiency and hence their grades.

CHAPTER 3

Demand, Supply, and Market Equilibrium

According to an old joke, if you teach a parrot to say "demand and supply," you have an economist. There is much truth in this quip. The tools of demand and supply can take us far in understanding both specific economic issues and how individual markets work.

Markets bring together buyers ("demanders") and sellers ("suppliers"), and exist in many forms. The corner gas station, an e-commerce site, the local music store, a farmer's roadside stand—all are familiar markets. The Toronto Stock Exchange and the Chicago Board of Trade are markets where buyers and sellers of stocks and bonds and farm commodities from all over the world communicate with one another to buy and sell. Auctioneers bring together potential buyers and sellers of art, livestock, used farm equipment, and, sometimes, real estate. In labour markets, new college or university graduates "sell" and employers "buy" specific labour services.

Some markets are local, while others are national or international. Some are highly personal, involving face-to-face contact between demander and supplier; others are faceless, with buyer and seller never seeing or knowing each other.

To keep things simple, we will focus in this chapter on markets consisting of large numbers of buyers and sellers of standardized products. These are the highly competitive

IN THIS CHAPTER
YOU WILL LEARN:

3.1 What demand is and what affects it

3.2 What supply is and what affects it

3.3 How demand and supply together determine market equilibrium

3.4 What government-set

- *In This Chapter You Will Learn*   We set out the learning objectives at the start of each chapter so the chapter's main concepts can be easily recognized. We have also tied the learning objectives to each of the numbered sections in each chapter and the Study Questions at the end of each chapter. In addition, the chapter summaries are organized by number.

- *Terminology*   A significant portion of any introductory course is terminology. Key terms are highlighted in bold type the first time they appear in the text. Key terms are defined in the margin and a comprehensive list appears at the end of each chapter. A glossary of definitions can also be found at the end of the book and on the Web site.

- *Ten Key Concepts*   Ten Key Concepts have been identified to help students organize the main principles. The Ten Key Concepts are introduced in Chapter 1 and each one is reinforced throughout the textbook by an icon.

FACING TRADEOFFS   **CONCEPT 3** ("Choosing a Little More or Less"): Choices are usually made at the margin; we choose a "little" more or a "little" less of something.

OPPORTUNITY COSTS   **CONCEPT 4** ("The Influence of Incentives"): The choices you make are influenced by incentives.

- **Data Updates** Data updates for selected graphs and tables can be found on the McConnell Web site **www.mcgrawhill connect.ca**.

- **Graphics with Supporting Data** Where possible we have tried to provide data to support our graphs. In such cases a data table now appears in the same figure with the graph.

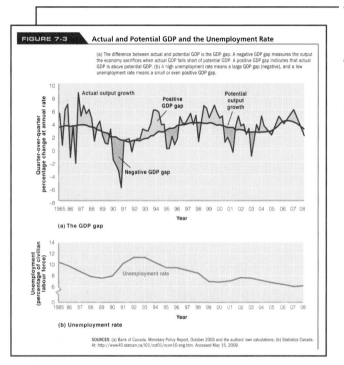

FIGURE 7-3   Actual and Potential GDP and the Unemployment Rate

(a) The difference between actual and potential GDP is the GDP gap. A negative GDP gap measures the output the economy sacrifices when actual GDP falls short of potential GDP. A positive GDP gap indicates that actual GDP is above potential GDP. (b) A high unemployment rate means a large GDP gap (negative), and a low unemployment rate means a small or even positive GDP gap.

(a) The GDP gap

(b) Unemployment rate

SOURCES: (a) Bank of Canada. Monetary Policy Report, October 2005 and the authors' own calculations; (b) Statistics Canada. At: http://www40.statcan.ca/l01/cst01/econ10-eng.htm. Accessed May 15, 2009.

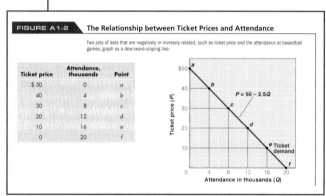

FIGURE A1-2   The Relationship between Ticket Prices and Attendance

Two sets of data that are negatively or inversely related, such as ticket price and the attendance at basketball games, graph as a downward-sloping line.

Ticket price	Attendance, thousands	Point
$50	0	a
40	4	b
30	8	c
20	12	d
10	16	e
0	20	f

$P = 50 - 2.5Q$

- **Key Graphs** We have labelled graphs having special relevance as Key Graphs. There is a quick quiz of four questions related to each Key Graph, with answers provided at the bottom of the graph.

- **Reviewing the Chapter** Important things should be said more than once. You will find a Chapter Summary at the conclusion of every chapter as well as two or three Quick Reviews within each chapter. The summary at the end of each chapter is presented by numbered chapter section. These review statements will help the student to focus on the essential ideas of each chapter and also to study for exams.

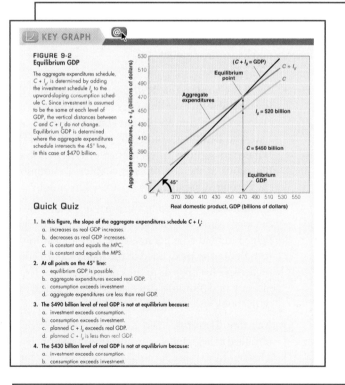

KEY GRAPH @

**FIGURE 9-2
Equilibrium GDP**

The aggregate expenditures schedule, $C + I_g$, is determined by adding the investment schedule I_g to the upward-sloping consumption schedule C. Since investment is assumed to be the same at each level of GDP, the vertical distances between C and $C + I_g$ do not change. Equilibrium GDP is determined where the aggregate expenditures schedule intersects the 45° line, in this case at $470 billion.

$(C + I_g = GDP)$

Equilibrium point

$C + I_g$

C

Aggregate expenditures

$I_g = $20 billion$

$C = $450 billion$

Equilibrium GDP

45°

Quick Quiz

1. In this figure, the slope of the aggregate expenditures schedule $C + I_g$:
   a. increases as real GDP increases.
   b. decreases as real GDP increases.
   c. is constant and equals the MPC.
   d. is constant and equals the MPS.

2. At all points on the 45° line:
   a. equilibrium GDP is possible.
   b. aggregate expenditures exceed real GDP.
   c. consumption exceeds investment
   d. aggregate expenditures are less than real GDP.

3. The $490 billion level of real GDP is not at equilibrium because:
   a. investment exceeds consumption.
   b. consumption exceeds investment.
   c. planned $C + I_g$ exceeds real GDP.
   d. planned $C + I_g$ is less than real GDP.

4. The $430 billion level of real GDP is not at equilibrium because:
   a. investment exceeds consumption.
   b. consumption exceeds investment.

QUICK REVIEW

▸ The main determinant of exports is the GDP of our trading partners. The main determinant of imports is our own GDP.

▸ Positive net exports increase aggregate expenditures on domestic output and increase equilibrium GDP; negative net exports decrease aggregate expenditures on domestic output and reduce equilibrium GDP.

▸ The multiplier for an open economy is smaller than the multiplier for a closed economy. The higher the marginal propensity to import, the smaller the open economy multiplier.

▸ In the open economy changes in (a) prosperity abroad, (b) tariffs, and (c) exchange rates can affect Canadian net exports and therefore Canadian aggregate expenditures and equilibrium GDP.

17.2 GLOBAL PERSPECTIVE

Exchange Rates: foreign currency per Canadian dollar

The amount of foreign currency that a dollar will buy varies greatly from nation to nation. These amounts are for May 2009 and fluctuate in response to supply and demand changes in the foreign exchange market.

$1 will buy
0.56 British pounds
0.90 U.S. dollars
11.8 Mexican pesos
0.64 Euros
87 Japanese yen
6.1 Chinese renminbi
42 Indian rupees

- **Global Perspective Boxes** Each nation increasingly functions in a global economy. To help the student gain appreciation of this wider economic environment, we provide Global Perspective features, which compare Canada to other nations.

- ***Consider This Boxes*** Consider This boxes are used to provide analogies, examples, or stories that help drive home central economic ideas in a student-oriented, real-world manner. These brief vignettes illustrate key points in a lively, colourful, and easy-to-remember way. See the list of Consider This boxes inside the front cover of the text.

CONSIDER THIS | The Ratchet Effect

A ratchet analogy is a good way to think about effects of changes in aggregate demand on the price level. A ratchet is a tool or mechanism such as a winch, car jack, or socket wrench that cranks a wheel forward but does not allow it to go backward. Properly set, each allows the operator to move an object (boat, car, or nut) in one direction while preventing it from moving in the opposite direction.

Product prices, wage rates, and per-unit production costs are highly flexible upward when aggregate demand increases along the aggregate supply curve. In Canada, the price level has increased in 57 of the 58 years since 1950.

But when aggregate demand decreases, product prices, wage rates, and per-unit production costs are inflexible downward. The price level has declined in only a single year (1953) since 1950, even though aggregate demand and real output have declined in a number of years, such as 1946, 1954, 1982, and 1991.

In terms of our analogy, increases in aggregate demand ratchet the Canadian price level upward. Once in place, the higher price level remains until it is ratcheted up again. The higher price level tends to remain even with declines in aggregate demand.

- ***The Last Word*** The Last Word features are lengthier applications and case studies located toward the end of each chapter. In this edition, we have included photos to pique student interest. See list of Last Word features inside the front cover of the text.

The LAST WORD Do Tax Increases Reduce Real GDP?*

Determining the relationship between changes in taxes and permanent changes in real GDP is fraught with complexities and difficulties. University of California–Berkeley economists Christina Romer and David Romer have recently devised a novel new way to approach the topic. Their findings suggest that tax increases reduce real GDP.**

How do changes in the level of taxation affect the level of economic activity? The simple correlation between taxation and economic activity shows that, on average, when economic activity rises more rapidly, tax revenues also are rising more rapidly. But this correlation almost surely does not reflect a positive effect of tax increases on output. Rather, under our tax system, any positive shock to output raises tax revenues by increasing income. In "The Macroeconomic Effects of Tax Changes: Estimates Based on a New Measure of Fiscal Shocks," authors Christina Romer and David Romer observe that this difficulty is just one of many manifestations of a more general problem. Changes in taxes occur for many reasons. And, because the factors that give rise to tax changes often are correlated with other developments in the economy, disentangling the effects of the tax changes from the other effects of these underlying factors is inherently difficult. To address this problem, Romer and Romer use the narrative record—Presidential speeches, executive branch documents, Congressional reports, and so on—to identify the size, timing, and principal motivation for all major tax policy actions in the post–World War II United States. This narrative analysis allows them to separate revenue changes resulting from legislation from changes occurring for other reasons. It also allows them to classify legislated changes according to their primary motivation. Romer and Romer find that despite the complexity of the legislative process, most significant tax changes have been motivated by one of four factors: counteracting other influences in the economy; paying for increases in government spending (or lowering taxes in conjunction with reductions in spending); addressing an inherited budget deficit; and promoting long-run growth. They observe that legislated tax changes taken to counteract other influences on the economy, or to pay for increases in government spending, are very likely to be correlated with other factors affecting the economy. As a result these observations are likely to lead to unreliable estimates of the effect of tax changes. Tax changes that are made to promote long-run growth, or to reduce an inherited budget deficit, in contrast, are undertaken for reasons essentially unrelated to other factors influencing output. Thus, examining the behaviour of output following these tax changes is likely to provide more reliable estimates of the output effects of tax changes. *The results of this more reliable test indicate that tax changes have very large effects: a tax increase of 1 percent of GDP lowers real GDP by roughly 2 to 3 percent.* These output effects are highly persistent. The behaviour of inflation and unemployment suggests that this persistence reflects long-lasting departures of output from previous levels. Romer and Romer also find that output effects of tax changes are much more closely tied to the actual changes in taxes than news about future changes, and that investment falls sharply in response to tax changes. Indeed, the strong response of investment helps to explain why the output consequences of tax increases are so large. Romer and Romer find suggestive evidence that tax increases to reduce an inherited budget deficit have much smaller output costs than other tax increases. This is consistent with the idea that deficit-driven tax increases may have important expansionary effects through [improved] expectations and [lower] long-term interest rates, or through [enhanced] confidence. There is good reason to believe that these general results may also apply to the Canadian economy.

*Abridged from Les Picker, "Tax Increases Reduce GDP," *The NBER Digest*, February/March 2008. The *Digest* provides synopses of research papers in progress by economists affiliated with the National Bureau of Economic Research (NBER).

**Christina Romer and David Romer, "The Macroeconomic Effects of Tax Changes: Estimates Based on a New Measure of Fiscal Shocks," National Bureau of Economic Research Working Paper No. 13264, 2007.

Question

On average, does an increase in taxes raise or lower real GDP? If taxes as a percentage of GDP go up 1 percent, by how much does real GDP change? Are the decreases in real GDP caused by tax increases temporary or permanent? Does the intention of a tax increase matter?

- ***Appendix on Graphs*** Being comfortable with graphical analysis and a few related quantitative concepts will be a big advantage to students in understanding the principles of economics. The appendix to Chapter 1, which reviews graphing, line slopes, and linear equations, should not be skipped.

Appendix to Chapter 1

A1.1 GRAPHS AND THEIR MEANINGS

If you glance quickly through this text, you will find many graphs. Some seem simple, others more complicated. All are included to help you visualize and understand economic relationships. Physicists and chemists sometimes illustrate their theories by building arrangements of multicoloured wooden balls, representing protons, neutrons, and electrons, which are held in proper relation to one another by wires or sticks. Economists use graphs to illustrate their models. By understanding these "pictures," you can more readily make sense of economic relationships. Most of our principles or models explain relationships between just two sets of economic facts, which can be conveniently represented with two-dimensional graphs.

Construction of a Graph

A *graph* is a visual representation of the relationship between two variables. Figure A1-1 is a hypothetical illustration showing the relationship between income and consumption for the economy as a whole. Without even studying economics, we would logically expect that people would buy more goods and services when their incomes go up. Thus it is not surprising to find in Figure A1-1 that total consumption in the economy increases as total income increases.

The information in Figure A1-1 is expressed both graphically and in table form. Here is how it is done: We want to show graphically how consumption changes as income changes. We therefore represent income on the **horizontal axis** of the graph and consumption on the **vertical axis**.

Now we arrange the vertical and horizontal scales of the graph to reflect the ranges of values of consumption and income, and mark the scales in convenient increments. As you can see in Figure A1-1, the values marked on the scales cover all the values in the table. The increments on both scales are $100 for approximately each centimetre.

Because the graph has two dimensions, each point within it represents an income value and its associated consumption value. To find a point that represents one of the five income–consumption combinations in the table, we draw straight lines from the appropriate values on the vertical and horizontal axes. For example, to plot point ***c*** (the $200 income, $150 consumption), straight lines are drawn up from the horizontal (income) axis at $200 and across from the vertical (consumption) axis at $150.These straight lines intersect at point ***c***, which represents this particular income–consumption combination. You should verify that the other income–consumption combinations shown in the table are properly located in the graph. Finally, by assuming

- ***Study Questions*** A comprehensive list of questions is located at the end of each chapter. The old cliché that you "learn by doing" is very relevant to economics. Use of these questions will enhance your understanding. We designate several of them as "Key Questions" and answer them in the Study Guide. For the twelfth Canadian edition of *Macroeconomics* we have added a total of five new Study Questions and connected every question with a Learning Objective.

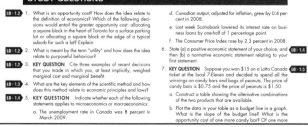

STUDY QUESTIONS

LO 1.2 1. What is an opportunity cost? How does the idea relate to the definition of economics? Which of the following decisions would entail the greater opportunity cost: allocating a square block in the heart of Toronto for a surface parking lot or allocating a square block at the edge of a typical suburb for such a lot? Explain.

LO 1.2 2. What is meant by the term "utility" and how does the idea relate to purposeful behaviour?

LO 1.2 3. **KEY QUESTION** Cite three examples of recent decisions that you made in which you, at least implicitly, weighed marginal cost and marginal benefit.

LO 1.3 4. What are the key elements of the scientific method and how does this method relate to economic principles and laws?

LO 1.4 5. **KEY QUESTION** Indicate whether each of the following statements applies to microeconomics or macroeconomics:

a. The unemployment rate in Canada was 8 percent in March 2009.

d. Canadian output, adjusted for inflation, grew by 0.4 percent in 2008.

e. Last week Scotiabank lowered its interest rate on business loans by one-half of 1 percentage point.

f. The Consumer Price Index rose by 2.3 percent in 2008.

6. State (a) a positive economic statement of your choice, and then (b) a normative economic statement relating to your first statement. LO 1.4

7. **KEY QUESTION** Suppose you won $15 on a Lotto Canada ticket at the local 7-Eleven and decided to spend all the winnings on candy bars and bags of peanuts. The price of candy bars is $0.75 and the price of peanuts is $1.50. LO 1.5

a. Construct a table showing the alternative combinations of the two products that are available.

b. Plot the data in your table as a budget line in a graph. What is the slope of the budget line? What is the opportunity cost of one more candy bar? Of one more

- ***Internet Application Questions*** Students are presented with questions to explore on the Internet relevant to the topic discussed in the chapter. From the McConnell Web site, **www.mcgrawhill connect.ca**, students will find direct links to the Web sites included in these questions.

INTERNET APPLICATION QUESTIONS @

1. **More Labour Resources—What Is the Evidence for Canada and France?** Use the links on the McConnell-Brue-Flynn-Barbiero Web site (Chapter 1) to compare the growth in employment in Canada and France. In which of the two countries did "more labour resources" (in percentage terms) have the greatest impact in shifting the nation's production possibilities curve outward over the 10-year period?

2. **Normative Economics—Canadian Politics.** Many economic policy statements made by the Liberal Party, the Conservative Party, and the New Democratic Party can be considered normative rather than positive economic statements. Use the links on the McConnell-Brue-Flynn-Barbiero Web site (Chapter 1) and compare and contrast their views on how to achieve economic goals. How much of the disagreement is based on positive statements and how much on normative statements? Give an example of loaded terminology from each site.

Comprehensive Learning and Teaching Package

The Twelfth Canadian Edition is also accompanied by a variety of high-quality supplements that help students master the subject and help instructors implement customized courses.

For the Students

LYRYX LEARNING INC
Online Learning and Assessment
lyryx.com

Lyryx Assessment for Economics is a leading-edge online assessment system, designed to support both students and instructors. The assessment takes the form of a homework assignment called a Lab. The assessments are algorithmically generated and automatically graded so that students get instant grades and feedback. New Labs are randomly generated each time, providing the student with unlimited opportunities to try a type of question. After they submit a Lab for marking, students receive extensive feedback on their work, thus promoting their learning experience.

Lyryx for the student offers algorithmically generated and automatically graded assignments. Students get instant grades and instant feedback—no need to wait until the next class to find out how well they did! Grades are instantly recorded in a grade book that the student can view.

Students are motivated to do their labs for two reasons: first because it can be tied to assessment, and second because they can try the Lab as many times as they wish prior to the due date with only their best grade being recorded.

Instructors know from experience that if students do their economics homework, they will be successful in the course. Recent research regarding the use of Lyryx has shown that when Labs are tied to assessment, even if worth only a small percentage of the total grade of the course, students WILL do their homework—and MORE THAN ONCE!

Please contact your *i*Learning Sales Specialist for additional information on the Lyryx Assessment Economics system.

Visit *http://lyryx.com*

- *Online Learning Centre* This electronic learning aid, located at **www.mcgrawhill.ca/olc/mcconnell**, offers materials including chapter highlights, key terms, the Origin of the Idea, and access to the Statistics Canada free database. Highly visible Web icons in the text margins alert students to points in the book where they can springboard to the site to learn more. There also are regular news updates and an interactive glossary—all specific to *Macroeconomics*. For the math-minded student, there is a "Math" section, where they can explore the mathematical details of the concepts in the text. There are also three optional bonus Web chapters.

- Developed in partnership with Youthography, a Canadian youth research company, and hundreds of students from across Canada, McGraw-Hill Connect™ embraces diverse study behaviours and preferences to maximize active learning and engagement.

  With McGraw-Hill Connect™, written by Lance Shandler of Kwantlen Polytechnic University, students complete pre- and post-diagnostic assessments that identify knowledge gaps and point them to concepts they need to learn. McGraw-Hill Connect™ provides students the option to work through recommended learning exercises and create their own personalized study plan using multiple sources of content, including a searchable e-book, multiple-choice and true/false quizzes, chapter-by-chapter learning goals, interactivities, personal notes, videos, and more. Using the copy, paste, highlight, and sticky note features, students collect, organize, and customize their study plan content to optimize learning outcomes.

For the Instructor

- *The Instructor Online Learning Centre* The Instructor Online Learning Centre (OLC) at **www.mcgrawhill.ca/olc/mcconnell** includes a password-protected Web site for instructors. The site offers downloadable Instructor supplements.

All Instructor supplements are available at the OLC:

- **Instructor's Manual**   The Instructor's Manual is prepared by Thomas Barbiero of Ryerson University, and Shawn D. Knabb of Western Washington University. Available again in this edition as a Microsoft® Office Word document, the manual includes: Chapter Overview, What's New, Instructional Objectives, Comments and Teaching Suggestions, Student Stumbling Blocks, Lecture Notes, Last Word, and answers to end-of-chapter questions.

- **Microsoft® PowerPoint® Presentation Software**   Prepared by Bruno Fullone of George Brown College, this presentation system is found on the Instructor's Site of the Online Learning Centre. It offers visual presentations that may be edited and manipulated to fit a particular course format.

- **Computerized Test Banks**   Prepared by Nargess Kayhani, Mount St. Vincent University, Computerized Test Bank I contains about 6000 multiple-choice and true/false questions. Rob Moir, University of New Brunswick, has prepared over 30 short-answer questions with suggested answers for each chapter. Also included is U.S. Test Bank II. This test bank contains around 6300 multiple choice and true/false questions. All questions are categorized according to level and difficulty.

In addition, content cartridges are available for the course management systems **WebCT** and **Blackboard**. These platforms provide instructors with user-friendly, flexible teaching tools. Please contact your local McGraw-Hill Ryerson *i*Learning Sales Specialist for details.

- McGraw-Hill Connect™ assessment activities don't stop with students! There is material for instructors to leverage as well, including a personalized teaching plan where instructors can choose from a variety of quizzes to use in class, assign as homework, or add to exams. They can edit existing questions and add new ones; track individual student performance—by question, assignment, or in relation to the class overall—with detailed grade reports; integrate grade reports easily with Learning Management Systems such as WebCT and Blackboard; and much more. Instructors can also browse or search teaching resources and text specific supplements and organize them into customizable categories. All the teaching resources are now located in one convenient place.
    McGraw-Hill Connect™ — helping instructors and students Connect, Learn, Succeed!

Superior Service

Integrated Learning

Your **Integrated Learning Sales Specialist** is a McGraw-Hill Ryerson representative who has the experience, product knowledge, training, and support to help you assess and integrate any of the above-noted products, technology, and services into your course for optimum teaching and learning performance. Whether it's using our test bank software, helping your students improve their grades, or putting your entire course online, your *i*Learning Sales Specialist is there to help you do it. Contact your local *i*Learning Sales Specialist today to learn how to maximize all of McGraw-Hill Ryerson's resources!

*i*Learning Services Program

McGraw-Hill Ryerson offers a unique *i*Services package designed for Canadian faculty. Our mission is to equip providers of higher education with superior tools and resources required for excellence in teaching. For additional information visit **www.mcgrawhill.ca/highereducation/iservices**.

Teaching, Technology, and Learning Conference Series

The educational environment has changed tremendously in recent years, and McGraw-Hill Ryerson continues to be committed to helping you acquire the skills you need to succeed in this new milieu. Our innovative Teaching, Technology, and Learning Conference Series brings together faculty from across Canada with winners of the 3M Teaching Excellence award to share teaching and learning best practices in a collaborative and stimulating environment. Pre-conference workshops on general topics, such as teaching large classes and technology integration, will also be offered. We will also work with you at your own institution to customize workshops that best suit the needs of your faculty.

Acknowledgements

The Twelfth Canadian Edition of *Macroeconomics* has benefitted from a number of perceptive reviewers, who were a rich source of suggestions for this revision. To each of you, and others we may have inadvertently overlooked, thank you for your considerable help in improving *Macroeconomics*. Reviewers include:

Morris Altman, University of Saskatchewan

Alka Bhushan, Seneca College

Tatjana Brkic, Red River College

Ida Ferrara, York University

Bruno Fullone, George Brown College School of Business

Susan Kamp, University of Alberta

Stephen Rakoczy, Humber College Business School

Neil Ridler, University of New Brunswick

Sheila Ross, SAIT

Jim Sentance, University of Prince Edward Island

Chandan Shirvaikar, Red Deer College

Javid Taheri, Saint Mary's University

Brennan Thompson, Ryerson University

Brian VanBlarcom, Acadia University

We are greatly indebted to an all-star group of professionals at McGraw-Hill Ryerson—in particular Bruce McIntosh and James Booty, Sponsoring Editors; Daphne Scriabin and Andria Fogarty, Developmental Editors; Joy Armitage Taylor, Executive Marketing Manager; and Stephanie Hess, Editorial Associate—for their publishing and marketing expertise. We thank Kelli Howey for her thorough and sensitive editing, Jacques Cournoyer for his vivid Last Word illustrations, Sarah Orr/ArtPlus Limited for the cover and interior design, Gianluigi Pelloni of the University of Bologna (Rimini Campus) for his helpful suggestions and insights, and Michael Lindsay of Humber College for his technical checks.

We also strongly acknowledge the McGraw-Hill Ryerson sales staff, who greeted this edition with wholehearted enthusiasm.

Campbell R. McConnell
Stanley L. Brue
Sean M. Flynn
Thomas P. Barbiero

An Introduction to Economics and the Economy

PART 1

CHAPTER 1

Limits, Alternatives, and Choices

(An appendix on understanding graphs follows this chapter. If you need a quick review of this mathematical tool, you might benefit by reading the appendix first.)

People's wants are numerous and varied. Biologically, people need only air, water, food, clothing, and shelter. But in modern society people also desire goods and services that provide a more comfortable or affluent standard of living. We want bottled water, soft drinks, and fruit juices, not just water from the creek. We want salads, burgers, and pizzas, not just berries and nuts. We want jeans, suits, and coats, not just woven reeds. We want apartments, condominiums, or houses, not just mud huts. And, as the saying goes, "that is not the half of it." We also want flat-panel TVs, Internet service, education, cell phones, health care, and much more.

Fortunately, society possesses productive resources, such as labour and managerial talent, tools and machinery, and land and mineral deposits. These resources, employed in the economic system (or simply the economy), help us produce goods and services that satisfy many of our economic wants. But the blunt reality is that our economic wants far exceed the productive capacity of our scarce (limited) resources. We are forced to make choices. This unyielding truth underlies the definition of **economics,** which is the social science concerned with how individuals, institutions, and society make optimal (best) choices under conditions of scarcity.

Numerous problems and issues arise from the challenge of making optimal choices under conditions of scarcity. Although it is tempting to plunge into them, that sort of analysis must wait until we discuss some important preliminaries.

IN THIS CHAPTER YOU WILL LEARN:

1.1 Ten key concepts to retain for a lifetime

1.2 The features of the economic way of thinking

1.3 The role of theories, principles, and models in economics

1.4 The distinction between microeconomics and macroeconomics

1.5 The nature of the economic problem and the categories of scarce resources

1.6 The production possibilities model and the nature of increasing opportunity costs

1.7 What economic growth is, and how present choices determine future production possibilities

A1.1 (Appendix) About graphs, curves, and slopes as they relate to economics

ORIGIN 1.1
Economics

economics
The social science concerned with how individuals, institutions, and society make optimal (best) choices under conditions of scarcity.

Economics is concerned with the efficient use of scarce resources to obtain the maximum satisfaction of society's unlimited wants.

 FACING TRADEOFFS

 OPPORTUNITY COSTS

 CHOOSING A LITTLE MORE OR LESS

 THE INFLUENCE OF INCENTIVES

 SPECIALIZATION & TRADE

 THE EFFECTIVENESS OF MARKETS

 THE ROLE OF GOVERNMENTS

 PRODUCTION & THE STANDARD OF LIVING

 MONEY & INFLATION

INFLATION– UNEMPLOYMENT TRADEOFF

1.1 | Ten Key Concepts to Retain for a Lifetime

Suppose you unexpectedly meet your introductory economics professor on the street five or ten years after you complete this course. What will you be able to tell her you retained from the course? More than likely you will not be able to remember very much. To help you retain the main ideas that economics has to offer, we have come up with **10 key concepts** we believe are essential to understand the world around you and will help you in your chosen career. These key concepts will be reinforced throughout the textbook so that you will hopefully retain them long after the course is over. When a key concept is about to be discussed you will be alerted with an icon and the concept description.

The 10 key concepts are simply listed here; you will find elaboration on each key concept as we progress through the textbook. At the end of the course you should review these 10 key concepts. They will help you organize and better understand the materials you have studied. We have divided the 10 key concepts into three categories: (a) concepts that pertain to the individual; (b) concepts that explain the interaction among individuals; and (c) concepts that deal with the economy as a whole and the standard of living.

The Individual

CONCEPT 1 ("Facing Tradeoffs"): Scarcity in relation to wants means you face **tradeoffs;** therefore, you have to make choices.

CONCEPT 2 ("Opportunity Costs"): The cost of the choice you make is what you give up for it, or the **opportunity cost.**

CONCEPT 3 ("Choosing a Little More or Less"): Choices are usually made at the margin; we choose a "little" more or a "little" less of something.

CONCEPT 4 ("The Influence of Incentives"): The choices you make are influenced by incentives.

Interaction among Individuals

CONCEPT 5 ("Specialization and Trade"): Specialization and trade will improve the well-being of all participants.

CONCEPT 6 ("The Effectiveness of Markets"): Markets usually do a good job of coordinating trade among individuals, groups, and nations.

CONCEPT 7 ("The Role of Governments"): Governments can occasionally improve the coordinating function of markets.

The Economy as a Whole and the Standard of Living

CONCEPT 8 ("Production and the Standard of Living"): The standard of living of the average person in a particular country is dependent on its production of goods and services. A rise in the standard of living requires a rise in the output of goods and services.

CONCEPT 9 ("Money and Inflation"): If the monetary authorities of a country annually print money in excess of the growth of output of goods and services it will eventually lead to inflation.

CONCEPT 10 ("Inflation–Unemployment Tradeoff"): In the short run, society faces a short-run **tradeoff** between **inflation** and its level of **unemployment**.

As you read the text, be on the lookout for the icon that alerts you that one of these concepts is being discussed. We now turn to our first topic, the economic way of thinking.

1.2 | The Economic Way of Thinking

Close your eyes for a minute and pretend you are in paradise, a place where you can have anything you want whenever you desire it. On a particular day you may decide you want a new pair of jeans, a new notebook computer, a cellular phone, tickets to see Avril Lavigne, and a new red Ferrari sports car to cruise around in. Your friends may have a completely different list of wants, but in paradise all of their desires also will be satisfied. Indeed, everyone's desires are satisfied. The following day you can start all over and make any request you have, and it will be fulfilled. And so it will continue, forever. Your body will never get old or sick, you will have all the friends and love you want, etc., etc.

Of course, paradise may be waiting for us in the afterlife, but in this world our wants greatly outstrip our ability to satisfy them. Anytime there is a situation in which wants are greater than the resources to meet those desires, we have an economic problem. It is this reality that gives economists their unique perspective. This **economic perspective** or *economic way of thinking* has several critical and closely interrelated features.

economic perspective
A viewpoint that envisions individuals and institutions making rational decisions by comparing the marginal benefits and marginal costs associated with their actions.

Scarcity and Choice

From our definition of economics, it is easy to see why economists view the world through the lens of scarcity. Since resources are scarce (limited), it follows that the goods and services we produce must also be limited. Scarcity limits our options and necessitates that we make choices. Because we "can't have it all," we must decide what we will have, and what we must forgo.

At the core of economics is the idea that "there is no free lunch." You may get treated to lunch, making it "free" to you, but there is a cost to someone—ultimately, society (see the Consider This box). Scarce inputs of land, equipment, farm labour, the labour of cooks and waiters, and managerial talent are required. Because these resources could be used in other production activities, they and the other goods and services they could have produced are sacrificed in making the lunch available. Economists call these sacrifices **opportunity costs.** To get more of one thing, you forgo the opportunity of getting the next best thing. That sacrifice is the opportunity cost of the choice. For example, you have $100 that you can spend on a pair of jeans or shoes. The opportunity cost of buying the shoes is the jeans you could have purchased, and vice versa.

 OPPORTUNITY COSTS

opportunity cost
The amount of other products that must be forgone or sacrificed to produce a unit of a product.

CONSIDER THIS | Free for All?

Free products are seemingly everywhere. Sellers from time to time offer free software, free cell phones, and no-fee chequing accounts. Dentists give out free toothbrushes. At provincial visitors' centres, there are free brochures and maps.

Does the presence of so many free products contradict the economist's assertion that "there is no free lunch"? No! Scarce resources are used to produce each of these products, and because those resources have alternative uses, society gives up something else to get the "free" good. Where resources are used to produce goods and services, there is no free lunch.

So why are these goods offered for free? In a word: marketing. Firms sometimes offer free products to entice people to

try them, hoping they will then purchase them later. The free version of software may eventually entice you to buy the next upgraded version, in other instances free brochures contain advertising for shops and restaurants, and free access to the Internet is filled with ads. In still other cases, the product is free only in conjunction with a purchase. To get the soft drink you must buy the large pizza. To get the free cell phone you need to sign up for a year (or more) of cell phone service.

So free products may or may not be truly free to individuals. They are never free to society.

ORIGIN 1.2
Utility

utility
The satisfaction a person gets from consuming a good or service.

Purposeful Behaviour

Economics assumes that human behaviour reflects "rational self-interest." Individuals look for and pursue opportunities to increase their **utility**—the pleasure, happiness, or satisfaction obtained from consuming a good or service. They allocate their time, energy, and money to maximize their satisfaction. Because they weigh costs and benefits, their decisions are purposeful or rational, not random or chaotic.

Consumers are purposeful in deciding what goods and services to buy. Business firms are purposeful in deciding what products to produce and how to produce them. Government entities are purposeful in deciding what public services to provide and how to finance them.

"Purposeful behaviour" does not assume that people and institutions are immune from faulty logic and therefore are perfect decision makers. They sometimes make mistakes. Nor does it mean that people's decisions are unaffected by emotion or the decisions of those around them. "Purposeful behaviour" simply means that people make decisions with some desired outcome in mind.

Rational self-interest is not the same as selfishness. In the economy, increasing one's own wage, rent, interest, or profit normally requires identifying and satisfying *somebody else's* wants! Also, people make personal sacrifices for others. They contribute time and money to charities because they derive pleasure from doing so. Parents help pay for their children's education for the same reason. These self-interested, but unselfish, acts help maximize the giver's satisfaction as much as any personal purchase of goods or services. Self-interested behaviour is simply behaviour designed to increase personal satisfaction, however it may be derived.

ORIGIN 1.3
Marginal Analysis

marginal analysis
The comparison of marginal ("extra" or "additional") benefits and marginal costs, usually for decision making.

Marginal Analysis: Benefits and Costs

The economic perspective focuses largely on **marginal analysis**—comparisons of *marginal benefits* and *marginal costs*. To economists, "marginal" means "extra," "additional," or "a change in." Most choices or decisions involve changes in the status quo (the existing state of affairs). Should you attend school for another year or not? Should you study an extra hour for an exam? Should you add fries to your fast-food order? Similarly, should a business expand or reduce its output? Should government increase or decrease health care funding?

CONSIDER THIS | Fast Food Lines

The economic perspective is useful in analyzing all sorts of behaviours. Consider an everyday example: the behaviour of customers at a fast-food restaurant. When customers enter the restaurant, they go to the shortest line, believing that line will minimize their time cost of obtaining food. They are acting purposefully; time is limited, and people prefer using it in some way other than standing in line.

If one fast-food line is temporarily shorter than other lines, some people will move to that line. These movers apparently view the time saving from the shorter line (marginal benefit) as exceeding the cost of moving from their present line (marginal cost). The line switching tends to equalize line lengths. No further movement of customers between lines occurs once all lines are about equal.

Fast-food customers face another cost-benefit decision when a clerk opens a new station at the counter. Should they move to the new station or stay put? Those who shift to the new line decide that the time saving from the move exceeds the extra cost of physically moving. In so deciding, customers

must also consider just how quickly they can get to the new station compared with others who may be contemplating the same move. (Those who hesitate in this situation are lost!)

Customers at the fast-food establishment do not have perfect information when they select lines. Thus, not all decisions turn out as expected. For example, you might enter a short line and find someone in front of you is ordering hamburgers and fries for 40 people in the Greyhound bus parked out back (and the employee is a trainee!). Nevertheless, at the time you made your decision, you thought it was optimal.

Finally, customers must decide what food to order when they arrive at the counter. In making their choices, they again compare marginal costs and marginal benefits in attempting to obtain the greatest personal satisfaction for their expenditure.

Economists believe that what is true for the behaviour of customers at fast-food restaurants is true for economic behaviour in general. Faced with an array of choices, consumers, workers, and businesses rationally compare marginal costs and marginal benefits in making decisions.

CHOOSING A LITTLE MORE OR LESS

Each option will have marginal benefits and marginal costs. In making choices, the decision maker will compare those two amounts. Example: You and your fiancé are shopping for an engagement ring. Should you buy a ¼-carat diamond, a ½-carat diamond, a ¾-carat diamond, or a larger one? The marginal cost of the larger diamond is the added expense beyond the smaller diamond. The marginal benefit is the greater lifetime pleasure (utility) from the larger stone. If the marginal benefit of the larger diamond exceeds its marginal cost, you buy the larger stone. But if the marginal cost is more than the marginal benefit, buy the smaller diamond instead, even if you can afford the larger stone.

In a world of scarcity, the marginal benefit associated with some specific option always includes the marginal cost of forgoing something else. Spending money on the larger diamond may mean forgoing a honeymoon to an exotic location. Opportunity costs, the value of the next best thing forgone, is always present whenever a choice is made. *(Key Question 3)*

1.3 | Theories, Principles, and Models

scientific method
The systematic pursuit of knowledge through formulating a problem, collecting data, and formulating and testing hypotheses to obtain theories, principles, and laws.

Like the physical and life sciences, as well as other social sciences, economics relies on the **scientific method.** That procedure consists of several elements:

- Observing real-world behaviour and outcomes.

- Based on those observations, formulating a possible explanation of cause and effect (hypothesis).

- Testing this explanation by comparing the outcomes of specific events to the outcome predicted by the hypothesis.

- Accepting, rejecting, or modifying the hypothesis based on these comparisons.

- Continuing to test the hypothesis against the facts. As favourable results accumulate, the hypothesis evolves into a theory. A very well tested and widely accepted theory is referred to as an economic law or an **economic principle**—a statement about economic behaviour or the economy that enables prediction of the probable effects of certain actions. Combinations of such laws or principles are incorporated into models, which are simplified representations of how parts of the economy work, such as a market or segment of the economy.

economic principle
A statement about economic behaviour or the economy that enables prediction of the probable effects of certain actions.

Economists develop theories of the behaviour of individuals (consumers, workers) and institutions (businesses, governments) engaged in the production, exchange, and consumption of goods and services. Theories, principles, and models are "purposeful simplifications." The full scope of economic reality itself is too complex and bewildering to be understood as a whole. In developing theories, principles, and models, economists remove the clutter and simplify.

Economic principles and models are highly useful in analyzing economic behaviour and understanding how the economy operates. They are the tools for ascertaining cause and effect (or action and outcome) within the economic system. Good theories do a good job of explaining and predicting. They are supported by facts concerning how individuals and institutions actually behave in producing, exchanging, and consuming goods and services.

There are some other things you should know about economic principles.

- *Generalizations*   Economic principles are generalizations relating to economic behaviour or to the economy itself. Economic principles are expressed as the tendencies of typical or average consumers, workers, or business firms. For example, economists say that consumers buy more of a particular product when its price falls. Economists recognize that some consumers may increase their purchases by a large amount, others by a small amount, and a few not at all. This "price–quantity" principle, however, holds for the typical consumer and for consumers as a group.

 ORIGIN 1.4
Ceteris Paribus

other-things-equal assumption
The assumption that factors other than those being considered are held constant.

- *Other-Things-Equal Assumption*   In constructing their theories, economists use the *ceteris paribus* or **other-things-equal assumption**—the assumption that factors other than those being considered do not change. They assume that all variables except those under immediate consideration are held constant for a particular analysis. For example, consider the relationship between the price of Pepsi and the amount of it purchased. Assume that of all the factors that might influence the amount of Pepsi purchased (for example, the price of Pepsi, the price of Coca-Cola, and consumer incomes and preferences), only the price of Pepsi varies. This is helpful because the economist can then focus on the relationship between the price of Pepsi and purchases of Pepsi in isolation without being confused by changes in other variables.

MATH 1.1
Ceteris Paribus

- *Graphical Expression*   Many economic models are expressed graphically. Be sure to read the appendix at the end of this chapter as a review of graphs.

1.4 | Microeconomics and Macroeconomics

Economists develop economic principles and models at two levels, microeconomics and macroeconomics.

Microeconomics

microeconomics
The part of economics concerned with such individual units as industries, firms, and households.

Microeconomics is the part of economics concerned with individual units such as a household, a firm, or an industry. At this level of analysis, the economist observes the details of an economic unit, or very small segment of the economy, under a figurative microscope. In microeconomics we look at decision making by individual customers, workers, households, and business firms. We measure the price of a specific product, the number of workers employed by a single firm, the revenue or income of a particular firm or household, or the expenditures of a specific firm, government entity, or family. In microeconomics, we examine the grains of sand, the rocks, and the shells, not the beach.

Macroeconomics

macroeconomics
The part of economics concerned with the economy as a whole.

aggregate
A collection of specific economic units treated as if they were one unit.

Macroeconomics examines either the economy as a whole or its basic subdivisions or aggregates, such as the government, household, and business sectors. An **aggregate** is a collection of specific economic units treated as if they were one unit. Therefore, we might lump together the millions of consumers in the Canadian economy and treat them as if they were one huge unit called "consumers."

In using aggregates, macroeconomics seeks to obtain an overview, or general outline, of the structure of the economy and the relationships of its major aggregates. Macroeconomics speaks of such economic measures as total output, total employment, total income, aggregate expenditures, and the general level of prices in analyzing various economic problems. No or very little attention is given to specific units making up the various aggregates. Figuratively, macroeconomics looks at the beach, not the grains of sand, the rocks, and the shells.

The micro–macro distinction does not mean that economics is so highly compartmentalized that every topic can be readily labelled as either macro or micro; many topics and subdivisions of economics are rooted in both. Example: While the problem of unemployment is usually treated as a macroeconomic topic (because unemployment relates to aggregate production), economists recognize that the decisions made by *individual* workers on how long to search for jobs and the way *specific* labour markets encourage or impede hiring are also critical in determining the unemployment rate. *(Key Question 5)*

Positive and Normative Economics

positive economics
The analysis of facts to establish cause-and-effect relationships.

normative economics
The part of economics involving value judgments about what the economy should be like.

Both microeconomics and macroeconomics contain elements of positive economics and normative economics. **Positive economics** focuses on facts and cause-and-effect relationships. It includes description, theory development, and theory testing (theoretical economics). Positive economics avoids value judgments, tries to establish scientific statements about economic behaviour, and deals with what the economy is actually like. Such scientific-based analysis is critical to good policy analysis.

Economic policy, on the other hand, involves **normative economics,** which incorporates value judgments about what the economy *should* be like or what particular policy actions *should* be recommended to achieve a desirable goal (policy economics). Normative economics looks at the desirability of certain aspects of the economy. It underlies expressions of support for particular economic policies.

Positive economics concerns *what is,* while normative economics embodies subjective feelings about *what ought to be.* Examples: Positive statement: "The unemployment rate in France is higher than that in Canada." Normative statement: "France ought to undertake policies to make its labour market more flexible to reduce unemployment rates." When you see words such as "ought" or "should" in a sentence, there is a strong chance you are encountering a normative statement.

Most of the disagreement among economists involves normative, value-based policy questions. Of course, there is often some disagreement about which theories or models best represent the economy and its parts. But economists agree on a full range of economic principles. Most economic controversy thus reflects differing opinions or value judgments about what society should be like.

QUICK REVIEW

▶ Economics examines how individuals, institutions, and society make choices under conditions of scarcity.

▶ The economic way of thinking stresses (a) resource scarcity and the necessity of making choices, (b) the assumption of purposeful (or rational) behaviour, and (c) comparisons of marginal benefit and marginal cost. In choosing among alternatives, people incur opportunity costs.

▶ Economists use the scientific method to establish economic theories—cause–effect generalizations about the economic behaviour of individuals and institutions.

▶ Microeconomics focuses on specific units of the economy; macroeconomics examines the economy as a whole.

▶ Positive economics deals with factual statements ("what is"); normative economics involves value judgments ("what ought to be").

1.5 | The Economic Problem

economic problem
The need to make choices because society's material wants for goods and services are unlimited but the resources available to satisfy these wants are limited (scarce).

Both individuals and society face an **economic problem,** which is the need to make choices because economic wants are virtually unlimited but the means (income, time, resources) for satisfying those wants are limited. We will construct a simple microeconomic model to look at the general economic problem faced by an individual.

Limited Income

We all have a finite amount of income, even the wealthiest among us. Even members of the Thompson and Weston families—Canada's richest—have to decide how to spend their money! And the majority of us have much more limited means. Our income comes to us in the form of wages, interest, rent, and profit, although we may also receive money from government programs or from family members. As Global Perspective 1.1 shows, the average income of Canadians in 2007 was $39,420 ($US). In the poorest nations, it was less than $500.

Unlimited Wants

For better or worse, most people have virtually unlimited wants. We desire various goods and services that provide utility. Our wants extend over a wide range of products, from *necessities* (food, shelter, clothing) to *luxuries* (perfumes, yachts, sports cars). Some wants such as basic food, shelter, and clothing have biological roots. Other wants—for example, specific kinds of food, shelter, and clothing—arise from the conventions and customs of society.

1.1 | GLOBAL PERSPECTIVE

Average Income, Selected Nations

Average income (total income/population) and therefore typical individual budget constraints vary greatly among nations.

Country	Per Capita Income, 2007 (U.S. dollars, based on exchange rates)
Switzerland	59,880
United States	46,040
Canada	39,420
France	38,500
Japan	37,670
South Korea	19,690
Mexico	8,340
Brazil	5,910
China	2,360
Nigeria	930
Pakistan	870
Rwanda	320
Liberia	150

Source: World Bank, www.worldbank.org.

Over time, as new and improved products are introduced, economic wants tend to change and multiply, fuelled by new products. Only recently have people wanted iPods, Internet service, digital cameras, or camera phones, because those products did not exist a few decades ago. Also, the satisfaction of certain wants may trigger others: the acquisition of a Ford Focus or a Honda Civic has been known to whet the appetite for a Lexus or a Mercedes.

Services, as well as goods, satisfy our wants. Car repair work, the removal of an inflamed appendix, legal and accounting advice, and haircuts all satisfy human wants. Actually, we buy many goods, such as automobiles and washing machines, for the services they render. The differences between goods and services are often smaller than they appear to be.

For most people, the desires for goods and services cannot be fully satisfied. Bill Gates may have all that he wants for himself but it is clear from his massive charitable giving that he keenly wants better health care for the world's poor. Our desires for a particular good or service can be satisfied; over a short period of time we can surely get enough toothpaste or pasta. And one appendectomy is plenty. But our broader desire for more goods and services and higher-quality goods and services seems to be another story.

Because we have only limited income (usually through our work) but seemingly insatiable wants, it is in our self-interest to pick and choose goods and services that maximize our satisfaction.

The Budget Line

budget line
A schedule or curve that shows various combinations of two products a consumer can purchase with a specific money income.

We can depict the economic problem facing individuals via a **budget line** (or, more technically, *budget constraint*). It is a schedule or curve that shows various combinations of two products a consumer can purchase with a specific money income.

To understand this idea, suppose that you received a Chapters (or Indigo) gift card as a birthday present. The $120 card is soon to expire. You take the card to the store and confine your purchase decisions to two alternatives: DVDs and paperback books. DVDs are $20 each and paperback books are $10 each. Your purchase options are shown in the table in Figure 1-1.

FIGURE 1-1 — A Consumer's Budget Line

The budget line (or budget constraint) shows all the combinations of any two products that can be purchased, given the prices of the products and the consumer's money income.

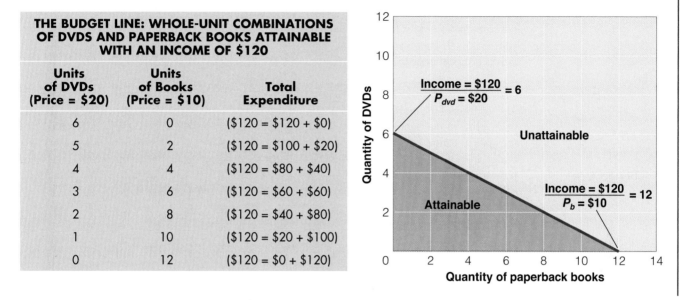

THE BUDGET LINE: WHOLE-UNIT COMBINATIONS OF DVDS AND PAPERBACK BOOKS ATTAINABLE WITH AN INCOME OF $120

Units of DVDs (Price = $20)	Units of Books (Price = $10)	Total Expenditure
6	0	($120 = $120 + $0)
5	2	($120 = $100 + $20)
4	4	($120 = $80 + $40)
3	6	($120 = $60 + $60)
2	8	($120 = $40 + $80)
1	10	($120 = $20 + $100)
0	12	($120 = $0 + $120)

At one extreme, you might spend all of your $120 "income" on 6 DVDs at $20 each and have nothing left to spend on books. Or, by giving up 2 DVDs and thereby gaining $40, you can have 4 DVDs at $20 each and 4 books at $10 each. And so on to the other extreme, at which you could buy 12 books at $10 each, spending your entire gift card on books with nothing left to spend on DVDs.

The graph in Figure 1-1 shows the budget line. Note that the graph is not restricted to whole units of DVDs and books as is the table. Every point on the graph represents a possible combination of DVDs and books, including fractional quantities. The slope of the graphed budget line measures the ratio of the price of books (P_b) to the price of DVDs (P_{dvd}); more precisely, the slope is $P_b/P_{dvd} = \$-10/\$+20 = -\frac{1}{2}$ or -0.5. So you must forgo 1 DVD (measured on the vertical axis) to buy 2 books (measured on the horizontal axis). This yields a slope of $-\frac{1}{2}$ or -0.5.

The budget line illustrates several ideas.

ATTAINABLE AND UNATTAINABLE COMBINATIONS

All the combinations of DVDs and books on or inside the budget line are *attainable* from the $120 of money income. You can afford to buy, for example, 3 DVDs at $20 each and 6 books at $10 each. You also can obviously afford to buy 2 DVDs and 5 books, if you so desire, and not use up the value on the gift card. But, to achieve maximum utility you will want to spend the full $120.

In contrast, all combinations beyond the budget line are *unattainable*. The $120 limit simply does not allow you to purchase, for example, 5 DVDs at $20 each and 5 books at $10 each. That $150 expenditure would clearly exceed the $120 limit. In Figure 1-1 the attainable combinations are on and within the budget line; the unattainable combinations are beyond the budget line.

TRADEOFFS AND OPPORTUNITY COSTS

The budget line in Figure 1-1 illustrates the idea of tradeoffs arising from limited income. To obtain more DVDs, you have to give up some books. For example, to obtain the first DVD you trade off 2 books. So the opportunity cost of the first DVD is 2 books. To obtain the second DVD the opportunity cost is also 2 books. The straight-line budget constraint, with its constant slope, indicates

ORIGIN 1.5
Opportunity Costs

constant opportunity cost. That is, the opportunity cost of 1 extra DVD remains the same (= 2 books) as more DVDs are purchased. And, in reverse, the opportunity cost of 1 extra book does not change (= ½ DVD) as more books are bought.

CHOICE

Limited income forces people to choose what to buy and what to forgo to fulfill wants. You will select the combination of DVDs and paperback books that you think is "best." That is, you will evaluate your marginal benefits and marginal costs (here, product price) to make choices that maximize your satisfaction. Other people, with the same $120 gift card, would undoubtedly make different choices.

INCOME CHANGES

**WORKED
PROBLEM 1.1**
Budget Line

The location of the budget line varies with money income. An increase in money income shifts the budget line to the right; a decrease in money income shifts it to the left. To verify this, recalculate the table in Figure 1-1, assuming the card value (income) is (a) $240 and (b) $60, and plot the new budget lines in the graph. No wonder people like to have more income: that shifts their budget lines outward and enables them to buy more goods and services. But even with more income, people will still face spending tradeoffs, opportunity costs, and choices. *(Key Question 7)*

Society's Economic Problem

Society must also make choices under conditions of scarcity. It, too, faces the economic problem. Should it devote more of its limited resources to the criminal justice system (police, courts, and prisons) or to education (teachers, books, and schools)? If it decides to devote more resources to both, what other goods and services does it forgo? Health care? Energy development?

Scarce Resources

economic resources
The land, labour, capital, and entrepreneurial ability that are used in the production of goods and services.

Society has limited or scarce **economic resources**, meaning all natural, human, and manufactured resources that go into the production of goods and services. That includes the entire set of factory and farm buildings and all the equipment, tools, and machinery used to produce manufactured goods and agricultural products; all transportation and communication facilities; all types of labour; and land and mineral resources.

Resource Categories

Economists classify economic resources into four general categories.

LAND

land
Natural resources used to produce goods and services.

Land means much more to the economist than it does to most people. To the economist, **land** includes all natural resources ("gifts of nature") used in the production process, such as arable land, forests, mineral and oil deposits, and water resources.

LABOUR

labour
The physical and mental talents of individuals used in producing goods and services.

The resource **labour** consists of the physical and mental talents of individuals used in producing goods and services. The services of a logger, retail clerk, machinist, teacher, professional hockey player, and nuclear physicist all fall under the general heading "labour."

CAPITAL

capital
Human-made resources (buildings, machinery, and equipment) used to produce goods and services.

For economists, **capital** (or capital goods) includes all manufactured aids used in producing consumer goods and services: tools and machinery, as well as all factory, storage, transportation, and distribution facilities. Note that the term "capital" does not refer to money; because money produces nothing, economists do not include it as an economic resource. Money (or money capital or financial capital) is simply a means for purchasing capital goods.

investment
Spending for the production and accumulation of capital.

Economists refer to the purchase of capital goods as **investment.** The amount of training and education that a person acquires through his or her lifetime is referred to as *human capital*, since it is similar to an investment in capital goods in that it can enhance output. But you should note that human capital is normally categorized under labour resources.

Capital goods differ from consumer goods because consumer goods satisfy wants directly, while capital goods do so indirectly by aiding the production of consumer goods.

ENTREPRENEURIAL ABILITY

entrepreneurial ability
The human talents that combine the other resources to produce a product, make non-routine decisions, innovate, and bear risks.

Finally, there is the special human resource, distinct from labour, called **entrepreneurial ability.** The entrepreneur performs several functions:

- The entrepreneur takes the initiative in combining the resources of land, labour, and capital to produce a good or a service. Both a sparkplug and a catalyst, the entrepreneur is the driving force behind production and the agent who combines the other resources in what is hoped will be a successful business venture.

- The entrepreneur makes the strategic business decisions that set the course of an enterprise.

- The entrepreneur is an innovator. He or she commercializes new products, new production techniques, or even new forms of business organization.

- The entrepreneur is a risk bearer. He or she has no guarantee of profit. The reward for the entrepreneur's time, efforts, and abilities may be profits or losses. The entrepreneur risks not only his or her invested funds but those of associates and shareholders as well.

factors of production
Economic resources: land, labour, capital, and entrepreneurial ability.

Because land, labour, capital, and entrepreneurial ability are combined to produce goods and services, they are called the **factors of production,** or simply "inputs."

QUICK REVIEW

▶ Because wants exceed incomes, individuals face an economic problem: they must decide what to buy and what to forgo.

▶ A budget line (budget constraint) shows the various combinations of two goods that a consumer can purchase with a specific money income.

▶ Straight-line budget constraints imply constant opportunity costs associated with obtaining more of either of the two goods.

▶ Economists categorize economic resources as land, labour, capital, and entrepreneurial ability.

1.6 | Production Possibilities Model and Increasing Opportunity Costs

Society uses its scarce resources to produce goods and services. The alternatives and choices it faces can best be understood through a macroeconomic model of production possibilities. To keep things simple, let's initially assume:

- *Full Employment* The economy is employing all its available resources.

- *Fixed Resources* The quantity and quality of the factors of production are fixed.

- *Fixed Technology* The state of technology (the methods used to produce output) is constant.

consumer goods
Products and services that satisfy human wants directly.

capital goods
Goods that do not directly satisfy human wants.

- *Two Goods* The economy is producing only two goods: pizzas and industrial robots. Pizzas symbolize **consumer goods,** products that satisfy our wants directly; industrial robots (for example, the kind used to weld automobile frames) symbolize **capital goods,** products that satisfy our wants indirectly by making possible more efficient production of consumer goods.

TABLE 1-1	Production Possibilities of Pizzas and Robots with Full Employment and Productive Efficiency				
	PRODUCTION ALTERNATIVES				
Type of Product	**A**	**B**	**C**	**D**	**E**
Pizzas (in hundred thousands)	0	1	2	3	4
Robots (in thousands)	10	9	7	4	0

Production Possibilities Table

A production possibilities table lists the different combinations of two products that can be produced with a specific set of resources, assuming full employment. Table 1-1 contains such a simple economy that is producing pizzas and industrial robots; the data are, of course, hypothetical. At alternative A, this economy would be devoting all its available resources to the production of industrial robots (capital goods); at alternative E, all resources would go to pizza production (consumer goods). Those alternatives are unrealistic extremes; an economy typically produces both capital goods and consumer goods, as in B, C, and D. As we move from alternative A to E, we increase the production of pizzas at the expense of the production of industrial robots.

Because consumer goods satisfy our wants directly, any movement toward E looks tempting. In producing more pizzas, society increases the current satisfaction of its wants. But there is a cost: More pizzas mean fewer industrial robots. This shift of resources to consumer goods catches up with society over time because the stock of capital goods does not expand, with the result that some potential for greater future production is lost. By moving toward alternative E, society chooses "more now" at the expense of "much later."

By moving toward A, society chooses to forgo current consumption, thereby freeing up resources that can be used to increase the production of capital goods. By building up its stock of capital this way, society will have greater future production and, therefore, greater future consumption. By moving toward A, society is choosing "more later" at the cost of "less now."

Generalization: At any point in time, a fully employed economy must sacrifice some of one good to obtain more of another good. Scarce resources prohibit such an economy from having more of both goods. Society must choose among alternatives. There is no such thing as a free pizza, or a free industrial robot. Having more of one thing means having less of something else. For example, if Canadians want more spending on health care, they will have to be satisfied with less spending on education.

Production Possibilities Curve

production possibilities curve
A curve showing the different combinations of goods or services that can be produced in a full-employment, full-production economy where the available supplies of resources and technology are fixed.

The data presented in a production possibilities table are shown graphically as a **production possibilities curve.** Such a curve displays the different combinations of goods and services that society can produce in a fully employed economy, assuming a fixed availability of supplies of resources and constant technology. We arbitrarily represent the economy's output of capital goods (here, industrial robots) on the vertical axis and the output of consumer goods (here, pizzas) on the horizontal axis, as shown in **Figure 1-2 (Key Graph).**

Each point on the production possibilities curve represents some maximum output of the two products. The curve is a "constraint" because it shows the limit of attainable outputs. Points on the curve are attainable as long as the economy uses all its available resources. Points lying inside the curve are also attainable, but they reflect less total output and therefore are not as desirable as points on the curve. Points inside the curve imply that the economy could have more of both industrial robots and pizzas if it achieved full employment. Points lying beyond the production possibilities curve, like W, would represent a greater output than the output at any point on the curve. Such points, however, are unattainable with the current availability of resources and technology.

KEY GRAPH

FIGURE 1-2 The Production Possibilities Curve

Each point on the production possibilities curve represents some maximum combination of two products that can be produced if full employment and full production are achieved. When operating on the curve, more robots means fewer pizzas, and vice versa. Limited resources and a fixed technology make any combination of robots and pizzas lying outside the curve (such as at W) unattainable. Points inside the curve are attainable, but they indicate that full employment and productive efficiency are not being realized.

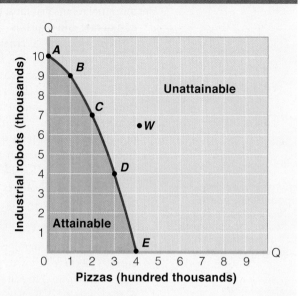

PRODUCTION ALTERNATIVES

Type of Product	A	B	C	D	E
Pizzas (in hundred thousands)	0	1	2	3	4
Robots (in thousands)	10	9	7	4	0

Quick Quiz

1. **Production possibilities curve *ABCDE* is bowed out from the origin because:**
   a. the marginal benefit of pizzas declines as more pizzas are consumed.
   b. the curve gets steeper as we move from *E* to *A*.
   c. it reflects the law of increasing opportunity costs.
   d. resources are scarce.

2. **The marginal opportunity cost of the second unit of pizzas is:**
   a. 2 units of robots.
   b. 3 units of robots.
   c. 7 units of robots.
   d. 9 units of robots.

3. **The total opportunity cost of 7 units of robots is:**
   a. 1 unit of pizzas.
   b. 2 units of pizzas.
   c. 3 units of pizzas.
   d. 4 units of pizzas.

4. **All points on this production possibilities curve necessarily represent:**
   a. society's optimal choice.
   b. less than full use of resources.
   c. unattainable levels of output.
   d. full employment.

Answers: 1. c; 2. a; 3. b; 4. d

Law of Increasing Opportunity Costs

Figure 1-2 clearly shows that more pizzas mean fewer industrial robots. The number of units of industrial robots that must be given up to obtain another unit of pizzas, of course, is the opportunity cost of that unit of pizzas.

In moving from alternative A to alternative B in Table 1-1, the cost of 1 additional unit of pizzas is 1 less unit of industrial robots. But when additional units are considered—B to C, C to D, and D to E—an important economic principle is revealed: For society, the opportunity cost of each additional unit of pizzas is greater than the opportunity cost of the preceding one. When we move from A to B, just 1 unit of industrial robots is sacrificed for 1 more unit of pizzas; but in going from B to C we sacrifice 2 additional units of industrial robots for 1 more unit of pizzas; then 3 more of industrial robots for 1 more of pizzas; and finally 4 for 1. Conversely, confirm that as we move from E to A, the cost of an additional unit of industrial robots (on average) is ¼, ⅓, ½, and 1 unit of pizzas, respectively, for the four successive moves.

Our example illustrates the **law of increasing opportunity costs.** As the production of a particular good increases, the opportunity cost of producing an additional unit rises.

SHAPE OF THE CURVE

The law of increasing opportunity costs is reflected in the shape of the production possibilities curve: The curve is bowed out from the origin of the graph. Figure 1-2 shows that when the economy moves from *A* to *E*, it must give up successively larger amounts of industrial robots (1, 2, 3, and 4) to acquire equal increments of pizzas (1, 1, 1, and 1). This is shown in the slope of the production possibilities curve, which becomes steeper as we move from *A* to *E*.

ECONOMIC EXPLANATION

The economic explanation for the law of increasing opportunity costs is that *economic resources are not completely adaptable to alternative uses.* Many resources are better at producing one type of good than at producing others. Some land is highly suited to growing the ingredients necessary for pizza production, but as pizza production expands society has to start using land that is less bountiful for farming. Other land is rich in mineral deposits and therefore well-suited to producing the materials needed to make industrial robots. As society steps up the production of robots, it must use land that is less and less adaptable to making their components.

If we start at *A* and move to *B* in Figure 1-2, we can shift resources whose productivity is relatively high in pizza production and low in industrial robots. But as we move from *B* to *C*, *C* to *D*, and so on, resources highly productive of pizzas become increasingly scarce. To get more pizzas, resources whose productivity in industrial robots is relatively great will be needed. It will take increasingly more of such resources, and hence greater sacrifices of industrial robots, to achieve each 1-unit increase in pizzas. This lack of perfect flexibility, or interchangeability, on the part of resources is the cause of increasing opportunity costs for society. *(Key Question 10)*

Optimal Allocation

Of all the attainable combinations of pizzas and industrial robots on the curve in Figure 1-2, which is optimal (best)? That is, what specific quantities of resources should be allocated to pizzas and what specific quantities to industrial robots in order to maximize satisfaction?

Recall that economic decisions centre on comparisons of marginal benefit (MB) and marginal cost (MC). Any economic activity should be expanded as long as marginal benefit exceeds marginal cost and should be reduced if marginal cost exceeds marginal benefit. The optimal amount of the activity occurs where MB = MC. Society needs to make a similar assessment about its production decision.

Consider pizzas. We already know from the law of increasing opportunity costs that the marginal costs of additional units of pizzas will rise as more units are produced. At the same time, we need to recognize that the extra or marginal benefits that come from producing and consuming pizza decline with each successive unit of pizza. Consequently, each successive unit of pizza brings with it both increasing marginal costs and decreasing marginal benefits.

law of increasing opportunity costs
As the production of a good increases, the opportunity cost of producing an additional unit rises.

WORKED PROBLEM 1.2
Production Possibilities

FIGURE 1-3   Optimal Allocation: MB = MC

Optimal allocation requires the expansion of a good's output until its marginal benefit (MB) and marginal cost (MC) are equal. No resources beyond that point should get allocated to the product. Here, allocative efficiency occurs when 200,000 pizzas are produced.

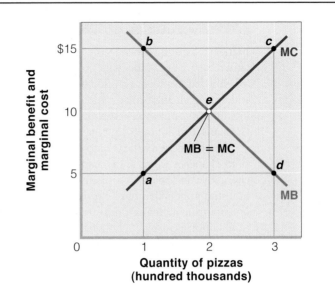

The optimal quantity of pizza production is indicated by point *e* at the intersection of the MB and MC curves: 200,000 units in Figure 1-3. Why is this amount the optimal quantity? If only 100,000 units of pizzas were produced, the marginal benefit of an extra unit of them (point *a*) would exceed its marginal cost (point *b*). In money terms, MB is $15, while MC is only $5. When society gains something worth $15 at a marginal cost of only $5, it is better off. In Figure 1-3, net gains can continue to be realized until pizza-product production has been increased to 200,000.

In contrast, the production of 300,000 units of pizzas is excessive. There the MC of an added unit is $15 (point *c*) and its MB is only $5 (point *d*). This means that 1 unit of pizzas is worth only $5 to society but costs it $15 to obtain. This is a losing proposition for society!

So resources are being efficiently allocated to any product when the marginal benefit and marginal cost of its output are equal (MB = MC). Suppose that by applying the above analysis to industrial robots, we find its optimal (MB = MC) output is 7000. This would mean that alternative *C* (200,000 units of pizzas and 7000 units of industrial robots) on the production possibilities curve in Figure 1-2 would be optimal for this economy. *(Key Question 11)*

QUICK REVIEW

▶ The production possibilities curve illustrates (a) scarcity of resources, implied by the area of unattainable combinations of output lying outside the production possibilities curve; (b) choice among outputs, reflected in the variety of attainable combinations of goods lying along the curve; (c) opportunity cost, illustrated by the downward slope of the curve; and (d) the law of increasing opportunity costs, implied by the bowed-outward shape of the curve.

▶ A comparison of marginal benefits and marginal costs is needed to determine the best or optimal output mix on a production possibilities curve.

1.7 | Economic Growth, Present Choices, and Future Possibilities

In the depths of the Great Depression of the 1930s, almost 20 percent of workers were unemployed and one-quarter of Canadian production capacity was idle. Canada has suffered a number of considerably milder downturns since then, one occurring in 1991. Almost all nations have experienced widespread unemployment and unused production capacity from business downturns at one time or another. Since 1995, for example, several nations—including Argentina, Japan, Mexico, Germany, and South Korea—have had economic downturns and unemployment.

How do these realities relate to the production possibilities model? Our analysis and conclusions change if we relax the assumption that all available resources are fully employed. The five alternatives in Table 1-1 represent maximum outputs; they illustrate the combinations of pizzas and industrial robots that can be produced when the economy is operating at full employment. With unemployment, this economy would produce less than each alternative shown in the table.

Graphically, we represent situations of unemployment by points inside the original production possibilities curve (reproduced here in Figure 1-4). Point *U* is one such point. Here the economy is falling short of the various maximum combinations of pizzas and industrial robots represented by the points on the production possibilities curve. The arrows in Figure 1-4 indicate three possible paths back to full employment. A move toward full employment would yield a greater output of one or both products.

A Growing Economy

When we drop the assumptions that the quantity and quality of resources and technology are fixed, the production possibilities curve shifts position and the potential maximum output of the economy changes.

INCREASES IN FACTOR SUPPLIES

Although factor supplies are fixed at any specific moment, they change over time via more education and training. Historically, the economy's stock of capital has increased at a significant, though

Unemployment, Productive Inefficiency, and the Production Possibilities Curve

FIGURE 1-4

Any point inside the production possibilities curve, such as U, represents unemployment or a failure to achieve productive efficiency. The arrows indicate that, by realizing full employment and productive efficiency, the economy could operate on the curve. This means it could produce more of one or both products than it is producing at point U.

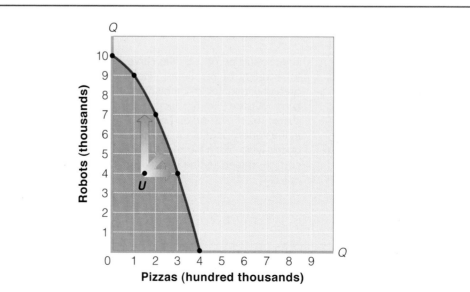

unsteady, rate. And although some of our energy and mineral resources are being depleted, new sources are also being discovered. The development of irrigation programs, for example, adds to the supply of arable land.

The net result of these increased supplies of the factors of production is the ability to produce more of both consumer goods and capital goods. Thus, 20 years from now the production possibilities may supersede those shown in Table 1-1. The new production possibilities might look like those in the table in Figure 1-5. The greater abundance of resources will result in a greater potential output of one or both products at each alternative. The economy will have achieved economic growth in the form of expanded potential output. Thus, when an increase in the quantity or quality of resources occurs, the production possibilities curve shifts outward and to the right, as illustrated by the move from the inner curve to curve A′B′C′D′E′ in Figure 1-5. This sort of shift represents growth of economic capacity, which when used means **economic growth:** a larger total output.

economic growth
An outward shift in the production possibilities curve that results from an increase in factor supplies or quality or an improvement in technology

ADVANCES IN TECHNOLOGY

An advancing technology brings both new and better goods and improved ways of producing them. For now, let's think of technological advance as being only improvements in the methods of production; for example, the introduction of computerized systems to manage inventories and schedule production. These advances alter our previous discussion of the economizing problem by allowing society to produce more goods with available resources. As with increases in resource supplies, technological advances make possible the production of more industrial robots and more pizzas.

A real-world example of improved technology is the recent surge of new technologies relating to computers, communications, and biotechnology. Technological advances have dropped the prices of computers and greatly increased their speed. Improved software has greatly increased the everyday usefulness of computers. Cellular phones and the Internet have increased communications capacity, enhancing production and improving the efficiency of markets. Advances in biotechnology have

---

FIGURE 1-5   ## Economic Growth and the Production Possibilities Curve

The increase in supplies of resources, the improvements in resource quality, and the technological advances that occur in a dynamic economy move the production possibilities curve outward and to the right, allowing the economy to have larger quantities of both types of goods.

PRODUCTION ALTERNATIVES					
Type of Product	**A′**	**B′**	**C′**	**D′**	**E′**
Pizzas (in hundred thousands)	0	2	4	6	8
Robots (in thousands)	14	12	9	5	0

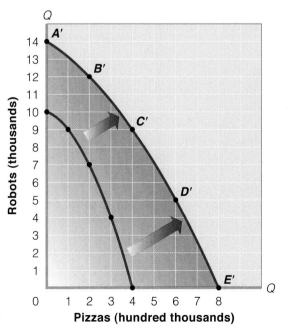

resulted in important agricultural and medical discoveries. These and other new and improved technologies have contributed to both global and Canadian economic growth (outward shifts of the nation's production possibilities curve).

Conclusion: Economic growth is the result of (1) increases in supplies of factors of production, (2) improvements in factor quality, and (3) technological advances. The consequence of growth is that a full-employment economy can enjoy a greater output of both consumption goods and capital goods. While static, no-growth economies must sacrifice some of one good to obtain more of another, dynamic, growing economies can have larger quantities of both goods. *(Key Question 13)*

Present Choices and Future Possibilities

An economy's current choice of positions on its production possibilities curve helps determine the future location of that curve. Let's designate the two axes of the production possibilities curve as "goods for the future" and "goods for the present," as in Figure 1-6. Goods for the future are such things as capital goods, research and education, and preventive medicine. They increase the quantity and quality of property resources, enlarge the stock of technological information, and improve the quality of human resources. As we have already seen, goods for the future, such as capital goods, are the ingredients of economic growth. Goods for the present are consumer goods, such as food, clothing, and entertainment.

Now suppose there are two hypothetical economies, Presentville and Futureville, which are initially identical in every respect except one: Presentville's current choice of positions on its production possibilities curve strongly favours present goods over future goods. Point *P* in Figure 1-6a indicates that choice. It is located quite far down the curve to the right, indicating a high priority for goods for the present, at the expense of fewer goods for the future. Futureville, in contrast, makes a current choice that stresses larger amounts of future goods and smaller amounts of present goods, as shown by point *F* in Figure 1-6b.

Now, other things equal, we can expect the future production possibilities curve of Futureville to be farther to the right than Presentville's curve. By currently choosing an output more favourable to technological advances and to increases in the quantity and quality of resources, Futureville will achieve greater economic growth than Presentville. In terms of capital goods, Futureville is choosing to make larger current additions to its "national factory" by devoting more of its current output to capital than Presentville. The payoff from this choice for Futureville is greater future production capacity and economic growth. The opportunity cost is fewer consumer goods in the present for Futureville to enjoy.

Is Futureville's choice thus necessarily "better" than Presentville's? That, we cannot say. The different outcomes simply reflect different preferences and priorities in the two countries. But each country will have to live with the economic consequences of its choice. *(Key Question 14)*

CONSIDER THIS | Women, the Workforce, and Production Possibilities

We have seen that more factors of production and better-quality factors and improved technology shift a nation's production possibilities curve outward. An example of more resources is the large increase in the number of employed women in Canada in the past 40 years. Sixty percent of adult Canadian women work full-time or part-time in paid jobs today, compared to only 40 percent in 1965.

Over recent decades, women have greatly increased their productivity in the workplace, mostly by becoming better educated and professionally trained. As a result, they can earn higher wages. Because those higher wages have increased the opportunity cost—the forgone wage earnings—of staying at home, women have substituted employment in the labour market for the now more "expensive" traditional home activities. This substitution has been particularly pronounced among married women. Along with other factors such as changing attitudes and expanded job access, the rising earnings of women have produced a substantial increase in the number of women workers in Canada. This increase in the quantity of available resources has helped push the Canadian production possibilities curve outward.

 **KEY GRAPH** @

FIGURE 1-6 Present Choices and Future Locations of a Production Possibilities Curve

A nation's current choice favouring "present goods," as made by Presentville in (a), will cause a modest outward shift of the curve in the future. A nation's current choice favouring "future goods," as made by Futureville in (b), will result in a greater outward shift of the curve in the future.

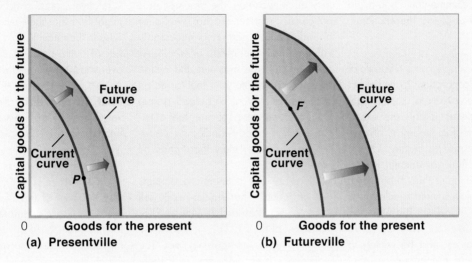

A Qualification: International Trade

Production possibilities analysis implies that an individual nation is limited to the combinations of output indicated by its production possibilities curve. But we must modify this principle when international specialization and trade exist.

You will see in later chapters that an economy can circumvent, through international specialization and trade, the output limits imposed by its domestic production possibilities curve. *International specialization* means directing domestic resources to output that a nation is highly efficient at producing. *International trade* involves the exchange of these goods for goods produced abroad. Specialization and trade enable a nation to get more of a desired good at less sacrifice of some other good. Rather than sacrifice three units of robots to get a third unit of pizza, as in Table 1-1, a nation might be able to obtain the third unit of pizza by trading only two units of robots for it. Specialization and trade have the same effect as having more and better resources or discovering improved production techniques; both increase the quantities of capital and consumer goods available to society. Expansion of domestic production possibilities and international trade are two separate routes for obtaining greater output.

 **QUICK REVIEW**

▶ Unemployment causes an economy to operate at a point inside its production possibilities curve.

▶ Increases in resource supplies, improvements in resource quality, and technological advances cause economic growth, which is depicted as an outward shift of the production possibilities curve.

▶ An economy's present choice of capital and consumer goods helps determine the future location of its production possibilities curve.

▶ International specialization and trade enable a nation to obtain more goods than its production possibilities curve indicates.

The **LAST WORD**   Pitfalls to Sound Economic Reasoning

Because they affect us so personally, we often have difficulty thinking accurately and objectively about economic issues.

Here are some common pitfalls to avoid in successfully applying the economic perspective.

Biases Most people bring a bundle of biases and preconceptions to the field of economics. For example, some might think that corporate profits are excessive or that lending money is always superior to borrowing money. Others might believe that government is necessarily less efficient than businesses, or that more government regulation is always better than less. Biases cloud thinking and interfere with objective analysis. All of us must be willing to shed biases and preconceptions that are not supported by facts.

Loaded Terminology The economic terminology used in newspapers and broadcast media is sometimes emotionally biased, or loaded. The writer or spokesperson may have a cause to promote or an axe to grind and may slant comments accordingly. High profits may be labelled "obscene," low wages may be called "exploitive," or self-interested behaviour may be identified as "greed." Government workers may be referred to as "mindless bureaucrats" and those favouring stronger government regulations may be called "socialists." To objectively analyze economic issues, you must be prepared to reject or discount such terminology.

Fallacy of Composition Another pitfall in economic thinking is the assumption that what is true for one individual or part of a whole is necessarily true for a group of individuals or the whole. This is a logical fallacy called the *fal-*

lacy of composition; the assumption is not correct. A statement that is valid for an individual or part is not necessarily valid for the larger group or whole. As an example, you may see the action better if you leap to your feet to see an outstanding play at a football game. But if everyone leaps to their feet at the same time, nobody—including you—will have a better view than when all remained seated.

Here are two economic examples: An individual shareholder can sell shares of, say, Research In Motion (RIM, the maker of the BlackBerry) stock without affecting the price of the stock. The individual's sale will not noticeably reduce the share price because the sale is a negligible fraction of the total shares of RIM being bought and sold. But if all the RIM shareholders decide to sell their shares on the same day, the market will be flooded with shares and the stock price will fall precipitously. Similarly, a single cattle ranch can increase its revenue by expanding the size of its livestock herd. The extra cattle will not affect the price of cattle when they are brought to market. But if all ranchers as a group expand their herds, the total output of cattle will increase so much that the price of cattle will decline when the cattle are sold. If the price reduction

is relatively large, ranchers as a group might find that their income has fallen despite their having sold a greater number of cattle because the fall in price overwhelms the increase in quantity.

Post Hoc Fallacy You must think very carefully before concluding that because event A precedes event B, A is the cause of B. This kind of faulty reasoning is known as the *post hoc, ergo propter hoc*, or "after this, therefore because of this" fallacy. To give a noneconomic example: The Calgary Flames team hires a new coach and the team's record improves. Is the new coach the cause? Maybe. Perhaps the presence of more experienced and talented players or an easier schedule is the true cause. Another example is that the rooster crows before dawn, but does not cause the sunrise.

Correlation But Not Causation Do not confuse correlation, or connection, with causation. Correlation between two events or two sets of data indicates only that they are associated in some systematic and dependable way. For example, we may find that when variable X increases, Y also increases. But this correlation does not necessarily mean that there is causation—that increases in X cause increases in Y. The relationship could be purely coincidental or dependent on some other factor, Z, not included in the analysis.

Here is an example: Economists have found a positive correlation between education and income. In general, people with more education earn higher incomes than those with less education.

Common sense suggests education is the cause and higher incomes are the effect; more education implies a more knowledgeable and productive worker, and such workers receive larger salaries.

But causation could also partly run the other way. People with higher incomes could buy more education, just as they buy more furniture and steaks. Or is part of the relationship explainable in still other ways? Are education and income correlated because the characteristics required for succeeding in education—ability and motivation—are the same ones required to be a productive and highly paid worker? If so, then people with those traits will probably both obtain more education and earn higher incomes. But greater education will not be the sole cause of the higher income.

Question

Studies indicate that married men on average earn more income than unmarried men of the same age and education level. Why must we be cautious in concluding that marriage is the cause and higher income is the effect?

CHAPTER SUMMARY

1.1 ▶ TEN KEY CONCEPTS TO RETAIN FOR A LIFETIME

- There are 10 key concepts to remember: four deal with the individual, three with the interaction among individuals, and three with the economy as a whole.

1.2 ▶ THE ECONOMIC WAY OF THINKING

- Economics is the social science that examines how individuals, institutions, and society make choices under conditions of scarcity. Central to economics is the idea of opportunity cost: the value of the good, service, or time forgone to obtain something else.

- The economic perspective includes three elements: scarcity and choice, purposeful behaviour, and marginal analysis. It sees individuals and institutions making rational decisions based on comparisons of marginal benefits and marginal costs.

1.3 ▶ THEORIES, PRINCIPLES, AND MODELS

- Economists employ the scientific method, in which they form and test hypotheses of cause-and-effect relationships to generate theories, principles, and laws. Economists often combine principles and laws into representations called models.

1.4 ▶ MICROECONOMICS AND MACROECONOMICS

- Microeconomics examines specific economic units or institutions. Macroeconomics looks at the economy as a whole or its major aggregates.

- Positive economics deals with facts; normative economics reflects value judgments.

1.5 ▶ THE ECONOMIC PROBLEM

- Individuals face an economic problem. Because their wants exceed their incomes, they must decide what to purchase and what to forgo. Society also faces the economic problem. Societal wants exceed the available resources necessary to fulfill them. Society therefore must decide what to produce and what to forgo.

- Graphically, a budget line (or budget constraint) illustrates the economic problem for individuals. The line shows the various combinations of two products that a consumer can purchase with a specific money income, given the prices of the two products.

- Economic resources are inputs into the production process and can be classified as land, labour, capital, and entrepreneurial ability. Economic resources are also known as factors of production or inputs.

1.6 ▶ PRODUCTION POSSIBILITIES MODEL AND INCREASING OPPORTUNITY COSTS

- Economists illustrate society's economic problem through production possibilities analysis. Production possibilities tables and curves show the different combinations of goods and services that can be produced in a fully employed economy, assuming that resource quantity, resource quality, and technology are fixed.

- An economy that is fully employed and thus operating on its production possibilities curve must sacrifice the output of some types of goods and services to increase the production of others. The gain of one type of good or service is always accompanied by an opportunity cost in the form of the loss of some of the other type.

www.mcgrawhillconnect.ca

- Because resources are not equally productive in all possible uses, shifting resources from one use to another creates increasing opportunity costs. The production of additional units of one product requires the sacrifice of increasing amounts of the other product.

- The optimal (best) point on the production possibilities curve represents the most desirable mix of goods and is determined by expanding the production of each good until its marginal benefit (MB) equals its marginal cost (MC).

1.7 ▶ ECONOMIC GROWTH, PRESENT CHOICES, AND FUTURE POSSIBILITIES

- Over time, technological advances and increases in the quantity and quality of resources enable the economy to produce more of all goods and services; that is, to experience economic growth. Society's choice as to the mix of consumer goods and capital goods in current output is a major determinant of the future location of the production possibilities curve and thus of the extent of economic growth. International trade enables nations to obtain more goods from their limited resources than their production possibilities curve indicates.

TERMS AND CONCEPTS

economics, p. 2
economic perspective, p. 3
opportunity cost, p. 3
utility, p. 4
marginal analysis, p. 4
scientific method, p. 5
economic principle, p. 5
other-things-equal assumption, p. 5
microeconomics, p. 6

macroeconomics, p. 6
aggregate, p. 6
positive economics, p. 6
normative economics, p. 6
economic problem, p. 7
budget line, p. 8
economic resources, p. 10
land, p. 10
labour, p. 10

capital, p. 10
investment, p. 11
entrepreneurial ability, p. 11
factors of production, p. 11
consumer goods, p. 11
capital goods, p. 11
production possibilities curve, p. 12
law of increasing opportunity costs, p. 14
economic growth, p. 17

STUDY QUESTIONS

LO ▶ 1.2 1. What is an opportunity cost? How does the idea relate to the definition of economics? Which of the following decisions would entail the greater opportunity cost: allocating a square block in the heart of Toronto for a surface parking lot or allocating a square block at the edge of a typical suburb for such a lot? Explain.

LO ▶ 1.2 2. What is meant by the term "utility" and how does the idea relate to purposeful behaviour?

LO ▶ 1.2 3. **KEY QUESTION** Cite three examples of recent decisions that you made in which you, at least implicitly, weighed marginal cost and marginal benefit.

LO ▶ 1.3 4. What are the key elements of the scientific method and how does this method relate to economic principles and laws?

LO ▶ 1.4 5. **KEY QUESTION** Indicate whether each of the following statements applies to microeconomics or macroeconomics:

a. The unemployment rate in Canada was 8 percent in March 2009.

b. A Canadian software firm discharged 15 workers last month and transferred the work to India.

c. An unexpected freeze in central Florida reduced the citrus crop and caused the price of oranges to rise.

d. Canadian output, adjusted for inflation, grew by 0.4 percent in 2008.

e. Last week Scotiabank lowered its interest rate on business loans by one-half of 1 percentage point.

f. The Consumer Price Index rose by 2.3 percent in 2008.

6. State (a) a positive economic statement of your choice, and then (b) a normative economic statement relating to your first statement. **LO ▶ 1.4**

7. **KEY QUESTION** Suppose you won $15 on a Lotto Canada ticket at the local 7-Eleven and decided to spend all the winnings on candy bars and bags of peanuts. The price of candy bars is $0.75 and the price of peanuts is $1.50. **LO ▶ 1.5**

a. Construct a table showing the alternative combinations of the two products that are available.

b. Plot the data in your table as a budget line in a graph. What is the slope of the budget line? What is the opportunity cost of one more candy bar? Of one more bag of peanuts? Do these opportunity costs rise, fall, or remain constant as each additional unit of the product is purchased?

c. How, in general, would you decide which of the available combinations of candy bars and bags of peanuts to buy?

d. Suppose that you had won $30 on your ticket, not $15. Show the $30 budget line in your diagram. Why would this budget line be preferable to the old one?

LO ▶ 1.5 8. What are economic resources? What categories do economists use to classify them? Why are resources also called factors of production? Why are they called inputs?

LO ▶ 1.5 9. Why is money not considered to be a capital resource in economics? Why is entrepreneurial ability considered a category of economic resource, distinct from labour? What are the major functions of the entrepreneur?

LO ▶ 1.6 10. **KEY QUESTION** Below is a production possibilities table for consumer goods (automobiles) and capital goods (forklifts):

PRODUCTION ALTERNATIVES

Type of production	A	B	C	D	E
Automobiles	0	2	4	6	8
Forklifts	30	27	21	12	0

a. Show these data graphically. Upon what specific assumptions is this production possibilities curve based?

b. If the economy is at point C, what is the cost of one more automobile? Of one more forklift? Explain how the production possibilities curve reflects the law of increasing opportunity costs.

c. If the economy characterized by this production possibilities table and curve were producing 3 automobiles and 20 forklifts, what could you conclude about its use of its available resources?

d. What would production at a point outside the production possibilities curve indicate? What must occur before the economy can attain such a level of production?

11. **KEY QUESTION** Specify and explain the typical shapes **LO ▶ 1.6** of marginal benefit and marginal cost curves. How are these curves used to determine the optimal allocation of resources to a particular product? If current output is such that marginal cost exceeds marginal benefit, should more or fewer resources be allocated to this product? Explain.

12. Explain how (if at all) each of the following events affects **LO ▶ .6** the location of a country's production possibilities curve:

a. The quality of education increases.

b. The number of unemployed workers increases.

c. A new technique improves the efficiency of extracting iron from ore.

d. A devastating earthquake destroys numerous production facilities.

13. **KEY QUESTION** Suppose improvement occurs in the **LO ▶ 1.6** technology of producing forklifts but not in the technology of producing automobiles. Draw the new production possibilities curve. Now assume that a technological advance occurs in producing automobiles but not in producing forklifts. Draw the new production possibilities curve. Now draw a production possibilities curve that reflects technological improvement in the production of both goods.

14. **KEY QUESTION** On average, households in China save **LO ▶ .7** 40 percent of their annual income each year, whereas households in Canada save less than 5 percent. Production possibilities are growing at roughly 9 percent annually in China and 3.5 percent in Canada. Use graphical analysis of "present goods" versus "future goods" to explain the difference in growth rates.

15. Suppose that, on the basis of a nation's production possi- **LO ▶ 1.7** bilities curve, an economy must sacrifice 10,000 pizzas domestically to get the 1 additional industrial robot it desires, but that it can get the robot from another country in exchange for 9000 pizzas. Relate this information to the following statement: "Through international specialization and trade, a nation can reduce its opportunity cost of obtaining goods and thus move outside its production possibilities curve."

INTERNET APPLICATION QUESTIONS @

1. **More Labour Resources—What Is the Evidence for Canada and France?** Use the links on the McConnell-Brue-Flynn-Barbiero Web site (Chapter 1) to compare the growth in employment in Canada and France. In which of the two countries did "more labour resources" (in percentage terms) have the greatest impact in shifting the nation's production possibilities curve outward over the 10-year period?

2. **Normative Economics—Canadian Politics.** Many economic policy statements made by the Liberal Party, the Conservative Party, and the New Democratic Party can be considered normative rather than positive economic statements. Use the links on the McConnell-Brue-Flynn-Barbiero Web site (Chapter 1) and compare and contrast their views on how to achieve economic goals. How much of the disagreement is based on positive statements and how much on normative statements? Give an example of loaded terminology from each site.

Appendix to Chapter 1

A1.1 | GRAPHS AND THEIR MEANINGS

If you glance quickly through this text, you will find many graphs. Some seem simple, others more complicated. All are included to help you visualize and understand economic relationships. Physicists and chemists sometimes illustrate their theories by building arrangements of multicoloured wooden balls, representing protons, neutrons, and electrons, which are held in proper relation to one another by wires or sticks. Economists use graphs to illustrate their models. By understanding these "pictures," you can more readily make sense of economic relationships. Most of our principles or models explain relationships between just two sets of economic facts, which can be conveniently represented with two-dimensional graphs.

Construction of a Graph

A *graph* is a visual representation of the relationship between two variables. Figure A1-1 is a hypothetical illustration showing the relationship between income and consumption for the economy as a whole. Without even studying economics, we would logically expect that people would buy more goods and services when their incomes go up. Thus it is not surprising to find in Figure A1-1 that total consumption in the economy increases as total income increases.

The information in Figure A1-1 is expressed both graphically and in table form. Here is how it is done: We want to show graphically how consumption changes as income changes. We therefore represent income on the **horizontal axis** of the graph and consumption on the **vertical axis**.

Now we arrange the vertical and horizontal scales of the graph to reflect the ranges of values of consumption and income, and mark the scales in convenient increments. As you can see in Figure A1-1, the values marked on the scales cover all the values in the table. The increments on both scales are $100 for approximately each centimetre.

Because the graph has two dimensions, each point within it represents an income value and its associated consumption value. To find a point that represents one of the five income–consumption combinations in the table, we draw straight lines from the appropriate values on the vertical and horizontal axes. For example, to plot point *c* (the $200 income, $150 consumption), straight lines are drawn up from the horizontal (income) axis at $200 and across from the vertical (consumption) axis at $150. These straight lines intersect at point *c*, which represents this particular income–consumption combination. You should verify that the other income–consumption combinations shown in the table are properly located in the graph. Finally, by assuming

FIGURE A1-1 | The Relationship between Income and Consumption

Two sets of data that are positively or directly related, such as consumption and income, graph as an upsloping line.

Income per week	Consumption per week	Point
$ 0	$ 50	a
100	100	b
200	150	c
300	200	d
400	250	e

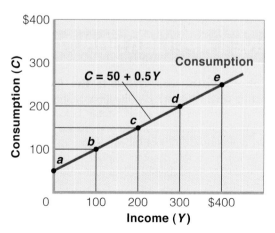

that the same general relationship between income and consumption prevails for all other incomes, we draw a line or smooth curve to connect these points. That line or curve represents the income–consumption relationship.

If the curve is a straight line, as in Figure A1-1, we say the relationship is *linear*. (It is permissible, and even customary, to call straight lines in graphs "curves.")

Direct and Inverse Relationships

The line in Figure A1-1 slopes upward to the right, depicting a direct relationship between income and consumption. By a **direct relationship** (or positive relationship) we mean that two variables—in this case, consumption and income—change in the *same* direction. An increase in consumption is associated with an increase in income; a decrease in consumption accompanies a decrease in income. When two sets of data are positively or directly related, they always graph as an *upward-sloping* line, as in Figure A1-1.

In contrast, two sets of data may be inversely related. Consider Figure A1-2, which shows the relationship between the price of basketball tickets and game attendance at Informed University (IU). Here we have an **inverse relationship** (or negative relationship) because the two variables change in *opposite* directions. When ticket prices decrease, attendance increases. When ticket prices increase, attendance decreases. The six data points in the table are plotted in the graph. Observe that an inverse relationship always graphs as a *downward-sloping* line.

Dependent and Independent Variables

Although it is not always easy, economists seek to determine which variable is the "cause" and which is the "effect." Or, more formally, they seek the independent variable and the dependent variable. The **independent variable** is the cause or source; it is the variable that changes first. The **dependent variable** is the effect or outcome; it is the variable that changes because of the change in the independent variable. As in our income–consumption example, income generally is the independent variable and consumption the dependent variable. Income causes consumption to be what it is rather than the other way around. Similarly, ticket prices (set in advance of the season and printed on the ticket) determine attendance at Informed University basketball games; attendance at games does not determine the printed ticket prices for those games. Ticket price is the independent variable, and the quantity of tickets purchased is the dependent variable.

You may recall from your high school courses that mathematicians put the independent variable (cause) on the horizontal axis and the dependent variable (effect) on the vertical axis. Economists are less tidy; their graphing of independent and dependent variables is more arbitrary. Their conventional graphing of the income–consumption relationship is consistent with mathematical presentation, but economists put price and cost data on the vertical axis. Hence, economists' graphing of IU's ticket price–attendance data differs from the normal mathematical procedure. This does not present a problem, but we want you to be aware of this fact to avoid possible confusion.

FIGURE A1-2   ## The Relationship between Ticket Prices and Attendance

Two sets of data that are negatively or inversely related, such as ticket price and the attendance at basketball games, graph as a downward-sloping line.

Ticket price	Attendance, thousands	Point
$ 50	0	a
40	4	b
30	8	c
20	12	d
10	16	e
0	20	f

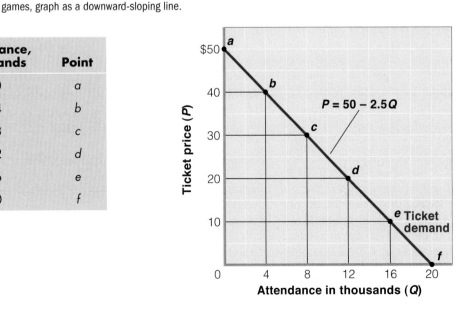

Other Things Equal

Our simple two-variable graphs purposely ignore many other factors that might affect the amount of consumption occurring at each income level or the number of people who attend IU basketball games at each possible ticket price. When economists plot the relationship between any two variables, they employ the *ceteris paribus* (other-things-equal) assumption. Thus, in Figure A1-1 all factors other than income that might affect the amount of consumption are held constant. Similarly, in Figure A1-2 all factors other than ticket price that might influence attendance at IU basketball games are assumed constant. In reality, "other things" are not equal; they often change and when they do, the relationship represented in our two tables and graphs will change. Specifically, the lines we have plotted will shift to new locations.

Consider a stock market "crash." The dramatic drop in the value of stocks might cause people to feel less wealthy and therefore less willing to consume at each level of income. The result might be a downward shift of the consumption line. To see this, you should plot a new consumption line in Figure A1-1, assuming that consumption is, say, $20 less at each income level. Note that the relationship remains direct; the line merely shifts downward to reflect less consumption spending at each income level.

Similarly, factors other than ticket prices might affect IU game attendance. If IU loses most of its games, attendance at IU games might fall at each ticket price. To see this, redraw the graph in Figure A1-2, assuming that 2000 fewer fans attend IU games at each ticket price. *(Key Appendix Question 2)*

Slope of a Line

Lines can be described in terms of their slopes and their intercepts. The **slope of a straight line** is the ratio of the vertical change (the rise or drop) to the horizontal change (the run) between any two points of the line, or "rise" over "run."

POSITIVE SLOPE

Between point *c* and point *d* in Figure A1-1 the rise or vertical change (the change in consumption) is +$50 and the run or horizontal change (the change in income) is +$100. Therefore

$$\text{Slope} = \frac{\text{vertical change}}{\text{horizontal change}} = \frac{+50}{+100} = \frac{1}{2} = 0.5$$

Note that our slope of ½ or 0.5 is positive because consumption and income change in the same direction; that is, consumption and income are directly or positively related.

The slope of 0.5 tells us there will be a $1 increase in consumption for every $2 increase in income. Similarly, it indicates that for every $2 decrease in income there will be a $1 decrease in consumption.

NEGATIVE SLOPE

Between any two of the identified points in Figure A1-2, say point *c* and point *d*, the vertical change is –10 (the drop) and the horizontal change is +4 (the run). Therefore

$$\text{Slope} = \frac{\text{vertical change}}{\text{horizontal change}} = \frac{-10}{+4} = -2\frac{1}{2} = -2.5$$

This slope is negative because ticket price and attendance have an inverse or negative relationship.

Note that on the horizontal axis attendance is stated in thousands of people. So the slope of –10/+4 or –2.5 means that lowering the price by $10 will increase attendance by 4000 people. This is the same as saying that a $2.50 price reduction will increase attendance by 1000 people.

SLOPES AND MEASUREMENT UNITS

The slope of a line will be affected by the choice of units for either variable. If, in our ticket-price illustration, we had chosen to measure attendance in individual people, our horizontal change would have been 4000 and the slope would have been

$$\text{Slope} = \frac{-10}{+4000} = \frac{-1}{+400} = -0.0025$$

The slope depends on the units by which variables are measured.

SLOPES AND MARGINAL ANALYSIS

Recall that economics largely deals with changes from the status quo. The concept of slope is important in economics because it reflects marginal changes—those involving one more (or one less) unit. For example, in Figure A1-1 the 0.5 slope shows that $0.50 of extra or marginal consumption is associated with each $1 change in income. In this example, people collectively will consume $0.50 of any $1 increase in their incomes and reduce their consumption by $0.50 for each $1 decline in income.

INFINITE AND ZERO SLOPES

Many variables are unrelated or independent of one another. For example, the quantity of digital cameras purchased is not related to the price of bananas. In Figure A1-3a we represent the price of bananas on the vertical axis and the quantity of digital cameras demanded on the horizontal axis. The graph of their relationship is the line parallel to the vertical axis, indicating that the same quantity of cameras is purchased no matter what the price of bananas. The slope of such a line is *infinite*.

Similarly, aggregate consumption is completely unrelated to the nation's divorce rate. In Figure A1-3b we put consumption on the vertical axis and the divorce rate on the horizontal axis. The line parallel to the horizontal axis represents this lack of relatedness. This line has a slope of *zero*.

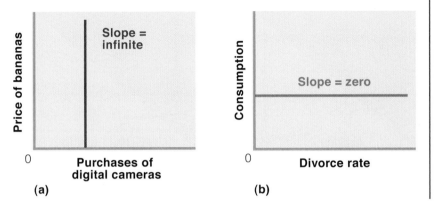

FIGURE A1-3   Infinite and Zero Slopes

(a) A line parallel to the vertical axis has an infinite slope. Here, purchases of digital cameras remain the same no matter what happens to the price of bananas.

(b) A line parallel to the horizontal axis has a slope of zero. In this case, consumption remains the same no matter what happens to the divorce rate. In both (a) and (b), the two variables are totally unrelated to one another.

(a)   **(b)**

Vertical Intercept

A line can be located on a graph (without plotting points) if we know its slope and its vertical intercept. The **vertical intercept** of a line is the point where the line meets the vertical axis. In Figure A1-1 the intercept is $50. This intercept means that if current income were zero, consumers would still spend $50. They might do this through borrowing or by selling some of their assets. Similarly, the $50 vertical intercept in Figure A1-2 shows that at a $50 ticket price, IU's basketball team would be playing in an empty arena.

Equation of a Linear Relationship

If we know the vertical intercept and slope, we can describe a line succinctly in equation form. In its general form the equation of a straight line is

$$y = a + bx$$

where y = dependent variable
a = *vertical* intercept
b = slope of line
x = independent variable

For our income–consumption example, if C represents consumption (the dependent variable) and Y represents income (the independent variable), we can write $C = a + bY$. By substituting the known values of the intercept and the slope, we get

$$C = 50 + 0.5Y$$

This equation also allows us to determine the amount of consumption C at any specific level of income. You should use it to confirm that at the $250 income level, consumption is $175.

When economists reverse mathematical convention by putting the independent variable on the vertical axis and the dependent variable on the horizontal axis, then y stands for the independent variable, rather than the dependent variable in the general form. We noted previously that this case is relevant for our IU ticket price–attendance data. If P represents the ticket price (independent variable) and Q represents attendance (dependent variable), their relationship is given by

$$P = 50 - 2.5Q$$

where the vertical intercept is 50 and the negative slope is $-2\frac{1}{2}$ or -2.5. Knowing the value of P lets us solve for Q, our dependent variable. You should use this equation to predict IU ticket sales when the ticket price is $15. (***Key Appendix Question 3***)

Slope of a Non-linear Curve

We now move from the simple world of linear relationships (straight lines) to the more complex world of non-linear relationships. The slope of a straight line is the same at all its points. The slope of a line representing a non-linear relationship changes from one point to another. Such lines are always referred to as *curves*.

Consider the downward-sloping curve in Figure A1-4. Its slope is negative throughout, but the curve flattens as we move down along it. Thus, its slope constantly changes; the curve has a different slope at each point.

To measure the slope at a specific point, we draw a straight line tangent to the curve at that point. A line is *tangent* at a point if it touches, but does not intersect, the curve at that point. Thus line aa' is tangent to the curve in Figure A1-4 at point A. The slope of the curve at that point is equal to the slope of the tangent line. Specifically, the total vertical change (drop) in the tangent line aa' is -20 and the total horizontal change (run) is $+5$. Because the slope of the tangent line aa' is $-20/+5$, or -4, the slope of the curve at point A is also -4.

Line bb' in Figure A1-4 is tangent to the curve at point B. Following the same procedure, we find the slope at B to be $-5/+15$, or $-\frac{1}{3}$. Thus, in this flatter part of the curve, the slope is less negative. (***Key Appendix Question 7***)

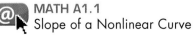

MATH A1.1
Slope of a Nonlinear Curve

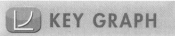 **KEY GRAPH**

FIGURE A1-4 Determining the Slopes of Curves

The slope of a non-linear curve changes from point to point on the curve. The slope at any point (say, B) can be determined by drawing a straight line that is tangent to that point (line bb') and calculating the slope of that line.

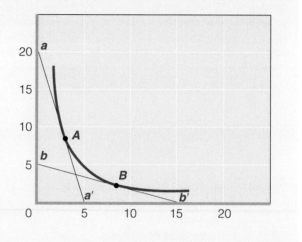

APPENDIX | SUMMARY

A1.1 GRAPHS AND THEIR MEANING

- Graphs are a convenient and revealing way to represent economic relationships.

- Two variables are positively or directly related when their values change in the same direction. The line (curve) representing two directly related variables slopes upward.

- Two variables are negatively or inversely related when their values change in opposite directions. The curve representing two inversely related variables slopes downward.

- The value of the dependent variable (the "effect") is determined by the value of the independent variable (the "cause").

- When the "other factors" that might affect a two-variable relationship are allowed to change, the graph of the relationship will likely shift to a new location.

- The slope of a straight line is the ratio of the vertical change to the horizontal change between any two points. The slope of an upward-sloping line is positive; the slope of a downward-sloping line is negative.

- The slope of a line or curve depends on the units used in measuring the variables. It is especially relevant for economics because it measures marginal changes.

- The slope of a horizontal line is zero; the slope of a vertical line is infinite.

- The vertical intercept and slope of a line determine its location; they are used in expressing the line—and the relationship between the two variables—as an equation.

- The slope of a curve at any point is determined by calculating the slope of a straight-line tangent to the curve at that point.

APPENDIX | TERMS AND CONCEPTS

horizontal axis   The "left-right" or "west-east" axis on a graph or grid. (p. 24)

vertical axis   The "up-down" or "north-south" axis on a graph or grid. (p. 24)

direct relationship   The (positive) relationship between two variables that change in the same direction, for example, product price and quantity supplied. (p. 25)

inverse relationship   The (negative) relationship between two variables that change in opposite directions, for example, product price and quantity demanded. (p. 25)

independent variable   The variable causing a change in some other (dependent) variable. (p. 25)

dependent variable   A variable that changes as a consequence of a change in some other (independent) variable; the "effect" or outcome. (p. 25)

slope of a line   The ratio of the vertical change (the rise or fall) to the horizontal change (the run) between any two points on a line. The slope of an upward sloping line is positive, reflecting a direct relationship between two variables; the slope of a downward sloping line is negative, reflecting an inverse relationship between two variables. (p. 26)

vertical intercept   The point at which a line meets the vertical axis of a graph. (p. 27)

APPENDIX | STUDY QUESTIONS

LO ▸ A1.1 1. Briefly explain the use of graphs as a way to represent economic relationships. What is an inverse relationship? How does it graph? What is a direct relationship? How does it graph? Graph and explain the relationships you would expect to find between (a) the number of centimetres of rainfall per month and the sale of umbrellas, (b) the amount of tuition and the level of enrollment at a college or university, and (c) the popularity of a music artist and the price of her concert tickets.

In each case cite and explain how variables other than those specifically mentioned might upset the expected relationship. Is your graph in part (b), above, consistent with the fact that, historically, enrollments and tuition have both increased? If not, explain any difference.

LO ▸ A1.1 2. **KEY APPENDIX QUESTION**   Indicate how each of the following might affect the data shown in Figure A1-2 of this appendix:

a. IU's athletic director schedules higher-quality opponents.

b. A National Basketball Association (NBA) team locates in the city where IU also plays.

c. IU contracts to have all its home games televised.

LO ▸ A1.1 3. **KEY APPENDIX QUESTION**   The following table contains data on the relationship between saving and income. Rearrange these data into a meaningful order and graph them on the accompanying grid. What is the slope of the line? The vertical intercept? Interpret the meaning of both the slope and the intercept. Write the equation that represents this line. What would you predict saving to be at the $12,500 level of income?

Income (per year)	Saving (per year)
$15,000	$1,000
0	−500
10,000	500
5,000	0
20,000	1,500

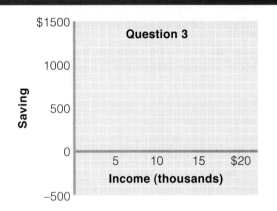

4. Construct a table from the data shown on the graph below. Which is the dependent variable and which the independent variable? Summarize the data in equation form.   **LO ▸ A1.1**

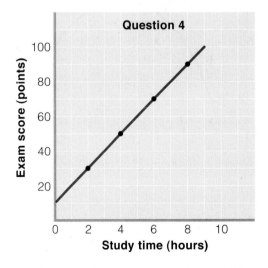

5. Suppose that when the interest rate on loans is 16 percent, **LO ▸ A1.1** businesses find it unprofitable to invest in machinery and equipment. However, when the interest rate is 14 percent, $5 billion worth of investment is profitable. At 12 percent interest, a total of $10 billion of investment is profitable. Similarly, total investment increases by $5 billion for each successive 2-percentage-point decline in the interest rate.

Describe the relevant relationship between the interest rate and investment in words, in a table, graphically, and as an equation. Put the interest rate on the vertical axis and investment on the horizontal axis. In your equation use the form $i = a - bI$, where i is the interest rate, a is the vertical intercept, $-b$ is the slope of the line (which is negative), and I is the level of investment. Comment on the advantages and disadvantages of the verbal, tabular, graphical, and equation forms of description.

LO ▸ A1.1 6. Suppose that $C = a + bY$, where C = consumption, a = consumption at zero income, b = slope, and Y = income.

    a. Are C and Y positively related or are they negatively related?

    b. If graphed, would the curve for this equation slope upward or slope downward?

    c. Are the variables C and Y inversely related or directly related?

    d. What is the value of C if $a = 10$, $b = 0.50$, and $Y = 200$?

    e. What is the value of Y if $C = 100$, $a = 10$, and $b = 0.25$?

LO ▸ A1.1 7. **KEY APPENDIX QUESTION** The accompanying graph shows curve XX′ and tangents at points A, B, and C. Calculate the slope of the curve at these three points.

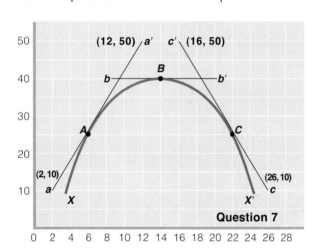

Question 7

8. In the accompanying graph, is the slope of curve AA′ positive or negative? Does the slope increase or decrease as we move along the curve from A to A′? Answer the same two questions for curve BB′. **LO ▸ A1.1**

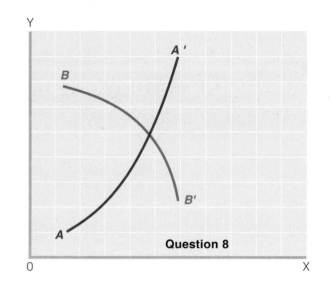

Question 8

CHAPTER 2

The Market System and the Circular Flow

You are at a mall in Halifax. Suppose you were assigned to compile a list of all the individual goods and services there, including the different brands and variations of each type of product. That task would be daunting and the list would be long! And even though a single shopping mall in Vancouver contains a remarkable quantity and variety of goods, it is only a tiny part of the Canadian economy.

Who decided that the particular goods and services available at the mall and in the broader Canadian economy should be produced? How did the producers determine which technology and types of factors to use in producing these particular goods? Who will obtain these products? What accounts for the new and improved products among these goods? This chapter will answer these and related questions.

2.1 | Economic Systems

Every society needs to develop an **economic system**—a particular set of institutional arrangements and a coordinating mechanism—to respond to the economic problem. The economic system determines what goods are produced, how they are produced, who gets them, how to accommodate change, and how to promote technological progress.

Economic systems differ as to (1) who owns the factors of production and (2) the method used to motivate, coordinate, and direct economic activity. There are two general types of economic systems: the command system and the market system.

The Command System

The **command system** is also known as *socialism* or *communism*. In that system, government owns most property resources and economic decision making occurs through a central economic plan. A central planning board appointed by the government makes nearly all the major decisions concerning the use of resources, the composition and distribution of output, and the organization of production. The government owns most of the business firms, which produce according to government directives. The central planning

economic system
A particular set of institutional arrangements and a coordinating mechanism for producing goods and services.

command system
An economic system in which most property resources are owned by the government and economic decisions are made by a central government body.

board determines production goals for each enterprise and specifies the amount of resources to be allocated to each enterprise so that it can reach its production goals. The division of output between capital and consumer goods is centrally decided, and capital goods are allocated among industries on the basis of the central planning board's long-term priorities.

A pure command economy would rely exclusively on a central plan to allocate the government-owned property resources. But, in reality, even the pre-eminent command economy—the Soviet Union—tolerated some private ownership and incorporated some markets before its collapse in 1992. Recent reforms in Russia and most of the eastern European nations have to one degree or another transformed their command economies to market-oriented systems. China's reforms have not gone as far, but they have greatly reduced the reliance on central planning. Although there is still extensive government ownership of resources and capital in China, the nation has increasingly relied on free markets to organize and coordinate its economy. North Korea and Cuba are the last remaining examples of largely centrally planned economies. Later in this chapter, we will explore the main reasons for the general demise of the command systems.

The Market System

market system
An economic system in which property resources are privately owned and markets and prices are used to direct and coordinate economic activities.

The polar alternative to the command system is the **market system,** or *capitalism.* The system is characterized by the private ownership of resources and the use of markets and prices to coordinate and direct economic activity. Participants act in their own self-interest. Individuals and businesses seek to achieve their economic goals through their own decisions regarding work, consumption, or production. The system allows for the private ownership of capital, communicates through prices, and coordinates economic activity through *markets*—places where buyers and sellers come together. Goods and services are produced and resources are supplied by whoever is willing and able to do so at the prevailing prices. The result is competition among independently acting buyers and sellers of each product and resource. Thus, economic decision making is widely dispersed. Also, the high potential for monetary rewards creates powerful incentives for existing firms to innovate and entrepreneurs to pioneer new products and processes.

ORIGIN 2.1
Laissez-faire

In *pure* capitalism—or *laissez-faire* capitalism—government's role is limited to protecting private property and establishing an environment appropriate to the operation of the market system. The term "laissez-faire" means "let it be"; that is, keep government from interfering with the economy. The idea is that such interference will inhibit the efficient working of the market system.

But in the capitalism practised in Canada and most other countries, government plays a significant role in the economy. It not only provides the rules for economic activity but also attempts to promote economic stability and growth, provides certain goods and services that would otherwise be underproduced or not produced at all, and modifies the distribution of income. The government, however, is not the dominant economic force in deciding what to produce, how to produce it, and who will get it. That force is the market.

2.2 | Characteristics of the Market System

An examination of some of the key features of the market system in detail will be instructive.

Private Property

private property
The right of private persons and firms to obtain, own, control, employ, dispose of, and bequeath land, capital, and other property.

In a market system, private individuals and firms, not the government, own most of the property resources (land and capital). It is this extensive private ownership of capital that gives capitalism its name. This right of **private property,** coupled with the freedom to negotiate binding legal contracts, enables individuals and businesses to obtain, use, and dispose of property resources as they see fit. The right of property owners to designate who will receive their property when they die sustains the institution of private property.

Property rights encourage investment, innovation, exchange, maintenance of property, and economic growth. No one would stock a store, build a factory, or clear land for farming if someone else, or the government itself, could take that property for his or her own benefit.

Property rights also extend to intellectual property through patents, copyrights, and trademarks. Such long-term protection encourages people to write books, music, and computer programs and to invent new products and production processes without fear that others will steal them and the rewards they may bring.

Moreover, property rights facilitate exchange. The title to an automobile or the deed to a cattle ranch assures the buyer that the seller is the legitimate owner. Also, property rights encourage owners to maintain or improve their property so as to preserve or increase its value. Finally, property rights enable people to use their time and resources to produce more goods and services, rather than using them to protect and retain the property they have already produced or acquired.

Freedom of Enterprise and Choice

Closely related to private ownership of property is freedom of enterprise and choice. The market system requires that various economic units make certain choices, which are expressed and implemented in the economy's markets:

- **Freedom of enterprise** ensures that entrepreneurs and private businesses are free to obtain and use economic resources to produce their choice of goods and services and to sell them in their chosen markets.

- **Freedom of choice** enables owners to employ or dispose of their property and money as they see fit. It also allows workers to enter any line of work for which they are qualified. Finally, it ensures that consumers are free to buy the goods and services that best satisfy their wants.

These choices are free only within broad legal limitations, of course. Illegal choices such as selling human organs or buying illicit drugs are punished through fines and imprisonment. (Global Perspective 2.1 reveals that the degree of economic freedom varies greatly from economy to economy.)

Self-Interest

In the market system, **self-interest** is the motivating force of the various economic units as they express their free choices. Self-interest simply means that each economic unit tries to achieve its own particular goal, which usually requires delivering something of value to others. Entrepreneurs try to maximize profit or minimize loss. Property owners try to get the highest price for the sale or rent of their resources. Workers try to maximize their utility (satisfaction) by finding jobs that offer the best combination of wages, hours, fringe benefits, and working conditions. Consumers try to obtain the products they want at the lowest possible price and apportion their expenditures to maximize their utility. The motive of self-interest gives direction and consistency to what might otherwise be a chaotic economy.

Competition

The market system depends on **competition** among economic units. The basis of this competition is freedom of choice exercised in pursuit of a monetary return. Very broadly defined, competition requires:

- independently acting sellers and buyers operating in a particular product or factor market
- freedom of sellers and buyers to enter or leave markets, on the basis of their economic self-interest

Competition among buyers and sellers diffuses economic power within the businesses and households that make up the economy. When there are independently acting sellers and buyers in a market, no one buyer or seller is able to dictate the price of the product or factor because others can undercut that price.

---

freedom of enterprise
The freedom of firms to obtain economic resources, to use these resources to produce products of the firm's own choosing, and to sell their products in markets of their choice.

freedom of choice
The freedom of owners of property resources to employ or dispose of them as they see fit, and of consumers to spend their incomes in a manner that they think is appropriate.

ORIGIN 2.2
Self-Interest

self-interest
That which each firm, property owner, worker, and consumer believes is best for itself.

competition
The presence in a market of a large number of independent buyers and sellers competing with one another and the freedom of buyers and sellers to enter and leave the market.

2.1 | GLOBAL PERSPECTIVE

Index of Economic Freedom, Selected Nations

The Index of Economic Freedom measures economic freedom using 10 broad categories, such as trade policy, property rights, and government intervention, with each category containing more than 50 specific criteria. The Index then ranks 157 nations according to the degree of economic freedom. A few selected rankings for 2009 are listed here.

Source: Heritage Foundation (www.heritage.org) and the *Wall Street Journal*.

FREE

1 Hong Kong
3 Australia
6 United States
7 Canada

MOSTLY FREE

20 Belgium
29 Spain
64 France

MOSTLY UNFREE

105 Brazil
132 China
146 Russia

REPRESSED

174 Venezuela
177 Cuba
179 North Korea

Competition also implies that producers can enter or leave an industry; there are no insurmountable barriers to an industry's expanding or contracting. This freedom of an industry to expand or contract provides the economy with the flexibility needed to remain efficient over time. Freedom of entry and exit enables the economy to adjust to changes in consumer tastes, technology, and factor availability.

The diffusion of economic power inherent in competition limits the potential abuse of that power. A producer that charges more than the competitive market price will lose sales to other producers. An employer who pays less than the competitive market wage rate will lose workers to other employers. A firm that fails to exploit new technology will lose profits to firms that do. Competition is the basic regulatory force in the market system.

Markets and Prices

We may wonder why an economy based on self-interest does not collapse in chaos. If consumers want breakfast cereal but businesses choose to produce running shoes and resource suppliers decide to make computer software, production would seem to be deadlocked by the apparent inconsistencies of free choices.

In reality, the millions of decisions made by households and businesses are highly coordinated with one another. Markets and prices are key components of the market system. They give the system its ability to coordinate millions of daily economic decisions. A **market** is an institution or mechanism that brings buyers ("demanders") and sellers ("suppliers") into contact. A market system conveys the decisions made by buyers and sellers of products and factors. The decisions made on each side of the market determine a set of product and factor prices that guide resource owners, entrepreneurs, and consumers as they make and revise their choices and pursue their self-interest.

market
Any institution or mechanism that brings together buyers and sellers of particular goods, services, or resources for the purpose of exchange.

Just as competition is the regulatory mechanism of the market system, the market system itself is the organizing and coordinating mechanism. It is an elaborate communication network through which innumerable individual free choices on the part of consumers and producers are recorded, summarized, and balanced. Those who respond to market signals and heed market dictates are rewarded with greater profit and income; those who do not respond to those signals and choose to ignore market dictates are penalized. Through this mechanism society decides what the economy should produce, how production can be organized efficiently, and how the fruits of production are to be distributed among the various units that make up the economy.

> ## QUICK REVIEW
>
> ▶ The market system rests on the private ownership of property and on freedom of enterprise and freedom of choice.
>
> ▶ The market system permits consumers, resource suppliers, and businesses to pursue and further their self-interest.
>
> ▶ Competition diffuses economic power and limits the actions of any single seller or buyer.
>
> ▶ The coordinating mechanism of capitalism is a system of markets and prices.

Technology and Capital Goods

In the market system, competition, freedom of choice, self-interest, and personal reward provide the opportunity and motivation for technological advance. The monetary rewards for new products or production techniques accrue directly to the innovator. The market system therefore encourages extensive use and rapid development of complex capital goods: tools, machinery, large-scale factories, and facilities for storage, communication, transportation, and marketing.

Advanced technology and capital goods are important because the most direct methods of production are often the least efficient. The only way to avoid that inefficiency is to rely on capital goods. It would be ridiculous for a farmer to go at production with bare hands. There are huge benefits to be derived from creating and using such capital equipment as plows, tractors, storage bins, and so on. More efficient production means much more abundant output.

Specialization

specialization
The use of the resources of an individual, a firm, a region, or a nation to produce one or a few goods and services.

The extent to which market economies rely on **specialization** is astonishing. Specialization is the use of resources of an individual, region, or nation to produce one or a few goods or services rather than the entire range of goods and services. Those goods and services are then exchanged for a full range of desired products. The majority of consumers produce virtually none of the goods and services they consume, and they consume little or nothing of the items they produce. The person working nine-to-five installing windows in commercial aircraft may rarely fly. Many farmers sell their milk to the local dairy and then buy margarine at the local grocery store. Society learned long ago that self-sufficiency breeds inefficiency. The jack-of-all-trades may be a very colourful individual but is certainly not an efficient producer.

DIVISION OF LABOUR

division of labour
Dividing the work required to produce a product into a number of different tasks that are performed by different workers.

Human specialization—called the **division of labour**—contributes to a society's output in several ways:

- *Specialization Makes Use of Differences in Ability*   Specialization enables individuals to take advantage of existing differences in their abilities and skills. If Peyton is strong, athletic, and good at throwing a football and Beyoncé is beautiful, agile, and can sing, their distribution of talents can be most efficiently used if Peyton plays professional football and Beyoncé records songs and gives concerts.

ORIGIN 2.3
Specialization:
Division of Labour

- **Specialization Fosters Learning by Doing**   Even if the abilities of two people are identical, specialization may still be advantageous. By devoting time to a single task, a person is more likely to develop the skills required and to improve techniques than by working at a number of different tasks. You learn to be a good lawyer by studying and practising law.

- **Specialization Saves Time**   By devoting time to a single task, a person avoids the loss of time incurred in shifting from one job to another. Also, time is saved by not "fumbling around" with a task that one is not trained to do.

For all these reasons, specialization increases the total output society derives from limited resources.

GEOGRAPHIC SPECIALIZATION

Specialization also works on a regional and international basis. It is conceivable that apples could be grown in Saskatchewan, but because of the unsuitability of the land, rainfall, and temperature, the costs would be very high. And it is conceivable that wheat could be grown in British Columbia, but such production would be costly for similar geographical reasons. So, Saskatchewan farmers produce products—wheat in particular—for which their resources are best suited, and British Columbians (especially in the Okanagan Valley) do the same, producing apples and other fruits. By specializing, both regional economies produce more than is needed locally. Then, very sensibly, Saskatchewan and British Columbia exchange some of their surpluses—wheat for apples, apples for wheat.

Similarly, on an international scale, Canada specializes in producing such items as commercial aircraft (Bombardier) and communication equipment (Research In Motion), which it sells abroad in exchange for digital video recorders from China, bananas from Honduras, and woven baskets from Thailand. Both human specialization and geographic specialization are needed to achieve efficiency in the use of limited resources.

Use of Money

A rather obvious characteristic of any economic system is the extensive use of money. Money performs several functions, but first and foremost it is a **medium of exchange.** It makes trade easier.

Specialization requires exchange. Exchange can, and sometimes does, occur through **barter**—swapping goods for goods; say, exchanging wheat for apples. But barter poses serious problems because it requires a *coincidence of wants* between the buyer and the seller. In our example, we assumed that Saskatchewan had excess wheat to trade and wanted apples. And we assumed that British Columbia had excess apples to trade and wanted wheat. So an exchange occurred. But if such a coincidence of wants is missing, trade will not occur.

Suppose that Saskatchewan has no interest in British Columbia's apples but wants potatoes from Prince Edward Island. And suppose that Prince Edward Island wants British Columbia's apples but not Saskatchewan's wheat. And, to complicate matters, suppose that British Columbia wants some of Saskatchewan's wheat but none of Prince Edward Island's potatoes. We summarize the situation in Figure 2-1.

In none of the cases shown in the figure is there a coincidence of wants. Trade by barter would obviously be difficult. Instead, people in each province use **money,** which is simply a convenient social invention to facilitate exchanges of goods and services. Historically, people have used cattle, cigarettes, shells, stones, pieces of metal, and many other commodities, with varying degrees of success, as a medium of exchange. But to serve as money, an item needs to pass only one test: It must be generally acceptable to sellers in exchange for their goods and services. Money is socially defined: whatever society accepts as a medium of exchange *is* money.

Today, most economies use pieces of paper as money. The use of paper dollars (currency) as a medium of exchange is what enables Saskatchewan, British Columbia, and Prince Edward Island to overcome their trade stalemate, as demonstrated in Figure 2-1.

medium of exchange
Items sellers generally accept and buyers generally use to pay for a good or service.

barter
The exchange of one good or service for another good or service.

money
Any item that is generally acceptable to sellers in exchange for goods and services.

FIGURE 2-1   **Money Facilitates Trade When Wants Do Not Coincide**

The use of money as a medium of exchange permits trade to be accomplished despite a non-coincidence of wants. (1) Saskatchewan trades the wheat that B.C. wants for money; (2) Saskatchewan trades the money it receives from B.C. for the potatoes it wants from P.E.I.; (3) P.E.I. trades the money it receives from Saskatchewan for the apples it wants from B.C.

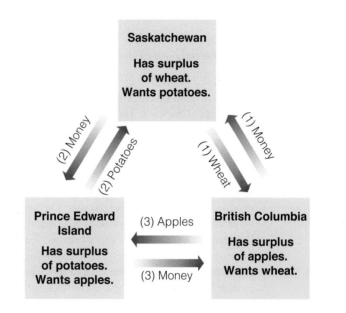

On a global basis different nations have different currencies, which complicates specialization and exchange. But swapping dollars, yen, euros, pounds, and pesos for one another in markets in which currencies are bought and sold makes it possible for Canadians, Japanese, Germans, Britons, and Mexicans to exchange goods and services without resorting to barter.

Active, But Limited, Government

An active, but limited, government is the final characteristic of market systems in modern advanced industrial economies. Although a market system promotes a high degree of efficiency in the use of its resources, it has certain inherent shortcomings called "market failures." We will discover in subsequent chapters that government can increase the overall efficiency of the economic system in several ways.

QUICK REVIEW

▸ The market systems of modern industrial economies are characterized by extensive use of technologically advanced capital goods. Such goods help these economies achieve greater efficiency in production.

▸ Specialization is extensive in market systems; it enhances efficiency and output by enabling individuals, regions, and nations to produce the goods and services for which their resources are best suited.

▸ The use of money in market systems facilitates the exchange of goods and services that specialization requires.

2.3 | Five Fundamental Questions

The key features of the market system help explain how market economies respond to five fundamental questions:

- What goods and services will be produced?
- How will the goods and services be produced?
- Who will get the goods and services?
- How will the system accommodate change?
- How will the system promote progress?

These five questions highlight the economic choices underlying the production possibilities curve discussed in Chapter 1. They reflect the reality of scarce resources in a world of unlimited wants. All economies, whether market or command, must address these five questions.

What Will Be Produced?

How will a market system decide on the specific types and quantities of goods and services to be produced? The simple answer is this: The goods and services produced at a continuing profit will be produced, and those produced at a continuing loss will not. Profits and losses are the difference between the total revenue (TR) a firm receives from the sale of its products and the total cost (TC) of producing those products. (For economists, economic costs include not only wage and salary payments to labour, and interest and rental payments for capital and land, but also payments to the entrepreneur for organizing and combining the other resources to produce a commodity.)

Continuing economic profit (TR > TC) in an industry results in expanded production and the movement of resources toward that industry. Existing firms grow and new firms enter. The industry expands. Continuing losses (TC > TR) in an industry leads to reduced production and the departure of resources from that industry. Some existing firms shrink in size; others go out of business. The industry contracts.

consumer sovereignty
Determination by consumers of the types and quantities of goods and services that will be produced with the scarce resources of the economy.

In the market system, consumers are sovereign (in command). **Consumer sovereignty** is crucial in determining the types and quantities of goods produced. Consumers spend their income on the goods they are most willing and able to buy. Through these "**dollar votes**" they register their wants in the market. If the dollar votes for a certain product are large enough to create a profit, businesses will produce that product and offer it for sale. In contrast, if the dollar votes do not create sufficient revenues to cover costs, businesses will not produce the product. So the consumers are sovereign. Through their dollar votes they collectively direct resources to industries that are meeting consumer wants and away from industries that are not meeting consumer wants.

dollar votes
The "votes" that consumers and entrepreneurs cast for the production of consumer and capital goods, respectively, when they purchase them in product and resource markets.

The dollar votes of consumers determine not only which industries will continue to exist but also which products will survive or fail. Only profitable industries, firms, and products survive. So firms are not as free to produce whatever products they want. Consumers' buying decisions make the production of some products profitable and the production of other products unprofitable, thus restricting the choice of businesses in deciding what to produce. Businesses must match their production choices with consumer choices or else face losses and eventual bankruptcy.

The same holds true for resource (factor) suppliers. The employment of resources derives from the sale of the goods and services that the resources help produce. Autoworkers are employed because automobiles are sold. There are few remaining professors of early Latin because there are few people who want to learn the Latin language. Resource suppliers that want to earn income are not truly free to allocate their resources to the production of goods or services that consumers do not value highly. Consumers register their preferences in the market; producers and resource suppliers, prompted by their own self-interest, try to satisfy those preferences. *(Key Question 8)*

How Will the Goods and Services Be Produced?

What combinations of resources and technologies will be used to produce goods and services? How will the production be organized? The answer: in combinations and ways that minimize the cost per unit of output. Because competition eliminates high-cost producers, profitability for firms requires that they produce their output at minimum cost per unit. Achieving this least-cost production necessitates that firms use the right mix of labour and capital, given the prices and productivity of those resources. It also means locating production facilities in such a way as to minimize production and transportation costs.

Least-cost production also means that firms must employ the most economically efficient technique of production in producing their output. The most efficient production technique depends on:

- The available technology; that is, the various combinations of resources that will produce the most output.

- The prices of the needed resources.

WORKED PROBLEM 2.1
Least Cost Production

A technique that requires just a few inputs of resources to produce a specific output may be highly inefficient economically if those resources are valued very highly in the market. Economic efficiency requires obtaining a particular output of product with the least input of scarce resources, when both output and resource inputs are measured in dollars and cents.

Who Will Get the Output?

The market system enters the picture in two ways when determining the distribution of total output. Generally, any product will be distributed to consumers on the basis of their ability and willingness to pay its existing market price. If the price of some product, say a small sailboat, is $3000, then buyers who are willing and able to pay that price will get it; those unwilling or unable to pay the price will not.

The ability to pay the prices for sailboats and other products depends on the amount of income that consumers have, along with the prices of, and preferences for, various goods. If consumers have sufficient income and want to spend their money on a particular good, they can have it. And the amount of income they have depends on (1) the quantities of the property and human resources they supply and (2) the prices those resources command in the factor market. Factor prices (wages, interest, rent, profit) are crucial in determining the size of each person's income and therefore each person's ability to buy part of the economy's output. If a lawyer earning $300 an hour and a recreational worker earning $10 an hour both work the same number of hours each year, the lawyer will be able to take possession of 30 times as much of society's output as the recreational worker that year.

How Will the System Accommodate Change?

Market systems are dynamic: consumer preferences, technology, and supplies of resources can all change at the same time. This means that the particular allocation of resources that is now the most efficient for a specific pattern of consumer tastes, range of technological alternatives, and amount of available resources will become obsolete and inefficient as consumer preferences change, new techniques of production are discovered, and resource supplies change over time. Can the market economy adjust to such changes?

Suppose consumer tastes change. For instance, assume that consumers decide they want more fruit juice and less milk than the economy currently provides. Those changes in consumer tastes will be communicated to producers through an increase in spending on fruit juice and a decline in spending on milk. Other things equal, prices and profits in the fruit juice industry will rise and those in the milk industry will fall. Self-interest will induce existing competitors to expand output and entice new competitors to enter the prosperous fruit juice industry and will in time force firms to scale down—or even exit—the depressed milk industry.

The higher prices and greater economic profit in the fruit juice industry not only will induce that industry to expand but also will give it the revenue needed to obtain the resources necessary to its growth. Higher prices and profits will permit fruit juice producers to draw more resources from less urgent alternative employment. The reverse occurs in the milk industry, where fewer workers and other resources are employed. These adjustments in the economy are automatic responses to the changes in consumer tastes. This is consumer sovereignty at work.

The market system is a gigantic communications system. Through changes in prices and profits it communicates changes in consumer demand and elicits appropriate responses from businesses and resource suppliers. By affecting price and profits, changes in consumer demand direct the expansion of some industries and the contraction of others. Those adjustments are conveyed to the factor market. As expanding industries employ more factors of production and contracting industries employ fewer, the resulting changes in factor prices (wages and salaries, for example) and income flows steer resources from the contracting industries to the expanding industries.

This *directing* or guiding function of prices and profits is a core element of the market system. Without such a system, a government planning board or some other administrative agency would have to direct businesses and resources into the appropriate industries. A similar analysis shows that the system can and does adjust to other fundamental changes—for example, to changes in technology and in the prices of various resources.

How Will the System Promote Progress?

Society desires economic growth (greater output) and higher standards of living (greater income per person). How does the market system promote technological improvements and capital accumulation, both of which contribute to a higher standard of living for society?

TECHNOLOGICAL ADVANCE

The market system provides a strong incentive for technological advance and enables better products and processes to supplant inferior ones. An entrepreneur or firm that introduces a popular new product will gain revenue and economic profit at the expense of rivals.

Technological advance also includes new and improved methods that reduce production or distribution costs. By passing on part of its cost reduction to the consumer through a lower product price, the firm can increase sales and obtain economic profit at the expense of rival firms.

Moreover, the market system promotes the *rapid spread* of technological advance throughout an industry. Rival firms must follow the lead of the most innovative firm or else suffer immediate losses and eventual failure. In some cases, the result is **creative destruction**: the creation of new products and production methods completely destroys the market positions of firms that are wedded to existing products and older ways of doing business. For example, the advent of compact discs largely demolished long-play vinyl records, and iPods and other digital technologies are now supplanting CDs.

CAPITAL ACCUMULATION

Most technological advances require additional capital goods. The market system provides the resources necessary to produce those goods through increased dollar votes for capital goods.

But who will register votes for capital goods? Answer: entrepreneurs and owners of businesses. As receivers of profit income, they often use part of that income to purchase capital goods. Doing so yields even greater profit income in the future if the technological innovation is successful. Also, by paying interest or selling ownership shares, the entrepreneur and firm can attract some of the income of households to cast dollar votes for the production of more capital goods. *(Key Question 9)*

creative destruction
The hypothesis that the creation of new products and production methods simultaneously destroys the market power of firms that are wedded to existing products and older ways of doing business.

▶ The output mix of the market system is determined by profits, which in turn depend heavily on consumer preferences. Economic profits cause industries to expand; losses cause industries to contract.

▶ Competition forces industries to use the least costly production methods.

▶ In a market economy, consumer income and product prices determine how output will be distributed.

▶ Competitive markets reallocate resources in response to changes in consumer tastes, technological advances, and changes in availability of resources.

▶ Competitive markets create incentives for technological advance and capital accumulation, both of which contribute to increases in standards of living.

The "Invisible Hand"

invisible hand
The tendency of firms and resource suppliers seeking to further their own self-interests in competitive markets to also promote the interest of society as a whole.

In his 1776 book *The Wealth of Nations,* Adam Smith first noted that the operation of a market system creates a curious unity between private interests and social interests. Firms and resource suppliers, seeking to further their own self-interest and operating within the framework of a highly competitive market system, will simultaneously, as though guided by an "**invisible hand**," promote the public or social interest. For example, we have seen that in a competitive environment, businesses seek to build new and improved products to increase profits. Those enhanced products increase society's well-being. Businesses also use the least costly combination of resources to produce a specific output because it is in their self-interest to do so. To act otherwise would be to forgo profit or even to risk business failure. But, at the same time, to use scarce resources in the least costly way is clearly in the social interest as well. It "frees up" resources to produce something else that society desires.

Self-interest, awakened and guided by the competitive market system, is what induces responses appropriate to the changes in society's wants. Businesses seeking to make higher profits and to avoid losses, and resource suppliers pursuing greater monetary rewards, negotiate changes in the allocation of resources and end up with the output that society wants. Competition guides self-interest such that self-interest automatically and quite unintentionally furthers the best interest of society. The invisible hand ensures that when firms maximize their profits and resource suppliers maximize their incomes, these groups also help maximize society's output and income.

Of the various virtues of the market system, three merit re-emphasis:

- *Efficiency*   The market system promotes the efficient use of resources, by guiding them into the production of the goods and services most wanted by society. It forces the use of the most efficient techniques in organizing resources for production, and it encourages the development and adoption of new and more efficient production techniques.

- *Incentives*   The market system encourages skill acquisition, hard work, and innovation. Greater work skills and effort mean greater production and higher incomes, which usually translate into a higher standard of living. Similarly, the assumption of risks by entrepreneurs can result in substantial profit incomes. Successful innovations generate economic rewards.

- *Freedom*   The major noneconomic argument for the market system is its emphasis on personal freedom. In contrast to central planning, the market system coordinates economic activity without coercion. The market system permits—indeed, it thrives on—freedom of enterprise and choice. Entrepreneurs and workers are free to further their own self-interest, subject to the rewards and penalties imposed by the market system itself.

Of course, no economic system, including the market system, is flawless. The global financial crisis that gripped most economies in 2008–09 highlighted some of the shortcomings of unfettered financial markets. In Chapter 15 of *Microeconomics* we will explain several well-known shortcomings of the market system and examine the government policies that try to remedy them.

2.4 | The Demise of the Command System

Our discussion of how a market system answers the five fundamental questions provides insights on why command systems of the Soviet Union, eastern Europe, and China (prior to its market reforms) failed. Those systems encountered two insurmountable problems.

The Coordination Problem

The first difficulty was the coordination problem. The central planners had to coordinate the millions of individual decisions by consumers, resource suppliers, and businesses. Consider the setting up of a factory to produce tractors. The central planners had to establish a realistic annual production target; for example, 1000 tractors. They then had to make available all the necessary inputs—labour, machinery, electric power, steel, tires, glass, paint, transportation—for the production and delivery of those 1000 tractors.

Because the outputs of many industries serve as inputs to other industries, the failure of any single industry to achieve its output target caused a chain reaction of repercussions. For example, if iron mines, for want of machinery or labour or transportation, did not supply the steel industry with the required inputs of iron ore, the steel mills were unable to fulfill the input needs of the many industries that depended on steel. Steel-using industries that produced capital goods (such as factory equipment and modes of transportation) were unable to fulfill their planned production goals. Eventually the chain reaction spread to all firms that used steel as an input and from there to other input buyers or final consumers.

The coordination problem became more difficult as the economies expanded. Products and production processes grew more complex, and the number of industries requiring planning increased. Planning techniques that worked for the simpler economy proved highly inadequate and inefficient for the larger economy. Bottlenecks and production stoppages became the norm, not the exception. In trying to cope, planners further suppressed product variety, focusing on one or two products in each product category.

A lack of a reliable success indicator added to the coordination problem in the Soviet Union and China (prior to its market reforms). We have seen that market economies rely on profit as a success indicator. Profit depends on consumer demand, production efficiency, and product quality. In contrast, the major success indicator for the command economies usually was a quantitative production target that the central planners assigned. Production costs, product quality, and product mix were secondary considerations. Managers and workers often sacrificed product quality because

CONSIDER THIS | The Two Koreas

North Korea is one of the few command economies still standing. After the Second World War, Korea was divided into North Korea and South Korea. North Korea, under the influence of the Soviet Union, established a command economy that emphasized government ownership and central government planning. South Korea established a market economy based upon private ownership and the profit motive. Today, the differences in the economic outcomes of the two systems are striking:

	North Korea	**South Korea**
GDP	$40 billion*	$1.2 trillion*
GDP per capita	$1,800*	$24,500*
Exports	$1.3 billion	$326 billion
Imports	$2.7 billion	$309.3 billion
Agriculture as % of GDP	30 %	3 %

*Based on purchasing power equivalencies to the U.S. dollar.

Source: *CIA World Fact Book*, 2008, www.cia.gov.

they were being awarded bonuses for meeting quantitative, not qualitative, targets. If meeting production goals meant sloppy assembly work, so be it.

It was difficult at best for planners to assign quantitative production targets without unintentionally producing distortions in output. If the plan specified a production target for producing nails in terms of *weight* (tons of nails), the enterprise made only large nails. But if it specified the target as a *quantity* (thousands of nails), the firm made all small nails, and lots of them! That is precisely what happens in centrally planned economies.

The Incentive Problem

The command economies also faced an incentive problem. Central planners determined the output mix. When they misjudged how many automobiles, shoes, shirts, and chickens were wanted at the government-determined prices, persistent shortages and surpluses of those products often arose. But as long as the managers who oversaw the production of those goods were rewarded for meeting their assigned production goals, they had no incentive to adjust production in response to the shortages and surpluses. And there were no fluctuations in prices and profitability to signal that more or less of certain products was desired. Thus, many products were unavailable or in short supply, while other products were overproduced and sat for months or years in warehouses.

CONSIDER THIS | Market Failure and the Need for Government

Suppose a municipality, say Brandon, Manitoba, requires a new road. In the absence of a government request that a private firm build it, it is unlikely that a private firm will build the required road on its own initiative. Or, to express it in another way, private markets will not make available public goods. The citizens of Brandon have to elect a government to either direct a private firm to build the road, or hire the people and buy the capital equipment needed to construct the road on its own.

Why would a private firm not undertake to build a road on its own? The obstacle is common property rights. The land on which the road is to be built must be owned by the firm before it would consider building the road. Lands used by all citizens are most often held publicly. The firm would thus need to get the consent of all the citizens affected. Such unanimity would be difficult to achieve. Indeed, it is the difficulty of making collective decisions that makes government action essential in the creation of an infrastructure—such as roads and airports—necessary to facilitate the functioning of markets. Not only must a decision be made to build the road, but then the decision must be made as to who should bear the cost. The free-rider problem arises here. Every individual hopes someone will pay for the needed road. This way he or she can have the benefits without contributing to its cost. The free-rider problem can potentially arise in all situations where collective action must be taken. Unless we have a central authority—government—with the monopoly power to impose costs on all members of a society, many socially useful projects will not be undertaken.

In a pathbreaking book, *The Logic of Collective Action*,[1] Mancur Olson pointed out 40 years ago that contrary to popular belief, groups of individuals with common interest do not necessarily attempt to further those common interests. In many instances group members attempt to further their own personal interests. A few years later, the political scientist Garrett Hardin popularized the term "the tragedy of the commons"[2] to describe the problems that arise when there are common property rights. For example, where there are common property rights to a natural resource, it is typically overexploited. The cod stocks on Canada's east coast have suffered just that fate.

Where collective action is required, or where there are common property rights, governments are needed because markets fail to bring together the interests of the individual and those of society. The federal government has had to impose mandatory fishing restrictions to save the cod stocks from dwindling further. Similarly, governments must make decisions to construct a road, otherwise the road might never get built.

But we do not want to leave the impression that all government interventions to rectify market failure succeed. Some individuals point to the failure of the Canadian federal government to properly manage the cod stocks off the eastern seaboard as a case in point.

[1] Mancur Olson, *The Logic of Collective Action* (Cambridge: Cambridge University Press, 1965).

[2] Garrett Hardin, "The Tragedy of the Commons," *Science* 162 (1968): 1243–48.

The command systems of the Soviet Union and China before its market reforms also lacked entrepreneurship. Central planning did not trigger the profit motive, nor did it reward innovation and enterprise. The route for getting ahead was through participation in the political hierarchy of the Communist Party. Moving up the hierarchy meant better housing, better access to health care, and the right to shop in special stores. Meeting production targets and manoeuvring through the minefields of party politics were measures of success in "business." But a definition of business success based solely on political savvy is not conducive to technological advance, which is often disruptive to existing products, production methods, and organizational structures.

2.5 | The Circular Flow Model

 ORIGIN 2.4
Circular Flow
Diagram

circular flow diagram
The flow of resources from households to firms and of products from firms to households. These flows are accompanied by reverse flows of money from firms to households and from households to firms.

factor market
A market in which households sell and firms buy factors of production.

product market
A market in which products are sold by firms and bought by households.

The dynamic market economy creates continuous, repetitive flows of goods and services, resources, and money. The **circular flow diagram,** shown in **Figure 2-2 (Key Graph),** illustrates those flows. Observe that in the diagram we group private decision makers into *businesses* and *households* and group markets into the *factor market* and the *product market.*

Factor Market

The upper part of the circular flow diagram represents the **factor market:** the place where resources or the services of resource suppliers are bought and sold. In the factor market, households sell resources and businesses buy them. Households (that is, people) own all economic resources either directly as workers or entrepreneurs or indirectly through their ownership of business corporations. They sell their resources to businesses, which buy them because they are necessary for producing goods and services. The funds that businesses pay for resources are costs to businesses but are flows of wage, rent, interest, and profit income to the households. Productive resources therefore flow from households to businesses, and money flows from businesses to households.

Product Market

Next consider the lower part of the diagram, which represents the **product market:** the place where goods and services produced by businesses are bought and sold. In the product market, businesses combine resources to produce and sell goods and services. Households use the (limited) income they have received from the sale of resources to buy goods and services. The monetary flow of consumer spending on goods and services yields sales revenues for businesses. Businesses compare those revenues to their costs in determining profitability and whether or not a particular good or service should continue to be produced.

The circular flow model depicts a complex, interrelated web of decision making and economic activity involving businesses and households. For the economy, it is the circle of life. Businesses and households are both buyers and sellers. Businesses buy resources and sell products. Households buy products and sell resources. As shown in Figure 2-2, there is a counterclockwise *real flow* of economic resources and finished goods and services and a clockwise *money flow* of income and consumption expenditures.

KEY GRAPH   @

FIGURE 2-2
The Circular Flow Diagram

Factors of production flow from households to businesses through the factor market and products flow from businesses to households through the product market. Opposite these real flows are monetary flows. Households receive income from businesses (their costs) through the factor market and businesses receive revenue from households (their expenditures) through the product market.

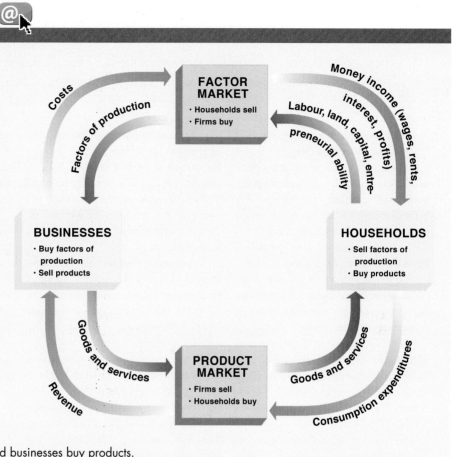

Quick Quiz

1. The factor market is where:
   a. households sell products and businesses buy products.
   b. businesses sell factors of production and households sell products.
   c. households sell factors of production and businesses buy factors of production (or the services of factors).
   d. businesses sell factors of production and households buy factors of production (or the services of factors).

2. Which of the following would be determined in the product market?
   a. a manager's salary
   b. the price of equipment used in a bottling plant
   c. the price of 80 hectares of farmland
   d. the price of a new pair of athletic shoes

3. In this circular flow diagram:
   a. money flows counterclockwise.
   b. resources flow counterclockwise.
   c. goods and services flow clockwise.
   d. households are on the selling side of the product market.

4. In this circular flow diagram:
   a. households spend income in the product market.
   b. firms sell resources to households.
   c. households receive income through the product market.
   d. households produce goods.

Answers: 1. c; 2. d; 3. b; 4. a

The LAST WORD   Shuffling the Deck

Economist Donald Boudreaux marvels at the way the market system systematically and purposefully arranges the world's tens of billions of individual resources.

In *The Future and Its Enemies*, Virginia Postrel notes the astonishing fact that if you thoroughly shuffle an ordinary deck of 52 playing cards, chances are practically 100 percent that the resulting arrangement of cards has never before existed. Never. Every time you shuffle a deck, you produce an arrangement of cards that exists for the first time in history.

The arithmetic works out that way. For a very small number of items, the number of possible arrangements is small. Three items, for example, can be arranged only six different ways. But the number of possible arrangements grows very quickly. The number of different ways to arrange five items is 120...for ten items it's 3,628,800...for fifteen items it's 1,307,674,368,000.

The number of different ways to arrange 52 items is 8.066×10^{67}. This is a big number. No human can comprehend its enormousness. By way of comparison, the number of possible ways to arrange a mere 20 items is 2,432,902,008,176,640,000—a number larger than the total number of seconds that have elapsed since the beginning of time ten billion years ago—and this number is Lilliputian compared to 8.066×10^{67}.

What's the significance of these facts about numbers? Consider the number of different resources available in the world—my labour, your labour, your land, oil, tungsten, cedar, coffee beans, chickens, rivers, the Empire State Build-

ing, [Microsoft] Windows, the wharves at Houston, the classrooms at Oxford, the airport at Miami, and on and on and on. No one can possibly count all of the different, productive resources available for our use. But we can be sure that this number is at least in the tens of billions.

When you reflect on how incomprehensibly large is the number of ways to arrange a deck containing a mere 52 cards, the mind boggles at the number of different ways to arrange all the world's resources.

If our world were random—if resources combined together haphazardly, as if a giant took them all into his hands and tossed them down like so many [cards]—it's a virtual certainty that the resulting combination of resources would be useless. Unless this chance arrangement were quickly rearranged according to some productive logic, nothing worthwhile would be produced. We would all starve to death. Because only a tiny fraction of possible arrangements serves human

ends, any arrangement will be useless if it is chosen randomly or with inadequate knowledge of how each and every resource might be productively combined with each other.

And yet, we witness all around us an arrangement of resources that's productive and serves human goals. Today's arrangement of resources might not be perfect, but it is vastly superior to most of the trillions upon trillions of other possible arrangements.

How have we managed to get one of the minuscule number of arrangements that works? The answer is private property—a social institution that encourages mutual accommodation.

Private property eliminates the possibility that resource arrangements will be random, for each resource owner chooses a course of action only if it promises rewards to the owner that exceed the rewards promised by all other available courses.

[The result] is a breathtakingly complex and productive arrangement of countless resources. This arrangement emerged over time (and is still emerging) as the result of billions upon billions of individual, daily, small decisions made by people seeking to better employ their resources and labor in ways that other people find helpful.

Source: Abridged from Donald J. Boudreaux, "Mutual Accommodation," *Ideas on Liberty*, May 2000, pp. 4–5. Reprinted with permission.

Question

What explains why millions of economic resources tend to get arranged logically and productively rather than haphazardly and unproductively?

CHAPTER SUMMARY

2.1 ▶ ECONOMIC SYSTEMS

- The command system and the market system are the two broad types of economic systems used to address the economic problem. In the command system (or socialism or communism), government owns most resources, and central planners coordinate most economic activity. In the market system (or capitalism), private individuals own most resources, and markets coordinate most economic activity.

2.2 ▶ CHARACTERISTICS OF THE MARKET SYSTEM

- The market system is characterized by the private ownership of resources, including capital, and the freedom of individuals to engage in economic activities of their choice to advance their material well-being. Self-interest is the driving force of such an economy, and competition functions as a regulatory or control mechanism.

- In the market system, markets, prices, and profits organize and make effective the many millions of individual economic decisions that occur daily.

- The use of advanced technology, specialization, and the extensive use of capital goods are common features of market systems. Functioning as a medium of exchange, money eliminates the problems of bartering and permits easy trade and greater specialization, both domestically and internationally.

2.3 ▶ FIVE FUNDAMENTAL QUESTIONS

- Every economy faces five fundamental questions: (1) What goods and services will be produced? (2) How will the goods and services be produced? (3) Who will get the goods and services? (4) How will the system accommodate change? (5) How will the system promote progress?

- The market system produces products whose production and sale yield total revenue sufficient to cover total cost. It does not produce products for which total revenue continuously falls short of total cost. Competition forces firms to use the lowest-cost production techniques.

- Positive economic profit (total revenue minus total cost) indicates that an industry is prosperous and promotes its expansion. Losses signify that an industry is not prosperous and hasten its contraction.

- Consumer sovereignty means that both businesses and resource suppliers are subject to the wants of consumers. Through their dollar votes, consumers decide on the composition of output.

- The prices that a household receives for the resources it supplies to the economy determine that household's income. This income determines the household's claim on the economy's output. Those who have income to spend get the products produced in the market system.

- By communicating changes in consumer tastes to entrepreneurs and resource suppliers, the market system prompts appropriate adjustments in the allocation of the economy's resources. The market system also encourages technological advance and capital accumulation, both of which raise a nation's standard of living.

- Competition, the primary mechanism of control in the market economy, promotes a unity of self-interest and social interests. As directed by an invisible hand, competition harnesses the self-interest motives of businesses and resource suppliers to further the social interest.

2.4 ▶ THE DEMISE OF THE COMMAND SYSTEM

- The command systems of the Soviet Union and pre-reform China met their demise because of coordination difficulties under central planning and the lack of profit incentives that encourage product improvement, produce new products, and give rise to entrepreneurship.

2.5 ▶ THE CIRCULAR FLOW MODEL

- The circular flow model illustrates the flows of resources and products from households to businesses and from businesses to households, along with the corresponding monetary flows. Businesses are on the buying side of the resource market and the selling side of the product market. Households are on the selling side of the resource market and the buying side of the product market.

TERMS AND CONCEPTS

economic system, p. 32
command system, p. 32
market system, p. 32
private property, p. 32
freedom of enterprise, p. 33
freedom of choice, p. 33
self-interest, p. 33

competition, p. 33
market, p. 34
specialization, p. 35
division of labour, p. 35
medium of exchange, p. 36
barter, p. 36
money, p. 36

consumer sovereignty, p. 38
dollar votes, p. 38
creative destruction, p. 40
invisible hand, p. 41
circular flow diagram, p. 44
factor market, p. 44
product market, p. 44

www.mcgrawhillconnect.ca

STUDY QUESTIONS

LO 2.1 1. Contrast how a market system and a command economy try to cope with economic scarcity.

LO 2.2 2. How does self-interest help achieve society's economic goals? Why is there such a wide variety of desired goods and services in a market system? In what way are entrepreneurs and businesses at the helm of the economy but commanded by consumers?

LO 2.2 3. Why is private property, and the protection of property rights, so critical to the success of the market system?

LO 2.2 4. What are the advantages of using capital in the production process? What is meant by the term "division of labour"? What are the advantages of specialization in the use of human and material resources? Explain why exchange is the necessary consequence of specialization.

LO 2.2 5. What problem does barter entail? Indicate the economic significance of money as a medium of exchange. What is meant by the statement "We want money only to part with it"?

LO 2.2 6. Evaluate and explain the following statements:

a. The market system is a profit-and-loss system.

b. Competition is the disciplinarian of the market economy.

LO 2.3 7. In the 1990s thousands of dot-com companies emerged with great fanfare to take advantage of the Internet and new information technologies. A few, like Yahoo, eBay, and Amazon, have generally thrived and prospered, but many others struggled and eventually failed. Explain these varied outcomes in terms of how the market system answers the question "What goods and services will be produced?"

LO 2.3 8. **KEY QUESTION** With current technology, suppose a firm is producing 400 loaves of banana bread daily. Also, assume that the least-cost combination of resources in producing those loaves is 5 units of labour, 7 units of land, 2 units of capital, and 1 unit of entrepreneurial ability, selling at prices of $40, $60, $60, and $20, respectively. If the firm can sell these 400 loaves at $2 per unit, will it continue to produce banana bread? If this firm's situation is typical for the other makers of banana bread, will factors of production flow to or away from this bakery good?

9. **KEY QUESTION** Some large hardware stores such as Canadian Tire boast of carrying as many as 20,000 different products in each store. What motivated the producers of those individual products to make them and offer them for sale? How did the producers decide on the best combinations of factors to use? Who made those factors available, and why? Who decides whether these particular hardware products should continue to be produced and offered for sale? **LO 2.3**

10. What is meant by the term "creative destruction"? How does the emergence of MP3 (iPod) technology relate to this idea? **LO 2.3**

11. In a sentence, describe the meaning of the phrase "invisible hand." **LO 2.3**

12. In market economies, firms rarely worry about the availability of inputs to produce their products, whereas in a command economies input availability is a constant concern. Why the difference? **LO 2.4**

13. Distinguish between the factor market and the product market in the circular flow model. In what way are businesses and households both sellers and buyers in this model? What are the flows in the circular flow model? **LO 2.5**

INTERNET APPLICATION QUESTIONS @

1. **Diamonds—Interested in Buying One?** Use the links on the McConnell-Brue-Flynn-Barbiero Web site (Chapter 2) to access the Internet auction site eBay. Select the category Jewelry and Watches, followed by Loose Diamonds and Gemstones, and then Loose Diamonds. How many loose diamonds are for sale at the moment? Note the wide array of sizes and prices of the diamonds. In what sense is there competition among the sellers in this market? How does that competition influence prices? In what sense is there competition among buyers? How does that competition influence prices?

2. **Barter and the Canada Revenue Agency.** Bartering occurs when goods or services are exchanged without the exchange of money. For some, barter's popularity is that it enables them to avoid paying taxes to the government. How might such avoidance occur? Use the links on the McConnell-Brue-Flynn-Barbiero Web site (Chapter 2) to access the Canada Revenue Agency's (CRA) interpretation of barter transactions. Does the CRA treat barter as taxable or nontaxable income? How is the value of a barter transaction determined?

CHAPTER 3

Demand, Supply, and Market Equilibrium

According to an old joke, if you teach a parrot to say "demand and supply," you have an economist. There is much truth in this quip. The tools of demand and supply can take us far in understanding both specific economic issues and how individual markets work.

Markets bring together buyers ("demanders") and sellers ("suppliers"), and exist in many forms. The corner gas station, an e-commerce site, the local music store, a farmer's roadside stand—all are familiar markets. The Toronto Stock Exchange and the Chicago Board of Trade are markets where buyers and sellers of stocks and bonds and farm commodities from all over the world communicate with one another to buy and sell. Auctioneers bring together potential buyers and sellers of art, livestock, used farm equipment, and, sometimes, real estate. In labour markets, new college or university graduates "sell" and employers "buy" specific labour services.

Some markets are local, while others are national or international. Some are highly personal, involving face-to-face contact between demander and supplier; others are faceless, with buyer and seller never seeing or knowing each other.

To keep things simple, we will focus in this chapter on markets consisting of large numbers of buyers and sellers of standardized products. These are the highly competitive markets such as a central grain exchange, a stock market, or a market for foreign currencies in which the price is "discovered" through the interacting decisions of buyers and sellers. All such markets involve demand, supply, price, and quantity.

3.1 | Demand

Demand is a schedule or a curve that shows the various amounts of a product that consumers are willing and able to purchase at each of a series of possible prices during a specified period of time.[1] Demand shows the quantities of a product that will be purchased at various possible prices, other things equal. Demand can easily be shown in table form. Figure 3-1 shows a hypothetical demand schedule for a single consumer purchasing bushels of corn.

---

[1] This definition obviously is worded to apply to product markets. To adjust it to apply to factor markets, substitute the word *factor* for *product* and the word *businesses* for *consumers*.

FIGURE 3-1   **An Individual Buyer's Demand for Corn**

Because price and quantity demanded are inversely related, an individual's demand schedule graphs as a downward-sloping curve such as *D*. Specifically, the law of demand says that, other things equal, consumers will buy more of a product as its price declines. Here and in later figures, *P* stands for price, and *Q* stands for quantity (either demanded or supplied).

Price per bushel	Quantity demanded (bushels per week)
$5	10
4	20
3	35
2	55
1	80

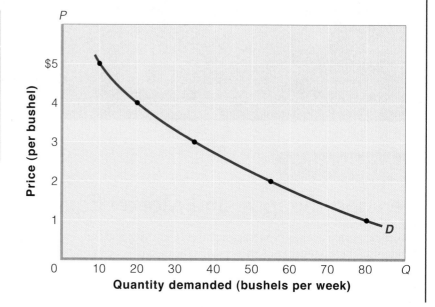

 ORIGIN 3.1
Demand
and Supply

demand
A schedule or curve that shows the various amounts of a product that consumers are willing and able to purchase at each of a series of possible prices during a specified period of time.

As price falls, the quantity demanded rises, and as price rises, the quantity demanded falls.

 ORIGIN 3.2
Law of Demand

law of demand
Other things equal, as price falls the quantity demanded rises, and vice versa.

The table in Figure 3-1 reveals the relationship between the various prices of corn and the quantity of corn a particular consumer would be willing *and able* to purchase at each of these prices. We say willing *and able* because willingness alone is not effective in the market. You may be willing to buy a plasma television set, but if that willingness is not backed by the necessary dollars, it will not be effective and, therefore, will not be reflected in the market. If the price of corn were $5 per bushel, our consumer would be willing and able to buy 10 bushels per week; if it were $4, the consumer would be willing and able to buy 20 bushels per week, and so forth.

The table in Figure 3-1 does not tell us which of the five possible prices will actually exist in the corn market. That depends on the interaction between demand and supply. Demand is simply a statement of a buyer's plans, or intentions, with respect to the purchase of a product.

To be meaningful, the quantities demanded at each price must relate to a specific period—a day, a week, a month. Saying "a consumer will buy 10 bushels of corn at $5 per bushel" is meaningless. Unless a specific time period is stated, we do not know whether the demand for a product is large or small.

Law of Demand

A fundamental characteristic of demand is this: *Other things equal, as price falls the quantity demanded rises, and as price rises the quantity demanded falls.* There is a negative or *inverse* relationship between price and quantity demanded. This inverse relationship is called the **law of demand.**

The "other-things-equal" assumption is critical here (see Chapter 1). Many factors other than the price of the product being considered affect the amount purchased. The quantity of Nikes purchased will depend not only on the price of Nikes but also on the prices of substitutes such as Reeboks, Adidas, and New Balances. The law of demand in this case says that fewer Nikes will be purchased if the price of Nikes rises *and if the prices of Reeboks, Adidas, and New Balances all remain constant.* Another way of stating it is that if the *relative price* of Nikes rises, fewer Nikes will be bought.

ORIGIN 3.3
Diminishing
Marginal Utility

diminishing marginal utility
As a consumer increases
the consumption of a good
or service, the marginal
utility obtained from each
additional unit of the good
or service decreases.

ORIGIN 3.4
Income and
Substitution Effect

income effect
A change in the price of a
product changes a consumer's
real income (purchasing
power) and thus the quantity
of the product purchased.

substitution effect
A change in the price of a
product changes the relative
expensiveness of that good
and hence changes the
willingness to buy it rather
than other goods.

MATH 3.1
The Demand
Function

demand curve
A curve illustrating the inverse
(negative) relationship between
the quantity demanded of a
good or service and its price,
other things equal.

Why the inverse relationship between price and quantity demanded? Let's look at two explanations:

- In any specific time period, each buyer of a product will derive less satisfaction (or benefit, or utility) from each successive unit of the product consumed. The second Big Mac will yield less additional satisfaction to the consumer than the first, and the third still less than the second. That is, consumption is subject to **diminishing marginal utility.** And because successive units of a particular product yield less and less marginal utility, consumers will buy additional units only if the price of those units is progressively reduced.

- We can also explain the law of demand in terms of *income* and *substitution* effects. The **income effect** indicates that a lower price increases the purchasing power of a buyer's money income, enabling the buyer to purchase more of the product than she or he could buy before. A higher price has the opposite effect. The **substitution effect** suggests that at a lower price, buyers have the incentive to substitute what is now a less expensive product for similar products that are now *relatively* more expensive. The product whose price has fallen is now "a better deal" relative to the other products.

For example, a decline in the price of chicken will increase the purchasing power of consumer incomes, enabling them to buy more chicken (the income effect). At a lower price, chicken is relatively more attractive and consumers tend to substitute it for pork, beef, and fish (the substitution effect). The income and substitution effects combine to make consumers able and willing to buy more of a product at a low price than at a high price.

The Demand Curve

The inverse relationship between price and quantity demanded for any product can be represented on a simple graph, in which, by convention, we measure *quantity demanded* on the horizontal axis and *price* on the vertical axis. In Figure 3-1 we have plotted the five price–quantity data points listed in the table and connected the points with a smooth curve, labelled *D*. Such a curve is called a **demand curve.** Its downward slope reflects the law of demand—people buy more of a product, service, or factor as its price falls. The relationship between price and quantity demanded is inverse (or negative). We also refer to the demand curve as the *marginal benefit curve*, a concept first introduced in Chapter 1. The demand curve tells us the extra benefit the consumer derives from one more unit of a good or service.

The table and the graph in Figure 3-1 contain exactly the same data and reflect the same relationship between price and quantity demanded. But the graph shows that relationship more simply and clearly than a table or a description in words.

Market Demand

So far, we have concentrated on just one consumer. By adding the quantities demanded by all consumers at each of the various possible prices, we can get from *individual* demand to *market* demand. If there are just three buyers in the market, as represented in Figure 3-2, it is relatively easy to determine the total quantity demanded at each price. Figure 3-2 shows the graphical summing procedure: At each price we sum horizontally the individual quantities demanded to obtain the total quantity demanded at that price; we then plot the price and the total quantity demanded as one point of the market demand curve.

Competition, of course, ordinarily entails many more than three buyers of a product. To avoid hundreds or thousands or millions of additions, we suppose that all the buyers in a market are willing and able to buy the same amounts at each of the possible prices. Then we just multiply those amounts by the number of buyers to obtain the market demand. This is how we arrived at the demand schedule and demand curve D_1, in Figure 3-3, for a market with 200 corn buyers. The table in Figure 3-3 shows the calculations for 200 corn buyers.

FIGURE 3-2	Market Demand for Corn, Three Buyers

The market demand curve D is the horizontal summation of the individual demand curves (D_1, D_2, and D_3) of all the consumers in the market. At the price of $3, for example, the three individual curves yield a total quantity demanded of 100 bushels.

Price per bushel	Quantity demanded							Total quantity demanded per week
	Joe		Jen		Jay			
$5	10	+	12	+	8	=		30
4	20	+	23	+	17	=		60
3	35	+	39	+	26	=		100
2	55	+	60	+	39	=		154
1	80	+	87	+	54	=		221

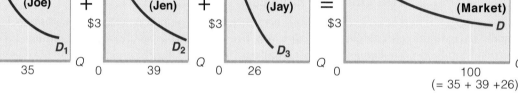

Determinants of Demand

In constructing a demand curve such as D_1 in Figure 3-3, we assume that price is the most important influence on the amount of any product purchased, even though other factors can and do affect purchases. These factors, called **determinants of demand,** are assumed to be constant when a demand curve like D_1 is drawn. They are the "other things equal" in the relationship between price and quantity demanded. When any of these determinants changes, the demand curve will shift to the right or left.

determinants of demand
Factors other than price that determine the quantities demanded of a good or service.

The basic determinants of demand are (1) consumers' tastes (preferences), (2) the number of consumers in the market, (3) consumers' incomes, (4) the prices of related goods, and (5) consumers' expectations.

Changes in Demand

A change in one or more of the determinants of demand will change the demand data (the demand schedule) in the table accompanying Figure 3-3, and therefore the location of the demand curve there. A change in the demand schedule—or, graphically, a shift in the demand curve—is called a *change in demand.*

If consumers desire to buy more corn at each possible price than is reflected in column 2 of the table in Figure 3-3, that *increase in demand* is shown as a shift of the demand curve to the right, say from D_1 to D_2. Conversely, a *decrease in demand* occurs when consumers buy less corn at each possible price than is indicated in column 2 of the table in Figure 3-3. The leftward shift of the demand curve from D_1 to D_3 in Figure 3-3 shows that situation.

Now let's see how changes in each determinant affect demand.

FIGURE 3-3 — Changes in the Demand for Corn

A change in one or more of the determinants of demand causes a change in demand. An increase in demand is shown as a shift of the demand curve to the right, as from D_1 to D_2. A decrease in demand is shown as a shift of the demand curve to the left, as from D_1 to D_3. These changes in demand are to be distinguished from a change in quantity demanded, which is caused by a change in the price of the product, as shown by a movement from, say, point a to point b on fixed demand curve D_1.

Market Demand for Corn, 200 Buyers, D_1	
(1) Price per bushel	(2) Total quantity demanded per week
$5	2,000
4	4,000
3	7,000
2	11,000
1	16,000

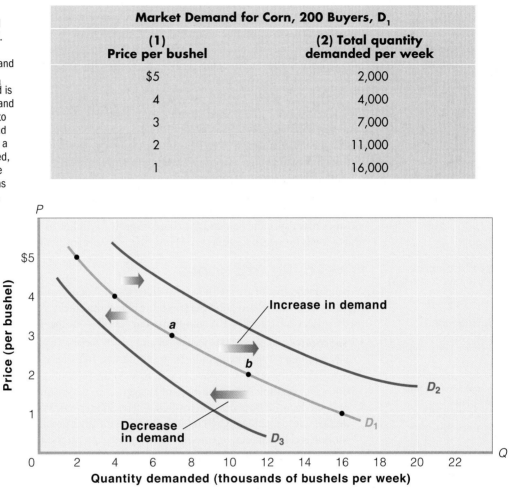

TASTES

A favourable change in consumer tastes (preferences) for a product—a change that makes the product more desirable—means that more of it will be demanded at each price. Demand will increase; the demand curve will shift rightward. An unfavourable change in consumer preferences will decrease demand, shifting the demand curve to the left.

New products may affect consumer tastes; for example, the introduction of digital cameras has greatly decreased demand for film cameras. Consumers' concern over the health hazards of cholesterol and obesity have increased the demand for broccoli, low-calorie sweeteners, and fresh fruit, while decreasing the demand for beef, veal, eggs, and whole milk. Over the past several years, the demand for coffee drinks and table wine has greatly increased, driven by changes in tastes. So, too, has the demand for DVDs and iPhones.

NUMBER OF BUYERS

An increase in the number of buyers in a market increases product demand; a decrease in the number of buyers decreases demand. For example, the rising number of older persons in Canada in recent years has increased the demand for motor homes, medical care, and retirement communities.

Immigration to Canada from many parts of the world has greatly increased the demand for a whole range of ethnic goods and services in southern Ontario and British Columbia. Improvements in communications have given financial markets international range and have thus increased the demand for stocks and bonds. International trade agreements have reduced foreign trade barriers to Canadian farm commodities, increasing the number of buyers and the demand for those products.

In contrast, the emigration (out-migration) from many small rural communities has reduced the population and thus the demand for housing, home appliances, and auto repair in those towns.

INCOME

How changes in income affect demand is more complex. For most products, a rise in income causes an increase in demand. Consumers typically buy more steaks, furniture, and electronic equipment as their incomes increase. Conversely, the demand for such products declines as income falls. Products for which demand varies directly with money income are called **normal goods.**

Although most products are normal goods, there are some exceptions. As incomes increase beyond some point, the demand for used clothing, retread tires, and third-hand automobiles may decrease, because the higher incomes enable consumers to buy new versions of those products. Similarly, rising incomes may cause the demand for charcoal grills to decline as wealthier consumers switch to gas grills. Goods for which demand varies *inversely* with money income are called **inferior goods.**

PRICES OF RELATED GOODS

A change in the price of a related good may either increase or decrease the demand for a product, depending on whether the related good is a substitute or a complement. A **substitute good** is one that can be used in place of another good. A **complementary good** is one that is used together with another good.

- *Substitutes*   Häagen-Dazs ice cream and Ben & Jerry's ice cream are substitute goods or, simply, *substitutes*. When two products are substitutes, an increase in the price of one will increase the demand for the other. Conversely, a decrease in the price of one will decrease the demand for the other. For example, when the price of Häagen-Dazs ice cream rises, consumers will demand less of it and increase their demand for Ben & Jerry's ice cream. When the price of Colgate toothpaste declines, the demand for Crest declines. So it is with other product pairs such as Nikes and Reeboks, Molson and Labatt beer, or Chevrolet and Ford pickup trucks. They are *substitutes in consumption.*

- *Complements*   Because complementary goods (or, simply, *complements*) are used together, they are typically demanded jointly. Examples include computers and software, cell phones and cellular service, and snowboards and lift tickets. If the price of a complement (for example, lettuce) goes up, the demand for the related good (salad dressing) will decline. Conversely, if the price of a complement (for example, tuition) falls, the demand for a related good (textbooks) will increase.

- *Unrelated Goods*   The vast majority of goods that are not related to one another are called *independent goods*. Examples are butter and golf balls, potatoes and automobiles, and bananas and wristwatches. A change in the price of one does not affect the demand for the other.

CONSUMER EXPECTATIONS

Changes in consumer expectations may shift demand. A newly formed expectation of higher future prices may cause consumers to buy now in order to "beat" the anticipated price rises, thus increasing current demand. That is often what happens in so-called hot real estate markets. Buyers rush in because they think the price of new homes will continue to escalate rapidly. Some buyers fear being "priced out of the market" and therefore not obtaining the home they desire. Other buyers— speculators—believe they will be able to sell the houses later at a higher price. Whichever their motivation, these buyers increase the demand for houses.

Similarly, a change in expectations concerning future income may prompt consumers to change their current spending. For example, first-round NHL draft choices may splurge on new luxury cars in anticipation of a lucrative professional hockey contract. Or workers who become fearful of losing their jobs may reduce their demand for, say, vacation travel.

---

normal good
A good or service whose consumption rises when income increases and falls when income decreases, price remaining constant.

inferior good
A good or service whose consumption declines as income rises (and conversely).

substitute goods
Products or services that can be used in place of each other.

complementary goods
Products and services that are used together.

TABLE 3-1   Determinants of Demand Curve Shifts

Determinant	Examples
Change in buyer tastes	Physical fitness rises in popularity, increasing the demand for jogging shoes and bicycles; cell phone popularity rises, reducing the demand for traditional phones.
Change in number of buyers	A decline in the birthrate reduces the demand for children's toys.
Change in income	A rise in incomes increases the demand for such normal goods as restaurant meals, sports tickets, and MP3 players while reducing the demand for such inferior goods as cabbage, turnips, and inexpensive wine.
Change in the prices of related goods	A reduction in airfares reduces the demand for bus transportation (substitute goods); a decline in the price of DVD players increases the demand for DVD movies (complementary goods).
Change in consumer expectations	Political instability in South America creates an expectation of higher future prices of coffee beans, thereby increasing today's demand for coffee beans.

In summary, an *increase* in demand—the decision by consumers to buy larger quantities of a product at each possible price—may be caused by:

- a favourable change in consumer tastes
- an increase in the number of buyers
- rising incomes if the product is a normal good
- falling incomes if the product is an inferior good
- an increase in the price of a substitute good
- a decrease in the price of a complementary good
- a new consumer expectation that prices and income will be higher in the future

You should "reverse" these generalizations to explain a *decrease* in demand. Table 3-1 provides additional illustrations of the determinants of demand. *(Key Question 3)*

Changes in Quantity Demanded

change in demand
A change in the quantity demanded of a good or service at every price.

A *change in demand* must not be confused with a *change in quantity demanded*. A **change in demand** is a shift of the entire demand curve to the right (an increase in demand) or to the left (a decrease in demand). It occurs because the consumer's state of mind about purchasing the product has been altered in response to a change in one or more of the determinants of demand. Recall that *demand* is a schedule or a curve; therefore, a *change in demand* means a change in the schedule and a shift of the curve.

change in quantity demanded
A movement from one point to another on a demand curve.

In contrast, a **change in quantity demanded** is a movement from one point to another point— from one price–quantity combination to another—on a fixed demand schedule or demand curve. The cause of such a change is an increase or decrease in the price of the product under consideration. In Figure 3-3, for example, a decline in the price of corn from $5 to $4 will increase the quantity of corn demanded from 2000 to 4000 bushels.

In Figure 3-3, the shift of the demand curve D_1 to either D_2 or D_3 is a change in demand. But the movement from point *a* to point *b* on curve D_1 represents a change in quantity demanded: Demand has not changed; it is the entire curve, and it remains fixed in place.

QUICK REVIEW

▶ A market is any arrangement that facilitates the purchase and sale of goods, services, or resources.

▶ Demand is a schedule or a curve showing the amount of a product that buyers are willing and able to purchase at each possible price in a series of prices, in a particular time period.

▶ The law of demand states that, other things equal, the quantity of a good purchased varies inversely with its price.

▶ The demand curve shifts because of changes in (a) consumer tastes, (b) the number of buyers in the market, (c) consumer income, (d) the prices of substitute or complementary goods, and (e) consumer expectations.

▶ A change in demand is a shift of the demand curve; a change in quantity demanded is a movement from one point to another on a fixed demand curve.

3.2 | Supply

supply
A schedule or curve that shows the amounts of a product that producers are willing and able to make available for sale at each of a series of possible prices during a specific period.

Supply is a schedule or curve that shows the amounts of a product that producers are willing and able to make available for sale at each of a series of possible prices during a specific period.[2] Figure 3-4 is a hypothetical supply schedule for a single producer of corn. It shows the quantities of corn that will be supplied at various prices, other things equal. We also refer to the supply curve as the *marginal cost curve*, a concept first introduced in Chapter 1. The supply curve tells us the extra cost incurred by a producer in producing one more unit of a good or service.

Law of Supply

The table in Figure 3-4 shows a direct relationship between price and quantity supplied. As price rises, the quantity supplied rises; as price falls, the quantity supplied falls. This relationship is called the **law of supply**. A supply schedule tells us that, other things equal, firms will produce and offer for sale more of their product at a high price than at a low price. The higher the price, the greater the incentive and the greater the quantity supplied.

law of supply
The principle that, other things equal, an increase in the price of a product will increase the quantity of it supplied, and conversely for a price decrease.

Price is an obstacle from the standpoint of the consumer, who is on the paying end. The higher the price, the less the consumer will buy. But the supplier is on the receiving end of the product's price. To the supplier, price represents revenue, which serves as an incentive to produce and sell a product. The higher the price, the greater is the incentive and greater the quantity supplied.

Consider a farmer in Ontario who is deciding on how much corn to plant. As corn prices rise, as shown in the table in Figure 3-4, the farmer finds it profitable to plant more. And the higher corn prices enable the Ontario farmer to cover the increased costs associated with more intensive cultivation and the use of more seed, fertilizer, and pesticides. The overall result is more corn.

Now consider a manufacturer. Beyond some quantity of production, manufacturers usually encounter increasing *marginal cost*—the added cost of producing one more unit of output. Certain productive resources—in particular, the firm's plant and machinery—cannot be expanded quickly, so the firm uses more of other resources, such as labour, to produce more output. But as labour becomes more abundant relative to the fixed plant and equipment, the additional workers have relatively less space and access to equipment. For example, the added workers may have to wait to gain access to machines. As a result, each added worker produces less added output, and the marginal cost of successive units of output rises accordingly. The firm will not produce the more costly units unless it receives a higher price for them. Again, price and quantity supplied are directly related.

---

[2] This definition is worded to apply to product markets. To adjust it to apply to factor markets, substitute the word *factor* for *product* and the word *owner* for *producer*.

FIGURE 3-4   ## An Individual Producer's Supply of Corn

Because price and quantity supplied are positively related, a firm's supply schedule is an upward-sloping curve such as S. Specifically, the law of supply says that, other things equal, firms will supply more of a product as its price rises.

Price per bushel	Quantity supplied (bushels per week)
$5	60
4	50
3	35
2	20
1	5

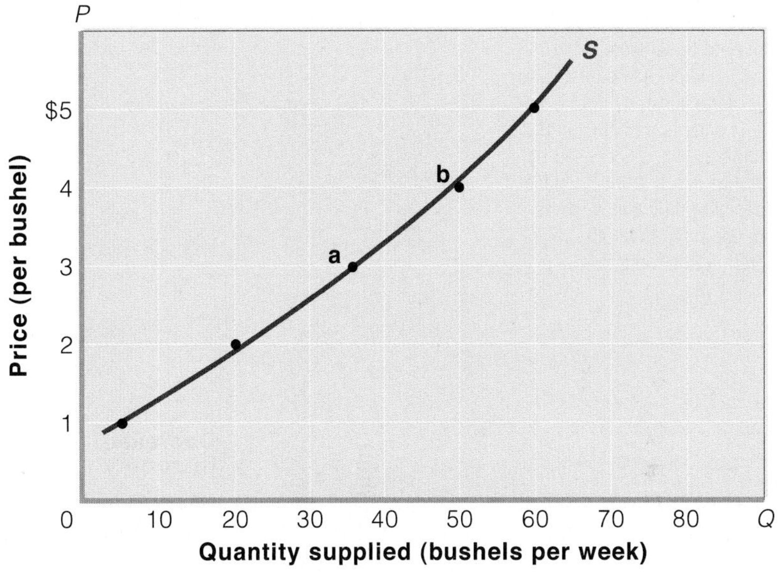

The Supply Curve

supply curve
A curve illustrating the positive (direct) relationship between the quantity supplied of a good or service and its price, other things equal.

As with demand, it is convenient to represent individual supply graphically. In Figure 3-4, curve S is the **supply curve** that corresponds with the price–quantity data in the accompanying table. The upward slope of the curve reflects the law of supply—a producer will offer more of a good, service, or factor for sale as its price rises. The relationship between price and quantity supplied is positive or direct.

 MATH 3.2
The Supply Function

Market Supply

Market supply is derived from individual supply in exactly the same way that market demand is derived from individual demand. We sum the quantities supplied by each producer at each price. That is, we obtain the market supply curve by "horizontally adding" the supply curves of the individual producers. The price–quantity supplied data in the table in Figure 3-5 are for an assumed 200 identical producers in the market, each willing to supply corn according to the supply schedule shown in Figure 3-4. Curve S_1 in Figure 3-5 is a graph of the market supply data. Note that the axes in Figure 3-5 are the same as those used in our graph of market demand (Figure 3-2). The only difference is that we change the label on the horizontal axis from "quantity demanded" to "quantity supplied."

Determinants of Supply

determinants of supply
Causes other than price that determine the quantities supplied of a good or service.

In constructing a supply curve, we assume that price is the most significant influence on the quantity supplied of any product. But other factors (the "other things equal") can and do affect supply. The supply curve is drawn on the assumption that these other things are fixed and do not change. If one of them does change, a *change in supply* will occur, meaning that the entire supply curve will shift.

The basic **determinants of supply** are (1) factor prices, (2) technology, (3) taxes and subsidies, (4) prices of other goods, (5) price expectations, and (6) the number of sellers in the market. A change in any one or more of these determinants of supply will move the supply curve for a product

FIGURE 3-5   **Changes in the Supply of Corn**

A change in one or more of the determinants of supply causes a shift in supply. An increase in supply is shown as a rightward shift of the supply curve, as from S_1 to S_2. A decrease in supply is depicted as a leftward shift of the curve, as from S_1 to S_3. In contrast, a change in the quantity supplied is caused by a change in the product's price and is shown by a movement from one point to another, as from *a* to *b*, on a fixed supply curve.

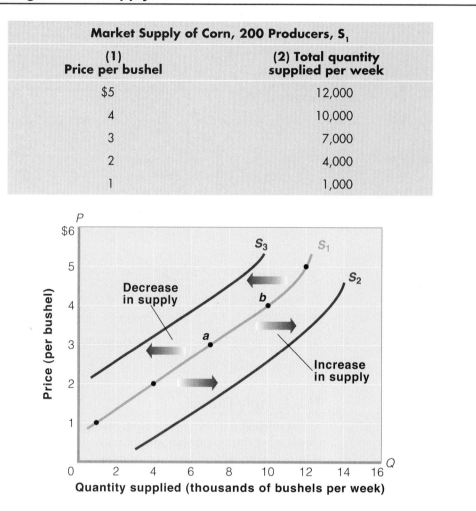

Market Supply of Corn, 200 Producers, S_1	
(1) Price per bushel	(2) Total quantity supplied per week
$5	12,000
4	10,000
3	7,000
2	4,000
1	1,000

either to the right or to the left. A shift to the *right,* as from S_1 to S_2 in Figure 3-5, signifies an *increase* in supply: Producers supply larger quantities of the product at each possible price. A shift to the *left,* as from S_1 to S_3, indicates a *decrease* in supply.

Changes in Supply

Let's consider how changes in each of the determinants affect supply. The key idea is that costs are a major factor underlying supply curves; anything that affects costs (other than changes in output itself) usually shifts the supply curve.

FACTOR PRICES

The prices of the factors used as inputs in the production process determine the costs of production. Higher *factor* prices raise production costs and, assuming a particular *product* price, squeeze profits. That reduction in profits reduces the incentive for firms to supply output at each product price. For example, an increase in the prices of iron ore and coke will increase the cost of producing steel for Dofasco and reduce its supply.

In contrast, lower *factor* prices reduce production costs and increase profits. So, when input prices fall, firms supply greater output at each product price. For example, a decrease in the prices of flat-panel glass will increase the supply of big-screen television sets.

TECHNOLOGY

Improvements in technology (techniques of production) enable firms to produce units of output with fewer inputs. Because inputs are costly, using fewer of them lowers production costs and increases supply. Example: Technological advances in producing flat-panel LCD (liquid crystal display) computer monitors have greatly reduced their cost. The manufacturers will now offer more such monitors than previously at various prices: the supply of flat-panel LCD monitors has increased.

TAXES AND SUBSIDIES

Businesses treat most taxes as costs. An increase in sales or property taxes will increase production costs and reduce supply. In contrast, subsidies are "taxes in reverse." If the government subsidizes the production of a good, it in effect lowers the producers' costs and increases supply. Government subsidies will, for example, help increase the number of rural medical practitioners.

PRICES OF OTHER GOODS

Firms that produce a particular product, say, soccer balls, can sometimes use their plant and equipment to produce alternative goods, say, basketballs and volleyballs. The higher prices of these "other goods" may entice soccer ball producers to switch production to those other goods to increase profits. This substitution in production results in a decline in the supply of soccer balls. Alternatively, when the prices of basketballs and volleyballs decline relative to the price of soccer balls, producers of those goods may decide to produce more soccer balls instead, increasing their supply.

PRODUCER EXPECTATIONS

Changes in expectations about the future price of a product may affect the producer's current willingness to supply that product. Ontario farmers anticipating a higher corn price in the future might withhold some of their current corn harvest from the market, thereby causing a decrease in the current supply of corn. In contrast, in many types of manufacturing industries, newly formed expectations that price will increase may induce firms to add another shift of workers or to expand their production facilities, causing current supply to increase.

NUMBER OF SELLERS

Other things equal, the larger the number of suppliers, the greater the market supply. As more firms enter an industry, the supply curve shifts to the right. Conversely, the smaller the number of firms in the industry, the less the market supply. This means that as firms leave an industry, the supply curve shifts to the left. Example: Canada and the United States have imposed restrictions on haddock fishing to replenish dwindling stocks. As part of that policy, the federal government has bought the boats of some of the haddock fishers as a way of putting them out of business and decreasing the catch. The result has been a decline in the market supply of haddock.

Table 3-2 is a checklist of the determinants of supply, along with further illustrations. *(Key Question 6)*

Changes in Quantity Supplied

The distinction between a *change in supply* and a *change in quantity supplied* mirrors the distinction between a change in demand and a change in quantity demanded. Because supply is a schedule or curve, a **change in supply** means a change in the entire schedule and a shift of the entire curve. An increase in supply shifts the curve to the right; a decrease in supply shifts it to the left. The cause of a change in supply is a change in one or more of the determinants of supply.

change in supply
A change in the quantity supplied of a good or service at every price; a shift of the supply curve to the left or right.

TABLE 3-2	Determinants of Supply Curve Shifts

Determinant	Examples
Change in factor prices	A decrease in the price of microchips increases the supply of computers; an increase in the price of crude oil reduces the supply of gasoline.
Change in technology	The development of more effective wireless technology increases the supply of cell phones.
Changes in taxes and subsidies	An increase in the excise tax on cigarettes reduces the supply of cigarettes; a decline in subsidies to universities reduces the supply of higher education.
Change in prices of other goods	An increase in the price of cucumbers decreases the supply of watermelons.
Change in producer expectations	An expectation of a substantial rise in future log prices decreases the supply of logs today.
Change in number of sellers	An increase in the number of Internet service providers increases the supply of such services; the formation of women's professional basketball leagues increases the supply of women's professional basketball games.

change in quantity supplied
A movement from one point to another on a fixed supply curve.

In contrast, a **change in quantity supplied** is a movement from one point to another on a fixed supply curve. The cause of such a movement is a change in the price of the specific product being considered. Consider supply curve S_1 in Figure 3-5. A decline in the price of corn from $4 to $3 decreases the quantity of corn supplied per week from 10,000 to 7000 bushels. This movement from point b to point a along S_1 is a change in quantity supplied, not a change in supply. Supply is the full schedule of prices and quantities shown, and this schedule does not change when the price of corn changes.

QUICK REVIEW

▶ A supply schedule or curve shows that, other things equal, the quantity of a good supplied varies directly with its price.

▶ The supply curve shifts because of changes in (a) factor prices, (b) technology, (c) taxes and subsidies, (d) prices of other goods, (e) producer expectations, and (f) the number of sellers.

▶ A change in supply is a shift of the supply curve; a change in quantity supplied is a movement from one point to another on a fixed supply curve.

3.3 | Market Equilibrium

With our understanding of demand and supply, we can now show how the decisions of buyers of corn interact with the decisions of the sellers to determine the price and quantity of corn. In the table in **Figure 3-6 (Key Graph)**, columns 1 and 2 repeat the market supply of corn (from Figure 3-5), and columns 2 and 3 repeat the market demand for corn (from the table in Figure 3-3). We assume this is a competitive market, so that neither buyers nor sellers can set the price.

Equilibrium Price and Quantity

equilibrium price
The price in a competitive market at which the quantity demanded and the quantity supplied are equal.

We are looking for the equilibrium price and equilibrium quantity. The **equilibrium price** (or "market-clearing price") is the price where the intentions of buyers and sellers match. It is the price where quantity demanded equals quantity supplied. The table in Figure 3-6 reveals that at $3, *and only at that price,* the number of bushels of corn that sellers wish to sell (7000) is identical to

KEY GRAPH

FIGURE 3-6
Equilibrium Price and Quantity

The intersection of the downward-sloping demand curve *D* and the upward-sloping supply curve *S* indicates the equilibrium price and quantity, here $3 and 7000 bushels of corn. The shortages of corn at below-equilibrium prices (for example, 7000 bushels at $2) drive up price. These higher prices increase the quantity supplied and reduce the quantity demanded until equilibrium is achieved. The surpluses caused by above-equilibrium prices (for example, 6000 bushels at $4) push price down. As price drops, the quantity demanded rises and the quantity supplied falls until equilibrium is established. At the equilibrium price and quantity, there are neither shortages nor surpluses of corn.

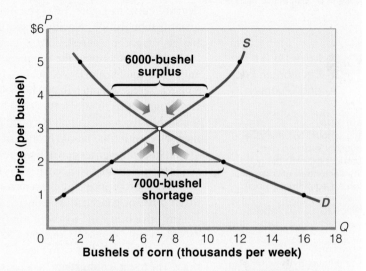

(1) Total quantity supplied per week	(2) Price per bushel	(3) Total quantity demanded per week	(4) Surplus (+) or shortage (–)
12,000	$5	2,000	+10,000↓
10,000	4	4,000	+ 6,000↓
7,000	3	7,000	0
4,000	2	11,000	– 7,000↑
1,000	1	16,000	–15,000↑

The arrows indicate the effect on price.

Quick Quiz

1. Demand curve *D* in Figure 3-6 is downward-sloping because:
   a. producers offer less product for sale as the price of the product falls.
   b. lower prices of a product create income and substitution effects, which lead consumers to purchase more of it.
   c. the larger the number of buyers in a market, the lower the product price.
   d. price and quantity demanded are directly (positively) related.

2. Supply curve *S*:
   a. reflects an inverse (negative) relationship between price and quantity supplied.
   b. reflects a direct (positive) relationship between price and quantity supplied.
   c. depicts the collective behaviour of buyers in this market.
   d. shows that producers will offer more of a product for sale at a low product price than at a high product price.

3. At the $3 price:
   a. quantity supplied exceeds quantity demanded.
   b. quantity demanded exceeds quantity supplied.
   c. the product is abundant and a surplus exists.
   d. there is no pressure on price to rise or fall.

4. At price $5 in this market:
   a. there will be a shortage of 10,000 units.
   b. there will be a surplus of 10,000 units.
   c. quantity demanded will be 12,000 units.
   d. quantity demanded will equal quantity supplied.

Answers: 1.b; 2.b; 3.d; 4.b

the number consumers want to buy (also 7000). At $3 and 7000 bushels of corn, there is neither a shortage nor a surplus of corn. So 7000 bushels of corn is the **equilibrium quantity:** the quantity demanded and quantity supplied at the equilibrium price in a competitive market.

Graphically, the equilibrium price is indicated by the intersection of the supply curve and the demand curve in Figure 3-6. (The horizontal axis now measures both quantity demanded and quantity supplied.) With neither a shortage nor a surplus at $3, the market is in equilibrium, mean-ing "in balance" or "at rest."

To better understand the uniqueness of the equilibrium price, let's consider other prices. At any above-equilibrium price, quantity supplied exceeds quantity demanded. For example, at the $4 price, sellers will offer 10,000 bushels of corn, but buyers will purchase only 4000. The $4 price encourages sellers to offer lots of corn but discourages many consumers from buying it. The result is a **surplus** (or *excess supply*) of 6000 bushels. If corn sellers produced them all, they would find themselves with 6000 unsold bushels of corn.

Surpluses drive prices down. Even if the $4 price existed temporarily, it could not persist. The large surplus would prompt competing sellers to lower the price to encourage buyers to take the surplus off their hands. As the price fell, the incentive to produce corn would decline and the incentive for consumers to buy corn would increase. As shown in Figure 3-6, the market would move to its equilibrium at $3.

Any price below the $3 equilibrium price would create a shortage; quantity demanded would exceed quantity supplied. Consider a $2 price, for example. We see both from column 2 of the table and from the demand curve in Figure 3-6 that quantity demanded exceeds quantity supplied at that price. The result is a **shortage** (or *excess demand*) of 7000 bushels of corn. The $2 price discourages sellers from devoting resources to corn and encourages consumers to desire more bushels than are available. The $2 price cannot persist as the equilibrium price. Many consumers who want to buy corn at this price will not obtain it. They will express a willingness to pay more than $2 to get corn. Competition among these buyers will drive up the price, eventually to the $3 equilibrium level. Unless disrupted by supply or demand changes, this $3 price of corn will continue to prevail.

Rationing Function of Prices

The ability of the competitive forces of supply and demand to establish a price at which selling and buying decisions are consistent is called the **rationing function of prices.** In our case, the equilib-rium price of $3 clears the market, leaving no burdensome surplus for sellers and no inconvenient shortage for potential buyers. It is the combination of freely made individual decisions that sets this market-clearing price. In effect, the market outcome says that all buyers who are willing and able to pay $3 for a bushel of corn will obtain it; all buyers who cannot or will not pay $3 will go without corn. Similarly, all producers who are willing and able to offer corn for sale at $3 a bushel will sell it; all producers who cannot or will not sell for $3 per bushel will not sell their product. *(Key Question 8)*

Efficient Allocation

A competitive market such as that we have described not only rations goods to consumers but also allo-cates society's resources efficiently to the particular product. Competition among corn producers forces them to use the best technology and right mix of productive resources. Otherwise, their costs will be too high relative to the market price and they will be unprofitable. The result is **productive efficiency:** the production of any particular good in the least costly way. When society produces corn at the lowest achievable per-unit cost, it is expending the smallest amount of resources to produce that product and therefore is making available the largest amount of resources to produce other desired goods. Suppose society has only $100 worth of resources available. If it can produce a bushel of corn using $3 of those resources, then it will have available $97 of resources remaining to produce other goods. This is clearly better than producing the corn for $5 and having only $95 of resources available for the alternative uses.

Competitive markets also produce **allocative efficiency:** the *particular mix* of goods and services most highly valued by society (minimum-cost production assumed). For example, society wants land suitable for growing corn used for that purpose, not to grow dandelions. It wants diamonds to

CONSIDER THIS | Ticket Scalping: A Bum Rap!

Ticket prices for athletic events and musical concerts are usually set far in advance of the events. Sometimes the original ticket price is too low to be the equilibrium price. Lines form at the ticket window, and a severe shortage of tickets occurs at the printed price. What happens next? Buyers who are willing to pay more than the original price bid up the ticket price in resale ticket markets.

Tickets sometimes get resold for much greater amounts than the original price—in a market transaction known as "scalping." For example, an original buyer may resell a $75 ticket to a concert for $200, $250, or more. The media sometimes denounces scalpers for "ripping off" buyers by charging "exorbitant" prices.

But is scalping really a rip-off? We must first recognize that such ticket resales are voluntary transactions. If both buyer and seller did not expect to gain from the exchange, it would not occur! The seller must value the $200 more than seeing the event, and the buyer must value seeing the event at $200 or more. So there are no losers or victims

here: Both buyer and seller benefit from the transaction. The "scalping" market simply redistributes assets (game or concert tickets) from those who would rather have the money (and the other things money can buy) to those who would rather have the tickets.

Does scalping impose losses or injury on the sponsors of the event? If the sponsors are injured, it is because they initially priced tickets below the equilibrium level. Perhaps they did this to create a long waiting line and the attendant media publicity. Alternatively, they may have had a genuine desire to keep tickets affordable for lower-income, ardent fans. In either case, the event sponsors suffer an opportunity cost in the form of less ticket revenue than they might have otherwise received. But such losses are self-inflicted and quite separate and distinct from the fact that some tickets are later resold at a higher price.

So is ticket scalping undesirable? Not on economic grounds! It is an entirely voluntary activity that benefits both sellers and buyers.

MATH 3.4
Allocative
Efficiency

be used for jewellery, not crushed up and used as an additive to give concrete more sparkle. It wants MP3 players and iPods, not cassette players and tapes. Moreover, society does not want to devote all its resources to corn, diamonds, and portable digital music players. It wants to assign some resources to wheat, gasoline, and cell phones. Competitive markets make those proper assignments.

The equilibrium price and quantity in competitive markets usually produce an assignment of resources that is "right" from an economic perspective. Demand essentially reflects the marginal benefit (MB) of the good (the extra benefit received from consuming one more unit of a good or service) and supply reflects the marginal cost (MC) of the good (the extra cost associated with producing one more unit of a good or service). The market ensures that firms produce all units of goods for which MB exceeds MC, and no units for which MC exceeds MB. At the intersection of the demand and supply curves, MB equals MC and allocative efficiency results. As economists say, there is neither an underallocation of resources nor an overallocation of resources to the product. We say more about productive and allocative efficiency in later chapters of *Microeconomics*.

Changes in Supply, Demand, and Equilibrium

We know that demand might change because of fluctuations in consumer tastes or incomes, changes in consumer expectations, or variations in the prices of related goods. Supply might change in response to changes in resource prices, technology, or taxes. What effects will such changes in supply and demand have on equilibrium price and quantity?

CHANGES IN DEMAND

Suppose that the supply for some good (for example, potatoes) is constant and demand increases, as shown in Figure 3-7a. As a result, the new intersection of the supply and demand curves is at higher values on both the price and quantity axes. An increase in demand raises both equilibrium price and equilibrium quantity. Conversely, a decrease in demand, such as that shown in Figure 3-7b, reduces

FIGURE 3-7 **Changes in Demand and Supply and the Effects on Price and Quantity**

The increase in demand from D_1 to D_2 in panel (a) increases both equilibrium price and quantity. The decrease in demand from D_1 to D_2 in panel (b) decreases both equilibrium price and quantity. The increase in supply from S_1 to S_2 in panel (c) decreases equilibrium price and increases equilibrium quantity. The decline in supply from S_1 to S_2 in panel (d) increases equilibrium price and decreases equilibrium quantity. The boxes in the top right corners summarize the respective changes and outcomes. The upward arrows in those boxes signify increases in demand (D), supply (S), equilibrium price (P), and equilibrium quantity (Q); the downward arrows signify decreases in these items.

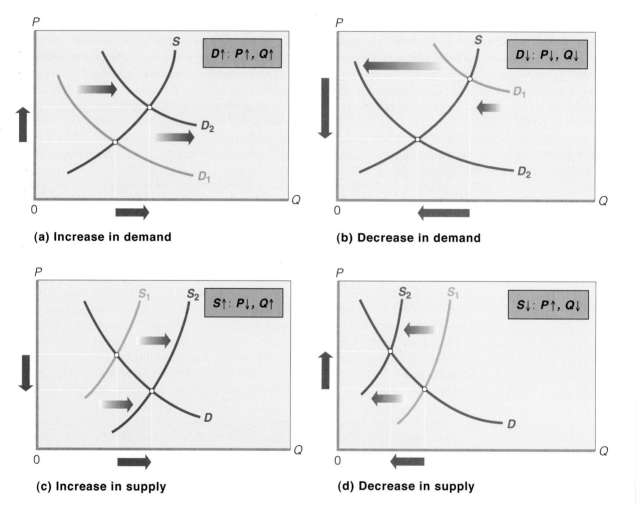

(a) Increase in demand

(b) Decrease in demand

(c) Increase in supply

(d) Decrease in supply

both equilibrium price and equilibrium quantity. (The value of graphical analysis is now apparent: We need not fumble with columns of figures to determine the outcomes; we need only compare the new and the old points of intersection on the graph.)

CHANGES IN SUPPLY

What happens if demand for some good (for example, flash drives) is constant but supply increases, as in Figure 3-7c? The new intersection of supply and demand is located at a lower equilibrium price but at a higher equilibrium quantity. An increase in supply reduces equilibrium price but increases equilibrium quantity. In contrast, if supply decreases, as in Figure 3-7d, the equilibrium price rises while the equilibrium quantity declines.

COMPLEX CASES

When both supply and demand change, the effect is a combination of the individual effects. As you study the following cases, keep in mind that each effect on the demand and supply curves has to be considered independently.

1. *Supply Increase; Demand Decrease*   What effect will a supply increase and a demand decrease for some good (for example, apples) have on equilibrium price? Both changes decrease price, so the net result is a price drop greater than that resulting from either change alone.

   What about equilibrium quantity? Here the effects of the changes in supply and demand are opposed: The increase in supply increases equilibrium quantity, but the decrease in demand reduces it. The direction of the change in quantity depends on the relative sizes of the changes in supply and demand. If the increase in supply is larger than the decrease in demand, the equilibrium quantity will increase. But if the decrease in demand is greater than the increase in supply, the equilibrium quantity will decrease.

2. *Supply Decrease; Demand Increase*   A decrease in supply and an increase in demand for some good (for example, gasoline) both increase price. Their combined effect is an increase in equilibrium price greater than that caused by either change separately. But their effect on equilibrium quantity is again indeterminate, depending on the relative sizes of the changes in supply and demand. If the decrease in supply is larger than the increase in demand, the equilibrium quantity will decrease. In contrast, if the increase in demand is greater than the decrease in supply, the equilibrium quantity will increase.

3. *Supply Increase; Demand Increase*   What if supply and demand both increase for some good (for example, cell phones)? A supply increase drops equilibrium price, while a demand increase boosts it. If the increase in supply is greater than the increase in demand, the equilibrium price will fall. If the opposite holds, the equilibrium price will rise.

   The effect on equilibrium quantity is certain: The increases in supply and in demand each raise equilibrium quantity. Therefore, the equilibrium quantity will increase by an amount greater than that caused by either change alone.

   MATH 3.5
   Changes in supply, demand, and equilibrium.

4. *Supply Decrease; Demand Decrease* What about decreases in both supply and demand? If the decrease in supply is greater than the decrease in demand, equilibrium price will rise. If the reverse is true, equilibrium price will fall. Because decreases in supply and in demand each reduce equilibrium quantity, we can be sure that equilibrium quantity will fall.

CONSIDER THIS | Salsa and Coffee Beans

If you forget the other-things-equal assumption, you can encounter situations that seem to be in conflict with the laws of demand and supply. For example, suppose salsa manufacturers sell 1 million bottles of salsa at $4 a bottle in one year; 2 million bottles at $5 in the next year; and 3 million at $6 in the year thereafter. Price and quantity purchased vary directly, and these data seem to be at odds with the law of demand.

But there is no conflict here; the data do not refute the law of demand. The catch is that the law of demand's other-things-equal assumption has been violated over the three years in the example. Specifically, because of changing tastes and rising incomes, the demand for salsa has increased sharply, as in Figure 3-7a. The result is higher prices and larger quantities purchased.

Another example: The price of coffee beans occasionally has shot upward at the same time that the quantity of coffee beans harvested has declined. These events seemingly contradict the direct relationship between price and quantity denoted by supply. The other-things-equal assumption underlying the upsloping supply curve was violated. Poor coffee harvests decreased supply, as in Figure 3-7d, increasing the equilibrium price of coffee and reducing the equilibrium quantity.

The laws of demand and supply are not refuted by observations of price and quantity made over periods of time in which either demand or supply changes.

TABLE 3-3	Effects of Changes in Both Supply and Demand		
	Change in supply	**Change in demand**	**Effect on equilibrium price**	**Effect on equilibrium quantity**
1	Increase	Decrease	Decrease	Indeterminate
2	Decrease	Increase	Increase	Indeterminate
3	Increase	Increase	Indeterminate	Increase
4	Decrease	Decrease	Indeterminate	Decrease

Table 3-3 summarizes these four cases. To understand them fully you should draw supply and demand diagrams for each case to confirm the effects listed in Table 3-3.

Special cases arise when a decrease in demand and a decrease in supply, or an increase in demand and an increase in supply, exactly cancel out. In both cases, the net effect on equilibrium price will be zero; price will not change. *(Key Question 9)*

The optional appendix accompanying this chapter provides examples of situations in which both supply and demand change over the same period of time.

3.4 | Application: Government-Set Prices

Prices in most markets are free to rise or fall to their equilibrium levels, no matter how high or low that might be. However, government sometimes concludes that supply and demand will produce prices that are unfairly high for buyers or unfairly low for sellers. So government may place legal limits on how high or low a price or prices may go. Is that a good idea?

Price Ceilings

price ceiling
A legally established maximum price for a good or service.

A **price ceiling** is the maximum legal price a seller may charge for a product or service. A price at or below the ceiling is legal; a price above it is not. The rationale for establishing price ceilings (or ceiling prices) on specific products is that they purportedly enable consumers to obtain some essential good or service that they could not afford at the equilibrium price. Examples are rent controls and usury laws, which specify maximum prices in the forms of rent and interest that can be charged to borrowers.

GRAPHICAL ANALYSIS

We can easily demonstrate the effects of price ceilings graphically using the example of gasoline. Let's suppose that rapidly rising world income boosts the purchase of automobiles and shifts the demand for gasoline to the right so that the equilibrium or market price reaches $1.25 per litre, shown as P_0 in Figure 3-8. The rapidly rising price of gasoline greatly burdens low-income and moderate-income households, who pressure the federal government to "do something." To keep gasoline affordable for these households, the government imposes a ceiling price, P_c, of $0.75 per litre. To be effective, a price ceiling must be below the equilibrium price. A ceiling price of $1.50, for example, would have no immediate effect on the gasoline market.

To be effective, a price ceiling on gasoline must be below the equilibrium price.

What are the effects of this $0.75 ceiling price? The rationing ability of the free market is rendered ineffective. Because the ceiling price, P_c, is below the market-clearing price, P_0, there is a shortage of gasoline. The quantity of gasoline demanded at P_c is Q_d and the quantity supplied is only Q_s; an excess demand or shortage of amount $Q_d - Q_s$ occurs.

The price ceiling, P_c, prevents the usual market adjustment in which competition among buyers bids up price, inducing more production and rationing some buyers out of the market. That process would continue until the shortage disappeared at the equilibrium price and quantity, P_0 and Q_0.

FIGURE 3·8 — A Price Ceiling Results in a Shortage

A price ceiling is a maximum legal price, such as P_c. When the ceiling price is below the equilibrium price a persistent product shortage results. Here that shortage is shown by the horizontal distance between Q_d and Q_s.

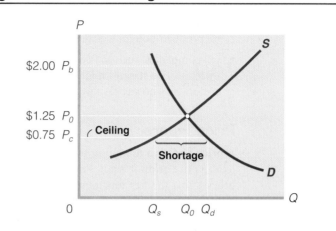

RATIONING PROBLEM

How will the government apportion the available supply, Q_s, among buyers who want the greater amount Q_d? Should gasoline be distributed on a first-come, first-served basis—that is, to those willing and able to get in line the soonest and to stay in line? Or should gas stations distribute it on the basis of favouritism? Since an unregulated shortage does not lead to an equitable distribution of gasoline, the federal government must establish some formal system for rationing it to consumers. One option is to issue ration coupons, which allow coupon-holders to purchase a fixed amount of gasoline per month. The rationing system might require the printing of coupons for Q_s litres of gasoline and then the equal distribution of the coupons among consumers so that the wealthy family of four and the poor family of four both receive the same number of coupons.

BLACK MARKETS

Ration coupons would not prevent a second problem from arising. The demand curve in Figure 3-8 tells us that many buyers are willing to pay more than the ceiling price P_c, and, of course, it is more profitable for gasoline stations to sell at prices above the ceiling. For example, at Q_s in Figure 3-8 some consumers would be willing to pay a price of up to $2.00 ($P_b$) to acquire some gasoline. Thus, despite the sizable enforcement bureaucracy that will accompany the price controls, *black markets* in which gasoline is illegally bought and sold at prices above the legal limits will flourish. Counterfeiting of ration coupons will also be a problem, and since the price of gasoline is now set by the federal government, there would be political pressure to set the price even lower.

CREDIT CARD INTEREST CEILINGS

Over the years there have been many calls in Canada for interest-rate ceilings on credit card accounts. The usual rationale for interest-rate ceilings is that the chartered banks and retail stores issuing such cards are presumably taking unfair advantage of users—and, in particular, lower-income users—by charging interest rates that average about 18 percent per year.

What might be the responses if the Canadian government imposed a below-equilibrium interest rate on credit cards? The lower interest income associated with a legal interest ceiling would require the issuers of cards to reduce their costs or enhance their revenues:

• Card issuers might tighten credit standards to reduce losses due to non-payment and collection costs. Then, low-income and young Canadians who have not yet established their creditworthiness would find it more difficult to obtain credit cards.

• The annual fee charged to cardholders might be increased, as might the fee charged to merchants for processing credit card sales. Similarly, card users might be charged a fee for every transaction.

- Card users now have a post-purchase grace period during which the credit provided is interest-free. That period might be shortened or eliminated.

- Certain "enhancements" that accompany some credit cards (for example, extended warranties on products bought with a card) might be eliminated.

- Oil companies, such as Petro-Canada, that issue their own cards to consumers who buy from their gasoline stations might increase their prices to help offset the decline of interest income; customers who pay cash would in effect be subsidizing customers who use credit cards.

Price Floors

price floor
A legally established price above an equilibrium price.

A **price floor** is a minimum price fixed by the government. A price at or above the price floor is legal; a price below it is not. Price floors above equilibrium prices are usually invoked when society believes that the free functioning of the market system has not provided a sufficient income for certain groups of resource suppliers or producers. Supported prices for some agricultural products and current minimum wages are two examples of price (or wage) floors. Let's analyze the results of imposing a price floor on wheat.

Suppose the equilibrium price for wheat is $3 per bushel and, because of that low price, many Prairie farmers have extremely low incomes. The federal government decides to help by establishing a legal price floor or price support of $4 per bushel.

What will be the effects? At any price above the equilibrium price, quantity supplied will exceed quantity demanded—that is, there will be an excess supply or surplus of the product. Prairie farmers will be willing to produce and offer for sale more than private buyers are willing to purchase at the price floor. As we saw with a price ceiling, an imposed legal price disrupts the rationing ability of the free market.

Supported prices for some agricultural products are an example of price floors.

GRAPHICAL ANALYSIS

Figure 3-9 illustrates the effect of a price floor on wheat. Suppose that S and D are the supply and demand curves for wheat. Equilibrium price and quantity are P_0 and Q_0, respectively. If the federal government imposes a price floor of P_f, farmers will produce Q_s, but private buyers will purchase only Q_d. The surplus is the excess of Q_s over Q_d.

FIGURE 3-9   **A Price Floor Results in a Surplus**

A price floor is a minimum legal price, such as P_f. When the price floor is above the equilibrium price, a persistent product surplus results. Here that surplus is shown by the horizontal distance between Q_s and Q_d.

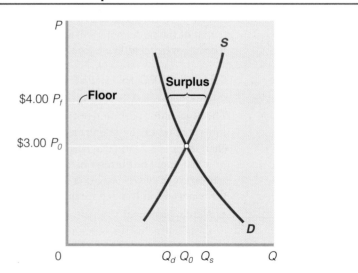

The government can cope with the surplus resulting from a price floor in only two ways:

1. It can restrict supply (for example, by asking farmers in Alberta, Saskatchewan, and Manitoba to agree to take a certain amount of land out of production) or increase demand (for example, by researching new uses for the product involved). These actions may reduce the difference between the equilibrium price and the price floor and thereby reduce the size of the resulting surplus.

2. The federal government can purchase the surplus output at the $4 price (thereby subsidizing Prairie farmers) and store or otherwise dispose of it.

ADDITIONAL CONSEQUENCES

Price floors such as P_f in Figure 3-9 not only disrupt the rationing ability of prices but also distort resource allocation. Without the price floor, the $3 equilibrium price of wheat would cause financial losses and force high-cost wheat producers to plant other crops or abandon farming altogether. But the $4 price floor allows them to continue to grow wheat and remain farmers. So society devotes too many of its scarce resources to wheat production and too few to producing other, more valuable, goods and services. It fails to achieve allocative efficiency.

That's not all. Consumers of wheat-based products pay higher prices because of the price floor. Taxpayers pay higher taxes to finance the government's purchase of the surplus. Also, the price floor causes potential environmental damage by encouraging wheat farmers to bring "marginal land" into production. The higher price also prompts imports of wheat. But, since such imports would increase the quantity of wheat supplied and thus undermine the price floor, the government needs to erect tariffs (taxes on imports) to keep the foreign wheat out. Such tariffs usually prompt other countries to retaliate with their own tariffs against Canadian agricultural or manufacturing exports.

It is easy to see why economists "sound the alarm" when politicians advocate imposing price ceilings or price floors such as price controls, interest-rate lids, or agricultural price supports. In all these cases, good intentions lead to bad economic outcomes. Government-controlled prices cause shortages or surpluses, distort resource allocation, and produce negative side effects. *(Key Question 14)*

QUICK REVIEW

▶ In competitive markets, prices adjust to the equilibrium level at which quantity demanded equals quantity supplied.

▶ The equilibrium price and quantity are those indicated by the intersection of the supply and demand curves for any product or resource.

▶ An increase in demand increases equilibrium price and quantity; a decrease in demand decreases equilibrium price and quantity.

▶ An increase in supply reduces equilibrium price but increases equilibrium quantity; a decrease in supply increases equilibrium price but reduces equilibrium quantity.

▶ Over time, equilibrium price and quantity may change in directions that seem at odds with the laws of demand and supply because the other-things-equal assumption is violated.

▶ Government-controlled prices in the form of ceilings and floors stifle the rationing functions of prices, distort resource allocations, and cause negative side effects.

The LAST WORD   A Legal Market for Human Organs?

A legal market might eliminate the present shortage of human organs for transplant. But many serious objections exist to turning human body parts into commodities for purchase and sale.

It has become increasingly commonplace in medicine to transplant kidneys, lungs, livers, eye corneas, pancreases, and hearts from deceased individuals to those whose organs have failed or are failing. But surgeons and many of their patients face a growing problem: Too few donated organs are available for transplant. Not everyone who needs a transplant can get one. Indeed, an inadequate supply of donated organs causes an estimated 400 Canadian deaths per year.

Why Shortages? Seldom do we hear of shortages of desired goods in market economies. What is different about organs for transplant? One difference is that no legal market exists for human organs. To understand this situation, observe the demand curve D_1 and supply curve S_1 in the accompanying figure. The downward slope of the demand curve tells us that if there were a market for human organs, the quantity of organs demanded would be greater at lower prices than at higher prices. Vertical supply curve S_1 represents the fixed quantity of human organs now donated via consent before death. Because the price of these donated organs is in effect zero, quantity demanded, Q_3, exceeds quantity supplied, Q_1. The shortage of $Q_3 - Q_1$ is rationed through a waiting list of those in medical need of transplants. Many people die while still on the waiting list.

Use of a Market A market for human organs would increase the incentive to donate organs. Such a market might work like this: An individual might specify in a legal document a willingness to sell one or more usable human organs on death or brain death. The person could specify where the money from the sale would go, for example, to family, a church, an educational institution, or a charity. Firms would then emerge to purchase organs and resell them where needed for profit. Under such a system, the supply curve of usable organs would take on the normal upward slope of typical supply curves. The higher the expected price of an organ, the greater the number of people willing to have their organs sold at death. Suppose that the supply curve is S_2 in the figure. At the equilibrium price P_1, the number of organs made available for transplant (Q_2) would equal the number purchased for transplant (also Q_2). In this generalized case, the shortage of organs would be eliminated and,

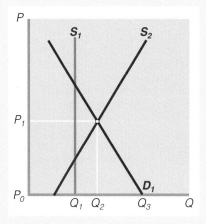

of particular importance, the number of organs available for transplanting would rise from Q_1 to Q_2. More lives would be saved and enhanced than under the present donor system.

Objections In view of this positive outcome, why is there no such market for human organs? Critics of market-based solutions have two main objections. The first is a moral objection: Critics feel that turning human organs into commodities commercializes human beings and diminishes the special nature of human life. They say there is something unseemly about selling and buying body organs as if they were bushels of wheat or ounces of gold. Moreover, critics note that the market would ration the available organs (as represented by Q_2 in the figure) to people who either can afford them (at P_1) or have health insurance for transplants. Second, a health cost objection suggests that a market for body organs would greatly increase the cost of health care. Rather than obtaining freely donated (although too few) body organs, patients would have to pay market prices for them, increasing the cost of medical care.

Rebuttal Supporters of market-based solutions to organ shortages point out that the market is simply being driven underground. Worldwide, an estimated $1 billion annual illegal market in human organs has emerged. As in other illegal markets, the unscrupulous tend to thrive.

Question

How many organ transplants were done in Canada in the latest year for which statistics are available? What is the current overall number of Canadian candidates waiting for an organ transplant? (For the answer, visit the London Health Sciences Centre Web site, www.lhsc.on.ca/About_Us/MOTP/). Do you favour the establishment of a legal market for transplant organs? Why or why not?

CHAPTER SUMMARY

3.1 ▶ DEMAND

- Demand is a schedule or curve representing the willingness of buyers in a specific period to purchase a particular product at each of various prices. The law of demand implies that consumers will buy more of a product at a low price than at a high price. Therefore, other things equal, the relationship between price and quantity demanded is negative or inverse and is graphed as a downward-sloping curve.

- Market demand curves are found by summing up (horizontally) the demand curves of the many individual consumers in the market.

- Changes in one or more of the determinants of demand (consumer tastes, the number of buyers in the market, the money incomes of consumers, the prices of related goods, and consumer expectations) shift the market demand curve. A shift to the right is an increase in demand; a shift to the left is a decrease in demand. A change in demand is different from a change in the quantity demanded, the latter being a movement from one point to another point on a fixed demand curve because of a change in the product's price.

3.2 ▶ SUPPLY

- Supply is a schedule or curve showing the amounts of a product that producers are willing to offer in the market at each possible price during a specific period. The law of supply states that, other things equal, producers will offer more of a product at a high price than at a low price. Thus, the relationship between price and quantity supplied is positive or direct, and supply is graphed as an upward-sloping curve.

- The market supply curve is the horizontal summation of the supply curves of the individual producers of the product.

- Changes in one or more of the determinants of supply (factor prices, technology, taxes and subsidies, price expectations, or the number of sellers in the market) shift the supply curve of a product. A shift to the right is an increase in supply; a shift to the left is a decrease in supply. In contrast, a change in the price of the product being considered causes a change in the quantity supplied, which is shown as a movement from one point to another point on a fixed supply curve.

3.3 ▶ MARKET EQUILIBRIUM

- The equilibrium price and quantity are established at the intersection of the supply and demand curves. The interaction of market demand and market supply adjusts the price to the point at which the quantity demanded and supplied are equal. This is the equilibrium price. The corresponding quantity is the equilibrium quantity.

- The ability of market forces to synchronize selling and buying decisions to eliminate potential surpluses and shortages is known as the rationing function of prices.

- A change in either demand or supply changes the equilibrium price and quantity. Increases in demand raise both equilibrium price and equilibrium quantity; decreases in demand lower both equilibrium price and equilibrium quantity. Increases in supply lower equilibrium price and raise equilibrium quantity; decreases in supply raise equilibrium price and lower equilibrium quantity.

- Simultaneous changes in demand and supply affect equilibrium price and quantity in various ways, depending on their direction and relative magnitudes.

3.4 ▶ APPLICATION: GOVERNMENT-SET PRICES

- A price ceiling is a maximum price set by government and is designed to help consumers.

- A price floor is a minimum price set by government and is designed to aid producers.

- Government-set prices stifle the rationing function of prices and distort the allocation of resources.

TERMS AND CONCEPTS

demand, p. 50
law of demand, p. 50
diminishing marginal utility, p. 51
income effect, p. 51
substitution effect, p. 51
demand curve, p. 51
determinants of demand, p. 52
normal good, p. 54
inferior good, p. 54
substitute goods, p. 54

complementary goods, p. 54
change in demand, p. 55
change in quantity demanded, p. 55
supply, p. 56
law of supply, p. 56
supply curve, p. 57
determinants of supply, p. 57
change in supply, p. 59
change in quantity supplied, p. 60
equilibrium price, p. 60

equilibrium quantity, p. 62
surplus, p. 62
shortage, p. 62
rationing function of prices, p. 62
productive efficiency, p. 62
allocative efficiency, p. 62
price ceiling, p. 66
price floor, p. 68

STUDY QUESTIONS

LO ▸ 3.1 1. Explain the law of demand. Why does a demand curve slope downward? How is a market demand curve derived from individual demand curves?

LO ▸ 3.1 2. What are the determinants of demand? What happens to the demand curve when any of these determinants change? Distinguish between a change in demand and a change in the quantity demanded, noting the cause(s) of each.

LO ▸ 3.1 3. **KEY QUESTION** What effect will each of the following have on the demand for small automobiles such as the Mini Cooper and Smart Car?

   a. Small automobiles become more fashionable.

   b. The price of large automobiles rises (with the price of small autos remaining the same).

   c. Income declines and small autos are an inferior good.

   d. Consumers anticipate that the price of small autos will greatly come down in the near future.

   e. The price of gasoline substantially drops.

LO ▸ 3.2 4. Explain the law of supply. Why does the supply curve slope upward? How is the market supply curve derived from the supply curves of individual producers?

LO ▸ 3.2 5. What are the determinants of supply? What happens to the supply curve when any of these determinants change? Distinguish between a change in supply and a change in the quantity supplied, noting the cause(s) of each.

LO ▸ 3.2 6. **KEY QUESTION** What effect will each of the following have on the supply of auto tires?

   a. A technological advance in the methods of producing tires.

   b. A decline in the number of firms in the tire industry.

   c. An increase in the price of rubber used in the production of tires.

   d. The expectation that the equilibrium price of auto tires will be lower in the future than currently.

   e. A decline in the price of the large tires used for semi-trailers and earth-hauling rigs (with no change in the price of auto tires).

   f. The levying of a per-unit tax on each auto tire sold.

   g. The granting of a subsidy of 50 cents per unit for each auto tire produced.

LO ▸ 3.3 7. "In the corn market, demand often exceeds supply and supply sometimes exceeds demand." "The price of corn rises and falls in response to changes in supply and demand." In which of these two statements are the terms "supply" and "demand" used correctly? Explain.

LO ▸ 3.3 8. **KEY QUESTION** Suppose the total demand for wheat and the total supply of wheat per month in the Winnipeg grain market are as follows:

Thousands of bushels demanded	Price per bushel	Thousands of bushels supplied	Surplus (+) or shortage (–)
85	$3.40	72	_____
80	$3.70	73	_____
75	$4.00	75	_____
70	$4.30	77	_____
65	$4.60	79	_____
60	$4.90	81	_____

   a. What is the equilibrium price? What is the equilibrium quantity? Fill in the surplus/shortage column and use it to explain why your answers are correct.

   b. Graph the demand for wheat and the supply of wheat. Be sure to label the axes of your graph correctly. Label equilibrium price P and equilibrium quantity Q.

   c. Why will $3.40 not be the equilibrium price in this market? Why not $4.90? "Surpluses drive prices up; shortages drive them down." Do you agree?

9. **KEY QUESTION** How will each of the following changes **LO ▸ 3.3** in demand and/or supply affect equilibrium price and equilibrium quantity in a competitive market; that is, do price and quantity rise, fall, or remain unchanged, or are the answers indeterminate because they depend on the magnitudes of the shifts? Use supply and demand diagrams to verify your answers.

   a. Supply decreases and demand is constant.

   b. Demand decreases and supply is constant.

   c. Supply increases and demand is constant.

   d. Demand increases and supply increases.

   e. Demand increases and supply is constant.

   f. Supply increases and demand decreases.

   g. Demand increases and supply decreases.

   h. Demand decreases and supply decreases.

10. In 2001, an outbreak of foot-and-mouth disease in Europe **LO ▸ 3.3** led to the burning of millions of cattle carcasses. What impact do you think this had on the supply of cattle hides, hide prices, the supply of leather goods, and the price of leather goods? In 2004, millions of chickens were culled in British Columbia due to the avian flu. What impact do you think this had on the supply of eggs, and the price of eggs?

11. Critically evaluate: "In comparing the two equilibrium **LO ▸ 3.3** positions in Figure 3-7b, I note that a smaller amount is actually demanded at a lower price. This refutes the law of demand."

LO 3.3 12. For each stock in the stock market, the number of shares sold daily equals the number of shares purchased. That is, the quantity of each firm's shares demanded equals the quantity supplied. So, if this equality always occurs, why do the prices of stocks ever change?

LO 3.3 13. Using the schedules given, plot the demand curve and the supply curve on the below graph. Label the axes and indicate for each axis the units being used to measure price and quantity. Then answer the questions.

Price	Quantity demanded (bushels of wheat)	Price	Quantity supplied (bushels of wheat)
$4.20	125,000	$4.20	230,000
4.00	150,000	4.00	220,000
3.80	175,000	3.80	210,000
3.60	200,000	3.60	200,000
3.40	225,000	3.40	190,000
3.20	250,000	3.20	180,000
3.00	275,000	3.00	170,000

a. Give the equilibrium price and quantity for wheat.

b. Indicate the equilibrium price and quantity on a graph by drawing lines from the intersection of the supply and demand curves to the price and quantity axes.

c. If the federal government decided to support the price of wheat at $4.00 per bushel, explain whether there would be a surplus or shortage and how much it would be.

d. Demonstrate your answer to part (c) on your graph being sure to label the quantity you designated as the shortage or surplus.

LO 3.4 14. **KEY QUESTION** Refer to the table in Question 8. Suppose that the government establishes a price ceiling of $3.70 for wheat. What might prompt the government to establish this price ceiling? Explain carefully the main

effects. Demonstrate your answer graphically. Next, suppose that the government establishes a price floor of $4.60 for wheat. What will be the main effects of this price floor? Demonstrate your answer graphically.

LO 3.4 15. What do economists mean when they say that "price floors and ceilings stifle the rationing function of prices and distort resource allocation"?

LO 3.4 16. Use data in the following table to explain the economic effects of a price ceiling at $6, at $5, and at $4.

Price	Quantity demanded	Quantity supplied
$7	4500	4500
6	5000	3500
5	5500	2500
4	6000	1500

LO 3.4 17. Use data in the following table to explain the economic effects of a price floor at $8, at $9, and at $10.

Price	Quantity demanded	Quantity supplied
$10	3000	7500
9	3500	6500
8	4000	5500
7	4500	4500

LO 3.3 18. **Advanced analysis:** Assume that demand for a commodity is represented by the equation $P = 10 - 0.2Q_d$ and supply by the equation $P = 2 + 0.2Q_s$, where Q_d and Q_s are quantity demanded and quantity supplied, respectively, and P is price. Using the equilibrium condition $Q_s = Q_d$, solve the equations to determine equilibrium price. Now determine equilibrium quantity. Graph the two equations to substantiate your answers.

INTERNET APPLICATION QUESTIONS @

1. **Farm Commodity Prices—Supply and Demand in Action.** Use the links on the McConnell-Brue-Flynn-Barbiero Web site (Chapter 3) to access data on the prices of farm products. Choose three farm products of your choice and determine whether their prices (as measured by "prices received by farmers") have generally increased, decreased, or stayed the same over the past three years. In which of the three cases, if any, do you think that supply has increased more rapidly than demand? In which of the three cases, if any, do you think that demand has increased more rapidly than supply? Explain your reasoning.

2. **Changes in Demand—Baby Diapers and Retirement Villages.** Other things equal, an increase in the number of buyers for a product or service will increase

demand. Baby diapers and retirement villages are two products designed for different population groups. The McConnell-Brue-Flynn-Barbiero Web site (Chapter 3) provides links to population pyramids (graphs that show the distribution of population by age and sex) for countries for the current year, 2025, and 2050. View the population pyramids for Mexico, Japan, and Canada by selecting International Data Base and then Population Pyramids. Which country would you expect to have the greatest percentage increase in demand for baby diapers in the year 2050? For retirement villages? Which country would you expect to have the greatest absolute increase in demand for baby diapers? For retirement villages?

Appendix: Additional Examples of Supply and Demand

Our discussion has clearly demonstrated that supply and demand analysis is a powerful tool for understanding equilibrium prices and quantities. The information provided is fully sufficient for moving forward in the book, but you may find that additional examples of supply and demand are helpful. This optional appendix provides several concrete illustrations of changes in supply and demand. It also applies supply and demand analysis to non-priced goods (goods owned in common and not bought and sold in markets).

Your instructor may assign all, some, or none of this appendix, depending on time availability and preferences.

Changes in Supply and Demand

As Figure 3-6 demonstrates, changes in supply and demand cause changes in price, quantity, or both. The following applications illustrate this fact in several real-world markets. The simplest situations are those in which either supply changes while demand remains constant, or demand changes while supply remains constant. Let's consider two such simple cases first, before looking at more complex applications.

Lettuce

Every now and then, we hear on the news that extreme weather has severely reduced the size of some crop such as lettuce, apples, or cherries. Suppose, for example, that a severe freeze destroys a sizable portion of the lettuce crop. This unfortunate situation implies a significant decline in supply, which we represent in Figure A3-1 as a leftward shift of the supply curve from S_1 to S_2. At each price, consumers desire as much lettuce as before, so the freeze does not affect the demand for lettuce. That is, demand curve D_1 does not shift.

What are the consequences of the reduced supply of lettuce for equilibrium price and quantity? As shown in Figure A3-1, the leftward shift of the supply curve disrupts the previous equilibrium in the market for lettuce and drives the equilibrium price up from P_1 to P_2.

Consumers respond to that price hike by reducing the quantity of lettuce demanded from Q_1 to Q_2. Equilibrium in the market is restored, now at P_2 and Q_2. Consumers who are willing and able to pay price P_2 obtain lettuce; consumers unwilling or

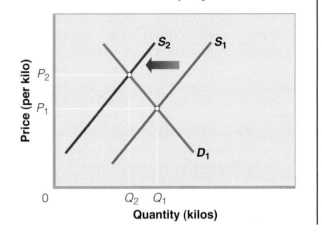

FIGURE A3-1 **The Market for Lettuce**

The decrease in the supply of lettuce, shown here by the shift from S_1 to S_2, increases the equilibrium price of lettuce from P_1 to P_2 and reduces the equilibrium quantity from Q_1 to Q_2.

unable to pay that price do not. Some consumers continue to buy as much lettuce as before, even at the higher price. Others buy some lettuce but not as much as before, and still others forgo lettuce altogether. The latter two groups use the money they would have spent on lettuce to obtain other products, say, carrots, whose price has not gone up.

Corn and Ethanol

Between the beginning of 2006 and middle of 2007, the price of corn doubled. Did people suddenly demand more corn flakes? Not hardly! The demand for cereals, beef, and other food products that use corn as inputs was relatively stable. Instead, the driving force was a rapid increase in the price of oil and gasoline (one of our following examples). This increase boosted the demand for ethanol, an alcohol-like substance that is blended with conventional gasoline. In North America, producers refine ethanol mainly from corn, although ethanol can also be refined from sugar and other agricultural commodities. So the increase in the demand for ethanol drove up the demand for corn and raised its equilibrium price.

We depict this situation in Figure A3-2 as the rightward shift of the demand curve from D_1 to D_2. This demand increase

FIGURE A3-2   The Market for Corn

The increase in the demand for corn, shown here by the shift from D_1 to D_2, increases the equilibrium price of corn from P_1 to P_2 and expands the equilibrium quantity from Q_1 to Q_2.

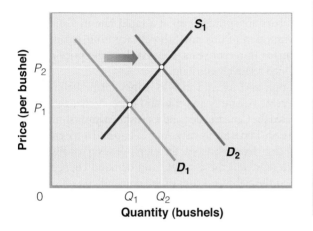

FIGURE A3-3   The Market for Pink Salmon

In the last two decades, the supply of pink salmon has increased and the demand for pink salmon has decreased. As a result, the price of pink salmon has declined, as from P_1 to P_2. Because supply has increased more than demand has decreased, the equilibrium quantity of pink salmon has increased, as from Q_1 to Q_2.

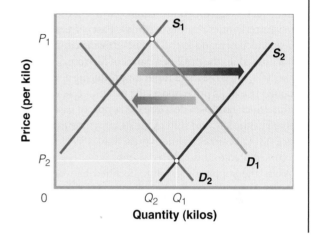

raised the equilibrium price of corn, in this case from P_1 to P_2. Producers responded accordingly by increasing the quantity of corn supplied, as from Q_1 to Q_2. At the higher price and quantity, the market achieved a new equilibrium.

Notice that the demand for corn, the price of corn, and the quantity of corn demanded and supplied all increased. But in the period depicted, the supply of corn—the entire curve S_1—remained securely fixed in place. Eventually, of course, the potential for high profits will encourage more farmers to plant more corn and therefore shift the supply curve rightward. Depending on what happens to demand, the price of corn may drop closer to P_1.

The rapid rise in the price of corn had a host of other effects that are easily understood through demand and supply analysis. The costs of producing corn-fed beef went up, which reduced the supply of beef and increased the price of hamburger and steak. The higher corn price caused the price of corn syrup (fructose) used in soft drinks to increase rapidly and led some soft-drink makers to use cane sugar instead of corn syrup in the production process. In Mexico, large numbers of angry people gathered in cities to protest the higher price of tortillas, which are made from corn and consumed in large quantities by many Mexicans.

Pink Salmon

Now let's see what happens when both supply and demand change at the same time. Several decades ago, people who caught salmon earned as much as $2 for each kilo of pink salmon—the type used mainly for canning—brought to the buyer. In Figure A3-3 that price is represented as P_1, at the intersection of supply

curve S_1 and demand curve D_1. The corresponding quantity of pink salmon is shown as Q_1 kilos. As time passed, supply and demand changed in the market for pink salmon. On the supply side, improved technology in the form of larger, more efficient fishing boats greatly increased the catch and lowered the cost of obtaining it. Also, high profits at price P_1 encouraged many new fishers to enter the industry. As a result of these changes, the supply of pink salmon greatly increased and the supply curve shifted to the right, as from S_1 to S_2 in Figure A3-3.

Over the same years, the demand for pink salmon declined, as represented by the leftward shift from D_1 to D_2 in Figure A3-3. That decrease resulted from increases in consumer income and reductions of the price of substitute products. As buyers' incomes rose, consumers shifted demand away from canned fish and toward higher-quality fresh or frozen fish, including more-valued Atlantic, Chinook, Sockeye, and Coho salmon. Moreover, the emergence of fish farming, in which salmon are raised in ocean net pens, lowered the prices of these substitute species. That, too, reduced the demand for pink salmon.

The altered supply and demand reduced the price of pink salmon to as low as $.20 per kilo, as represented by the drop in price from P_1 to P_2 in Figure A3-3. Both the supply increase and the demand decrease helped reduce the equilibrium price. However, in this particular case the equilibrium quantity of pink salmon increased, as represented by the move from Q_1 to Q_2. Both shifts of the curves reduced the equilibrium price, but equilibrium quantity increased because the increase in supply exceeded the decrease in demand.

www.mcgrawhillconnect.ca

Gasoline

The price of gasoline has increased rapidly in Canada over the past several years. For example, the average price of a litre of gasoline rose from around $.60 in 2004 to about $1.05 in 2007. What caused this more than 50 percent rise in the price of gasoline? How would we diagram this increase?

We begin in Figure A3-4 with the price of a litre of gasoline at P_1, representing the $.60 price. Simultaneous supply and demand factors disturbed this equilibrium. On the supply side, supply uncertainties relating to Middle East politics and warfare and expanded demand for oil by fast-growing countries such as China pushed up the price of a barrel of oil from $37 in 2004 to $80 in 2007. Oil is the main input for producing gasoline, so any sustained rise in its price boosts the per-unit cost of producing gasoline. Such cost rises decrease the supply of gasoline, as represented by the leftward shift of the supply curve from S_1 to S_2 in Figure A3-4. At times, refinery breakdowns in North America also contributed to this reduced supply.

While the supply of gasoline declined between 2004 and 2007, the demand for gasoline increased, as depicted by the rightward shift of the demand curve from D_1 to D_2. Incomes in general were rising over these years because the Canadian economy was rapidly expanding. Rising incomes raise demand for all normal goods, including gasoline. An increased number of low-gas-mileage SUVs and light trucks on the road also contributed to growing gas demand.

The combined decline in gasoline supply and increase in gasoline demand boosted the price of gasoline from $.60 to $1.05, as represented by the rise from P_1 to P_2 in Figure A3-4.

Because the demand increase outweighed the supply decrease, the equilibrium quantity expanded here, from Q_1 to Q_2.

In other periods the price of gasoline has *declined* as the demand for gasoline has increased. Test your understanding of the analysis by explaining how such a price decrease could occur.

Sushi

Sushi bars are springing up at a rapid rate in Canadian cities. Consumption of this raw-fish delicacy from Japan has soared in Canada in recent years. Nevertheless, the price of sushi has remained relatively constant.

Supply and demand analysis helps explain this circumstance of increased quantity and constant price. A change in tastes has increased the Canadian demand for sushi. Many first-time consumers of sushi find it highly tasty. And, as implied by the growing number of sushi bars in Canada, the supply of sushi has also expanded.

We represent these supply and demand changes in Figure A3-5 as the rightward shift of the demand curve from D_1 to D_2 and the rightward shift of the supply curve from S_1 to S_2. Observe that the equilibrium quantity of sushi increases from Q_1 to Q_2 and equilibrium price remains constant at P_1. The increase in supply, which taken alone would reduce price, has perfectly offset the increase in demand, which taken alone would raise price. The price of sushi does not change, but the equilibrium quantity greatly rises. That happens because both the increase in demand and the increase in supply expand purchases and sales.

Simultaneous increases in demand and supply can cause price to rise, fall, or remain constant, depending on the relative magnitudes of the supply and demand increases. In this case, price remained constant.

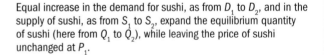

FIGURE A3-4 **The Market for Gasoline**

An increase in the demand for gasoline, as shown by the shift from D_1 to D_2, coupled with a decrease in supply, as shown by the shift from S_1 to S_2, boosts equilibrium price (here from P_1 to P_2). In this case, equilibrium quantity increases from Q_1 to Q_2 because the increase in demand outweighs the decrease in supply.

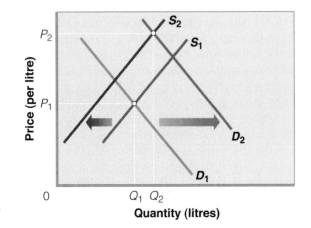

FIGURE A3-5 **The Market for Sushi**

Equal increase in the demand for sushi, as from D_1 to D_2, and in the supply of sushi, as from S_1 to S_2, expand the equilibrium quantity of sushi (here from Q_1 to Q_2), while leaving the price of sushi unchanged at P_1.

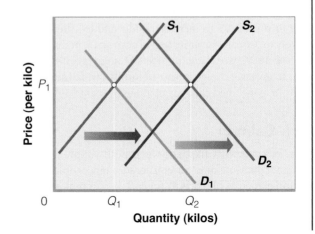

Preset Prices

In the body of this chapter we saw that an effective government-imposed price ceiling (legal maximum price) causes quantity demanded to exceed quantity supplied—a shortage. An effective government-imposed price floor (legal minimum price) causes quantity supplied to exceed quantity demanded—a surplus. Put simply: Shortages result when prices are set below equilibrium prices, and surpluses result when prices are set above equilibrium prices. We now want to establish that shortages and surpluses can occur in markets other than those in which government imposes price floors and ceilings. Such market imbalances happen when the seller or sellers set prices in advance of sales and the prices selected turn out to be below or above equilibrium prices. Consider the following two examples.

Olympic Figure Skating Finals

Tickets for the women's figure skating championship at the Olympics are among the world's hottest tickets. The popularity of this event and the high incomes of buyers translate into tremendous ticket demand. Olympic officials set the price for the tickets in advance. Invariably, the price, although high, is considerably below the equilibrium price that would equate quantity demanded and quantity supplied. A severe shortage of tickets therefore occurs in this *primary market*—the market involving the official ticket office. The shortage, in turn, creates a *secondary market* in which buyers bid for tickets held by initial purchasers rather than the original seller. Scalping tickets—selling them above the ticket price—may be legal or illegal,

depending on local laws. Figure A3-6 shows how the shortage in the primary ticket market looks in terms of supply and demand analysis. Demand curve D represents the strong demand for tickets, and supply curve S represents the supply of tickets. The supply curve is vertical because a fixed number of tickets are printed to match the capacity of the arena. At the printed ticket price of P_1, the quantity of tickets demanded, Q_2, exceeds the quantity supplied, Q_1. The result is a shortage of ab—the horizontal distance between Q_2 and Q_1 in the primary market. If the printed ticket price had been the higher equilibrium price P_2, no shortage of tickets would have occurred. But at the lower price P_1, a shortage and secondary ticket market will emerge among those buyers willing to pay more than the printed ticket price and those sellers willing to sell their purchased tickets for more than the printed price. Wherever there are shortages and secondary markets, we can safely assume that price was set below the equilibrium price.

Olympic Curling Preliminaries

Contrast the shortage of tickets for the women's figure skating finals at the Olympics to the surplus of tickets for one of the preliminary curling matches. Curling is a sport in which participants slide a heavy round object called a stone down the ice toward a target while people called sweepers use brooms to alter the course of the stone when desired. Curling is a popular spectator sport in a few nations such as Canada, but it does not draw many fans in most countries. So the demand for tickets to most of the preliminary curling events is not very strong. We demonstrate this weak demand as D in Figure A3-7. As in our previous example, the supply of tickets is fixed by the size of the arena and is shown as vertical line S.

FIGURE A3-6   **The Market for Tickets to Olympic Women's Figure Skating Finals**

The demand curve D and the supply curve S produce an equilibrium price above the P_1 price printed on the ticket. At price P_1 the quantity of tickets demanded, Q_2, greatly exceeds the quantity of tickets available (Q_1). The resulting shortage of ab (= Q_2Q_1) gives rise to a legal or illegal secondary market.

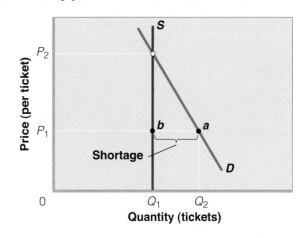

FIGURE A3·7 **The Market for Tickets to the Olympic Curling Preliminaries**

The demand curve D and the supply curve S produce an equilibrium price below the P_1 price printed on the ticket. At price P_1 the quantity of tickets demanded is less than the quantity of tickets available. The resulting surplus of ba ($= Q_1Q_2$) means the event is not sold out.

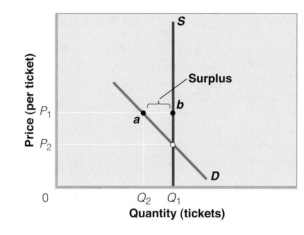

We represent the printed ticket price as P_1 in Figure A3-7. In this case the printed price is much higher than the equilibrium price of P_2. At the printed ticket price, quantity supplied is Q_1 and quantity demanded is Q_2. So a surplus of tickets of ba (= Q_1Q_2) occurs. No ticket scalping occurs and there are numerous empty seats. Only if Olympic officials had priced the tickets at the lower price P_2 would the event have been a sell-out. (Actually, Olympic officials try to adjust to demand realities for curling contests by holding them in smaller arenas than used for figure skating and by charging less for tickets. Nevertheless, the stands are rarely full for the preliminary contests, which compete against final events in other winter Olympic sports.)

APPENDIX | SUMMARY

- A decrease in the supply of a product increases its equilibrium price and reduces its equilibrium quantity. In contrast, an increase in the demand for a product boosts both its equilibrium price and its equilibrium quantity.

- Simultaneous changes in supply and demand affect equilibrium price and quantity in various ways, depending on the relative magnitudes of the changes in supply and demand. Equal increases in supply and demand, for example, leave equilibrium price unchanged.

- Sellers set prices of some items such as tickets in advance of the event. These items are sold in the primary market that involves the original seller and buyers. If preset prices turn out to be below the equilibrium prices, shortages occur and scalping in legal or illegal secondary markets arises. The prices in the secondary market then rise above the preset prices. In contrast, surpluses occur when the preset prices happen to exceed the equilibrium prices.

- Non-priced goods such as fish in public waters and game on public lands are owned in common and therefore not bought and sold in markets. A surplus of a non-priced good occurs when the sustainable quantity of the good exceeds the quantity demanded. A shortage of a non-priced good occurs when the quantity demanded exceeds the sustainable quantity. In this latter case, the good tends to be overconsumed and, without protection, may eventually be exhausted.

APPENDIX | STUDY QUESTIONS

LO ▶ A3.1 1. Suppose the supply of apples sharply increases because of perfect weather conditions throughout the growing season. Assuming no change in demand, explain the effect on the equilibrium price and quantity of apples. Explain why quantity demanded increases even though demand does not change.

LO ▶ A3.1 2. Assume the demand for lumber suddenly rises because of a rapid growth of demand for new housing. Assume no change in supply. *Why* does the equilibrium price of lumber rise? What would happen if the price did not rise under the demand and supply circumstances described?

LO ▶ A3.1 3. Suppose both the demand for olives and the supply of olives decline by equal amounts over some time period. Use graphical analysis to show the effect on equilibrium price and quantity.

LO ▶ A3.1 4. Assume that both the supply of bottled water and the demand for bottled water rise during the summer but that supply increases more rapidly than demand. What can you conclude about the directions of the impacts on equilibrium price and equilibrium quantity?

LO ▶ A3.1 5. Why are shortages or surpluses more likely with preset prices, such as those on tickets, than flexible prices, such as those on gasoline?

LO ▶ A3.1 6. Use this table to answer the questions that follow:

Quantity demanded, (thousands)	Price ($)	Quantity supplied, (thousands)
80	25	60
75	35	60
70	45	60
65	55	60
60	65	60
55	75	60
50	85	60

a. If this table reflects the supply of and demand for tickets to a particular World Cup soccer game, what is the stadium capacity?

b. If the preset ticket price is $45, would we expect to see a secondary market for tickets? Explain why or why not. Would the price of a ticket in the secondary market be higher than, the same as, or lower than the price in the primary (original) market?

c. Suppose for some other World Cup game the quantities of tickets demanded are 20,000 lower at each ticket price than shown in the table. If the ticket price remains $45, would the event be a sell-out? Explain why or why not.

7. Most scalping laws make it illegal to sell—but not to buy— **LO ▶ A3.1** tickets at prices above those printed on the tickets. Assuming that is the case, use supply and demand analysis to explain why the equilibrium ticket price in an illegal secondary market tends to be higher than in a legal secondary market.

8. Gasoline prices—how high (or low) now? Go to **Gasticker.** **LO ▶ A3.1** **com** or **www.garnetknight.com/gas** and follow the links to find the current retail price of gasoline in your area. How does the current price of regular gasoline compare with the price a year ago? What must have happened to either supply, demand, or both to explain the observed price change?

Math Appendix to Chapter 3

A3.1 | THE MATHEMATICS OF MARKET EQUILIBRIUM

A market equilibrium is the price and the quantity, denoted as the pair (Q^*, P^*), of a commodity bought or sold at price P^*. The following mathematical note provides an introduction of how a market equilibrium (Q^*, P^*) is derived.

The market equilibrium is found by using the market demand (buyers' behaviour), the market supply (sellers' behaviour), and the negotiating process (to find the agreed upon price and quantity, namely P^* and Q^*, on which to transact). The market equilibrium is identified by the condition reached at the end of the negotiating process that at the price they negotiated, P^*, the quantity of the commodity that buyers are willing to buy, denoted as Q_d, and the quantity sellers are willing to sell, denoted as Q_s, matches exactly.

The Demand Curve

The equation describing the downward-sloping demand when the demand curve is a straight line, in which Q_d represents the quantity demanded by buyers and P the price, is

$$P = a - bQ_d$$

The demand equation and curve below tell us that if the price is higher than a then the buyers will not buy; thus, for a transaction to occur the price must be lower. The demand equation and curve also tell us that at a price lower than a the quantity demanded by the buyers increases. Buyers' behaviour, as described by the demand equation, is that at lower prices buyers buy more quantity.

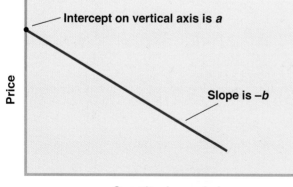

Intercept on vertical axis is *a*

Slope is *−b*

Quantity demanded

The Supply Curve

The equation describing the upward-sloping market supply function when the supply curve is a straight line, in which Q_s represents the quantity supplied by sellers and P the price, is

$$P = c + dQ_s$$

If the price is lower than c then the sellers will sell nothing, as the figure below shows. If the price is c or higher, then the supply equation states that sellers facing higher prices sell more quantity. Sellers' behaviour, as described by the supply curve and equation, is that at higher prices sellers make more quantity available.

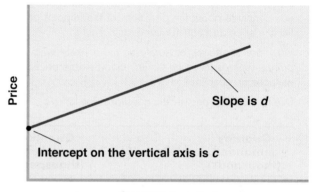

Slope is *d*

Intercept on the vertical axis is *c*

Quantity supplied

The Market Equilibrium

The negotiating process (in which price and quantity or both adjust) provides the mechanism by which, eventually, buyers and sellers agree upon a price, P^*, and a quantity, Q^*, at which they can buy and sell and thus complete the transaction. At the end of the negotiating process, the quantity demanded by the buyers, Q_d, is equal to the quantity supplied by the sellers, Q_s (at the agreed-upon price), and thus the market is in equilibrium. The mathematical representation of such a negotiating process is described as follows.

At the agreed price, P^*, the equilibrium condition of the negotiating process, the equality in the quantity demanded and supplied, is

$$Q_d = Q_s$$

Having denoted Q^* as the equilibrium quantity, then it must be that $Q^* = Q_d = Q_s$. To solve for the equilibrium quantity Q^* and the equilibrium price P^* the demand and supply functions are used. With Q^* the equilibrium quantity, for the buyers

$$P^* = a - bQ^*,$$

and for the sellers

$$P^* = c + dQ^*.$$

Now, since P^* is the same agreed-upon price by both buyer and seller, then

$$a - bQ^* = c + dQ^*,$$

giving the equilibrium quantity, Q^*, as

$$Q^* = \frac{(a-c)}{(b+d)}$$

To find P^* substitute $\frac{(a-c)}{(b+d)}$ in the supply (or demand) function.

$$P^* = c + d = \frac{(a-c)}{(b+d)}, \text{ thus}$$

$$P^* = \frac{(ad-bc)}{(b+d)}$$

The equilibrium is $(Q^*, P^*) = \left[\frac{(a-c)}{(b+d)}, \frac{(ad-bc)}{(b+d)}\right].$

The market equilibrium may also be represented diagrammatically, as shown below.

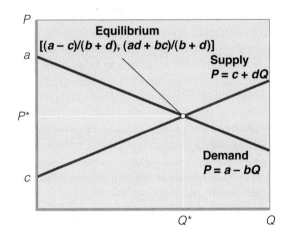

Example

Assume the demand for a pair of jeans is represented by the equation:

$$P = 100 - 0.2Q_d$$

Assume the supply of a pair of jeans is represented by the equation:

$$P = 20 + 0.2Q_s$$

Assume quantities are expressed in jeans per day, and the price in dollars.

To find the equilibrium price P^*, and equilibrium quantity Q^*, substitute Q^* for Q_d and Q_s and P^* for P in the demand and supply equations. To solve for Q^*:

$$100 - 0.2Q^* = 20 + 0.2Q^*$$
$$0.4Q^* = 80$$
$$Q^* = 200$$

To solve for P^*:

$$P^* = 100 - 0.2(200)$$
$$= 60$$

The equilibrium quantity of jeans is 200 per day, and the equilibrium price is $60 per pair of jeans.

GDP, Growth, and Fluctuations

CHAPTER 4

Introduction to Macroeconomics

As you know from Chapter 1, macroeconomics studies the behaviour of the economy as a whole. It is primarily concerned with two topics: long-run economic growth, and the short-run fluctuations in output and employment that are often referred to as **the business cycle.** These phenomena are closely related because they happen simultaneously: Economies show a distinct growth trend that leads to higher output and higher standards of living in the long run, but in the short run there is a great deal of variability. Sometimes growth proceeds more rapidly and sometimes it proceeds more slowly. It may even turn negative for a while so that output and living standards actually decline, a situation referred to as a **recession.** This chapter provides an overview of the data macroeconomists use to measure the status and growth of an entire economy as well as a preview of the models they use to help explain both long-run growth and short-run fluctuations.

4.1 | Assessing the Health of the Economy: Performance and Policy

In order to understand how economies operate and how their performance might be improved, economists collect and analyze economic data. An almost infinite number of data items can be looked at, including the amount of new construction taking place each month, how many ships laden with cargo are arriving at Canadian ports each year, and how many new inventions have been patented in the last few weeks. But macroecono-

the business cycle
Recurring increase and decrease in the level of economic activity over periods of years.

recession
A period of decline in total output, income, and employment.

real GDP (real gross domestic product)
Measures the value of final goods and services produced within the borders of a given country during a given time period, typically a year.

nominal GDP
The dollar value of all goods and services produced within the borders of a given country using the country's current prices during the year the goods and services were produced.

unemployment
A failure of the economy to fully employ its labour force.

inflation
An increase in the overall price level.

mists tend to focus on just a few statistics when trying to assess the health and development of an economy. Chief among these are real GDP, unemployment, and inflation.

Real GDP (or **real gross domestic product**) measures the value of final goods and services produced within the borders of a given country during a given time period, typically a year. This statistic is very useful because it can tell us whether an economy's output is growing. For instance, if Canada's real GDP in 2010 is larger than Canada's real GDP in 2009, then we know that Canada's output increased from 2009 to 2010. To get real GDP, government statisticians first calculate **nominal GDP,** which totals the dollar value of all goods and services produced within the borders of a given country using the country's *current prices during the year the goods and services were produced.* But because nominal GDP uses current prices it suffers from a major problem: it can increase from one year to the next even if no increase in output has occurred. To see how, consider a sculptor who produces 10 sculptures this year and 10 sculptures next year, in an economy where sculpture is the only item produced. Clearly, output in this hypothetical economy does not change from this year to next year. But if the price of sculptures rises from $10,000 this year to $20,000 next year, nominal GDP will rise from $100,000 (= 10 × $10,000) this year to $200,000 (= 10 × $20,000) next year because of the increase in prices. Real GDP corrects for price changes. As a result, we can compare real GDP numbers from one year to the next and really know if there has been a change in output (rather than prices). Because more output means greater consumption possibilities—including the chance to consume not only more fun things like movies, vacations, and video games, but also more serious things like better health care and safer roads—economists and policymakers are deeply concerned with encouraging a large and growing real GDP.

Unemployment occurs when a person cannot get a job despite being willing to work and actively seeking work. High unemployment rates indicate that a nation is not using a large fraction of its most important resource—the talents and skills of its people. Unemployment is a waste because we must count as a loss all the goods and services that unemployed workers could have produced if they had been working. Furthermore, researchers have drawn links between higher rates of unemployment and major social problems like higher crime rates and greater political unrest, as well as higher rates of depression, heart disease, and other illnesses among unemployed individuals.

Inflation is an increase in the overall level of prices. As an example, consider all the goods and services bought by a typical family over the course of one year. If the economy is experiencing inflation, it will cost the family more money to buy those goods and services this year than it cost to buy them last year. This can be problematic for several reasons. First, if the family's income does not rise as fast as the prices of the goods and services that it consumes, it won't be able to purchase as much as it used to and its standard of living will fall. Along the same lines, a surprise jump in inflation reduces the purchasing power of people's savings. Savings a family believed would buy a given amount of goods and services will turn out to buy less than expected due to the higher-than-expected prices.

Because these statistics are the standards by which economists keep track of long-run growth and short-run fluctuations, we spend substantial time in the next few chapters examining how these statistics are computed, how accurately they capture the well-being of actual people, and how they vary both across countries and over time. Once these statistics are understood, we will build upon them in subsequent chapters by developing macroeconomic models of both long-run growth and short-run fluctuations. These models help us understand how policymakers attempt to maximize growth while minimizing unemployment and inflation.

Macroeconomic models also clarify many important questions about the powers and limits of government economic policy, including the following:

• Can governments promote long-run economic growth?

• Can governments reduce the severity of recessions by smoothing out short-run fluctuations?

• Are certain government policy tools, such as manipulating interest rates (monetary policy), more effective at mitigating short-run fluctuations than other government policy tools, such as making changes to tax rates or government spending (fiscal policy)?

- Is there a trade-off between lower rates of unemployment and higher rates of inflation?
- Does government policy work best when it is announced in advance or when it is a surprise?

The answers to these questions are of crucial importance because of the vast differences in economic performance seen across various economies at different times. For instance, the output generated by the Canadian economy grew at an average rate of 3.1 percent per year between 1998 and 2008, while the output generated by the Japanese economy grew at an average rate of only about 1.0 percent per year over the same period. Could Japan have done as well as Canada if it had pursued different economic policies? Similarly, in 2008 unemployment in Canada was only 6.1 percent of the labour force, while it was 7.8 percent in Germany, 6.8 percent in India, 9.8 percent in Poland, and 80 percent in Zimbabwe. At the same time the inflation rate in Canada was 2.3 percent, compared with over 10 million percent in Zimbabwe! Our models will help us understand why such large differences in rates of growth, unemployment, and inflation exist and how government policies influence them.

4.2 | The Miracle of Modern Economic Growth

Rapid and sustained economic growth is a relatively recent phenomenon. Before the Industrial Revolution began in the late 1700s in England, standards of living showed virtually no growth over hundreds or even thousands of years. For instance, the standard of living of the average Roman peasant was virtually the same at the start of the Roman Empire around the year 500 B.C. as it was at the end of the Roman Empire about 1000 years later. Similarly, historians and archaeologists have estimated that the standard of living enjoyed by the average Chinese peasant was essentially the same in the year 1800 A.D. as it was in the year 100 A.D.

This is not to say that the Roman and Chinese economies did not expand over time. They did. In fact, their total outputs of goods and services increased many times over. The problem was that as output increased, their populations went up by similar proportions so that the amount of output *per person* remained virtually unchanged. This historical pattern continued until the start of the Industrial Revolution, which ushered in not only factory production and automation but also increases in research and development so that new and better technologies were constantly being invented. The result was that output began to grow faster than the population, and living standards began to rise as the amount of output *per person* increased.

modern economic growth
The historically recent phenomenon in which nations for the first time have experienced sustained increases in real GDP per capita.

PRODUCTION &
THE STANDARD
OF LIVING

Not all countries experienced this phenomenon, but those that did were experiencing **modern economic growth** (in which output per person rises) as compared with earlier times in which output (but not output per person) increased. Under modern economic growth, the annual increase in output per person is often not large, perhaps 2 percent per year in the countries such as England that were the first to industrialize. But when compounded over time, an annual growth rate of 2 percent adds up very rapidly. Indeed, it implies that standards of living will double every 35 years. So if the average citizen of a country enjoying 2 percent growth begins this year with an income of $10,000, in 35 years that person will have an income of $20,000. And 35 years after that there will be another doubling so that the income of the average citizen in 70 years will be $40,000. And 35 years after that, income will double again to $80,000. Such high rates of growth are amazing when compared to the period before modern economic growth, when standards of living remained unchanged century after century.

The vast differences in living standards seen today between rich and poor countries are almost entirely the result of the fact that only some countries have experienced modern economic growth. Indeed, before the start of the Industrial Revolution in the late 1700s, living standards around the world were very similar—so much so that the average standard of living in the richest parts of the world was at most only two or three times higher than the standard of living in the poorest parts of the world. By contrast, the citizens of the richest nations today have material standards of living that

4.1 | GLOBAL PERSPECTIVE

GDP per capita, selected countries

Country	GPD per capita, 2008 (U.S. dollars based on purchasing power parity)
United States	46,859
Canada	39,183
United Kingdom	36,523
France	34,208
Japan	34,100
South Korea	27,647
Saudi Arabia	23,834
Russia	15,922
Mexico	14,560
China	5,963
India	2,762
North Korea	1,700
Tanzania	1,352
Burundi	389

Source: International Monetary Fund, www.imf.org, for all countries except North Korea, the data for which come from the *CIA World Factbook*, www.cia.gov.

are on average more than 50 times higher than those experienced by citizens of the poorest nations, as can be seen by the GDP per person data for the year 2005 given in Global Perspective 4.1.

Global Perspective 4.1 facilitates international comparisons of living standards by making three adjustments to each country's GDP. First, it converts each country's GDP from its own currency into U.S. dollars so no confusion exists about the values of different currencies. Second, it divides each country's GDP measured in dollars by the size of its population. The resulting number, *GDP per capita,* is the average amount of output each person in each country could have if each country's total output were divided equally among its citizens; it is a measure of each country's average standard of living. Third, the table uses a method called *purchasing power parity* to adjust for the fact that prices are much lower in some countries than others. By making this adjustment, we can trust that $1 of GDP per person in Canada represents about the same quantity of goods and services as $1 of GDP per person in any of the other countries. The resulting numbers—GDP per capita adjusted for purchasing power parity—are presented in Global Perspective 4.1. *(Key Question 2)*

4.3 | Savings, Investment, and Modern Economic Growth

At the heart of economic growth is the principle that in order to raise living standards over time an economy must devote at least some fraction of its current output to increasing future output. As implied in Chapter 1 this process requires both savings and investment, which we will define before returning to discuss why they are so important for economic growth.

- **Savings** are generated when current consumption is less than current output.

savings
The accumulation of funds that results when people in an economy spend (consume) less than their incomes during a given time period.

investment
Spending for the production and accumulation of capital and additions to inventories.

financial investment
Purchasing financial assets (stocks, bonds, mutual funds) or real assets (houses, land, factories), or building such assets, in the expectation of financial gain.

economic investment
Spending for the production and accumulation of capital and additions to inventories.

- **Investment** occurs when resources are devoted to increasing future output—for instance, by building a new research facility in which scientists invent the next generation of fuel-efficient automobiles, or by constructing a super-efficient factory.

Economics students are often confused about the way the word "investment" is used in economics. This is because only economists draw a distinction between "financial investment" and "economic investment." **Financial investment** captures what ordinary people mean when they say investment, namely the purchase of assets like stocks, bonds, and real estate in the hope of reaping a financial gain in the future. Anything of monetary value is an asset and, in everyday usage, people purchase—or "invest in"—assets hoping to receive a financial gain, either by eventually selling the asset at a higher price than they paid or by receiving a stream of payments as the asset's owner (as is the case with landlords who rent the property they own to tenants). By contrast, when economists say "investment" they are referring to the much more specific concept of **economic investment,** which has to do with the creation and expansion of business enterprises. Specifically, economic investment includes only money spent purchasing *newly created* capital goods such as machinery, tools, factories, and warehouses.

Indeed, as defined and measured by economists, purely financial transactions such as swapping cash for a stock or a bond are not "investment." Neither is a firm's purchase of a factory built several years ago and used previously by another company. Both types of transactions simply transfer the ownership of old assets from one party to another; they do not pay for *newly created* capital goods. As such, they are great examples of *financial investment,* but are not examples of the narrower idea of *economic investment.* So, now that you know the difference, remember that purely financial transactions like buying Scotiabank stock or a five-year-old factory are indeed referred to as "investment"—except in economics!

The key point to understanding why savings and investment are so important for economic growth is that the amount of economic investment (hereafter, simply "investment") is ultimately limited by the amount of savings. The only way that more output can be directed at investment activities is if savings increases. But that, in turn, implies that individuals and society as a whole must make trade-offs between current and future consumption.

This is true because the only way to pay for more investment—and the higher levels of future consumption that more investment can generate—is to increase savings in the present. But increased savings can come only at the price of reduced current consumption. Individuals and society as a whole must therefore wrestle with a choice between present consumption and future consumption, deciding how to balance the reductions in current consumption that are necessary to fund current investment against the higher levels of future consumption that can result from more current investment.

Banks and Other Financial Institutions

Households are the principal source of savings, but businesses are the main economic investors. So how do the savings generated by households when they spend less than they consume get transferred to businesses so that they can purchase newly created capital goods? The answer is through banks and other financial institutions such as mutual funds, pension plans, and insurance companies. These institutions collect the savings of households, rewarding savers with interest and dividends and sometimes capital gains (increases in asset values). The banks and other financial institutions then lend the funds to businesses, which invest in equipment, factories, and other capital goods.

Macroeconomics devotes considerable attention to money, banking, and financial institutions because a well-functioning financial system helps to promote economic growth and stability by encouraging savings and by properly directing that savings into the most productive possible investments. In the 2008–09 period, the financial system was certainly *not* well functioning. Quite the contrary! Lending from banks to households, banks to businesses, and banks to banks slowed down considerably. In the United States, where the financial crisis began, the Federal Reserve (its central bank) and U.S. Treasury intervened with huge infusions of money to keep the financial system from completely freezing up. In Canada, the economic contraction was not as severe but lending also dried up, if to a lesser extent, and the Bank of Canada also intervened in the money market to help maintain lending to businesses and consumers.

4.4 | Uncertainty, Expectations, Shocks, and Short-Run Fluctuations

Decisions about savings and investment are complicated by the fact that the future is uncertain. Investment projects sometimes produce disappointing results or even fail totally. As a result, firms spend considerable time trying to predict future trends so that they can, hopefully, invest only in projects that are likely to succeed. This implies that macroeconomics has to take into account **expectations** about the future.

expectations
The anticipations of consumers, firms, and others about future economic conditions.

Expectations are hugely important for two reasons. The more obvious reason involves the effect that changing expectations have on current behaviour. If firms grow more pessimistic about the future returns likely to come from current investments, they are going to invest less today than they would if they were more optimistic. Expectations therefore have a large effect on economic growth since increased pessimism will lead to less current investment and, subsequently, less future consumption.

The less obvious reason why expectations are so important has to do with what happens when expectations are unmet. Firms are often forced to cope with **shocks**—situations in which they were expecting one thing to happen but then something else happens. For instance, consider a situation in which a firm decides to build a high-speed railroad that will shuttle passengers between Windsor and Toronto. They do so expecting it to be very popular and make a handsome profit. But if it unexpectedly turns out to be unpopular and loses money, the railroad must figure out how to respond. Should the railroad go out of business completely? Should it attempt to see if it can turn a profit by hauling cargo instead of passengers? Is there a possibility that the venture might succeed if the firm borrows $30 million from a bank to pay for a massive advertising campaign? These sorts of decisions are necessitated by the shock and surprise of having to deal with an unexpected situation.

shocks
Situations in which one thing is expected to occur but in reality something different occurs.

Economies are exposed to both demand shocks and supply shocks. **Demand shocks** are unexpected changes in the demand for goods and services. **Supply shocks** are unexpected changes in the supply of goods and services. The word "shock" tells us only that something unexpected has happened, not whether it is unexpectedly good or unexpectedly bad. Economists use even more specific terms. For instance, a *positive demand shock* refers to a situation in which demand turns out to be higher than expected, while a *negative demand shock* refers to a situation in which demand turns out to be lower than expected.

demand shocks
Sudden, unexpected changes in demand.

supply shocks
Sudden, unexpected changes in aggregate supply.

Economists believe that most short-run fluctuations are the result of demand shocks. Supply shocks do happen in some cases and are very important when they occur. But we will focus most of our attention in this chapter and subsequent chapters on demand shocks, how they affect the economy, and how government policy may be able to help the economy adjust to them. But why are demand shocks such a big problem? Why would we have to consider calling in the government to help deal with them? And why can't firms deal with demand shocks on their own?

The answer to these questions is that the prices of many goods and services are inflexible (slow to change, or "sticky") in the short run. As we will explain, this implies that price changes do not quickly equalize the quantities demanded of such goods and services with their respective quantities supplied. Instead, because prices are inflexible, the economy is forced to respond in the short run to demand shocks primarily through changes in output and employment rather than through changes in prices.

Although an economy as a whole is much more complex than a single firm, an analogy that uses a single car factory will be helpful in explaining why demand shocks and inflexible prices are so important to understanding most of the short-run fluctuations that affect the entire economy. Consider a car manufacturing company named Buzzer Auto. Like most companies, Buzzer Auto is in business to try to make a profit. Part of turning a profit involves trying to develop accurate expectations about future market conditions. Consequently, Buzzer constantly does market research to estimate future demand conditions so that it will, hopefully, only build cars that people are going to want to buy.

After extensive market research, Buzzer concludes that it could earn a modest profit if it builds and staffs an appropriately sized factory to build an environmentally friendly car, which it decides to call the Prion. Buzzer's marketing economists collaborate with Buzzer's engineers and conclude that expected profits will be maximized if the firm builds a factory that has an optimal output rate of 900 cars per week. If the factory operates at this rate, it can produce Prions for only $36,500 per vehicle. This is terrific because the firm's estimates for demand indicate that a supply of 900 vehicles per week can be sold at a price of $37,000 per vehicle—meaning that if everything goes according to plan, Buzzer Auto should make an accounting profit of $500 on each Prion that it produces and sells. Expecting these future conditions, Buzzer decides to build the factory, staff it with workers, and begin making the Prion.

Look at Figure 4-1a, which shows the market for Prions when the vertical supply curve for Prions is fixed at the factory's optimal output rate of 900 cars per week. Notice that we have drawn three possible demand curves. D_L corresponds to low demand for the Prion; D_M corresponds to the medium level of demand that Buzzer's marketing economists are expecting to materialize; and D_H corresponds to high demand for the Prion. Figure 4-1a is consistent with the marketing economists' expectations; if all goes according to plan and the actual demand that materializes is D_M, the equilibrium price will in fact be $37,000 per Prion and the equilibrium quantity demanded will be 900 cars per week. Thus, if all goes according to expectations, the factory will have exactly the right capacity to meet the expected quantity demanded at the sales price of $37,000 per vehicle. In addition, the firm's books will show a profit of $500 per vehicle on each of the 900 vehicles that it builds and expects to sell each week at that price.

Here is the key point: If expectations are always fulfilled, Buzzer Auto will never contribute to any of the short-run fluctuations in output and unemployment that affect real-world economies. First, if everything always goes according to plan and Buzzer Auto's expectations always come true, then the factory will always produce and sell at its optimal output rate of 900 cars per week. This would mean that it would never experience any fluctuations in output—either in the short run or in the long run. At the same time, since producing a constant output of 900 cars each week will always require the same number of workers, the factory's labour demand and employment should

FIGURE 4-1 — The Effect of Unexpected Changes in Demand under Flexible and Fixed Prices

(a) If prices are flexible, then no matter what demand turns out to be, Buzzer Auto can continue to sell its optimal output of 900 cars per week since the equilibrium price will adjust to equalize the quantity demanded with the quantity supplied. (b) By contrast, if Buzzer Auto sticks with a fixed price policy, then the quantity demanded will vary with the level of demand. At the fixed price of $37,000 per vehicle, the quantity demanded will be 700 cars per week if demand is D_L, 900 cars per week if demand is D_M, and 1150 cars per week if demand is D_H.

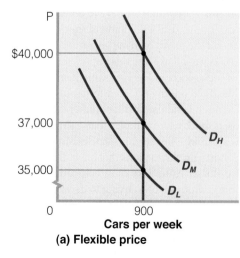

(a) Flexible price

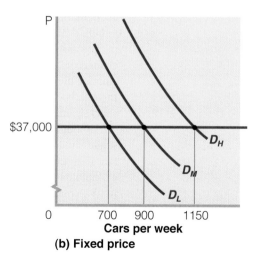

(b) Fixed price

never vary. So if everything always goes according to plan, Buzzer Auto will never have any effect on unemployment because it will always hire a constant number of workers.

These facts imply that the short-run fluctuations in output and unemployment that we see in the real world must be the result of shocks and things *not* going according to plan. In particular, business cycle fluctuations typically arise because the actual demand that materializes ends up being either lower or higher than what firms were expecting. When this occurs, some adjustments will be necessary to bring the quantity demanded and the quantity supplied back into alignment. As we are about to explain, the nature of these adjustments varies hugely depending upon whether prices are flexible or inflexible.

Demand Shocks and Flexible Prices

Figure 4-1a illustrates the case of adjusting to unexpected changes in demand *when prices are flexible.* Here, if demand is unexpectedly low at D_L, the market price can adjust downward to \$35,000 per vehicle so that the quantity demanded at that price will still be equal to the factory's optimal output rate of 900 cars per week. On the other hand, if demand is unexpectedly high at D_H, the market price can adjust upward to \$40,000 per vehicle so that the quantity demanded will still be equal to the factory's optimal output rate of 900 cars per week. These adjustments imply that *if* the price of Prions is free to quickly adjust to new equilibrium levels in response to unexpected changes in demand, the factory could always operate at its optimal output rate of 900 cars per week. Only the amount of profit or loss will vary with demand.

Applying this logic to the economy as a whole, *if* the prices of goods and services could always adjust quickly to unexpected changes in demand, then the economy could always produce at its optimal capacity since prices would adjust to ensure that the quantity demanded of each good and service would always equal the quantity supplied. Simply put, if prices were fully flexible there would be no short-run fluctuations: output would remain constant and unemployment levels would not change because firms would always need the same number of workers to produce the same amount of output.

Demand Shocks and Inflexible Prices

In reality, many prices in the economy are inflexible and are not able to change rapidly when demand changes unexpectedly. Consider the extreme case shown in Figure 4-1b, in which the price of Prions is totally inflexible, fixed at \$37,000 per Prion. Here, if demand unexpectedly falls from D_M to D_L, the quantity demanded at the fixed price of \$37,000 will be only 700 cars per week, which is 200 cars fewer than the factory's optimal output of 900 cars per week. On the other hand, if demand is unexpectedly high at D_H, the quantity demanded at the fixed price of \$37,000 will be 1150 cars per week, which is 250 cars more than the factory's optimal output of 900 cars per week.

One way for companies to deal with these unexpected shifts in quantity demanded would be to try to adjust the factory's output to match them. That is, during weeks of low demand Buzzer Auto could attempt to produce only 700 Prions while during weeks of high demand it could try to produce 1150 Prions. But this sort of flexible output strategy is very expensive because factories operate at their lowest costs when they are producing constantly at their optimal output levels; operating at either a higher or a lower production rate results in higher per-unit production costs.[1]

Knowing this, manufacturing firms typically attempt to deal with unexpected changes in demand by maintaining an inventory. An **inventory** is a store of output that has been produced but not yet sold. Inventories are useful because they can be allowed to grow or decline in periods when demand is unexpectedly low or high—thereby allowing production to proceed smoothly even when demand is variable. In our example, Buzzer Auto would maintain an inventory of unsold Prions. In weeks when demand is unexpectedly low, the inventory will increase by 200 Prions as the quantity

inventory
Goods that have been
produced but remain unsold.

---

[1] If you have studied microeconomics, you will recognize that the firm's optimal output level of 900 cars per week is the level that minimizes the factory's average total cost (ATC) per vehicle of producing the Prion. Producing either more or fewer Prions will result in higher per-vehicle production costs.

demanded falls 200 vehicles short of the factory's optimal output. By contrast, during weeks when demand is unexpectedly high, the inventory will decrease as the quantity demanded exceeds the factory's optimal output by 250 cars. By allowing inventory levels to fluctuate with changes in demand, Buzzer Auto can respond to unexpected changes in demand by adjusting inventory levels rather than output levels. In addition, with any luck, the overall inventory level will stay roughly constant over time as unexpected increases and decreases roughly cancel each other out.

But consider what will happen if the firm experiences many successive weeks of unexpectedly low demand. For each such week, the firm's inventory of unsold Prions will increase by 200 cars. The firm's managers will not mind if this happens for a few weeks, but if it continues for many weeks the managers will be forced to cut production—because, among other things, there simply will be no place to park so many unsold vehicles. More importantly, holding large numbers of unsold cars in inventory is unprofitable because while costs must be incurred to build an unsold car, an unsold car obviously brings in no revenue. Constantly rising inventories hurt firm profits, and management will want to reduce output if it sees inventories rising week after week due to unexpectedly low demand.

This simplified story about a single car company explains why economists believe that a combination of unexpected changes in demand and inflexible prices is the key to understanding the short-run fluctuations that affect real-world economies. If prices were flexible, then the firm could always operate at the factory's optimal output level because prices would always adjust to ensure that it could sell its optimal output of 900 cars per week no matter what happens to demand. But if prices are inflexible, then an unexpected decline in demand that persists for any length of time will result in increasing inventories that will eventually force the firm's management to cut production to less than the optimal output level of 900 cars per week. When this happens, not only will output fall, but unemployment will also rise. The firm will lay off workers because fewer employees will be needed to produce fewer cars.

Generalizing this story to the economy as a whole, if demand falls for many goods and services across the entire economy for an extended period of time, then many firms will find inventories piling up and will be forced to cut production. As they do, the economy will go into recession, with GDP falling and unemployment rising.

On the other hand, if demand is unexpectedly high for a prolonged period of time, the economy will boom and unemployment will fall. In the case of our Prion example, for each week that demand is unexpectedly high inventories will fall by 250 cars. If this keeps happening week after week, inventories will start to run out and the firm will have to react by increasing production to more than the optimal output rate of 900 cars per week so that orders do not go unfilled. When this happens, GDP will increase as more cars per week are produced and unemployment will fall because the factory will have to hire more workers in order to produce the larger number of cars. (***Key Question 7***)

How Sticky Are Prices?

inflexible prices (sticky prices)
Product prices that remain in place (at least for a while) even though supply or demand has changed; also called sticky prices.

flexible prices
Product prices that react within seconds to changes in supply and demand.

We have just shown that **inflexible prices**—or **"sticky" prices,** as economists are fond of saying—help to explain how unexpected changes in demand lead to the fluctuations in GDP and employment that occur over the course of the business cycle. Of course, not all prices are sticky. Indeed, the markets for many commodities and raw materials such as corn, oil, and natural gas feature extremely **flexible prices** that react within seconds to changes in supply and demand. By contrast, the prices of most of the final goods and services people consume are quite sticky, with the average good or service going 4.3 months between price changes. To get a better appreciation for the fact that price stickiness varies greatly by product or service look at Table 4-1, which gives the average number of months between price changes for various common goods and services. The prices of some products like gasoline and airline tickets change very rapidly—about once a month or even less than once a month. By contrast, haircuts and newspapers average more than two years between price changes. And coin-operated laundry machines average nearly four years between price changes!

TABLE 4·1	Average Number of Months between Price Changes for Selected Goods and Services

Item	Months
Coin-operated laundry machines	46.4
Newspapers	29.9
Haircuts	25.5
Taxi fares	19.7
Veterinary services	14.9
Magazines	11.2
Computer software	5.5
Beer	4.3
Microwave ovens	3.0
Milk	2.4
Electricity	1.8
Airline tickets	1.0
Gasoline	0.6

Source: Mark Bils and Peter J. Klenow, "Some Evidence on the Importance of Sticky Prices," *Journal of Political Economy*, October 2004, pp. 947–85.

In later chapters, we will discuss several factors that increase short-run price stickiness. But to keep the current discussion brief, let's focus on just two factors here. One factor is that companies selling final goods and services know that consumers prefer stable, predictable prices that do not fluctuate rapidly with changes in demand. Consumers would be annoyed if the same bottle of soda or shampoo cost one price one day, a different price the next day, and yet another price a week later. Volatile prices make planning more difficult, and, in addition, consumers who come in to buy the product on a day when the price happens to be high will likely feel they are being taken advantage of.

To avoid this, most firms try to maintain stable prices that do not change very often. Firms do have occasional sales where they lower prices, but on the whole they tend to try to keep prices stable and predictable—the result being price inflexibility.

Another factor that causes sticky prices has to do with the fact that in certain situations a firm may be afraid that cutting its price may be counterproductive because its rivals might simply match the price cut—a situation often referred to as a price war. This possibility is common among firms that have only one or two major rivals. Consider Coca-Cola and Pepsi. If Coca-Cola faces unexpectedly low demand for its product, it might be tempted to reduce its price in the hope that it can steal business away from Pepsi. But such a strategy would work only if Pepsi left its price alone when Coca-Cola cut its price. That, of course, is not likely. If Coca-Cola cuts its price, Pepsi will very likely cut its price in retaliation, doing its best to make sure that Coca-Cola doesn't steal away any of its customers. Thus, if Pepsi retaliates, Coca-Cola will only be made worse off by its decision to cut its price; it will not pick up any more business (due to the fact that Pepsi also cut its price) and it will also be receiving less money for each bottle of Coke that it sells because it cut its price. Thus, firms that have to deal with the possibility of price wars often have sticky prices.

CONSIDER THIS | Price-Level Changes during the Recession of 2008–09

Figure 4-1 is helpful in demonstrating the story of the economic contraction that resulted from the financial crisis of 2008–09. First, consider Figure 4-1b where the price of Buzzer's autos is fixed. Like actual auto producers such as GM and Ford, Buzzer established its production capacity and its expectations of product demand on the basis of normal times. But suppose that demand in this example unexpectedly fell from D_M to D_L because of a general decline in household income, greater difficulty in getting auto loans, and declining consumer confidence. With the price stuck at P, sales of cars would fall from 1150 to 700 per week. Because fewer workers would be needed to produce fewer cars, Buzzer would need to lay off a large portion of its workforce.

The analysis roughly fits the facts of the relatively severe recession of 2008–09. Between the start of the recession and May 2009, the economy's price level (essentially a weighted average of prices) was quite sticky. In fact, the price level in May 2009 looked very much like the price level at the start of the recession in the fall of 2008. Therefore, real output took the full brunt of the decline of total demand in the economy. In April 2009, the severe economic contraction forced Chrysler, one of the major North American Automobile manufacturers, to file for bankruptcy protection. General Motors followed Chrysler into bankruptcy two months later.

Categorizing Macroeconomic Models Using Price Stickiness

We have now demonstrated why price stickiness is believed to have such a large role in short-run economic fluctuations. Note, however, that price stickiness moderates over time. This is true because firms that choose to use a fixed-price policy in the short run do not have to stick with that policy permanently. In particular, if unexpected changes in demand begin to look permanent, many firms will allow their prices to change so that price changes (in addition to quantity changes) can help to equalize quantities supplied with quantities demanded.

For this reason, economists speak of "sticky prices" rather than "stuck prices." Only in the very short run are prices totally inflexible. As time passes and prices are revised, the world looks much more like Figure 4-1a, in which prices are fully flexible, rather than Figure 4-1b, in which prices are totally inflexible. Indeed, the totally inflexible case shown in the right graph can be thought of as the extremely short-run response to an unexpected change in demand, while the fully flexible case shown in the left graph can be thought of as a longer-run response to an unexpected change in demand. In terms of time durations, the extreme short run can be thought of as the first few weeks and months after a demand shock, while the long run can be thought of as extending from many months to several years after a demand shock happens.

This realization is very useful in categorizing and understanding the differences between the various macroeconomic models that we will be presenting in subsequent chapters. For instance, the aggregate expenditures model presented in Chapter 9 assumes perfectly inflexible prices (and wages) and thus is a model in which prices are not just sticky but completely stuck. By contrast, the aggregate demand–aggregate supply model presented in Chapter 10 allows for flexible prices (with or without flexible wages) and is therefore useful for understanding how the economy behaves over longer periods of time.

As you study these various models, keep in mind that we need different models precisely because the economy behaves so differently depending on how much time has passed after a demand shock. The differences in behaviour result from the fact that prices go from stuck in the extreme short run to fully flexible in the long run. Using different models for different stages in this process gives us much better insights into not only how economies actually behave but also how various government and central bank policies may have different effects in the short run, when prices are fixed, versus the long run, when prices are flexible.

Where will we go from here? In the remainder of Part 2, we examine how economists measure GDP and why GDP has expanded over time. Then, we discuss the terminology of business cycles and explore the measurement and types of unemployment and inflation. At that point you will be well-prepared to examine the economic models, monetary considerations, and stabilization policies that lie at the heart of macroeconomics.

The **LAST WORD** | Will Better Inventory Management Mean Fewer Recessions?

Computerized inventory tracking has greatly accelerated how quickly companies can respond to unexpected changes in demand.

Before computers made it possible to track inventory changes in real time, firms could only react to unexpected shifts in demand very slowly. This was true because before computers tracking inventory was a painful, slow process that basically involved hiring people to physically count the items held in inventory—one at a time. Since this process was both costly and annoying, firms typically counted their inventories only a few times per year.

An unfortunate side effect of counting inventory so infrequently was that unexpected shifts in demand could cause large changes in inventory levels before anyone could find out about them. To see why this is true, consider a firm that counts its inventory just twice per year, for example once in January and once in July. If the demand for its product suddenly falls in February and then remains low, the decline in demand will not be discovered until the July inventory count is taken. Only then will a high inventory level alert the firm's management that the demand for its product must have unexpectedly declined.

The long delay between when the shift in demand happens and when it is discovered means that the firm will very likely feel pressed to reduce its production of new output since the fastest way to reduce its high inventory level will be to sharply reduce its output rate (so that new sales will exceed the reduced output rate). Following this policy, however, implies not only a large cut in output but also a substantial increase in unemployment since fewer workers will be needed to produce less output. As a result, infrequent inventory counting leads to strong fluctuations in output *and* employment, because by the time an unexpected change in demand is discovered it will have had plenty of time to cause a large change in inventory levels that will very likely be rectified by a large change in production levels.

By contrast, many economists believe that economic fluctuations may have become much less severe during the last 20 years because of the introduction of computerized inventory tracking systems that allow companies to track their inventory levels in real time. These systems keep continuous track of inventory levels by means of technologies like bar codes and laser scanners. This allows firms to tell almost immediately if demand has changed unexpectedly. As a result, the firms that have adopted these systems can make much more subtle changes to output and employment because they can discover the unexpected changes in demand before those unexpected changes have caused large shifts in inventory levels.

While it is not possible to "prove" that inventory management systems have led to smaller business cycle fluctuations, the behaviour of the Canadian economy over the past 30 years is suggestive. The last severe recession happened in 1981–82. Up to that point, recessions appeared to happen in Canada every five or so years and were often quite punishing, with high levels of unemployment and significant declines in output. But computerized inventory management systems began to be widely adopted during the 1980s, and since that time the Canadian economy has experienced only one mild recession, in 1991–92. Since this recession was mild by historical standards, some economists have taken this performance as evidence that from now on recessions will be less frequent and less severe due to the recent improvements in inventory management.

Opinions vary, however, as to how much credit computerized inventory management should be given for the apparent reduction in the frequency and severity of the business cycle. Indeed, several other explanations have been put forward to explain why things seem to have improved. One hypothesis is that we may have just been lucky in recent years in that there simply have not been that many significant demand shocks. Indeed, the severe global economic contraction of 2008–09, one of the worst since the Great Depression, may strengthen the credibility of this argument. Another explanation is that governments may have learned from past mistakes and implemented better economic policies. Taking the various competing explanations into account, it is safe to say that while no economist would give *all* the credit for the more moderate business cycle fluctuations of the past 25 years to computerized inventory management systems, nearly all would give at least some of the credit to these systems and the fact that they allow firms to rapidly react to unexpected changes in demand.

Question

Why do some economists believe that better inventory control software may help to reduce the frequency and severity of recessions? Could differences in technology explain why recessions appear to be more frequent and more severe in poorer countries?

CHAPTER SUMMARY

4.1 ▶ ASSESSING THE HEALTH OF THE ECONOMY: PERFORMANCE AND POLICY

- Macroeconomics studies long-run economic growth and short-run economic fluctuations.

- Macroeconomists focus their attention on three key economic statistics: GDP, unemployment, and inflation. GDP is the dollar amount of all final goods and services produced in a country during a given period of time. The unemployment rate measures the percentage of all workers who are not able to find paid employment despite being willing and able to work. The inflation rate measures the extent to which the overall level of prices is rising in the economy.

4.2 ▶ THE MIRACLE OF MODERN ECONOMIC GROWTH AND ITS COMPONENTS

- Before the Industrial Revolution, living standards did not show any sustained increases over time. Economies grew, but any increase in output tended to be offset by an equally large increase in population, so that the amount of output per person did not rise. By contrast, since the Industrial Revolution began in the late 1700s many nations have experienced modern economic growth in which output grows faster than population—so that standards of living rise over time.

4.3 ▶ SAVINGS, INVESTMENT, AND MODERN ECONOMIC GROWTH

- Macroeconomists believe that one of the keys to modern economic growth is the promotion of savings and investment (for economists, the purchase of capital goods). Investment activities increase the economy's future potential output level. But investment must be funded by saving, which is possible only if people are willing to reduce current consumption. Consequently, individuals and society face a trade-off between current consumption and future consumption. Banks and other financial institutions help to convert saving into investment by taking the savings generated by households and lending it to businesses that wish to make investments.

4.4 ▶ UNCERTAINTY, EXPECTATIONS, SHOCKS, AND SHORT-RUN FLUCTUATIONS

- Expectations have an important effect on the economy for two reasons. First, if people and businesses are more positive about the future, they will save and invest more. Second, individuals and firms must adjust to shocks—situations in which expectations are unmet and the future does not turn out the way people were expecting. In particular, shocks often imply situations where the quantity supplied of a given good or service does not equal the quantity demanded of that good or service.

- If prices were always flexible and capable of rapid adjustment, then dealing with situations in which quantities demanded did not equal quantities supplied would always be easy since prices could simply adjust to the market equilibrium price at which quantities demanded equal quantities supplied. Unfortunately, real-world prices are often inflexible (or "sticky") in the short run so that the only way for the economy to adjust is through changes in output levels.

- "Sticky" prices combine with shocks to drive short-run fluctuations in output and employment. Consider a negative demand shock in which demand is unexpectedly low. Because prices are fixed, the lower-than-expected demand will result in unexpectedly slow sales. This will cause inventories to increase. If demand remains low for an extended period of time, inventory levels will become too high and firms will have to cut output and lay off workers. Thus, when prices are inflexible, the economy adjusts to unexpectedly low demand through changes in output and employment rather than through changes in prices (which are not possible when prices are inflexible).

- Prices are inflexible in the short run for various reasons, two of which are discussed in this chapter. First, firms often attempt to set and maintain stable prices in order to please

customers who like predictable prices because they make for easy planning (and who might become upset if prices were volatile). Second, a firm with just a few competitors may be reluctant to cut its price due to the fear of starting a price war, a situation in which its competitors retaliate by cutting their prices as well—thereby leaving the firm worse off than it was to begin with.

TERMS AND CONCEPTS

the business cycle, p. 83
recession, p. 83
real GDP (real gross domestic product), p. 83
nominal GDP, p. 83
unemployment, p. 83
inflation, p. 83

modern economic growth, p. 84
savings, p. 85
investment, p. 86
financial investment, p. 86
economic investment, p. 86
expectations, p. 87

shocks, p. 87
demand shocks, p. 87
supply shocks, p. 87
inventory, p. 89
inflexible prices ("sticky prices"), p. 90
flexible prices, p. 90

STUDY QUESTIONS

LO 4.1 1. Why do you think macroeconomists focus on just a few key statistics when trying to understand the health and trajectory of an economy? Would it be better to try to make use of all possible data?

LO 4.2 2. **KEY QUESTION** Consider a nation in which the volume of goods and services is growing by 5 percent per year. What is the likely impact of this high rate of growth on the power and influence of its government relative to other countries experiencing slower rates of growth? What about the effect of this 5 percent growth on the nation's living standards? Will these also necessarily grow by 5 percent per year, given population growth? Why or why not?

LO 4.2 3. A mathematical approximation called the *rule of 70* tells us that the number of years it will take something that is growing to double in size is approximately equal to the number 70 divided by its percentage rate of growth. Thus, if Mexico's real GDP per person is growing at 7 percent per year, it will take about 10 years (= 70 ÷ 7) to double. Apply the rule of 70 to solve the following problem. If real GDP per person in Mexico was $11,000 in 2008, while it was $44,000 per person in Canada, and if real GDP per person in Mexico grows at a rate of 5 percent a year, how long will it take Mexico's real GDP per person to reach the level that Canada was at in 2008? (*Hint:* How many times would Mexico's 2008 real GDP per person have to double to reach Canada's 2008 real GDP per person?)

LO 4.3 4. Why is there a trade-off between the amount of consumption that people can enjoy today and the amount of consumption that they can enjoy in the future? Why can't people enjoy

more of both? How does saving relate to investment and thus to economic growth? What role do banks and other financial institutions play in aiding the growth process?

5. How does investment as defined by economists differ from **LO 4.3** investment as defined by the general public? What would happen to the amount of investment made today if firms expected the future returns to such investment to be very low? What if firms expected future returns to be very high?

6. Why, in general, do shocks force people to make changes? **LO 4.4** Give at least two examples from your own experience.

7. **KEY QUESTION** Catalogue companies are the classic **LO 4.4** example of perfectly inflexible prices because once they print and ship out their catalogues, they are committed to selling at the prices as printed. If a catalogue company finds its inventory of sweaters rising, what does that tell you about the demand for sweaters? Was it unexpectedly high, unexpectedly low, or as expected? If the company *could* change the price of sweaters, would it raise the price, lower the price, or keep the price the same? Given that the company cannot change the price of sweaters, consider the number of sweaters it orders each month from the company that makes them. If inventories become very high, will the catalogue company increase, decrease, or keep orders the same? Given what the catalogue company does with its orders, what is likely to happen to employment and output at the sweater manufacturer?

8. Why are prices sticky? Explain the two reasons given in **LO 4.4** this chapter and then try to think of two more.

INTERNET APPLICATION QUESTIONS @

1. **Do All Poor Countries Grow Fast?** Go to the McConnell-Brue-Flynn-Barbiero Web site (Chapter 4), where you can access economic, political, and social data for nearly every country in the world. Click on the link and scroll down to the Economy section and click on "GDP—real growth rate." Write down the growth rates of the countries with the five highest real GDP growth rates and the five lowest real GDP growth rates. Go back to the Economy section and click on "GDP—per capita" (*per capita* is Latin for *per person*). Look up GDP per person for each of the countries whose growth rates you have just written down. Can we say that *all* poor countries grow fast? Should we assume that countries with lower levels of GDP per person will *automatically* be able to catch up with living standards in rich countries?

2. **Is Real GDP per Person a Sufficient Measure of Well-Being?** Economists tend to focus on real GDP per capita as their primary way of comparing living standards among countries. But they are also aware that real GDP per capita does not capture many factors that affect the quality of life. Go to the McConnell-Brue-Flynn-Barbiero Web site (Chapter 4), and click on the link. Scroll down to the People section and click on "Infant mortality rate." Write down the rank and the infant mortality rate for the following four countries: Canada, France, Mexico, and China. (You may want to use your web browser's search feature to find these countries more quickly.) Go back to the People section and click on "Life expectancy at birth—total." For each of the four countries, write down its rank and life expectancy at birth. Now compare the data you just wrote down for infant mortality and life expectancy at birth with the GDP per person data shown in Global Perspective 4.1. Does the country with the highest GDP per person have the lowest infant mortality or the highest life expectancy? Can poorer countries do well on these alternative measures of well being? Could people be misled about differences in living standards if they only compared different countries' levels of GDP per person?

CHAPTER 5

Measuring the Economy's Output

Disposable Income Flat. Personal Consumption Surges. Investment Spending Stagnates. GDP Up 4 Percent. These headlines, typical of those found on Yahoo Finance or in the *Globe and Mail*, give knowledgeable readers valuable information on the state of the economy. This chapter will help you interpret such headlines and understand the stories reported under them. Specifically, it will help you become familiar with the vocabulary and methods of national income accounting. The terms and ideas in this chapter provide a foundation for the macroeconomic analysis in subsequent chapters.

5.1 | Measuring the Economy's Performance: GDP

National income accounting measures the economy's overall performance. It does for the economy as a whole what private accounting does for the individual firm or household. A firm measures its flows of income and expenditures regularly—usually every three months or once a year—to gauge its economic health. If things are going well and profits are good, the accounting data can be used to explain that success. Were costs down? Was output up? Have market prices risen? If things are going badly and profits are poor, the firm may be able to identify the reason by studying the record over several accounting periods. All this information helps the firm's managers to plot their future strategy.

National income accounting operates in much the same way for the economy as a whole. Statistics Canada compiles the national income accounts for the Canadian economy. This accounting allows economists and policymakers to:

- Assess the health of the economy by comparing levels of production at regular intervals.
- Track the long-run course of the economy to see whether it has grown, been constant, or declined.
- Formulate policies that will maintain and improve the economy's health.

national income accounting
The techniques used to measure the overall production of the economy and other related variables for the nation as a whole.

gross domestic product (GDP)
The total market value of all final goods and services produced annually within the boundaries of Canada.

Gross Domestic Product

The main measure of the economy's performance is its annual total output of goods and services—or, as it is called, *aggregate output*. Aggregate output can be measured in several ways depending upon how one wishes to define "an economy." For instance, should the value of the cars produced at a Toyota plant in Ontario count as part of the output of the Canadian economy because they are made within Canada, or as part of the Japanese economy because Toyota is a Japanese company? The most common measure of aggregate output, **gross domestic product (GDP),** clarifies this and other issues since it defines aggregate output as the dollar value of all final goods and services produced within the borders of a given country during a given period of time, typically a year. Under this definition, the value of the cars produced at the Toyota factory in Ontario clearly count as part of Canadian aggregate output rather than Japanese aggregate output.

A Monetary Measure

If the economy produces three sofas and two computers in year 1 and two sofas and three computers in year 2, in which year is output greater? We can't answer that question until we attach a price tag to each of the two products to indicate how society evaluates their relative worth.

That's what GDP does. It is a *monetary measure of a nation's output.* Without such a measure we would have no way of comparing the relative values of the vast number of goods and services produced in different years. In Table 5-1 the price of sofas is $500 and the price of computers is $2000. GDP gauges the output of year 2 ($7000) as greater than the output of year 1 ($5500), because society places a higher monetary value on the output of year 2. Society is willing to pay $1500 more for the combination of goods produced in year 2 than for the combination of goods produced in year 1.

Avoiding Multiple Counting

intermediate goods
Products purchased for resale or further processing or manufacturing.

final goods
Goods and services purchased for final use and not for resale or further processing or manufacturing.

multiple counting
Wrongly including the value of intermediate goods in the GDP.

To measure aggregate output accurately, all goods and services produced in a particular year must be counted only once. Because most products go through a series of production stages before they reach the market, some of their components are bought and sold many times. To avoid counting those components more than once, GDP includes only the market value of *final goods* and ignores *intermediate goods* altogether. **Intermediate goods** are goods and services that are purchased for resale or for further processing or manufacturing. **Final goods** include both consumption goods and capital goods that are purchased by their final users, rather than for resale or for further processing or manufacturing.

Why is the value of final goods included in GDP, but the value of intermediate goods excluded? Because the value of final goods includes the value of all intermediate goods used in producing them. To include the value of intermediate goods would amount to **multiple counting,** and that would distort the value of GDP.

To see why, suppose there are five stages to manufacturing a wool suit and getting it to the consumer—the final user. Table 5-2 shows that firm A, a sheep ranch, sells $120 worth of wool to firm B, a wool processor. Firm A pays out the $120 in wages, rent, interest, and profit. Firm B processes the

	Comparing Heterogeneous Outputs by Using Money Prices
TABLE 5-1	

Year	Annual output	Market value
1	3 sofas and 2 computers	3 at $500 + 2 at $2000 = $5500
2	2 sofas and 3 computers	2 at $500 + 3 at $2000 = $7000

TABLE 5·2	Value Added in a Five-Stage Production Process	
(1) **Stage of production**	**(2)** **Sales value of** **materials or product**	**(3)** **Value added**
	0	
Firm A, sheep ranch	$ 120	$120 (= $120 – $ 0)
Firm B, wool processor	180	60 (= 180 – 120)
Firm C, suit manufacturer	220	40 (= 220 – 180)
Firm D, clothing wholesaler	270	50 (= 270 – 220)
Firm E, retail clothier	350	80 (= 350 – 270)
Total sales value	$1140	
Value added (total income)		$350

wool and sells it to firm C, a suit manufacturer, for $180. What does firm B do with the $180 it receives? It pays $120 to firm A for the wool and uses the remaining $60 to pay wages, rent, interest, and profit for the resources used in processing the wool. Firm C, the manufacturer, sells the suit to firm D, a wholesaler, who sells it to firm E, a retailer. Then at last a consumer, the final user, comes in and buys the suit for $350.

How much of these amounts should we include in GDP to account for the production of the suit? Just $350, the value of the final product. The $350 includes all the intermediate transactions leading up to the product's final sale. To include the sum of all the intermediate sales, $1140, in GDP would amount to multiple counting. The production and sale of the final suit generated just $350, not $1140.

Alternatively, we could avoid multiple counting by measuring and cumulating only the *value added* at each stage. **Value added** is the market value of a firm's output *less* the value of the inputs the firm bought from others. At each stage, the difference between what a firm pays for inputs and what it receives from selling the product made from those inputs is paid out as wages, rent, interest, and profit. Column 3 of Table 5-2 shows that the value added by firm B is $60, the difference between the $180 value of its output and the $120 it paid for the input from firm A. We find the total of the suit by adding together all the values added by the five firms. Similarly, by calculating and summing the values added to all the goods and services produced by all firms in the economy, we can find the market value of the economy's total output—its GDP.

value added
The value of the product sold by a firm, less the value of the products purchased and used by the firm to produce the product.

GDP Excludes Nonproduction Transactions

Although many monetary transactions in the economy involve final goods and services, many others do not. These nonproduction transactions must be excluded from GDP because they have nothing to do with the production of final goods. *Nonproduction transactions* are of two types: purely financial transactions and second-hand sales.

FINANCIAL TRANSACTIONS

Purely financial transactions include the following:

- *Public Transfer Payments* These are the social insurance payments—for example, welfare and employment insurance—the government makes directly to households. Since the recipients contribute nothing to *current production* in return, including such payments in GDP would overstate the year's output.

- ***Private Transfer Payments***   Such payments include, for example, money that parents give their children or the cash gifts given at Christmas time. They produce no output. They simply transfer funds from one individual to another and consequently do not enter into GDP.

- ***Stock-Market Transactions***   The buying and selling of stocks (and bonds) is just a matter of swapping bits of paper. Stock-market transactions do not directly contribute to current production and are not included in GDP. Payments for the services provided by a stockbroker *are* included, however, because their services are currently provided and are thus a part of the economy's current output of goods and services.

SECOND-HAND SALES

Second-hand sales contribute nothing to current production and for that reason are excluded from GDP. Suppose you sell your 2002 Ford Mustang to a friend; that transaction would not be included in calculating this year's GDP because it generates no current production. The same would be true if you sold a brand-new Mustang to a neighbour a week after you purchased it. *(Key Question 3)*

Two Ways of Calculating GDP: Expenditures and Income

Let's look again at how the market value of total output is measured. Given the data listed in Table 5-2, how can we measure the market value of a suit? One way is to see how much the final user paid for it. That will tell us the market value of the final product. Or we can add up the entire wage, rental, interest, and profit incomes that were created in producing the suit.

The expenditures and income approaches are two ways of looking at the same thing: What is spent on making a product is income to those who helped to make it. If $350 is spent on manufacturing a suit, then $350 is the total income derived from its production. (See this chapter's Last Word for a third way Statistics Canada computes GDP: the value-added approach.)

We can look at GDP in the same two ways. We can view GDP as the sum of all the money spent in buying final goods and services, called the **expenditures approach.** Or we can view GDP in terms of the income derived or created from producing final goods and services, called the **income approach.** Buying (spending money) and selling (receiving income) are two aspects of the same transaction. On the expenditures side of GDP, all final goods produced by the economy are bought either by three domestic sectors (households, businesses, and government) or by buyers abroad. On the income side (once certain statistical adjustments are made), the total receipts from the sale of that total output go to the suppliers of factors of production as wages, rent, interest, and profit.

The Expenditures Approach

To determine GDP using the expenditures approach, we add up all the spending on final goods and services that has taken place throughout the year. Precise terms for the types of spending are listed in Table 5-3.

PERSONAL CONSUMPTION EXPENDITURES (*C*)

The term **personal consumption expenditures** covers all expenditures by households on *durable consumer goods* (automobiles, refrigerators, DVD players), *nondurable consumer goods* (bread, milk, vitamins, pencils, toothpaste), and *consumer expenditures for services* (of lawyers, doctors, mechanics, barbers). The symbol *C* is used to designate this component of GDP.

GROSS INVESTMENT (I_g)

The term **gross investment** (I_g) includes (1) all final purchases of machinery, equipment, and tools by firms; (2) all construction; and (3) changes in inventories.

Notice that except for the first item, this list includes more than we have meant by "investment" so far. The second item includes residential construction as well as the construction of new factories, warehouses, and stores. Why is residential construction regarded as investment rather than consumption?

---

expenditures approach
The method to measure GDP that adds up all the expenditures made for final goods and services.

income approach
The method to measure GDP that adds up all the income generated by the production of final goods and services.

personal consumption expenditures
The expenditures of households for durable and nondurable consumer goods and services.

gross investment
Expenditures for newly produced capital goods (such as machinery, equipment, tools, and buildings) and for additions to inventories.

TABLE 5-3	Calculating GDP in 2008: The Expenditures Approach (billions of dollars)

	% of GDP
Personal consumption expenditures (C)	891
Gross investment (I_g)	309
Government current purchases of goods and services (G)	375
Net exports (X_n)	25
Gross domestic product at market prices*	1600

Source: Statistics Canada Gross Domestic Product, expenditure-based. Accessed May 1, 2009.
Updates at http://www40.statcan.ca/l01/cst01/econ04-eng.htm.

*Includes adjustments and statistical discrepancy.

Increases in inventories (unsold goods) are considered to be investment because they are unconsumed output.

Because apartment buildings and houses, like factories and stores, earn income when they are rented or leased. Owner-occupied houses are treated as investment goods because they *could be* rented to bring in an income return. So, the national income accountants treat all residential construction as investment. Finally, increases in inventories (unsold goods) are considered to be investment because they represent, in effect, "unconsumed output." For economists, all new output that is not consumed is, by definition, capital. An increase in inventories is an addition (although perhaps temporary) to the stock of capital goods, and such additions are precisely how we define investment.

Positive and Negative Changes in Inventories   Inventories can either increase or decrease over some period. Suppose they increased by $10 billion between December 31, 2007 and December 31, 2008. That means the economy produced $10 billion more output than was purchased in 2008. We need to count all output produced in 2008 as part of that year's GDP, even though some of it remained unsold at the end of the year. This is accomplished by including the $10 billion increase in inventories as investment in 2008. That way the expenditures in 2008 will correctly measure the output produced that year.

Alternatively, suppose that inventories decreased by $10 billion in 2008. This "drawing down of inventories" means that the economy sold $10 billion more of output in 2008 than it produced that year. It did this by selling goods produced in prior years—goods already counted as GDP in those years. Unless corrected, expenditures in 2008 will overstate GDP for 2008. So, in 2008 we consider the $10 billion decline in inventories as "negative investment" and subtract it from total investment that year. Thus, expenditures in 2008 will correctly measure the output produced in 2008.

Non-Investment Transactions   So much for what investment is. You need to know what it isn't. Investment does not include the transfer of paper assets (stocks, bonds) or the resale of tangible assets (houses, jewellery, boats). Such transactions merely transfer the ownership of existing assets. Investment has to do with the creation of new, physical capital assets. The transfer (sale) of claims to existing capital goods does not create new capital.

Gross Investment versus Net Investment   As we have seen, the category gross investment, or *gross capital formation,* includes (1) all final purchases of machinery, equipment, and tools; (2) all construction; and (3) changes in inventories. The word *gross* means that we are referring to all investment goods—both those that replace machinery, equipment, and buildings that were used up (worn out or made obsolete) in producing the current year's output and any net additions to the economy's stock of capital. Gross investment includes investment in replacement capital *and* in added capital.

FIGURE 5·1   **Gross Investment, Depreciation, Net Investment, and the Stock of Capital**

When gross investment exceeds depreciation during a year, net investment occurs. This net investment expands the stock of private capital from the beginning of the year to the end of the year by the amount of the net investment. Other things equal, the economy's production capacity expands.

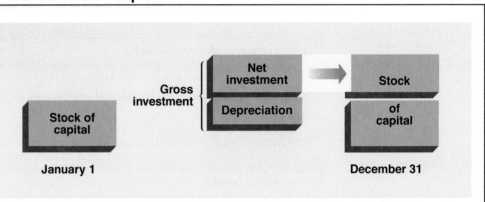

net investment
Gross investment less consumption of fixed capital.

capital consumption allowance
Estimate of the amount of capital worn out or used up (consumed) in producing the GDP; also called *depreciation*.

In contrast, **net investment** includes *only* investment of added capital. The amount of capital that is used up over the course of a year is called **capital consumption allowance,** or simply *depreciation.* So:

Net investment = gross investment – depreciation

In typical years, gross investment exceeds depreciation. Thus net investment is positive and the nation's stock of capital rises by the amount of net investment. As illustrated in Figure 5-1, the stock of capital at the end of the year exceeds the stock of capital at the beginning of the year by the amount of net investment.

CONSIDER THIS | Stock Answers about Flows

An analogy of a reservoir may be helpful in thinking about a nation's capital stock, investment, and depreciation. Picture a reservoir that has water flowing in from a river and flowing out from an outlet after it passes through turbines. The volume of water in the reservoir *at any particular time* is a "stock." In contrast, the inflow from the river and outflow from the outlet are "flows." Such flows are always measured over *some period of time.* Suppose that we measure these inflows and outflows at the end of each week and compare them with our measurements at the beginning of the week.

The volume or "stock" of water in the reservoir will rise if the weekly inflow exceeds the weekly outflow. It will fall if the inflow is less than the outflow. And it will remain constant if the two flows are equal.

We could simplify further by thinking in terms of the *net inflow* (inflow *minus* outflow) into the reservoir, where the net inflow can be positive or negative. The volume of water in the reservoir will rise if the net inflow is positive, decline if it is negative, and remain constant if it is zero.

Now let's apply this analogy to the stock of capital, gross investment, and depreciation. The stock of capital is the total capital in place at any time. Changes in this stock over some period of time, for example one year, depend on gross *investment* and *depreciation* (capital consumption allowance). Gross investment (the addition of capital goods) adds to the stock of capital and depreciation (the using up of capital goods) subtracts from it. The capital stock increases when gross investment exceeds depreciation, declines when gross investment is less than depreciation, and remains the same when gross investment and depreciation are equal.

Alternatively, the stock of capital increases when *net investment* (gross investment *minus* depreciation) is positive. When net investment is negative, the stock of capital declines, and when net investment is zero, the stock of capital remains constant.

Gross investment need not always exceed depreciation, however. When gross investment and depreciation *are equal,* net investment is zero and there is no change in the size of the capital stock. When gross investment *is less than* depreciation, net investment is negative. The economy then is *disinvesting*—using up more capital than it is producing—and the nation's stock of capital shrinks. That happened in the Great Depression of the 1930s.

National income accountants use the symbol *I* for private domestic investment spending. To differentiate between gross investment and net investment, they add either the subscript *g* or the subscript *n*. But it is gross investment, I_g, that they use when tallying up GDP.

GOVERNMENT PURCHASES (*G*)

government purchases
The expenditures of all governments in the economy for final goods and services.

The third category of expenditures in the national income accounts is **government purchases,** expenditures for the goods and services governments consume in providing public services. Government purchases (federal, provincial, and municipal) include all government expenditures on final goods, investment goods, and all direct purchases of resources, including labour. Government purchases do *not* include government transfer payments, because, as we have seen, they merely transfer government receipts to certain households and generate no production of any sort. Examples of government transfer payments are employment insurance benefits, welfare payments, and Canada Pension Plan benefits. National income accountants use the symbol *G* to signify government purchases.

NET EXPORTS (X_n)

International trade transactions are a significant item in national income accounting. But when calculating Canadian GDP, we must keep in mind that we want to total up only those expenditures used to purchase goods and services produced within Canada. Thus, we must add in the value of exports, *X*, since exports are by definition goods and services produced *within the borders of Canada*. Don't be confused by the fact that the expenditures to buy our exports are made by foreigners. The definition of GDP does not care about who is making expenditures on Canadian-made goods and services—only that the goods and services they buy are made within Canada. Thus, foreign spending on our exports must be included in GDP.

At this point, you might incorrectly think that GDP should be equal to the sum of $C + I_g + G + X$. But this sum overstates GDP. The problem is that, once again, we must consider only expenditures made on *domestically produced* goods and services. As it stands, C, I_g, and G count up expenditures on consumption, investment, and government purchases *regardless* of where those goods and services are made. Crucially, not all of the C, I_g, or G expenditures are for domestically produced goods and services. Some of the expenditures are for imports—goods and services produced outside of Canada. Thus, since we wish to count *only* the part of C, I_g, and G that goes to purchasing domestically produced goods and services, we must subtract the spending that goes to imports, *M*. Doing so yields the correct formula for calculating gross domestic product: $GDP = C + I_g + G + X - M$.

net exports
Exports minus imports.

Accountants simplify this formula for GDP by defining **net exports,** X_n, to be equal to exports minus imports:

Net exports (X_n) = exports (*X*) – imports (*M*)

Using this definition of net exports, the formula for gross domestic product simplifies to

GDP = $C + I_g + G + X_n$

Table 5-3 shows that in 2008 people from other countries spent $25 billion more on Canadian exports than Canadians spent on imports. That is, net exports in 2008 were a *positive* $25 billion. In another year net exports could be *negative:* imports would be greater than exports in that case.

PUTTING IT ALL TOGETHER: GDP = $C + I_g + G + X_n$

Taken together, the four categories of expenditures provide a measure of the market value of a certain year's total output—its GDP.

For Canada in 2008 (Table 5-3):

GDP = $891 + 309 + 375 + 25 = 1600

Global Perspective 5.1 lists the GDPs of several countries (values are converted to U.S. dollars using international exchange rates).

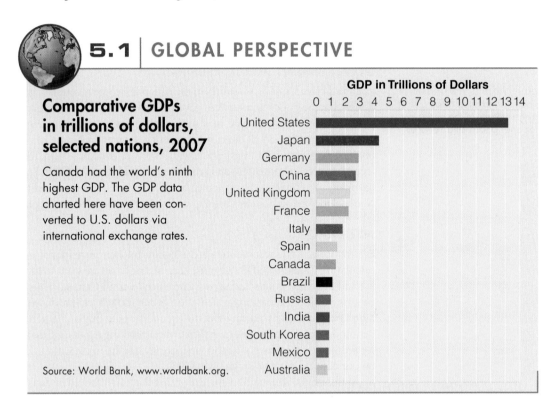

5.1 | GLOBAL PERSPECTIVE

Comparative GDPs in trillions of dollars, selected nations, 2007

Canada had the world's ninth highest GDP. The GDP data charted here have been converted to U.S. dollars via international exchange rates.

Source: World Bank, www.worldbank.org.

The Income Approach

Table 5-4 shows how 2008's $1600 billion of expenditures were allocated as income to those producing the output. It would be simple if we could say that the entire amount of expenditures flowed back to them in the form of wages, rent, interest, and profit. But some expenditures flow to other recipients (such as the government) or to other uses (such as paying to replace the capital goods that have worn out while producing this year's GDP). These must be accounted for in order to balance the expenditures and income sides of the account. We will begin by looking at the items that make up *national income.*

WAGES, SALARIES, AND SUPPLEMENTARY LABOUR INCOME

The largest income category is made up primarily of the wages and salaries paid by businesses and government to suppliers of labour. It also includes wage and salary supplements, in particular payments by employers of employment insurance premiums, workers' compensation premiums, and employer contributions to a variety of private and public pension funds for workers. Economists abbreviate all these as "wages."

PROFITS OF CORPORATIONS AND GOVERNMENT ENTERPRISES BEFORE TAXES

Corporate profits are the earnings of government enterprises and the owners of corporations. Private corporations' profits are divided into three categories:

TABLE 5·4	Calculating GDP in 2008: The Income Approach (billions of dollars)
Wages, salaries, and supplementary labour income	$823
Profits of corporations and government enterprises before taxes	231
Interest and investment income	81
Net income of farm and unincorporated businesses	93
Taxes less subsidies on factors of production	70
Indirect taxes less subsidies on products*	93
Capital consumption allowances	208
Statistical discrepancy	1
Gross domestic product at market prices	1600

Source: Statistics Canada Gross Domestic Product, expenditure-based.
Updates at http://www40.statcan.ca/l01/cst01/econ03-eng.htm. Accessed May 1, 2009.

* Includes inventory valuation adjustment, which adjusts for price changes to corporate inventories carried from one year to the next.

- *Corporate Income Taxes* These taxes are levied on the corporation's net earnings and flow to the government.

- *Dividends* These are the part of corporate profits that are paid to the corporate shareholders and thus flow to households—the ultimate owners of all corporations.

- *Undistributed Corporate Profits* This is money saved by the corporation to be invested later in new plants and equipment; also called *retained earnings*.

INTEREST AND INVESTMENT INCOME

Interest income consists of money paid by private businesses to the suppliers of capital. This income includes interest on bonds and loans of capital. Investment income includes rental income received by households and imputed rent; that is, the estimated rent on housing that households use for their own purpose.

NET INCOME FROM FARMS AND UNINCORPORATED BUSINESSES

This is the earnings of farmers and proprietors from their own businesses. These earnings represent a mixture of labour income and investment income that is impossible to segregate. Farm and non-farm proprietors supplying their own capital earn profits (or losses), interest, and rents mixed in with their labour income.

ADDING UP DOMESTIC INCOME

When we add up wages, salaries and supplementary labour income, corporate and government enterprise profits, interest and investment income, and income of farm and nonfarm unincorporated businesses, and make the appropriate inventory valuation adjustment, we get the *net domestic income at factor cost,* which is all the income earned by Canadian-supplied factors of production as wages, interest, rent, and profit. But to arrive at GDP we have to make two adjustments.

indirect taxes
Sales taxes, business property taxes, and customs duties, which firms treat as costs of producing a product.

Indirect Taxes The first adjustment is to add to net domestic income indirect taxes, less subsidies, which include general sales taxes (including GST), business property taxes, and customs duties.

Why do national income accountants add these indirect business taxes to wages, rent, interest, and profit in determining national income? The answer is, "to account for expenditures that are diverted to the government." Consider an item that would otherwise sell for $1, but costs $1.05 because the government has imposed a 5 percent sales tax. When this item is purchased, consumers will expend $1.05 to buy it. But only $1 will go to the seller (who will then distribute it as income in the form of wages, rent, interest, and profit in order to compensate resource providers). The remaining 5 cents will flow as revenue to the government. The GDP accountants handle the extra 5 cents by placing it in the category called "Taxes on Production and Imports" and loosely consider it to be "income" to government.

Depreciation: Capital Consumption Allowance   The useful life of capital equipment (such as bakery ovens or automobile assembly lines) extends far beyond the year in which it was produced. To avoid understating profit and income in the year of purchase, and to avoid overstating profit and income in succeeding years, the cost of such capital must be allocated over its lifetime. The amount allocated is an estimate of the capital being used up each year in production, called *depreciation*.

The depreciation charge against gross investment is the capital consumption allowance—the allowance for capital goods "consumed" in producing this year's GDP. It is the portion of GDP that must be set aside to pay for the replacement of the capital goods used up in production. That part of this charge is the difference between gross investment, I_g, and net investment, I_n.

The money allocated to consumption of fixed capital (the depreciation allowance) is a cost of production and thus included in the gross value of output. But this money is not available for other purposes, and, unlike other costs of production, it does not add to anyone's income. So it is not included in national income. We must therefore add it to national income to achieve balance with the economy's expenditures, as in Table 5-4.

Finally, national income accountants add a statistical discrepancy to make the income approach match the outcome of the expenditures approach. In 2008, the discrepancy was about $1 billion. *(Key Question 8)*

QUICK REVIEW

▶ Gross domestic product (GDP) measures the total market value of all final goods and services produced within a nation in a specific year.

▶ The expenditures approach to GDP sums total spending on final goods and services: $GDP = C + I_g + G + X_n$.

▶ When net investment is positive, the economy's production capacity increases; when net investment is negative, the economy's production capacity decreases.

▶ The income approach to GDP sums the total income earned by a nation's resource suppliers, then adds in indirect taxes and capital consumption allowance.

5.2 | Other National Accounts

Several other national accounts provide additional useful information about the economy's performance. We can derive these accounts by making various adjustments to GDP.

Gross National Product (GNP)

Until 1986, *gross national product (GNP)* was the main aggregate in the national accounts published by Statistics Canada. GNP is the total income that residents of a country earn within the year. The change to GDP was made because in Canada foreign investment is significant, and GDP would give us a better indication of output *produced* in Canada and the total income derived from that output.

GNP measures output by Canadians here and abroad, but excludes the contribution to Canadian output from investments of nonresidents. For example, the production of cars in the Honda factory in Alliston, Ontario is included in both Canadian GDP and GNP. But GNP excludes profit (referred to as net investments from nonresidents) sent to foreign shareholders of Honda, while this profit is included in Canadian GDP. Because there are many foreign-owned firms in Canada (compared to Canadian-owned firms abroad), GNP is less than GDP. Canadian GNP for 2008 totalled $1585 billion, whereas GDP was $1600 billion.

Net Domestic Product (NDP)

net domestic product (NDP)
GNP less the part of the year's output needed to replace the capital goods worn out in producing the output.

As a measure of total output, GNP does not make allowances for replacing the capital goods used up in each year's production. As a result, it does not tell us how much new output was available for consumption and for additions to the stock of capital. To determine that, we must subtract from GNP the capital that was consumed in producing the GNP and that had to be replaced. That is, we need to subtract consumption of fixed capital (depreciation) from GNP. The result is a measure of **net domestic product** (NDP). NDP measures the total annual output that the entire economy—households, businesses, government, and foreigners—can consume without impairing its capacity to produce in ensuing years. For 2008, NDP totalled $1296 billion.

Net National Income at Basic Prices (NNI)

net national income (NNI)
Total income earned by resource suppliers for their contribution to GDP.

Sometimes it is useful to know how much Canadians earned for their contributions of land, labour, capital, and entrepreneurial talent. Canadian **net national income** (NNI) includes all income earned through the use of Canadian-owned factors, whether they are located at home or abroad. To derive NNI from NDP, we must *subtract indirect business taxes*. Because government is not an economic resource, the indirect business taxes it collects do not qualify as payments to productive resources and thus are not included in national income. In 2008, NNI at basic prices amounted to $1201 billion.

Personal Income (PI)

personal income (PI)
The earned and unearned income available to resource suppliers and others before the payment of personal income taxes.

WORKED PROBLEM 5.1
Measuring Output and Income

Personal income (PI) includes all income *received* by households, earned or unearned. It is likely to differ from NNI because some income that is earned—corporate income taxes, undistributed corporate profits, government investment income, and social insurance contributions—is not actually received by households, and conversely, some income that is received—transfer payments—is not currently earned. Transfer payments are made up of such items as (1) Canada and Quebec Pension Plan payments, old age security pension payments, and employment insurance benefits; (2) welfare payments; and (3) a variety of veterans' payments. To arrive at personal income, we must subtract from NNI income that is earned but not received and add in income received but not currently earned. For 2008, PI totalled $1145 billion.

Disposable Income (DI)

disposable income (DI)
Personal income less personal taxes.

Disposable income (DI) is personal income less personal taxes and other personal transfers to government. *Personal taxes* are made up of personal income taxes and personal property taxes. In 2008, DI amounted to $952 billion.

Households use their disposable income in two ways—consumption (C) and savings (S):

$$DI = C + S$$

QUICK REVIEW

- Gross national product (GNP) is derived by subtracting net investments from non-residents from GDP.

- Net domestic product (NDP) is equal to GNP minus capital consumption allowances (depreciation).

- Net national income (NNI) is all income earned through the use of Canadian-owned factors, whether located at home or abroad.

- Personal income (PI) is all income received by households, whether earned or not.

- Disposable income (DI) is all income received by households minus personal taxes.

5.3 | Nominal GDP versus Real GDP

Recall that GDP is a measure of the market or money value of all final goods and services produced by the economy in a given year. We use money or nominal values to sum that heterogeneous output into a meaningful total. But that creates a problem: How can we compare the market values of GDP from year to year if the value of money itself changes because of inflation (rising prices) or deflation (falling prices)? After all, we determine the value of GDP by multiplying total output (Q) by market prices (P).

Whether there is a 5 percent increase in output (Q) with no change in prices (P) or a 5 percent increase in prices (P) with no change in output (Q), the change in the value of GDP will be the same. And yet it is the *quantity* (Q) of goods that gets produced and distributed to households that affects our standard of living, not the price (P) of the goods. The hamburger that sold for $3 in 2008 yields the same satisfaction as an identical hamburger that sold for 50 cents in 1970.

The way around this problem is to *deflate* GDP when prices rise and to *inflate* GDP when prices fall. These adjustments give us a measure of GDP for various years as if the value of the dollar had always been the same as it was in some reference (base) year. A GDP based on prices when the output was produced is called unadjusted GDP, or **nominal GDP.** A GDP that has been deflated or inflated to reflect changes in the price level is called adjusted GDP, or **real GDP.**

nominal GDP
GDP measured in terms of the price level at the time of measurement (unadjusted for inflation).

real GDP
Nominal GDP adjusted for inflation.

Adjustment Process in a One-Product Economy

There are two ways we can adjust nominal GDP to reflect price changes. For simplicity, let's assume that the economy produces only one good, pizza, in the amount indicated in Table 5-5 for years 1, 2, and 3. Suppose we gather revenue data directly from the financial reports of the pizza business to measure nominal GDP in various years. After completing our effort we would have calculated nominal GDP for each year, as shown in column 4 of Table 5-5. But we would have no way of

TABLE 5-5   Calculating Real GDP (base year = year 1)

Year	(1) Units of output (Q)	(2) Price of pizza per unit (P)	(3) Price index (year 1 = 100)	(4) Unadjusted, or nominal, GDP (Q) × (P)	(5) Adjusted, or real, GDP
1	5	$10	100	$ 50	$50
2	7	20	200	140	70
3	8	25	250	200	80
4	10	30	_____	_____	_____
5	11	28	_____	_____	_____

knowing to what extent changes in price and/or changes in quantity of output have accounted for the increases or decreases in nominal GDP that we observe.

PRICE INDEX

How can we calculate real GDP in our pizza economy? One way is to assemble data on the price changes that occurred over various years (column 2) and use them to establish an overall price index for the entire period. Then we can use the index in each year to adjust nominal GDP to real GDP for that year.

A **price index** is a measure of the price of a specified collection of goods and services, called a "market basket," in a specific year as compared to the price of an identical (or highly similar) collection of goods and services in a reference year. That point of reference, or benchmark, is known as the base period or base year. More formally,

price index
An index number that shows how the weighted average price of a "market basket" of goods and services changes through time.

$$\text{Price index in specific year} = \frac{\text{price of market basket in specific year}}{\text{price of same market basket in base year}} \times 100 \qquad (1)$$

By convention, the price ratio between a given year and the base year is multiplied by 100 to facilitate computation. For example, a price ratio of 2/1 (= 2) is expressed as a price index of 200. A price ratio of 1/3 (= 0.33) is expressed as a price index of 33.

In our pizza-only example, of course, our market basket consists of only one product. Column 2 of Table 5-5 reveals that the price of pizza was $10 in year 1, $20 in year 2, $25 in year 3, and so on. Let's select year 1 as our base year. Now we can express the successive prices of the contents of our market basket in, say, years 2 and 3 as compared to the price of the market basket in year 1:

$$\text{Price index, year 2} = \frac{\$20}{\$10} \times 100 = 200$$

$$\text{Price index, year 3} = \frac{\$25}{\$10} \times 100 = 250$$

For year 1, the base year, the price index is 100.

The index numbers tell us that the price of pizza rose from year 1 to year 2 by 100 percent [= (200 − 100)/100 × 100] and from year 1 to year 3 by 150 percent [= (250 − 100)/100 × 100].

DIVIDING NOMINAL GDP BY THE PRICE INDEX

We can now use the index numbers shown in column 3 to deflate or inflate the nominal GDP figures in column 4. The simplest and most direct method of deflating (or inflating) is to divide the price index into the corresponding nominal GDP. That gives us real GDP:

$$\text{Real GDP} = \frac{\text{nominal GDP}}{\text{price index}} \times 100 \qquad (2)$$

Column 5 of Table 5-5 shows the results. These figures for real GDP measure the market value of the output of pizza in years 1, 2, and 3 as though the price of pizza had been a constant $10 throughout the three-year period.

To test your understanding, extend Table 5-5 to years 4 and 5, using equation (2). Then run through the entire deflating procedure, using year 3 as the base period. This time you will have to inflate some of the nominal GDP data, using the same procedure as we used in the examples.

An Alternative Method

Another way to calculate real GDP is to gather separate data on physical outputs (Q) (as in column 1 of Table 5-5) and their prices (P) (as in column 2). We could then determine the market value of outputs in successive years *if the base-year price ($10) had prevailed*. In year 2, the seven units of pizza would have a value of $70 (= 7 units × $10). As column 5 confirms, that $70 worth of output is year 2's real GDP. Similarly, we could determine the real GDP for year 3 by multiplying the eight units of output that year by the $10 price in the base year.

Once we have determined real GDP through this method, we can identify the *implicit price index,* or **GDP deflator,** for a given year simply by dividing the nominal GDP by the real GDP for that year.

GDP deflator
An implicit price index calculated by dividing nominal GDP by real GDP and multiplying by 100.

 WORKED PROBLEM 5.2
Real GDP and Price Indexes

$$\text{GDP deflator} = \frac{\text{nominal GDP}}{\text{real GDP}} \times 100 \qquad (3)$$

Example: In year 2 we get a GDP deflator of 200, which equals the nominal GDP of $140 divided by the real GDP of $70 (× 100). Note that equation (3) is simply a rearrangement of equation (2). Table 5-6 summarizes the two methods of determining real GDP in our single-good economy. *(Key Question 12)*

Real-World Considerations and Data

In the real world of many goods and services, of course, determining GDP and constructing a reliable price index are far more complex matters than in our pizza-only economy. The national income accountants must assign a "weight" to each of the 380 categories of goods and services based on the relative proportion of each category in total output. They update the weights as expenditure patterns change.

Table 5-7 shows some of the real-world relationships between nominal GDP, real GDP, and the GDP price index. Here the reference year is 2002, the base year Statistics Canada currently uses, and the index is set at 100. Because the price level has been rising over the long run, the pre-2002 values of real GDP (column 3) are higher than the nominal values of GDP for those years (column 2). This upward adjustment means that prices were lower in the years before 2002, and thus nominal GDP understated the real output of those years and must be inflated.

Conversely, the rising price level on the post-2002 years caused nominal GDP figures for those years to overstate real output. So statisticians deflate those figures to determine what real GDP would have been in other years if 2002 prices had prevailed. Doing so reveals that real GDP has been less than nominal GDP since 2002.

By inflating the nominal pre-2002 GDP data and deflating the post-2002 data, government accountants determine annual real GDP, which can then be compared with the real GDP of any other year in the series of years. So the real GDP values in column 3 are directly comparable with one another.

Once we have determined nominal GDP and real GDP, we can calculate the GDP deflator. And once we have determined nominal GDP and the price index, we can calculate real GDP.

TABLE 5·6   Steps for Deriving Real GDP from Nominal GDP

Method 1

1. Find nominal GDP for each year.

2. Compute a price index.

3. Divide each year's nominal GDP by that year's price index, then multiply by 100 to determine real GDP.

Method 2

1. Break down nominal GDP into physical quantities of output and prices for each year.

2. Find real GDP for each year by determining the dollar amount that each year's physical output would have sold for if base-year prices had prevailed. (The implicit price index, or GDP deflator, can then be found by dividing nominal GDP by real GDP, and then multiplying by 100.)

TABLE 5-7	Nominal GDP, Real GDP, and the GDP Deflator*, Selected Years		
(1) Year	(2) Nominal GDP	(3) Real GDP	(4) GDP deflator 2002 = 100
1980	314.4	625.0	——
1985	485.7	716.4	67.8
1990	679.9	825.1	82.4
1995	810.4	——	90.2
1997	882.7	1032.6	——
2000	1076.6	——	97.8
2002	1152.9	1152.9	100.0
2008	1600.1	1321.4	121.1

* Chain-type annual-weights price index.

Source: Statistics Canada. Gross GDP at: http://www40.statcan.ca/l01/cst01/econ03-eng.htm and Real GDP, expenditure-based, at: http://www40.statcan.ca/l01/cst01/econ05-eng.htm, various years. Accessed May 5, 2009.

Example: Nominal GDP in 2008 was $1600.1 billion and real GDP was $1321.4 billion. So the price level in 2008 was 121.1 (= $1600.1/$1321.4 × 100), or 21.1 percent higher than in 2002. To find real GDP for 2008 we divide the nominal GDP of $1600.1 by the 2008 GDP deflator, and multiply by 100.

To test your understanding of the relationships between nominal GDP, real GDP, and the GDP deflator, determine the values of the GDP deflator for 1980 and 1997 in Table 5-7 and determine real GDP for 1995 and 2000. We have left those figures out on purpose. (*Key Question 14*)

Chain-Weighted Index

Up to 2001 Statistics Canada established weights, based on price, for a base year for the 380 categories it uses in calculating the implicit price index, and changed these weights approximately every 10 years. Statistics Canada currently uses 2002 as the base year. This *fixed based price index* method, which we just studied, worked well as long as the weights remained relatively constant from year to year. But with the rapid expansion of the information technology (IT) sector, many prices for the outputs of this sector fell dramatically. Using 2002 prices as weights for the outputs of the IT sector would result in "overweighting" these goods and services. Since the output of the IT sector has grown rapidly in the last 20 years, such overweighting in essence overestimated GDP growth during this time period. Thus, in May 2001 Statistics Canada began to calculate a *chain-weighted index,* or chain Fisher index, which is adjusted annually to better represent the weight of each category, particularly the IT sector.

To better understand why Statistics Canada now calculates a chain-weighted index, let's look at an example. Consider an economy that has only two sectors, computers and pears, and consumers spend half of their income on pears and the other half on computers. We assume that the output of computers is rising at a very rapid 10 percent per year, while pear production is stagnant, remaining the same from year to year. We further assume that the price of computers falls relative to the price of pears over time due to the rapid expansion of computer production. If we construct a fixed weighted index using prices (weights) prevailing in, say, 2008, the rapid output growth of computers will also translate into a very rapid growth rate of GDP. But that very rapid GDP growth rate is actually overstated because the price (the weight) of computers is falling. Moreover, consumers have not changed the proportion of their income they spend on pears and computers. So, in situations where prices of some goods in the economy are falling, as has been the case in Canada in the IT sector in the last 20 years or so, the traditional fixed weight index to calculate real GDP is inadequate.

Rather than using only a base year, the new Statistics Canada method of calculating GDP considers both quantities and prices in the base year and the following year, and then averages the two. For example, if using 2008 prices as weights yields a real GDP increase of 4 percent in 2009, but using 2009 prices yields a GDP increase of 3 percent because some prices in the economy declined, the new chain-weighted index would give an increase of real GDP in 2009 of 3.5 percent (= (4 + 3)/2). You can see in this simple example that falling prices for some output in 2009 have reduced the growth rate of GDP compared to the fixed weighted method of calculating GDP.

The new index used by Statistics Canada is referred to as a chain-weighted index because it links each year to the previous year through the use of both the prior-year prices and current-year prices. For example, the calculation of the chain-weighted index would use both 2007 and 2008 prices to calculate real GDP growth in 2008. Since the 2007 chain-weighted index was arrived at using both 2006 and 2007 prices, the year 2008 is linked back—as the links of a chain are—to 2007, 2006, and previous years as well.

QUICK REVIEW

▸ Nominal GDP is output valued at current prices. Real GDP is output valued at constant base-year prices.

▸ A price index compares the price (market value) of a basket of goods and services in a given year to the price of the same market basket in a reference year.

▸ Nominal GDP can be transformed into real GDP by dividing the nominal GDP by the GDP deflator and then multiplying by 100.

5.4 | Shortcomings of GDP

GDP is a reasonably accurate and highly useful measure of how well or how poorly the economy is performing. But it has several shortcomings as a measure of total output and of well-being (total utility).

Measurement Shortcomings

Although GDP is the best measure of overall output in an economy, it suffers from a number of omissions that tend to understate total output.

NONMARKET TRANSACTIONS

Certain production transactions do not take place in any market—the services of homemakers, for example, and the labour of carpenters who repair their own homes. Such activities never show up in GDP because the accountants who tally up GDP only get data on economic transactions involving *market activities*—that is, transactions in which output or resources are traded for money. Consequently, GDP understates a nation's total output because it does not count *unpaid work*.

THE UNDERGROUND ECONOMY

In the Canadian economy there is a flourishing, productive underground sector. Some of the people who conduct business there are gamblers, smugglers, prostitutes, "fences" of stolen goods, drug growers, and drug dealers. They have good reason to conceal their income.

Most participants in the underground economy, however, engage in perfectly legal activities but choose (illegally) not to report their full income to the Canada Revenue Agency. A barista at a coffee shop may report just a portion of the tips received from customers. Storekeepers may

5.2 | GLOBAL PERSPECTIVE

The underground economy as a percentage of GDP, selected nations

Underground economies vary in size worldwide. Three factors that help explain the variation are (1) the extent and complexity of regulation, (2) the type and degree of taxation, and (3) the effectiveness of law enforcement.

Source: Friedrich Schneider and Dominik H. Enste, "Shadow Economies: Size, Causes, and Consequences," *Journal of Economic Literature* (March 2000), p. 104. The figure for Canada is from David E. A. Giles and Lindsay M. Tedds, *Taxes and the Canadian Underground Economy*, Toronto: Canadian Tax Foundation, 2002.

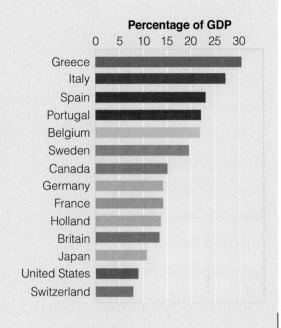

Percentage of GDP

report only a portion of their sales receipts. Unemployed workers who want to hold on to their employment insurance benefits may take an "off the books" or "cash only" job. A brick mason may agree to rebuild a neighbour's fireplace in exchange for the neighbour's repairing his boat engine. The value of such transactions does not show up in GDP, but is estimated to be about 15 percent of the recorded GDP in Canada—meaning that GDP in 2008 was understated by more than $240 billion. Global Perspective 5.2 shows estimates of the relative sizes of underground economies in selected nations.

LEISURE

The average workweek in Canada has declined since the turn of the twentieth century—from about 53 hours to about 35 hours. Moreover, the greater frequency of paid vacations, holidays, and leave time has shortened the work year itself. This increase in leisure time has had a positive effect on overall well-being. But our system of national income accounting understates well-being by ignoring leisure's value. Nor does the system measure the satisfaction—the "psychic income"—that many people derive from their work.

IMPROVED PRODUCT QUALITY

Because GDP is a quantitative measure rather than a qualitative measure, it fails to capture the full value of improvements in product quality. There is a very real difference in quality between a $200 cell phone purchased today and a cell phone that cost that same amount just five years ago. Today's cell phone is digital, has greater storage capacity, a clearer screen, and quite likely a camera and an MP3 player.

Obviously quality improvement has a great effect on economic well-being, as does the quantity of goods produced. Although Statistics Canada adjusts GDP for quality improvements for selected items, the vast majority of such improvements for the entire range of goods and services do not get reflected in GDP.

Shortcomings of the Well-Being Measure

Although the output of goods and services is an important aspect of the well-being of the citizens of a nation, it is not the only factor. We must also consider environmental degradation caused by the production of goods and services, the composition and distribution of that output, and the importance of nonmaterial sources of well-being, which are not captured by GDP.

GDP AND THE ENVIRONMENT

The growth of GDP is inevitably accompanied by "gross domestic by-products," including dirty air and polluted water, toxic waste, congestion, and noise. The social costs of those negative by-products reduce our economic well-being. And since those costs are not deducted from total output, GDP overstates our national well-being. Ironically, when money is spent to clean up pollution and reduce congestion, those expenses are added to the GDP!

COMPOSITION AND DISTRIBUTION OF OUTPUT

The composition of output is undoubtedly important for well-being. But GDP does not tell us whether the mix of goods and services is enriching or potentially detrimental to society. GDP assigns equal weight to an assault rifle and a computer, so long as both sell for the same price. Moreover, GDP reveals nothing about the way the output is distributed. Does 90 percent of the output go to 10 percent of the households, for example, or is the output more evenly distributed? The distribution of output may make a big difference for society's overall well-being.

NONMATERIAL SOURCES OF WELL-BEING

Finally, the connection between GDP and well-being is problematic for another reason. Just as a household's income does not measure its total happiness, a nation's GDP does not measure its total well-being. Many things could make a society better off without necessarily raising GDP: a reduction of crime and violence, peaceful relations with other countries, greater civility toward one another, better understanding between parents and children, and a reduction of drug and alcohol abuse.

The **LAST WORD**   Value Added and GDP

The third method by which Statistics Canada arrives at GDP is through the value-added approach. In this piece, Statistics Canada compares and contrasts the value-added approach with the expenditure-and-income approach in computing GDP in Canada.

Gross domestic product (GDP) by industry is one of the three GDP series produced by the Canadian System of National Accounts (CSNA). It is also known as the output-based GDP, because it sums the value added (output less intermediate consumption of goods and services) of all industries in Canada. This GDP series is published on a monthly basis and thus delivers the earliest and most up-to-date information on current developments in the economy. The other two GDP series are the income-based GDP, which tallies earnings that are generated by productive activity, and the expenditure-based GDP, which is equal to final expenditure on goods and services produced. Both the income-based and expenditure-based GDP measures are published on a quarterly basis.

The meaning of the word "output" in the output-based GDP needs to be elaborated to avoid any confusion between its present definition in the international System of National Accounts 1993 (SNA 1993) and its earlier use. The output of an economy was always meant to be equal to "net output" ("gross output" of goods and services less the intermediate use of goods and services in its production).

This "net output" is now called "value added" and the terms "gross output" and "net output" are no longer used in the SNA 1993. The three alternative GDPs are designed to independently but equivalently portray the production activity of the country, seen from different perspectives. With information on the sources of goods, services, and incomes generated by processes of production, the output-based GDP and the income-based GDP provide a comprehensive and detailed description of the supply side of domestic production. Expenditure-based GDP, on the other hand, traces the disposition of the output produced among the various categories of demand, and thus offers a demand-side view of the Canadian economy. Changes in the level of production are key indicators of economic activity. Evaluating production therefore is fundamental in monitoring the behaviour of the economy. For this reason GDP is an indispensable tool for a broad range of analytical, modelling, and policy-formulation purposes. Governments, businesses, trade and labour organizations, academic researchers, journalists and the general public use GDP figures to evaluate the performance of the economy, to appraise the success of monetary and industrial policies, to explore past trends in production, to forecast future prospects for economic growth, to carry out international comparisons, and so on. Since economic activity is one of the several major factors influencing welfare policy, movements in GDP may also play a role in the assessment of the general well-being of the country. Estimates of the three GDP series are produced within the highly integrated conceptual and statistical framework of the CSNA, sharing a consistent set of concepts, definitions, and classifications. On an annual basis, the growth rates of the income-based and expenditure-based GDP are identical, and the year-to-year movements of the output-based GDP deviate only slightly. The small discrepancies in growth rates (less than two-tenths of one percent in any of the years between 1990 and 1998) are caused primarily by differences in the treatment of taxes and subsidies.

Source: Statistics Canada, Gross Domestic Product by Industry: Sources and Methods, 2002, p. 7, Catalogue No. at-547-XIE.

Question

Distinguish among (a) the value-added approach, (b) the expenditure approach, and (c) the income approach to calculating GDP.

CHAPTER SUMMARY

5.1 ▸ MEASURING THE ECONOMY'S PERFORMANCE: GDP

- Gross domestic product (GDP), a basic measure of economic performance, is the market value of all final goods and services produced within the borders of a nation in a year.

- Intermediate goods, nonproduction transactions, and second-hand sales are purposely excluded in calculating GDP.

- GDP may be calculated by summing total expenditures on all final output or by summing the income derived from the production of that output.

- By the expenditures approach, GDP is determined by adding consumer purchases of goods and services, gross investment spending by businesses, government purchases, and net exports: $GDP = C + I_g + G + X_n$.

- Gross investment is divided into (a) replacement investment (required to maintain the nation's stock of capital at its existing level), and (b) net investment (the net increase in the stock of capital). Positive net investment is associated with an expanding production capacity; negative net investment with a declining production capacity.

- By the income approach, GDP is calculated as the sum of wages and salaries, profits of corporations and government enterprises before taxes, interest and investment income, net income of farmers and unincorporated businesses, and the two non-income charges (indirect taxes less subsidies and capital consumption allowances).

5.2 ▸ OTHER NATIONAL ACCOUNTS

- Other national income accounting measures are derived from the GDP. Gross national product (GNP) is the total income that residents of a country earn each year. Net domestic product (NDP) is GDP less the consumption of fixed capital. Net national income (NNI) is total income earned by resource suppliers; it is found by subtracting indirect taxes and capital consumption allowances from GDP. Personal income (PI) is the total income paid to households prior to any allowance for personal taxes. Disposable income (DI) is personal income after personal taxes have been paid; it measures the amount of income households have available to consume or save.

5.3 ▸ NOMINAL GDP VERSUS REAL GDP

- Price indexes are computed by dividing the price of a specific collection or market basket of output in a particular period by the price of the same market basket in a base period and multiplying the result (the quotient) by 100.

- The implicit price index, or GDP deflator, is used to adjust nominal GDP for inflation or deflation and thereby obtain real GDP.

- Nominal (current-dollar) GDP measures each year's output valued in terms of the prices prevailing in that year. Real (constant-dollar) GDP measures each year's output in terms of the prices that prevailed in a selected base year. Because real GDP is adjusted for price-level changes, differences in real GDP are due only to differences in production activity.

- A chain-weighted index to compute real GDP is constructed using an average of current and past prices as weights. It is particularly useful in an economy in which the prices of some outputs are declining.

5.4 ▸ SHORTCOMINGS OF GDP

- GDP is a reasonably accurate and very useful indicator of a nation's economic performance, but it has limitations. It fails to account for nonmarket and illegal transactions, changes in leisure and in product quality, the environmental effects of production, and the composition and distribution of output. GDP should not be interpreted as a complete measure of well-being.

TERMS AND CONCEPTS

STUDY QUESTIONS

LO ▶ 5.1 1. In what ways are national income statistics useful?

LO ▶ 5.1 2. Explain why an economy's output, in essence, is also its income.

LO ▶ 5.1 3. **KEY QUESTION** Why do national income accountants include only final goods in measuring GDP for a particular year? Why don't they include the value of the stocks and bonds bought and sold? Why don't they include the value of the used furniture bought and sold?

LO ▶ 5.1 4. What is the difference between gross investment and net investment?

LO ▶ 5.1 5. Why are changes in inventories included as part of investment spending? Suppose inventories declined by $1 billion during 2004. How would this affect the size of gross investment and gross domestic product in 2004? Explain.

LO ▶ 5.1 6. Use the concepts of gross and net investment to distinguish between an expanding, a static, and a declining economy. "In 1933 net investment was minus $324 million. This means in that particular year the economy produced no capital goods at all." Do you agree? Explain: "Though net investment can be positive, negative, or zero, it is quite impossible for gross investment to be less than zero."

LO ▶ 5.1 7. Define net exports. Explain how Canadian exports and imports each affect domestic production. Suppose foreigners spend $7 billion on Canadian exports in a given year and Canadians spend $5 billion on imports from abroad in the same year. What is the amount of Canada's net exports? Explain how net exports might be a negative amount.

LO ▶ 5.1 8. **KEY QUESTION** Following is a list of national income figures for a certain year. All figures are in billions. Calculate GDP by both the expenditure and income methods. The answers derived by each approach should be the same.

Personal consumption expenditures	$120
Capital consumption allowances (depreciation)	20
Interest and investment income	10
Net income of farms and unincorporated businesses	17
Net exports	+13
Profits of corporations and government enterprises before taxes	42
Wages, salaries, and supplementary labour income	113
Indirect business taxes less subsidies	11
Government current purchases of goods and services	40
Net investment (net capital formation)	30
Taxes less subsidies on factors of production	10

LO ▶ 5.1 9. Using the following national income accounting data, compute GDP by the expenditures approach. All figures are in billions.

Wages, salaries, and supplementary labour income	$194.2
Canadian exports of goods and services	17.8
Capital consumption allowances (depreciation)	11.8
Government current purchases of goods and services	59.4
Net investment (net capital formation)	52.1
Canadian imports of goods and services	16.5
Personal consumption expenditures	219.1

LO ▶ 5.1 10. Using the following national income accounting data, compute GDP by both the expenditures and income approaches. All figures are in billions.

Profits of corporations and government enterprises before taxes	$ 46
Exports	94
Capital consumption allowances	65
Government current purchases of goods and services	113
Net income of farm and unincorporated businesses	24
Taxes less subsidies on factors of production	75
Wages, salaries, supplementary labour income	371
Gross investment	167
Indirect taxes less subsidies on products	11
Interest and investment income	59
Personal consumption expenditures	284
Imports	7

LO ▶ 5.3 11. Why do national income accountants compare the market value of the total outputs in various years rather than actual physical volumes of production? Explain. What problem is posed by any comparison, over time, of the market values of various total outputs? How is this problem resolved?

LO ▶ 5.3 12. **KEY QUESTION** Suppose that in 1984 the total output in a single-good economy was 7000 buckets of chicken. Also suppose that in 1984 each bucket of chicken was priced at $10. Finally, assume that in 1996 the price per bucket of chicken was $16 and that 22,000 buckets were purchased. Determine the GDP price index for 1984, using 1996 as the base year. By what percentage did the price level, as measured by this index, rise between 1984 and 1996? Use the two methods listed in Table 5-6 to determine real GDP for 1984 and 1996.

LO ▶ 5.3 13. Distinguish between a fixed-base price index and a chain-weighted index. Why can a fixed-base price index exaggerate GDP growth?

LO ▶ 5.3 14. **KEY QUESTION**   The following table shows nominal GDP and an appropriate price index group of selected years. Compute real GDP. Indicate in each calculation whether you are inflating or deflating the nominal GDP data.

Year	Nominal GDP (billions)	GDP deflator (2002 = 100)	Real GDP (billions)
1962	44.8	15.8	$_____
1974	173.9	30.1	$_____
1984	449.6	65.8	$_____
1994	770.9	88.2	$_____
2004	1290.9	106.6	$_____
2007	1532.9	116.4	$_____

15. Which of the following are actually included in deriving **LO ▶ 5.4** this year's GDP? Explain your answer in each case.

a. Interest on a Bell Canada bond.

b. Canada Pension Plan payments received by a retired factory worker.

c. The services of a painter in painting the family home.

d. The income of a dentist.

e. The money received by Smith when she resells her economics textbook to a book buyer.

f. The monthly allowance a college student receives from home.

g. Rent received on a two-bedroom apartment.

h. The money received by Mac when he resells this year's Ford Mustang to Stan.

i. Interest received on government bonds.

j. A two-hour decline in the length of the workweek.

k. The purchase of a Quebec Hydro bond.

l. A $2 billion increase in business inventories.

m. The purchase of 100 Research In Motion common shares.

n. The purchase of an insurance policy.

INTERNET APPLICATION QUESTIONS @

1. **Nominal and Real GDP** Visit Statistics Canada through the McConnell-Brue-Flynn-Barbiero Web site (Chapter 5) and select *Economic Accounts*. Under *Gross Domestic Product, Expenditure Based*, identify the current-dollar GDP (nominal GDP) for the past four years. Return to the original site and choose *Real Gross Domestic Product at 2002 Prices (expenditure based)* and identify real GDP data for the last four years. Why was nominal GDP higher than real GDP in each of those years? What were the percentage changes in nominal GDP and real GDP for the most recent year? How do those percentage changes compare to those for the prior three years?

CHAPTER 6

Economic Growth

People living in rich countries tend to take economic growth and rising standards of living for granted. Recessions—periods during which growth declines—are normally infrequent and temporary, usually lasting less than a year. Once they pass, market economies return to growing and living standards continue their seemingly inexorable rise.

But a look back at history or around the world today quickly dispels any confidence that economic growth and rising standards of living are automatic or routine. Looking back at history reveals that continually rising living standards are a recent phenomenon, seen only during the last century or two; before then living standards barely rose from one generation to the next, if at all. And looking around the world today reveals huge differences in standards of living resulting from the disturbing fact that some countries have enjoyed decades or even centuries of steadily rising per capita income levels while others have experienced hardly any growth at all.

This chapter investigates the causes of economic growth, what government policies appear to promote economic growth, and the controversies surrounding the benefits and costs of economic growth. As you will see, economic growth has been perhaps the most revolutionary and powerful force in history. Consequently, no study of economics is complete without a thorough understanding of the causes and consequences of economic growth.

6.1 | Economic Growth

Economists define and measure **economic growth** as either:

- An increase in real GDP occurring over some time period.
- An increase in real GDP per capita occurring over some time period.

With either definition, economic growth is calculated as a percentage rate of growth per quarter (three-month period) or per year. For the first definition, for example, real GDP in Canada was $1315.9 billion in 2007 and $1321.4 billion in 2008. So the rate of economic growth in Canada for 2007 was 0.4 percent, calculated as follows:

economic growth
An increase either in real output (GDP) or in real output per capita.

real GDP per capita
The real GDP per person, found by dividing real GDP by a country's population.

% change in growth = [(2008 real GDP – 2007 real GDP) / 2007 GDP] × 100

= [($1321.4 billion – $1315.9 billion)/$1315.9 billion] × 100

= 0.4 %

The second definition takes into consideration the size of the population. **Real GDP per capita** (or per capita output) is found by dividing real GDP by population. The resulting number is then compared in percentage terms with that of the previous period. For example, real GDP in Canada was $1283.4 billion in 2006 and population was 32.65 million. So, its real GDP per capita was $39,308. In 2007, real GDP per capita rose to $40,419. Therefore Canada's rate of growth of real GDP per capita for 2007 was 2.7 percent {= [$40,419 – $39,308/$39,308] × 100}.

Unless specified otherwise, growth rates reported in the news and by international agencies use the growth of real GDP. For comparing living standards, however, the second definition is superior. While China's GDP in 2006 was U.S. $2644 billion compared with Denmark's $275 billion, Denmark's real GDP per capita was $52,110 compared with China's meagre $2000. And in some cases, growth of real GDP can be misleading. Madagascar's real GDP grew at a rate of 1.7 percent per year from 1990 to 2004. But over the same period its annual population growth was 2.9 percent, resulting in a decline in real GDP per capita of approximately 1.2 percent per year. *(Key Question 2)*

Growth as a Goal

Growth is a widely held economic goal. The expansion of total output relative to population results in rising real wages and incomes and thus higher standards of living. An economy that is experiencing economic growth is better able to meet people's wants and resolve socioeconomic problems. Rising real wages and income provide richer opportunities to individuals and families—a vacation trip, a personal computer, a higher education—without sacrificing other opportunities and pleasures. With a growing economy a government can undertake new programs to alleviate poverty, embrace diversity, cultivate the arts, and protect the environment without impairing existing levels of consumption, investment, and public goods production. In short, *growth lessens the burden of scarcity.*

Arithmetic of Growth

Why do economists pay so much attention to small changes in the rate of growth? Because such changes really matter! For Canada, with a current real GDP of over $1 trillion, the difference between a 3 percent and a 4 percent rate of growth is more than $10 billion of output each year. For a poor country, a difference of one-half percentage point in the rate of growth may mean the difference between hunger and starvation.

rule of 70
A method for determining the number of years it will take for some measure to double, given its annual percentage increase, by dividing that percentage increase into 70.

The mathematical approximation called the **rule of 70** provides a quantitative grasp of the effect of economic growth. It tells us that we can find the number of years it will take for some measure to double, given its annual percentage increase, by dividing that percentage increase into the number 70. So,

$$\text{Approximate number of years required to double real GDP} = \frac{70}{\text{annual percentage rate of growth}}$$

 WORKED PROBLEM 6.1
GDP Growth

Examples: A 3 percent annual rate of growth will double real GDP in about 23 years (= 70 ÷ 3). Growth of 8 percent per year will double real GDP in about 9 years (= 70 ÷ 8). The rule of 70 is applicable generally. For example, it works for estimating how long it will take a price level or a savings account to double at various percentage rates of inflation or interest. When compounded over many years, an apparently small difference in the rate of growth thus becomes highly significant. Suppose China and Italy start with identical GDPs, but then China grows at an 8 percent yearly rate, while Italy grows at 2 percent. China's GDP would double in about 9 years but Italy's GDP would double in 35 years.

Growth in Canada

Table 6-1 gives an overview of economic growth in Canada over past years. Column 2 reveals strong growth as measured by increases in real GDP. Note that between 1961 and 2008 real GDP increased fivefold. But the Canadian population also increased. Nevertheless, in column 4 we find that real GDP per capita rose almost threefold over these years.

What has been the *rate* of growth in Canada? Real GDP grew at an annual rate of almost 3.5 percent between 1961 and 2008. Real GDP per capita increased at 2.1 percent per year over that time. But we must qualify these numbers in several ways:

- ***Improved Products and Services***   Since the numbers in Table 6-1 do not fully account for the improvements in products and services, they understate the growth of economic well-being. Such purely quantitative data do not fully compare an era of vacuum-tube computers and low-efficiency V8 hotrods with an era of digital cell phone networks and fuel-sipping hybrid-drive vehicles.

- ***Added Leisure***   The increases in real GDP and per capita GDP identified in Table 6-1 were accomplished despite large increases in leisure. The standard workweek, once 50 hours, is now about 35 hours. Again, the raw-growth numbers understate the gain in economic well-being.

- ***Other Impacts***   These measures of growth do not account for any effects growth may have had on the environment and the quality of life. If growth debases the physical environment and creates a stressful work environment, the bare growth numbers will overstate the gains in well-being that result from growth. On the other hand, if growth leads to stronger environmental protections or a more secure and stress-free lifestyle, these numbers will understate the gains in well-being.

Two other points should be made about Canadian growth rates. First, they are not constant or smooth over time. Like those of other countries, Canadian growth rates vary quarterly and annually depending on a variety of factors such as the introduction of major new inventions and the economy's

TABLE 6-1   Real GDP and Per Capita GDP, 1961–2008

(1) Year	(2) GDP (billions of 2002 $)	(3) Population (millions)	(4) Per capita GDP (2002 $) (2) ÷ (3)
1961	263.9	18.2	14,500
1966	360.1	20.0	18,005
1971	437.5	21.6	20,255
1976	547.9	23.0	23,822
1981	647.2	24.8	26,097
1986	733.2	26.1	28,092
1991	808.2	28.0	28,864
1996	913.6	29.7	30,761
2001	1120.4	31.0	36,142
2005	1246.0	32.3	38,576
2008	1321.4	33.5	39,445

Source: Statistics Canada. GDP, income-based at: http://www40.statcan.ca/l01/cst01/econ03-eng.htm, and Real GDP, expenditure-based at: http://www40.statcan.ca/l01/cst01/econ05-eng.htm, various years. Accessed May 6, 2009.

current position in the business cycle. Second, although many countries share the Canadian experience of positive and ongoing economic growth, sustained growth is both a historically new occurrence and also one that is not shared equally by all countries.

6.2 | Modern Economic Growth

modern economic growth The historically recent phenomenon in which nations have experienced sustained increases in real GDP per capita.

PRODUCTION & THE STANDARD OF LIVING

We live in an era of wireless high-speed Internet connections, genetic engineering, and space exploration. New inventions and new technologies drive continual economic growth and ongoing increases in living standards. But it wasn't always like this. Economic growth and sustained increases in living standards are a historically recent phenomenon that started with the Industrial Revolution of the late 1700s—before the Industrial Revolution living standards were basically flat over long periods of time, so that, for instance, Greek peasants living in the year 300 B.C. had about the same material standard of living as Greek peasants living in the year 1500 A.D. By contrast, our current era of **modern economic growth** is characterized by sustained and ongoing increases in living standards that can cause dramatic increases in the standard of living within less than a single human lifetime.

Economic historians informally date the start of the Industrial Revolution to the 1770s, when the Scottish inventor James Watt perfected a powerful and efficient steam engine. The steam engine, which could be used to drive industrial factory equipment, steamships, and steam locomotives, inaugurated the modern era. New industrial factories mass-produced goods for the first time, with nearly all manufacturing shifting to factories rather than being produced by hand by local craftsmen. The new steamships and steam locomotives meant that resources could easily flow to factories, and that the products of factories could be shipped to distant consumers at low cost. The result was a huge increase in long-distance trade and a major population shift as people left farms to go work in the towns and cities where the new industrial factories were concentrated. Steam power later would largely be replaced by electric power, and many more inventions followed the steam engine. But the key point to remember is that the last 200 or so years of history have been fundamentally different from anything that went before.

The biggest change has been change itself. Whereas in earlier times material standards of living and the goods and services that people produced and consumed changed very little over the course of an entire human lifespan, nowadays people living in countries experiencing economic growth are constantly exposed to new technologies, new products, and new services.

What is more, economic growth has vastly affected cultural, social, and political arrangements:

• Culturally, the vast increases in wealth and living standards have for the first time in history allowed ordinary people to have significant time for leisure activities and the arts.

• Socially, countries experiencing modern economic growth have instituted universal public education, and have largely eliminated ancient social norms and legal restrictions against women and minorities doing certain jobs or holding certain positions.

• Politically, countries experiencing modern economic growth have tended to move toward democracy, a form of government that was extremely rare before the start of the Industrial Revolution.

In addition, the average human lifespan has more than doubled, from an average of less than 30 years before economic growth began in the late 1700s to a worldwide average of over 67 years today. Thus, for the first time in world history the average person can expect to live into old age.

These and other changes speak to the truly revolutionary power of economic growth and naturally lead economists to consider the causes of economic growth and what policies could be pursued to sustain and promote it. Their desire is intensified by the reality that economic growth is distributed so unevenly around the world.

The Uneven Distribution of Growth

Modern economic growth has spread only slowly from its British birthplace. It first advanced to France, Germany, and other parts of Western Europe in the early 1800s before spreading to Canada, the United States, and Australia by the late 1800s. Japan began to industrialize in the 1870s but the rest of Asia did not follow until the early to mid 1900s, at which time large parts of Central and South America as well as the Middle East also began to experience economic growth. Africa for the most part did not experience sustained economic growth until the past 20 years. Some parts of the world have yet to experience economic growth at all.

The different starting dates for modern economic growth in different parts of the world are the main cause of the vast differences in per capita GDP levels seen today. The huge divergence in living standards caused by the fact that different countries started modern economic growth at different times is best seen in Figure 6-1, which shows how GDP per capita has evolved since 1820 in Canada and the United States, Western Europe, Latin America, Asia, and Africa.

To make comparisons easy to interpret, income levels have been converted into 1990 U.S. dollars. Using this convention, it is clear that in 1820 per capita incomes in all areas were quite similar, with the richest area in the world in 1820, Western Europe, having an average per capita income of $1232, while the poorest area of the world at that time, Africa, had an average per capita income of $418. Thus, in 1820, average incomes in the richest area were only about three times larger than those in the poorest area.

But because Western Europe and North America started experiencing modern economic growth earlier than other areas, they have now ended up vastly richer than other areas, despite the fact that per capita incomes in nearly all places have increased at least a bit. For instance, per capita GDP in Canada in 1998 was $20,559, while it was only $1368 in Africa. Thus, because economic growth has occurred for nearly two centuries in Canada compared to a few decades in Africa, average living standards in Canada in 1998 were 15 times higher than those in Africa.

Catching Up Is Possible

Do not get the wrong impression looking at Figure 6-1. Countries that began modern economic growth more recently are *not* doomed to be permanently poorer than the countries that began earlier. This is true because people can adopt technology more quickly than they can invent it. Broadly speaking, the richest countries today have achieved that status because they have the most advanced technology. But because rich countries already have the most advanced technology, they must invent new technology to get even richer. Because inventing and implementing new technology is slow and costly, real GDP per capita in the richest **leader countries** typically grows by an average annual rate of just 2 or 3 percent per year.

By contrast, poorer **follower countries** can grow much faster because they can simply adopt existing technologies from rich leader countries. For instance, in many places in Africa today, the first telephones most people have ever been able to use are cell phones. That is, these countries have not even bothered to install the copper wires necessary for land-line telephones, which are basically a 19th-century technology. Instead, they have gone directly for internet-capable mobile phone networks, a 21st-century technology. By doing so, follower countries can skip past many stages of technology and development that Canada and other currently rich countries had to pass through. In effect, follower countries jump directly to the most up-to-date, most highly productive technology. The result is that, under the right circumstances, it is possible for poorer countries to experience extremely rapid increases in living standards. Rising living standards can continue until follower

leader countries
As it relates to economic growth, countries that develop and use advanced technologies, which then become available to follower countries.

follower countries
As it relates to economic growth, countries that adopt advanced technologies that previously were developed and used by leader countries.

FIGURE 6-1   The Great Divergence

Income levels around the world were very similar in 1820. But they are now very different because certain areas including Canada, the United States, and Western Europe began experiencing modern economic growth much earlier than other areas.

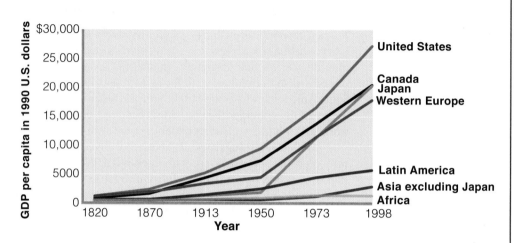

SOURCE: Angus Maddison, *The World Economy: A Millennial Perspective* (Paris: OECD, 2001), p. 264.

countries are caught up with the leader countries and become leader countries themselves. Once that happens, their growth rates typically fall down to the 2 or 3 percent rate typical of leader countries. This happens because once follower countries become rich and are using the latest technology, their growth rates are limited by the rate at which new technology can be invented and applied.

Table 6-2 shows both how the growth rates of leader countries are constrained by the rate of technological progress and how certain follower countries have been able to catch up by adopting more advanced technologies and growing rapidly. Table 6-2 shows real GDP per capita in 1960 and 2004 as well as the average annual growth rate of real GDP per capita between 1960 and 2004 for four countries—the United States, Canada, the United Kingdom, and France—that were already rich leader countries in 1960 as well as for five other nations that were relatively poor follower countries at that time. To make comparisons easy, the GDP and GDP per capita for all countries are expressed in terms of 1996 U.S. dollars. The countries are ordered by their respective GDP per capita in 1960, so that the richest country in the world at the time, the United States, is listed first while the poorest of the eight selected countries at the time, South Korea, is listed last.

First, notice that the average annual growth rates of the four leader countries have all been between 2.2 and 2.7 percent per year; their growth is limited by the rate at which new technologies can be invented and applied. By contrast, the five countries that were follower countries in 1960 have been able to grow much faster, between 3.9 percent per year and 5.8 percent per year. This has had remarkable effects on their standards of living relative to the leader countries. For instance, Ireland's GDP per capita was only about half that of its neighbour, the United Kingdom, in 1960. But because Ireland grew at a 3.9 percent rate for the next 44 years while the United Kingdom grew at only a 2.2 percent rate, by 2004 Irish GDP per capita was actually higher than United Kingdom GDP per capita. Ireland had become a leader country, too.

The growth experiences of the other four nations that were poor in 1960 have been even more dramatic. Hong Kong, for instance, moved from a GDP per capita that was less than one-third of that enjoyed by the United Kingdom in 1960 to a GDP per capita nearly 10 percent higher than that of the United Kingdom in 2004. The Consider This box emphasizes how quickly small differ-

TABLE 6·2

Real GDP per Capita in 1960 and 2004 (plus average annual growth rates of GDP per capita 1960–2004 for eight selected countries, 1996 dollars)

Country	Real GDP per capita, 1960	Real GDP per capita, 2004	Average annual growth rate, 1960–2004
United States	12,892	36,098	2.3
Canada	10,576	28,398	2.7
United Kingdom	10,323	26,762	2.2
France	8,531	26,168	2.5
Ireland	5,294	28,957	3.9
Japan	4,509	24,661	3.9
Singapore	4,219	29,404	4.4
Hong Kong	3,322	29,642	5.0
South Korea	1,458	18,424	5.8

Source: Penn World Table version 6.2, http://pwt.econ.upenn.edu/php_site/pwt62/pwt62_form.php

Note: GDP figures for all countries are measured in "international dollars" of equal value to U.S. dollars in 1996.

ences in growth rates can change both the level of real GDP per capita and how countries stand in relation to each other in terms of real GDP per capita. This chapter's Last Word, on China, also reinforces our point.

Institutional Structures That Promote Growth

Table 6-2 demonstrates that poor follower countries can catch up and become rich leader countries by growing rapidly. But how does a country start that process and enter into modern economic growth? And once it has started experiencing economic growth, how does it keep the process going?

CONSIDER THIS | Economic Growth Rates Matter!

When compounded over many decades, small differences in rates of economic growth add up to substantial differences in real GDP and standards of living. Consider three hypothetical countries—Slogo, Sumgo, and Speedo. Suppose that in 2009 these countries had identical levels of real GDP ($1 trillion), population (32 million), and real GDP per capita ($30,000). Also assume that annual real GDP growth is 2 percent in Slogo, 3 percent in Sumgo, and 4 percent in Speedo.

How will these alternative growth rates affect real GDP and real GDP per capita over a long period, say, a 70-year life span? By 2078 the 2 percent, 3 percent, and 4 percent growth rates would boost real GDP from $1 trillion to approximately:

- $4 trillion in Slogo,
- $7.9 trillion in Sumgo, and
- $15.6 trillion in Speedo.

For illustration, let's assume that each country experienced an average annual population growth of 1 percent over the 70 years. Then, in 2073 real GDP per capita would be about:

- $66,435 in Slogo,
- $131,519 in Sumgo, and
- $258,652 in Speedo.

Economic growth rates matter!

CONSIDER THIS | Patents and Innovation

It costs North American and European drug companies about $1 billion to research, patent, and safety-test a new drug because literally thousands of candidate drugs fail for each drug that succeeds. The only way to cover these costs is by relying on patent protections that give a drug's developer the exclusive monopoly right to market and sell the new drug for 20 years after it is developed. The revenues over that time period will hopefully be enough to cover the drug's development costs and—if the drug is popular—generate a profit for the drug company. Once the 20 years are over, however, the drug will go "off patent" and anyone will be able to manufacture and sell it.

Leader and follower countries have gotten into heated disputes in recent years, however, because the follower countries have often refused to recognize the patents granted to pharmaceutical companies in rich countries. India, for instance, has allowed local drug companies to copy and sell drugs that were developed by American companies and which are still under patent protection in the United States.

This benefits Indian citizens because the local drug companies compete with each other and end up charging much less for a given drug than the drug's patent holder would if it could enforce its monopoly patent and act as the drug's only seller. On the other hand, the weak patent protections found in India also make it completely unprofitable for local drug companies to try to develop innovative new drugs because, without patent protections, they too will be unable to prevent rivals from copying their new drugs and selling them for extremely low prices. As a result, India has recently moved to strengthen its patent protections, realizing that unless it does so, it will never be able to provide the financial incentive that can transform its local drug companies from copycats to innovators. But note that the innovative new drugs that may result from the increased patent protections are not without a cost. As patent protections in India are improved, cheap copycat drugs will no longer be available to Indian consumers.

Economic historians have identified several institutional structures that promote and sustain economic growth. Some structures increase the savings and investment that are needed to fund the construction and maintenance of the huge amounts of infrastructure required to run economies. Other institutional structures promote the development of new technologies. And still others act to ensure that resources flow efficiently to their most productive uses. These growth-promoting institutional structures include:

- **Strong Property Rights**   These appear to be absolutely necessary for rapid and sustained economic growth. People will not invest if they believe that thieves, bandits, or a rapacious and tyrannical government will steal their investments or their expected returns.

- **Patents and Copyrights**   These are necessary if a society wants a constant flow of innovative new technologies and sophisticated new ideas. Before patents and copyrights were first issued and enforced, inventors and authors usually saw their ideas stolen before they could profit from them. By giving inventors and authors the exclusive right to market and sell their creations, patents and copyrights give a strong financial incentive to invent and create.

- **Efficient Financial Institutions**   These are needed to channel the savings generated by households toward the businesses, entrepreneurs, and inventors that do most of society's investing and inventing. Banks as well as stock and bond markets appear to be institutions crucial to economic growth.

- **Literacy and Education**   Without highly educated inventors, new technologies do not get developed. And without a highly educated workforce, it is impossible to implement those technologies and put them to productive use.

- **Free Trade**   Free trade promotes economic growth by allowing countries to specialize so that different types of output can be produced in the countries where they can be made most efficiently. In addition, free trade promotes the rapid spread of new ideas so that innovations made in one country quickly spread to other countries.

- *Competitive Market System*   Under a market system, prices and profits serve as the signals that tell firms what to make, and in what quantity. Rich leader countries vary substantially in terms of how much government regulation they impose on markets, but in all cases, firms have substantial autonomy to follow market signals not only in terms of current production but also in terms of the investments they will currently make to produce what they believe consumers will demand in the future.

Several other difficult-to-measure factors also influence a nation's capacity for economic growth. For example, Canada's overall social-cultural-political environment has encouraged economic growth. Beyond the market system that has prevailed, Canada has also had a stable political system characterized by democratic principles, internal order, the right of property ownership, the legal status of enterprise, and the enforcement of contracts. Economic freedom and political freedom have been "growth-friendly."

In addition, and unlike some nations, virtually no social or moral taboos on production and material progress exist in Canada. The nation's social philosophy has embraced wealth creation as an attainable and desirable goal and the inventor, the innovator, and the business person are accorded high degrees of prestige and respect in Canadian society. Finally, Canadians have a positive attitude toward work and risk taking, resulting in an ample supply of willing workers and innovative entrepreneurs. A flow of energetic immigrants has greatly augmented that supply.

The Consider This box deals with how fast-growing follower countries such as India sometimes alter their growth-related institutional structures as they grow richer. Chapter 17W looks at the special problems of economic growth in developing nations.

QUICK REVIEW

▶ Before the advent of modern economic growth starting in England in the late 1700s, living standards showed no sustained increases over time. Modern economic growth brings with it not only ongoing increases in GDP per capita but also profound cultural, social, and political changes.

▶ Large differences in standards of living exist today because certain areas of the world have experienced nearly 200 years of economic growth while other areas have had only a few decades of economic growth.

▶ Poor follower countries can catch up with and even surpass the living standards of rich leader countries. The growth rates of rich-country GDPs per capita are limited to about 2 percent per year because, in order to further increase their standards of living, rich countries must invent and apply new technologies. By contrast, poor follower countries can grow much faster because they can simply adopt the cutting-edge technologies and institutions already developed by rich leader countries.

▶ Institutional structures that promote growth include strong property rights, patents and copyrights, efficient financial institutions, literacy and education, free trade, and a competitive market system.

6.3 | Ingredients of Growth

PRODUCTION & THE STANDARD OF LIVING

Our discussion of economic growth and the institutional structures that promote it has purposely been general. We now want to focus our discussion on six factors that directly affect the *rate* of economic growth. These six "ingredients" of economic growth can be grouped into four supply factors, one demand factor, and one efficiency factor.

Supply Factors

Four of the ingredients of economic growth relate to the physical ability of the economy to expand. They are

- increases in the quantity and quality of natural resources,
- increases in the quantity and quality of human resources,
- increases in the supply (or stock) of capital goods, and
- improvements in technology.

These **supply factors**—changes in the physical and technical agents of production—enable an economy to expand.

supply factor
An increase in the availability of a resource, an improvement in its quality, or an expansion of technological knowledge that makes it possible for an economy to produce a greater output of goods and services.

Demand Factor

The fifth ingredient of economic growth is the **demand factor.** To achieve the higher production potential created by the supply factors, households and businesses either domestically or abroad must *purchase* the economy's expanding output of goods and services. Economic growth requires increases in total spending to realize the output gains made available by increased production capacity.

demand factor
The increase in the level of aggregate demand that brings about the economic growth made possible by an increase in the production potential of the economy.

Efficiency Factor

The sixth ingredient of economic growth is the **efficiency factor.** To reach its full production potential, an economy must achieve economic efficiency as well as full employment. The economy must use its resources in the least costly way (productive efficiency) to produce the specific mix of goods and services that maximize people's well-being (allocative efficiency). The ability to expand production, together with the full use of available resources, is not sufficient for achieving maximum possible growth. Also required is the efficient use of those resources.

efficiency factor
The capacity of an economy to combine resources effectively to achieve growth of real output that the supply factors make possible.

The supply, demand, and efficiency factors in economic growth are interrelated. Unemployment caused by insufficient total spending (the demand factor) may lower the rate of new capital accumulation (a supply factor) and delay expenditures on research (also a supply factor). Conversely, low spending on investment (a supply factor) may cause insufficient spending (the demand factor) and unemployment. Widespread inefficiency in the use of resources (the efficiency factor) may translate into higher costs of goods and services and thus lower profits, which in turn may slow innovation and reduce the accumulation of capital (supply factors). Economic growth is a dynamic process in which the supply, demand, and efficiency factors all interact.

Production Possibilities Analysis

To put the six factors affecting the rate of economic growth into better perspective, let's use the production possibilities analysis introduced in Chapter 1.

GROWTH AND PRODUCTION POSSIBILITIES

Recall that a curve like *AB* in Figure 6-2 is a production possibilities curve. It indicates the various *maximum* combinations of products an economy can produce with its fixed quantity and quality of natural, human, and capital resources and its associated stock of technological knowledge. An improvement in any of the supply factors will push the production possibilities curve outward, as from *AB* to *CD*.

But the demand factor reminds us that an increase in total spending is needed to move the economy from a point like *a* on curve *AB* to any of the points on the higher curve *CD*. And the efficiency factor reminds us that the location on *CD* must be optimal for the resources to make their maximum possible dollar contribution to total output. You will recall from Chapter 1 that this "best

FIGURE 6-2   Economic Growth and the Production Possibilities Curve

Economic growth is made possible by the four supply factors that shift the production possibilities curve outward, as from AB to CD. Economic growth is realized when the demand factor and the efficiency factor move the economy from point *a* to *b*.

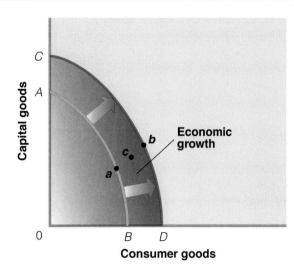

allocation" is determined by expanding production of each good until its marginal benefit equals its marginal cost. Here, we assume that this optimal combination of capital and consumer goods occurs at point *b*.

For example, the net increase in the size of the labour force in Canada in recent years has been 250,000 to 300,000 workers per year. That increment raises the economy's production capacity. But obtaining the extra output that these added workers could produce depends on their success in finding jobs. It also depends on whether the jobs are in firms and industries where the workers' talents are fully and optimally used. Society does not want new labour-force entrants to be unemployed. Nor does it want pediatricians working as plumbers, or pediatricians producing services for which marginal costs exceed marginal benefits.

Normally, increases in total spending match increases in production capacity and the economy moves from a point on the previous production possibilities curve to a point on the expanded curve. Moreover, the competitive market system tends to drive the economy toward productive and allocative efficiency. Occasionally the curve may shift outward but leave the economy behind at some level of operation such as *c* in Figure 6-2. Because *c* is inside the new production possibilities curve *CD*, the economy has not realized its potential for economic growth. **(Key Question 5)**

LABOUR AND PRODUCTIVITY

Although demand and efficiency factors are important, discussions of economic growth focus primarily on supply factors. Society can increase its real output and income in two fundamental ways: (1) by increasing its inputs of resources, and (2) by raising the productivity of those inputs. Figure 6-3 focuses on the input of *labour* and provides a useful framework for discussing the role of supply factors in growth. A nation's real GDP in any year depends on the input of labour (measured in worker-hours) multiplied by **labour productivity** (measured as real output per worker per hour).

labour productivity
The average product of labour; output per worker per hour.

Real GDP = worker-hours × labour productivity

Or, expressed in terms of percentage change:

% change in GDP = % change in worker-hours + % change in productivity

 WORKED PROBLEM 6.1
Productivity and Economic Growth

So, thought of in this way, a nation's economic growth from one year to the next depends on its *increase* in labour inputs (if any) and its *increase* in labour productivity (if any). Illustration:

FIGURE 6-3	The Supply Determinants of Real Output

Real GDP is usefully viewed as the product of the quantity of labour inputs (worker-hours) multiplied by labour productivity.

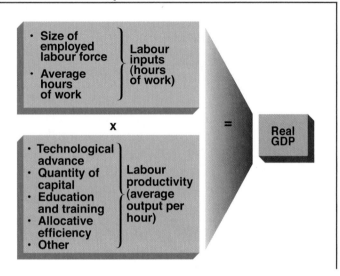

Suppose the hypothetical economy of Ziam has 10 workers in year 1, each working 2000 hours per year (50 weeks at 40 hours per week). The total input of labour therefore is 20,000 hours. If productivity (average real output per worker-hour) is $10 per hour, then real GDP in Ziam will be $200,000 (= 20,000 × $10) per year. If worker-hours rise to 20,200 and labour productivity rises to $10.40 per hour, Ziam's real GDP will increase to $210,080 in year 2. Ziam's rate of economic growth will be about 5 percent [= ($210,080 − $200,000)/$200,000)] for the year.

CONSIDER THIS | Negative Growth Rates during Severe Economic Downturns

During the economic downturn of 2008–09, economic growth became negative (real GDP declined). In the last quarter of 2008, GDP declined at an average annual rate of 3.4 percent per annum, while during the first quarter of 2009 it shrank by a steep average annual rate of 5.4 percent. (The adjustment from a quarterly basis to an annual basis simply shows what the three-month decline would equate to if it were to continue for an entire year.) That contrasts with the long-term 3.5 percent annual increase of real GDP since 1961. The recession reduced real output, not the economy's production capacity. The production of goods and services simply dropped well below the level of production that the economy was capable of producing.

Figure 6-2 helps clarify this distinction. The nation's production possibilities curve shifted rightward during the recession, reflecting ongoing improvements in labour productivity and an increasing labour force. But due to the recession, the economy did not reach its new, higher potential. It moved from producing at a point like *a* on production possibilities curve *AB* to a point like *c*, which

is to the left of production possibilities curve *CD*. Then, the economy declined from point *c* to some point (not shown) even further inside curve *CD*. This latter decline in both the production of consumer goods and capital goods illustrates the recession.

If economic downturns are long enough and deep enough, however, they can negatively affect the subsequent growth of production possibilities. Long periods of idle capital and labour can have carryover effects on the growth rate in subsequent years through the adverse effects they have on the supply factors of growth. For example, recessions depress investment and capital accumulation. Furthermore, the expansion of research budgets may be slowed by recession so that technological advance diminishes, union resistance to technological advance may stiffen, public support for free international trade may weaken, and the skills of idle workers may erode. Although it is difficult to quantify the impact of these considerations on the long-term growth trend, they could take on considerable importance if the current recession carries on for a long time.

labour force participation rate
The percentage of the working-age population that is actually in the labour force.

- **Worker-Hours**   What determines the number of hours worked each year? As shown in Figure 6-3, the hours of labour input depend on the size of the employed labour force and the length of the average workweek. Not shown, labour-force size depends on the size of the working-age population and the **labour force participation rate**—the percentage of the working-age population actually in the labour force. The length of the average workweek is governed by legal and institutional considerations and by collective bargaining agreements negotiated between unions and employers.

- **Labour Productivity**   Figure 6-3 tells us that labour productivity is determined by technological progress, the quantity of capital goods available to workers, the quality of the labour itself, and the efficiency with which inputs are allocated, combined, and managed. Productivity rises when the health, training, education, and motivation of workers improve; when workers have more and better machinery and natural resources with which to work; when production is better organized and managed; and when labour is reallocated from less efficient industries to more efficient industries.

6.4 | Accounting for Growth in Canada

Output growth in Canada has been considerably greater in the last half century than can be attributed solely to increases in the inputs of labour and capital. Two other factors are involved. The first is interindustry shifts from lower- to higher-productivity occupations. The best-known example is the shift of workers out of relatively low-productivity farming to higher-productivity urban industry. The second factor is multifactor productivity (MFP), the efficiency with which factors are used together in the production process. It includes technological progress, organizational structure, economies of scale, regulation, entrepreneurship and risk taking, labour–management relations, capacity utilization, and the efficiency with which resources are allocated. MFP growth is output growth less input growth. Table 6-3 shows the sources of growth of real GDP between 1981 and 2007. During that period multifactor productivity increased almost 4 percent, or at an average annual growth rate of 0.1 percent.

Inputs versus Productivity

About two-thirds of Canada's growth rate since 1981 has been due to the use of more inputs and about one-third to rising productivity—getting more output per unit of labour and capital input. Thus, productivity growth has been a significant force underlying the growth of our real GDP. Table 6-3 shows that between 1981 and 2007, output per unit of labour (labour productivity) increased at an average annual rate of 1.7 percent while that of capital advanced at a rate of 0.8 percent.

TABLE 6-3   Sources of Growth of Real GDP, 1981–2007*

Annual average growth of real GDP	Annual average growth of multifactor productivity (MFP)	Annual average growth of labour productivity	Annual average growth of output per unit of capital services	Annual average growth of capital input	Annual average growth of labour input
4.4	0.1	1.7	0.8	6.4	2.8

* The business sector

Source: Statistics Canada, The Canadian Productivity Accounts, http://www.statcan.gc.ca/bsolc/olc-cel/olc-cel?lang=eng&catno=15-003-X.

CONSIDER THIS | Women, the Labour Force, and Economic Growth

The substantial rise in the number of women working in the paid workforce in Canada has been one of the major labour market trends of the past half-century. In 1965, some 40 percent of women worked full-time or part-time in paid jobs. Today, that number is about 62 percent. Women have greatly increased their productivity in the workplace, mostly by becoming better educated and professionally trained. Rising productivity has increased women's wage rates. Those higher wages have raised the opportunity costs—the forgone wage earnings—of staying at home. Women have therefore substituted employment in the labour market for traditional home activities. This substitution has been particularly pronounced among married women. (Single women have always had high labour-force participation rates.)

Furthermore, changing lifestyles and the widespread availability of birth control have freed up time for greater labour force participation by women. Women not only have fewer children, but those children are spaced closer together in age. Thus women who leave their jobs during their children's early years return to the labour force sooner.

Greater access to jobs by women also has been a significant factor in the rising labour-force participation of women. Service industries—teaching, nursing, and office work, for instance—that traditionally have employed many women have expanded rapidly in the past several decades. Also, the population in general has shifted from farms and rural regions to urban areas, where jobs for women are more abundant and more geographically accessible. An increased availability of part-time jobs also has made it easier for women to combine labour market employment with child-rearing and household activities. Also, anti-discrimination laws and enforcement efforts have reduced barriers that previously discouraged or prevented women from taking traditional male jobs such as business managers, lawyers, professors, and physicians. More jobs are open to women today than a half-century ago.

In summary, women in Canada are better educated, more productive, and more efficiently employed than ever before. Their increased presence in the labour force has contributed greatly to economic growth in Canada.

Quantity of Labour

The Canadian population and the size of the labour force have both expanded significantly. Between 1929 and 2008, total population grew from 10 million to over 33 million, and the labour force increased from 4 million to over 17 million workers. Reductions in the length of the workweek reduced the growth of labour inputs before World War II, but the workweek has remained relatively stable since then. Falling birth rates over the past 30 years have slowed the growth of the native population, but increased immigration has offset that slowdown. Of greatest significance has been the surge of women's participation in the labour force. Partly because of that increased participation, Canadian labour force growth has averaged about 238,000 workers per year during the past 25 years. Table 6-3 shows that between 1981 and 2007 the quantity of labour input increased about 73 percent, or at an average annual growth rate of 2.8 percent.

Because increases in labour productivity are so important to economic growth, economists go to the trouble of investigating and assessing the relative importance of the factors that contribute to productivity growth. Five factors appear to explain changes in productivity growth rates: technological advance, the amount of capital each worker has to work with, education and training, economies of scale, and resource allocation. We will examine each factor in turn, noting how much each factor contributes to productivity growth.

Technological Advance

The largest contributor to productivity growth is technological advance, which is thought to account for about 40 percent of productivity growth. As economist Paul Romer stated, "Human history teaches us that economic growth springs from better recipes, not just from more cooking."

Technological advance includes not only innovative production techniques, but also new managerial methods and new forms of business organization that improve the process of production.

Generally, technological advance is generated by the discovery of new knowledge, which allows for resources to be combined in new ways that increase output. Once discovered and implemented, new knowledge soon becomes available to entrepreneurs and firms at relatively low cost. Technological advance therefore eventually spreads through the entire economy, boosting productivity and economic growth.

Technological advance and capital formation (investment) are closely related, since technological advance usually promotes investment in new machinery and equipment. In fact, technological advance is often *embodied* within new capital. For example, the purchase of new computers brings into industry speedier, more powerful computers that incorporate new technology.

Technological advance has been both rapid and profound. Gas and diesel engines, conveyor belts, and assembly lines were significant developments of the past. So, too, were fuel-efficient commercial aircraft, integrated microcircuits, personal computers, digital photography, and containerized shipping. More recently, technological advance has exploded, particularly in the areas of wireless communication, computers, photography, and the Internet. Other fertile areas of recent innovation are medicine and biotechnology. Government investment in basic research has facilitated technological advance in Canada.

Quantity of Capital

infrastructure
The capital goods usually provided by the public sector for the use of its citizens and firms.

A key determinant of productivity growth is the amount of capital goods available *per worker*. If both the aggregate stock of capital goods and the size of the labour force increase rapidly over a given period, the individual worker is not necessarily better equipped and productivity will not necessarily rise. But the quantity of capital equipment available per worker in Canada has increased greatly over time. Table 6-3 shows that between 1981 and 2007 capital input increased almost 170 percent, or at an annual average growth rate of 6.4.

Public investment in Canada's **infrastructure** (highways and bridges, public transit systems, waste-water treatment facilities, water systems, airports, educational facilities, and so on) has also grown. This publicly owned capital complements private capital. Investments in new highways promote private investment in new factories and retail stores along their routes. Industrial parks developed by local governments attract manufacturing and distribution firms.

Education and Training

human capital
The accumulation of prior investments in education, training, health, and other factors that increase productivity.

Education and training contribute to a worker's stock of **human capital**—the knowledge and skill that make for a productive worker. Perhaps the simplest measure of labour quality is the level of educational attainment. Investment in human capital includes not only formal education but also on-the-job training. Like investment in physical capital, investment in human capital is an important means of increasing labour productivity and earnings. An estimated 15 percent of productivity growth derives from investments in people's education and skills. Global Perspective 6.1 shows that Canada ranks in the top 10 countries of the world in science and mathematics on standardized tests. Another indication of educational attainment is the number of students attending university in Canada. In the academic year 2005–06 the number of students enrolled at Canadian universities surpassed the 1 million mark for the first time. The fact that post-secondary education is subsidized in Canada is certainly a contributing factor for the rapid increase in the number of university students.

Education and training contribute to a worker's stock of human capital.

economies of scale
Reductions in the average total cost of producing a product as the firm expands the size of plant (its output) in the long run.

Economies of Scale and Resource Allocation

Economies of scale and improved resource allocation are a fourth and fifth source of productivity growth, and together are estimated to explain about 15 percent of productivity growth.

ECONOMIES OF SCALE

Reductions in per-unit production costs that result from the increases in output levels are called **economies of scale.** Markets have increased in size over time, allowing firms to increase output

6.1 | GLOBAL PERSPECTIVE

Average test scores of eighth-grade students in math and science, top 10 countries and the United States

The test performance of Canadian eighth-grade students ranked favourably with that of eighth graders in several other nations in the Trends in International Mathematics and Science Study (TIMSS) (2003).

Mathematics		Science	
Rank	**Score**	**Rank**	**Score**
1. Singapore	605	1. Singapore	578
2. South Korea	589	2. Taiwan	571
3. Hong Kong (China)	586	3. South Korea	558
4. Taiwan	585	4. Hong Kong (China)	556
5. Japan	570	5. Estonia	552
6. Belgium	537	5. Japan	552
7. Netherlands	536	6. Hungary	543
8. Canada	533*	7. Netherlands	536
9. Estonia	531	8. Canada	532*
10. Hungary	529	9. United States	527
15. United States	504	9. Australia	527
		10. Sweden	524

*Average of Ontario and Quebec.

levels and thereby achieve production advantages associated with greater size. As firms expand, they use more efficient plant, equipment, and methods of manufacturing and delivery that result in greater productivity. They also are better able to recoup substantial investments in developing new products and production methods. Examples: A large manufacturer of autos can use elaborate assembly lines with computerization and robotics, while smaller producers must settle for less advanced technologies using more labour inputs. And large pharmaceutical firms greatly reduce the average amount of labour (researchers, production workers) needed to produce each pill as they increase the number of pills produced. Accordingly, economies of scale enable greater real GDP and thus contribute to economic growth.

IMPROVED RESOURCE ALLOCATION

Improved resource allocation means that workers have moved over time from low-productivity employment to high-productivity employment. Historically, many workers have shifted from agriculture, where labour productivity is low, to manufacturing, where it is quite high. More recently, labour has shifted away from manufacturing industries to even higher-productivity industries such as computer software, business consulting, and pharmaceuticals. As a result of such shifts, the average productivity of Canadian workers has increased.

Also, discrimination in education and the labour market has historically deterred some women and minorities from entering high-productivity jobs. With the decline of such discrimination over time, many members of those groups have shifted from low-productivity jobs to higher-productivity jobs. The result has been higher overall labour productivity and real GDP.

Finally, tariffs, import quotas, and other barriers to international trade tend to relegate resources to relatively unproductive pursuits. Both here and abroad, the long-run movement toward liberalized international trade has improved the allocation of resources, increased labour productivity, and expanded real output. *(Key Question 8)*

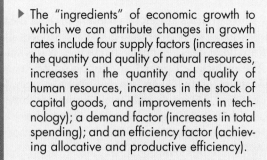

QUICK REVIEW

▶ The "ingredients" of economic growth to which we can attribute changes in growth rates include four supply factors (increases in the quantity and quality of natural resources, increases in the quantity and quality of human resources, increases in the stock of capital goods, and improvements in technology); a demand factor (increases in total spending); and an efficiency factor (achieving allocative and productive efficiency).

▶ Improvements in labour productivity have been an important contributor to increases in Canadian real GDP.

▶ Improved technology, more capital, greater education and training, economies of scale, and better resource allocation have been the main contributors to Canadian productivity growth and thus to Canadian economic growth.

6.5 | Recent Productivity Acceleration

The pickup in productivity in the last decade has led many economists to believe that this higher productivity growth resulted from a significant new wave of technological advance coupled with global competition. Some economists are hopeful that the higher trend rates of productivity growth may be permanent.

This increase in productivity growth is important because real output, real income, and real wages are linked to labour productivity. To see why, suppose you are alone on an uninhabited island. The number of fish you can catch or coconuts you can pick per hour—your productivity— is your real wage (or real income) per hour. By *increasing* your productivity, you can improve your standard of living because greater output per hour means there are more fish and coconuts (goods) available to consume.

So it is for the economy as a whole: Over long periods, the economy's labour productivity determines its average real hourly wage. The economy's income per hour is equal to its output per hour. Productivity growth therefore is its main route for increasing its standard of living. It allows firms to pay higher wages without lowering their business profits.

Reasons for the Productivity Acceleration

Why has productivity growth increased relative to earlier periods?

THE MICROCHIP AND INFORMATION TECHNOLOGY

The core element of the productivity speedup is an explosion of entrepreneurship and innovation based on the microprocessor, or *microchip*, which bundles transistors on a piece of silicon. Some observers liken the invention of the microchip to that of electricity, the automobile, air travel, the telephone, and television in importance and scope.

The microchip has found its way into thousands of applications. It has helped create a wide array of new products and services and new ways of doing business. Its immediate results were the pocket calculator, the bar code scanner, the personal computer, the laptop computer, and more powerful business computers. But the miniaturization of electronic circuits also advanced the development of other products such as the cell phone and pager, computer-guided lasers, the deciphered genetic codes, global positioning equipment, energy conservation systems, Doppler radar, digital cameras, and machines to decipher the human genome.

Perhaps of greatest significance, the widespread availability of personal and notebook computers stimulated the desire to tie them together. That desire promoted rapid development of the Internet and all its many manifestations such as business-to-household and business-to-business electronic commerce (e-commerce). The combination of the computer, fibre-optic cable, wireless technology, and the Internet constitute a spectacular advance in **information technology,** which has been used to connect all parts of the world.

information technology
New and more efficient methods of delivering and receiving information using computers, fax machines, wireless phones, and the Internet.

NEW FIRMS AND INCREASING RETURNS

start-up firm
A new firm focused on creating and introducing a particular new product or employing a specific new production or distribution method.

Hundreds of new **start-up firms** advanced various aspects of the new information technology. Many of these firms created more hype than goods and services and quickly fell by the wayside. But a number of firms flourished, eventually to take their places among the nation's largest firms. Examples of those firms include Research In Motion (mobile communications), Rogers Communications (cable Internet provider and wireless phone service), Intel (microchips), Apple and Dell (personal computers), Microsoft and Oracle (computer software), Cisco Systems (Internet switching systems), Yahoo and Google (Internet search engines), and Amazon.com (electronic commerce). There are scores more! Most of these firms were not on the radar—or were just a small blip on the radar—30 years ago.

increasing returns
An increase in a firm's output by a larger percentage than the percentage increase in its inputs.

Successful new firms often experience **increasing returns,** a situation in which a given percentage increase in the amount of inputs a firm uses leads to an even larger percentage increase in the amount of output the firm produces. For example, suppose that a company called Techco decides to double the size of its operations to meet the growing demand for its services. After doubling its plant and equipment and doubling its workforce—say, from 100 workers to 200 workers—it finds that its total output has tripled, from 8000 units to 24,000 units. Techco has experienced increasing returns; its output has increased by 200 percent while its inputs have increased by only 100 percent. Consequently, its labour productivity has gone up from 80 units per worker (= 8000 units/100 workers) to 120 units per worker. Increasing returns boost labour productivity and lower per-unit production costs. Since these cost reductions result from increases in output levels, they are examples of economies of scale.

Both emerging firms and established firms can exploit several different sources of increasing returns and economies of scale:

- *More Specialized Inputs*   Firms can use more specialized and thus more productive capital and workers as they expand their operations. A growing new e-commerce business, for example, can purchase highly specialized inventory management systems and hire specialized personnel, such as accountants, marketing managers, and system maintenance experts.

- *Spreading of Development Costs*   Firms can spread high product development costs over greater output. For example, suppose that a new software product cost $100,000 to develop and only $2 per unit to manufacture and sell. If the firm sells 1000 units of the software its per-unit cost will be $102 [= ($100,000 + $2000)/1000], but if it sells 500,000 units that cost will drop to only $2.20 [= $100,000 + $1 million)/500,000].

- *Simultaneous Consumption*   Many recently developed products and services can satisfy large numbers of customers at the same time. Unlike a litre of gas that needs to be produced for each buyer, a software program needs to be produced only once. It then becomes available at very low expense to thousands or even millions of buyers. The same is true of entertainment delivered on CDs, movies distributed on DVDs, and information disseminated through the Internet.

network effects
Increases in the value of a product to each user, including existing users, as the total number of users rises.

- *Network Effects*   Software and Internet services become more beneficial to a buyer the greater the number of households and businesses that also buy them. When others have Internet service you can send email messages to them. When they also have software to display documents and photos, you can attach those items to your email messages. These systems advantages are called **network effects,** increases in the value of the product to each user, including existing users, as the total number of users rises. The domestic and global expansion of the Internet in particular has produced network effects, as have cell phones, pagers, handheld computers, and other aspects of wireless communication. Network effects magnify the value of output well beyond the costs of inputs.

learning-by-doing
Achieving greater productivity and lower average total cost through gains in knowledge and skill that accompany repetition of a task; a source of economies of scale.

- *Learning-by-Doing*   Finally, firms that produce new products or pioneer new ways of doing business ultimately experience increasing returns through **learning-by-doing.** Tasks that initially may have taken hours may take only minutes once the methods are perfected.

Whatever the particular source of increasing returns, the result is higher productivity, which tends to reduce the per-unit cost of producing and delivering products. Table 6-4 lists a number of specific U.S. examples of cost reduction from technology in recent years; the magnitude can be expected to be the same in Canada.

GLOBAL COMPETITION

The Canadian economy is now characterized not only by information technology and increasing returns, but also by heightened global competition. The collapse of the socialist economies in the late 1980s and early 1990s together with the success of market systems have led to a reawakening of capitalism throughout the world. The new information technologies have "shrunk the globe" and made it imperative for all firms to lower their costs and prices and to innovate to remain competitive. Free-trade zones such as NAFTA and the European Union (EU), along with trade liberalization through the World Trade Organization (WTO), have also heightened competition internationally by removing trade protection from domestic firms. The larger geographic markets, in turn, have enabled firms to expand beyond the borders of Canada. Global Perspective 6.2 shows the global competitiveness index for 2008.

Implication: More-Rapid Economic Growth

Other things equal, stronger productivity growth and heightened global competition allow the economy to achieve a higher rate of economic growth. A glance back at Figure 6-2 will help make this point. Suppose the shift of the production possibilities curve from *AB* to *CD* reflects annual changes in potential output levels before the recent increase in growth rates. Then the higher growth rates of the more recent period of accelerated productivity growth would be depicted by a *larger* outward shift of the economy's production possibilities from *AB* to a curve beyond *CD*. When coupled with economic efficiency and increased total spending, the economy's real GDP would rise by more than that shown.

A caution: Economists who believe that the higher productivity growth rates experienced in recent years are likely to continue do not believe that the business cycle is dead. The relatively deep

---

TABLE 6-4   **Examples of Cost Reduction from Technology**

- The cost of storing one megabyte of information—enough for a 320-page book—fell from $5257 in 1975 to 17¢ in 1999.

- Prototyping each part of a car once took Ford weeks and cost $20,000 on average. Using an advanced 3-D object printer, Ford cut the time to just hours and the cost to less than $20.

- Studies show that telecommuting saves businesses about $20,000 annually for a worker earning $44,000—a saving in lost work time and employee retention costs, plus gains in worker productivity.

- Using scanners and computers, Weyerhaeuser increased the lumber yield and value from each log by 30 percent.

- Amoco has used 3-D seismic exploration technology to cut the cost of finding oil from nearly $10 per barrel in 1991 to under $1 per barrel in 2000.

- Wal-Mart reduced the operating cost of its delivery trucks by 20 percent through installing computers, global positioning gear, and cell phones in 4300 vehicles.

- Banking transactions on the Internet cost 1¢ each, compared with $1.14 for face-to-face and pen-and-paper communication.

Source: Compiled and directly quoted from W. Michael Cox and Richard Alm, "The New Paradigm." *Federal Reserve Bank of Dallas Annual Report*, May 2000, various pages. Amounts are in U.S. dollars.

Global competitiveness index, 2009–2010

The World Economic Forum annually compiles a global competitiveness index, which uses various factors (such as innovativeness, effective transfer of technology among sectors, efficiency of the financial system, rates of investment, and degree of integration with the rest of the world) to measure the ability of a country to achieve economic growth over time. Here is its latest top 10 list.

Source: World Economic Forum, www.weforum.org.

Country	Global competitiveness ranking
Switzerland	1
United States	2
Singapore	3
Sweden	4
Denmark	5
Finland	6
Germany	7
Japan	8
Canada	9
Netherlands	10

recession of 2008–09 brought about by the global financial crisis lends credence to the doubt about the supposed end of the business cycle. Their contention is limited to the belief that the *trend lines* of productivity growth and economic growth have become steeper. Real output may periodically deviate below and above the steeper trend.

Skepticism about Permanence

Although most macroeconomists have revised their forecasts for long-term productivity growth upward, at least slightly, others are still skeptical and urge a wait-and-see approach. These macroeconomists acknowledge that the economy has experienced a rapid advance of new technology, some new firms have experienced increasing returns, and global competition has increased. But they wonder if these factors are sufficiently profound to produce a 15- to 20-year period of substantially higher rates of productivity growth and real GDP growth.

What Can We Conclude?

Given the different views on the recent productivity acceleration, what should we conclude? Perhaps the safest conclusions are these:

- The prospects for a lasting increase in productivity growth are good. Studies indicate that productivity increases related to information technology have spread to a wide range of industries, including services.

- Time will tell. It will be several more years before economists can declare the recent productivity acceleration a long-run, sustainable trend. *(Key Question 11)*

QUICK REVIEW

▶ Over long time periods, labour productivity growth determines an economy's growth of real wages and its standard of living.

▶ Many economists believe that Canada has entered a period of faster productivity growth and higher rates of economic growth.

▶ The productivity speedup is based on rapid technological change in the form of the microchip and information technology, increasing returns and lower per-unit costs, and heightened global competition that helps hold down prices.

▶ Faster productivity growth means the economy can grow more rapidly than previously without producing inflation. Nonetheless, many economists caution that it is still too early to determine whether the higher rates of productivity growth are a lasting long-run trend or a short-lived occurrence.

6.6 | Is Economic Growth Desirable and Sustainable?

Economists usually take for granted that economic growth is desirable and sustainable. But not everyone agrees.

The Anti-Growth View

Critics of growth say industrialization and growth result in pollution, global warming, ozone depletion, and other environmental problems. These adverse spillover costs occur because inputs in the production process re-enter the environment as some form of waste. The more rapid our growth and the higher our standard of living, the more waste the environment must absorb—or attempt to absorb. In an already wealthy society, further growth usually means satisfying increasingly trivial wants at the cost of mounting threats to the ecological system.

Critics also argue there is little compelling evidence that economic growth has solved sociological problems such as poverty, homelessness, and discrimination. Consider poverty. In the anti-growth view, Canadian poverty is a problem of distribution, not production. The solution to the problem requires commitment and political courage to redistribute wealth and income, not further increases in output.

Anti-growth sentiment also says that although growth may permit us to "make a better living," it does not give us "the good life." We may be producing more and enjoying it less. Growth means assembly-line jobs, worker burnout, and alienated employees who have little or no control over decisions affecting their lives. High-growth economies are high-stress economies, which may impair our physical and mental health.

Finally, critics of high rates of growth doubt that they are sustainable. The planet Earth has finite amounts of natural resources available, and they are being consumed at alarming rates.

In Defence of Growth

The primary defence of growth is that it is the path to the greater material abundance and higher living standards desired by the vast majority of people. Rising output and incomes allow people to buy more of the goods and services they want. Growth also enables society to improve the nation's infrastructure, improve the care of the sick and elderly, provide greater access for the disabled, and provide more police and fire protection. Economic growth may be the only realistic way to reduce poverty, since little political support exists for greater redistribution of income. The way to improve the economic position of the poor is to increase household incomes through higher productivity and economic growth. Also, a no-growth policy among industrial nations might severely limit growth in poor nations. Foreign investment and development assistance in those nations would fall, keeping the world's poor in poverty longer.

Economic growth has not made labour more unpleasant or hazardous, as critics suggest. New machinery is usually less taxing and less dangerous than the machinery it replaces. Air-conditioned workplaces are more pleasant than steamy workshops.

Does growth threaten the environment? The connection between growth and environment is tenuous, say growth proponents. Increases in economic growth need not mean increases in pollution. Pollution is not so much a by-product of growth as it is a "problem of the commons." Much of the environment—streams, lakes, oceans, and the air—is treated as "common property," with insufficient or no restrictions on its use. The commons have become our dumping grounds; we have overused and debased them. Environmental pollution is a case of spillover or external costs, and correcting this problem involves regulatory legislation or specific taxes ("effluent charges") to remedy misuse of the environment.

Those who support growth admit there are serious environmental problems. But they say that limiting growth is the wrong solution. Growth has allowed economies to reduce pollution, be more sensitive to environmental considerations, set aside wilderness, create national parks, and clean up hazardous waste, while still enabling rising household incomes.

Is growth sustainable? Yes, say its proponents. If we were depleting natural resources faster than their discovery, we would see the prices of those resources rise. That has not been the case for most natural resources, and in fact the prices of many of them have declined. And if one natural resource becomes too expensive, another resource will be substituted for it. Moreover, say economists, economic growth has more to do with the expansion and application of human knowledge and information than extractable natural resources. Economic growth is limited only by human imagination.

The **LAST WORD**   Economic Growth in China

China's economic growth rate in the past 25 years is among the highest
recorded for any country during any period of world history.

Propelled by market reforms, China has experienced nearly 9 percent annual growth rates over the past 25 years. Real output has more than quadrupled over that period. In 2006, China's growth rate was 10.7 percent and in 2007 it was 11.3 percent. Expanded output and income have boosted domestic saving and investment, and the expansion in capital goods has further increased productivity, output, and income. The rising income, together with inexpensive labour, has attracted more foreign direct investment: a total of over U.S. $170 billion between 2005 and 2007.

China's real GDP and real income have grown much more rapidly than China's population. Per capita income has increased at a high annual rate of 8 percent since 1980. This is particularly noteworthy because China's population has expanded by 14 million a year (despite a policy that encourages one child per family). China's per capita income is now about U.S. $2500 annually. But because the prices of many basic items in China are still low and are not totally reflected in exchange rates, Chinese per capita purchasing power is estimated to be equivalent to about $5300 of income in Canada. The rapid rate of growth in China has been accompanied by significant reduction in poverty levels.

The growth of per capita income in China has resulted from increased use of capital, improved technology, and shifts of labour away from lower-productivity toward higher-productivity uses. One such shift of employment has been from agriculture toward rural

and urban manufacturing. Another shift has been from state-owned enterprises toward private firms. Both shifts have raised the productivity of Chinese workers.

Chinese economic growth had been accompanied by a huge expansion of China's international trade. Chinese exports rose from $5 billion in 1978 to $1.2 trillion in 2007. These exports have provided the foreign currency needed to import consumer goods and capital goods. Imports of capital goods from industrially advanced countries have brought with them highly advanced technology that is embodied in, for example, factory design, industrial machinery, office equipment, and telecommunications systems.

China still faces some significant problems in its transition to the market economy, however. At times, investment booms in China have resulted in too much spending relative to production capacity. The result has been some periods of 15 to 25 percent annual rates of inflation. China has successfully confronted the inflation problem by giving its central bank more power so that, when appropriate, the bank can raise interest rates to cool down investment spending. This greater monetary control has reduced inflation sig-

nificantly. China's inflation rate was a relatively mild 1.2 in 2003, 4.1 in 2004, and 1.9 in 2005. More vigilance may be required, however, as inflation rebounded over the next two years, reaching 7.1 percent in 2007.

In addition, the overall financial system in China remains weak and inadequate. Many unprofitable state-owned enterprises owe colossal sums of money on loans made by the Chinese state-owned banks (an estimate is nearly $100 billion). Because most of these loans are not collectible, the government may need to bail out the banks to keep them in operation.

Unemployment is also a problem. Even though the transition from an agriculture-dominated economy to a more urban, industrial economy has been gradual, considerable displacement of labour has occurred. There is substantial unemployment and underemployment in the interior regions of China.

China still has much work to do to fully integrate its economy into the world's system of international finance and trade. As a condition of joining the World Trade Organization in 2001, China agreed to reduce its high tariffs on imports and remove restrictions on foreign ownership. In addition, it agreed to change its poor record of protecting intellectual property rights such as copyrights, trademarks, and patents. Unauthorized copying of products is a major source of trade friction between China and the rest of the world. So, too, is China's trade surplus with many developed countries, as well as a currency that is set at an artificially low international value.

China's economic development has been very uneven geographically. Hong Kong is a wealthy capitalist city with per capita income of about U.S. $29,000. The standard of living is also relatively high in China's southern provinces and coastal cities, although not nearly as high as it is in Hong Kong. In fact, people living in these special economic zones have been the major beneficiaries of China's rapid growth. In contrast, the majority of people living elsewhere in China have very low incomes. Despite its remarkable recent economic successes, China remains a relatively low-income nation. But that status is quickly changing.

Question

Based on the information in this chapter, contrast the economic growth rates of Canada and China over the 25 years. How does the real GDP per capita of China compare with that of Canada? Why is there such a huge disparity in per capita income between China's coastal cities and its interior regions?

CHAPTER SUMMARY

6.1 ▶ ECONOMIC GROWTH

- A nation's economic growth can be measured either as an increase in real GDP over time or as an increase in real GDP per capita over time. Real GDP in Canada has grown at an average annual rate of about 2.7 percent since 1960; real GDP per capita has grown at roughly a 2.3 percent annual rate over that same period.

- Sustained increases in real GDP per capita did not happen until the past two centuries, when England and then other countries began to experience modern economic growth, which is characterized by institutional structures that encourage savings, investment, and the development of new technologies. Institutional structures that promote growth include strong property rights, patents, efficient financial institutions, education, and a competitive market system.

6.2 ▶ MODERN ECONOMIC GROWTH

- Because some nations have experienced nearly two centuries of economic growth while others have begun to experience economic growth only recently, some countries today are much richer than other countries.

- It is possible, however, for countries that are currently poor to grow faster than countries that are currently rich because the growth rates of rich-country GDPs per capita are limited to about 2 percent per year. In order to continue growing, rich countries must invent and apply new technologies. By contrast, poor countries can grow much faster because they can simply adopt the institutions and cutting-edge technologies already developed by the rich countries.

6.3 ▶ INGREDIENTS OF GROWTH

- The "ingredients" of economic growth to which we can attribute changes in growth rates include four supply factors (increases in the quantity and quality of natural resources, increases in the quantity and quality of human resources, increases in the stock of capital goods, and improvements in technology); a demand factor (increases in total spending); and an efficiency factor (increases in how well an economy achieves allocative and productive efficiency).

- The growth of a nation's capacity to produce output can be illustrated graphically by an outward shift of its production possibilities curve.

- Growth accounting attributes increases in real GDP either to increases in the amount of labour being employed or to increases in the productivity of the labour being employed. Increases in Canada's real GDP are mostly the result of increases in labour productivity. The increases in labour productivity can be attributed technological progress, increases in the quantity of capital per worker, improvements in the education and training of workers, the exploitation of economies of scale, and improvements in the allocation of labour across different industries.

- Over long time periods, the growth of labour productivity underlies an economy's growth of real wages and its standard of living.

6.4 ▸ ACCOUNTING FOR GROWTH IN CANADA

- Canada's real GDP has grown partly because of increased inputs of labour and primarily because of increases in the productivity of labour. The increases in productivity have resulted mainly from technological progress, increases in the quantity of capital per worker, improvements in the quality of labour, economies of scale, and an improved allocation of labour.

- Over long time periods, the growth of labour productivity underlies an economy's growth of real wages and its standard of living.

6.5 ▸ RECENT PRODUCTIVITY ACCELERATION

- The recent productivity acceleration is based on rapid technological change in the form of the microchip and information technology; increasing returns and lower per-unit costs; and heightened global competition that holds down prices.

- The main sources of increasing returns in recent years are (a) use of more specialized inputs as firms grow, (b) the spreading of development costs, (c) simultaneous consumption by consumers, (d) network effects, and (e) learning-by-doing. Increasing returns means higher productivity and lower per-unit production costs.

- Skeptics wonder if the recent productivity speedup is permanent. They point out that surges in productivity and real GDP growth have previously occurred during vigorous economic expansions but do not necessarily represent long-lived trends.

6.6 ▸ IS ECONOMIC GROWTH DESIRABLE AND SUSTAINABLE?

- Critics of rapid growth say that it adds to environmental degradation, increases human stress, and exhausts the earth's finite supply of natural resources. Defenders of rapid growth say that it is the primary path to the rising living standards nearly universally desired by people, that it need not debase the environment, and that there are no indications we are running out of resources. Growth is based on the expansion and application of human knowledge, which is limited only by human imagination.

TERMS AND CONCEPTS

economic growth, p. 120
real GDP per capita, p. 120
rule of 70, p. 120
modern economic growth, p. 122
leader countries, p. 123
follower countries, p. 123

supply factor, p. 128
demand factor, p. 128
efficiency factor, p. 128
labour productivity, p. 129
labour force participation rate, p. 131
infrastructure, p. 133

human capital, p. 133
economies of scale, p. 133
information technology, p. 135
start-up firm, p. 136
increasing returns, p. 136
network effects, p. 136
learning-by-doing, p. 136

STUDY QUESTIONS

LO 6.1 1. Why is economic growth important? Why could the difference between a 2.5 percent and a 3 percent annual growth rate be of great significance over several decades?

LO 6.1 2. **KEY QUESTION** Suppose an economy's real GDP is $30,000 in year 1 and $31,200 in year 2. What is the growth rate of its real GDP? Assume that population is 100 in year 1 and 102 in year 2. What is the growth rate of GDP per capita?

LO 6.2 3. When and where did modern economic growth first happen? What are the major institutional factors that form the foundation for modern economic growth? What do they have in common?

4. Why are some countries today much poorer than other **LO 6.2** countries? Are today's poor countries destined to always be poorer than today's rich countries? If so, explain why. If not, explain how today's poor countries can catch up or even pass today's rich countries.

5. **KEY QUESTION** What are the four supply factors of **LO 6.3** economic growth? What is the demand factor? What is the efficiency factor? Illustrate these factors in terms of the production possibilities curve.

6. Suppose that Alpha and Omega have identically sized **LO 6.3** working-age populations but that annual hours of work are much greater in Alpha than in Omega. Provide two possible explanations.

LO ▶ 6.3 7. Suppose that work hours in New Zombie are 200 in year 1 and productivity is $8 per hour worked. What is New Zombie's real GDP? If work hours increase to 210 in year 2 and productivity rises to $10 per hour, what is New Zombie's rate of economic growth?

LO ▶ 6.4 8. **KEY QUESTION** To what extent have increases in Canadian real GDP resulted from more labour inputs? From higher labour productivity?

LO ▶ 6.4 9. True or false? If false, explain why.

  a. Technological advance, which to date has played a relatively small role in Canadian economic growth, is destined to play a more important role in the future.

  b. Many public capital goods are complementary to private capital goods.

  c. Immigration has slowed economic growth in Canada.

LO ▶ 6.5 10. Explain why there is such a close relationship between changes in a nation's rate of productivity growth and changes in its average real hourly wage.

11. **KEY QUESTION** Relate each of the following to the recent productivity acceleration: **LO ▶ 6**

  a. Information technology

  b. Increasing returns

  c. Network effects

  d. Global competition

12. Provide three examples of products or services that can be simultaneously consumed by many people. Explain why labour productivity greatly rises as the firm sells more units of the product or service. Explain why the higher level of sales greatly reduces the per-unit cost of the product. **LO ▶ 6.**

13. Productivity often rises during economic expansions and falls during economic recessions. Can you think of reasons why? Briefly explain. (Hint: Remember that the level of productivity involves both levels of output and levels of labour input.) **LO ▶ 6.**

INTERNET APPLICATION QUESTIONS @

1. **Economic Growth in Canada—What Are the Latest Rates?** Visit the Statistics Canada Web site through the McConnell-Brue-Flynn-Barbiero Web site (Chapter 6). What are the annual growth rates for the Canadian economy for the last five years? Is the average of those rates above or below the long-run Canadian annual growth rate of about 3.5 percent?

2. **Productivity and Technology—Examples of Innovations** Recent innovations are increasing productivity. Go to the McConnell-Brue-Flynn-Barbiero Web site (Chapter 6) to link to the Timeline of Historic Inventions. Scroll down until you find the inventions made starting in the 1940s. Look at them and later inventions. Cite five technological "home runs" (for example, the transistor in 1947) and five technological "singles" (for example, the personal stereo in 1977). Which one innovation do you think has increased productivity the most? List two innovations since 1990. How might they have boosted productivity?

CHAPTER 7

Business Cycles, Unemployment, and Inflation

Between 1996 and 2000, real GDP in Canada expanded quickly and price level rose only slowly. The economy experienced neither significant unemployment nor inflation. Some observers felt that the Canadian economy, along with that of the United States, had entered a new era in which the business cycle was dead. But that wishful thinking came to an end in 2001 when Canada's economy slowed down, though it did not slip into recession as the American economy did. Within approximately the past six decades, real GDP has declined in Canada in five periods: 1945–46, 1954, 1981–82, 1991–92, and during the global crisis of 2008–09.

Although the Canadian economy has experienced remarkable economic growth over time, high unemployment or inflation has sometimes been a problem. For example, between August 2008 and August 2009 unemployment rose by over 400,000 workers, and the unemployment rate rose to 8.7 percent from 6.2 percent of the labour force. The rate of inflation in Canada was 10.2 percent in 1980 and 4.8 percent in 1990. Other nations also have suffered high unemployment rates or inflation rates in recent years. For example, the unemployment rate in Germany reached 10.7 percent in 2005. The inflation rate was 26,000 percent in Zimbabwe in 2007.

In this chapter we provide an introductory look at the trend of macroeconomic fluctuations. Our specific topics are the business cycle, unemployment, and inflation.

7.1 | The Business Cycle

The long-run trend of the Canadian economy is one of economic growth. But growth has been interrupted by periods of economic fluctuations usually associated with business cycles. The term **business cycle** refers to alternating rises and declines in the level of economic activity, sometime over several years. Individual cycles (one "up" followed by one "down") vary substantially in duration and intensity.

ORIGIN 7.1
Business Cycles

business cycle
Recurring increase and decrease in the level of economic activity over periods of years.

peak
A phase in the business cycle during which the economy is at full employment and the level of real output is at or very close to the economy's capacity.

recession
A period of decline in total output, income, and employment.

trough
The point during a recession or depression when output and employment reach their lowest levels.

expansion
The phase of the business cycle during which output and employment rise toward full employment.

Phases of the Business Cycle

Figure 7-1 shows the four phases of a generalized business cycle. At a **peak,** such as the middle peak shown in Figure 7-1, business activity has reached a temporary maximum. Here the economy is near or at full employment and the level of real output is at or very close to the economy's capacity. The price level is likely to rise during this phase.

A **recession** is a period of decline in total output, income, and employment. This downturn, which lasts six months or more, is marked by the widespread contraction of business activity in many sectors of the economy. Along with declines in real GDP, significant increases in unemployment occur. Table 7-1 documents the six recessions that have occurred in Canada since 1930.

In the **trough** of the recession or depression, output and employment "bottom out" at their lowest levels. The trough phase may be either short-lived or quite long. A recession is usually followed by a recovery and **expansion,** a period in which real GDP, income, and employment rise. At some point, the economy again approaches full employment. If spending then expands more rapidly than does production capacity, prices of nearly all goods and services will rise. In other words, inflation will occur.

Although business cycles all pass through the same phases, they vary greatly in duration and intensity. That is why many economists prefer to talk of business *fluctuations* rather than cycles, because cycles imply regularity but fluctuations do not. The Great Depression of the 1930s resulted in a 27.5 percent decline in real GDP over a three-year period in Canada and seriously impaired business activity for a decade. By comparison, more recent Canadian recessions, detailed in Table 7-1, were relatively mild in both intensity and duration, including the recession of 2008–09 brought about by a global financial crisis.

Recessions, of course, occur in other countries, too. At one time or another during the past 10 years, Argentina, Brazil, Colombia, Indonesia, Japan, Mexico, South Korea, and the United States experienced recessions.

Provincial Variations

National GDP data for Canada conceal significant differences in economic fluctuations among Canada's provinces and territories. Table 7-2 gives a breakdown of economic growth.

FIGURE 7-1   **The Business Cycle**

Economists distinguish four phases of the business cycle; the duration and strength of each phase may vary.

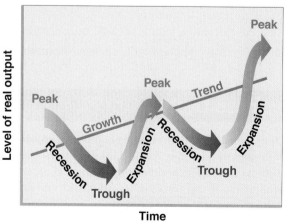

TABLE 7-1	**Canadian Recessions Since 1930**

Year	Depth (decline in real GDP, %)
1930–33	– 27.5
1945	– 2.4
1946	– 2.2
1954	– 1.1
1982	– 3.2
1991	– 1.7
2008–09*	– 2.2

Source: Statistics Canada. Updates at: http://www40.statcan.ca/l01/cst01/media01-eng.htm. Accessed May 7, 2009.

* Fourth quarter 2008 and first quarter 2009

TABLE 7-2	**Percentage Change in Real GDP for Provinces and Territories, 2008**

	2008
CANADA	0.5
Newfoundland and Labrador	– 0.1
Prince Edward Island	0.9
Nova Scotia	2.0
New Brunswick	0.0
Quebec	1.0
Ontario	– 0.4
Manitoba	2.4
Saskatchewan	4.4
Alberta	– 0.2
British Columbia	– 0.3
Yukon	5.2
Northwest Territories	– 6.5
Nunavut	5.5

Source: Statistics Canada. Updates at: http://www.statcan.gc.ca/daily-quotidien/090427/dq090427a-eng.htm. Accessed May 11, 2009.

Causation: a First Glance

The long-run trend of the Canadian economy is expansion and growth. That is why the stylized business cycles in Figure 7-1 are drawn against a trend of economic growth. A key issue in macro-economics is why business cycles fluctuate around the long-run growth trend. Economists have come up with several theories. But before turning to them, it is important to recall that in Chapter 4 we explained that if all the expectations in an economy were fulfilled or if all the prices in an economy were fully flexible and could respond rapidly to unexpected changes, there would be no cyclical variations in output or employment. In terms of Figure 7-1, the economy would stay on the long-run growth trend rather than fluctuating around it. Viewed in this light, the fundamental problem underlying business cycles is that unexpected changes (shocks) occasionally occur in the economy and many prices do not adjust quickly to them.

That being said, economists fall into several different camps when it comes to the types of shocks they believe are responsible for business cycles. One group, for instance, says that momentous innovations—the railroad, the automobile, synthetic fibres, microchips—have great impact on investment and consumption spending and therefore on output, employment, and the price level. Such major innovations occur irregularly and unexpectedly, thus contributing to the variability of economic activity.

Another school of thought sees major shocks to productivity as causes of business cycles. When productivity unexpectedly increases, the economy booms; when productivity unexpectedly falls, the economy recedes. Others view the business cycle as a purely monetary phenomenon. When government creates more money than people were expecting, they say, an inflationary boom occurs. By contrast, printing less money than people were expecting triggers a decline in output and employment and, eventually, in the price level. Still others say that business cycles result from financial bubbles and bursts, which spill over through optimism or pessimism to affect the production of goods and services.

But whatever they see as the initiating force, most economists agree that the *immediate* cause of the large majority of cyclical changes in the levels of real output and employment is unexpected changes in the level of total spending. If total spending unexpectedly sinks and firms cannot lower prices, firms will find themselves selling fewer units of output (since with prices fixed, a decreased amount of spending implies fewer items purchased). Slower sales will cause firms to cut back on production. As they do, GDP will fall. And since fewer workers are needed to produce less output, employment will also fall. The economy will contract and enter a recession.

By contrast, if the level of spending unexpectedly rises, output, employment, and incomes will rise. This is true because with sticky prices the increased spending will mean that consumers will be buying a larger volume of goods and services (since, with prices fixed, more spending means more items purchased). Firms will respond by increasing output, and thus GDP will also rise. And

CONSIDER THIS | The Cause of the Recession of 2008–09

The recession of 2008–09 originated from an unexpected financial bubble that burst in the U.S., which adversely affected U.S. production of goods and services. Through a fall in our exports to the U.S., the recession spilled into Canada. The economic contraction in the U.S. was precipitated by a severe financial crisis involving overvalued real estate and unsustainable mortgage debt. This debt was bundled into new securities ("derivatives"), which were then sold to financial investors. The investors in turn bought insurance against losses that might arise from the securities. As real estate prices in the U.S. plummeted and mortgage defaults rocketed to levels much higher than expected, the securitization and insurance structure buckled and nearly collapsed. The financial crisis that followed curtailed lending by commercial banks, and the U.S. economy experienced a severe economic contraction—and Canada saw our exports fall precipitously.

because firms will need to hire more workers to produce the larger volume of output, employment will also increase. The economy will boom and enjoy an expansion. Eventually, as time passes and prices become more flexible, prices are also likely to rise as a result of the increased spending.

Cyclical Impact: Durables and Nondurables

Although the business cycle is felt everywhere in the economy, it affects different segments in different ways and to different degrees.

Firms and industries producing *capital goods* (for example, housing, commercial buildings, heavy equipment, and farm implements) and *consumer durables* (for example, automobiles and refrigerators) are affected most by the business cycle. Within limits, firms can postpone the purchase of capital goods. As the economy recedes, producers frequently delay the purchase of new equipment and the construction of new plants. The business outlook simply does not warrant increases in the stock of capital goods. In good times, capital goods are usually replaced before they depreciate completely. But when recession strikes, firms patch up their old equipment and make do. As a result, investment in capital goods declines sharply. Firms that have excess plant capacity may not even bother to replace all the capital that is depreciating. For them, net investment may be negative. The pattern is much the same for consumer durables such as automobiles and major appliances. When recession occurs and households must trim their budgets, purchases of these goods are often deferred. Families repair their old cars and appliances rather than buy new ones, and the firms producing these products suffer. (Of course, producers of capital goods and consumer durables also benefit most from expansions.)

In contrast, *service* industries and industries that produce *nondurable consumer goods* are somewhat insulated from the most severe effects of recession. People find it difficult to cut back on needed medical and legal services, for example. And a recession actually helps some service firms, such as pawnbrokers and law firms that specialize in bankruptcies. Nor are the purchases of many nondurable goods such as food and clothing easy to postpone. The quantity and quality of purchases of nondurables will decline, but not as much as will purchases of capital goods and consumer durables. *(Key Question 1)*

QUICK REVIEW

▸ The typical business cycle goes through four phases: peak, recession, trough, and expansion.

▸ Fluctuations in output and employment are caused by economic shocks combined with sticky prices.

▸ Sources of shocks include unexpected innovations, unexpected changes in produc-

tivity, unexpected changes in the money supply, unexpected changes in the level of total spending in the economy, and financial crises.

▸ During recessions, industries that produce capital goods and consumer durables normally suffer greater output and employment declines than industries that produce services and nondurable consumer goods.

7.2 | Unemployment

Two problems arise over the course of the business cycle: unemployment and inflation. Let's look at unemployment first.

Measurement of Unemployment

To measure the unemployment rate we must first determine who is eligible and available to work. Figure 7-2 provides a helpful starting point. It divides the total Canadian population into three groups. One group is made up of people under 15 years of age and people who are institutionalized, for example in psychiatric hospitals or correctional institutions. Such people are not considered potential members of the labour force.

A second group, labelled "Not in labour force," is composed of adults who are potential workers but are not employed and are not seeking work. For example, they are homemakers, full-time students, or retirees.

The third group is the **labour force,** which constituted just over 50 percent of the total population in 2008. The labour force consists of people who are able and willing to work, and includes both those who are employed and those who are unemployed but actively seeking work. The labour force *participation rate* is defined as the percentage of the population 15 years and over (about 67.8 percent in 2008) that is currently employed. The **unemployment rate** is the percentage of the labour force that is unemployed:

$$\text{Unemployment rate} = \frac{\text{unemployed}}{\text{labour force}} \times 100$$

The statistics included in Figure 7-2 show that in 2008 the unemployment rate was $1{,}119{,}300/18{,}245{,}100 \times 100 = 6.1\%$.

Each month, Statistics Canada conducts a nationwide random survey of some 50,000 households to determine who is employed and who is not employed. In a series of questions, it asks which members of the household are working, unemployed and looking for work, not looking for work, and so on. From the answers it determines an unemployment rate for the entire nation. Despite the use of scientific sampling and interviewing techniques, the data collected in this survey are subject to criticism.

labour force
Persons 15 years of age and older who are not in institutions and who are employed, or are unemployed and seeking work.

unemployment rate
The percentage of the labour force that is unemployed at any time.

WORKED PROBLEM 7.1
Unemployment Rate

FIGURE 7-2   **The Labour Force, Employment, and Unemployment, 2008**

The labour force consists of persons 15 years of age or older who are not in institutions and who are (1) employed or (2) unemployed but seeking employment.

SOURCE: Statistics Canada. The Labour Force, Employment, and Unemployment, 2008. At: http://www40.statcan.ca/l01/cst01/econ10-eng.htm. Accessed May 11, 2009.

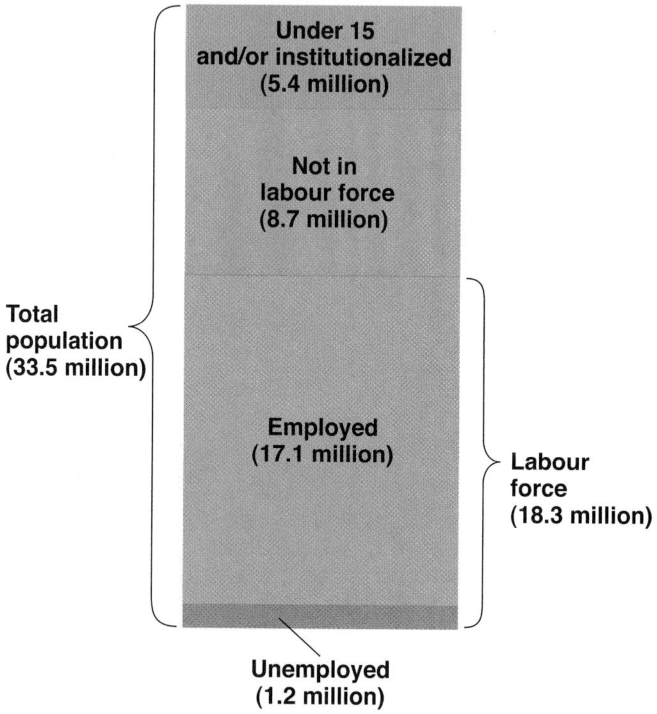

Total population (33.5 million)

Under 15 and/or institutionalized (5.4 million)

Not in labour force (8.7 million)

Employed (17.1 million)

Labour force (18.3 million)

Unemployed (1.2 million)

- *Part-Time Employment Statistics*　Canada fails to distinguish between fully and partially employed workers. In 2008 about 3.15 million people worked part-time. By counting them as fully employed, say critics, the official Statistics Canada data understate the unemployment rate.

- *Discouraged Workers*　An individual must be actively seeking employment to be counted as unemployed. An unemployed person who is not actively seeking work is classified as "not in the labour force." The problem is that many people, after unsuccessfully seeking employment for a time, become discouraged and drop out of the labour force. The number of such **discouraged workers** is larger during recession than during prosperity. By not counting discouraged workers as unemployed, say critics, the official Statistics Canada data understate the unemployment problem. *(Key Question 3)*

discouraged workers
People who have left the labour force because they have not been able to find employment.

Types of Unemployment

There are four types of unemployment: frictional, structural, cyclical, and seasonal.

FRICTIONAL UNEMPLOYMENT

At any particular time some workers are "between jobs." Some are moving voluntarily from one job to another. Others have been fired and are seeking re-employment. Still others have been laid off temporarily because of seasonal demand. In addition to those between jobs, many young workers are searching for their first job. As these unemployed people find jobs or are called back from temporary layoffs, other job seekers and laid-off workers will replace them in the unemployment pool. A crucial point to keep in mind is that while the pool itself persists because there are always newly unemployed workers flowing into it, most workers do not stay in the pool for very long. Indeed most unemployed workers find new jobs within a couple of months. Do not make the mistake of confusing the permanence of the pool itself with the false idea that the pool's membership is permanent, too.

Economists use the term **frictional unemployment** for workers who are either searching for jobs or waiting to take jobs in the near future. The word frictional implies that the labour market does not operate perfectly and instantaneously (without friction) in matching workers and jobs.

Frictional unemployment is inevitable and, at least in part, desirable. Many workers who are voluntarily between jobs are moving from low-paying, low-productivity jobs to higher-paying, higher-productivity positions. That means greater income for the workers, a better allocation of labour resources, and a larger real GDP for the economy.

frictional unemployment
A type of unemployment caused by workers voluntarily changing jobs and by temporary layoffs; unemployed workers between jobs.

STRUCTURAL UNEMPLOYMENT

Frictional unemployment blurs into a category called **structural unemployment.** Here, economists use *structural* in the sense of *compositional*. Changes over time in consumer demand and in technology alter the "structure" of the total demand for labour, both occupationally and geographically.

Occupationally, the demand for certain skills (for example, sewing clothes or working on farms) may decline or even vanish. The demand for other skills (for example, designing software or maintaining computer systems) will intensify. Unemployment results because the composition of the labour force does not respond immediately or completely to the new structure of job opportunities. Workers whose skills and experience have become obsolete thus find that they have no marketable talents. They are structurally unemployed until they adapt or develop skills that employers want.

Geographically, the demand for labour also changes over time. For example, industry and thus employment opportunities have migrated from the Maritimes to Central Canada over the past few decades. Migration of labour has also occurred in western Canada to Alberta.

What distinguishes frictional from structural unemployment? The key difference is that *frictionally* unemployed workers have saleable skills and either live in areas where jobs exist or are able to move to areas where they do. *Structurally* unemployed workers find it hard to find new jobs without retraining, gaining additional education, or relocating. Frictional unemployment is short-term; structural unemployment is more likely to be long-term and consequently more serious.

structural unemployment
Unemployment of workers whose skills are not demanded by employers, who lack sufficient skills to obtain employment, or who cannot easily move to locations where jobs are available.

CYCLICAL UNEMPLOYMENT

cyclical unemployment
Unemployment caused by a decline in total spending (or by insufficient aggregate demand).

Unemployment caused by a decline in total spending is called **cyclical unemployment** and typically begins in the recession phase of the business cycle. As the demand for goods and services decreases, employment falls and unemployment rises. Cyclical unemployment results from insufficient demand for goods and services. The 20 percent unemployment rate in the depth of the Great Depression in 1933 reflected mainly cyclical unemployment, as did significant parts of the 11 percent unemployment rate during the recession year 1982 and the 11.3 percent rate in the recession year 1991. More recently, the unemployment rate rose from 6.1 percent in the early fall of 2008 to 8.4 percent in May 2009.

Cyclical unemployment is a very serious problem when it occurs. We will say more about its high costs later, after we define "full employment."

SEASONAL UNEMPLOYMENT

seasonal unemployment
Unemployment caused by seasonal factors.

Most parts of Canada have quite severe winters during which some sectors, for example building construction and farming, come to a virtual stop. These sectors experience substantial **seasonal unemployment,** as many workers are temporarily laid off due to seasonal factors. Another example of seasonal unemployment is ski resort workers laid off during summer months.

Definition of Full Employment

Because frictional and structural unemployment is largely unavoidable in a dynamic economy, *full employment* is something less than 100 percent employment of the labour force. Economists say that the economy is "fully employed" when it is experiencing only frictional, structural, and seasonal unemployment. That is, full employment occurs when no cyclical unemployment exists.

natural rate of unemployment (NRU)
The unemployment rate that occurs when no cyclical unemployment exists and the economy is achieving its potential output.

Economists describe the unemployment rate that is consistent with full employment as the *full-employment rate of unemployment,* or the **natural rate of unemployment (NRU)**, sometimes referred to as the *non-inflationary rate of unemployment.* At the NRU, the economy is said to be producing its non-inflationary **potential GDP.** This is the real GDP that the economy would produce at full employment.

potential GDP
The real output an economy can produce when it fully employs its available resources.

When the economy is operating at NRU, the number of *job seekers* equals the number of *job vacancies.* Also, it takes time for the structurally unemployed to achieve the skills and geographic relocation needed for re-employment.

However, "natural" does not mean the economy will always operate at this rate and thus realize its potential output. When cyclical unemployment occurs, the economy has much more unemployment than that which would occur at the NRU. Moreover, the economy can operate for a while at an unemployment rate *below* the NRU. At times, the demand for labour may be so great that firms take a stronger initiative to hire and train the structurally unemployed. Also, some homemakers, teenagers, college and university students, and retirees who were casually looking for just the right part-time or full-time jobs may quickly find them. Thus the unemployment rate temporarily falls below the natural rate.

The NRU also can vary over time. In the 1980s, the NRU was about 7.5 percent. Today, it is estimated to be 6 to 7 percent. Why the decline?

- The proportion of younger workers in the labour force has declined as the baby boom generation has aged. The labour force now has a larger proportion of middle-aged workers, who traditionally have lower unemployment rates, perhaps because of less turnover.

- The growth of temporary-help agencies and the improved information sharing of the Internet have lowered the NRU by enabling workers to find jobs more quickly.

A decade ago, a 6 to 7 percent rate of unemployment would have reflected excessive spending, an unbalanced labour market, and rising inflation; today, that same rate is consistent with a balanced labour market and a stable, low rate of inflation.

Economic Costs of Unemployment

Unemployment that is above the natural rate involves great economic and social costs.

GDP GAP AND OKUN'S LAW

The basic economic cost of unemployment is forgone output. When the economy fails to create enough jobs for all who are able and willing to work, potential production of goods and services is irretrievably lost. In terms of the analysis in Chapter 1, unemployment above the natural rate means that society is operating at some point inside its production possibilities curve. Economists call this sacrifice of output a **GDP gap**—the difference between actual and potential GDP. That is,

> GDP gap = actual GDP – potential GDP

The GDP gap can be either negative (actual GDP < potential GDP) or positive (actual GDP > potential GDP). In the case of unemployment above the natural rate, it is negative because actual GDP falls short of potential GDP.

Potential GDP is determined by assuming that the natural rate of unemployment prevails. The growth of potential GDP is simply projected forward on the basis of the economy's "normal" growth rate of real GDP. Figure 7-3 shows the GDP gap for recent years in Canada. It also indicates the close correlation between the actual unemployment rate (Figure 7-3b) and the GDP gap (Figure 7-3a). The higher the unemployment rate, the larger the GDP gap.

Macroeconomist Arthur Okun was the first to quantify the relationship between the unemployment rate and the GDP gap. Based on recent estimates, **Okun's law** indicates that *for every one percentage point by which the actual unemployment rate exceeds the natural rate, a GDP gap (shortfall) of about 2 percent occurs.* With this information, we can calculate the absolute loss of output associated with any above-natural unemployment rate. For example, in 1992 the unemployment rate was 11.3 percent, or 3.8 percentage points above the then 7.5 percent natural rate of unemployment. Multiplying this 3.8 percent by Okun's 2 percent indicates that 1992's GDP gap was 7.6 percent of potential GDP (in real terms). By applying this 7.6 percent loss to 1992's potential GDP of $770 billion, we find that the economy sacrificed $59 billion of real output because the natural rate of unemployment was not achieved. *(Key Question 5)*

Sometimes the economy's actual output will exceed its potential GDP, or full-employment GDP, creating a "positive" GDP gap. Potential GDP can occasionally be exceeded, but the excess of actual over potential GDP eventually causes inflation and cannot be sustained indefinitely.

UNEQUAL BURDENS

An increase in the unemployment rate—say, from 8 to 9 or 10 percent—might be more tolerable to society if every worker's hours of work and wage income were reduced proportionately. But this is not the case. Part of the burden of unemployment is that its cost is unequally distributed.

Table 7-3 examines unemployment rates for various labour market groups for two years. Recession pushed the 1992 unemployment rate to 11.3 percent. In 2008 the Canadian economy was close to full employment for most of the year, with an annual average rate of 6.1 percent unemployment. By observing the large variations in unemployment rates for the different groups within each year and comparing the rates between the two years, we can generalize as follows.

- *Occupation* Workers in lower-skilled occupations have higher unemployment rates than workers in higher-skilled occupations. Lower-skilled workers have more and longer spells of structural unemployment than higher-skilled workers. Moreover, lower-skilled workers usually bear the brunt of recessions. Businesses usually retain most of their higher-skilled workers, in whom they have invested the expense of training.

- *Age* Teenagers have much higher unemployment rates than adults. Teenagers have lower skill levels, quit their jobs more frequently, are more frequently fired, and have less geographic mobility than adults. Many unemployed teenagers are new in the labour market, searching for their first job. Male aboriginal teenagers, in particular, have very high unemployment rates.

GDP gap
The amount by which actual GDP falls below potential GDP.

Okun's law
The generalization that any one-percentage-point rise in the unemployment rate above the natural rate of unemployment will decrease GDP by 2 percent of the economy's potential GDP.

WORKED PROBLEM 7.2
Okun's Law

FIGURE 7-3   Actual and Potential GDP and the Unemployment Rate

(a) The difference between actual and potential GDP is the GDP gap. A negative GDP gap measures the output the economy sacrifices when actual GDP falls short of potential GDP. A positive GDP gap indicates that actual GDP is above potential GDP. (b) A high unemployment rate means a large GDP gap (negative), and a low unemployment rate means a small or even positive GDP gap.

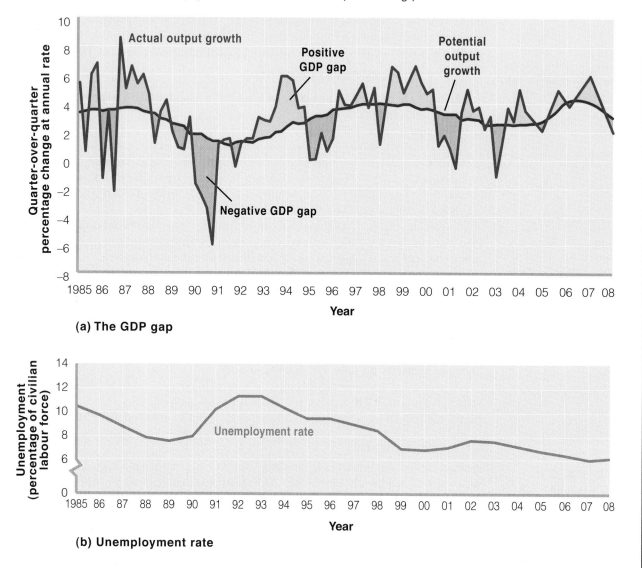

(a) The GDP gap

(b) Unemployment rate

SOURCES: (a) Bank of Canada, Monetary Policy Report, October 2005 and the authors' own calculations; (b) Statistics Canada, at: http://www40.statcan.ca/l01/cst01/econ10-eng.htm. Accessed May 15, 2009.

- *Gender*   The unemployment rates for men and women are usually very similar. (The lower unemployment rate for women in 1992 occurred because of the greater incidence of male workers in such cyclically vulnerable industries as automobiles, steel, and construction.)

- *Education*   Less-educated workers, on average, have higher unemployment rates than workers with more education. Less education is usually associated with lower-skilled, less permanent jobs, more time between jobs, and jobs that are more vulnerable to cyclical layoff.

TABLE 7-3	Unemployment by Demographic Group: Recession (1992) and Full Employment (2008)	

Demographic group	Unemployment rate, March 1992	Unemployment rate, March 2008
Overall	11.3 %	6.0 %
Age		
15–24 years	19.1	11.0
25 years and over	11.1	5.1
Sex		
Male	13.9	5.2
Female	10.8	4.9

Source: Statistics Canada. Table: Employment by age, sex, type of work, class of worker and province (monthly). Updates at: http://www40.statcan.ca/l01/cst01/labr66a-eng.htm. Accessed May 18, 2009.

Non-Economic Costs of Unemployment

Severe cyclical unemployment is more than an economic malady; it is a social catastrophe. Unemployment means idleness. And idleness means loss of skills, loss of self-respect, plummeting morale, family disintegration, and sociopolitical unrest. Widespread joblessness increases poverty, heightens racial and ethnic tensions, and reduces hope for material advancement. History demonstrates that severe unemployment can lead to rapid and sometimes violent social and political change. At the individual level, research links higher unemployment to increases in suicide, homicide, fatal heart attacks and strokes, and mental illness.

Regional Variations

The national unemployment rate in Canada does not reveal the significant diversity in regional unemployment. Table 7-4 gives both the national unemployment rate and a provincial breakdown. For 2008 the national rate was 6.1 percent, but rates went as high as 13.2 percent in Newfoundland and Labrador and as low as 3.6 percent in Alberta.

International Comparisons

Unemployment rates differ greatly among nations at any given time. One reason is that nations have different natural rates of unemployment. Another is that nations may be in different phases of their business cycles. Global Perspective 7.1 shows unemployment rates for five industrialized

CONSIDER THIS | Unemployment during the Global Financial Crisis of 2008–09

During the global financial crisis in 2008–09, the Canadian unemployment rate climbed to 8.4 percent—an 11-year high—in a period of only eight months. From October 2008 to May 2009 the Canadian economy lost 406,000 full-time jobs, and a total of 1.55 million workers were unemployed. The sudden increase in the unemployment rate was the result of the recession that began in Canada in September 2008 as

fallout from the global financial crisis. However, the national unemployment rate masked the large provincial differences, which varied from a high of 15.1 percent in Newfoundland and Labrador to only 4.9 percent in both Manitoba and Alberta. The recession hit Ontario, with the largest manufacturing sector in the country, particularly hard: 363,000 jobs were lost between October 2008 and May 2009.

TABLE 7-4	Provincial Breakdown of the Unemployment Rate, 2008

	%
CANADA	6.1
Newfoundland and Labrador	13.2
Prince Edward Island	10.8
Nova Scotia	7.7
New Brunswick	8.6
Quebec	7.2
Ontario	6.5
Manitoba	4.2
Saskatchewan	4.1
Alberta	3.6
British Columbia	4.6

Source: Statistics Canada. Updates at: http://www40.statcan.gc.ca/daily-quotidien/090427a-eng.htm. Accessed May 18, 2009.

7.1 | GLOBAL PERSPECTIVE

Unemployment rates in five industrial nations, 1998–2008

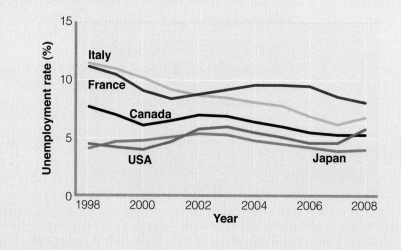

Source: Bureau of Labour Statistics, www.bls.gov

nations in recent years. Between 1998 and 2008 the Canadian unemployment rate came down steadily, to reach a 30-year low of 6.0 percent by early 2008. However, in autumn 2008 Canada entered a recession that saw the unemployment rate rise to 8.4 percent by May 2009. Still, Canada's economy did relatively well during the global recession of 2008–09. While Canada has had a higher unemployment rate compared to the United States in the last 30 years, by May 2009 it was lower by a full percentage point. (See the Consider This box on the rapid rise in the unemployment rate during the global financial crisis of 2008–09.) In recent years the unemployment rate in Canada has been lower than in most European countries.

QUICK REVIEW

▶ Unemployment is of four general types: frictional, structural, cyclical, and seasonal.

▶ The natural unemployment rate (frictional plus structural) is currently 6 to 7 percent.

▶ Society loses real GDP when cyclical unemployment occurs: according to Okun's law, for each one percentage point of unemployment above the natural rate, the Canadian economy suffers a 2-percent shortfall in real GDP below its potential GDP.

▶ Lower-skilled workers, teenagers, and less well-educated workers bear a disproportionate burden of unemployment.

7.3 | Inflation

MONEY & INFLATION

We now turn to inflation, another aspect of macroeconomic fluctuations. The problems inflation poses are more subtle than those posed by unemployment.

Meaning of Inflation

inflation
A continual rise in the general level of prices in an economy.

Inflation is a continual rise in the *general level of prices*. When inflation occurs, each dollar of income will buy fewer goods and services than before. Inflation reduces the purchasing power of money. But inflation does not mean that *all* prices are rising. Even during periods of rapid inflation, some prices may be relatively constant and others may even fall. For example, although Canada experienced high rates of inflation in the 1970s and early 1980s, the price of digital watches and calculators declined.

Measurement of Inflation

Consumer Price Index (CPI)
An index that measures the prices of a fixed market basket of goods and services that is bought by a typical consumer.

The main measure of inflation in Canada is the **Consumer Price Index (CPI)**, compiled by Statistics Canada. The government uses this index to report inflation rates each month and each year. It also uses the CPI to adjust social benefits and income tax brackets for inflation. The CPI reports the price of a "market basket" of over 600 consumer goods and services that are purchased by a typical Canadian consumer. (The GDP price index discussed in Chapter 5 is a much broader measure of inflation, since it includes not only consumer goods and services but also capital goods, goods and services purchased by government, and goods and services that enter world trade.)

The composition of the CPI market basket is based on spending patterns of Canadian consumers in a specific period, currently 2002. (See this chapter's Last Word for more detailed information about the eight main categories.) Statistics Canada sets the CPI for 2002 equal to 100. So, the CPI for any particular year is found as follows:

$$\text{CPI} = \frac{\text{Price of the 2002 basket in the particular year}}{\text{Price of the same basket in the base year (2002)}} \times 100$$

The rate of inflation for a certain year (say, 2008) is found by comparing, in percentage terms, that year's index with the index in the previous year. For example, the CPI was 114.1 in 2008, up from 111.5 in 2007. So the rate of inflation for 2008 is calculated as follows:

$$\text{Rate of inflation} = \frac{114.1 - 111.5}{111.5} \times 100 = 2.3\%$$

In Chapter 6, we discussed the mathematical approximation called *the rule of 70*, which tells us that we can find the number of years it will take for some measure to double, given its annual percentage increase, by dividing that percentage increase into the number 70. So, with a 3 percent annual rate of inflation the price level will double in about 23 years (= 70 ÷ 3). Inflation of 8 percent per year will double the price level in about 9 years (= 70 ÷ 8). *(Key Question 8)*

Facts of Inflation

Figure 7-4 shows the annual rates of inflation in Canada between 1960 and 2008. Observe that inflation reached double-digit rates in the 1970s and early 1980s, but has since declined and recently has been relatively mild.

In recent years inflation in Canada has been unusually low relative to inflation in several other industrial countries (see Global Perspective 7.2); some nations (not shown) have had double-digit, triple-digit, or even higher annual rates of inflation. In 2008, for example, the annual inflation rate in Venezuela was 30 percent; in Kenya, 26 percent; and in Tajikistan, 20 percent. Recall from the chapter opener that inflation was 26,000 percent in Zimbabwe in 2007.

FIGURE 7-4 Annual Inflation Rates in Canada, 1960–2008

The major periods of inflation in Canada in the past half century were in the 1970s and 1980s.

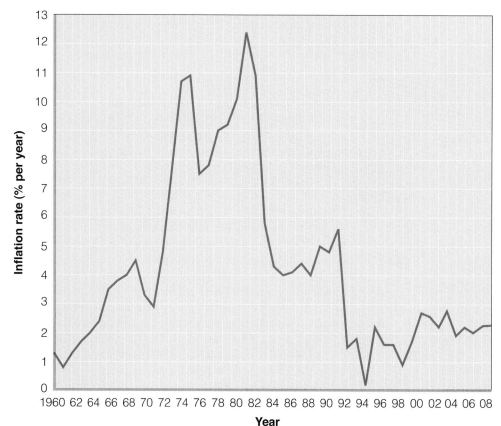

SOURCE: Statistics Canada. Updates at: http://www40.statcan.ca/l01/cst01/econ163a-eng.htm. Accessed May 18, 2009.

7.2 | GLOBAL PERSPECTIVE

Inflation rates in five industrial nations, 1998–2008

Inflation rates in Canada in recent years were neither extraordinarily high nor extraordinarily low compared to rates in other industrial nations.

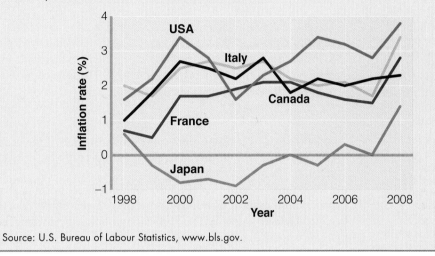

Source: U.S. Bureau of Labour Statistics, www.bls.gov.

CONSIDER THIS | The Consumer Price Index during Recession

While in most years the Canadian CPI advances anywhere between 1 and 3 percent, during severe recessions it can actually drop. Consider what happened to the CPI during the recession that started in Canada in the fall of 2008. For the entire year of 2008 the CPI rose 2.3 percent. But this annual rate hides the deflationary pressures experienced by the Canadian economy as a result of the financial crisis that swept across the globe in the latter half of 2008.

The CPI in April 2009 was 113.9, down from the 114.1 average for 2008. On an annual basis, however, the CPI was up 0.4 percent between April 2008 and April 2009. As we noted in Chapter 4, even during recession, which usually slows the growth of general price increases in the economy, prices rarely fall from one year to the next because they are inflexible downward. An actual fall in prices year over year would require a very severe recession.

The recession of 2008–09 caused by the global financial crisis sparked concern about deflation. The Bank of Canada, which wants to prevent deflation, took aggressive steps to prevent it.

Why the concern about deflation? First, it typically occurs only when the economy is falling deeper into a recession. It therefore reflects an underlying malady of deficient aggregate spending and confirms that public policy has failed to halt the decline in the economy.

Deflation also can worsen a recession by further undermining the already diminished willingness of households and businesses to borrow and spend. When the price level is falling, dollars borrowed do not have as much purchasing power as the dollars needed to pay back the loans. Borrowing is thus discouraged, even though nominal interest rates may sink to zero. Also, expectations of falling prices cause households and businesses to wait for prices to fall farther before purchasing consumer and capital goods. This behaviour reduces current demand—and thus makes the recession worse.

Types of Inflation

Nearly all prices in an economy are set by supply and demand. Consequently, if the economy is experiencing inflation and the overall level of prices is rising, we need to look for an explanation in terms of demand and supply. *Demand-pull inflation* explains situations in which inflation is caused by an increase in demand. *Cost-push inflation* explains situations in which inflation is caused by a decrease in supply.

DEMAND-PULL INFLATION

demand-pull inflation
Increases in the price level caused by an excess of total spending beyond the economy's capacity to produce.

Usually, increases in the price level are caused by an excess of total spending beyond the economy's capacity to produce. When resources are already fully employed, the business sector cannot respond to this excess demand by expanding output. So the excess demand bids up the prices of the limited real output, causing **demand-pull inflation.** The essence of this type of inflation is "too much spending chasing too few goods."

COST-PUSH INFLATION

cost-push inflation
Increases in the price level resulting from an increase in resource costs and hence in per-unit production costs.

per-unit production cost
The average production cost of a particular level of output; total input cost divided by units of output.

Inflation may also arise on the supply, or cost, side of the economy. During some periods in Canadian economic history, including the mid-1970s, the price level increased even though total spending was not excessive.

The theory of **cost-push inflation** explains rising prices in terms of factors that raise **per-unit production costs** at each level of spending. A per-unit production cost is the average cost of a particular level of output. This average cost is found by dividing the total cost of all resource inputs by the amount of output produced. That is,

$$\text{Per-unit production cost} = \frac{\text{total input cost}}{\text{units of output}}$$

CONSIDER THIS | Clipping Coins

Loosely defined, demand-pull inflation is "too much money chasing too few goods." Some interesting early episodes of demand-pull inflation occurred in Europe during the ninth to the fifteenth centuries, under feudalism. In that economic system *lords* (or *princes*) ruled individual fiefdoms and their *vassals* (or *peasants*) worked the fields. The peasants initially paid parts of their harvest as taxes to the princes. Later, when the princes began issuing "coins of the realm," peasants began paying their taxes with gold coins.

Some princes soon discovered a way to transfer purchasing power from their vassals to themselves without explicitly increasing taxes. As gold coins came into the treasury, princes clipped off parts, making them slightly smaller. From the clippings they minted new coins and used them to buy more goods for themselves. This practice of clipping coins was a subtle form of taxation. The quantity of goods being produced in the fiefdom remained the same, but the number of gold coins increased.

With "too much money chasing too few goods," inflation occurred. Each gold coin earned by the peasants therefore had less purchasing power than previously because prices were higher. The increase of the money supply shifted purchasing power away from the peasants and toward the princes just as surely as if the princes had increased taxation of the peasants.

In more recent eras some dictators have simply printed money to buy more goods for themselves, their relatives, and their key loyalists. These dictators, too, have levied hidden taxes on their populations by creating inflation.

The moral of the story is quite simple: A society that values price-level stability should not entrust the control of its money supply to people who benefit from inflation.

Rising per-unit production costs reduce profits and reduce the amount of output firms are willing to supply at the existing price level. As a result, the economy's supply of goods and services declines and the price level rises. In this scenario costs are *pushing* the price level upward, whereas in demand-pull inflation demand is *pulling* it upward.

The major sources of cost-push inflation have been so-called *supply shocks.* Specifically, abrupt increases in the costs of raw materials or energy inputs have on occasion driven up per-unit production costs and thus product prices. The rocketing prices of imported oil in 1973–74 and again in 1979–80 are good illustrations. As energy prices surged upward during these periods, the costs of producing and transporting virtually every product in the economy rose, and cost-push inflation ensued.

Complexities

It is often difficult to distinguish between demand-pull and cost-push inflation unless the original source of inflation is known. For example, suppose a significant increase in total spending occurs in a fully employed economy, causing demand-pull inflation. But as the demand-pull stimulus works its way through various product and factor markets, individual firms find their wage costs, material costs, and fuel prices rising. Firms must raise their prices because production costs (someone else's prices) have risen. Although this inflation is clearly demand-pull in origin, it may mistakenly appear to be cost-push inflation to business firms and to government. Without proper identification of the source of the inflation, the Bank of Canada may be slow to enact policies to reduce excessive total spending.

Another complexity is that cost-push inflation and demand-pull inflation differ in their persistence. Demand-pull inflation will continue as long as there is excess total spending. Cost-push inflation is automatically self-limiting; it will die out by itself. Increased per-unit costs will reduce supply, which means lower real output and employment. Those decreases will constrain further per-unit cost increases. In other words, cost-push inflation generates a recession. And in a recession, households and businesses concentrate on keeping their resources employed, not on pushing up the prices of those resources.

QUICK REVIEW

▸ Inflation is a rising general level of prices and is measured as percentage change in a price index such as the Consumer Price Index (CPI).

▸ The CPI measures changes in the prices of a fixed market basket of goods and services bought by the typical urban consumer.

▸ The inflation rate in Canada has been within the lower range of rates compared to other advanced industrial nations and far below the rates experienced by some nations.

▸ Demand-pull inflation occurs when total spending exceeds the economy's ability to provide goods and services at the existing price level; total spending pulls the price level upward.

▸ Cost-push inflation occurs when factors such as rapid increases in the price of raw materials drive up per-unit production costs at each level of output; higher costs push the price level upward.

7.4 | Redistribution Effects of Inflation

Inflation hurts some people, leaves others unaffected, and actually helps still others by redistributing real income from some people to other people. Who gets hurt? Who benefits? Before we can answer, we need to discuss some terminology.

Nominal Income and Real Income

nominal income
The number of current dollars received as wages, rent, interest, or profits.

real income
The amount of goods and services nominal income can buy.

There is a difference between money (or nominal) income and real income. **Nominal income** is the number of dollars received as wages, rent, interest, or profits. **Real income** is a measure of the amount of goods and services nominal income can buy; it is the purchasing power of nominal income, or income adjusted for inflation. That is,

$$\text{Real income} = \frac{\text{nominal income}}{\text{price index}} \times 100$$

Inflation need not alter an economy's overall real income. It is evident from the above equation that real income will remain the same when nominal income rises at the same rate as the price index.

But when inflation occurs, not everyone's nominal income rises at the same pace as the price level. Therein lies the potential for redistribution of real income from some to others. If the change in the price level differs from the change in a person's nominal income, his or her real income will be affected. The following approximation (shown by the ≅ sign) tells us roughly how much real income will change:

WORKED PROBLEM 7.3
Nominal and Real Income

Percentage change in real income	≅	Percentage change in nominal income	−	Percentage change in price income

For example, suppose the price level rises by 6 percent in some period. If Bob's nominal income rises by 6 percent, his real income will *remain unchanged.* But if his nominal income instead rises by 10 percent, his real income will *increase* by about 4 percent. And if Bob's nominal income rises by only 2 percent, his real income will *decline* by about 4 percent.[1]

Expectations

unanticipated inflation
Increases in the price level that occur at a rate greater than expected.

anticipated inflation
Increases in the price level that occur at the expected rate.

The redistribution effects of inflation depend upon whether or not it is expected. We will first discuss situations involving **unanticipated inflation.** As you will see, these cause real income and wealth to be redistributed, harming some and benefitting others. We will then discuss situations involving **anticipated inflation.** These are situations in which people see an inflation coming in advance. With the ability to plan ahead, people are able to avoid or lessen the redistribution effects associated with inflation.

Who Is Hurt by Inflation?

Unanticipated inflation hurts people with fixed incomes, savers, and creditors. It redistributes real income away from them and toward others.

- ***Those with Fixed Incomes***   People whose income is fixed see their real income fall when inflation occurs. The classic case is the elderly couple living on a private pension or annuity that provides a fixed amount of nominal income each month. They may have retired in, say, 1991 on what appeared to be an adequate pension. However, by 2008 they would have discovered that inflation has cut the purchasing power of that pension—their real income—by about one-third. Similarly, landlords who receive lease payments of fixed dollar amounts will be hurt by inflation as they receive dollars of declining value over time. Public-sector workers whose incomes are dictated by fixed pay schedules

---

[1] A more precise calculation uses our equation for real income. In our first illustration above, if nominal income rises by 10 percent from $100 to $110 and the price level (index) rises by 6 percent from 100 to 106, then real income has increased as follows:

$$\frac{\$110}{106} \times 100 = \$103.77$$

The 4 percent increase in real income shown by the simple formula in the text is a reasonable approximation of the 3.77 percent yielded by our more precise formula.

may also suffer under inflation. The fixed "steps" (the upward yearly increases) in their pay schedules may not keep up with inflation. Minimum-wage workers and families living on fixed welfare incomes will also be hurt by inflation.

- **Savers**   Unanticipated inflation hurts savers. As prices rise, the real value, or purchasing power, of an accumulation of savings deteriorates. Paper assets such as savings accounts, insurance policies, and annuities that were once adequate to meet rainy-day contingencies or provide for a comfortable retirement decline in real value during inflationary periods. Example: A household may save $1000 in a guaranteed investment certificate (GIC) in a chartered bank at 6 percent annual interest. But if inflation is 13 percent, the real value or purchasing power of that $1000 will be cut to about $938 by the end of the year. Although the saver will receive $1060 (equal to $1000 plus $60 of interest), deflating that $1060 for 13 percent inflation means that its real value is only about $938 (= $1060 ÷ 1.13).

- **Creditors**   Unanticipated inflation harms creditors (lenders). Suppose Manitoba Bank lends Bob $1000, to be repaid in two years. If in that time the price level doubles, the $1000 that Bob repays will have only half the purchasing power of the $1000 he borrowed. Because of inflation, each of those dollars will buy only half as much as it did when the loan was negotiated. As prices go up, the value of the dollar goes down. Thus, the borrower is lent "dear" dollars but, because of inflation, pays back "cheap" dollars. The owners of Manitoba Bank suffer a loss of real income.

Who Is Unaffected or Helped by Inflation?

Some people are unaffected by inflation and others may actually be helped by it. For the second group, inflation redistributes real income toward them and away from others.

- **Those with Flexible Incomes**   Individuals who derive their income solely from social programs are largely unaffected by inflation, because payments are indexed to the CPI. Benefits automatically increase when the CPI increases, preventing erosion of benefits from inflation. Some union workers also get automatic **cost-of-living adjustments (COLAs)** in their pay when the CPI rises, although such increases rarely equal the full percentage rise in inflation.

    Rapid inflation may cause some nominal incomes to spurt ahead of the price level, thereby enhancing their real incomes. For some, the 3 percent increase in nominal income that occurs when inflation is 2 percent may become a 7 percent increase when inflation is 5 percent. As an example, property owners faced with an inflation-induced real-estate boom may be able to raise rents more rapidly than the rate of inflation. Also, some business owners may benefit from inflation. If product prices rise faster than factor prices, business revenues will grow more rapidly than costs. In those cases, the growth rate of profit incomes will outpace the rate of inflation.

- **Debtors**   Unanticipated inflation benefits debtors (borrowers). In our previous example, Manitoba Bank's loss of real income from inflation is Bob's gain of real income. Debtor Bob borrows "dear" dollars but, because of inflation, pays back the principal and interest with "cheap" dollars of which purchasing power has been eroded by inflation. Real income is redistributed away from the owners of Manitoba Bank toward borrowers such as Bob.

cost-of-living adjustment (COLA)
An automatic increase in the income (wages) of workers when inflation occurs.

Anticipated Inflation

The redistribution effects of inflation are less severe or are eliminated altogether if people anticipate inflation and can adjust their nominal incomes to reflect the expected price-level rises. The prolonged inflation that began in the late 1960s prompted many labour unions in the 1970s to insist on labour contracts with cost-of-living adjustment clauses.

Similarly, if inflation is anticipated, the redistribution of income from lender to borrower may be altered. Suppose a lender (perhaps a chartered bank or a credit union) and a borrower (a household) both agree that 5 percent is a fair rate of interest on a one-year loan provided the price level

FIGURE 7·5   The Inflation Premium, and Nominal and Real Interest Rates

The inflation premium—the expected rate of inflation—gets built into the nominal interest rate. Here, the nominal interest rate of 11 percent comprises the real interest rate of 5 percent plus the inflation premium of 6 percent.

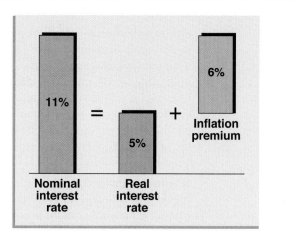

is stable. But assume that inflation has been occurring and is expected to be 6 percent over the next year. If the bank lends the household $100 at 5 percent interest, the bank will be paid back $105 at the end of the year. But if 6 percent inflation does occur during that year, the purchasing power of the $105 will have been reduced to about $99. The lender will in effect have paid the borrower $1 for the use of the lender's money for a year.

The lender can avoid this subsidy by charging an *inflation premium*—that is, by raising the interest rate by 6 percent, the amount of the anticipated inflation. By charging 11 percent, the lender will receive back $111 at the end of the year. Adjusted for the 6 percent inflation, that amount will have the purchasing power of today's $105. The result then will be a mutually agreeable transfer of purchasing power from borrower to lender of $5, or 5 percent, for the use of $100 for one year. Financial institutions have also developed variable-interest-rate mortgages to protect themselves from the adverse effects of inflation. (Incidentally, this example points out that, rather than being a *cause* of inflation, high nominal interest rates are a *consequence* of inflation.)

ORIGIN 7.2
Real Interest Rates

real interest rate
The interest rate expressed in dollars of constant value (adjusted for inflation).

nominal interest rate
The interest rate expressed in terms of annual amounts currently charged for interest and not adjusted for inflation.

deflation
A decline in the economy's price level.

Our example reveals the difference between the real rate of interest and the nominal rate of interest. The **real interest rate** is the percentage increase in *purchasing power* that the borrower pays the lender. In our example the real interest rate is 5 percent. The **nominal interest rate** is the percentage increase in *money* that the borrower pays the lender, including that resulting from the built-in expectation of inflation, if any. In equation form:

Nominal interest rate = real interest rate + inflation premium (the expected rate of inflation)

As illustrated in Figure 7-5, the nominal interest rate in our example is 11 percent.

Other Redistribution Issues

We end our discussion of the redistribution effects of inflation by making three final points.

- *Deflation* The effects of unanticipated **deflation**—declines in the price level—are the reverse of those of inflation. People with fixed nominal incomes will find their real incomes enhanced. Creditors will benefit at the expense of debtors. As prices and wages fall, fixed debt obligations actually rise as a percentage of disposable income. And savers will discover that the purchasing power of their savings has grown because of the falling prices.

- *Mixed Effects* A person who is simultaneously an income earner, a holder of financial assets, and a debtor will probably find that the redistribution impact of inflation is cushioned. If the person owns fixed-value monetary assets (savings accounts, bonds, and insurance policies), inflation will lessen their real value. But that same inflation may produce an increase in the person's nominal wage. Also, if the person holds a fixed-interest-rate mortgage, the real burden of that debt will decline. In short, many individuals are simultaneously hurt and benefitted by inflation. All these effects must be considered before we can conclude that any particular person's net position is better or worse because of inflation.

- *Arbitrariness*   The redistribution effects of inflation occur regardless of society's goals and values. Inflation lacks a social conscience and takes from some and gives to others, whether they are rich, poor, young, old, healthy, or infirm.

QUICK REVIEW

▸ Inflation harms those who receive relatively fixed nominal incomes and either leaves unaffected or helps those who receive flexible nominal incomes.

▸ Unanticipated inflation hurts savers and creditors while benefitting debtors.

▸ The nominal interest rate equals the real interest rate plus the inflation premium (the expected rate of inflation).

7.5 | Effects of Inflation on Output

MONEY & INFLATION

Thus far, our discussion has focused on how inflation redistributes a given level of total real income. But inflation may also affect an economy's level of real output (and thus its level of real income). The direction and significance of this effect on output depends on the type of inflation and its severity.

Cost-Push Inflation and Real Output

Recall that abrupt and unexpected rises in key resource prices can drive up overall production costs sufficiently to cause cost-push inflation. As prices rise, the quantity of goods and services demanded falls. So, firms respond by producing less output, and unemployment goes up.

Demand-Pull Inflation and Real Output

Economists do not fully agree on the effects of mild inflation (less than 3 percent) on real output. One perspective is that even low levels of inflation reduce real output, because inflation diverts time and effort toward activities designed to hedge against inflation. Examples:

- Businesses must incur the cost of changing thousands of prices on their shelves and in their computers simply to reflect inflation.

- Households and businesses must spend time and effort obtaining the information they need to distinguish between real and nominal values such as prices, wages, and interest rates.

- To limit the loss of purchasing power from inflation, people try to limit the amount of money they hold in their wallets and chequing accounts at any one time and instead put more money into interest-bearing accounts and stock and bond funds. But cash and cheques are needed in even greater amounts to buy the higher-priced goods and services, so banking transactions become more frequent.

Without inflation, these uses of resources, time, and effort would not be needed and they could be diverted toward producing more valuable goods and services. Proponents of "zero inflation" bolster their case by pointing to cross-country studies that indicate lower rates of inflation are associated with higher rates of economic growth.

In contrast, other economists point out that full employment and economic growth depend on strong levels of total spending. Such spending creates high profits, strong demand for labour, and a powerful incentive for firms to expand their plant and equipment. In this view, the mild inflation that is a by-product of this strong spending is a small price to pay for full employment and continued economic growth. Moreover, a little inflation may have positive effects because it makes it easier for firms to adjust real wages downward when the demands for their products fall. With mild inflation, firms can reduce real wages by holding nominal wages steady. With zero inflation, firms would need to cut nominal wages to reduce real wages. Such cuts in nominal wages are highly visible and may cause considerable worker resistance and labour strife.

Finally, defenders of mild inflation say that it is much better for an economy to err on the side of strong spending, full employment, economic growth, and mild inflation than on the side of weak spending, unemployment, recession, and deflation.

Hyperinflation

hyperinflation
A very rapid rise in the general price level.

All economists agree that **hyperinflation,** which is extraordinarily rapid inflation, can have a devastating impact on real output and employment.

As prices shoot up sharply and unevenly during hyperinflation, people begin to anticipate even more rapid inflation, and normal economic relationships are disrupted. Business owners do not know what to charge for their products. Consumers do not know what to pay. Resource suppliers want to be paid with actual output, rather than with rapidly depreciating money. Money eventually becomes almost worthless and ceases to do its job as a medium of exchange. To hedge against inflation, businesses and individual savers may decide to buy nonproductive wealth—jewels, gold and other precious metals, real estate, and so forth—rather than invest in capital equipment. The economy may be thrown into a state of barter, and production and exchange drop further. The net result is economic collapse and, often, political chaos.

Examples of hyperinflation are Germany after World War I and Japan after World War II. In Germany, "prices increased so rapidly that waiters changed the prices on the menu several times during the course of a lunch. Sometimes customers had to pay double the price listed on the menu when they ordered."[2] In post-war Japan, in 1947 "fisherman and farmers…used scales to weigh currency and change, rather than bothering to count it."[3]

There are also more recent examples: Between June 1986 and March 1991 the cumulative inflation in Nicaragua was 11,895,866,143 percent. From November 1993 to December 1994 the cumulative inflation rate in the Democratic Republic of Congo was 69,502 percent. From February 1993 to January 1994 the cumulative inflation rate in Serbia was 156,312,790 percent.[4]

Such dramatic hyperinflations are always the consequence of highly imprudent expansions of the money supply by government. The rocketing money supply produces frenzied total spending and severe demand-pull inflation. Zimbabwe's 26,000 percent in 2007 is just the latest example.

---

[2] Theodore Morgan, *Income and Employment*, 2nd ed. (Englewood Cliffs, NJ: Prentice-Hall, 1952), p. 361.

[3] Raburn M. Williams, *Inflation! Money, Jobs, and Politicians* (Arlington Heights, IL: AHM Publishing Corporation, 1980), p. 2.

[4] Stanley Fischer, Ratna Sahay, and Carlos Végh, "Modern Hyper- and High Inflations," *Journal of Economic Literature* (September 2002), p. 840.

The LAST WORD   The Stock Market and the Economy

How, if at all, do changes in stock prices relate to macroeconomic fluctuations?

Every day, the individual stocks (ownership shares) of thousands of corporations are bought and sold in the stock market. The owners of the individual stocks receive dividends—a portion of that firm's profit. Supply and demand in the stock market determine the price of each firm's stock, with individual stock prices generally rising and falling in concert with the collective expectations for each firm's profits. Greater profits normally result in higher dividends to the shareholders, and in anticipation of higher dividends people are willing to pay a higher price for the stock.

The media closely monitor and report stock market averages such as the weighted-average price of the stocks of 100 major Canadian firms, called the S&P/TSX composite index (TSX refers to the Toronto Stock Exchange and S&P refers to Standard & Poor's). It is common for these price averages to change over time, or even to rise or fall sharply during a single day.

On "Black Monday," October 19, 1987, the S&P/TSX composite fell by 20 percent. A sharp drop in stock prices also occurred in October 1997, mainly in response to rapid declines in stock prices in Hong Kong and other Southeast Asian stock markets. In contrast, the stock market averages rose in 1999 and 2000, with the S&P/TSX composite rising, respectively, 31 percent and 6 percent in those two years. Between early September 2008 and early March 2009, stock markets around the world dropped precipitously with the spreading global financial crisis. The S&P/TSX

lost almost 42 percent during that period, but by June 2009 had recovered all of that loss.

The volatility of the stock market raises this question: Do changes in stock price averages and thus stock market wealth cause macroeconomic instability? There are linkages between the stock market and the economy that might lead us to answer yes. Consider a sharp increase in stock prices. Feeling wealthier, shareholders respond by increasing their spending (the *wealth effect*). Firms react by increasing their purchases of new capital goods, because they can finance such purchases through issuing new shares of high-valued stock (the *investment effect*). Of course, sharp declines in stock prices would produce the opposite results.

Studies find that changes in stock prices do affect consumption and investment, but that these consumption and investment impacts are relatively weak. For example, a 10 percent sustained increase in stock market values in one year is associated with a 4 percent increase in consumption spending over the next three years. The investment response is even weaker. So, typical day-to-day and year-to-year changes in stock market values have little impact on the macroeconomy.

In contrast, *stock market bubbles* can be detrimental to an economy. Such bubbles are huge run-ups of overall stock prices, caused by excessive optimism and frenzied buying. The rising stock values are unsupported by realistic prospects of the future strength of the economy and the firms operating in it. Rather than slowly decompressing, such bubbles may burst and cause harm to the economy. The freefall of stock values, if long lasting, causes reverse wealth effects. The stock market crash may also create an overall pessimism about the economy that undermines consumption and investment spending even further.

A related question: Even though typical changes in stock prices do not cause recession or inflation, might they predict such maladies? That is, since stock market values are based on expected profits, wouldn't we expect rapid changes in stock price averages to forecast changes in future business conditions? Indeed, stock prices often do fall prior to recessions and rise prior to expansions. For this reason stock prices are among a group of 10 variables that constitute an index of leading indicators (The Last Word, Chapter 10). Such an index may provide a useful clue to the future direction of the economy. But taken alone, stock market prices are not a reliable predictor of changes in GDP. Stock prices have fallen rapidly in some instances with no recession following. Black Monday itself did not produce a recession during the following two years. In other instances, recessions have occurred with no prior decline in stock market prices.

Question

Why might substantial, unexpected changes in real GDP have more impact on stock market values than substantial, unexpected changes in stock market values have on real GDP?

CHAPTER SUMMARY

7.1 ▶ THE BUSINESS CYCLE

- Canada and other industrial economies have gone through periods of fluctuations in real GDP, employment, and price level. Although they have certain phases in common—peak, recession, trough, expansion—business cycles vary greatly in duration and intensity.

- Although economists explain the business cycle in terms of underlying causal factors such as major innovations, productivity shocks, money creation, and financial crises, they generally agree that the level of total spending is the immediate determinant of real output and employment.

- The business cycle affects all sectors of the economy, though in varying ways and degrees. The cycle has greater effects on output and employment in the capital goods and durable consumer goods industries than in the services and nondurable goods industries.

7.2 ▶ UNEMPLOYMENT

- Economists distinguish among frictional, structural, cyclical, and seasonal unemployment. The full-employment or natural rate of unemployment, which is made up of frictional and structural unemployment, is currently between 6 and 7 percent. The presence of part-time and discouraged workers makes it difficult to measure unemployment accurately.

- The GDP gap, which can be either a positive or a negative value, is found by subtracting potential GDP from actual GDP. The economic cost of unemployment, as measured by the GDP gap, consists of the goods and services forgone by society when its resources are involuntarily idle. Okun's law suggests that every increase in unemployment by 1 percent above the natural rate causes an additional 2 percent negative GDP gap.

- Unemployment rates vary widely globally. Unemployment rates differ because nations have different natural rates of unemployment and often are in different phases of their business cycles.

7.3 ▶ INFLATION

- Inflation is a rise in the general price level and is measured in Canada by the Consumer Price Index (CPI). When inflation occurs, each dollar of income will buy fewer goods and services than before. That is, inflation reduces the purchasing power of money.

- Economists distinguish between demand-pull and cost-push (supply-side) inflation. Demand-pull inflation results from an excess of total spending relative to the economy's capacity to produce. The main source of cost-push inflation is abrupt and rapid increases in the prices of key resources. These supply shocks push up per-unit production costs and ultimately the prices of consumer goods.

7.4 ▶ REDISTRIBUTION EFFECTS OF INFLATION

- Unanticipated inflation arbitrarily redistributes real income at the expense of people with a fixed income, creditors, and savers. If inflation is anticipated, individuals and businesses may be able to take steps to lessen or eliminate adverse redistribution effects.

- When inflation is anticipated, lenders add an inflation premium to the interest rate charged on loans. The nominal interest rate thus reflects the real interest rate plus the inflation premium (the expected rate of inflation).

7.5 ▶ EFFECTS OF INFLATION ON OUTPUT

- Cost-push inflation reduces real output and employment. Proponents of zero inflation argue that even mild demand-pull inflation (1 to 3 percent) reduces the economy's real output. Other economists say that mild inflation may be a necessary by-product of the high and growing spending that produces high levels of output, full employment, and economic growth.

- Hyperinflation, caused by highly imprudent expansions of the money supply, may undermine the monetary system and cause severe declines in real output.

TERMS AND CONCEPTS

business cycle, p. 146
peak, p. 146
recession, p. 146
trough, p. 146
expansion, p. 146
labour force, p. 150
unemployment rate, p. 150
discouraged workers, p. 151
frictional unemployment, p. 151
structural unemployment, p. 151
cyclical unemployment, p. 152

seasonal unemployment, p. 152
natural rate of unemployment (NRU), p. 152
potential GDP, p. 152
GDP gap, p. 153
Okun's law, p. 153
inflation, p. 157
Consumer Price Index (CPI), p. 157
demand-pull inflation, p. 160
cost-push inflation, p. 160

per-unit production cost, p. 160
nominal income, p. 162
real income, p. 162
unanticipated inflation, p. 162
anticipated inflation, p. 162
cost-of-living adjustment (COLA), p. 163
real interest rate, p. 164
nominal interest rate, p. 164
deflation, p. 164
hyperinflation, p. 166

STUDY QUESTIONS

LO 7.1 1. **KEY QUESTION**   What are the four phases of the business cycle? How long do business cycles last? How do seasonal variations and long-run trends complicate measurement of the business cycle? Why does the business cycle affect output and employment in capital goods industries and consumer durable goods industries more severely than in industries producing consumer nondurables?

LO 7.2 2. What factors make it difficult to determine the unemployment rate? Why is it difficult to distinguish among frictional, structural, and cyclical unemployment? Why is unemployment an economic problem? What are the consequences of a GDP gap? What are the non-economic effects of unemployment?

LO 7.2 3. **KEY QUESTION**   Use the following data to calculate (a) the size of the labour force and (b) the official unemployment rate: total population, 500; population under 15 years of age or institutionalized, 120; not in labour force, 150; unemployed, 23; part-time workers looking for full-time jobs, 10.

LO 7.2 4. Since Canada has an employment insurance program that provides income for those out of work, why should we worry about unemployment?

LO 7.2 5. **KEY QUESTION**   Assume that in a particular year the natural rate of unemployment is 5 percent and the actual rate of unemployment is 9 percent. Use Okun's law to determine the size of the GDP gap in percentage-point terms. If the nominal GDP is $500 billion in that year, how much output is being forgone because of cyclical unemployment?

LO 7.3 6. Explain how an increase in your nominal income and a decrease in your real income might occur simultaneously. Who loses from inflation? Who loses from unemployment? If you had to choose between (a) full employment with a 6 percent annual rate of inflation and (b) price stability with an 8 percent unemployment rate, which would you choose? Why?

7. What is the Consumer Price Index (CPI) and how is it determined each month? How does Statistics Canada calculate the rate of inflation from one year to the next? What effect does inflation have on the purchasing power of a dollar? On the gap, if any, between nominal and real interest rates? How does deflation differ from inflation? **LO 7.3**

8. **KEY QUESTION**   If the CPI was 110 last year and is **LO 7.3** 121 this year, what is this year's rate of inflation? What is the "rule of 70"? How long would it take for the price level to double if inflation persisted at (a) 2 percent, (b) 5 percent, and (c) 10 percent per year?

9. Distinguish between demand-pull and cost-push inflation. **LO 7.4** Which of the two types is most likely to be associated with a (negative) GDP gap? Which with a positive GDP gap (in which actual GDP exceeds potential GDP)?

10. Evaluate as accurately as you can how each of the **LO 7.4** following individuals would be affected by unanticipated inflation of 10 percent per year:

   a. A pensioned railroad worker

   b. A department-store clerk

   c. A unionized automobile assembly-line worker

   d. A heavily indebted farmer

   e. A retired business executive whose current income comes entirely from interest on government bonds

   f. The owner of an independent small-town department store

11. Explain how hyperinflation might lead to a severe decline **LO 7.5** in total output.

INTERNET APPLICATION QUESTIONS

1. **What Is the Current Canadian Unemployment Rate?** Use the links on the McConnell-Brue-Flynn-Barbiero Web site (Chapter 7) to access Statistics Canada's Web site. What is the unemployment rate for the current month? How does it compare to the unemployment rate in the previous month? In what provinces did the unemployment increase or decrease?

2. **What Is the Current Canadian Inflation Rate?** Use the links on the McConnell-Brue-Flynn-Barbiero Web site (Chapter 7) to access Statistics Canada's Web site. What is the change in the CPI for the current month? How does it compare to the inflation rate in the previous month? Which of the sub-categories experienced the highest rise in prices?

www.mcgrawhillconnect.ca

Macroeconomic Models and Fiscal Policy

CHAPTER 8

Basic Macroeconomic Relationships*

In Chapter 7 we discussed the business cycle, unemployment, and inflation. Our eventual goal is to build economic models that can explain these phenomena. This chapter begins that process by examining basic relationships that exist between three different pairs of economic aggregates. (Recall that to economists "aggregate" means "total" or "combined.") Specifically, this chapter looks at the relationships between:

- income and consumption (and income and saving),
- the interest rate and investment, and
- changes in spending and changes in output.

What explains the trends in consumption (consumer spending) and saving reported in the news? How do changes in interest rates affect investment? How can initial changes in spending ultimately produce multiplied changes in GDP? The basic macroeconomic relationships discussed in this chapter answer these questions.

---

* Note to instructors: If you wish to bypass the aggregate expenditures model covered in full in Chapter 9, assigning the present chapter will provide a seamless transition to the AD–AS model of Chapter 10 and the chapters beyond. If you want to cover the aggregate expenditures model, this chapter provides the necessary building blocks.

8.1 | The Income-Consumption and Income-Saving Relationships

The other-things-equal relationship between income and consumption is one of the best-established relationships in macroeconomics. In examining that relationship, we are also exploring the relationship between income and saving. Economists define *personal saving* as "not spending" or as "that part of disposable (after-tax) income not consumed." Saving (*S*) equals disposable income (DI) *minus* consumption (*C*).

Many factors determine a nation's levels of consumption and saving, but the most significant is disposable income. Consider some recent historical data for Canada. In Figure 8-1 each dot represents

FIGURE 8-1 | Consumption and Disposable Income, 1985–2008

Each dot in this figure shows consumption and disposable income in a specific year. The line *C*, which generalizes the relationship between consumption and disposable income, indicates a direct relationship and shows that households consume most of their income.

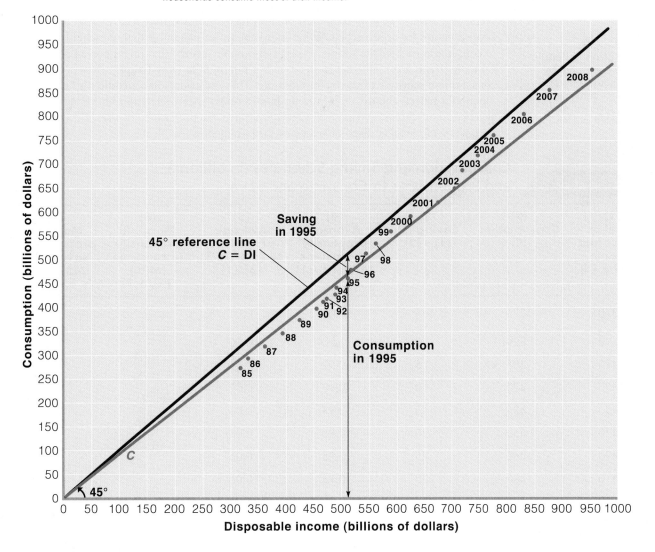

SOURCE: Statistics Canada, *National Income and Expenditure Accounts*, various years.

consumption and disposable income for one year since 1985. The line *C* fitted to these points shows that consumption is directly (positively) related to disposable income; moreover, households spend a large part of their income.

But we can say more. The **45° (degree) line** is a reference line. Because it bisects the 90° angle formed by the two axes of the graph, each point on it is equidistant from the two axes. At each point on the 45° line, consumption equals disposable income, or $C = DI$. Therefore the vertical distance between the 45° line and any point on the horizontal axis measures either consumption *or* disposable income. If we let it measure disposable income, the vertical distance between it and the line labelled *C* represents the amount of saving (*S*) in that year.

Saving is the amount by which actual consumption in any year falls short of the 45° line ($S = DI - C$). For example, in 2008 disposable income was $952 billion and consumption was $891 billion, so saving was $61 billion. Observe that the vertical distance between the 45° line and line *C* increases as we move rightward along the horizontal axis and decreases as we move leftward. Like consumption, saving varies directly with the level of disposable income: as DI rises, saving increases; as DI falls, saving decreases.

The Consumption Schedule

The dots in Figure 8-1 represent the actual amounts of DI, *C*, and *S* in Canada over a period of years. But, because we want to understand how the economy would behave under different possible scenarios, we need a schedule that shows the various amounts that households would plan to consume at each of the various levels of disposable income that might prevail at some time. Columns 1 and 2 of Table 8-1, represented in **Figure 8-2a (Key Graph)**, show a hypothetical consumption schedule of the type we require. This **consumption schedule** (or "consumption function") reflects the direct consumption–disposable income relationship. Note that, in the aggregate, households increase their spending as their disposable income rises and spend a larger proportion of a smaller disposable income than a larger disposable income.

Margin notes

45° (degree) line
A reference line that bisects the 90° angle formed by the two axes, and along which consumption equals disposable income.

ORIGIN 8.1
Income-Consumption Relationship

consumption schedule
A schedule showing the amounts households plan to spend for consumer goods at different levels of disposable income.

TABLE 8-1

Consumption and Saving Schedules (in billions) and Propensities to Consume and Save

(1) Level of output and income (GDP = DI)	(2) Consumption (C)	(3) Saving (S) (1) – (2)	(4) Average propensity to consume (APC) (2)/(1)	(5) Average propensity to save (APS) (3)/(1)	(6) Marginal propensity to consume (MPC) Δ(2)/Δ(1)*	(7) Marginal propensity to save (MPS) Δ(3)/Δ(1)*
(1) $370	$375	$–5	1.01	–0.01		
					0.75	0.25
(2) 390	390	0	1.00	0.00		
					0.75	0.25
(3) 410	405	5	0.99	0.01		
					0.75	0.25
(4) 430	420	10	0.98	0.02		
					0.75	0.25
(5) 450	435	15	0.97	0.03		
					0.75	0.25
(6) 470	450	20	0.96	0.04		
					0.75	0.25
(7) 490	465	25	0.95	0.05		
					0.75	0.25
(8) 510	480	30	0.94	0.06		
					0.75	0.25
(9) 530	495	35	0.93	0.07		
					0.75	0.25
(10) 550	510	40	0.93	0.07		

* The Greek letter Δ, delta, means "the change in."

KEY GRAPH

FIGURE 8-2 Consumption and Saving Schedules

The two parts of this figure show the income-consumption and income-saving relationships in Table 8-1 graphically. The saving schedule in (b) is found by subtracting the consumption schedule in (a) vertically from the 45° line. Consumption equals disposable income (and saving thus equals zero) at $390 billion for these hypothetical data.

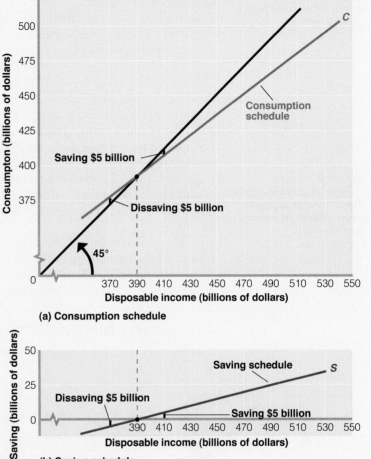

(a) Consumption schedule

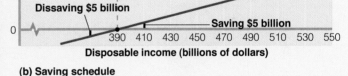

(b) Saving schedule

Quick Quiz

1. **The slope of the consumption schedule in this figure is 0.75. Thus the**
   a. slope of the saving schedule is 1.33.
   b. marginal propensity to consume is 0.75.
   c. average propensity to consume is 0.25.
   d. slope of the saving schedule is also 0.75.

2. **In this figure, when consumption is a positive amount, saving**
   a. must be a negative amount.
   b. must also be a positive amount.
   c. can be either a positive or a negative amount.
   d. is zero.

3. **In this figure,**
   a. the marginal propensity to consume is constant at all levels of income.
   b. the marginal propensity to save rises as disposable income rises.
   c. consumption is inversely (negatively) related to disposable income.
   d. saving is inversely (negatively) related to disposable income.

4. **When consumption equals disposable income,**
   a. the marginal propensity to consume is zero.
   b. the average propensity to consume is zero.
   c. consumption and saving must be equal.
   d. saving must be zero.

Answers: 1. b; 2. c; 3. a; 4. d

The Saving Schedule

saving schedule
A schedule that shows the amounts households plan to save at different levels of disposable income.

It is relatively simple to derive a **saving schedule** (or "saving function"). Because saving equals disposable income less consumption ($S = DI - C$), we need only subtract consumption (Table 8-1, column 2) from disposable income (column 1) to find the amount saved (column 3) at each DI. Thus, columns 1 and 3 in Table 8-1 are the saving schedule, represented in Figure 8-2b. The graph shows there is a direct relationship between saving and DI but that saving is a smaller proportion of a small DI than of a large DI.

Since at each point on the 45° line consumption equals DI, we see dissaving at relatively low DIs, such as $370 billion (row 1, Table 8-1), at which consumption is $375 billion. Households can consume more than their current income by liquidating (selling for cash) accumulated wealth or by borrowing. Graphically, dissaving is shown as the vertical distance of the consumption schedule above the 45° line or as the vertical distance of the saving schedule below the horizontal axis. We have marked the dissaving at the $370 billion level of income in Figures 8-2a and b. Both vertical distances measure the $5 billion of dissaving that occurs at $370 billion of income.

break-even income
The level of disposable income at which households plan to consume all their income and to save none of it.

In our example, the **break-even income** is $390 billion (row 2). This is the income level at which households plan to consume their entire incomes ($C = DI$). Graphically, the consumption schedule cuts the 45° line, and the saving schedule cuts the horizontal axis (saving is zero) at the break-even income level.

At all higher incomes, households plan to save part of their income. Graphically, the vertical distance that the consumption schedule lies below the 45° line measures this saving, as does the vertical distance that the saving schedule lies above the horizontal axis. For example, at the $410 billion level of income (row 3), both these distances indicate $5 billion of saving (also see Figures 8-2a and b).

Average and Marginal Propensities

Columns 4 to 7 in Table 8-1 show additional characteristics of the consumption and saving schedules.

8.1 | GLOBAL PERSPECTIVE

Average propensities to consume, selected nations

There are surprisingly large differences in average propensities to consume (APCs) among nations. Canada and the United States in particular have substantially higher APCs, and thus lower APSs, than other advanced economies.

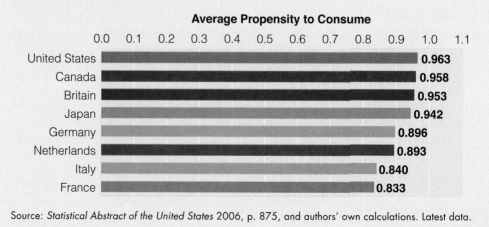

Average Propensity to Consume

United States	0.963
Canada	0.958
Britain	0.953
Japan	0.942
Germany	0.896
Netherlands	0.893
Italy	0.840
France	0.833

Source: *Statistical Abstract of the United States* 2006, p. 875, and authors' own calculations. Latest data.

APC AND APS

average propensity to consume (APC)
The fraction (or percentage) of disposable income that households plan to spend for consumer goods and services.

The fraction, or percentage, of total income that is consumed is the **average propensity to consume (APC)**. The fraction of total income that is saved is the **average propensity to save (APS)**. That is,

$$APC = \frac{consumption}{income}$$

and

average propensity to save (APS)
The fraction (or percentage) of disposable income that households save.

$$APS = \frac{saving}{income}$$

For example, at $470 billion of income (row 6) in Table 8-1, the APC is 450/470 = 45/47, or about 96 percent, and the APS is 20/470 = 2/47, or about 4 percent. Columns 4 and 5 in Table 8-1 show the APC and APS at each of the 10 levels of DI; note in the table that the APC falls and the APS rises as DI increases, as was implied in our previous comments.

Because disposable income is either consumed or saved, the fraction of any DI consumed plus the fraction saved (not consumed) must exhaust that income. Mathematically, APC + APS = 1 at any level of disposable income, as columns 4 and 5 in Table 8-1 illustrate.

Global Perspective 8.1 shows APCs for several countries.

MPC AND MPS

marginal propensity to consume (MPC)
The fraction (or percentage) of any change in disposable income spent for consumer goods.

The proportion, or fraction, of any change in income consumed is called the **marginal propensity to consume (MPC)**, *marginal* meaning "extra" or "a change in." The MPC is the ratio of a change in consumption to the change in the income that caused the consumption change:

$$MPC = \frac{change\ in\ consumption}{change\ in\ income}$$

marginal propensity to save (MPS)
The fraction (or percentage) of any change in disposable income that households save.

Similarly, the fraction of any change in income saved is the **marginal propensity to save (MPS)**. The MPS is the ratio of a change in saving to the change in income that brought it about:

$$MPS = \frac{change\ in\ saving}{change\ in\ income}$$

If disposable income is $470 billion (row 6 horizontally in Table 8-1) and household income rises by $20 billion to $490 billion (row 7), households will consume $^{15}/_{20}$, or $^{3}/_{4}$, and save $^{5}/_{20}$, or $^{1}/_{4}$, of that increase in income. In other words, the MPC is $^{3}/_{4}$ or 0.75, and the MPS is $^{1}/_{4}$ or 0.25, as shown in columns 6 and 7.

The sum of the MPC and the MPS for any change in disposable income must always be 1. Consuming or saving out of extra income is an either/or proposition; the fraction of any change in income not consumed is, by definition, saved. Therefore the fraction consumed (MPC) plus the fraction saved (MPS) must exhaust the whole change in income: MPC + MPS = 1. In our example, 0.75 plus 0.25 equals 1.

MPC AND MPS AS SLOPES

WORKED PROBLEM 8.1
Consumption and Saving

The MPC is the numerical value of the slope of the consumption schedule, and the MPS is the numerical value of the slope of the saving schedule. We know from the appendix to Chapter 1 that the slope of any line is the ratio of the vertical change to the horizontal change.

Figure 8-3 shows how the slopes of the consumption and saving lines are calculated, using enlarged portions of Figures 8-2a and 8-2b. Observe that consumption changes by $15 billion (vertical change) for each $20 billion change in disposable income (horizontal change). The slope of the consumption line is thus 0.75 (= $15/$20)—the value of the MPC. Saving changes by $5 billion (vertical change) for every $20 billion change in disposable income (horizontal change). The slope of the saving line therefore is 0.25 (= $5/$20), which is the value of the MPS. *(Key Question 5)*

Non-Income Determinants of Consumption and Saving

The amount of disposable income is the main determinant of the amounts households will consume and save. But certain determinants other than income will cause households to consume more or less at each possible level of income and thereby shift the consumption and saving schedules. Those other determinants are wealth, borrowing, expectations, and real interest rates.

WEALTH

wealth effect
A downward shift of the saving schedule and an upward shift of the consumption schedule due to higher asset wealth.

A household's wealth is the dollar amount of all the assets that it owns minus the dollar amount of its liabilities (all the debt that it owes). Households build wealth by saving money out of current income. The point of building wealth is to increase consumption possibilities. The larger the stock of wealth that a household can build up, the larger will be its present and future consumption possibilities.

Events sometimes suddenly boost the value of existing wealth. When this happens, households tend to increase their spending and reduce their saving. This so-called **wealth effect** shifts the consumption schedule upward and the saving schedule downward. They move in response to households taking advantage of the increased consumption possibilities afforded by the sudden increase in wealth. Examples: In the late 1990s, skyrocketing stock values expanded the value of household wealth by increasing the value of household assets. Predictably, households spent more and saved less. In contrast, a modest "reverse wealth effect" occurred in 2000 and 2001, when stock prices dropped.

BORROWING

Household borrowing also affects consumption. When a household borrows, it can increase current consumption beyond what would be possible if its spending were limited to its DI.[1] By allowing households to spend more, borrowing shifts the current consumption schedule upward. But note that "there's no free lunch." While borrowing in the present allows for higher consumption in the present, it necessitates lower consumption in the future when the debts must be repaid. Stated a bit differently, increased borrowing increases debt (liabilities), which in turn reduces household wealth (since wealth = assets – liabilities). This reduction in wealth reduces future consumption possibilities

---

FIGURE 8-3   **The Marginal Propensity to Consume and the Marginal Propensity to Save**

The MPC is the slope (ΔC/ΔDI) of the consumption schedule, and MPS is the slope (ΔS/ΔDI) of the saving schedule. The Greek letter delta (Δ) means "the change in."

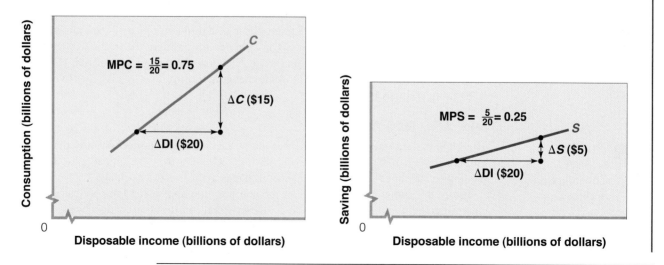

---

[1] Households can also maintain or increase current consumption by dipping into past savings.

in much the same way that a decline in asset values would. But note that the term "reverse wealth effect" is reserved for situations in which wealth unexpectedly changes because asset values unexpectedly change. It is not used to refer to situations such as the one being discussed here, where wealth is intentionally reduced by households through borrowing and piling up debt in order to increase current consumption.

EXPECTATIONS

Household expectations about future prices and income affect current spending and saving. For example, expectations of rising prices tomorrow may trigger more spending and less saving today. Thus, the current consumption schedule shifts up and the current saving schedule shifts down. Or, expectations of lower income in the future may result in less consumption and more saving today. If so, the consumption schedule will shift down and the saving schedule will shift up.

REAL INTEREST RATES

When real interest rates (those adjusted for inflation) fall, households tend to borrow more, consume more, and save less. A lower interest rate, for example, induces consumers to purchase automobiles and other goods bought on credit. A lower interest rate also diminishes the incentive to save because of the reduced interest "payment" to the saver. These effects on consumption and saving, however, are very modest. Lower interest rates shift the consumption schedule slightly upward and the saving schedule slightly downward. Higher interest rates do the opposite.

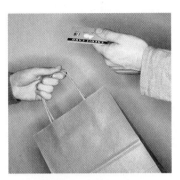

Expectations of rising prices tomorrow may trigger more spending and less saving today

More on Consumption and Saving Schedules

We need to make several additional points about the consumption and saving schedules:

- **Switch to Real GDP**   When developing macroeconomic models, economists change their focus from the relationship between consumption (and saving) and disposable income to the relationship between consumption (and saving) and real domestic output (real GDP). That modification is reflected in Figures 8-4a and 8-4b, where the horizontal axes measure real GDP.

- **Changes along Schedules**   The movement from one point to another on a consumption schedule (for example, from a to b on C_0 in Figure 8-4a)—a change in the amount consumed— is solely caused by a change in disposable income (or GDP). On the other hand, an upward or downward shift of the entire schedule—for example, a shift from C_0 to C_1 or C_2 in Figure 8-4a—is a shift of the consumption schedule and is caused by changes in any one or more of the four non-income determinants of consumption just discussed. A similar distinction in terminology applies to the saving schedule in Figure 8-4b.

- **Schedule Shifts**   Changes in wealth, borrowing, expectations, and real interest rates will shift the consumption schedule in one direction and the saving schedule in the opposite direction. If households decide to consume more at each possible level of real GDP they must save less, and vice versa. (Even when they spend more by borrowing, they are in effect reducing their current saving by the amount borrowed since borrowing is, effectively, "negative saving.") Graphically, if the consumption schedule shifts from C_0 to C_1 in Figure 8-4a, the saving schedule will shift downward, from S_0 to S_1 in Figure 8-4b. Similarly, a downward shift of the consumption schedule from C_0 to C_2 means an upward shift of the saving schedule from S_0 to S_2.

- **Taxation**   In contrast, a change in taxes shifts the consumption and saving schedules in the same direction. Taxes are paid partly at the expense of consumption and partly at the expense of saving. So an increase in taxes will reduce both consumption and saving, shifting the consumption schedule in Figure 8-4a and the saving schedule in Figure 8-4b downward. Conversely, households will partly consume and partly save any decrease in taxes. Both the consumption schedule and saving schedule will shift upward.

⌐ KEY GRAPH   @

FIGURE 8-4 Shifts in the Consumption and Saving Schedules

Normally, if households consume more at each level of real GDP, they are necessarily saving less. Graphically this means that an upward shift of the consumption schedule (C_0 to C_1) entails a downward shift of the saving schedule (S_0 to S_1). If households consume less at each level of real GDP, they are saving more. A downward shift of the consumption schedule (C_0 to C_2) is reflected in an upward shift of the saving schedule (S_0 to S_2). (This pattern breaks down, however, when taxes change; then the consumption and saving schedules shift in the same direction—opposite to the direction of the tax change.)

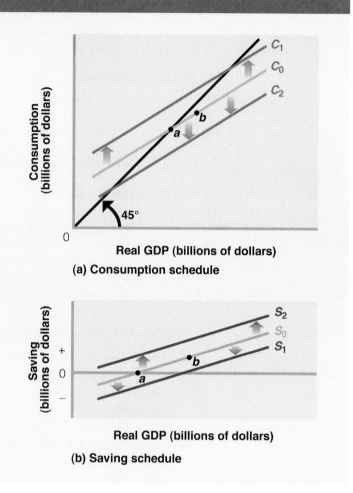

(a) Consumption schedule

(b) Saving schedule

The consumption schedule is relatively stable even during rather extraordinary times. Between March 2000 and July 2002, the Canadian stock market lost hundreds of billions of value. Yet consumption spending was greater at the end of that period than at the beginning. How can that be? Why didn't a "reverse wealth effect" reduce consumption? There are a number of reasons. Of greatest importance, the amount of consumption spending in the economy depends mainly on the *flow* of income, not the *stock* of wealth. Disposable income (DI) in Canada is almost $1 trillion annually, and consumers spend a large portion

of it. Even though the economy slowed down in 2001, DI and consumption spending were both greater in July 2002 than in March 2000. Second, household wealth did not fall by the full amount of the stock market loss because the market value of houses increased over this period. Finally, lower interest rates during this period enabled many households to refinance their mortgages, reduce monthly loan payments, and increase their current consumption. For all these offsetting reasons, the general consumption-income relationship of Figure 8-2 held steady in the face of extraordinary loss of stock market value.

- *Stability*   The consumption and saving schedules are usually relatively stable unless altered by major tax increases or decreases. Their stability may be because consumption–saving decisions are strongly influenced by long-term considerations such as saving to meet emergencies or saving for retirement. It may also be because changes in the non-income determinants frequently work in opposite directions and therefore may cancel each other out.

QUICK REVIEW

▶ Consumption spending and saving both rise when disposable income increases; both fall when disposable income decreases.

▶ The average propensity to consume (APC) is the fraction of disposable income that is spent on consumer goods; the average propensity to save (APS) is the fraction of disposable income that is saved. The APC falls and the APS rises as disposable income increases.

▶ The marginal propensity to consume (MPC) is the fraction of a change in disposable income that is consumed and is the slope of the consumption schedule; the marginal propensity to save (MPS) is the fraction of a change in disposable income that is saved and is the slope of the saving schedule.

▶ Changes in consumer wealth, borrowing, expectations, and real interest rates can shift the consumption and saving schedules (as they relate to real GDP).

8.2 | The Interest Rate–Investment Relationship

Recall that investment consists of expenditures on new plants, capital equipment, machinery, inventories, and so on. The investment decision is a marginal-benefit–marginal-cost decision: The marginal benefit from investment is the expected rate of return businesses hope to realize. The marginal cost is the interest rate that must be paid for borrowing funds. Business will invest in all projects for which the expected rate of return exceeds the interest rate. Expected returns (profits) and the interest rate therefore are the two basic determinants of investment spending.

Expected Rate of Return

Investment spending is guided by the profit motive; businesses buy capital goods only when such purchases will be profitable. Suppose the owner of a small cabinet-making shop is considering whether to invest in a new sanding machine that costs $1000 and has a useful life of only one year. The new machine will increase the firm's output and sales revenue. Suppose the net expected revenue from the machine (that is, after such operating costs as power, lumber, labour, and certain taxes have been subtracted) is $1100. Then, after the $1000 cost of the machine is subtracted from the net expected revenue of $1100, the firm will have an expected profit of $100. Dividing this $100 profit by the $1000 cost of the machine, we find that the **expected rate of return,** r, on the machine is 10 percent (= $100/$1000). Note that this is an *expected* rate of return, not a *guaranteed* rate of return. The investment may or may not generate as much revenue or as much profit as anticipated. Investment involves risk.

expected rate of return
The increase in profit a firm anticipates it will obtain by purchasing capital.

The Real Interest Rate

One important cost associated with investing that our example has ignored is interest—the financial cost of borrowing the *money* capital required to purchase the *real* capital (the sanding machine).

The interest cost is computed by multiplying the interest rate, i, by the $1000 amount borrowed to buy the machine. If the interest rate is, say, 7 percent, the total interest cost will be $70. This compares favourably with the net expected return of $100, which produced the 10 percent rate of return. We can generalize as follows: If the expected rate of return (say, 10 percent) exceeds the interest rate (say, 7 percent), the investment will be profitable. But if the interest rate (say, 12 percent) exceeds the expected rate of return (10 percent), the investment will be unprofitable. The firm undertakes all profitable investment projects. That means it invests up to the point where $r = i$, because then it has undertaken all investment for which r exceeds i.

The *real* rate of interest, rather than the *nominal* rate, is crucial in making investment decisions. Recall from Chapter 7 that the nominal interest rate is expressed in dollars of current value, but the real interest rate is stated in dollars of constant or inflation-adjusted value. The *real interest rate* is the nominal rate less the rate of inflation. In our sanding machine illustration, our implicit assumption of a constant price level ensures that all our data, including the interest rate, are in real terms. *(Key Question 7)*

Investment Demand Curve

We now move from a single firm's investment decision to total demand for investment goods by the entire business sector. Assume that every firm has estimated the expected rates of return from all investment projects and has recorded those data. We can cumulate—successively sum—these data by asking: How many dollars' worth of investment projects have an expected rate of return of, say, 16 percent or more? Of 14 percent or more? Of 12 percent or more? And so on.

Suppose no prospective investments yield an expected return of 16 percent or more. But suppose there are $5 billion of investment opportunities with expected rates of return between 14 and 16 percent; an additional $5 billion yielding between 12 and 14 percent; still an additional $5 billion yielding between 10 and 12 percent; and an additional $5 billion in each successive 2 percent range of yield down to and including the 0 to 2 percent range.

To cumulate these figures for each rate of return, r, we add the amounts of investment that will yield each particular rate of return r or higher. In this way we obtain the data in Table 8-2, shown graphically in **Figure 8-5 (Key Graph)**. In Table 8-2 the number opposite 12 percent, for example, tells us there are $10 billion of investment opportunities that will yield an expected rate of return of 12 percent or more. The $10 billion includes the $5 billion of investment expected to yield a return of 14 percent or more plus the $5 billion expected to yield between 12 and 14 percent.

 MATH 8.1 Investment Demand Curve

We know from our example of the sanding machine that an investment project will be profitable, and will be undertaken, if its expected rate of return, r, exceeds the real interest rate, i. Let's first suppose i is 12 percent. Businesses will undertake all investments for which r is equal to or exceeds 12 percent. Figure 8-5 reveals that $10 billion of investment spending will be undertaken at a 12 percent interest rate; that means $10 billion of investment projects have an expected rate of return of 12 percent or more.

TABLE 8-2	**Rates of Expected Return and Investment**
Expected rate of return (r)	**Cumulative amount of investment having this rate of return or higher, billions per year**
16%	$ 0
14	5
12	10
10	15
8	20
6	25
4	30
2	35
0	40

KEY GRAPH

FIGURE 8-5   The Investment Demand Curve

The investment demand curve is constructed by arraying all potential investment projects in descending order of their expected rates of return. The curve is downward-sloping, reflecting an inverse relationship between the real interest rate (the financial "price" of each dollar of investing) and the quantity of investment demanded.

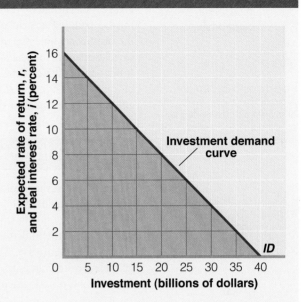

Quick Quiz

1. The investment demand curve:
   a. reflects a direct (positive) relationship between the real interest rate and investment.
   b. reflects an inverse (negative) relationship between the real interest rate and investment.
   c. shifts to the right when the real interest rate rises.
   d. shifts to the left when the real interest rate rises.

2. In this figure:
   a. greater cumulative amounts of investment are associated with lower expected rates of return on investment.
   b. lesser cumulative amounts of investment are associated with lower expected rates of return on investment.
   c. higher interest rates are associated with higher expected rates of return on investment, and therefore greater amounts of investment.
   d. interest rates and investment move in the same direction.

3. In this figure, if the real interest rate falls from 6 to 4 percent:
   a. investment will increase from 0 to $30 billion.
   b. investment will decrease by $5 billion.
   c. the expected rate of return will rise by $5 billion.
   d. investment will increase from $25 billion to $30 billion.

4. In this figure, investment will be:
   a. zero if the real interest rate is zero.
   b. $40 billion if the real interest rate is 16 percent.
   c. $30 billion if the real interest rate is 4 percent.
   d. $20 billion if the real interest rate is 12 percent.

Answers: 1. b; 2. a; 3. d; 4. c

ORIGIN 8.2
Interest-Rate–
Investment
Relationship

investment demand curve
A curve that shows the amount of investment demanded by an economy at a series of real interest rates.

By applying the marginal-benefit–marginal-cost rule that investment projects should be undertaken up to the point where $r = i$, we see that we can add the real interest rate to the vertical axis in Figure 8-5. The curve in Figure 8-5 shows not only rates of return, but also the quantity of investment demanded at each "price" i (interest rate) of investment. The vertical axis in Figure 8-5 shows the various possible real interest rates, and the horizontal axis shows the corresponding quantities of investment demanded. The inverse (downward-sloping) relationship between the interest rate (price) and dollar quantity of investment demanded conforms with the law of demand discussed in Chapter 3. The curve ID in Figure 8-5 is the economy's **investment demand curve.** It shows the amount of investment forthcoming at each real interest rate. *(Key Question 8)*

8.3 | Shifts in the Investment Demand Curve

Figure 8-5 shows the relationship between the interest rate and the amount of investment demanded, other things equal. When other things change, the investment demand curve shifts. In general, any factor that leads businesses collectively to expect greater rates of return on their investments increases investment demand; that factor shifts the investment demand curve to the right, as from ID_0 to ID_1 in Figure 8-6. Any factor that leads businesses collectively to expect lower rates of return on their investments shifts the curve to the left, as from ID_0 to ID_2. What are those non–interest rate determinants of investment demand?

Acquisition, Maintenance, and Operating Costs

The initial costs of capital goods, and the estimated costs of operating and maintaining those goods, affect the expected rate of return on investment. When costs fall, the expected rate of return from prospective investment projects rises, shifting the investment demand curve to the right. Example: Lower electricity costs associated with operating equipment shifts the investment demand curve to the right. Higher costs, in contrast, shift the curve to the left.

Business Taxes

When government is considered, firms look to expected returns *after taxes* in making their investment decisions. An increase in business taxes lowers the expected profitability of investments and shifts the investment demand curve to the left; a reduction of business taxes shifts it to the right.

FIGURE 8-6   Shifts in the Investment Demand Curve

Increases in investment demand are shown as rightward shifts in the investment demand curve; decreases in investment demand are shown as leftward shifts in the investment demand curve.

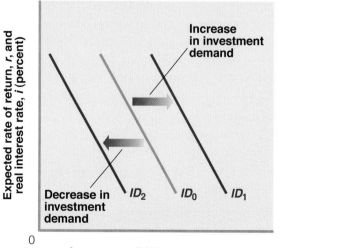

Technological Change

Technological progress stimulates investment.

Technological progress—the development of new products, improvements in existing products, and the creation of new machinery and production processes—stimulates investment. The development of a more efficient machine, for example, lowers production costs or improves product quality and increases the expected rate of return from investing in the machine. Profitable new products (for example, cholesterol medications, Internet services, high-resolution televisions, cellular phones, and so on) induce a flurry of investment as firms tool up for expanded production. A rapid rate of technological progress shifts the investment demand curve to the right.

Stock of Capital Goods on Hand

The stock of capital goods on hand, relative to output and sales, influences investment decisions by firms. When the economy is overstocked with production facilities and when firms have excessive inventories of finished goods, the expected rate of return on new investment declines. Firms with excess production capacity have little incentive to invest in new capital. Therefore, less investment is forthcoming at each real interest rate; the investment demand curve shifts leftward.

When the economy is understocked with production facilities and when firms are selling their output as fast as they can produce it, the expected rate of return on new investment increases and the investment demand curve shifts rightward.

Planned Inventory

Recall from Chapter 5 that the definition of investment includes changes in inventories of unsold goods. An increase in inventories is counted as positive investment, while a decrease is counted as negative investment. It is important to remember that some inventory changes are planned, while others are unplanned. Since the investment demand curve deals only with *planned* investment, it is affected only by *planned* changes that firms desire to make to their inventory levels. If firms plan to increase their inventories, the investment demand curve shifts to the right. If firms plan to decrease their inventories, the investment demand curve shifts to the left.

Firms make planned changes to their inventory levels mostly because they are expecting either faster or slower sales. A firm that expects its sales to double in the next year will want to keep more inventory in stock, thereby increasing its investment demand. By contrast, a firm that is expecting slower sales will plan on reducing its inventory, thereby reducing its overall investment demand. But because life often does not turn out as expected, firms often find that the actual amount of inventory investment that they end up making is either greater or less than what they had planned. The size of the gap is, naturally, the dollar amount of their *unplanned* inventory changes. These unplanned inventory adjustments will play a large role in the aggregate expenditures model studied in Chapter 9.

Expectations

We noted that business investment is based on expected returns (expected additions to profit). Most capital goods are durable, with a life expectancy of 10 or 20 years. Thus, the expected rate of return on capital investment depends on the firm's expectations of future sales, future operating costs, and future profitability of the product that the capital helps to produce. These expectations are based on forecasts of future business conditions as well as on such elusive and difficult-to-predict factors as changes in the domestic political climate, the thrust of foreign affairs, population growth, and consumer tastes. If executives become more optimistic about future sales, costs, and profits, the investment demand curve will shift to the right; a pessimistic outlook will shift it to the left.

Global Perspective 8.2 compares investment spending relative to GDP for several nations in a recent year. Domestic real interest rates and investment demand determine the levels of investment relative to GDP.

8.2 | GLOBAL PERSPECTIVE

Gross investment expenditures as a percentage of GDP, selected nations

As a percentage of GDP, investment varies widely by nation. These differences, of course, can change from year to year.

Source: *International Financial Statistics*, International Monetary Fund, www.imf.org. Used with permission.

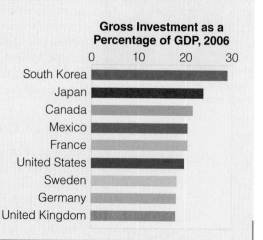

Gross Investment as a Percentage of GDP, 2006

South Korea
Japan
Canada
Mexico
France
United States
Sweden
Germany
United Kingdom

QUICK REVIEW

▸ A specific investment will be undertaken if the expected rate of return, *r*, equals or exceeds the real interest rate, *i*.

▸ The investment demand curve shows the total monetary amounts that will be invested by an economy at various possible real interest rates.

▸ The investment demand curve shifts when changes occur in (a) the costs of acquiring, operating, and maintaining capital goods, (b) business taxes, (c), technology, (d) the stock of capital goods on hand, and (e) business expectations.

Fluctuations of Investment

In contrast to the consumption schedule, the investment schedule fluctuates quite a bit. Investment, in fact, is the most volatile component of total spending—so much so that most of the fluctuations in output and employment that happen over the course of the business cycle can be attributed to increases and decreases in investment. Figure 8-7 shows just how volatile investment in Canada has been. Several factors explain the variability of investment.

DURABILITY

Because of their durability, capital goods have an indefinite useful lifespan. Within limits, purchases of capital goods are discretionary and therefore can be postponed. Firms can scrap or replace older equipment and buildings, or they can patch them up and use them for a few more years. Optimism about the future may prompt firms to replace their older facilities, and such modernizing will call for a high level of investment. A less optimistic view, however, may lead to smaller amounts of investment as firms repair older facilities and keep them in use.

IRREGULARITY OF INNOVATION

We know that technological progress is a major determinant of investment. New products and processes stimulate investment. But history suggests that major innovations such as railroads, electricity, automobiles, fibre optics, and computers occur quite irregularly. When they do happen, they induce a vast upsurge or "wave" of investment spending that in time recedes.

FIGURE 8-7 | **The Volatility of Investment**

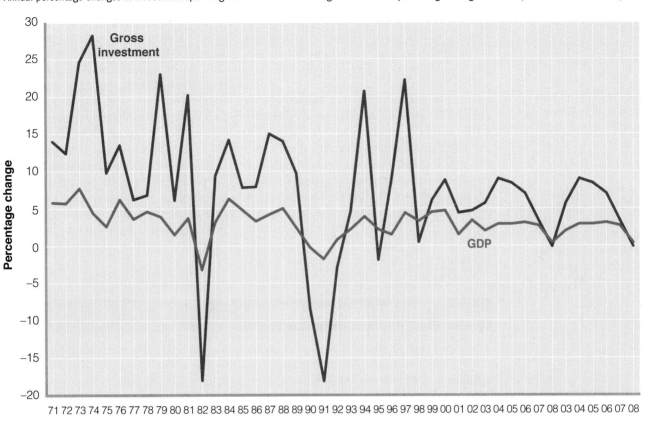

Annual percentage changes in investment spending are often several times greater than the percentage changes in GDP. (Data are in real terms.)

A contemporary example is the tremendous popularity of the personal computer and the Internet, which has caused a wave of investment in those industries and in many related industries such as fibre optics, computer software, and electronic commerce. Sometime in the future, this particular surge of investment undoubtedly will level off. For example, the rapid expansion of fibre optics networks came to a virtual halt in 2001 and 2002 as overcapacity dogged the sector, with dire consequences for such well-known Canadian firms as Nortel Networks and JDS Uniphase.

VARIABILITY OF PROFITS

When evaluating whether to undertake a given investment, a firm's expectations about the potential profitability of that investment are influenced to some degree by the size of the profits currently being earned by other firms that have made similar investments. Current profits, however, are themselves highly variable. Thus, the variability of profits contributes to the volatile nature of the incentive to invest.

Profit fluctuations may cause investment fluctuations in a second way. Profits are a major source of funds for business investment. Canadian businesses sometimes prefer this internal source of financing to increases in external debt or stock issue.

In short, expanding profits give firms both greater incentives and greater means to invest; declining profits have the reverse effects. The fact that actual profits are variable thus adds doubly to the fluctuation of investment.

VARIABILITY OF EXPECTATIONS

Firms tend to project current business conditions into the future. But expectations can change quickly when some event suggests a significant possible change in future business conditions. Changes in exchange rates, changes in the outlook for international peace, court decisions in key labour or anti-combines cases, legislative actions, changes in trade barriers, changes in governmental economic policies, and a host of similar considerations may cause substantial shifts in business expectations.

The stock market can also influence business expectations because firms look to it as one of several indicators of society's overall confidence in future business conditions. Rising stock prices tend to signify public confidence in the business future, whereas falling stock prices may imply a lack of confidence. The stock market, however, is often driven by "herd behaviour" in which financial investors follow the lead of others rather than think independently. When stock prices rise because others are buying, they also buy; when stock prices fall because others are selling, they also sell. This behaviour can greatly magnify the volatility of stock prices that otherwise would be much more stable. Business can easily confuse these large swings in stock prices for real changes in society's optimism or pessimism about future business conditions. If they do, businesses are likely to respond by overadjusting their investment plans one direction or the other. In this way, stock market volatility can add to the instability of investment spending. For all these reasons, changes in investment cause many of the fluctuations in output and employment that occur over the business cycle. In terms of Figures 8-5 and 8-6, we would represent volatility of investment as occasional and substantial shifts in the investment demand curve.

8.4 | The Multiplier Effect*

A final basic relationship that merits discussion is the relationship between changes in spending and changes in real GDP. Assuming that the economy has room to expand—so that increases in spending do not lead to increases in prices—a direct relationship exists between these two aggregates. More spending results in a higher GDP; less spending results in a lower GDP. But there is much more to this relationship. A change in spending—say, investment—ultimately changes output and income by more than the initial change in investment spending. That surprising result is called the *multiplier effect:* a change in a component of total spending leads to a larger change in GDP. The **multiplier** determines how much larger that change will be; it is the ratio of a change in GDP to the initial change in spending (in this case, investment). Stated generally,

multiplier
The ratio of a change in the equilibrium GDP to the change in investment or in any other component of aggregate expenditures.

$$\text{Multiplier} = \frac{\text{change in real GDP}}{\text{initial change in spending}}$$

By rearranging this equation, we can also say that

Change in GDP = multiplier × initial change in spending

Note these three points about the multiplier:

- The "initial change in spending" is usually associated with investment spending because of investment's volatility. But changes in consumption (unrelated to changes in income), net exports, and government purchases also lead to the multiplier effect.

- The "initial change in spending" associated with investment spending results from a change in the real interest rate and/or a shift of the investment demand curve.

---

* Note to instructors: If you cover the full aggregate expenditures model (Chapter 9) rather than moving directly to aggregate demand and aggregate supply (Chapter 10), you may choose to defer this discussion until after the analysis of equilibrium real GDP.

- Implicit in the preceding point is that the multiplier works in both directions. An increase in initial spending will create a multiple increase in GDP; a decrease in spending will create a larger decrease in GDP.

Rationale

The multiplier effect follows from two facts. First, the economy supports repetitive, continuous flows of expenditures and income through which dollars spent by Smith are received as income by Chin and then spent by Chin and received as income by Dubois, and so on. Second, any change in income will vary both consumption and saving in the same direction as, and by a fraction of, the change in income.

It follows that an initial change in spending will set off a spending chain throughout the economy. That chain of spending, although of diminishing magnitude at each successive step, will cumulate to a multiple change in GDP. Initial changes in spending produce magnified changes in output and income.

Table 8-3 illustrates the rationale underlying the multiplier effect. Suppose a $5 billion increase in investment spending occurs. We assume that the MPC is .75, the MPS is .25, and prices remain constant. That is, neither the initial increase in spending nor any of the subsequent increases in spending will cause prices to rise.

The initial $5 billion increase in investment generates an equal amount of wage, rent, interest, and profit income, because spending income and receiving income are two sides of the same transaction. How much consumption will be induced by this $5 billion increase in the incomes of households? We find the answer by applying the marginal propensity to consume of 0.75 to this change in income. Thus, the $5 billion increase in income initially raises consumption by $3.75 (= 0.75 × $5) billion and saving by $1.25 (= 0.25 × $5) billion, as shown in columns 2 and 3 in Table 8-3.

Other households receive as income (second round) the $3.75 billion of consumption spending. Those households consume 0.75 of this $3.75 billion, or $2.81 billion, and save 0.25 of it, or $0.94 billion. The $2.81 billion that is consumed flows to still other households as income to be spent or saved (third round). And the process continues, with the added consumption and income becoming less in each round. The process ends when there is no additional income to spend.

Figure 8-8 extends Table 8-3 and shows the cumulative effects of this full process. Each round adds an orange block to GDP. The accumulation of the additional income in each round—the sum of the orange blocks—is the total change in income or GDP. Although the spending and respending effects of the increase in investment diminish with each successive round, the cumulative increase in output and income will be $20 billion. Thus, the multiplier is 4 (= $20 billion/$5 billion).

TABLE 8-3	The Multiplier: A Tabular Illustration (in billions)		
	(1) Change in income	(2) Change in consumption (MPC = 0.75)	(3) Change in saving (MPS = 0.25)
Increase in investment of $5.00	$ 5.00	$ 3.75	$1.25
Second round	3.75	2.81	0.94
Third round	2.81	2.11	0.70
Fourth round	2.11	1.58	0.53
Fifth round	1.58	1.19	0.39
All other rounds	4.75	3.56	1.19
Total	$20.00	$15.00	$5.00

FIGURE 8-8 **The Multiplier Process (MPC = 0.75)**

An initial change in investment spending of $5 billion creates an equal $5 billion of new income in round 1. Households spend $3.75 (= 0.75 × $5) billion of this new income, creating $3.75 of added income in round 2. Of this $3.75 of new income, households spend $2.81 (= 0.75 × $3.75) billion, and income rises by that amount in round 3. The cumulation of such income increments over the entire process eventually results in a total change of income and GDP of $20 billion. The multiplier therefore is 4 (= $20 billion ÷ $5 billion).

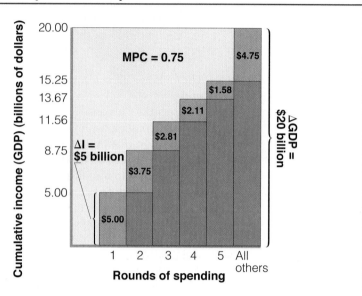

The Multiplier and the Marginal Propensities

You may have sensed from Table 8-3 that the fraction of an increase in income consumed (MPC) and saved (MPS) determines the cumulative respending effects of any initial change in spending and therefore determines the size of the multiplier. *The MPC and the multiplier are directly related and the MPS and the multiplier are inversely related.* The precise formulas are as shown in the next two equations:

$$\text{Multiplier} = \frac{1}{1 - \text{MPC}}$$

Recall, too, that MPC + MPS = 1. Therefore MPS = 1 − MPC, which means we can also write the multiplier formula as

$$\text{Multiplier} = \frac{1}{\text{MPS}}$$

This latter formula is a quick way to determine the multiplier. All you need to know is the MPS.

The smaller the fraction of any change in income saved, the greater the respending at each round and, therefore, the greater the multiplier. When the MPS is 0.25, as in our example, the multiplier is 4. If the MPS were 0.2, the multiplier would be 5. If the MPS were 0.33, the multiplier would be 3. Let's see why.

Suppose the MPS is 0.2 and businesses increase investment by $5 billion. In the first round of Table 8-3, consumption will rise by $4 billion (= MPC of 0.8 × $5 billion) rather than by $3.75 billion because saving will increase by $1 billion (MPS of 0.2 × $5 billion) rather than $1.25 billion. The greater rise in consumption in round one will produce a greater increase in income in round two. The same will be true for all successive rounds. If we worked through all rounds of the multiplier, we would find that the process ends when income has cumulatively increased by $25 billion, not the $20 billion shown in the table. When the MPS is 0.2 rather than 0.25, the multiplier is 5 (= $25 billion/$5 billion) as opposed to 4 (= $20 billion/$5 billion.)

If the MPS were 0.33 rather than 0.25, the successive increases in consumption and income would be less than those in Table 8-3. We would discover that the process ended with a $15 billion increase in income rather than the $20 billion shown. When the MPS is 0.33, the multiplier is 3 (= $15 billion/

$5 billion). The mathematics works such that the multiplier is equal to the reciprocal of the MPS. The reciprocal of any number is the quotient you obtain by dividing 1 by that number.

A large MPC (small MPS) means the succeeding rounds of consumption spending shown in Figure 8-9 diminish slowly and thereby cumulate to a large change in income. Conversely, a small MPC (a large MPS) causes the increases in consumption to decline quickly, so the cumulative change in income is small. The relationship between the MPC (and thus the MPS) and multiplier is summarized in Figure 8-9.

WORKED PROBLEM 8.2
Multiplier Effect

How Large Is the Actual Multiplier Effect?

The multiplier we have just described is based on simplifying assumptions. Consumption of domestic output rises by the increases in income minus the increases in saving. But in reality, consumption of domestic output increases in each round by a lesser amount than implied by the MPS alone. In addition to saving, households use some of the extra income in each round to purchase additional goods from abroad (imports) and pay additional taxes. Because spending on imports and taxes does not directly create new income in the Canadian economy, the 1/MPS formula for the multiplier overstates the actual size of the multiplier effect. We can correct this problem by changing the multiplier equation to read: "1 divided by the fraction of the change in income that is not spent on domestic output." Also, we will find in later chapters that an increase in spending may be partly dissipated as inflation rather than realized fully as an increase in real GDP. This happens when increases in spending drive up prices. The multiplier process still happens, but it induces a much smaller change in real output because at higher prices any given amount of spending buys less real output. Thus, the actual multiplier for the Canadian economy is well under 2 in magnitude. *(Key Question 9)*

FIGURE 8-9   **The MPC and the Multiplier**

The larger the MPC (the smaller the MPS), the greater the size of the multiplier.

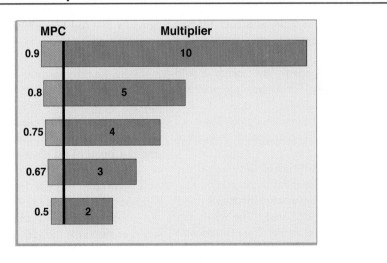

QUICK REVIEW

▸ The multiplier effect reveals that an initial change in spending can cause a larger change in domestic income and output. The multiplier is the factor by which the initial change is magnified: multiplier = change in real GDP/initial change in spending.

▸ The higher the marginal propensity to consume (the lower the marginal propensity to save), the larger the multiplier: multiplier = 1/MPS.

The LAST WORD   Squaring the Economic Circle

Humorist Art Buchwald examines the multiplier.

The recession hit so fast that nobody knows exactly how it happened. One day we were the land of milk and honey and the next day we were the land of sour cream and food stamps.

This is one explanation.

Hofberger, the Ford salesman, called up Littleton, of Littleton Menswear & Haberdashery, and said, "Good news, the new [Fords] have just come in and I've put one aside for you and your wife."

Littleton said, "I can't, Hofberger, my wife and I are getting a divorce."

"I'm sorry," Littleton said, "but I can't afford a new car this year. After I settle with my wife, I'll be lucky to buy a bicycle."

Hofberger hung up. His phone rang a few minutes later.

"This is Bedcheck the painter," the voice on the other end said. "When do you want us to start painting your house?"

"I changed my mind," said Hofberger, "I'm not going to paint the house."

"But I ordered the paint," Bedcheck said. "Why did you change your mind?"

"Because Littleton is getting a divorce and he can't afford a new car."

That evening when Bedcheck came home his wife said, "The new color television set arrived from Gladstone's TV shop."

"Take it back," Bedcheck told his wife.

"Why?" she demanded.

"Because Hofberger isn't going to have his house painted now that the Littletons are getting a divorce."

The next day Mrs. Bedcheck dragged the TV set in its carton back to Gladstone. "We don't want it."

Gladstone's face dropped. He immediately called his travel agent, Sandstorm. "You know that trip you had scheduled for me to the Virgin Islands?"

"Right, the tickets are all written up."

"Cancel it. I can't go. Bedcheck just sent back the color TV set because Hofberger didn't sell a car to Littleton because they're going to get a divorce and she wants all his money."

Sandstorm tore up the airline tickets and went over to see his banker, Gripsholm. "I can't pay back the loan this month because Gladstone isn't going to the Virgin Islands."

Gripsholm was furious. When Rudemaker came in to borrow money for a new kitchen he needed for his restaurant, Gripsholm turned him down cold. "How can I loan you money when Sandstorm hasn't repaid the money he borrowed?"

Rudemaker called up the contractor, Eagleton, and said he couldn't put in a new kitchen. Eagleton laid off eight men.

Meanwhile, Ford announced it was giving a rebate on its new models. Hofberger called up Littleton immediately. "Good news," he said, "even if you are getting a divorce, you can afford a new car."

"I'm not getting a divorce," Littleton said. "It was all a misunderstanding and we've made up."

"That's great," Hofberger said. "Now you can buy the [Ford]."

"No way," said Littleton. "My business has been so lousy I don't know why I keep the doors open."

"I didn't realize that," Hofberger said.

"Do you realize I haven't seen Bedcheck, Gladstone, Sandstorm, Gripsholm, Rudemaker or Eagleton for more than a month? How can I stay in business if they don't patronize my store?"

SOURCE: Art Buchwald, "Squaring the Economic Circle," *Cleveland Plain Dealer*, Feb. 22, 1975. Reprinted by permission.

Question

What is the central economic idea humorously demonstrated in Art Buchwald's piece, "Squaring the Economic Circle"? How does the central idea relate to recessions, on the one hand, and vigorous expansion on the other?

CHAPTER SUMMARY

8.1 ▶ THE INCOME-CONSUMPTION AND INCOME-SAVING RELATIONSHIPS

- Other things equal, there is a direct (positive) relationship between income and consumption and income and saving. The consumption and saving schedules show the various amounts that households intend to consume and save at the various income and output levels, assuming a fixed price level.

- The average propensities to consume and save show the fractions of any total income that are consumed and saved: APC + APS = 1. The marginal propensities to consume and save show the fractions of any change in total income that is consumed and saved: MPC + MPS = 1.

- The locations of the consumption and saving schedules (as they relate to real GDP) are determined by (a) the amount of wealth owned by households; (b) expectations of future income, future prices, and product availability; (c) the relative size of household debt; and (d) taxation. The consumption and saving schedules are relatively stable.

8.2 ▶ THE INTEREST RATE–INVESTMENT RELATIONSHIP

- The immediate determinants of investment are (a) the expected rate of return and (b) the real interest rate. The economy's investment demand curve is found by cumulating investment projects, arraying them in descending order according to their expected rates of return, graphing the result, and applying the rule that investment will be profitable up to the point at which the real interest rate, i, equals the expected rate of return, r. The investment demand curve reveals an inverse relationship between the interest rate and the level of aggregated investment.

8.3 ▶ SHIFTS IN THE INVESTMENT DEMAND CURVE

- Shifts in the investment demand curve can occur as the result of changes in (a) the acquisition, maintenance, and operating costs of capital goods; (b) business taxes; (c) technology; (d) the stocks of capital goods on hand; and (e) expectations.

- Either changes in interest rates or shifts in the investment demand curve can shift the investment schedule.

- The durability of capital goods, the variability of expectations, and the irregular occurrence of major innovations all contribute to the high fluctuations in investment spending.

8.4 ▶ THE MULTIPLIER EFFECT

- Through the multiplier effect, an increase in investment spending (or consumption spending, government purchases, or net export) ripples through the economy, ultimately creating a magnified increase in real GDP. The multiplier is the ultimate change in GDP divided by the initiating change in investment or some other component of spending.

- The multiplier is equal to the reciprocal of the marginal propensity to save: the greater the marginal propensity to save, the smaller the multiplier. Also, the greater the marginal propensity to consume, the larger the multiplier.

TERMS AND CONCEPTS

45° (degree) line, p. 172
consumption schedule, p. 172
saving schedule, p. 174
break-even income, p. 174
average propensity to consume (APC), p. 175

average propensity to save (APS), p. 175
marginal propensity to consume (MPC), p. 175
marginal propensity to save (MPS), p. 175

wealth effect, p. 176
expected rate of return, p. 179
investment demand curve, p. 182
multiplier, p. 186

STUDY QUESTIONS

LO 8.1 1. Very briefly summarize what relationships are shown by (a) the consumption schedule, (b) the saving schedule, (c) the investment demand curve, and (d) the investment schedule. Which of these relationships are direct relationships and which are inverse (negative) relationships? Why are consumption and saving in Canada greater today than they were a decade ago?

LO 8.1 2. Precisely how are the APC and the MPC different? Why must the sum of the MPC and the MPS equal 1? What are the basic determinants of the consumption and saving schedules? of your own level of consumption?

LO 8.1 3. Explain how each of the following will affect the consumption and saving schedules (as they relate to real GDP) or the investment schedule, other things being equal.

   a. A large increase in the value of real estate, including private houses.

   b. A decline in the real interest rate.

   c. A sharp, sustained decline in stock prices.

   d. An increase in the rate of population growth.

   e. The development of a cheaper method of manufacturing computer chips.

   f. A sizable increase in the age for collecting retirement benefits.

   g. An increase in the federal personal income tax.

LO 8.1 4. Explain why an upward shift of the consumption schedule typically involves an equal downward shift of the saving schedule. What is the exception to this relationship?

LO 8.1 5. **KEY QUESTION**   Complete the following table:

   a. Show the consumption and saving schedules graphically.

   b. Find the break-even level of income. Explain how it is possible for households to dissave at very low income levels.

   c. If the proportion of total income consumed (APC) decreases and the proportion saved (APS) increases as income rises, explain both verbally and graphically how the MPC and MPS can be constant at various levels of income.

6. What are the basic determinants of investment? Explain **LO 8.2** the relationship between the real interest rate and the level of investment. Why is investment spending less stable than consumption spending and saving?

7. **KEY QUESTION**   Suppose a handbill publisher can buy **LO 8.2** a new duplicating machine for $500 and the duplicator has a one-year life. The machine is expected to contribute $50 to the year's net revenue. What is the expected rate of return? If the real interest rate at which funds can be borrowed to purchase the machine is 8 percent, should the publisher choose to invest in the machine? Explain.

8. **KEY QUESTION**   Assume there are no investment projects **LO 8.3** in the economy that yield an expected rate of return of 25 percent or more. But suppose there are $10 billion of investment projects yielding expected returns of between 20 and 25 percent; another $10 billion yielding between 15 and 20 percent; another $10 billion between 10 and 15 percent; and so forth. Cumulate these data and present them graphically, putting the expected rate of return on the vertical axis and the amount of investment on the horizontal axis. What will be the equilibrium level of aggregate investment if the real interest rate is (a) 15 percent, (b) 10 percent, and (c) 5 percent? Explain why this curve is the investment demand curve.

Level of output and income (GDP = DI)	Consumption	Saving	APC	APS	MPC	MPS
$240	$____	$−4	___	___	___	___
260	____	0	___	___	___	___
280	____	4	___	___	___	___
300	____	8	___	___	___	___
320	____	12	___	___	___	___
340	____	16	___	___	___	___
360	____	20	___	___	___	___
380	____	24	___	___	___	___
400	____	28	___	___	___	___

LO ▸ 8.4 9. **KEY QUESTION**   What is the multiplier effect? What relationship does the MPC bear to the size of the multiplier? the MPS? What will the multiplier be when the MPS is 0, 0.4, 0.6, and 1? What will it be when the MPC is 1, 0.90, 0.67, 0.50, and 0? How much of a change in GDP will result if firms increase their level of investment by $8 billion and the MPC is 0.80? if the MPC is 0.67?

LO ▸ 8.4 10. **Advanced Analysis** Linear equations for the consumption and saving schedules take the general form $C = a + bY$ and $S = -a + (1 - b)Y$, where C, S, and Y are consumption, saving, and national income, respectively. The constant a represents the vertical intercept, and b the slope of the consumption schedule.

   a. Use the following data to determine numerical values for a and b in the consumption and saving equations:

National income (Y)	Consumption (C)
$ 0	$ 80
100	140
200	200
300	260
400	320

   b. What is the economic meaning of b? Of $(1 - b)$?

   c. Suppose the amount of saving that occurs at each level of national income falls by $20, but that the values of b and $(1 - b)$ remain unchanged. Restate the saving and consumption equations for the new numerical values, and cite a factor that might have caused the change.

11. **Advanced Analysis** Suppose the linear equation for consumption in a hypothetical economy is $C = 40 + 0.8Y$. Also suppose that income (Y) is $400. Determine (a) the marginal propensity to consume, (b) the marginal propensity to save, (c) the level of consumption, (d) the average propensity to consume, (e) the level of saving, and (f) the average propensity to save.   **LO ▸ 8.4**

INTERNET APPLICATION QUESTIONS @

1. **Investment Instability—Changes in Nonresidential Structures and Equipment.** Statistics Canada provides data for "nonresidential structures and equipment," which is a component of "business gross fixed capital formation." Access the data through the McConnell-Brue-Flynn-Barbiero Web site (Chapter 8). Have nonresidential structures and equipment been volatile (as measured by the percentage from the previous year)? Looking at the investment data, what investment forecast would you make for the forthcoming year?

CHAPTER 9

The Aggregate Expenditures Model

Two of the most critical questions in macroeconomics are: (1) What determines the level of GDP, given a nation's production capacity? (2) What causes real GDP to rise in one period and to fall in another? To answer these questions, we construct the aggregate expenditures (AE) model, which has its origins in the 1936 writings of the British economist John Maynard Keynes (pronounced "Caines"). The basic premise of the aggregate expenditures model—also known as the "Keynesian cross" model—is that the amount of goods and services produced, and therefore the level of employment, depends directly on the level of aggregate expenditures (total spending). Business will produce only a level of output it thinks it can profitably sell, and will idle workers and machinery when no markets exists for their goods and services. When aggregate expenditures fall, total output and employment decrease; when aggregate expenditures rise, total output and employment increase.

9.1 | The Aggregate Expenditures Model: Consumption and Saving

We now turn to investigate the details of the aggregate expenditures model. But first let's look at the assumptions underlying the model.

Assumptions and Simplifications

The simplifying assumptions underpinning the aggregate expenditures model reflect the economic conditions prevalent during the Great Depression. As discussed in this chapter's Last Word, Keynes created the model during the middle of the Great Depression in the hopes of understanding both why the Great Depression had happened and how it might be ended.

The most fundamental assumption behind the aggregate expenditures model is that prices in the economy are fixed. In the terminology of Chapter 4, the aggregate expenditures model is an extreme version of a sticky price model. In fact, it is a stuck price model, since prices cannot change at all.

ORIGIN 9.1
Aggregate
Expenditure Model

Keynes made this assumption because the economy during the Great Depression was operating far below its potential output. Real GDP in Canada declined by 25 percent from 1929 to 1933 and the unemployment rate rose to almost 20 percent. Thousands of factories sat idle, gathering dust and producing nothing because nobody wanted to buy their output. To Keynes, this massive unemployment of labour and capital meant that even if a sudden increase in demand occurred, prices were unlikely to rise at all because the massive oversupply of productive resources would keep prices low. Consequently, he focused his attention on how the economy might reach an equilibrium in a situation in which prices were likely to be stuck for a while.

According to Keynes, even if prices are stuck firms will still be able to receive feedback from the markets about how much they should produce. With prices stuck, this feedback obviously cannot come in the form of changing prices. Instead, it comes in the form of unplanned changes in firm inventory levels. As we will explain, these changes can guide firms to an equilibrium level of GDP. Crucially, this equilibrium level of GDP can be well below a nation's potential output—meaning that the aggregate expenditures model can explain the situation of massive unemployment the economy found itself in during the Great Depression.

But the aggregate expenditures model is not just of historical interest. It can be used fruitfully even today because, as we explained in Chapter 4, prices in the modern economy are very sticky and sometimes nearly stuck in the short run. As a result, the aggregate expenditures model can help us to understand how the modern economy is likely to adjust in the short run to various economic shocks including changes in things such as tax rates, government spending, consumption expenditure, and investment spending.

We will build up the aggregate expenditures model in simple stages. Let's first look at aggregate expenditures and equilibrium GDP in a *private closed economy*—one without international trade or government. Then we will open the closed economy to exports and imports, and also convert our private economy to a more realistic mixed economy that includes government purchases (or, more loosely, *government spending*) and taxes.

In addition, until we introduce taxes into the model, we will assume that real GDP equals disposable income (DI). For instance, if $500 billion of output is produced as GDP, households will receive exactly $500 billion of disposable income that they can then consume or save. And, finally, unless specified otherwise we will assume (as Keynes did) that the economy has excess production capacity and unemployed labour, so an increase in aggregate expenditures will increase real output and employment but not raise the price level.

Consumption and Investment Schedules

planned investment
The amount that firms plan or intend to invest.

In the private closed economy, the two components of aggregate expenditures are consumption, C, and gross investment, I_g. Because we examined the *consumption schedule* (Figure 8-2a) in the previous chapter, there is no need to repeat that analysis here. But to add the investment decisions of businesses to the consumption plans of households, we need to construct an investment schedule showing the amounts business firms collectively intend to invest—their **planned investment**—at each possible level of GDP. Such a schedule represents the investment plans of businesses in the same way the consumption schedule represents the consumption plans of households. In developing the investment schedule, we will assume that this planned investment is independent of the level of current disposable income or real output.

investment schedule
A curve or schedule that shows the amounts firms plan to invest at various possible values of real GDP.

Suppose the investment demand curve is as shown in Figure 9-1a and the current real interest rate is 8 percent. This means that firms will find it profitable to spend $20 billion on investment goods. The line I_g (*gross* investment) in Figure 9-1b shows the economy's **investment schedule.** Do not confuse this investment schedule I_g with the investment demand curve ID in Figure 9-1a. The investment schedule shows the amount of investment forthcoming at each level of GDP. As indicated in Figure 9-1, this amount ($20 billion) is determined by the real interest rate together with the location of the investment demand curve. Table 9-1 shows the investment schedule in tabular form. Note that investment (I_g) in column 2 is $20 billion at all levels of real GDP.

FIGURE 9-1   **The Investment Demand Curve and the Investment Schedule**

(a) The level of investment spending (here, $20 billion) is determined by the real interest rate (here, 8 percent) together with the investment demand curve *ID*. (b) The investment schedule I_g relates the amount of investment ($20 billion) determined in (a) to the various levels of GDP.

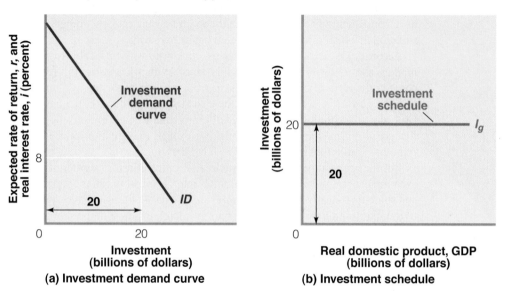

(a) Investment demand curve

(b) Investment schedule

Calculating GDP

Now let's combine the consumption and investment schedules to explain the equilibrium levels of output, income, and employment.

TABULAR ANALYSIS

Columns 2 through 5 in Table 9-2 repeat the consumption and saving schedules in Table 8-1 and the investment schedule in Table 9-1.

TABLE 9-1   **The Investment Schedule (in billions)**

(1) Level of real output and income	(2) Investment (I_g)
$370	$20
390	20
410	20
430	20
450	20
470	20
490	20
510	20
530	20
550	20

- **Real Domestic Output**   Column 2 in Table 9-2 lists the various possible levels of total output—of real GDP—that the private sector might produce. Producers are willing to offer any of these 10 levels of output if they can expect to receive an identical level of income from the sale of that output. For example, firms will produce $370 billion of output, incurring $370 billion of costs (wages, rents, interest, and normal profit costs) only if they believe they can sell that output for $370 billion. Firms will offer $390 billion of output if they think they can sell that output for $390 billion. And so it is for all other possible levels of output.

- **Aggregate Expenditures**   In the private closed economy of Table 9-2, aggregate expenditures consist of consumption (column 3) plus investment (column 5). Their sum is shown in column 6, which along with column 2 makes up the **aggregate expenditures schedule** for the economy. This schedule shows the amount $(C + I_g)$ that will be spent at each possible output or income level. At this point we are working with *planned investment*—the data in column 5, Table 9-2. These data show the amounts firms intend to invest, not the amounts they actually will invest if there are unplanned changes in inventories—more about that shortly.

aggregate expenditures schedule
A schedule or curve that shows the total amount spent for final goods and services at different levels of GDP.

- **Equilibrium GDP**   Of the 10 possible levels of GDP in Table 9-2, which is the equilibrium level? Which total output is the economy capable of sustaining? The equilibrium output is that output which creates total spending just sufficient to produce that output. So the equilibrium level of GDP is the level at which the total quantity of goods produced (GDP) equals the total quantity of goods purchased $(C + I_g)$. If you look at the domestic output levels in column 2 and the aggregate expenditures level in column 6, you will see that this equality exists only at $470 billion of GDP (row 6). There is no overproduction, which would result in a piling up of unsold goods and consequently cutbacks in the production rate. Nor is there an excess of total spending, which would draw down inventories of goods and prompt increases in the rate of production. In short, there is no reason for businesses to alter this rate of production; $470 billion is the **equilibrium GDP**.

equilibrium GDP
The level at which the total quantity of goods produced (GDP) equals the total quantity of goods purchased.

TABLE 9-2	Determination of the Equilibrium Levels of Employment, Output, and Income: A Private Closed Economy						
(1) Possible levels of employment (millions)	(2) Real domestic output (and income) (GDP = DI) (billions)	(3) Consumption (C) (billions)	(4) Saving (S) (billions)	(5) Invest-ment (I_g) (billions)	(6) Aggregate expend-itures (C + I_g) (billions)	(7) Unplanned changes in inventories (+) or (−)	(8) Tendency of employment, output, and income
(1) 2.5	$370	$375	$−5	$20	$395	$−25	Increase
(2) 5.0	390	390	0	20	410	−20	Increase
(3) 7.5	410	405	5	20	425	−15	Increase
(4) 10.0	430	420	10	20	440	−10	Increase
(5) 12.5	450	435	15	20	455	− 5	Increase
(6) 15.0	470	450	20	20	470	0	Equilibrium
(7) 17.5	490	465	25	20	485	+ 5	Decrease
(8) 20.0	510	480	30	20	500	+10	Decrease
(9) 22.5	530	495	35	20	515	+15	Decrease
(10) 25.0	550	510	40	20	530	+20	Decrease

- ***Disequilibrium***   No level of GDP other than the equilibrium level can be sustained. At levels of GDP less than equilibrium, spending always exceeds GDP. If, for example, firms produced $410 billion of GDP (row 3 in Table 9-2), they would find it would yield $405 billion in consumer spending. Supplemented by $20 billion of planned investment, aggregate expenditures $(C + I_g)$ would be $425 billion, as shown in column 6. The economy would provide an annual rate of spending more than sufficient to purchase the $410 billion of annual production. Because buyers would be taking goods off the shelves faster than firms could produce them, an unintended decline in business inventories of $15 billion would occur (column 7). But businesses can adjust to such an imbalance between aggregate expenditures and real output by stepping up production. Greater output will increase employment and total income. This process will continue until the equilibrium level of GDP is reached ($470 billion). The reverse is true at all levels of GDP greater than the $470 billion equilibrium level. Businesses will find that these total outputs fail to generate the spending needed to clear the shelves of goods.

GRAPHICAL ANALYSIS

We can demonstrate the same analysis graphically in **Figure 9-2 (Key Graph)**. Recall that at any point on the 45° line, the value of what is being measured on the horizontal axis (here, GDP) is equal to the value of what is being measured on the vertical axis (here, aggregate expenditures, or $C + I_g$). Having discovered in our tabular analysis that the equilibrium level of domestic output is determined where $C + I_g$ equals GDP, we can say that the 45° line in Figure 9-2 is a graphical statement of that equilibrium condition.

Now we must graph the aggregate expenditures schedule onto Figure 9-2. To do this we duplicate the consumption schedule C in Figure 8-2a and add to it vertically the constant $20 billion amount of investment I_g from Figure 9-1b. This $20 billion is the amount we assumed firms plan to invest at all levels of GDP. Or, more directly, we can plot the $C + I_g$ data in column 6, Table 9-2.

Observe in Figure 9-2 that the aggregate expenditures line $C + I_g$ shows that total spending rises with income and output (GDP), but not as much as income rises. That is true because the marginal propensity to consume—the slope of line C—is less than 1. A part of any increase in income will be saved rather than spent. And because the aggregate expenditures line $C + I_g$ is parallel to the consumption line C, the slope of the aggregate expenditures line also equals the MPC for the economy and is less than 1. For our particular data, aggregate expenditures rise by $15 billion for every $20 billion increase in real output and income because $5 billion of each $20 billion increment is saved. Therefore, the slope of the aggregate expenditures line is 0.75 (=Δ$15/Δ$20).

The equilibrium level of GDP is determined by the intersection of the aggregate expenditures schedule and the 45° line. This intersection locates the only point at which aggregate expenditures (on the vertical axis) are equal to GDP (on the horizontal axis). Because Figure 9-2 is based on the data in Table 9-2, we once again find that equilibrium output is $470 billion. Observe that consumption at this output is $450 billion and investment is $20 billion.

WORKED PROBLEM 9.1
Equilibrium GDP

It is evident from Figure 9-2 that no levels of GDP *above* the equilibrium level are sustainable because at those levels $C + I_g$ falls short of GDP. Underspending causes *inventories to rise*, prompting firms to readjust production downward, in the direction of the $470 billion output level.

Conversely, at levels of GDP *below* $470 billion, $C + I_g$ exceeds total output. This overspending causes inventories to decline, prompting firms to adjust production upward, in the direction of the $470 billion output level. Once production reaches that level, it will be sustained there indefinitely unless some change occurs in the location of the aggregate expenditures line.

Other Features of Equilibrium GDP

We have seen that $C + I_g$ = GDP at equilibrium in the private closed economy. A closer look at Table 9-2 reveals two more characteristics of equilibrium GDP: (1) saving and *planned* investment are equal, and (2) no *unplanned* changes in inventories occur.

KEY GRAPH @

FIGURE 9-2
Equilibrium GDP

The aggregate expenditures schedule, $C + I_g$, is determined by adding the investment schedule I_g to the upward-sloping consumption schedule C. Since investment is assumed to be the same at each level of GDP, the vertical distances between C and $C + I_g$ do not change. Equilibrium GDP is determined where the aggregate expenditures schedule intersects the 45° line, in this case at $470 billion.

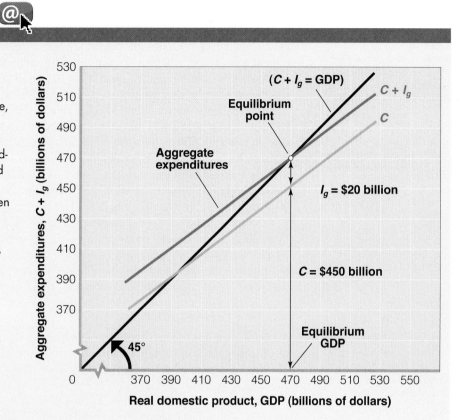

Quick Quiz

1. In this figure, the slope of the aggregate expenditures schedule $C + I_g$:
   a. increases as real GDP increases.
   b. decreases as real GDP increases.
   c. is constant and equals the MPC.
   d. is constant and equals the MPS.

2. At all points on the 45° line:
   a. equilibrium GDP is possible.
   b. aggregate expenditures exceed real GDP.
   c. consumption exceeds investment
   d. aggregate expenditures are less than real GDP.

3. The $490 billion level of real GDP is not at equilibrium because:
   a. investment exceeds consumption.
   b. consumption exceeds investment.
   c. planned $C + I_g$ exceeds real GDP.
   d. planned $C + I_g$ is less than real GDP.

4. The $430 billion level of real GDP is not at equilibrium because:
   a. investment exceeds consumption.
   b. consumption exceeds investment.
   c. planned $C + I_g$ exceeds real GDP.
   d. planned $C + I_g$ is less than real GDP.

Answers: 1. c; 2. a; 3. d; 4. c

SAVING EQUALS PLANNED INVESTMENT

As shown by row 6 in Table 9-2, saving and planned investment are both $20 billion at the $470 billion equilibrium level of GDP. Saving is a **leakage** or withdrawal of spending from the income-expenditures stream. Saving is what causes consumption to be less than total output or GDP. As a result of saving, consumption is insufficient to take all domestic output off the shelves, setting the stage for a decline in total output.

However, firms do not intend to sell their entire output to consumers; some domestic output will consist of capital goods sold within the business sector. Investment can therefore be thought of as an **injection** of spending into the income-expenditures stream. Investment is thus a potential replacement for the leakage of saving.

If the leakage of saving at a certain level of GDP exceeds the injection of investment, then $C + I_g$ will fall short of GDP and that level of GDP cannot be sustained. Any GDP for which saving exceeds investment is an above-equilibrium GDP. This spending deficiency will reduce real GDP.

Conversely, if the injection of investment exceeds the leakage of saving, then $C + I_g$ will be greater than GDP and drive GDP upward. Any GDP for which investment exceeds saving is a below-equilibrium GDP. Only where $S = I_g$—where the leakage of saving of $20 billion is exactly offset by the injection of investment of $20 billion—will aggregate expenditures equal real output. And that $C + I_g$ = GDP equality is what defines the equilibrium GDP. *(Key Question 2)*

NO UNPLANNED CHANGES IN INVENTORIES

As part of their investment plans, firms may decide to increase or decrease their inventories. But, as confirmed in row 6 in Table 9-2, no **unplanned changes in inventories** occur at equilibrium GDP. This fact, along with $C + I_g$ = GDP, and $S = I$, is a characteristic of equilibrium GDP in the private closed economy.

Unplanned changes in inventories play a major role in achieving equilibrium GDP. Consider, as an example, the $490 billion *above-equilibrium* GDP shown in row 7 of Table 9-2. What happens if firms produce that output, thinking they can sell it? Households save $25 billion of their $490 billion DI, so consumption is only $465 billion. Planned investment—which includes *planned* changes in inventories—is $20 billion (column 5). This means that aggregate expenditures ($C + I_g$) are $485 billion and sales fall short of production by $5 billion. Firms retain that extra $5 billion of goods as an *unplanned* increase in inventories (column 7). It results from total spending being less than the amount needed to remove total output from the shelves.

Because changes in inventories are a part of investment, we note that **actual investment** is $25 billion. It consists of $20 billion of planned investment *plus* the $5 billion unplanned increase in inventories. Actual investment exactly equals the saving of $25 billion, even though saving exceeds planned investment by $5 billion. Because firms cannot earn profits by accumulating unwanted inventories, they will cut back production. GDP will fall to its equilibrium level of $470, at which changes in inventories are zero.

Now look at the *below-equilibrium* $450 billion output (row 5, Table 9-2). Because households save only $15 billion of their $450 billion DI, consumption is $435 billion. Planned investment by firms is $20 billion, so aggregate expenditures are $455 billion. Sales exceed production by $5 billion. This is so only because a $5 billion unplanned decrease in business inventories has occurred. Firms must *disinvest* $5 billion in inventories (column 7). Note again that actual investment is $15 billion ($20 billion planned *minus* the $5 billion decline in inventory investment) and is equal to saving of $15 billion, even though planned investment exceeds saving by $5 billion. The unplanned decline in inventories, resulting from the excess of sales over production, will encourage firms to expand production. GDP will rise to $470 billion, at which unplanned changes in inventories are zero.

When economists say differences between investment and saving can occur and bring about changes in equilibrium GDP, they are referring to planned investment and saving. Equilibrium occurs only when planned investment and saving are equal. *But when unplanned changes in inventories are considered, investment and saving are always equal, regardless of the level of GDP.*

leakage
A withdrawal of potential spending from the income-expenditures stream via saving, tax payments, or imports.

injection
An addition of spending to the income-expenditures stream.

unplanned changes in inventory
Changes in inventories that firms did not anticipate.

actual investment
The amount that firms do invest; equal to planned investment plus unplanned investment.

That is true because actual investment consists of planned investment and unplanned investment (unplanned changes in inventories). Unplanned changes in inventories act as a balancing item that equates the actual amounts saved and invested in any period.

9.2 | Changes in Equilibrium GDP and the Multiplier

In the private closed economy, the equilibrium GDP will change in response to changes in either the investment schedule or the consumption schedule. Because changes in the investment schedule usually are the main source of fluctuations, we direct our attention to them.

Figure 9-3 shows the effect of changes in investment spending on the equilibrium real GDP. Suppose the expected rate of return on investment rises or that the real interest rate falls such that investment spending increases by $5 billion. We would show this increase as an upward shift of the investment schedule in Figure 9-1b. In Figure 9-3, the $5 billion increase of investment will shift the aggregate expenditures schedule upward from $(C + I_g)_0$ to $(C + I_g)_1$. Equilibrium real GDP will rise from $470 billion to $490 billion.

If the expected rate of return on investment decreases or if the real interest rate rises, investment spending will decline by, say, $5 billion. That would be shown as a downward shift of the investment schedule in Figure 9-1b and a downward shift of the aggregate expenditures schedule from $(C + I_g)_0$ to $(C + I_g)_2$ in Figure 9-3. Equilibrium GDP will fall from $470 billion to $450 billion.

FIGURE 9·3

Changes in the Equilibrium GDP Caused by Shifts in the Aggregate Expenditures Schedule and the Investment Schedule

An upward shift of the aggregate expenditures schedule from $(C + I_g)_0$ to $(C + I_g)_1$ will increase the equilibrium GDP. A downward shift from $(C + I_g)_0$ to $(C + I_g)_2$ will lower the equilibrium GDP.

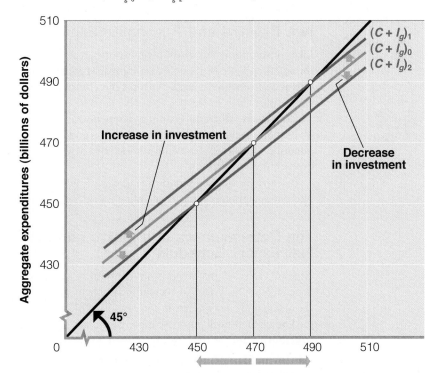

Real domestic product, GDP (billions of dollars)

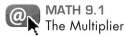

MATH 9.1
The Multiplier

In our examples, a $5 billion change in investment spending leads to a $20 billion change in output and income. So the *multiplier* is 4 (= $20/$5). Recall that the simple multiplier equals 1/MPS. In our example the MPS is 0.25, meaning that for every $1 billion of new income, $0.25 billion of new saving occurs. Therefore, $20 billion of new income is needed to generate $5 billion of new saving. Once that increase in income and saving occurs, the economy is back in equilibrium—$C + I_g$ = GDP; saving and investment are equal; and there are no unintended changes in inventories. You can see, then, that the multiplier process is an integral part of the aggregate expenditures model. (A brief review of Table 8-3 and Figure 8-8 will be helpful at this point.)

QUICK REVIEW

▶ In a private closed economy, equilibrium GDP occurs where aggregate expenditures equal real domestic output ($C + I_g$ = GDP).

▶ At equilibrium GDP, saving equals planned investment ($S = I_g$).

▶ At equilibrium GDP, unplanned changes in inventories are zero.

▶ Actual investment consists of planned investment plus unplanned changes in inventories (+ or –) and is always equal to saving in a private closed economy.

▶ Through the multiplier effect, an initial change in investment spending can cause a magnified change in domestic output.

9.3 | International Trade and Equilibrium Output

We next move from a "closed" economy to an "open" economy that incorporates exports (X) and imports (M). Our focus will be *net exports* (exports minus imports, or X_n), which may be positive or negative.

Net Exports and Aggregate Expenditures

Like consumption and investment, exports create domestic production, income, and employment for a nation. Foreign spending on Canadian goods and services increases production and creates jobs and incomes in Canada. We must therefore add exports as a component of Canada's aggregate expenditures.

Conversely, when an economy is open to international trade, part of its consumption and investment spending will be for imports—goods and services produced abroad rather than in domestic industries. To avoid overstating the value of domestic production, we must subtract expenditures on imports.

In short, for a closed economy, aggregate expenditures are $C + I_g$. But for an open economy with international trade, aggregate spending is $C + I_g + X_n$, where X_n represents ($X - M$).

The Determinants of Imports and Exports and the Net Export Schedule

Note in Table 9-3 that exports are constant at all levels of GDP. This is because our exports are dependent on the GDPs of our trading partners. *If GDP in other countries is growing, we can expect the demand for our exports to increase.* If GDP in the United States increases, we can expect that the United States will purchase more goods and services from Canada. For example, housing construction expands with the economy and, thus, if that sector were to expand in the United States it would translate into higher sales of Canadian lumber. If the United States experiences a recession, our exports would decrease.

TABLE 9-3	Net Export Schedule			
(1) Domestic output (and income) (GDP = DI) (billions)	(2) Exports (X) (billions)	(3) Imports (M) (billions)	(4) Net exports (X_n) (billions) (2) – (3)	(5) Marginal propensity to import (MPM) $\Delta(3)/\Delta(1)$
$370	$40	$15	$25	0.25
390	40	20	20	0.25
410	40	25	15	0.25
430	40	30	10	0.25
450	40	35	5	0.25
470	40	40	0	0.25
490	40	45	– 5	0.25
510	40	50	−10	0.25
530	40	55	−15	0.25
550	40	60	−20	0.25

Our imports are dependent on our own GDP. When the Canadian economy expands, imports also rise. As the Canadian business sector expands and GDP rises, it will require machines and materials from abroad. Likewise, as consumer spending rises, some of it will go to imports.

Imports and exports are also affected by trade policies and the rate at which the Canadian dollar can be exchanged for other currencies. More will be said about trade policy and exchange rates later in this chapter.

Imports and the Multiplier

marginal propensity to import (MPM)
The fraction (or percentage) of any change in GDP spent for imported goods and services.

A hypothetical *net export schedule* is shown in columns 1 to 4 of Table 9-3. Note that although exports are constant at all levels of GDP, imports, and therefore *net* exports (X – M), change by $5 billion for every $20 billion change in GDP. The change in imports divided by a change in GDP is called the **marginal propensity to import (MPM).** In our example the marginal propensity to import is 0.25 (= $5 billion/$20 billion). Just as the marginal propensity to consume is the slope of the consumption schedule, so the marginal propensity to import is the slope of the net export schedule.

For convenience, let's call this new multiplier an "open-economy multiplier." Why does it differ from the multiplier of 4 in the closed economy? Recall that for the closed economy the multiplier is 1/MPS—or, for our data, 1/0.25, or 4. The multiplier is the reciprocal of the MPS, where the MPS is the fraction of any change in national income that "leaks" into saving. Moving to an open economy we add a second leakage—expenditures on imports. Since the marginal propensity to import (MPM) is the fraction of any change in disposable income spent on imports, we must add the MPM to the MPS in the denominator of the multiplier formula. The multiplier for an open economy (without a government sector) is therefore

$$\text{Open economy multiplier} = \frac{1}{\text{MPS} + \text{MPM}}$$

For the data of Table 9-3, the MPM is 5/20, or 0.25, and the open-economy multiplier is

$$\frac{1}{\text{MPS} + \text{MPM}} = \frac{1}{0.25 + 0.25} = \frac{1}{0.5} = 2$$

Note that the open economy multiplier applies to any change in expenditure, whether it originates in the domestic economy, such as a change in I_g, or a change in net exports (X_n). In the next section we investigate the impact of government expenditures and taxation on equilibrium GDP, changes that originate in the domestic economy. Keep in mind that in an open economy any change in either government spending or taxation is subject to the open economy multiplier.

Net Exports and Equilibrium GDP

Let's now include exports and imports in our discussion of income determination. Columns 1 and 2 of Table 9-4 repeat columns 2 and 6 from Table 9-2, where the equilibrium GDP for a closed economy is $470 billion. Columns 3 to 5 of Table 9-4 repeat columns 2 to 4 of Table 9-3. In column 6, we have adjusted the domestic aggregate expenditures of column 2 for net exports, giving us aggregate expenditures for an open economy.

The export and import figures we have selected are such that foreign trade leaves the equilibrium GDP unchanged. Net exports are zero at the closed economy's equilibrium GDP of $470 billion, so aggregate expenditures for the open economy (column 6) equal domestic output (column 1) at $470 billion.

Figure 9-4 shows these results. The $(C + I_g + X_n)_0$ schedule is aggregate expenditures for the open economy. In this case, aggregate expenditures for the open economy intersect domestic output at the same point as do aggregate expenditures for the closed economy, and therefore the $470 billion equilibrium GDP is unchanged by world trade.

TABLE 9-4 — Determinants of the Equilibrium Levels of Output and Income in an Open Economy (without Government)

(1) Domestic output (and income) (GDP = DI) (billions)	(2) Aggregate expenditures for closed economy, without government $(C + I_g)$ (billions)	(3) Exports (X) (billions)	(4) Imports (M) (billions)	(5) Net exports (X_n) (billions) (3) – (4)	(6) Aggregate expenditures for open economy, without government $(C + I_g + X_n)$ (billions) (2) + (5)
$370	$395	$40	$15	$25	$420
390	410	40	20	20	430
410	425	40	25	15	440
430	440	40	30	10	450
450	455	40	35	5	460
470	470	40	40	0	470
490	485	40	45	– 5	480
510	500	40	50	– 10	490
530	515	40	55	– 15	500
550	530	40	60	– 20	510

FIGURE 9-4   Net Exports and the Equilibrium GDP

An increase in net exports raises the aggregate expenditures from $(C + I_g + X_n)_0$ to $(C + I_g + X_n)_2$ and increases the equilibrium GDP. Conversely, a decrease in net exports shifts the aggregate expenditures schedule downward from $(C + I_g + X_n)_0$ to $(C + I_g + X_n)_1$ and lowers the equilibrium GDP.

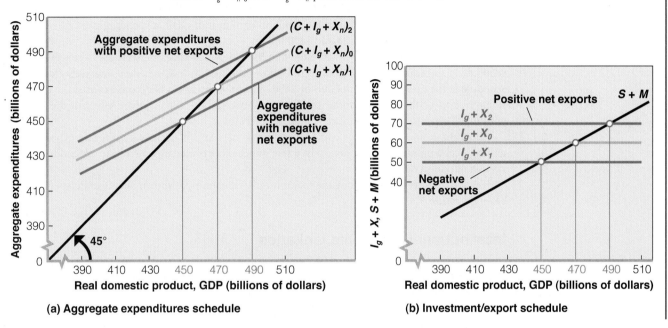

(a) Aggregate expenditures schedule

(b) Investment/export schedule

POSITIVE NET EXPORTS

But there is no reason why net exports will have a neutral effect on equilibrium GDP. For example, by either increasing exports by $10 billion (from $40 to $50 billion) or decreasing imports by $10 billion at each GDP level, net exports become plus $10 billion at the original $470 billion GDP. With an open economy multiplier of 2, an increase in net exports of $10 billion results in a $20 billion increase in GDP. The recalculation of aggregate expenditures in column 6 of Table 9-4 reveals that the equilibrium GDP will shift from $470 to $490 billion.

In Figure 9-4a, the new open economy aggregate expenditures line is $(C + I_g + X_n)_2$, which lies $10 billion above $(C + I_g + X_n)_0$ because of the $10 billion increase in net exports. This creates a $10 billion gap at the original $470 equilibrium GDP, and as a result the equilibrium GDP *increases* to $490 billion.

Figure 9-4b shows the same result. The new $I_g + X_2$ schedule (a $10 billion increase in exports: $I_g + X$ increases from $60 to $70 billion) intersects the $S + M$ schedule at the new equilibrium GDP of $490 billion.

Notice that the increase in GDP by $10 billion is the result of exports being larger than imports. This is true because exports and imports have opposite effects on domestic output. Exports increase real GDP by increasing expenditures on domestically produced output. Imports reduce real GDP by directing expenditures toward output produced abroad. It is only because net exports are positive in this example—so that the expansionary effect of exports outweighs the contractionary effect of imports—that we get the overall increase in real GDP. As the next section shows, if net exports are negative then the contractionary effect of imports will outweigh the expansionary effect of exports and domestic real GDP will decrease.

NEGATIVE NET EXPORTS

By reducing net exports by $10 billion, GDP will fall by $20 billion, given an open economy multiplier of 2. Recalculating aggregate expenditures in column 6 of Table 9-4, the resulting net equilibrium GDP will be $450 billion.

Graphically, the new open-economy aggregate expenditures schedule is shown by $(C + I_g + X_n)_1$ in Figure 9-4a. This schedule lies $10 billion below $(C + I_g + X_n)_0$, reflecting the $10 billion decline in net exports. Thus, at the original $470 billion equilibrium GDP, a spending gap of $10 billion exists, which causes GDP to *decline* to $450 billion.

Figure 9-4b shows the same result. Note that the $I_g + X_0$ schedule intersects the "leakages" $S + M$ schedule at the equilibrium GDP of $470 billion. The new $I_g + X_1$ schedule intersects the $S + M$ schedule at the new equilibrium GDP of $450 billion. When imports exceed exports, the contractionary effect of the larger amount of imports outweighs the expansionary effect of the smaller amount of exports, and equilibrium real GDP decreases.

Generalization: Other things equal, a decline in net exports decreases aggregate expenditures and reduces a nation's GDP; conversely, a rise in net exports increases aggregate expenditures and raises a nation's GDP.

Net exports vary greatly among the major industrial nations, as shown in Global Perspective 9.1. *(Key Question 9)*

International Economic Linkages

Our analysis of net exports and real GDP reveals how circumstances or policies abroad can affect Canadian GDP.

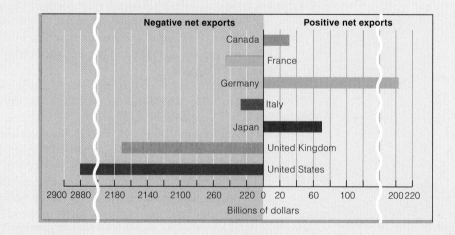

9.1 | GLOBAL PERSPECTIVE

Net exports of goods, selected nations, 2006

Some nations, such as Canada, Japan, and Germany, have positive net exports; other countries, such as the United States and the United Kingdom, have negative net exports.

Source: World Trade Organization, WTO Publications, www.wto.org. Used with permission.

PROSPERITY ABROAD

A rising level of real output and thus income among our trading partners enables Canada to sell more goods abroad, raising Canadian net exports and increasing our real GDP. We should be interested in the prosperity of our trading partners because if they do well they buy more of our exports, increasing our income and making it possible for us to buy more of their imports. Prosperity abroad transfers some of that prosperity to Canadians.

TARIFFS

Suppose our trading partners impose high tariffs on Canadian goods, such as softwood lumber, to reduce their imports and stimulate production in their economies. Their imports, however, are our exports. So when they restrict their imports to stimulate their economies, they are reducing Canadian exports and depressing *our* economy. We may retaliate by imposing trade barriers on their products. If so, their exports will decline and their net exports to us may fall. In the Great Depression of the 1930s various nations, including Canada, imposed trade barriers as a way to reduce domestic unemployment. But rounds of retaliation simply reduced world trade, worsened the depression, and increased unemployment.

EXCHANGE RATES

Depreciation of the Canadian dollar relative to other currencies means the price of Canadian goods in terms of these currencies will fall, stimulating purchases of our exports. Also, Canadian consumers will find foreign goods more expensive and, consequently, will reduce their spending on imports. The increased Canadian exports and decreased imports will increase Canada's net exports and expand the nation's GDP.

Whether depreciation of the dollar will actually raise real GDP or produce inflation depends on the initial position of the economy relative to its full-employment output. If the economy is operating below its full-employment level, prices are likely to be sticky or even stuck due to a large oversupply of unemployed labour and capital. In such a situation, depreciation of the Canadian dollar and the resulting rise in net exports will increase aggregate expenditures and expand real

CONSIDER THIS | The Transmission of the Recession during the Global Economic Downturn of 2008–09

The severe downturn in the United States reduced U.S. imports (other nations' exports). Countries such as Canada and Japan—whose economies depend highly on exports to the United States—therefore were negatively impacted by the U.S. recession. Canada, along with many other nations, suffered from its own financial crises, albeit much less severe than in the U.S. The ensuing domestic economic weaknesses, and the decline in export sales to the United States, helped push the Canadian economy into recession. As our own recessions made us poorer, we cut back on our purchases of U.S. exports. That, in turn, further lowered real GDP in the United States.

Global recessions typically shrink the volume of international trade. This reduces the output gains from specialization and exchange and therefore lowers global output and income. That

is precisely what happened during the recession of 2008–09. The World Trade Organization projected that world trade would shrink by 9 percent in 2009, the largest drop since the Second World War.

Nations experiencing painful declines in employment often are tempted to impose tariffs on imports to protect domestic production and employment. But when one trading partner increases trade barriers, other partners normally retaliate. To keep recessions from worsening, trading partners need to resist trade restrictions as well as other protectionist behaviours, such as enacting laws requiring their governments to buy goods only from domestic producers. These policies may for a time be good politics, but they are bad economics. They result in even greater unemployment and hardship.

GDP without increasing prices. But if the economy already has full employment, then there will not be a huge oversupply of unemployed labour and capital keeping prices sticky. In such a situation, prices will be flexible and the increase in net exports and aggregate expenditures will cause inflationary pressure. However, we caution you that evidence from the actual economy suggests that, even at full employment, the inflationary consequences of dollar depreciation are very small.

This last example has been cast only in terms of depreciation of the dollar. Now think through the impact that *appreciation* of the dollar would have on net exports and equilibrium GDP.

QUICK REVIEW

▸ The main determinant of exports is the GDP of our trading partners. The main determinant of imports is our own GDP.

▸ Positive net exports increase aggregate expenditures on domestic output and increase equilibrium GDP; negative net exports decrease aggregate expenditures on domestic output and reduce equilibrium GDP.

▸ The multiplier for an open economy is smaller than the multiplier for a closed economy. The higher the marginal propensity to import, the smaller the open economy multiplier.

▸ In the open economy changes in (a) prosperity abroad, (b) tariffs, and (c) exchange rates can affect Canadian net exports and therefore Canadian aggregate expenditures and equilibrium GDP.

9.4 | Adding the Public Sector

Our final step in constructing the aggregate expenditures model is to move the analysis from that of a private (no government) open economy to a mixed open economy that has a public sector. This means adding government spending and taxes to the model.

For simplicity, we assume that government purchases do not cause any upward or downward shifts in the consumption and investment schedules. Thus, government expenditures are independent of the level of GDP. Also, we assume that government's net tax revenues—total tax revenues less "negative taxes" in the form of transfer payments—are derived entirely from personal taxes. Finally, we assume that a fixed amount of taxes is collected regardless of the level of GDP.

Government Purchases and Equilibrium GDP

Suppose that government decides to purchase $40 billion of goods and services regardless of the level of GDP.

TABULAR EXAMPLE

Table 9-5 shows the impact of this purchase on the equilibrium GDP. Columns 1 to 7 are carried over from Tables 9-2 and 9-4 for the open economy in which the equilibrium GDP is $470 billion. The only new items are exports and imports in columns 5 and 6, and government purchases in column 8. By adding government purchases to private spending ($C + I_g + X_n$), we get a new, higher level of aggregate expenditures, as shown in column 9. Comparing columns 1 and 9, we find that aggregate expenditures and real output are equal at a higher level of GDP. Without government spending, equilibrium GDP is $470 billion (row 6); with government spending, aggregate expenditures and real output are equal at $550 billion (row 10). Increases in public spending, like increases in private spending, shift the aggregate expenditures schedule upward and result in a higher equilibrium GDP.

Note, too, that government spending is subject to the open economy multiplier. A $40 billion increase in government purchases has increased equilibrium GDP by $80 billion (from $470 billion

TABLE 9-5		The Impact of Government Purchases on Equilibrium GDP						
(1) Domestic output (and income) (GDP = DI) (billions)	(2) Consumption (C) (billions)	(3) Saving (S) (billions)	(4) Invest-ment (I_g) (billions)	(5) Exports (X) (billions)	(6) Imports (M) (billions)	(7) Net exports (X_n) (billions) (5) – (6)	(8) Government purchases (G) (billions)	(9) Aggregate expenditures (C + I_g + X_n + G) (billions) (2) + (4) + (7) + (8)
(1) $370	$375	$–5	$20	$40	$15	$25	$40	$460
(2) 390	390	0	20	40	20	20	40	470
(3) 410	405	5	20	40	25	15	40	480
(4) 430	420	10	20	40	30	10	40	490
(5) 450	435	15	20	40	35	5	40	500
(6) 470	450	20	20	40	40	0	40	510
(7) 490	465	25	20	40	45	– 5	40	520
(8) 510	480	30	20	40	50	–10	40	530
(9) 530	495	35	20	40	55	–15	40	540
(10) 550	510	40	20	40	60	–20	40	550

MATH 9.2
Government

to $550 billion). We have implicitly assumed the $40 billion in government expenditure has all gone to purchase domestic output.

This $40 billion increase in government spending is *not* financed by increased taxes. Soon we will find that increased taxes *reduce* equilibrium GDP.

GRAPHICAL ANALYSIS

In Figure 9-5 we add $40 billion of government purchases, G, vertically to the level of private spending, $C + I_g + X_n$. That increases the aggregate expenditures schedule (private plus public) to $C + I_g + X_n + G$, resulting in the $80 billion increase in equilibrium GDP shown from $470 to $550 billion.

A decline in government spending G will lower the aggregate expenditures schedule, and the result is a multiplied decline in the equilibrium GDP. Verify using Table 9-5 that if government spending were to decline from $40 billion to $20 billion, the equilibrium GDP would fall by $40 billion.

Taxation and Equilibrium GDP

lump-sum tax
A tax that yields the same amount of tax revenue at all levels of GDP.

Government also collects taxes. Suppose it imposes a **lump-sum tax,** which is a tax yielding the same amount of tax revenue at all levels of GDP. For simplicity, we suppose this lump-sum tax is $40 billion, so government obtains $40 billion of tax revenue at each level of GDP. Generally, government revenues rise with GDP.

TABULAR EXAMPLE

In Table 9-6, which continues our example, we find taxes in column 2, and we see in column 3 that disposable (after-tax) income is lower than GDP (column 1) by the $40 billion amount of the tax. Because disposable income is used for consumer spending and saving, the tax lowers both

FIGURE 9-5   **Government Spending and the Equilibrium GDP**

The addition of government purchases, G, raises the aggregate expenditures ($C + I_g + X_n + G$) schedule and increases the equilibrium level of GDP, as would an increase in C, I_g, or X_n.

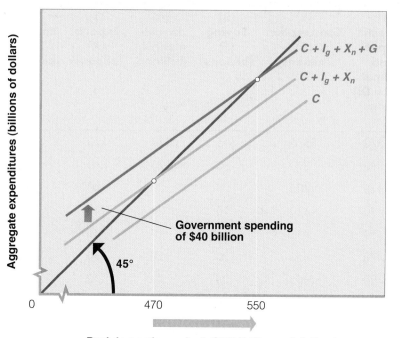

consumption and saving. But by how much will each decline as a result of the $40 billion in taxes? The MPC and MPS hold the answer: The MPC tells us what fraction of a decline in disposable income will come out of consumption, and the MPS indicates what fraction will come out of saving. Since the MPC is 0.75, if government collects $40 billion in taxes at each possible level of GDP, domestic consumption will drop by $30 billion (= 0.75 × $40 billion). Since the MPS is 0.25, saving will fall by $10 billion (= 0.25 × $40 billion).

We must make one more refinement to the new lower consumption level brought about by the tax increase. In an open economy such as Canada's, consumption consists of both domestic and imported commodities. Of the $30 billion drop in total consumption, there will be a $10 billion (= 0.25 × $40 billion) decrease in M since the MPM equals 0.25. The remaining $20 billion, therefore, comes out of domestic consumption.

Columns 4 and 5 of Table 9-6 list the amounts of consumption and saving *at each level of GDP*, which are $30 and $10 billion smaller, respectively, than those in Table 9-5. After taxes are imposed, DI is $410 billion, $40 billion short of the $450 billion GDP, with the result that consumption is only $405 billion, saving is $5 billion, and imports $25 billion (row 5 of Table 9-6).

Taxes reduce disposable income by the amount of the taxes. This decline in DI reduces consumption, saving, and imports at each level of GDP. The sizes of the declines in C, S, and M are determined by the MPC, the MPS, and the MPM, respectively.

To find out the effect of taxes on equilibrium GDP, we calculate aggregate expenditures once again, as shown in column 9 of Table 9-6. Aggregate spending is $20 billion less at each level of GDP than it was in Table 9-5. The reason is that after-tax consumption, C_a, is $30 billion less, and M_a is $10 billion less (therefore, X_{na} is $10 billion more) at each level of GDP. Comparing real output and aggregate expenditures in columns 1 and 9, we see that the aggregate amounts produced and

TABLE 9·6	Determination of the Equilibrium Levels of Employment, Output, and Income (in billions): Private and Public Sectors

(1) Real domestic output (and income) (GDP = DI)	(2) Taxes (T)	(3) Disposable income (DI) (1) – (2)	(4) Consumption - (C_a)	(5) Saving (S_a) (3) – (4)	(6) Investment (I_g)	(7) Net exports (X_n) X	M_a	X_{na}	(8) Government purchases (G)	(9) Aggregate expenditures ($C_a + I_g + X_{na} + G$) (4) + (6) + (8) + (9)
(1) $370	$40	$330	$345	$–15	$20	$40	$ 5	$35	$40	$440
(2) 390	40	350	360	–10	20	40	10	30	40	450
(3) 410	40	370	375	– 5	20	40	15	25	40	460
(4) 430	40	390	390	0	20	40	20	20	40	470
(5) 450	40	410	405	5	20	40	25	15	40	480
(6) 470	40	430	420	10	20	40	30	10	40	490
(7) 490	40	450	435	15	20	40	35	5	40	500
(8) 510	40	470	450	20	20	40	40	0	40	510
(9) 530	40	490	465	25	20	40	45	– 5	40	520
(10) 550	40	510	480	30	20	40	50	–10	40	530

purchased are equal only at the $510 billion level of GDP (row 8). The $40 billion lump-sum tax has reduced equilibrium GDP from $550 billion (row 10 in Table 9-5) to $510 billion (row 8 in Table 9-6), not back to $470 billion.

GRAPHICAL ANALYSIS

In Figure 9-6 the $40 billion increase in taxes shows up as a $20 billion (not $40 billion) decline in the aggregate expenditures ($C_a + I_g + X_{na} + G$) schedule. This decline in aggregate expenditures results solely from a decline in the consumption component C of the aggregate expenditures. The equilibrium GDP falls from $550 billion to $510 billion because of this tax-induced drop in consumption. Increases in taxes lower the aggregate expenditures schedule relative to the 45° line and reduce the equilibrium GDP.

In contrast to our previous case, a *decrease* in existing taxes will raise the aggregate expenditures schedule in Figure 9-6 as a result of an increase in the consumption at all GDP levels. You should confirm that a tax reduction of $20 billion (from the present $40 billion to $20 billion) will increase the equilibrium GDP from $510 billion to $530 billion. *(Key Question 12)*

DIFFERENTIAL IMPACTS

You may have noted that equal changes in government purchases and taxes do not have equivalent impacts on GDP. The $40 billion increase in G in our illustration, subject to the multiplier of 2, produced an $80 billion increase in real GDP. But the $40 billion increase in taxes reduced GDP by only $40 billion. Given an MPC of 0.75, the tax increase of $40 billion reduced consumption by only $30 billion (not $40 billion) and domestic consumption by $20 billion because savings fell by $10 billion and imports fell by $10 billion. Subjecting the $20 billion decline in consumption to the multiplier of 2, we find the tax increase of $40 billion reduced GDP by $40 billion (not $80 billion).

FIGURE 9·6   Taxes and Equilibrium GDP

If the MPC is 0.75, the $40 billion of taxes will lower the domestic consumption schedule by $20 billion and cause a decline in the equilibrium GDP. In the open economy with government, equilibrium GDP occurs where C_a (after-tax income) $+ I_g + X_n + G =$ GDP.

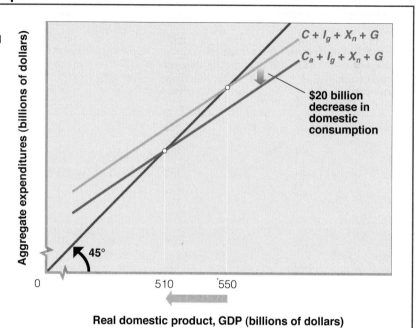

Table 9-6 and Figure 9-6 constitute the complete aggregate expenditures model for an open economy with government. When total spending equals total production, the economy's output is in equilibrium. In the open mixed economy, equilibrium GDP occurs where

$$C_a + I_g + X_n + G = \text{GDP}.$$

Injections, Leakages, and Unplanned Changes in Inventories

The related characteristics of equilibrium that we noted for the private closed economy also apply to the full model. In particular, it is still the case that injections into the income–expenditures stream equal leakages from the income stream. For the private closed economy, $S = I_g$. For the expanded economy, imports and taxes are added leakages. Saving, importing, and paying taxes are all uses of income that subtract from potential consumption. Consumption will now be less than GDP—creating a potential spending gap—in the amount of after-tax saving (S_a), imports (M), and taxes (T). But exports (X) and government purchases (G), along with investment (I_g), are injections into the income-expenditures stream. At the equilibrium GDP, the sum of the leakages equals the sum of the injections. In symbols:

$$S_a + M + T = I_g + X + G$$

 WORKED PROBLEM 9.2
Complete Aggregate Expenditure Model

Use the data in Table 9-6 to confirm this equality between leakages and injections at the equilibrium GDP of $510 billion. Also, verify that a lack of such an equality exists at all other possible levels of GDP.

Although not directly shown in Table 9-6, the equilibrium characteristic of "no unplanned changes in inventories" will also be fulfilled at the $510 billion GDP. Because aggregate expenditures equal GDP, all the goods and services produced will be purchased. No unplanned increase or decrease in inventories will occur.

CONSIDER THIS | Paradox of Thrift

In Chapter 1 we said that a higher rate of saving is *good* for society because it frees resources from consumption uses and directs them toward investment goods. More machinery and equipment means a greater capacity for the economy to produce goods and services.

But implicit within this "saving is good" proposition is the assumption that increased saving will be borrowed and spent for investment goods. If investment does not increase along with saving, a curious irony called the *paradox of thrift* may arise. The attempt to save more may simply reduce GDP and leave actual saving unchanged.

Our analysis of the multiplier process helps explain this possibility. Suppose an economy that has an MPC of 0.75, an MPS of 0.25, and a multiplier of 4 decides to save an additional $20 billion. From the social viewpoint, a penny

saved that is not invested is a penny not spent and therefore a decline in someone's income. Through the multiplier process, the $20 billion reduces consumption spending, and lowers real GDP by $80 billion (4 × $20 billion).

The $80 billion decline of real GDP, in turn, reduces saving by $20 billion (= MPS of 0.25 × $80 billion), which completely cancels the initial $20 billion increase of saving. Here, the attempt to increase saving is *bad* for the economy: It creates a recession and leaves saving unchanged.

For increased saving to be *good* for an economy, greater investment must accompany greater saving. If investment replaces consumption dollar-for-dollar, aggregate expenditures stay constant and the higher level of investment raises the economy's future growth rate

9.5 | Equilibrium versus Full-Employment GDP

A key point about the equilibrium GDP of the aggregate expenditures model is that it need not equal the economy's full-employment GDP. In fact, Keynes specifically designed the model so that it could explain situations like the Great Depression, during which the economy was seemingly stuck at a bad equilibrium where real GDP was far below potential output. As we will show you in a moment, Keynes also used the model to suggest policy recommendations for moving the economy back toward potential output and full employment.

The fact that equilibrium and potential GDP in the aggregate expenditures model need not match also reveals critical insights about the causes of demand-pull inflation. We will first examine the "expenditure gaps" that give rise to differences between equilibrium and potential GDP .

Recessionary Expenditure Gap

Suppose in **Figure 9-7a (Key Graph)** that the full-employment level of GDP is $530 billion and the aggregate expenditures schedule is AE_1. This schedule intersects the 45° line to the left of the full-employment output, so the economy's aggregate production is $20 billion short of its full-employment output of $530 billion. According to column 1 in Table 9-2, employment at full-employment GDP is 22.5 million workers. But the economy depicted in Figure 9-7a is employing only 20 million workers; 2.5 million workers are unemployed. For that reason, the economy is sacrificing $20 billion of output.

recessionary expenditure gap
The amount by which aggregate expenditures fall short of those required to achieve full-employment GDP.

The amount by which aggregate expenditures fall short of those required to achieve the full-employment GDP (also called potential GDP) is called the **recessionary expenditure gap.** In Table 9-6, assuming the full-employment GDP to be $530 billion, the corresponding recessionary expenditure gap is $10 billion. The aggregate expenditures schedule would have to shift upward to realize the full-employment GDP. Because the multiplier is 2, there is a $20 billion differential ($10 billion times the multiplier of 2) between aggregate expenditures at the equilibrium GDP and those required to attain full-employment GDP. This $20 billion difference is a negative *GDP gap*—an idea you first encountered in our discussion of cyclical unemployment (Chapter 7).

CONSIDER THIS | The Fallout of the Global Financial Crisis and the Keynesian Explanation

The recession in Canada of 2008–09 brought about by the global financial crisis is easily portrayed through the aggregate expenditures model, which John Maynard Keynes (1883–1946) created to explain the Great Depression of the 1930s. Examine Figure 9-7a. Recall that the AE_0 line in this figure consists of the combined amount of after-tax consumption expenditures (C_a), gross investment expenditures (I_g), net export expenditures (X_n), and government purchases (G) planned at each level of real GDP. During the relatively severe recession of 2008–09 both after-tax consumption and investment expenditures declined, with the largest drop being investment expenditures.

As viewed through the figure, aggregate expenditures thus declined, as from AE_0 to AE_1. This set off a multiple decline in real GDP, illustrated in the figure by the decline from $530 billion to $510 billion. In the language of the aggregate expenditures model, a recessionary expenditure gap produced a sizeable negative GDP gap. Employment sank, unemployment rose, and the unemployment rate bolted upward.

KEYNES'S SOLUTION TO A RECESSIONARY EXPENDITURE GAP

Keynes pointed to two different policies that a government might pursue to close a recessionary expenditure gap and achieve full employment. The first is to increase government spending. The second is to lower taxes. Both work by increasing aggregate expenditures.

Look back at Figure 9-5. There we showed how an increase in government expenditures G will increase overall aggregate expenditures and, consequently, the equilibrium real GDP. Applying this strategy to the situation in Figure 9-7a, government could completely close the $20 billion negative GDP gap between the initial equilibrium of $510 billion and the economy's potential output of $530 billion if it increased spending by the $10 billion amount of the recessionary expenditure gap. Given the economy's multiplier of 2, the $10 billion increase in G would create a $20 billion increase in equilibrium real GDP, thereby bringing the economy to full employment.

Government could also lower taxes to close the recessionary expenditure gap and thus eliminate the negative GDP gap. Look back at Figure 9-6 in which an *increase* in taxes resulted in lower after-tax consumption spending and a smaller equilibrium real GDP. Keynes simply suggested a reversal of this process: Since an increase in taxes lowers equilibrium real GDP, a decrease in taxes will raise equilibrium GDP. The decrease in taxes will leave consumers with higher after-tax income. That will lead to higher consumption expenditures and an increase in equilibrium real GDP.

But by how much should the government cut taxes? By $13.33 billion, because the MPC is .75. The tax cut of $13.33 billion will increase consumers' after-tax income by $13.33 billion. They will then increase consumption spending by .75 of that amount, or $10 billion. This will increase aggregate expenditures by the $10 billion needed to close the recessionary expenditure gap. The economy's equilibrium real GDP will rise to its potential output of $530 billion.

But a big warning is needed here: As the economy moves closer to its potential output, it becomes harder to justify Keynes's assumption that prices are stuck. As the economy closes its negative GDP gap, nearly all workers are employed and nearly all factories are operating at or near full capacity. In such a situation, there is no massive

Oversupply of productive resources to keep prices from rising. In fact, economists know from real-world experience that in such situations prices are not fully stuck. Instead, they become increasingly flexible as the economy moves nearer to potential output.

This fact is one of the major limitations of the aggregate expenditures model and is the reason why in the next chapter we develop a different model that can handle inflation. Nevertheless, the aggregate expenditures model is still very useful despite its inability to handle flexible prices. For instance, as we explained in Chapter 4, an economy operating near full employment will show sticky

KEY GRAPH   @

FIGURE 9-7   Recessionary and Inflationary Expenditure Gaps

The equilibrium and full-employment GDPs may not coincide. (a) A recessionary expenditure gap is the amount by which aggregate expenditures fall short of those required to achieve full-employment GDP. Here, the recessionary expenditure gap is $20 billion, caused by a $10 billion shortfall of aggregate expenditures. (b) An inflationary expenditure gap is the amount by which aggregate expenditures exceed those needed to achieve full-employment GDP. Here, the inflationary expenditure gap is $20 billion; this overspending brings about demand-pull inflation.

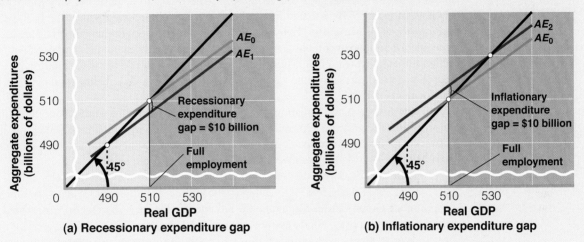

(a) Recessionary expenditure gap

(b) Inflationary expenditure gap

Quick Quiz

1. In the economy depicted,
   a. the MPS is 0.20.
   b. the multiplier is 2.
   c. the potential GDP level of real GDP is $510 billion.
   d. nominal GDP always equals real GDP.

2. The inflationary expenditure gap depicted will cause
   a. demand-pull inflation.
   b. cost-push inflation.
   c. cyclical unemployment.
   d. frictional unemployment.

3. The recessionary expenditure gap depicted will cause
   a. demand-pull inflation.
   b. cost-push inflation.
   c. cyclical unemployment.
   d. frictional unemployment.

4. In the economy depicted, the $20 billion inflationary expenditure gap
   a. expands full-employment real GDP to $550 billion.
   b. leaves full-employment real GDP at $530 billion, but causes inflation.
   c. could be remedied by equal $20 billion increases in taxes and government spending.
   d. implies that real GDP exceeds nominal GDP.

Answers: 1. b; 2. a; 3. c; 4. b

or even stuck prices in the short run. In such situations, the intuitions of the aggregate expenditures model will still hold true. The benefit of the aggregate demand–aggregate supply model that we develop in the next chapter is that it can also show us what happens in the longer run, as prices become more flexible and are increasingly able to adjust.

Inflationary Expenditure Gap

inflationary expenditure gap
The amount by which aggregate expenditures exceed those required to achieve full-employment GDP.

Economists use the term **inflationary expenditure gap** to describe the amount by which an economy's aggregate expenditures exceed those just necessary to achieve the full-employment level of GDP. In Figure 9-7b, a $10 billion inflationary expenditure gap exists at the $530 billion full-employment GDP. This is shown by the vertical distance between the actual aggregate expenditures schedule AE_2 and the hypothetical schedule AE_0, which would be just sufficient to achieve the $530 billion full-employment GDP. Thus, the inflationary expenditure gap is the amount by which the aggregate expenditures schedule would have to shift downward to realize equilibrium at the full-employment GDP.

But why does the name "inflationary expenditure gap" contain the word inflationary? In particular, what does the situation depicted in Figure 9-7b have to do with inflation? The answer lies in the answer to a different question: Could the economy actually achieve and maintain an equilibrium real GDP that is substantially above the full-employment output level?

The unfortunate answer is, no. It is unfortunate because if such a thing were possible, then the government could make real GDP as high as it wanted by simply increasing G to an arbitrarily high number. Graphically, it could raise the AE_2 curve in Figure 9-7b as far up as it wanted, thereby raising equilibrium real GDP up as high as it wanted. Living standards would skyrocket! But this is not possible because, by definition, all the workers in the economy are fully employed at the full-employment output level. Producing a bit more than the full-employment output level for a few months might be possible if you could convince all the workers to work overtime day after day. But there simply isn't enough labour to have the economy produce at much more than potential output for any extended period of time.

WORKED PROBLEM 9.3
Expenditure Gaps

So what *does* happen in situations in which aggregate expenditures are so high that the model predicts an equilibrium level of GDP beyond potential output? The answer is twofold. First, the economy ends up producing either at potential output or just above potential output due to the limited supply of labour. Second, the economy experiences demand-pull inflation. With the supply of output limited by the supply of labour, high levels of aggregate expenditures simply act to drive up prices. Nominal GDP will increase because of the higher price level, but real GDP will not. **(Key Question 13)**

Application: The Slowdown of the Canadian Economy in 2001

The Canadian economy grew at a healthy pace in the last half of the 1990s, with real GDP expanding at about 3.5 percent annually and the unemployment rate dropping from 9.6 percent of the labour force in 1996 to 6.8 percent in 2000. The economic expansion and falling rates of unemployment, however, did not spark inflation, as had been the case in prior business cycles. By increasing the economy's production capacity, exceptionally strong productivity growth in the late 1990s accommodated the growing aggregate expenditures. In terms of Figure 9-7b, it was as though the full-employment level of real GDP expanded from $530 billion to $550 billion at the same time as the aggregate expenditure curve rose from AE_0 to AE_2, so the inflationary expenditure gap of $20 billion never materialized. Inflation averaged less than 2.0 percent annually between 1995 and 2000.

But the booming economy of the second half of the 1990s produced notable excesses. A large number of ill-conceived Internet-related firms were born, attracting billions of investment dollars. Investment spending surged throughout the economy and added too much production capacity. A stock market bubble developed as stock investing became a national pastime. Consumers increased their household debt to expand their consumption.

The boom ended in the early 2000s. Hundreds of Internet-related start-up firms folded. Many firms, particularly those in telecommunications, such as Nortel Networks, and aircraft manufacturing, such as Bombardier, began to experience severe overcapacity. The stock market bubble burst, erasing billions of dollars of "paper" wealth. Firms significantly reduced their investment spending because of lower estimates of rates of return. The unemployment rate rose from 6.8 percent in February 2001 to 8.0 percent in December 2001. In terms of Figure 9-7a, a recessionary expenditure gap emerged, although not a full-fledged recession.

Application: Full-Employment Output without an Inflationary Gap

In 2007 the Canadian economy achieved full employment and relatively tame inflation. Real GDP increased by 2.7 percent, the unemployment rate dropped to a 30-year low of 6 percent, and the Consumer Price Index advanced by only 2.2 percent. The Canadian economy was buoyed by strong demand for natural resources from developing nations such as China and India, particularly for oil, the price of which began to rise rapidly. Ordinarily, one would have expected the Consumer Price Index to begin to increase at a more rapid rate than it did, given the fact that the Canadian economy was at full employment.

At least part of the reason for this happy outcome was the effective role of the Bank of Canada's monetary policy. As the economy approached full employment, the Bank of Canada raised short-term interest rates several times beginning in mid 2005, bringing the overnight lending rate from 2.5 percent to 4.5 percent by 2007. We say more about monetary policy in Chapter 13.

QUICK REVIEW

▶ Government purchases shift the aggregate expenditures schedule upward and raise the equilibrium GDP.

▶ Taxes reduce disposable income, lower consumption spending on domestically produced goods and saving, shift the imported and aggregate expenditures schedules downward, and reduce the equilibrium GDP.

▶ A recessionary expenditure gap is the amount by which GDP falls short of potential GDP; the inflationary expenditure gap is the amount by which GDP exceeds potential GDP.

The LAST WORD   Say's Law, the Great Depression, and Keynes

The aggregate expenditures theory emerged as a critique of classical economics and as a response to the Great Depression.

Until the Great Depression of the 1930s, many prominent economists, including David Ricardo (1772–1823) and John Stuart Mill (1806–73), believed that the market system would ensure full employment of an economy's resources. These so-called *classical* *economists* acknowledged that now and then abnormal circumstance such as wars, political upheavals, droughts, speculative crises, and gold rushes would occur, deflecting the economy from full-employment status. But when such deviations occurred, conditions would automatically adjust and soon restore the economy to full-employment output. For example, a slump in output and employment would result in lower prices, wages, and interest rates, which in turn would increase consumer spending, employment, and investment spending. Any excess supply of goods and workers would soon be eliminated.

Classical macroeconomists denied that the level of spending in an economy could be too low to bring about the purchase of the entire full-employment output. They based their denial of inadequate spending in part on *Say's law*, attributed to the nineteenth-century French economist J. B. Say (1767–1832). This law is the disarmingly simple idea that the very act of producing goods generates income equal to the value of the goods produced. The production of any output automatically provides the income needed to buy that output. More succinctly stated, *supply creates its own demand.*

Say's law can best be understood in terms of a barter economy. A woodworker, for example, produces or supplies furniture as a means of buying or demanding the food and clothing produced by other workers. The woodworker's supply of furniture is the income that he will "spend" to satisfy his demand for the other goods. The goods he buys (demands) will have a total value exactly equal to the goods he produces (supplies). And so it is for other producers and for the entire economy. Demand must be the same as supply!

Assuming that the composition of output is in accord with consumer preferences, all markets would be cleared of their outputs. It would seem that all firms need to do to sell a full-employment output is to produce that level of output. Say's law guarantees there will be sufficient spending to purchase it all.

The Great Depression of the 1930s called into question the theory that supply creates its own demand (Say's law). In Canada, real GDP declined by almost 30 percent and the unemployment rate rocketed to nearly 20 percent. Other nations experienced similar impacts. And cyclical unemployment lingered for a decade. An obvious inconsistency exists between a theory that says unemployment is virtually impossible and the actual occurrence of a 10-year siege of substantial unemployment.

In 1936 British economist John Maynard Keynes (1883–1946) explained why cyclical employment could occur in a market economy. In his *General Theory of Employment, Interest, and Money*, Keynes attacked the foundations of classical theory and developed the ideas underlying the aggregate expenditures model. Keynes disputed Say's law, pointing out that not all income need be spent in the same period that it is produced. Investment spending, in particular, is volatile, said Keynes. A substantial decline in investment will lead to insufficient total spending. Unsold goods will accumulate in producers' warehouses and producers will respond by reducing their output and discharging workers. A recession or depression will result, and widespread cyclical unemployment will occur. Moreover, said Keynes, recessions or depressions are not likely to correct themselves. In contrast to the more laissez-faire view of the classical economists, Keynes argued that government should play an active role in stabilizing the economy. Today, most economists embrace the idea of fiscal stimulus in an economic downturn. During the global financial crisis of 2008–09 governments around the world increased spending in an effort to combat the severe recession that ensued.

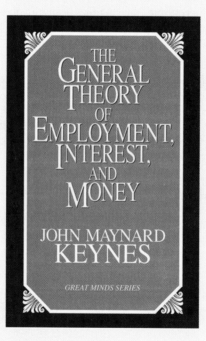

 ORIGIN 9.2
Say's Law

Question

What is Say's Law? How does it relate to the view held by classical economists that the economy generally will operate at a position on its production possibilities curve (Chapter 1)? Use production possibility analysis to demonstrate Keynes's view on this matter.

CHAPTER SUMMARY

9.1 ▶ THE AGGREGATE EXPENDITURES MODEL: CONSUMPTION AND SAVING

- The aggregate expenditures model views the total amount of spending in the economy as the primary factor determining the level of real GDP that the economy will produce. The model assumes that prices are fixed. Keynes made this assumption to reflect the reality of the Great Depression and the fact that there existed such huge oversupplies of labour and other productive resources that increases in spending were unlikely to drive up prices.

- For a private closed economy the equilibrium level of GDP occurs when aggregate expenditures and real output are equal—or, graphically, where the $C + I_g$ line intersects the 45° line. At any GDP greater than equilibrium GDP, real output will exceed aggregate spending, resulting in unintended investment in inventories and eventual declines in output and income (GDP). At any below-equilibrium GDP, aggregate expenditures will exceed real output, resulting in unintended declines in inventories and eventual increases in GDP.

- At equilibrium GDP, the amount households save (leakages) and the amount businesses plan to invest (injections) are equal. Any excess of saving over planned investment will cause a shortage of total spending, forcing GDP to fall. Any excess of planned investment over saving will cause an excess of total spending, inducing GDP to rise. The change in GDP will in both cases correct the discrepancy between saving and planned investment.

- At equilibrium GDP, no unplanned changes in inventories occur. When aggregate expenditures diverge from GDP, an unplanned change in inventories occurs. Unplanned increases in inventories are followed by a cutback in production and a decline of real GDP. Unplanned decreases in inventories result in an increase in production and a rise of GDP.

- Actual investment consists of planned investment plus unplanned changes in inventories and is always equal to saving.

9.2 ▶ CHANGES IN EQUILIBRIUM GDP AND THE MULTIPLIER

- The simple multiplier is equal to the reciprocal of the marginal propensity to save: the greater the marginal propensity to save, the smaller the multiplier. Also, the greater the marginal propensity to consume, the larger the multiplier.

- A shift in the investment schedule (caused by changes in expected rates of return or changes in interest rates) shifts the aggregate expenditures curve and causes a new equilibrium level of real GDP. Real GDP changes by more than the amount of the initial change in investment. This multiplier effect ($\Delta GDP/\Delta I_g$) accompanies both increases and decreases in aggregate expenditures and also applies to changes in net exports (X_n) and government purchases (G).

9.3 ▶ INTERNATIONAL TRADE AND EQUILIBRIUM OUTPUT

- The net export schedule relates net exports (exports minus imports) to levels of real GDP. For simplicity, we assume the level of exports is the same at all levels of real GDP.

- Positive net exports increase aggregate expenditures to a higher level than they would be if the economy were "closed" to international trade. They raise equilibrium real GDP by a multiple of the net exports. Negative net exports decrease aggregate expenditures relative to those in a closed economy, decreasing equilibrium real GDP by a multiple of their amount. Increases in exports or decreases in imports have an expansionary effect on real GDP, but decreases in exports or increases in imports have a contractionary effect.

9.4 ▶ ADDING THE PUBLIC SECTOR

- Government purchases shift the aggregate expenditures schedule upward and raise GDP.

- Taxation reduces disposable income, lowers consumption spending and saving, shifts the aggregate expenditures curve downward, and reduces equilibrium GDP.

- In the complete aggregate expenditures model, equilibrium GDP occurs where $C_a + I_g + X_n + G = $ GDP. At the equilibrium GDP, leakages of after-tax saving (S_a), imports (M), and taxes (T) equal injections of investment (I_g), exports (X), and government purchases (G). Also, there are no unplanned changes in inventories.

9.5 ▶ EQUILIBRIUM VERSUS FULL-EMPLOYMENT GDP

- The equilibrium GDP and the full-employment GDP may differ. The recessionary expenditure gap is the amount by which aggregate expenditures fall short of those required to achieve full-employment GDP. This gap produces a negative GDP gap (actual GDP minus potential GDP). The inflationary expenditure gap is the amount by which aggregate expenditures exceed those needed to achieve full-employment GDP. This gap causes demand-pull inflation.

- Keynes believed that prices during the Great Depression were stuck at low levels due to high unemployment. In such a situation, the government could increase real GDP (by increasing government expenditures or lowering taxes) without having to worry about inflation. By contrast, if an economy's GDP gap is more moderate so that there are not such high rates of unemployment, then it is less likely that prices will be sticky. The closer an economy is to its full-employment output level, the more likely it is that any increase in aggregate expenditures will lead to inflation rather than an increase in real GDP.

TERMS AND CONCEPTS

planned investment, p. 195
investment schedule, p. 195
aggregate expenditures schedule,
   p. 197
equilibrium GDP, p. 197

leakage, p. 200
injection, p. 200
unplanned changes in inventory, p. 200
actual investment, p. 200

marginal propensity to import (MPM),
   p. 203
lump-sum tax, p. 209
recessionary expenditure gap, p. 213
inflationary expenditure gap, p. 216

STUDY QUESTIONS

LO 9.1 1. What is the investment schedule and how does it differ from an investment demand curve?

LO 9.1 2. **KEY QUESTION**   Assuming the level of investment is $16 billion and independent of the level of total output, complete the following table and determine the equilibrium levels of output and employment that this private closed economy would provide. What are the sizes of the MPC and MPS?

Possible levels of employ-ment (millions)	Real domestic output (GDP = DI) (billions)	Consumption (billions)	Saving (billions)
40	$240	$244	$___
45	260	260	___
50	280	276	___
55	300	292	___
60	320	308	___
65	340	324	___
70	360	340	___
75	380	356	___
80	400	372	___

LO 9.1 3. Using the consumption and saving data in question 2 and assuming investment is $16 billion, what are saving and planned investment at the $380 billion level of domestic output? What are saving and actual investment at that level? What are saving and planned investment at the $300 billion level of domestic output? What are the levels of saving and actual investment? Use the concept of unplanned investment to explain adjustments toward equilibrium from both the $380 and $300 billion levels of domestic output.

4. Why is saving called a *leakage*? Why is planned investment called an *injection*? Why must saving equal planned investment at equilibrium GDP? Are unplanned changes in inventories rising, falling, or constant at equilibrium GDP? Explain. **LO 9.**

5. What effect will each of the changes listed in study question 3 of Chapter 8 have on the equilibrium level of GDP? Explain your answers. **LO 9.**

6. By how much will GDP change if firms increase their investment by $8 billion and the MPC is 0.80? if the MPC is 0.67? **LO 9.2**

7. Depict graphically the aggregate expenditures model for a private closed economy. Now show a decrease in the aggregate expenditures schedule and explain why the decline in real GDP in your diagram is greater than the initial decline in aggregated expenditures. What would be the ratio of a decline in real GDP to the initial drop in aggregate expenditures if the slope of your aggregate expenditures schedule was 0.8? **LO 9.2**

8. Suppose a certain country has an MPC of 0.9 and a real GDP of $400 billion. If its investment spending decreases by $4 billion, what will be its new level of real GDP in the aggregate expenditures model? **LO 9.2**

9. **KEY QUESTION**   The data in columns 1 and 2 in the table below are for a private closed economy: **LO 9.3**

   a. Use columns 1 and 2 to determine the equilibrium GDP for this hypothetical economy.

   b. Now open up this economy to international trade by including the export and import figures of columns 3 and 4. Fill in columns 5 and 6 and determine the equilibrium GDP for the open economy. Explain why this equilibrium GDP differs from that of the closed economy.

(1) Real domestic output (GDP = DI) (billions)	(2) Aggregate expenditures, private closed economy (billions)	(3) Exports (billions)	(4) Imports (billions)	(5) Net exports (billions)	(6) Aggregate expenditures, private open economy (billions)
$200	$240	$20	$30	$___	$___
250	280	20	30	___	___
300	320	20	30	___	___
350	360	20	30	___	___
400	400	20	30	___	___
450	440	20	30	___	___
500	480	20	30	___	___
550	520	20	30	___	___

c. Given the original $20 billion level of exports, what would be the equilibrium GDP if imports were $10 billion greater at each level of GDP?

d. What is the open-economy multiplier in these examples?

O ▶ 9.4 10. Assume that, without taxes, the consumption schedule of an economy is as follows:

GDP, billions	Consumption, billions
$100	$120
200	200
300	280
400	360
500	440
600	520
700	600

a. Graph this consumption schedule and determine the MPC.

b. Assume now that a lump-sum tax is imposed such that the government collects $10 billion in taxes at all levels of GDP. Graph the resulting consumption schedule, and compare the MPC and the multiplier with those of the pretax consumption schedule.

O ▶ 9.4 11. Explain graphically the determination of equilibrium GDP for a private economy through the aggregate expenditures model. Now add government spending (any amount you choose) to your graph, showing its impact on equilibrium GDP. Finally, add taxation (any amount of lump-sum tax that you choose) to your graph and show its effect on equilibrium GDP. Looking at your graph, determine whether equilibrium GDP has increased, decreased, or stayed the same given the sizes of the government spending and taxes that you selected.

12. **KEY QUESTION**   Refer to columns 1 and 6 in the table **LO ▶ 9.4** for question 9. Incorporate government into the table by assuming that it plans to tax and spend $20 billion at each possible level of GDP. Also assume that the tax is a personal tax and that government spending does not induce a shift in the private aggregate expenditures schedule. Compute and explain the change in equilibrium GDP caused by the addition of government.

13. **KEY QUESTION**   Refer to the table below in answering **LO ▶ 9.5** the questions that follow:

(1) Possible levels of employment (millions)	(2) Real domestic output (billions)	(3) Aggregate expenditures $(C_a + I_g + X_n + G)$ (billions)
9	$500	$520
10	550	560
11	600	600
12	650	640
13	700	680

a. If full employment in this economy is 13 million, will there be an inflationary or a recessionary expenditure gap? What will be the consequence of this gap? By how much would aggregate expenditures in column 3 have to change at each level of GDP to eliminate the inflationary or the recessionary gap? Explain. What is the multiplier in this example?

b. Will there be an inflationary expenditure gap or a recessionary expenditure gap if the full-employment level of output is $500 billion? Explain the consequences. By how much would aggregate expenditures in column 3 have to change at each level of GDP to eliminate the inflationary or the recessionary gap? What is the multiplier in this example?

c. Assuming that investment, net exports, and government expenditures do not change with changes in real GDP, what are the sizes of the MPC, the MPS, and the multiplier?

LO 9.4 14. **Advanced Analysis** Assume the consumption schedule for a private open economy is such that consumption $C = 50 + 0.8Y$. Assume further that planned investment I_g and net exports X_n are independent of the level of real GDP and constant at $I_g = 30$ and $X_n = 10$. Recall also that, in equilibrium, the real output produced (Y) is equal to aggregate expenditures: $Y = C + I_g + X_n$.

a. Calculate the equilibrium level of income or real GDP for this economy. Check your work by expressing the consumption, investment, and net export schedules in tabular form and determining the equilibrium GDP.

b. What happens to equilibrium Y if I_g changes to 10? What does this outcome reveal about the size of the multiplier?

15. Answer the following questions that relate to the aggregate **LO 9.5** expenditures model:

a. If C_a is $100, I_g is $50, X_n is $-10, and G is $30, what is the economy's equilibrium GDP?

b. If real GDP in an economy is currently $200, C_a is $100, I_g is $50, X_n is $-10, and G is $30, will its real GDP rise, fall, or stay the same?

c. Suppose that full-employment (and full-capacity) output in an economy is $200. If C_a is $150, I_g is $50, X_n is $-10, and G is $30, what will be the macroeconomic result?

INTERNET APPLICATION QUESTIONS @

1. **The Multiplier—Calculate a Change in GDP.** Use the links on the McConnell-Brue-Flynn-Barbiero Web site (Chapter 9) to access Statistics Canada's Web site. Find the most current values for GDP = $C + I + G + (X - M)$. Assume an MPC of 0.75, and that for each of the following, the values of the initial variables are those you just discovered. What would be the new value of GDP if (a) investment increased by 5 percent? (b) imports increased by 5 percent and exports increased by 5 percent? (c) consumption increased by 5 percent? (d) government spending increased by 5 percent? Which 5 percent increase caused GDP to change the most in absolute dollars?

2. **Net Exports—What Is the Current Economic Impact?** Use the links on the McConnell-Brue-Flynn-Barbiero Web site (Chapter 9) to access Statistics Canada's Web site. Positive net exports have an expansionary effect on domestic GDP; negative net exports have a contractionary effect. Check the latest figures at Statistics Canada for exports and imports of goods and services. Assume a multiplier of 4. Compared to the previous period, how much is GDP increased or decreased by a change in (a) net exports of goods, (b) net exports of services, and (c) net exports of goods and services? Which has the greatest impact? Should services be included or excluded from net exports?

Math Appendix to Chapter 9

A9.1 | THE MATH BEHIND THE AGGREGATE EXPENDITURES MODEL

We begin with an explanation of the symbols we use:

- Aggregate expenditures, AE
- Real GDP, Y
- Disposable income, Y_d
- Consumption expenditure, C
- Autonomous consumption expenditure, a
- Investment expenditure, I_a
- Government expenditure, G_a
- Exports, X_a
- Imports, M
- Autonomous taxes, T_a
- Marginal tax rate, t
- Marginal propensity to consume, b
- Marginal propensity to import, m
- Autonomous expenditure, A
- Marginal propensity to withdraw, W

AGGREGATE EXPENDITURES

We know that $AE = C + I + (X - M) + G$. Let's look at each component of aggregate expenditures in more detail.

CONSUMPTION EXPENDITURES

The consumption function is given by the linear equation $C = a + bY_d$. This means that consumption consists of an "autonomous" amount, a, plus a portion of disposable income Y_d, the portion being the product of Y_d and the marginal propensity to consume, b. To arrive at disposable income Y_d we must deduct net taxes. So far we have assumed that taxes are a lump sum, an assumption that made the exposition easier. We now assume that taxes consist of an autonomous amount T_a, plus an induced portion of Y, which is the marginal tax rate, t. So the consumption function becomes:

$$C = a + b(Y - T_a - tY)$$
$$= a - bT_a + b(1 - t)Y$$

INVESTMENT

We assume investment spending (I_a) to be autonomous, or a constant amount.

NET EXPORTS

Recall that in our expenditure model, exports (X_a) are determined abroad, so they are autonomous. Imports are determined by the level of our own GDP multiplied by the marginal propensity to import (m):

$$M = mY$$

GOVERNMENT EXPENDITURES

Our expenditure model assumes that government expenditures (G_a) are autonomous, or independent of GDP.

We can now put all the terms together to get:

$$AE = a - bT_a + b(1 - t)Y + I_a + G_a + X_a - mY \qquad (1)$$

AGGREGATE EXPENDITURES AND EQUILIBRIUM GDP

Equilibrium expenditures occur when planned aggregate expenditures (AE) equals real GDP (Y):

$$Y = AE \qquad (2)$$

Substituting (2) into (1), we get

$$Y = a - bT_a + b(1 - t)Y + I_a + G_a + X_a - mY$$

We now solve for the value of Y that satisfies both equations (1) and (2). To do so we group the Y terms that are on the right side of the previous equation:

$$Y = Y[b(1 - t) - m] + a - bT_a + I_a + G_a + X_a$$

Bringing the Y terms to the left side of the equation leads us to the equilibrium condition:

$$Y = \frac{a - bT_a + I_a + G_a + X_a}{1 - [b(1 - t) - m]} \qquad (3)$$

Note that in the denominator, $[b(1 - t) - m]$ is the equivalent of the marginal propensity to consume, but that this term refers to the marginal propensity to spend out of national income, rather than just consumption. Note that the denominator $1 - [b(1 - t) - m]$ is a leakage, or a withdrawal from domestic expenditures, which apart from savings also includes taxes and imports. We can simplify equation (3) by denoting the numerator, which consists of autonomous expenditures, by the letter A, and using the letter W for the marginal propensity to withdraw from domestic expenditures, to give us:

$$Y = A/W$$

GRAPHICAL ILLUSTRATION

In Figure A9-1 we portray important features of the aggregate expenditures model graphically. In Figure A9-1a the slope of the aggregate expenditure curve, equal to the term $b(1 - t) - m$, is the marginal propensity to spend. Autonomous expenditure, A, is equal to the sum of $a - bT_a + I_a + G_a + X_a$.

Figure A9-1b shows that equilibrium in the aggregate expenditures model occurs where planned expenditure is equal to actual output.

NUMERICAL EXAMPLE

Let's look at a concrete example to calculate equilibrium income. Suppose you are given the following information:

$$C = 60 + 0.6Y_d \qquad\qquad G_a = 70$$

$$T = 40 + 0.25Y \qquad\qquad X_a = 44$$

$$I_a = 60 \qquad\qquad M = 0.15Y$$

There are two ways you can arrive at the result. The first is to substitute the numbers into equation (1):

At equilibrium $Y = AE$, or

$$Y = C + I + (X - M) + G$$

Substituting each of the components into the equation, we get:

$$Y = 60 + 0.6(Y - 40 - 0.25Y) + 60 + (44 - 0.15Y) + 70$$

Collecting the terms gives us:

$$Y = 210 + 0.3Y$$

Subtracting $0.3Y$ from each side yields:

$$0.7Y = 210$$

Dividing both sides of the equation by 0.7 gives us the equilibrium real GDP:

$$Y = 300$$

The second way is to substitute the numbers into equation (3):

$$Y = \frac{a - bT_a + I_a + G_a + X_a}{1 - [b(1 - t) - m]}$$

$$Y = \frac{60 - 0.6(40) + 60 + 70 + 44}{1 - [0.6(1 - 0.25) - 0.15]}$$

$$Y = \frac{210}{1 - 0.3}$$

$$Y = \frac{210}{0.7}$$

$$Y = 300$$

FIGURE A9·1   **The Aggregate Expenditures Curve**

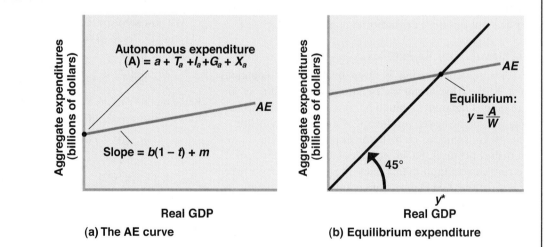

(a) The AE curve

(b) Equilibrium expenditure

CHAPTER 10

Aggregate Demand and Aggregate Supply

In an update of its *Monetary Policy Report* in October 2005, the Bank of Canada reported:

> In line with the Bank's outlook, and given that the Canadian economy now appears to be operating at capacity, some further reduction of monetary stimulus will be required to maintain a balance between aggregate supply and demand over the next four to six quarters, and to keep inflation on target. However, with risks to the global outlook tilted to the downside as we look to 2007 and beyond, the Bank will monitor international developments particularly closely.[1]

This is precisely the language of the **aggregate demand–aggregate supply model** (AD–AS model), which we will develop in this chapter. The AD–AS model enables us to analyze changes in both real GDP and the price level simultaneously. The AD–AS model therefore provides insights on inflation, unemployment, and economic growth. In later chapters, we will see that it also explains the logic of macroeconomic stabilization policies.

10.1 | Aggregate Demand

Aggregate demand is a schedule or curve that shows the amounts of real output (real GDP) that buyers collectively desire to purchase at each possible price level. The relationship between the price level (as measured by the GDP price index) and the amount of real GDP demanded is inverse or negative: When the price level rises, the quantity of real GDP demanded decreases; when the price level falls, the quantity of real GDP demanded increases.

Aggregate Demand Curve

The inverse relationship between the price level and real GDP is shown in Figure 10-1, where the aggregate demand curve AD slopes downward, as does the demand curve for an individual product. Why the downward slope? The explanation rests on three effects of a price-level change.

---

[1] http://www.bankofcanada.ca/en/mpr/pdf/mproct05.pdf

aggregate demand–aggregate supply model
The macroeconomic model that uses aggregate demand and aggregate supply to explain price level and real domestic output.

aggregate demand
A schedule or curve that shows the total quantity of goods and services demanded (purchased) at different price levels.

 ORIGIN 10.1
Real-Balances Effect

real-balances effect
The inverse relationship between the price level and the real value (or purchasing power) of financial assets with fixed money value.

interest-rate effect
The direct relationship between price level and the demand for money, which affects interest rates, and, as a result, total spending in the economy.

foreign-trade effect
The inverse relationship between the net exports of an economy and its price level relative to price levels in the economies of trading partners.

REAL-BALANCES EFFECT

A change in the price level produces a **real-balances effect.** Here is how it works. A higher price level reduces the purchasing power of the public's accumulated saving balances. In particular, the real value of assets with fixed money values, such as savings accounts or bonds, diminishes. Because a higher price level erodes the purchasing power of such assets, the public is poorer in real terms and will reduce its spending. A household might buy a new car or a plasma TV if the purchasing power of its financial asset balances is, say $50,000. But if inflation erodes the purchasing power of its asset balances to $30,000, the family may defer its purchase. So a higher price level means less consumption spending.

INTEREST-RATE EFFECT

The aggregate demand curve also slopes downward because of the **interest-rate effect.** When we draw an aggregate demand curve, we assume that the supply of money in the economy is fixed. But when the price level rises, consumers need more money for purchases, and businesses need more money to meet their payrolls and to buy other resources. A $10 bill will do when the price of an item is $10, but a $10 bill plus a loonie is needed when the item costs $11. In short, a higher price level increases the demand for money. So, given a fixed supply of money, an increase in money demand will drive up the price paid for its use. The price of money is the interest rate.

Higher interest rates restrain investment spending and interest-sensitive consumption spending. Firms that expect a 6 percent rate of return on a potential purchase of capital will find that investment profitable when the interest rate is, say, 5 percent. But the investment will be unprofitable and will not be made when the interest rate has risen to 7 percent. Similarly, consumers may decide not to purchase a new house or automobile when the interest rate on loans goes up. So, by increasing the demand for money and consequently the interest rate, a higher price level reduces the amount of real output demanded.

FOREIGN-TRADE EFFECT

The final reason why the aggregate demand curve slopes downward is the **foreign-trade effect.** When the Canadian price level rises relative to foreign price levels, foreigners buy fewer Canadian goods and Canadians buy more foreign goods. Therefore, Canadian exports fall and Canadian imports rise. In short, the rise in the price level reduces the quantity of Canadian goods demanded as net exports.

FIGURE 10-1   **The Aggregate Demand Curve**

The downward-sloping aggregate demand curve AD indicates an inverse relationship between the price level and the amount of real output purchased.

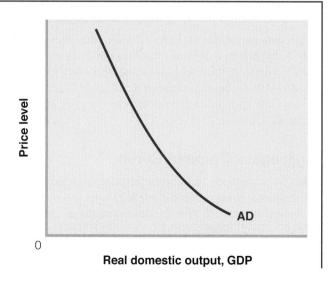

These three effects, of course, work in the opposite directions for a decline in the price level. A decline in the price level increases consumption through the real-balances effect and interest-rate effect; increases investment through the interest-rate effect; and raises net exports by increasing exports and decreasing imports through the foreign-trade effect.

Changes in Aggregate Demand

Other things equal, a change in the price level will change the amount of aggregate spending and therefore change the amount of real GDP demanded by the economy. Movements along a fixed aggregate demand curve represent these changes in real GDP. However, if one or more of those other things changes, the entire aggregate demand curve will shift. We call these "other things" **determinants of aggregate demand.** They are listed in Figure 10-2.

In Figure 10-2, the rightward shift of the curve from AD$_1$ to AD$_2$ shows an increase in aggregate demand. At each price level, the amount of real goods and services demanded is larger than before. The leftward shift of the curve from AD$_1$ to AD$_3$ shows a decrease in aggregate demand; the amount of real GDP demanded at each price level is lower.

Let's examine each determinant of aggregate demand that is listed in Figure 10-2.

CONSUMER SPENDING

Even when the Canadian price level is constant, domestic consumers may change their purchases of Canadian-produced real output. If those consumers decide to buy more output at each price level, the aggregate demand curve will shift to the right, as from AD$_1$ to AD$_2$ in Figure 10-2. If they decide to buy less output, the aggregate demand curve will shift to the left, as from AD$_1$ to AD$_3$.

Several factors other than a change in the price level may change consumer spending and thus shift the aggregate demand curve. As Figure 10-2 shows, those factors are real consumer wealth, consumer expectations, household borrowing, and taxes.

determinants of aggregate demand Factors (such as consumption spending, investment, government spending, and net exports) that shift the aggregate demand curve.

FIGURE 10-2   **Changes in Aggregate Demand**

A change in one or more of the listed determinants of aggregate demand will change aggregate demand. An increase in aggregate demand is shown as a rightward shift of the AD curve, here from AD$_1$ to AD$_2$; a decrease in aggregate demand is shown as a leftward shift, here from AD$_1$ to AD$_3$.

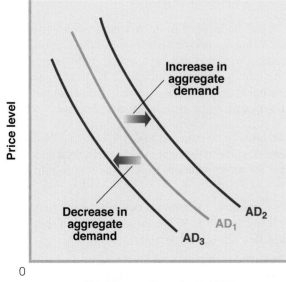

Determinants of aggregate demand: factors that shift the aggregate demand curve

1. Change in consumer spending
   a. Consumer wealth
   b. Consumer expectations
   c. Household borrowing
   d. Personal taxes
2. Change in investment spending
   a. Interest rates
   b. Expected returns
      • Expected future business conditions
      • Technology
      • Degree of excess capacity
      • Business taxes
3. Change in government spending
4. Change in net export spending
   a. National income abroad
   b. Exchange rates

Consumer Wealth   Consumer wealth is the total dollar value of all assets owned by consumers in the economy less the dollar value of their liabilities (debts). Assets include stocks, bonds, and real estate. Liabilities include mortgages, car loans, and credit card balances. Consumer wealth sometimes changes suddenly and unexpectedly due to surprising changes in asset values. An unforeseen increase in the stock market is a good example. The increase in wealth prompts pleasantly surprised consumers to save less and buy more out of their current incomes than they had previously been planning. The resulting increase in consumer spending—the so-called wealth effect—shifts the aggregate demand curve to the right. In contrast, an unexpected decline in asset values will cause an unanticipated reduction in consumer wealth at each price level. As consumers tighten their belts in response to the bad news, a "reverse wealth effect" sets in. Unpleasantly surprised consumers increase savings and reduce consumption, thereby shifting the aggregate demand curve to the left.

Consumer Expectations   Changes in expectations about the future may change consumer spending. When people expect their future real income to rise, they spend more of their current income. Thus current consumption spending increases (current saving falls), and the aggregate demand curve shifts to the right. Similarly, a widely held expectation of surging inflation in the near future may increase aggregate demand today because consumers will want to buy products before their prices rise. Conversely, expectations of lower future income or lower future prices may reduce current consumption and shift the aggregate demand curve to the left.

Household Borrowing   Consumers can increase their consumption spending by borrowing. Doing so shifts the aggregate demand curve to the right. By contrast, a decrease in borrowing for consumption purposes shifts the aggregate demand curve to the left. The aggregate demand curve will also shift to the left if consumers increase their savings rates in order to pay off their debts. With more money flowing to debt repayment, consumption expenditures decline and the AD curve shifts left.

Personal Taxes   A reduction in personal income tax rates raises take-home income and increases consumer purchases at each possible price level. Tax cuts shift the aggregate demand curve to the right. Tax increases reduce consumption spending and shift the curve to the left.

INVESTMENT SPENDING

Investment spending (the purchase of capital goods) is a second major determinant of aggregate demand. A decline in investment spending at each price level will shift the aggregate demand curve to the left. An increase in investment spending will shift it to the right.

Real Interest Rates   Other things equal, an increase in interest rates will lower investment spending and reduce aggregate demand. We are not referring here to the interest-rate effect resulting from a change in the price level. Instead, we are identifying a change in the interest rate that results from, say, a change in the nation's money supply. An increase in the money supply lowers the interest rate, thereby increasing investment and aggregate demand. A decrease in the money supply raises the interest rate, reduces investment, and decreases aggregate demand.

Expected Returns   Higher expected returns on investment projects will increase the demand for capital goods and shift the aggregate demand curve to the right. Alternatively, declines in expected returns will decrease investment and shift the curve to the left. Expected returns, in turn, are influenced by several factors:

- *Expectations about Future Business Conditions*   If firms are optimistic about future business conditions, they are more likely to invest more today. On the other hand, if they think the economy will deteriorate in the future, they will invest less today.

- *Technology*   New and improved technologies increase expected returns on investment and thus increase aggregate demand. For example, recent advances in microbiology have motivated pharmaceutical companies to establish new labs and production facilities.

- *Degree of Excess Capacity*   Other things equal, firms operating factories at well below capacity have little incentive to build new factories. But when firms discover that their excess capacity is dwindling or has completely disappeared, their expected returns on new investment in factories and capital equipment rises. Thus, they increase their investment spending and the aggregate demand curve shifts to the right.

- *Business Taxes*   An increase in business taxes will reduce after-tax profits from capital investment and lower expected returns. So investment and aggregate demand will decline. A decrease in business taxes will have the opposite effect.

The variability of interest rates and investment expectations makes investment quite volatile. In contrast to consumption, investment spending rises and falls quite often, independent of changes in total income. Investment, in fact, is the least stable component of aggregate demand.

GOVERNMENT SPENDING

Government purchases are the third determinant of aggregate demand. An increase in government purchases (for example, more computers for government agencies) will shift the aggregate demand curve to the right, provided tax collections and interest rates do not change as a result. In contrast, a reduction in government spending (for example, fewer transportation projects) will shift the curve to the left.

NET EXPORT SPENDING

The final determinant of aggregate demand is net export spending. Other things equal, a rise of Canadian *exports* means increased foreign demand for Canadian goods, whereas lower Canadian *imports* implies that Canadian consumers have decreased their demand for foreign-produced products. So, a rise in net exports (higher exports and/or lower imports) shifts the aggregate demand curve to the right. In contrast, a decrease in Canadian net exports shifts the aggregate demand curve leftward. (These changes in net exports are *not* those prompted by a change in the Canadian price level—those associated with the foreign-trade effect. The changes here explain shifts of the AD curve, not movements along the AD curve.)

What might cause net exports to change, other than the price level? Two possibilities are changes in national income abroad and changes in exchange rates.

National Income Abroad   Rising national income abroad encourages foreigners to buy more products, some of which are made in Canada. Canadian net exports thus rise and the Canadian aggregate demand curve shifts to the right. Declines in national income abroad, of course, do the opposite: They reduce Canadian net exports and shift the aggregate demand curve in Canada to the left. For example, in 2008 the U.S. economy, Canada's largest trading partner, slowed down perceptibly and our exports to the U.S. declined.

Exchange Rates   Changes in the dollar's exchange rate—the prices of foreign currencies in terms of the Canadian dollar—may affect Canadian net exports and therefore aggregate demand. Suppose the Canadian dollar depreciates in terms of the euro (the euro appreciates in terms of the dollar). The new relative lower value of dollars and higher value of euros make Canadian goods less expensive, so European consumers buy more Canadian goods and Canadian exports rise. But Canadian consumers now find European goods more expensive, so reduce their imports from Europe. Canadian exports rise and Canadian imports fall. Conclusion: Dollar depreciation increases net exports (imports go down; exports go up) and therefore increases aggregate demand. Dollar *appreciation* has the opposite effects: Net exports fall (imports go up; exports go down) and aggregate demand declines.

10.2 | Aggregate Supply

aggregate supply
A schedule or curve that shows the total quantity of goods and services supplied (produced) at different price levels.

Aggregate supply is a schedule or curve showing the relationship between the price level of output and the amount of real domestic output that firms in the economy produce. This relationship varies depending on the time horizon and how quickly output prices and input prices can change. We will define three time horizons.

- In the *immediate short run*, both input prices and output prices are fixed.
- In the *short run*, input prices are fixed but output prices can vary.
- In the *long run*, input prices as well as output prices can vary.

In Chapter 4, we discussed both the immediate short run and the long run in terms of how an automobile maker named Buzzer Auto responds to changes in the demand for its new car, the Prion. Here we extend the logic of that chapter to the economy as a whole in order to discuss how total output varies with the price level in the immediate short run, the short run, and the long run. As you will see, the relationship between the price level and total output is different in each of the three time horizons because input prices are stickier than output prices. While both become more flexible as time passes, output prices usually adjust more rapidly.

Aggregate Supply in the Immediate Short Run

Depending on the type of firm, the immediate short run can last anywhere from a few days to a few months. It lasts as long as *both* input prices and output prices stay fixed. Input prices are fixed in both the immediate short run and the short run by contractual agreements. In particular, 75 percent of the average firm's costs are wages and salaries—and these are almost always fixed by labour contracts for months or years at a time. As a result, they are usually fixed for a much longer duration than output prices, which can begin to change within a few days or a few months depending upon the type of firm.

Output prices are also typically fixed in the immediate short run. This is most often caused by firms setting fixed prices for their customers and then agreeing to supply whatever quantity demanded results at those fixed prices. For instance, once an appliance manufacturer sets its annual list prices for refrigerators, stoves, and microwaves, it is obligated to supply however many or few appliances customers want to buy at those prices. Similarly, a catalogue company is obliged to sell however many customers want to buy of its products at the prices listed in its current catalogue. And it is stuck supplying those quantities demanded until it sends out its next catalogue.

immediate-short-run aggregate supply curve (AS_{ISR})
An aggregate supply curve for which real output, but not the price level, changes when the aggregate demand curve shifts.

With output prices fixed and firms selling as much as customers want to purchase at those fixed prices, the **immediate-short-run aggregate supply curve** AS_{ISR} is a horizontal line, as shown in Figure 10-3. The AS_{ISR} curve is horizontal at the overall price level P_1, which is calculated from all of the individual prices set by the various firms in the economy. Its horizontal shape implies that the

| FIGURE 10-3 | Aggregate Supply in the Immediate Short Run |

In the immediate short run, the aggregate supply curve AS_{ISR} is horizontal at the economy's current price level, P_1. With output prices fixed, firms collectively supply the level of output that is demanded at those prices.

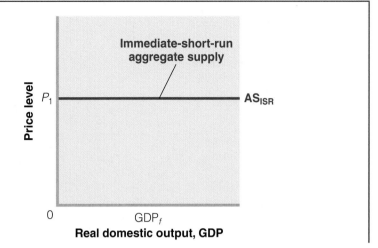

total amount of output supplied in the economy depends directly on the volume of spending that results at price level P_1. If total spending is low at price level P_1, firms will supply a small amount to match the low level of spending. If total spending is high at price level P_1, they will supply a high level of output to match the high level of spending. The amount of output that results may be higher than or lower than the economy's full-employment output level GDP_f.

Notice, however, that firms will respond in this manner to changes in total spending only as long as output prices remain fixed. As soon as firms are able to change their product prices, they can respond to changes in consumer spending not only by increasing or decreasing output but also by raising or lowering prices. This is the situation that leads to the upward-sloping short-run aggregate supply curve, which we discuss next.

Aggregate Supply in the Short Run

The short run begins after the immediate short run ends. As it relates to macroeconomics, the short run is a period of time during which output prices are flexible but input prices are either totally fixed or highly inflexible.

These assumptions about output prices and input prices are general—they relate to the economy in the aggregate. Naturally, some input prices are more flexible than others. Since gasoline prices are quite flexible, a package delivery firm like UPS that uses gasoline as an input will have at least one very flexible input price. On the other hand, wages at UPS are set by multi-year labour contracts negotiated with its drivers' union. Because wages are the firm's largest and most important input cost, it is the case that, overall, UPS faces input prices that are inflexible for several years at a time. Thus, its "short run"—during which it can change the shipping prices that it charges its customers but during which it must deal with substantially fixed input prices—is actually quite long. Keep this in mind as we derive the short-run aggregate supply for the entire economy. Its applicability does not depend on some arbitrary definition of how long the "short run" should be. Instead, the short run for which the model is relevant is any period of time during which output prices are flexible but input prices are fixed or nearly fixed.

short-run aggregate supply curve
An aggregate supply curve for which real output, but not the price level, changes when the aggregate demand curve shifts.

As illustrated in Figure 10-4, the **short-run aggregate supply curve** AS slopes upward because with input prices fixed, changes in the price level will raise or lower real firm profits. To see how this works, consider an economy that has only a single multi-product firm called Mega Buzzer and in which the firm's owners must receive a real profit of $20 in order to produce the full-employment output of 100 units. Assume the owner's only input (aside from entrepreneurial talent) is 10 units of

FIGURE 10-4 | **Short-Run Aggregate Supply Curve**

The upward-sloping aggregate supply curve AS indicates a direct (or positive) relationship between the price level and the amount of real output that firms will offer for sale. The AS curve is relatively flat below the full-employment output because unemployed resources and unused capacity allow firms to respond to price-level rises with large increases in real output. It is relatively steep beyond the full-employment output because resource shortages and capacity limitations make it difficult to expand real output as the price level rises.

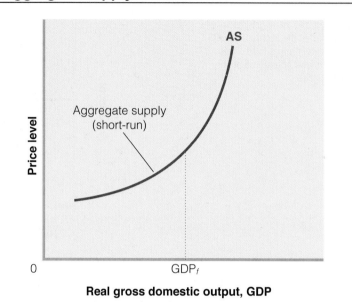

hired labour at $8 per worker, for a total wage cost of $80. Also assume that the 100 units of output sell for $1 per unit, so total revenue is $100. Mega Buzzer's nominal profit is $20 (= $100 − $80), and using the $1 price to designate the base-price index of 100 its real profit is also $20 (= $20/1.00). Well and good; the full-employment output is produced.

Next, consider what will happen if the price of Mega Buzzer's output doubles. The doubling of the price level will boost total revenue from $100 to $200, but since we are discussing the short run, during which input prices are fixed, the $8 nominal wage for each of the 10 workers will remain unchanged so that total costs stay at $80. Nominal profit will rise from $20 (= $100 − $80) to $120 (= $200 − $80). Dividing that $120 profit by the new price index of 200 (= 2.0 in hundredths), we find that Mega Buzzer's real profit is now $60. The rise in the real reward from $20 to $60 prompts the firm (economy) to produce more output. Conversely, price-level declines reduce real profits and cause the firm (economy) to reduce its output. So, in the short run, there is a direct, or positive, relationship between the price level and real output. When the price level rises, real output rises and when the price level falls, real output falls. The result is an upward-sloping short-run aggregate supply curve. Notice, however, that the slope of the short-run aggregate supply curve is not constant. It is relatively flat at outputs below the full-employment output level GDP$_f$ and relatively steep at outputs above it. This has to do with the fact that per-unit production costs underlie the short-run aggregate supply curve. Recall from Chapter 7 that

$$\text{Per-unit production cost} = \frac{\text{total input cost}}{\text{units of output}}$$

The per-unit production cost of any specific level of output establishes that output's price level because the associated price level must cover all the costs of production, including profit "costs."

As the economy expands in the short run, per-unit production costs generally rise because of reduced efficiency. But the extent of that rise depends on where the economy is operating relative to its capacity. When the economy is operating below its full-employment output, it has large amounts of unused machinery and equipment and large numbers of unemployed workers. Firms can put these idle human and property resources back to work with little upward pressure on per-unit production costs. And as output expands, few if any shortages of inputs or production bottlenecks will arise to raise per-unit production costs. That is why the slope of the short-run aggregate supply curve increases only slowly at output levels below the full-employment output level GDP_f.

On the other hand, when the economy is operating beyond GDP_f, the vast majority of its available resources are already employed. Adding more workers to a relatively fixed number of highly used capital resources such as plant and equipment creates congestion in the workplace and reduces the efficiency (on average) of workers. Adding more capital, given the limited number of available workers, leaves equipment idle and reduces the efficiency of capital. Adding more land resources when capital and labour are highly constrained reduces the efficiency of land resources. Under these circumstances, total input costs rise more rapidly than total output. The result is rapidly rising per-unit production costs that give the short-run aggregate supply curve its rapidly increasing slope at output levels beyond GDP_f.

Aggregate Supply in the Long Run

In macroeconomics, the long run is the time horizon over which both input prices and output prices are flexible. It begins after the short run ends. Depending on the type of firm and industry, this may be from a couple of weeks to several years in the future. But for the economy as a whole, it is the time horizon over which all output and input prices—including wage rates—are fully flexible.

long-run aggregate supply curve (AS_{LR})
The aggregate supply curve associated with a time period in which input prices (especially nominal wages) are fully responsive to changes in the price level.

The **long-run aggregate supply curve** AS_{LR} is vertical at the economy's full-employment output GDP_f, as shown in Figure 10-5. The vertical curve means that in the long run the economy will produce the full-employment output level no matter what the price level is. How can this be? Shouldn't higher prices cause firms to increase output? The explanation lies in the fact that in the long run when both input prices and output prices are flexible profit levels will always adjust to give firms exactly the right profit incentive to produce exactly the full-employment output level GDP_f.

To see why this is true, look back at the short-run aggregate supply curve AS shown in Figure 10-4. Suppose the economy starts out producing at the full-employment output level GDP_f and that the price level at that moment has an index value of 100. Now suppose that output prices double, so that the price index goes to 200. We previously demonstrated for our single-firm economy that this doubling of the price level would cause profits to rise in the short run and that the higher profits would motivate the firm to increase output.

This outcome, however, is totally dependent upon the fact that input prices are fixed in the short run. Consider what will happen in the long run when they are free to change. Firms can produce beyond the full-employment output level only by running factories and businesses at extremely high rates of utilization. This creates a great deal of demand for the economy's limited supply of productive resources. In particular, labour is in great demand because the only way to produce beyond full employment is if workers are working overtime.

FIGURE 10-5   **Aggregate Supply in the Long Run**

The long-run aggregate supply curve AS_{LR} is vertical at the full-employment level of real GDP (GDP_f) because in the long run wages and other input prices rise and match changes in the price level. So price-level changes do not affect firms' profits and thus they create no incentive for firms to alter their output.

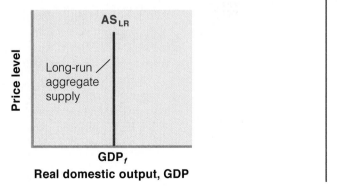

An aggregate supply curve identifies the relationship between the price level and real output.

As time passes and input prices are free to change, the high demand will start to raise input prices. In particular, overworked employees will demand and receive raises as employers scramble to deal with the labour shortages that arise when the economy is producing at above its full-employment output level. As input prices increase, firm profits will begin to fall. And as they decline, so does the motive firms have to produce more than the full-employment output level. This process of rising input prices and falling profits continues until the rise in input prices exactly matches the initial change in output prices (in our example, they both double). When that happens, firm profits in real terms return to their original level so that firms are once again motivated to produce at exactly the full-employment output level. This adjustment process means that in the long run the economy will produce at full employment regardless of the price level (in our example, at either P = 100 or P = 200). That is why the long-run aggregate supply curve AS_{LR} is vertical above the full-employment output level. Every possible price level on the vertical axis is associated with the economy producing at the full-employment output level in the long run once input prices adjust to exactly match changes in output prices.

Focusing on the Short Run

The immediate-short-run aggregate supply curve, the short-run aggregate supply curve, and the long-run aggregate supply curve are all important. Each curve is appropriate to situations that match its respective assumptions about the flexibility of input and output prices. In the remainder of the book, we will have several different opportunities to refer to each curve. But our focus in the rest of this chapter and the several chapters that immediately follow will be on short-run aggregate supply curves, such as the AS curve shown in Figure 10-4. Indeed, unless explicitly stated otherwise, all references to "aggregate supply" are to the AS curve in the short run.

Our emphasis on the short-run aggregate supply curve AS stems from our interest in understanding the business cycle in the simplest possible way. It is a fact that real-world economies typically manifest simultaneous changes in both their price levels and their levels of real output. The upward-sloping short-run AS curve is the only version of aggregate supply that can handle simultaneous movements in both of these variables. By contrast, the price level is assumed fixed in the immediate-short-run version of aggregate supply illustrated in Figure 10-3 and the economy's output is always equal to the full-employment output level in the long-run version of aggregate supply shown in Figure 10-5. This renders these versions of the aggregate supply curve less useful as part of a core model for analyzing business cycles and demonstrating the short-run government policies designed to deal with them. In our current discussion, we will reserve use of the immediate short run and the long run for specific, clearly identified situations. Later in the book we will explore how the short-run AS curve and long-run AS curve are linked, and how that linkage adds several additional macroeconomic insights about cycles and policy.

Changes in Aggregate Supply

An existing aggregate supply curve identifies the relationship between the price level and real output, other things equal. But when one or more of these "other things" change, the curve itself shifts. The rightward shift of the curve from AS_1 to AS_3 in Figure 10-6 represents an increase in aggregate supply, indicating that firms are willing to produce and sell more real output at each price level. The leftward shift of the curve from AS_1 to AS_2 represents a decrease in aggregate supply. At each price level, firms will not produce as much output as before.

determinants of aggregate supply
Factors such as input prices, productivity, and the legal-institutional environment that shift the aggregate supply curve.

Figure 10-6 lists the "other things" that shift the aggregate supply curve. Called the **determinants of aggregate supply,** they collectively determine the location of the aggregate supply curve and shift the curve when they change. Changes in these determinants cause per-unit production costs to be either higher or lower than before *at each price level*. These changes in per-unit production cost affect profits, which leads firms to alter the amount of output they are willing to produce *at each price level*. For example, firms may collectively offer $1 trillion of real output at a price level of 1.0 (100 in index value), rather than $900 billion. Or, they may offer $800 billion rather than $1 trillion.

FIGURE 10-6   Changes in Short-Run Aggregate Supply

A change in one or more of the listed determinants of aggregate supply will shift the aggregate supply curve. The rightward shift of the aggregate supply curve from AS$_1$ to AS$_3$ represents an increase in aggregate supply; the leftward shift of the curve from AS$_1$ to AS$_2$ shows a decrease in aggregate supply.

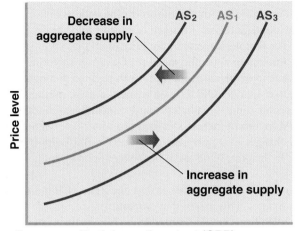

Determinants of the short-run aggregate supply: factors that shift the aggregate supply curve

1. Change in input prices
   a. Domestic resource price
   b. Price of imported resources
2. Change in productivity
3. Change in legal-institutional environment
   a. Business taxes and subsidies
   b. Government regulation

The point is that when one of the determinants listed in Figure 10-6 changes, the aggregate supply curve shifts to the right or left. Changes that reduce per-unit production cost shift the aggregate supply curve to the right, as from AS$_1$ to AS$_2$; changes that increase per-unit production costs shift it to the left, as from AS$_1$ to AS$_3$. When per-unit production costs change for reasons other than changes in real output, the aggregate supply curve shifts.

The determinants of aggregate supply listed in Figure 10-6 require more discussion.

INPUT PRICES

Input or resource prices—to be distinguished from the output prices that make up the price level—are a key determinant of aggregate supply. These resources can be either domestic or imported.

Domestic Resource Prices   As stated earlier, wages and salaries make up about 75 percent of all business costs. Other things equal, decreases in wages and salaries reduce per-unit production costs. So, the aggregate supply shifts to the right. Increases in wages and salaries shift the curve to the left. Examples:

- Labour supply increases because of substantial immigration. Wages and per-unit production costs fall, shifting the AS curve to the right.

- Labour supply decreases because a rapid increase in pension income causes many older workers to opt for early retirement. Wage rates and per-unit production costs rise, shifting the AS curve to the left.

Similarly, the aggregate supply curve shifts when the prices of land and capital inputs change. Examples:

- The price of capital (machinery and equipment) falls because of declines in the prices of steel and electronic components. Per-unit production costs decline and the AS shifts to the right.

- Land resources expand through discoveries of mineral deposits, irrigation of land, or technical innovations that transform "non-resources" (say, vast northern shrub lands) into valuable resources (productive lands). The price of land declines, per-unit production costs fall, and the AS curve shifts to the right.

Prices of Imported Resources Just as foreign demand for Canadian goods contributes to Canadian aggregate demand, resources imported from abroad (such as oil, tin, and coffee beans) add to Canadian aggregate supply. Added resources—whether domestic or imported—boost production capacity. Generally, a decrease in the price of imported resources increases Canadian aggregate supply, and an increase in their price reduces Canadian aggregate supply.

A good example of the major effect that changing resource prices can have on aggregate supply is the oil price hikes of the 1970s. At that time, a group of oil-producing nations called the Organization of the Petroleum Exporting Countries (OPEC) worked in concert to decrease oil production in order to raise the price of oil. The tenfold increase in the price of oil that OPEC achieved during the 1970s drove up per-unit production costs and jolted the Canadian aggregate supply curve leftward. By contrast, a sharp decline in oil prices in the mid-1980s resulted in a rightward shift of the Canadian aggregate supply curve. In 1999 OPEC again reasserted itself, raising oil prices and therefore per-unit production costs for some Canadian producers including airlines and shipping companies like FedEx and UPS. More recent increases in the price of oil have been mostly due to increases in demand rather than changes in supply caused by OPEC. But keep in mind that no matter what their cause, increases in the price of oil and other resources raise production costs and decrease aggregate supply.

Exchange-rate fluctuations are one factor that may change the price of imported resources. Suppose the Canadian dollar appreciates. This means that domestic producers face a lower *dollar* price of imported resources. Canadian firms would respond by increasing their imports of foreign resources, thereby lowering their per-unit production costs at each level of output. Falling per-unit production costs would shift the Canadian aggregate supply curve to the right.

A depreciation of the dollar will have the opposite effects and will shift the aggregate supply to the left.

PRODUCTIVITY

The second major determinant of aggregate supply is *productivity*, which is a measure of the relationship between a nation's level of real output and the amount of resources used to produce it. Productivity is a measure of real output per unit of input:

$$\text{Productivity} = \frac{\text{total output}}{\text{total input}}$$

An increase in productivity enables the economy to obtain more real output from its limited resources. It does this by reducing the per-unit cost of output (per-unit production cost). Suppose, for example, that real output is 10 units, that 5 units of input are needed to produce that quantity, and that the price of each input unit is $2. Then

$$\text{Productivity} = \frac{\text{total output}}{\text{total input}} = \frac{10}{5} = 2$$

and

$$\text{Per-unit production cost} = \frac{\text{total input cost}}{\text{total output}} = \frac{(\$2 \times 5)}{10} = \$1$$

Note that we obtain the total input cost by multiplying the unit input cost by the number of inputs used.

Now suppose productivity increases so that real output doubles to 20 units, while the price and quantity of the input remain constant at $2 and 5 units. Using the above equations, we see that productivity rises from 2 to 4 and that the per-unit production cost of the output falls from $1 to $0.50. The doubled productivity has reduced the per-unit production cost by half.

WORKED PROBLEM 10.1
Productivity and Costs

By reducing the per-unit production cost, an increase in productivity shifts the aggregate supply curve to the right. The main source of productivity advance is improved production technology, often embodied within new plant and equipment that replaces old plant and equipment. Other sources of productivity increases are a better-educated and a better-trained workforce, improved forms of business enterprises, and the reallocation of labour resources from lower productivity to higher productivity uses.

Much rarer, decreases in productivity increase per-unit production costs and therefore reduce aggregate supply (shift the curve to the left).

LEGAL-INSTITUTIONAL ENVIRONMENT

Changes in the legal-institutional setting in which businesses operate are the final determinant of aggregate supply. Such changes may alter the per-unit costs of output and, if so, shift the aggregate supply curve. Two changes of this type are (1) changes in business taxes and subsidies, and (2) changes in the extent of regulation.

Business Taxes and Subsidies   Higher business taxes—corporate income taxes and capital, sales, excise, and payroll taxes—increase per-unit costs and reduce aggregate supply in much the same way as a wage increase does. An increase in such taxes paid by businesses will increase per-unit production costs and shift the aggregate supply curve to the left. Similarly, a business subsidy—a payment or tax break by government to producers—lowers production costs and increases aggregate supply.

Government Regulation   It is usually costly for businesses to comply with government regulations. More regulation therefore tends to increase per-unit production costs and shift the aggregate supply curve to the left. "Supply-side" proponents of deregulation of the economy have argued forcefully that by increasing efficiency and reducing the paperwork associated with complex regulations deregulation will reduce per-unit costs and shift the aggregate supply curve to the right.

QUICK REVIEW

- The immediate-short-run aggregate supply curve is horizontal at the economy's current price level to reflect the fact that in the immediate short run input and output prices are fixed so that producers will supply whatever quantity of real output is demanded at the current output prices.

- The short-run aggregate supply curve (or simply the "aggregate supply curve") is upward-sloping because it reflects the fact that in the short run wages and other input prices remain fixed while output prices vary. Given fixed resource costs, higher output prices raise firm profits and encourage them to increase their output levels. The curve's upward slope reflects rising per-unit production costs as output expands.

- The long-run aggregate supply curve is vertical because, given sufficient time, wages and other input prices rise and fall to match price-level changes; because price-level changes do not change real rewards, they do not change production decisions.

- By altering the per-unit production cost independent of changes in the level of output, changes in one or more of the determinants of aggregate supply (Figure 10-6) shift the short-run aggregate supply curve.

- An increase in short-run aggregate supply is shown as a rightward shift of the curve; a decrease is shown as a leftward shift of the curve.

10.3 | Equilibrium and Changes in Equilibrium

equilibrium price level
The price level at which the aggregate demand curve intersects the aggregate supply curve.

equilibrium real domestic output
The real domestic output at which the aggregate demand curve intersects the aggregate supply curve.

Of all the possible combinations of price levels and levels of real GDP, which combination will the economy gravitate toward, at least in the short run? **Figure 10-7 (Key Graph)** and its accompanying table provide the answer. Equilibrium occurs at the price level that equalizes the amount of real output demanded and supplied. The intersection of the aggregate demand curve AD and the aggregate supply curve AS establishes the economy's **equilibrium price level** and **equilibrium real domestic output.** So, aggregate demand and aggregate supply jointly establish the price level and level of real GDP.

In Figure 10-7 the equilibrium price level and level of real output are 100 and $510 billion, respectively. To illustrate why, suppose the price level were 92 rather than 100. We see from the table that the lower price level would encourage businesses to produce real output of $502 billion. This is shown by point *a* on the AS curve in the graph. But, as revealed by the table and point *b* on the aggregate demand curve, buyers would want to purchase $514 billion of real output at price level 92. Competition among buyers to purchase the lesser available real output of $502 billion will eliminate the $12 billion (= $514 billion − $502 billion) shortage and pull up the price level to 100.

As the table and graph show, the excess demand for the output of the economy causes the price level to rise from 92 to 100, which encourages producers to increase their real output from $502 billion to $510 billion, thereby increasing GDP. In increasing their real output, producers hire more employees, reducing the unemployment level in the economy. When equality occurs between the amounts of real output produced and purchased, as it does at price level 100, the economy has achieved equilibrium (here at $510 billion of real GDP).

Now let's apply the AD–AS model to various situations that can confront the economy. For simplicity we will use *P* and GDP symbols rather than actual numbers. Remember that these symbols represent, respectively, price index values and real amounts of GDP.

Increases in AD: Demand-Pull Inflation

Suppose households and businesses decide to increase their consumption and investment spending—actions that shift the aggregate demand curve to the right. Our list of determinants of aggregate demand (Figure 10-2) provides several reasons why this shift might occur. Perhaps consumers feel wealthier because of large gains in their stock holdings. As a result, consumers would consume more (save less) of their current income. Perhaps firms boost their investment spending because they anticipate higher future profits from investments in new capital. Those profits are based on having new equipment and facilities that incorporate a number of new technologies. And perhaps government increases spending in health care.

inflationary gap
The amount by which equilibrium GDP exceeds potential GDP.

As shown by the rise in the price level from P_1 to P_2 in Figure 10-8, the increase in aggregate demand beyond the full-employment level of output causes inflation. This is *demand-pull inflation,* because the price level is being pulled up by the increase in aggregate demand. Also, observe that the increase in demand expands real output from the full-employment level GDP_f to GDP_1. The distance between GDP_1 and GDP_f is an **inflationary gap,** the amount by which equilibrium GDP exceeds potential GDP. An inflationary gap is also referred to as a positive GDP gap. *(Key Question 4)*

A careful examination of Figure 10-8 reveals an interesting point. The increase in aggregate demand from AD_1 to AD_2 increases real output only to GDP_1, not to GDP_2, because part of the increase in aggregate demand is absorbed as inflation as the price level rises from P_1 to P_2. Had the price level remained at P_1, the shift of aggregate demand from AD_1 to AD_2 would have increased real output to GDP_2. But in Figure 10-8 inflation reduced the increase in real output only to GDP_1. For any initial increase in aggregate demand, the resulting increase in real output will be smaller the greater the increase in the price level.

KEY GRAPH @

FIGURE 10-7   The Equilibrium Price Level and Equilibrium Real GDP

The intersection of the aggregate demand curve and the aggregate supply curve determines the economy's equilibrium price level. At the equilibrium price level of 100 (in index-value terms) the $510 billion of real output demanded matches the $510 billion of real output supplied. So the equilibrium GDP is $510 billion.

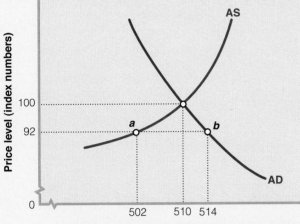

Real Output Demanded (billions)	Price Level (index number)	Real Output Supplied (billions)
$506	108	$513
508	104	512
510	**100**	**510**
512	96	505
514	92	502

Quick Quiz

1. **The AD curve slopes downward because**
   a. per-unit production costs fall as real GDP increases.
   b. the income and substitution effects are at work.
   c. changes in the determinants of AD alter the amounts of real GDP demanded at each price level.
   d. decreases in the price level give rise to real-balances, interest-rate, and foreign-trade effects, which increase the amounts of real GDP demanded.

2. **The AS curve slopes upward because**
   a. per-unit production costs rise as real GDP expands toward and beyond its full-employment level.
   b. the income and substitution effects are at work.
   c. changes in the determinants of AS alter the amounts of real GDP supplied at each price level.
   d. increases in the price level give rise to real-balances, interest-rate, and foreign-purchases effects, which increase the amounts of real GDP supplied.

3. **At price level 92**
   a. a GDP surplus of $12 billion occurs that drives the price level up to 100.
   b. a GDP shortage of $12 billion occurs that drives the price level up to 100.
   c. the aggregate amount of real GDP demanded is less than the aggregate amount of GDP supplied.
   d. the economy is operating beyond its capacity to produce.

4. **Suppose real output demanded rises by $4 billion at each price level. The new equilibrium price level will be:**
   a. 108.   c. 96.
   b. 104.   d. 92.

FIGURE 10-8 — An Increase in Aggregate Demand that Causes Demand-Pull Inflation

An increase in aggregate demand generally increases both the GDP and price level. The increase in aggregate demand from AD_1 to AD_2 is partly dissipated in inflation (P_1 to P_2) and real output increases only from GDP_f to GDP_1.

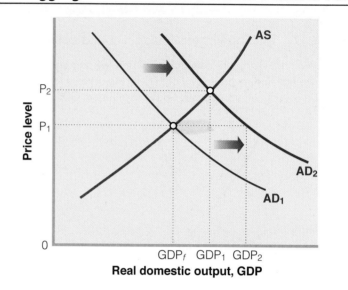

Decreases in AD: Recession and Cyclical Unemployment

Decreases in aggregate demand describe the opposite end of the business cycle: recession and cyclical unemployment (rather than above-full employment and demand-pull inflation). For example, in 2000 investment spending substantially declined in the wake of an overexpansion of capital during the second half of the 1990s. In Figure 10-9 we show the resulting decline in aggregate demand as a leftward shift from AD_1 to AD_2.

But now we add an important twist to the analysis—a twist that makes use of the fact that fixed prices lead to horizontal aggregate supply curves (a fact explained earlier in this chapter in the section on the immediate-short-run aggregate supply curve). What goes up—the price level—does not readily go down. *Deflation,* a decline in the price level, is a rarity in the Canadian economy.

FIGURE 10-9 — A Decrease in Aggregate Demand That Causes a Recession

If the price level is downwardly inflexible at P_1, a decline of aggregate demand from AD_1 to AD_2 will move the economy leftward from a to b along the horizontal broken-line segment (an immediate-short-run aggregate supply curve) and reduce real GDP from GDP_f to GDP_1. Idle production capacity, cyclical unemployment, and a recessionary GDP gap (of GDP_f minus GDP_1) will result. If the price level were flexible downward, the decline in aggregate demand would move the economy a to c instead of from a to b.

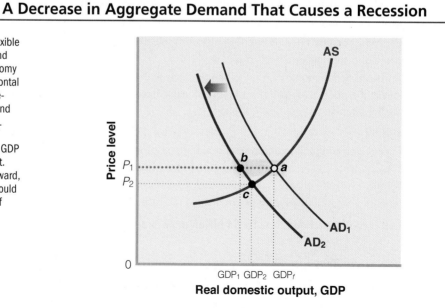

CONSIDER THIS | The Global Financial Crisis and the Decrease in Aggregate Demand

Figure 10-9 helps demonstrate the recession in Canada in 2008–09, brought about by the global financial crisis. A large unexpected decrease in aggregate demand (as from AD_1 to AD_2) occurred because private-sector spending suddenly declined. Viewed through the determinants of aggregate demand:

- *Consumer spending* declined because of (a) reduced consumer wealth due to reductions in stock market value, (b) fearful consumer expectations about future employment and income levels, and (c) increased emphasis on saving more and borrowing less.

- *Investment spending* declined because of lower expected returns on investment. These lower expectations resulted from the prospects of poor future business conditions and high degrees of excess capacity.

- *Net exports* declined because our major trading partner, the U.S., was in deep recession due to the burst of the housing bubble.

The decline in aggregate demand jolted the Canadian economy from a point such as *a* in Figure 10-9 leftward to a point such as *b*. Because the price level remained roughly constant, the decline in aggregate demand caused the economy to move leftward along the immediate-short-run aggregate supply curve (the dashed horizontal line). As a result, real GDP took the brunt of the blow, declining sharply (as from GDP_f to GDP_1). By contrast, if prices had been more flexible, then the economy could have slid down the downward-sloping AS curve (as from point *a* to point *c*), with the result being a smaller decrease in real GDP (as from GDP_f to GDP_2). But with the price level roughly constant, a full-strength multiplier occurred, as illustrated in Figure 10-9 by the decline of output from GDP_f to GDP_1, rather than from GDP_f to GDP_2. As of March 2009, the Canadian economy was experiencing a significant negative GDP gap (as illustrated by GDP_1 minus GDP_f in the figure), which was accompanied by a large reduction in employment, a large increase in unemployment, and a sharp rise in the unemployment rate. In August 2009, the unemployment rate reached an 11-year high of 8.7 percent.

The economy represented by Figure 10-9 moves from *a* to *b*, rather than from *a* to *c*. The outcome is a decline of real output from GDP_f to GDP_1, with no change in the price level. It is as though the aggregate supply curve in Figure 10-9 is horizontal at P_1 leftward from GDP_f, as indicated by the dashed line. This decline of real output from GDP_f to GDP_1 constitutes a *recession*, and since fewer workers are needed to produce the lower output, *cyclical unemployment* arises. The distance between GDP_1 and GDP_f is a **recessionary gap,** the amount by which actual output falls short of the full-employment output. A recessionary gap is also referred to as a *negative GDP gap.* Such a gap occurred in Canada during 2001 when unemployment rose to 7.7 percent of the labour force from 6.8 percent in 2000. But unlike the American economy, Canada did not slip into recession in 2001; economic growth slowed to 1.9 percent in 2001, from a strong 4.4 percent in 2000.

Close inspection of Figure 10-9 reveals that, with the price level stuck at P_1, real GDP decreases by the full leftward shift of the AD curve. Real output takes the full brunt of the decline in aggregate demand because product prices tend to be inflexible in a downward direction. There are numerous reasons for this.

- ***Fear of Price Wars***   Some large firms may be concerned that if they reduce their prices, rivals not only will match their price cuts but also may retaliate by making even deeper cuts. An initial price cut may touch off an unwanted *price war*—successively deeper and deeper rounds of price cuts. In such a situation, each firm eventually ends up with far less profit or higher losses than would be the case if it had simply maintained its prices. For this reason, each firm may resist making the initial price cut, choosing instead to reduce production and lay off workers.

- ***Menu Costs***   Firms that think a recession will be relatively short lived may be reluctant to cut their prices. One reason is what economists metaphorically call **menu costs,** named after their most obvious example: the cost of printing new menus when a restaurant decides to reduce its prices. But lowering prices also creates other costs, including (1) estimating the magnitude and

recessionary gap
The amount by which equilibrium GDP falls short of potential GDP.

menu costs
Costs associated with changing the prices of goods and services.

duration of the shift in demand to determine whether prices should be lowered, (2) re-pricing items held in inventory, (3) printing and mailing new catalogues, and (4) communicating new prices to customers, perhaps through advertising. When menu costs are present, firms may choose to avoid them by retaining current prices. That is, they may wait to see if the decline in aggregate demand is permanent.

ORIGIN 10.2
Efficiency Wages

efficiency wages
Wages that elicit maximum work effort and thus minimize labour cost per unit of output.

- *Wage Contracts*   It usually is not profitable for firms to cut their product prices if they cannot also cut their wage rates. Wages are usually inflexible downward because large parts of the labour force work under contracts prohibiting wage cuts for the duration of the contract. (It is not uncommon for collective bargaining agreements in major industries to run for three years.) Similarly, the wages and salaries of non-union workers are usually adjusted once a year, rather than quarterly or monthly.

- *Morale, Effort, and Productivity*   Wage inflexibility downward is reinforced by the reluctance of many employers to reduce wage rates. Some current wages may be so-called **efficiency wages**—wages that elicit maximum work effort and thus minimize labour costs per unit of output. If worker productivity (output per hour of work) remains constant, lower wages *do* reduce labour costs per unit of output. But lower wages might lower worker morale and work effort, thereby reducing productivity. Considered alone, lower productivity raises labour costs per unit of output because less output is produced. If the higher labour costs resulting from reduced productivity exceed the cost savings from the lower wage, then wage cuts will increase rather than reduce labour costs per unit of output. In such situations, firms will resist lowering wages when they are faced with a decline in aggregate demand.

- *Minimum Wage*   The minimum wage imposes a legal floor under the wages of the least skilled workers. Firms paying those wages cannot reduce that wage rate when aggregate demand declines.

But a major caution is needed here: although most economists agree that wages and prices tend to be inflexible downward in the short run, wages and prices are more flexible than in the past. Intense foreign competition and the declining power of unions in Canada have undermined the ability of workers and firms to resist price and wage cuts when faced with falling aggregate demand. This increased flexibility may be one reason for the relatively mild recessions in recent times. In 2002 and 2003 Canadian auto manufacturers, for example, maintained output in the face of falling demand by offering zero-interest loans on auto purchases. This, in effect, was a disguised price cut. But, our description in Figure 10-9 remains valid. In 2001 the overall price level did not decline although unemployment rose by 80,000 workers.

CONSIDER THIS | The Ratchet Effect

A ratchet analogy is a good way to think about effects of changes in aggregate demand on the price level. A ratchet is a tool or mechanism such as a winch, car jack, or socket wrench that cranks a wheel forward but does not allow it to go backward. Properly set, each allows the operator to move an object (boat, car, or nut) in one direction while preventing it from moving in the opposite direction.

Product prices, wage rates, and per-unit production costs are highly flexible upward when aggregate demand increases along the aggregate supply curve. In Canada, the price level has increased in 57 of the 58 years since 1950.

But when aggregate demand decreases, product prices, wage rates, and per-unit production costs are inflexible downward. The price level has declined in only a single year (1953) since 1950, even though aggregate demand and real output have declined in a number of years, such as 1946, 1954, 1982, and 1991.

In terms of our analogy, increases in aggregate demand ratchet the Canadian price level upward. Once in place, the higher price level remains until it is ratcheted up again. The higher price level tends to remain even with declines in aggregate demand.

Decreases in AS: Cost-Push Inflation

Suppose that tropical storms in areas where there are major oil facilities severely disrupt world oil supplies and drive up oil prices by, say, 300 percent. Higher energy prices would spread through the economy, driving up production and distribution costs on a wide variety of goods. The Canadian aggregate supply curve would shift to the left, say from AS_1 to AS_2 in Figure 10-10. The resulting increase in price level would be *cost-push inflation.*

The effects of a leftward shift in aggregate supply are doubly bad. When aggregate supply shifts from AS_1 to AS_2, the economy moves from *a* to *b*. The price level rises from P_1 to P_2 and real output declines from GDP_f to GDP_2. Along with the cost-push inflation, a recession (and negative GDP gap) occurs. That is exactly what happened in Canada in the mid-1970s when the price of oil rocketed upward. Then, oil expenditures were about 10 percent of Canadian GDP, compared to only 3 percent today. So, as indicated in this chapter's Last Word, the Canadian economy is now less vulnerable to cost-push inflation arising from such aggregate supply shocks.

Increases in AS: Full Employment with Price-Level Stability

For the first time in more than a decade, in early 2000 Canada experienced full employment, strong economic growth, and very low inflation. Specifically, in 2000 the unemployment rate fell below 7 percent—a level not seen since 1975—and real GDP grew at 4.3 percent, *without igniting inflation.* At first thought, this "macroeconomic bliss" seems to be incompatible with the AD–AS model. An upward-sloping aggregate supply curve suggests that increases in aggregate demand that are sufficient for full employment (or overfull employment) will raise the price level. Higher inflation, so it would seem, is the inevitable price paid for expanding output to and beyond the full-employment level.

But inflation remained very mild in the late 1990s and early 2000s. Figure 10-11 helps explain why. Let's first suppose that aggregate demand increased from AD_1 to AD_2 along the aggregate supply curve AS_1. Taken alone, that increase in aggregate demand would move the economy from *a* to *b*. Real output would rise from less than full-employment real output GDP_1 to full-capacity real output GDP_2. The economy would experience inflation as shown by the increase in the price level from P_1 to P_3. Such inflation had occurred at the end of previous vigorous expansions of aggregate demand in the late 1980s.

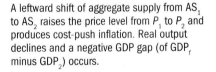

FIGURE 10-10   A Decrease in Aggregate Supply That Causes Cost-Push Inflation

A leftward shift of aggregate supply from AS_1 to AS_2 raises the price level from P_1 to P_2 and produces cost-push inflation. Real output declines and a negative GDP gap (of GDP_f minus GDP_2) occurs.

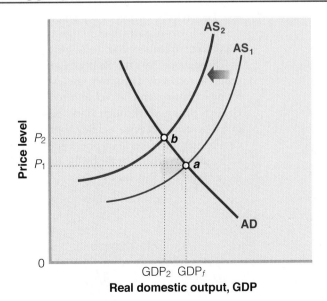

| FIGURE 10-11 | Growth, Full Employment, and Relative Price Stability |

Normally, an increase in aggregate demand from AD_1 to AD_2 would move the economy from a to b along AS_1. Real output would expand to its full-capacity level (GDP_2), and inflation would result (P_1 to P_3). But in the late 1990s, significant increases in productivity shifted the aggregate supply curve, as from AS_1 to AS_2. The economy moved from a to c rather than from a to b. It experienced strong economic growth (GDP_1 to GDP_3), full employment, and only very mild inflation (P_1 to P_2).

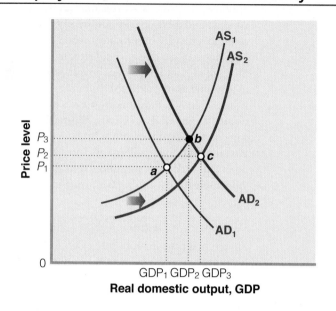

A shift of the aggregate supply curve to the right shifts the economy's full employment and its full capacity output.

In the more recent period, however, larger-than-usual increases in productivity occurred due to a burst of new technology relating to computers, the Internet, inventory management systems, electronic commerce, and so on. The quickened productivity growth reduced per-unit production cost and shifted the aggregate supply curve to the right, as from AS_1 to AS_2 in Figure 10-11. The relevant aggregate demand and aggregate supply curves thus became AD_2 and AS_2, not AD_2 and AS_1. Instead of moving from a to b, the economy moved from a to c. Real output increased from GDP_1 to GDP_3 and the price level rose only modestly (from P_1 to P_2). The shift of the aggregate supply curve from AS_1 to AS_2 increased the economy's full-employment output and its full-capacity output. That accommodated the increase in aggregate demand without causing inflation.

But in 2001 the macroeconomic bliss of the late 1990s came face to face with the old economic principles. Aggregate demand growth slowed because of a substantial fall in investment spending. The terrorist attacks of September 11, 2001 in the U.S. further dampened aggregate demand through lower exports to our largest trading partner. The unemployment rate inched up from 6.8 percent in January 2001 to 7.7 percent in mid-2002.

Throughout 2001 the Bank of Canada lowered interest rates to try to halt the slowdown and promote recovery. The lower interest rates spurred aggregate demand, particularly the demand for new housing, and helped spur recovery. The economy resumed its economic growth in 2002. Growth continued through 2008, during which the unemployment rate reached a 37-year low of 6.0 percent. Yet price stability continued as the core rate of inflation stayed at about 2 percent despite hefty increases in oil prices during 2008. We will examine government stabilization policies such as those carried out the by the Bank of Canada in the AD–AS context in chapters that follow. *(Key Questions 5, 6, and 7)*

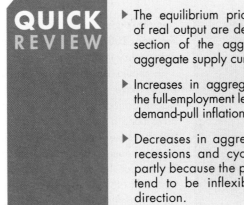

QUICK REVIEW

▶ The equilibrium price level and amount of real output are determined at the intersection of the aggregate demand and aggregate supply curves.

▶ Increases in aggregate demand beyond the full-employment level of real GDP cause demand-pull inflation.

▶ Decreases in aggregate demand cause recessions and cyclical unemployment, partly because the price level and wages tend to be inflexible in a downward direction.

▶ Decreases in aggregate supply cause cost-push inflation.

▶ Full employment, high economic growth, and price stability are compatible if productivity-driven increases in aggregate supply are sufficient to balance growing aggregate demand.

The LAST WORD   Has the Impact of Oil Prices Diminished?

Significant changes in oil prices historically have shifted the aggregate supply curve and greatly affected the Canadian economy. Have the effects of such changes weakened?

Canada has experienced several aggregate supply shocks—abrupt shifts of the aggregate supply curve—caused by significant changes in oil prices. In the mid-1970s the price of oil rose from $4 to $12 per barrel, and then again in the late 1970s it increased to $24 per barrel and eventually to $35. These oil price changes shifted the aggregate supply curve leftward, causing rapid inflation, rising unemployment, and a negative GDP gap.

In the late 1980s and through most of the 1990s oil prices fell, sinking to a low of $11 per barrel in late 1998. This decline created a positive aggregate supply shock beneficial to the Canadian economy. But in response to those low oil prices, in late 1999 OPEC teamed with Mexico, Norway, and Russia to restrict oil output and thus boost prices. That action, along with a rapidly growing international demand for oil, sent oil prices upward once again. By March 2000 the price of a barrel of oil reached $34, before

settling back to about $25 to $28 in 2001 and 2002.

Some economists feared that the rising price of oil would increase energy prices by so much that the Canadian aggregate supply curve would shift to the left, creating cost-push inflation. But inflation in Canada remained modest.

Then came a greater test: A "perfect storm"—continuing conflict in Iraq, the rising demand for oil in China and India, a pickup of economic growth in several industrial nations, disruption of oil production by hurricanes in the United States, and concern about political developments in Venezuela—pushed the price of oil to over $60 a barrel in 2005. (You can find the current daily basket price of oil at OPEC's Web site, www.opec.org.) The Canadian inflation rate rose in 2005, but core *inflation* (the inflation rate after subtracting changes in the prices of food and energy) remained steady. Why have rises in oil prices lost their inflationary punch?

In the early 2000s, other determinants of aggregate supply swamped the potential inflationary impacts of the oil price increases. The overall trend of lower production costs resulting from rapid productivity advances more than compensated for the rise in oil prices. Put simply, aggregate supply did not decline as it had in earlier periods.

Perhaps of greater importance, oil prices are a less significant factor in the Canadian economy than they were in the 1970s. Prior to 1980, changes in oil prices greatly affected core inflation in Canada. But since 1980 they have had very little effect on core inflation.[2] The main reason has been a significant decline in the amount of oil and gas used in producing each dollar of Canadian GDP. In 2005 producing a dollar of GDP required about 7000 BTUs of oil and gas, compared to 14,000 BTUs in 1970. (A BTU, or British Thermal Unit, is the amount of energy required to heat one pound of water by one degree Fahrenheit.)

Part of this decline resulted from new production techniques spawned by the higher oil and energy prices. But equally important has been the changing relative composition of the GDP; away from larger, heavier items (such as earth-moving equipment) that are energy-intensive to make and transport and toward smaller, lighter items (such as microchips and software). American experts on energy economics estimate that the U.S. economy is about 33 percent less sensitive to oil price fluctuations than it was in the early 1980s and 50 percent less sensitive than in the mid-1970s.[3] Given the similarities between the Canadian and U.S. economies, there is reason to believe that similar magnitudes also hold for the Canadian economy.

A final reason why changes in oil prices seem to have lost their inflationary punch is that the Bank of Canada has become more vigilant and adept at maintaining price stability through monetary policy. The Bank of Canada did not let the oil price increases of

1999–2000 become generalized as core inflation. The same turned out to be true with the dramatic rise in oil prices in 2007 and 2008, when the price of oil rose from just over $50 per barrel in January 2007 to over $140 per barrel in July 2008. But the onset of a world recession in the fall of 2008

sent the price of oil to below $40 in February 2009. (We will discuss monetary policy in depth in Chapter 13.)

It should be noted that higher oil prices have had differential impacts across Canada. The higher oil prices have been a boon to Alberta's economy because it made the exploitation of its oil sands economically feasible. To a much lesser extent, Newfoundland and Nova Scotia have also indirectly benefited from higher oil prices because of their offshore oil reserves. On the other hand, the higher oil prices have hardly been welcome by consumers (particularly low-income families) and businesses in provinces such as Ontario and Quebec.

[2]Mark A. Hooker, "Are Oil Shocks Inflationary? Asymmetric and Nonlinear Specifications versus Changes in Regimes," *Journal of Money, Credit and Banking*, May 2002, pp. 540–561.

[3]Stephen P., A. Brown, and Mine K. Yücel, "Oil Prices and the Economy," Federal Reserve Bank of Dallas, *Southwest Economy*, July–August 2000, pp. 1–6.

Question

Go to the OPEC website, www.opec.org, and find the current "OPEC basket price" of oil. By clicking on that amount, you will find the annual prices of oil for the past five years. By what percentage is the current price higher or lower than five years ago? Next, go to the Statistics Canada website (http://www40.statcan.ca/l01/cst01/econ05-eng.htm) and find Canada's real GDP for the past five years. By what percentage is real GDP higher or lower than it was five years ago? What if, anything, can you conclude about the relationship between the price of oil and the level of real GDP in Canada?

CHAPTER SUMMARY

10.1 ▶ AGGREGATE DEMAND

- The aggregate demand–aggregate supply model (AD–AS model) is a variable-price model that enables analysis of simultaneous changes of real GDP and the price level.

- The aggregate demand curve shows the level of real output that the economy will purchase at each price level.

- The aggregate demand curve is downward-sloping because of the real-balances effect, the interest-rate effect, and the foreign-trade effect. The real-balances effect indicates that inflation reduces the real value or purchasing power of fixed-value financial assets held by households, causing them to retrench on their consumer spending. The interest-rate effect means that, with a specific supply of money, a higher price level increases the demand for money, raising the interest rate and reducing consumption and investment purchases. The foreign-trade effect suggests that an increase in one country's price level relative to other countries' reduces the net exports component of that nation's aggregate demand.

- The determinants of aggregate demand are spending by domestic consumers, businesses, government, and foreign buyers. Changes in the factors listed in Figure 10-2 alter the spending by these groups and shift the aggregate demand curve.

10.2 ▶ AGGREGATE SUPPLY

- The aggregate supply curve shows the levels of real output that businesses will produce at various possible price levels. The slope of the aggregate supply curve depends upon the flexibility of input and output prices. Since these vary over time, aggregate supply curves are categorized into three time horizons that each have different underlying assumptions about the flexibility of input and output prices.

- The *immediate-short-run aggregate supply curve* assumes that both input prices and output prices are fixed. With output prices fixed, the aggregate supply curve is a horizontal line at the current price level. The *short-run aggregate supply curve* assumes nominal wages and other input prices remain fixed while output prices vary. The aggregate supply curve is generally upsloping because per-unit production costs, and hence the prices that firms must receive, rise as real output expands. The aggregate supply curve is relatively steep to the right of the full-employment output level and relatively flat to the left of it. The *long-run aggregate supply curve* assumes that nominal wages and other input prices fully match any change in the price level. The curve is vertical at the full-employment output level.

- Because the short-run aggregate supply curve is the only version of aggregate supply that can handle simultaneous changes in the price level and real output, it serves well as the core aggregate supply curve for analyzing the business cycle and economic policy. Unless stated otherwise, all references to "aggregate supply" refer to the immediate-short-run aggregate supply and the short-run aggregate supply curve.

- Figure 10-6 lists the determinants of aggregate supply: input prices, productivity, and the legal-institutional environment. A change in any one of these factors will change per-unit production costs at each level of output and therefore alter the location of the aggregate supply curve.

10.3 ▶ EQUILIBRIUM AND CHANGES IN EQUILIBRIUM

- The intersection of the aggregate demand and aggregate supply curves determines an economy's equilibrium price level and real GDP. At the intersection, the quantity of real GDP demanded equals the quantity of real GDP supplied.

- Increases in aggregate demand to the right of the full-employment output cause inflation and positive GDP gaps (actual GDP exceeds potential GDP). An upward-sloping aggregate supply curve weakens the effect of an increase in aggregate demand because a portion of the increase in aggregate demand is dissipated in inflation.

- Shifts of the aggregate demand curve to the left of the full-employment output cause recession, negative GDP gaps, and cyclical unemployment. The price level may not fall during recessions because of downwardly inflexible prices and wages. This inflexibility results from fear of price wars, menu costs, wage contracts, efficiency wages, and minimum wages. When the price level is fixed, in essence there is a horizontal portion of the aggregate supply curve, referred to as the immediate-short-run aggregate supply curve.

- Leftward shifts of the aggregate supply curve reflect increases in per-unit production costs and cause cost-push inflation, with accompanying negative GDP gaps.

- Rightward shifts of the aggregate supply curve, caused by large improvements in productivity, help explain the simultaneous achievement of full employment, economic growth, and price stability that Canada achieved between 1996 and 2000, and 2002 and 2008.

TERMS AND CONCEPTS

aggregate demand–aggregate supply model, p. 226
aggregate demand, p. 226
real-balances effect, p. 226
interest-rate effect, p. 226
foreign-trade effect, p. 226
determinants of aggregate demand, p. 227

aggregate supply, p. 230
immediate-short-run aggregate supply curve, p. 230
short-run aggregate supply curve, p. 231
long-run aggregate supply curve, p. 233
determinants of aggregate supply, p. 234
equilibrium price level, p. 238

equilibrium real domestic output, p. 238
inflationary gap, p. 238
recessionary gap, p. 241
menu costs, p. 241
efficiency wages, p. 242

STUDY QUESTIONS

LO ▶ 10.1 1. Why is the aggregate demand curve downward sloping? Specify how your explanation differs from that for the downward-sloping demand curve for a single product.

LO ▶ 10.1 2. Distinguish between the "real-balances effect" and the "wealth effect" as the terms are used in this chapter. How does each relate to the aggregate demand curve?

LO ▶ 10.2 3. What assumptions cause the immediate-short-run aggregate supply curve to be horizontal? Why is the long-run aggregate supply curve vertical? Explain the shape of the short-run aggregate supply curve. Why is the short-run curve relatively flat to the left of the full-employment output and relatively steep to its right?

LO ▶ 10.3 4. **KEY QUESTION** Suppose that the aggregate demand and the aggregate supply schedules for a hypothetical economy are as shown below:

Amount of real domestic output demanded (billions)	Price level (price index)	Amount of real domestic output supplied (billions)
$100	300	$400
200	250	400
300	200	300
400	150	200
500	150	100

a. Use these data to graph the aggregate demand and supply curves. Find the equilibrium price level and level of real output in this hypothetical economy. Is the equilibrium real output also the potential GDP? Explain.

b. Why will a price level of 150 not be an equilibrium price level in this economy? Why not 250?

c. Suppose that buyers desire to purchase $200 billion of extra real output at each price level. Sketch in the new aggregate demand curve as AD_1. What factors might cause this change in aggregate demand? What are the new equilibrium price level and level of real output?

5. **KEY QUESTION** Suppose that the hypothetical economy in question 4 has the following relationship between its real output and the input quantities necessary for producing that output: **LO ▶ 10**

Input quantity	Real domestic output
150.0	400
112.5	300
75.0	200

a. What is productivity in this economy?

b. What is the per-unit cost of production if the price of each input unit is $2?

c. Assume that the input price increases from $2 to $3 with no accompanying change in productivity. What is the new per-unit cost of production? In what direction would the $1 increase in input price push the aggregate supply curve? What effect would this shift in the short-run aggregate supply have on the price level and the level of real output?

d. Suppose that the increase in input price does not occur but instead that productivity increases by 100 percent. What would be the new per-unit cost of production? What effect would this change in per-unit production cost have on the short-run aggregate supply curve? What effect would this shift in the short-run aggregate supply have on the price level and the level of real output?

> 10.3 6. **KEY QUESTION** What effects would each of the following have on aggregate demand or short-run aggregate supply? In each case use a diagram to show the expected effects on the equilibrium price level and level of real output. Assume all other things remain constant.

a. A widespread fear of recession among consumers.

b. A $2 per pack increase in the excise tax on cigarettes.

c. A reduction in interest rates at each price level.

d. A major increase in federal spending for health care.

e. The expectation of rapid inflation.

f. The complete disintegration of OPEC, causing oil prices to fall by one-half.

g. A 10 percent reduction in personal income tax rates.

h. An increase in labour productivity (with no change in nominal wages).

i. A 12 percent increase in nominal wages (with no change in productivity).

j. Depreciation in the international value of the dollar.

> 10.3 7. **KEY QUESTION** Assume that (a) the price level is flexible upward but not downward and (b) the economy is currently operating at its full-employment output. Other things equal, how will each of the following affect the equilibrium price level and equilibrium level of real output in the short run?

a. An increase in aggregate demand.

b. A decrease in aggregate supply, with no change in aggregate demand.

c. Equal increases in aggregate demand and aggregate supply.

d. A decrease in aggregate demand.

e. An increase in aggregate demand that exceeds an increase in aggregate supply

> 10.3 8. Explain how an upward-sloping aggregate supply curve weakens the impact of a rightward shift of the aggregate demand curve.

> 10.3 9. Why does a reduction in aggregate demand reduce real output, rather than the price level?

> 10.3 10. Explain: "Unemployment can be caused by a decrease of aggregate demand or a decrease of aggregate supply." In each case, specify the price-level outcomes.

> 10.3 11. Use shifts in the AD and AS curves to explain (a) the Canadian experience of strong economic growth, full employment, and price stability in the late 1990s and early 2000s; and (b) how a strong negative wealth effect from, say, a precipitous drop in the stock market could cause a recession even though productivity is surging.

> 10.3 12. Suppose the aggregate demand and supply schedules for a hypothetical economy are as shown below:

Amount of real domestic output demanded (billions)	Price level (price index)	Amount of real domestic output supplied (billions)
$ 60	350	$240
120	300	240
180	250	180
240	200	120
300	150	60

a. What will be the equilibrium price and output level in this hypothetical economy? Is it also the full-employment level of output? Explain.

b. Why won't the 200 index be the equilibrium price level? Why won't the 300 index be the equilibrium price level?

c. Suppose demand increases by $120 billion at each price level. What will be the new equilibrium price and output levels?

d. List five factors that might cause a change in aggregate demand.

13. Use this aggregate demand–aggregate supply schedule for a hypothetical economy to answer the following questions.   LO 10.3

Real domestic output demanded (billions)	Price level (price index)	Real domestic output supplied (billions)
$3000	350	$9000
4000	300	8000
5000	250	7000
6000	200	6000
7000	150	5000
8000	100	4000

a. What will be the equilibrium price level and quantity of real domestic output?

b. If the quantity of real domestic output demanded increased by $2000 at each price level, what will be the new equilibrium price level and quantity of real domestic output?

c. Using the original data from the table, if the quantity of real domestic output demanded *increased* by $5000 and the quantity of real domestic output supplied *increased* by $1000 at each price level, what would be the new equilibrium price level and quantity of real domestic output?

INTERNET APPLICATION QUESTIONS @

1. **The Interest-Rate Effect—Price Levels and Interest Rates.** The interest-rate effect suggests that as the price level rises so do interest rates, and rising interest rates reduce certain kinds of consumption and investment spending. Use the links on the McConnell-Brue-Flynn-Barbiero Web site (Chapter 10) and compare price levels (all items) and interest rates (prime business loan rate) over the past five years. Do the data support the link between the price level and interest rates?

2. **Aggregate Demand and Supply—Equilibrium Prices and GDPs.** Go to the statistical section of the OECD through the McConnell-Brue-Flynn-Barbiero Web site (Chapter 10) to retrieve the data on inflation (see CPI under short-term indicators) and GDP for Canada, the United States, Germany, and Japan. Assume that these CPI and GDP figures represent the equilibrium price and real GDPs for their respective years. Plot the price/GDP levels for the past three years for each country using a graph similar to Figure 10-7. Are there any similarities across countries? Speculate on changes in aggregate demand and supply that most likely produced the succession of equilibrium points. (*Note:* AS usually moves rightward at a slow, steady annual pace.)

Appendix to Chapter 10

| A10.1 | THE RELATIONSHIP OF THE AGGREGATE DEMAND CURVE TO THE AGGREGATE EXPENDITURES MODEL* |

Derivation of the Aggregate Demand Curve from the Aggregate Expenditures Model

We can directly connect the downward-sloping aggregate demand curve of Figure 10-1 to the aggregate expenditures model discussed in Chapter 9 by relating the various possible price levels to corresponding equilibrium GDPs. In Figure A10-1 we have stacked the aggregate expenditures model (Figure A10-1a) and the aggregate demand curve (Figure A10-1b) vertically. We can do this because the horizontal axes of both models measure real GDP. Now let's derive the AD curve in three distinct steps (throughout this discussion, keep in mind that price level P_1 < price level P_2 < price level P_3):

- First suppose that the economy's price level is P_1 and its aggregate expenditures schedule is AE_1, the top schedule in Figure A10-1a. The equilibrium GDP is then GDP_1 at point 1. So in Figure A10-1b we can plot the equilibrium real output GDP_1 and the corresponding price level P_1. This gives us one point 1′ in Figure A10-1b.

- Now assume the price level rises from P_1 to P_2. Other things equal, this higher price level will (1) decrease the value of wealth, decreasing consumption expenditures; (2) increase the interest rate, reducing investment and interest-sensitive consumption expenditures; and (3) increase imports and decrease exports, reducing net export expenditures. The aggregate expenditures schedule will fall from AE_1 to, say, AE_2 in Figure A10-1a, giving us equilibrium GDP_2 at point 2. In Figure A10-1b we plot this new price-level–real-output combination, P_2 and GDP_2, as point 2′.

- Finally, suppose the price level rises from P_2 to P_3. The value of real wealth balances, the interest rate rises, exports fall, and imports rise. Consequently, the consumption, investment, and net export schedules fall, shifting the aggregate expenditures schedule downward from AE_2 to AE_3, which gives us equilibrium GDP_3 at point 3. In Figure A10-1b, this enables us to locate point 3′, where the price level is P_3 and real output is GDP_3.

In summary, increases in the economy's price level will successively shift its aggregate expenditures schedule downward and will reduce real GDP. The resulting price level–real GDP combination will yield various points such as 1′, 2′, and 3′ in Figure A10-1b. Together, such points locate the downward-sloping aggregate demand curve for the economy.

Aggregate Demand Shifts and the Aggregate Expenditures Model

The determinants of aggregate demand listed in Figure 10-2 are the components of the aggregate expenditures model discussed in Chapter 9. When one of those determinants changes, the aggregate expenditures schedule shifts too. We can easily link such shifts in the aggregate expenditures schedule to shifts of the aggregate demand curve.

Let's suppose the price level is constant. In Figure A10-2 we begin with the aggregate expenditures schedule at AE_1 in diagram (a), yielding real output of GDP_1. Assume now that investment spending increases in response to more optimistic business expectations, so that the aggregate expenditures schedule rises from AE_1 to AE_2. (The notation "at P_1" reminds us that the price level is assumed to be constant.) The result will be a multiplied increase in real output from GDP_1 to GDP_2.

In Figure A10-2b, the increase in investment spending is reflected in the horizontal distance between AD_1 and the broken curve to its right. The immediate effect of the increase in investment is an increase in aggregate demand by the exact amount of the new spending. But then the multiplier process magnifies the initial increase in investment into successive rounds of consumption spending and an ultimate multiplied increase in aggregate demand from AD_1 to AD_2. Equilibrium real output rises from GDP_1 to GDP_2, the same multiplied increase in real GDP as that in Figure A10-2a. The initial increase in investment in (a) has shifted the AD curve in (b) by a horizontal distance equal to the change in investment times the multiplier. This particular change in real GDP is still associated with the constant price level P_1. To generalize,

Shift of AD curve = initial change in spending × multiplier

---

*This appendix presumes knowledge of the aggregate expenditures model discussed in Chapter 9 and should be skipped if Chapter 9 was not assigned.

FIGURE A10·1   Deriving the Aggregate Demand Curve from the Expenditures Model

(a) Rising price levels from P_1 to P_2 to P_3 shift the aggregate expenditures curve downward from AE_1 to AE_2 to AE_3 and reduce real GDP from GDP_1 to GDP_2 to GDP_3. (b) The aggregate demand curve AD is derived by plotting the successively lower real GDPs from the upper graph against the P_1, P_2, and P_3 price levels.

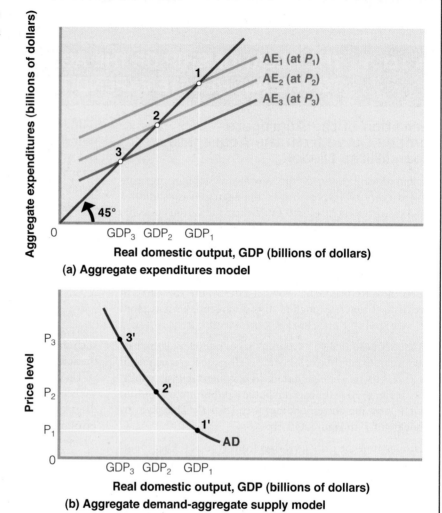

(a) Aggregate expenditures model

(b) Aggregate demand-aggregate supply model

FIGURE A10-2

Shifts in the Aggregate Expenditures Schedule and in the Aggregate Demand Curve

Panel (a): A change in some determinant of consumption, investment, or net exports (other than the price level) shifts the aggregate expenditures schedule upward from AE_1 to AE_2. The multiplier increases real output from GDP_1 to GDP_2. Panel (b): The counterpart of this change is an initial rightward shift of the aggregate demand curve by the amount of initial new spending (from AD_1 to the broken curve). This leads to a multiplied rightward shift of the curve to AD_2, which is just sufficient to show the same increase in GDP as in the aggregate expenditures model.

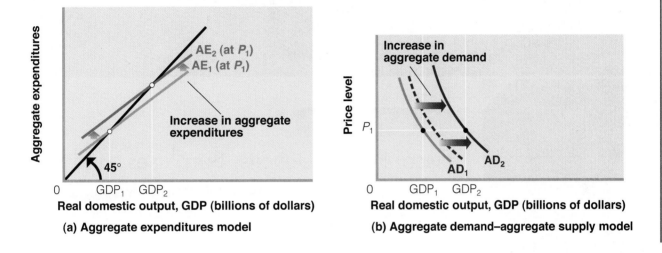

(a) Aggregate expenditures model

(b) Aggregate demand–aggregate supply model

APPENDIX SUMMARY

- A change in the price level alters the location of the aggregate expenditures schedule through the real-balances, interest-rate, and foreign-trade effects. The aggregate demand curve is derived from the aggregate expenditures model by allowing the price level to change and observing the effect on the aggregate expenditures schedule and thus on equilibrium GDP.

- With the price level held constant, increases in consumption, investment, government, and net export expenditures shift the aggregate expenditures schedule upward and the aggregate demand curve to the right. Decreases in these spending components reduce the opposite effects.

APPENDIX STUDY QUESTIONS

0 ▶ A10.1 1. Explain carefully: "A change in the price level shifts the aggregate expenditures curve but not the aggregate demand curve."

0 ▶ A10.1 2. Suppose the price level is constant and investment spending increases sharply. How would you show this increase in the aggregate expenditures model? What would be the outcome for real GDP? How would you show this rise in investment in

the aggregate demand–aggregate supply model, assuming the economy is operating in what, in effect, is a horizontal range of the aggregate supply curve?

3. How does the aggregate expenditures analysis differ from the aggregate demand–aggregate supply analysis? **LO ▶ A10.1**

CHAPTER 11

Fiscal Policy, Deficits, Surpluses, and Debt

In the previous chapter we saw that an excessive increase in aggregate demand can cause demand-pull inflation and that a significant decline in aggregate demand can cause recession and cyclical unemployment. For those reasons, central governments sometimes use budgetary actions to try to "stimulate the economy" or "rein in inflation." Such countercyclical *fiscal policy* consists of deliberate changes in government spending and tax collections designed to achieve full employment, control inflation, and encourage economic growth. (The adjective "fiscal" simply means "financial.") We begin this chapter by examining the logic behind fiscal policy, its current status, and its limitations. Then we examine a closely related topic: the Canadian public debt.

11.1 | Fiscal Policy and the AD–AS Model

Since 1945 one of the main tools used by government in stabilization policy has been **fiscal policy,** which includes changes in government spending and taxation designed to achieve full employment and a stable price level. In Canada, the idea that government fiscal actions can exert a stabilizing influence on the economy emerged from the Great Depression of the 1930s and the rise of Keynesian economics. Since then, macroeconomic theory has played a major role in the design of fiscal policy and the improved understanding of its limitations.

Fiscal policy is described as *discretionary* (or "active") if the changes in government spending and taxes are *at the option* of the government. They do not occur automatically, independent of parliamentary action. Those changes are *nondiscretionary* (or "passive" or "automatic"), and we will examine them in the next section of this chapter.

Expansionary Fiscal Policy

When recession occurs, an **expansionary fiscal policy** may be in order. Consider Figure 11-1, where we suppose a sharp decline in investment spending has shifted the economy's aggregate demand curve leftward from AD_1 to AD_2. (Disregard the arrows

FIGURE 11-1   Expansionary Fiscal Policy

Expansionary fiscal policy uses increases in government spending or tax cuts to push the economy out of recession. In an economy with an MPC of .75, a $5 billion increase in government spending or a $6.67 billion decrease in personal taxes (producing a $5 billion initial increase in consumption) expands aggregate demand from AD$_2$ to the downsloping dashed curve. The multiplier then magnifies this initial increase in spending to AD$_1$. So real GDP rises along the broken horizontal aggregate supply line by $20 billion.

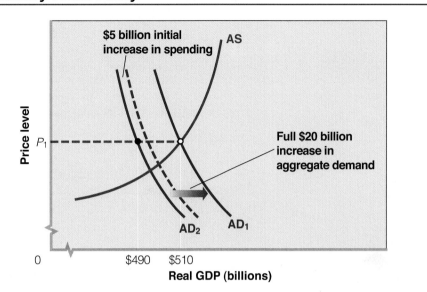

ORIGIN 11.1
Fiscal Policy

fiscal policy
Changes in government spending and tax collections designed to achieve a full-employment and non-inflationary domestic output.

expansionary fiscal policy
An increase in government spending, a decrease in net taxes, or some combination of the two, for the purpose of increasing aggregate demand and expanding real output.

budget deficit
The amount by which the expenditures of the federal government exceed its revenues in any year.

If government initiates new spending on highways, airports, education, and health care, the amount of real output demanded rises.

and dashed downsloping line for now.) Perhaps profit expectations on investment projects have dimmed, curtailing much investment spending and reducing aggregate demand.

Suppose the economy's potential or full-employment output is $510 billion in Figure 11-1. If the price level is inflexible downward at P_1, the broken horizontal line in effect becomes the relevant aggregate supply curve. The aggregate demand curve moves leftward and reduces real GDP from $510 billion to $490 billion. A negative GDP gap of $20 billion (= $490 billion − $510 billion) arises. An increase in unemployment accompanies this negative GDP gap because fewer workers are needed to produce the reduced output. In short, the economy depicted is suffering both recession and cyclical unemployment.

What fiscal policy should the federal government adopt to stimulate the economy? It has three main options: (1) increase government spending, (2) reduce taxes, or (3) some combination of the two. If the federal budget is balanced at the outset, expansionary fiscal policy will create a government **budget deficit**—annual government spending in excess of tax revenues.

INCREASED GOVERNMENT SPENDING

Other things equal, a sufficient increase in government spending will shift an economy's aggregate demand curve to the right, from AD$_2$ to AD$_1$ in Figure 11-1. To see why, suppose the recession prompts the government to initiate $5 billion of new spending on highways, education, and health care. We represent this new $5 billion of government spending as the horizontal distance between AD$_2$ and the dashed line immediately to its right. At each price level, the amount of real output that is demanded is now $5 billion greater than that demanded before the expansion of government spending.

But the initial increase in aggregate demand is not the end of the story. Through the multiplier effect, the aggregate demand curve shifts to AD$_1$, a distance that exceeds that represented by the originating $5 billion increase in government purchases. This greater shift occurs because the multiplier process magnifies the initial change in spending into successive rounds of new consumption spending. If the economy's marginal propensity to consume (MPC) is .75, then the simple multiplier is 4. So the aggregate demand curve shifts rightward by four times the distance between AD$_2$ and the broken line.

Because this *particular* increase in aggregate demand occurs along the horizontal broken-line segment of aggregate supply, real output rises by the full extent of the multiplier. Observe that real output rises to $510 billion, up $20 billion from its recessionary level of $490 billion. Concurrently, unemployment falls as firms increase their employment to the full-employment level that existed before the recession.

TAX REDUCTIONS

Alternatively, the government could reduce taxes to shift the aggregate demand curve to the right, as from AD_2 to AD_1. Suppose the government cuts personal income taxes by $6.67 billion, which increases disposable income by the same amount. Consumption will rise by $5 billion (= MPC of .75 × $6.67 billion) and saving will go up by $1.67 billion (= MPS of .25 × $6.67 billion). In this case the horizontal distance between AD_2 and the dashed downsloping line in Figure 11-1 represents only the $5 billion initial increase in consumption spending. Again, we call it "initial" consumption spending because the multiplier process yields successive rounds of increased consumption spending. The aggregate demand curve eventually shifts rightward by four times the $5 billion initial increase in consumption produced by the tax cut. Real GDP rises by $20 billion, from $490 billion to $510 billion, implying a multiplier of 4. Employment increases accordingly.

You may have noted that a tax cut must be somewhat larger than the proposed increase in government spending if it is to achieve the same amount of rightward shift in the aggregate demand curve. This is because part of a tax reduction increases saving, rather than consumption. To increase initial consumption by a specific amount, the government must reduce taxes by more than that amount. With an MPC of .75, taxes must fall by $6.67 billion for $5 billion of new consumption to be forthcoming because $1.67 billion is saved (not consumed). If the MPC had instead been, say, .6, an $8.33 billion reduction in tax collections would have been necessary to increase initial consumption by $5 billion. The smaller the MPC, the greater the tax cut needed to accomplish a specific initial increase in consumption and a specific shift in the aggregate demand curve.

COMBINED GOVERNMENT SPENDING INCREASES AND TAX REDUCTIONS

The government may combine spending increases and tax cuts to produce the desired initial increase in spending and eventual increase in aggregate demand and real GDP. In the economy depicted in Figure 11-1, the government might increase its spending by $1.25 billion while reducing taxes by $5 billion. As an exercise, explain why this combination will produce the targeted $5 billion initial increase in new spending.

If you were assigned Chapter 9, think through these three fiscal policy options in terms of the recessionary expenditure-gap analysis associated with the aggregate expenditures model (Figure 9-7). And recall from the appendix to Chapter 10 that rightward shifts of the aggregate demand curve relate directly to upward shifts of the aggregate expenditures schedule. *(Key Question 1)*

Contractionary Fiscal Policy

contractionary fiscal policy
A decrease in government spending, an increase in net taxes, or some combination of the two for the purpose of decreasing aggregate demand and thus controlling inflation.

When demand-pull inflation occurs, a restrictive or **contractionary fiscal policy** may help control it. Look at Figure 11-2, where the full-employment level of real GDP is $510 billion. The economy starts at equilibrium at point a, where the initial aggregate demand curve AD_3 intersects aggregate supply curve AS. Suppose that after going through the multiplier process, a $5 billion initial increase in investment and net export spending shifts the aggregate demand curve to the right by $20 billion, from AD_3 to AD_4. (Ignore the downsloping dashed line for now.) Given the upward-sloping AS curve, however, the equilibrium GDP does not rise by the full $20 billion. It rises by only $12 billion, to $522 billion, thereby creating an inflationary GDP gap of $12 billion ($522 billion − $510 billion). The upward slope of the AS curve means that some of the rightward movement of the AD curve ends up causing demand-pull inflation rather than increased output. As a result, the price level rises from P_1 to P_2 and the equilibrium moves to point b.

Without a government response, the inflationary GDP gap will cause further inflation (as input prices rise in the long run to meet the increase in output prices). If the government looks to fiscal policy to eliminate the inflationary GDP gap, its options are the opposite of those used to combat

FIGURE 11-2 @ Contractionary Fiscal Policy

Contractionary fiscal policy uses decreases in government spending or increases in taxes to close an inflationary gap. Contractionary fiscal policy must take the ratchet effect into account. To return the economy to producing at full employment, the government can either reduce government spending or increase taxes. Either policy will shift aggregate demand leftward, from AD$_3$ to AD$_4$. The inflationary GDP gap is eliminated while the price level remains at P_2.

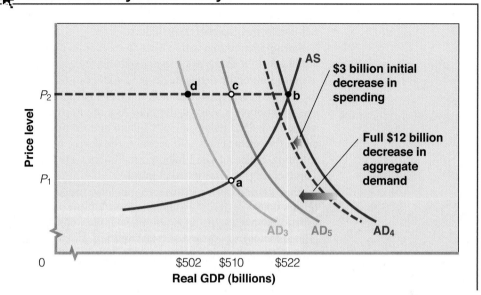

budget surplus
The amount by which the revenues of the federal government exceed its expenditures in any year.

recession. It can (1) decrease government spending, (2) raise taxes, or (3) use some combination of those two policies. When the economy faces demand-pull inflation, fiscal policy should move toward a government **budget surplus**—tax revenues in excess of government spending.

But before discussing how the government can either decrease government spending or increase taxes to move toward a government budget surplus and control inflation, we have to keep in mind that the price level is like a ratchet. While increases in aggregate demand that expand real output beyond the full-employment level tend to ratchet the price level upward, declines in aggregate demand do not seem to push the price level downward. This means that stopping inflation is a matter of halting the rise of the price level, not trying to lower it to the previous level. It also means that the government must take the ratchet effect into account when deciding how big a cut in spending or an increase in taxes it should undertake.

DECREASED GOVERNMENT SPENDING

Reduced government spending shifts the aggregate demand curve leftward to control demand-pull inflation. To see why the ratchet effect matters so much, look at Figure 11-2 and consider what would happen if the government ignored the ratchet effect and attempted to design a spending reduction policy to eliminate the inflationary GDP gap. Since the $12 billion gap was caused by the $20 billion rightward movement of the aggregate demand curve from AD$_3$ to AD$_4$, the government might naively think that it could solve the problem by causing a $20 billion leftward shift of the aggregate demand curve to move it back to where it originally was. It could attempt to do so by reducing government spending by $5 billion and then allowing the multiplier effect to expand that initial decrease into a $20 billion decline in aggregate demand. That would shift the aggregate demand curve leftward by $20 billion, putting it back at AD$_3$.

This policy would work fine if there were no ratchet effect and if prices were flexible. The economy's equilibrium would move back from point *b* to point *a*, with equilibrium GDP returning to the full-employment level of $510 billion and the price level falling from P_2 back to P_1. But because there *is* a ratchet effect, that scenario is not what will actually happen. Instead, the ratchet effect implies that the price level is stuck at P_2, so that the broken horizontal line at price level P_2 becomes the relevant aggregate supply curve. This means that when the government reduces spending by

$5 billion in order to shift the aggregate demand curve back to AD_3, it will actually cause a recession! The new equilibrium will not be at point *a*. It will be at point *d*, where aggregate demand curve AD_3 crosses the broken horizontal line. At point *d*, real GDP is only $502 billion, $8 billion below the full-employment level of $510 billion.

The problem is that with what is in essence an immediate-short-run AS curve, the multiplier is at full effect. With the price level fixed and the aggregate supply curve horizontal, the $20 billion leftward shift of the aggregate demand curve causes a full $20 billion decline in real GDP. None of the change in aggregate demand can be dissipated as a change in the price level (as it can be when aggregate supply is upward-sloping). As a result, equilibrium GDP declines by the full $20 billion, falling from $522 billion to $502 billion and putting it $8 billion below potential output. By not taking the ratchet effect into account, the government has overdone the decrease in government spending, replacing a $12 billion inflationary GDP gap with an $8 billion recessionary GDP gap. This is clearly not what it had in mind.

Here's how it can avoid this scenario. First, the government takes account of the size of the inflationary GDP gap. It is $12 billion. Second, it knows that with the price level fixed, aggregate supply will be horizontal so that the multiplier will be in full effect. Thus, it knows that any decline in government spending will be multiplied by a factor of 4. It then reasons that government spending will have to decline by only $3 billion rather than $5 billion. Why? Because the $3 billion initial decline in government spending will be multiplied by 4, creating a $12 billion decline in aggregate demand. Under the circumstances, a $3 billion decline in government spending is the correct amount to exactly offset the $12 billion GDP gap. This inflationary GDP gap is the problem that government wants to eliminate. To succeed, it need not undo the full increase in aggregate demand that caused the inflation in the first place.

Graphically, the horizontal distance between AD_4 and the dashed line to its left represents the $3 billion decrease in government spending. Once the multiplier process is complete, this spending cut will shift the aggregate demand curve leftward from AD_4 to AD_5. With the price level fixed at P_2 and aggregate supply in this area represented by the horizontal dashed line, the economy will come to equilibrium at point *c*. The economy will operate at its potential output of $510 billion. The inflationary GDP gap will be eliminated. And because the government took the ratchet effect correctly into account, the government will not accidentally push the economy into a recession by making an overly large initial decrease in government spending.

TAX INCREASES

Just as government can use tax cuts to increase consumption spending, it can use tax *increases* to *reduce* consumption spending. If the economy in Figure 11-2 has an MPC of .75, the government must raise taxes by $4 billion. The $4 billion tax increase reduces saving by $1 billion (= the MPS of .25 × $4 billion). This $1 billion reduction in saving, by definition, is not a reduction in spending. But the $4 billion tax increase also reduces consumption spending by $3 billion (= the MPC of .75 × $4 billion), as shown by the distance between AD_4 and the dashed line to its left in Figure 11-2. After the multiplier process is complete, this initial $3 billion decline in consumption will cause aggregate demand to shift leftward by $12 billion at each price level (multiplier of 4 × $3 billion). With the economy moving to point *c*, the inflationary GDP gap will be closed and the inflation will be halted.

COMBINED GOVERNMENT SPENDING DECREASES AND TAX INCREASES

The government may choose to combine spending decreases and tax increases in order to reduce aggregate demand and check inflation. To check your understanding, determine why a $1.5 billion decline in government spending combined with a $2 billion increase in taxes would shift the aggregate demand curve from AD_4 to AD_5. Also, if you were assigned Chapter 9, explain the three fiscal policy options for fighting inflation by referring to the inflationary-expenditure-gap concept developed with the aggregate expenditures model (Figure 9-7). And recall from the appendix to Chapter 10 that leftward shifts of the aggregate demand curve are associated with downshifts of the aggregate expenditures schedule.

Policy Options: *G* or *T*?

Which is preferable as a means of eliminating recession and inflation: the use of government spending or the use of taxes? The answer depends largely on one's view as to whether the government is too large or too small. Economists who believe there are many unmet social and infrastructure needs usually recommend that government spending be increased during recessions. In times of demand-pull inflation, they usually recommend tax increases. Both actions either expand or preserve the size of government. Economists who think the government is too large and inefficient usually advocate tax cuts during recessions and cuts in government spending during times of demand-pull inflation. Both actions either restrain the growth of government or reduce its size. The point is that discretionary fiscal policy designed to stabilize the economy can be associated with either an expanding government or with a contracting government. *(Key Question 2)*

QUICK REVIEW

▶ Discretionary fiscal policy is the deliberate change of government expenditures and tax collections by government to promote full employment, price stability, and economic growth.

▶ The government uses expansionary fiscal policy to shift the aggregate demand curve rightward to expand real output. This policy requires increases in government spending, reductions in taxes, or some combination of the two.

▶ The government uses contractionary fiscal policy to shift the aggregate demand curve leftward (or to constrain its rightward shift) in an effort to halt demand-pull inflation. This policy requires reductions in government spending, tax increases, or some combination of the two.

▶ To be implemented correctly, contractionary fiscal policy must account for the ratchet effect and the fact that prices will not fall as the government shifts the aggregate demand curve leftward.

11.2 | Built-in Stability

To some degree, government tax revenues change automatically over the course of the business cycle, in ways that stabilize the economy. This automatic response, or built-in stability, constitutes nondiscretionary budgetary policy. We did not include this built-in stability in our discussion of fiscal policy because we implicitly assumed the same amount of tax revenue was being collected at each level of GDP. But the actual Canadian tax system is such that *net tax revenues* vary directly with GDP. (Net taxes are tax revenues less transfers and subsidies. From here on, we will use the simpler "taxes" to mean "net taxes.")

Virtually any tax will yield more tax revenue as GDP rises. In particular, personal income taxes have progressive rates and thus generate more than proportionate increases in tax revenues as GDP expands. Furthermore, as GDP rises and more goods and services are purchased, revenues from corporate income taxes and from sales taxes also increase. And similarly, revenues from employment insurance and Canada pension (compulsory) contributions rise as economic expansion creates more jobs. Conversely, when GDP declines, tax revenues from all these sources also decline.

Transfer payments (or "negative taxes") behave in the opposite way from tax revenues. Unemployment compensation payments and welfare payments decrease during economic expansion and increase during economic contraction.

Automatic or Built-in Stabilizers

built-in stabilizer
A mechanism that increases government's budget deficit (or reduces its surplus) during a recession and increases government's budget surplus (or reduces its deficit) during inflation without any action by policymakers.

A **built-in stabilizer** is a structure of taxation and spending that increases the government's budget deficit (or reduces its budget surplus) during a recession and increases its budget surplus (or reduces its budget deficit) during an expansion without requiring explicit action by policymakers. As Figure 11-3 reveals, this is precisely what the Canadian tax system does.

Government expenditures G are fixed and assumed to be independent of the level of GDP. Parliament decides on a particular level of spending, but it does not determine the magnitude of tax revenues. Instead, it establishes tax rates, and then tax revenues vary directly with the level of GDP that the economy achieves. Line T represents that direct relationship between tax revenues and GDP.

ECONOMIC IMPORTANCE

The economic importance of this direct relationship between tax receipts and GDP becomes apparent when we consider that:

- Taxes reduce spending and aggregate demand.
- Reductions in spending are desirable when the economy is developing inflationary pressures, whereas increases in spending are desirable when the economy is slumping.

As shown in Figure 11-3, tax revenues automatically increase as GDP rises during prosperity, and, since taxes reduce household and business spending, they restrain the economic expansion. That is, as the economy moves toward a higher GDP, tax revenues automatically rise and move the budget from deficit toward surplus. In Figure 11-3, observe that the high and perhaps inflationary income level GDP_3 automatically generates a contractionary budget surplus. Conversely, as GDP falls during recession, tax revenues automatically decline, reducing the fall in spending and cushioning the economic contraction. With a falling GDP, tax receipts decline and move the government's budget from surplus toward deficit. In Figure 11-3, the low level of income GDP_1 will automatically yield an expansionary budget deficit.

TAX PROGRESSIVITY

Figure 11-3 reveals that the size of the automatic budget deficits or surpluses—and therefore built-in stability—depends on the responsiveness of tax revenues to changes in GDP. If tax revenues change sharply as GDP changes, the slope of line T in the figure will be steep and the vertical distances between T and G (the deficits or surpluses) will be large. If tax revenues change very little when GDP changes, the slope will be gentle and built-in stability will be low.

FIGURE 11-3   **Built-in Stability**

Tax revenues T vary directly with GDP, and government spending G is assumed to be independent of GDP. As GDP falls in a recession, deficits occur automatically and help alleviate the recession. As GDP rises during expansion, surpluses occur automatically and help offset possible inflation.

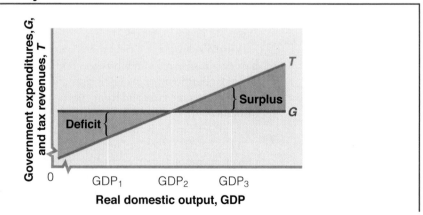

progressive tax
A tax with an average tax rate that increases as the taxpayer's income increases and decreases as the taxpayer's income decreases.

proportional tax
A tax with an average tax rate that remains constant as the taxpayer's income increases or decreases.

regressive tax
A tax with an average tax rate that decreases as the taxpayer's income increases and increases as the taxpayer's income decreases.

The steepness of T in Figure 11-3 depends on the tax system itself. In a **progressive tax** system, the average tax rate (= tax revenue/GDP) rises with GDP. In a **proportional tax** system, the average tax rate remains constant as GDP rises. In a **regressive tax** system, the average tax rate falls as GDP rises. The progressive tax system has the steepest tax line T of the three. However, tax revenues will rise with GDP under both the progressive and proportional tax systems, and they may rise, fall, or stay the same under a regressive tax system. The main point is this: The more progressive the tax system, the greater the economy's built-in stability.

So, changes in public policies or laws that alter the progressivity of the tax system affect the degree of built-in stability. For example, during the 1960s and 1970s the marginal tax rates were raised. These increases in tax rates raised the overall progressivity of the tax system, bolstering the economy's built-in stability. As the economy expanded vigorously in the late 1990s, the federal budget swung from deficit to surplus. That swing helped dampen private spending and forestall inflation.

The built-in stability provided by the Canadian tax system has reduced the severity of business fluctuations. But built-in stabilizers can only diminish, not eliminate, swings in real GDP. Discretionary fiscal policy (changes in tax rates and expenditures) or monetary policy (central bank–caused changes in interest rates) will be needed to correct a recession or inflation of any appreciable magnitude.

Evaluating Fiscal Policy

So, how can we determine whether a government's discretionary fiscal policy is expansionary or contractionary? We cannot simply examine the actual budget deficits or surpluses that take place under the current policy because they will necessarily include the automatic changes in tax revenues that accompany every change in GDP. In addition, the expansionary or contractionary strength of any change in discretionary fiscal policy depends not on its absolute size but on how large it is relative to the size of the economy. So, in evaluating the status of fiscal policy, we must adjust deficits and surpluses to eliminate automatic changes in tax revenues and also compare the sizes of the adjusted budget deficits and surpluses to the level of potential GDP.

Cyclically Adjusted Budget

cyclically adjusted budget
What the government budget balance would be if the economy were operating at full employment.

Economists use the **cyclically adjusted budget** (also called the *full-employment budget*) to adjust actual federal budget deficits and surpluses to account for the changes in tax revenues that happen automatically whenever GDP changes. The cyclically adjusted budget measures what the federal budget deficit or surplus would have been with existing tax rates and government spending levels if the economy had achieved its full-employment level of GDP (its potential output). The idea essentially is to compare *actual* government expenditures with the tax revenues *that would have occurred* if the economy had achieved full-employment GDP. That procedure removes budget deficits or surpluses that arise simply because of changes in GDP, which then tell us whether the government's current discretionary fiscal policy is fundamentally expansionary, neutral, or contractionary.

Consider Figure 11-4a, where line G represents government expenditures and line T represents tax revenues. In full-employment year 1, government expenditures of $500 billion equal tax revenues of $500 billion, as indicated by the intersection of lines G and T at point a. The cyclically adjusted budget deficit in year 1 is zero—government expenditures equal the tax revenues forthcoming at the full-employment output GDP_1. Obviously, the full-employment deficit *as a percentage of GDP* is also zero. The government's fiscal policy is neutral.

cyclical deficit
A federal budget deficit that is caused by a recession and the consequent decline in tax revenues.

Now, suppose that a recession occurs and GDP falls from GDP_1 to GDP_2, as shown in Figure 11-4a. Let's also assume that the government takes no discretionary action, so that lines G and T remain as shown in the figure. Tax revenues automatically fall to $450 billion (point c) at GDP_2, while government spending remains unaltered at $500 billion (point b). A $50 billion budget deficit (represented by distance bc) arises. But this **cyclical deficit** is simply a by-product of the economy's slide into recession, not the result of discretionary fiscal actions by the government. We would be wrong to conclude from this deficit that the government is engaging in an expansionary fiscal policy. The government's fiscal policy has not changed. It is still neutral.

That fact is highlighted when we consider the cyclically adjusted budget deficit for year 2 in Figure 11-4a. The $500 billion of government expenditures in year 2 are shown by *b* on line *G*. And, as shown by *a* on line *T*, $500 billion of tax revenues would have occurred if the economy had achieved its full-employment GDP. Because both *b* and *a* represent $500 billion, the cyclically adjusted budget deficit in year 2 is zero, as is this deficit as a percentage of GDP. Since the cyclically adjusted budget deficits are zero in both years, we know that government did not change its discretionary fiscal policy, even though a recession occurred and an actual deficit of $50 billion resulted.

Next, consider Figure 11-4b. Suppose that real output declined from full-employment GDP_3 to GDP_4. But also suppose the federal government responded to the recession by reducing tax rates in year 4, as represented by the downward shift of the tax line from T_1 to T_2. What has happened to the size of the cyclically adjusted deficit? Government expenditures in year 4 are $500 billion, as shown by *e*. We compare that amount with the $475 billion of tax revenues that would occur if the economy achieved its full-employment GDP. That is, we compare position *e* on line *G* with position *h* on line T_2. The $25 billion of tax revenues by which *e* exceeds *h* is the cyclically adjusted budget deficit for year 4. As a percentage of GDP, the cyclically adjusted budget deficit has increased from zero in year 3 (before the tax rate cut) to some positive percentage [= ($25 billion/$GDP_4 \times 100$] in year 4. This increase in the relative size of the cyclically adjusted deficit between the two years reveals that the new fiscal policy is *expansionary*.

FIGURE 11-4 **Cyclically Adjusted Deficits**

Panel (a): In the left-hand graph the cyclically adjusted deficit is zero at the full-employment output GDP_1. But it is also zero at the recessionary output GDP_2, because the $500 billion of government expenditures at GDP_2 equals the $500 of tax revenues that would be forthcoming at the full-employment GDP_1. There has been no change in fiscal policy. Panel (b): In the right-hand graph, discretionary fiscal policy, as reflected in the downward shift of the tax line from T_1 to T_2, has increased the cyclically adjusted budget deficit from zero in year 3 to $25 billion in year 4. This is found by comparing the $500 billion of government spending in year 4 with the $475 billion of taxes that would accrue at the full-employment GDP_3. Such a rise in cyclically adjusted deficits (as a percentage of GDP) identifies an expansionary fiscal policy.

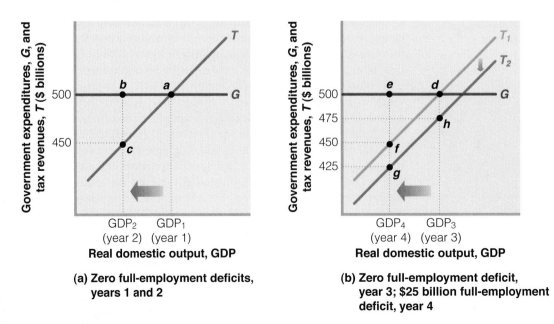

(a) Zero full-employment deficits, years 1 and 2

(b) Zero full-employment deficit, year 3; $25 billion full-employment deficit, year 4

CONSIDER THIS | Automatic Stabilizers and Budget Deficits during Severe Recession

The automatic stabilizers discussed in this section kicked in during the recession of 2008–09 as the number of unemployed workers increased from an average of 6.1 percent of the labour force in 2008 to 8.7 by August of 2009. Thus, the number of people receiving employment insurance rose rapidly, as did those receiving welfare payments. The decline in personal income automatically reduced income tax revenues. The decline in corporate profits automatically reduced the tax inflow to government from the corporate income tax. Falling consumer spending lowered sales tax revenues received by provincial and local governments. As viewed through Figure 11-3, the decline in taxes resulting from the reduction of GDP automatically increased the size of the federal budget deficit in 2009. Consequently, part of the rising federal budget deficit was cyclical.

In contrast, if we observed a full-employment deficit (as a percentage of GDP) of zero in one year, followed by a cyclically adjusted budget surplus in the next, we could conclude that fiscal policy has changed from being neutral to being contractionary. Because the cyclically adjusted budget adjusts for automatic changes in tax revenues, the increase in the cyclically adjusted budget surplus reveals that government either decreased its spending (G) or increased tax rates such that tax revenues (T) increased. These changes in G and T are precisely the discretionary actions that we have identified as elements of a *contractionary* fiscal policy.

TABLE 11-1 **Federal Deficits (–) and Surpluses (+) as Percentage of GDP, 1996–2007**

(1) Year	(2) Actual deficit or surplus	(3) Cyclically adjusted deficit or surplus
1996	–3.9	–3.4
1997	+0.7	+1.4
1998	+0.8	+1.3
1999	+0.9	+0.8
2000	+1.9	+1.3
2001	+1.1	+1.1
2002	+0.8	+0.8
2003	+0.3	+0.6
2004	+0.8	+0.9
2005	+0.1	+0.1
2006	+0.7	+0.6
2007	+1.0	+1.0

Source: Minister of Public Works and Government Services Canada, Department of Finance, *Fiscal Reference Tables*. http://www.fin.gc.ca/frt-trf/2008/frt08_8-eng.asp#46

Recent Canadian Fiscal Policy

Table 11-1 lists the actual federal budget deficits and surpluses (column 2) and the cyclically adjusted deficits and surpluses (column 3), as percentages of GDP, for recent years. The cyclically adjusted budget provides the information needed to assess discretionary fiscal policy and determine whether it is expansionary, neutral, or contractionary.

Column 3 shows that fiscal policy was mildly expansionary in 1996, but became contractionary in the later years shown. In this last regard, the cyclically adjusted budget moved from a deficit of 3.4 percent of GDP in 1996 to a surplus of 1.0 percent in 2007. This contractionary fiscal policy was appropriate in light of the rapidly growing Canadian economy over that period. This policy undoubtedly dampened the rapid growth of aggregate demand and contributed to price-level stability. Actual deficits have given way to actual surpluses, and cyclically adjusted (full-employment) deficits have given way to cyclically adjusted (full-employment) surpluses. Because of these surpluses, the federal government is better positioned to move toward an expansionary fiscal policy if the economy significantly weakens, as it did in the last quarter of 2008, with the onset of the financial crisis that swept across the globe. As of June 2009, the federal government projected a deficit of about $50 billion for the fiscal year 2009–10. *(Key Question 5)*

Global Perspective 11.1 shows the extent of the cyclically adjusted budget deficits or surpluses of a number of countries in a recent year.

11.1 │ GLOBAL PERSPECTIVE

Cyclically adjusted budget deficits or surpluses as a percentage of potential GDP, selected nations

In 2007 some nations had cyclically adjusted budget surpluses, while others had cyclically adjusted budget deficits. These surpluses and deficits varied as a percentage of each nation's potential GDP. Generally, the surpluses represented contractionary fiscal policy and the deficits expansionary fiscal policy.

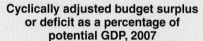

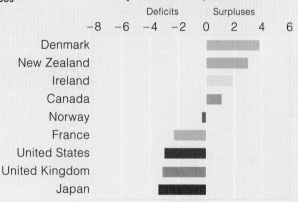

Cyclically adjusted budget surplus or deficit as a percentage of potential GDP, 2007

Source: Organisation for Economic Co-operation and Development, *OECD Economic Outlook*, www.oecd.org.

▶ Automatic changes in net taxes (taxes minus transfers) add a degree of built-in stability to the economy.

▶ The cyclically adjusted budget compares government spending to the tax revenues that would accrue if there were full employment; cyclically adjusted budget deficits or surpluses (as percentages of GDP) reveal whether fiscal policy is expansionary, neutral, or contractionary.

▶ Cyclically adjusted budget deficits and surpluses are distinct from actual cyclical deficits, which simply reflect changes in tax revenues resulting from changes in GDP.

11.3 | Problems, Criticisms, and Complications

Economists recognize that governments may encounter a number of significant problems in developing and applying fiscal policy.

Problems of Timing

Several problems of timing may arise in connection with fiscal policy:

- *Recognition Lag* The recognition lag is the time between the beginning of recession or inflation and the certain awareness that it is actually happening. This lag arises because the economy does not move smoothly through the business cycle. Even during good times, the economy has slow months interspersed with months of rapid growth and expansion. This makes recognizing a recession difficult since several slow months will have to happen in succession before people can conclude with any confidence that the good times are over and a recession has begun. The same is true with inflation. Even periods of moderate inflation have months of high inflation—so that several high-inflation months must come in sequence before people can confidently conclude that inflation has moved to a higher level. Attempts to get a jump on recognition lag by attempting to predict the future course of the economy have also proven to be largely futile (see this chapter's Last Word on the index of leading indicators). As a result, the economy is often four to six months into a recession or inflation before the situation is clearly discernible in the relevant statistics. Due to this recognition lag, the economic downslide or the inflation may become more serious than it would have if the situation had been identified and acted on sooner.

- *Administration Lag* The wheels of democratic government turn slowly. There will typically be a significant lag between the time the need for fiscal action is recognized and the time action is taken. The Canadian Parliament has on occasion taken so much time to adjust fiscal policy that the economic situation has changed in the interim, rendering the belated policy action inappropriate.

- *Operational Lag* A lag also occurs between the time fiscal action is taken and the time that action affects output, employment, or the price level. Although changes in tax rates can be put into effect relatively quickly once new laws are passed, government spending on public works—new dams, hospitals, and so on—requires long planning periods and even longer periods of construction. Such spending is of questionable use in offsetting short periods (for example, 6 to 18 months) of recession. Consequently, discretionary fiscal policy has increasingly relied on tax changes rather than on changes in spending as its main tool.

Political Considerations

Fiscal policy is conducted in a political arena. That reality may slow the enactment of fiscal policy, but it may also create the potential for political considerations swamping economic considerations in its formulation. It is a human trait to rationalize actions and policies that are in one's self-interest. Politicians are very human—they want to get re-elected. A strong economy at election time will certainly help them. So they may favour large tax cuts under the guise of expansionary fiscal policy even though that policy is economically inappropriate. Similarly, they may rationalize increased government spending on popular items such as farm subsidies, health care, highways, and education.

At the extreme, elected officials and political parties might collectively "hijack" fiscal policy for political purposes, cause inappropriate changes in aggregate demand, and thereby cause (rather than avert) economic fluctuations. For instance, before an election they may try to stimulate the economy to improve their re-election hopes. And then after the election they may try to use contractionary fiscal policy to dampen the excessive aggregate demand that they caused with their pre-election stimulus. In short, elected officials may cause so-called **political business cycles.** Such scenarios are difficult to document and prove, but there is little doubt that political considerations weigh heavily in the formulation of fiscal policy. The question is how often, if ever, do those political considerations run counter to "sound economics."

political business cycle
The alleged tendency of government to destabilize the economy by reducing taxes and increasing government expenditures before elections and to raise taxes and lower expenditures after elections.

Future Policy Reversals

Fiscal policy may fail to achieve its intended objectives if households expect future reversals of policy. Consider a tax cut, for example. If taxpayers believe the tax reduction is temporary, they may save a large portion of their tax cut, reasoning that rates will go up again in the future. They save more now so that they will be able draw on this extra savings to maintain their future consumption levels if taxes do indeed rise again in the future. The extra saving today will help them maintain their consumption at that time. But in the present, consumption spending and aggregate demand will not rise as much as our simple model (Figure 11-1) suggests.

The opposite may be true for a tax increase. If taxpayers think it is temporary, they may reduce their saving to pay the tax while maintaining their present consumption. They may reason that they can increase their saving when the tax rate again falls. So the tax increase will not reduce current consumption and aggregate demand by as much as policymakers intended.

To the extent that this so-called *consumption smoothing* occurs, fiscal policy will lose some of its strength. The lesson is that tax-rate changes viewed by households as permanent are more likely to alter consumption and aggregate demand than changes viewed as temporary.

Offsetting Provincial and Municipal Finance

The fiscal policies of provincial and municipal governments are frequently *pro-cyclical*, meaning that they worsen rather than correct recession or inflation. Like households and private businesses, provincial and municipal governments increase their expenditures during prosperity and cut them during recession. During the recession of 1990–91, some provincial and municipal governments had to increase tax rates, impose new taxes, and reduce spending to offset falling tax revenues resulting from the reduced personal income and spending of their citizens.

 ORIGIN 11.2
Crowding-Out

crowding-out effect
A rise in interest rates and a resulting decrease in planned investment caused by the federal government's increased borrowing in the money market.

Crowding-Out Effect

Another potential flaw of fiscal policy is the so-called **crowding-out effect:** An expansionary fiscal policy (deficit spending) may increase the interest rate and reduce investment spending, thereby weakening or cancelling the stimulus of the expansionary policy. The rising interest rate might also potentially crowd out interest-sensitive consumption spending (such as purchasing automobiles on credit). But since investment is the most volatile component of GDP, the crowding-out effect focuses its attention on investment and whether the stimulus provided by deficit spending may be partly or even fully neutralized by an offsetting reduction in investment spending.

To see the potential problem, note that whenever the government borrows money (as it must if it is deficit spending) it increases the overall demand for money. If the monetary authorities are holding the money supply constant, this increase in demand will raise the price paid for borrowing money: the interest rate. Because investment spending varies inversely with the interest rate, some investment will be choked off or "crowded out."

Economists vary in their opinions about how strong the crowding-out effect is. An important thing to keep in mind is that crowding out is likely to be less of a problem when the economy is in recession. This is true because investment demand tends to be low during recessions. Why? Because sales are slow during recessions, so that most businesses end up with substantial amounts of excess capacity. As a result, they do not have much incentive to add new machinery or build new factories. After all, why should they add capacity when some of the capacity they already have is sitting idle?

With investment demand low during a recession, the crowding-out effect is likely to be very small. Simply put, with investment demand at such a low level due to the recession, there isn't much investment for the government to crowd out. Even if deficit spending does increase the interest rate, investment spending cannot fall by that much for the simple reason that it is only a small number to begin with. By contrast, when the economy is operating at or near full capacity, investment demand is likely to be quite high so that crowding out is likely to be a much more serious problem. When the economy is booming, factories will be running at or near full capacity and firms will have high investment demand for two reasons. First, equipment running at full capacity wears out fast, so that firms will be doing a lot of investment just to replace machinery and equipment that wears out and depreciates. Second, the economy is likely to be growing overall so that firms will be investing not just to replace worn-out equipment in order to keep their productive capacity from deteriorating, but also so that they can make *additions* to their productive capacity.

GRAPHICAL PRESENTATION

An upward-sloping aggregate supply curve causes a part of the increase in aggregate demand, as in Figure 11-5, to be dissipated in higher prices, with the result that the increase in real GDP is diminished. The price level rises from P_0 to P_1 and real domestic output increases to only GDP_1, rather than GDP_f. As was noted earlier, the ratchet effect will mean that the price level will rise to P_1.

FIGURE 11-5   **Fiscal Policy: The Effects of Crowding Out and the Net Export Effect**

With an upward-sloping aggregate supply curve, a part of the impact of an expansionary policy will be reflected in a rise in the price level rather than an increase in real output and employment.

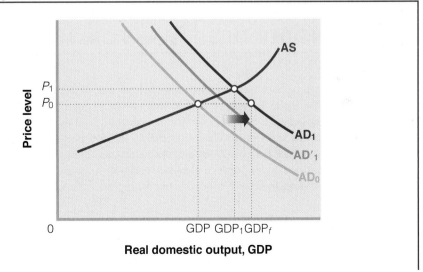

Fiscal Policy in the Open Economy

An additional complication when implementing fiscal policy arises from the fact that each national economy is a component of the world economy.

SHOCKS ORIGINATING FROM ABROAD

Events and policies abroad that affect a nation's net exports affect its own economy. Economies are open to unforeseen international *aggregate demand shocks* that can alter domestic GDP and make current domestic fiscal policy inappropriate. Suppose Canada is in a recession and has enacted an expansionary fiscal policy to increase aggregate demand and GDP without igniting inflation. Now suppose the economies of Canada's major trading partners unexpectedly expand rapidly. Greater employment and rising incomes in those nations mean more purchases of Canadian goods. Canadian net exports rise, aggregate demand increases rapidly and beyond its full-employment level, and Canada experiences demand-pull inflation. If Canadian policymakers had known in advance that net exports might rise significantly, less expansionary fiscal policy would have been enacted. We see, then, that participation in the world economy brings with it the complications of mutual interdependence along with the gains from specialization and trade.

NET EXPORT EFFECT

net export effect
The idea that the impact of a change in monetary or fiscal policy will be strengthened or weakened by the consequent change in net exports.

The **net export effect** may also work through international trade to reduce the effectiveness of fiscal policy. We concluded in our discussion of the crowding-out effect that an expansionary fiscal policy might boost interest rates, reducing investment and weakening fiscal policy. Now we want to know what effect an interest-rate increase might have on a nation's *net exports* (exports minus imports).

Suppose Canada undertakes an expansionary fiscal policy that causes a higher Canadian interest rate. The higher interest rate will attract financial capital from abroad, where we assume interest rates are unchanged. But foreign financial investors must acquire Canadian dollars to invest in Canadian securities. We know that an increase in the demand for a commodity—in this case, dollars—will raise its price. So the price of the Canadian dollar rises in terms of foreign currencies—that is, the Canadian dollar appreciates.

The impact of this dollar appreciation on Canadian net exports is that the rest of the world will see Canadian exports as being more expensive, and Canadian exports will decline. Canadians, who can now exchange their dollars for more units of foreign currencies, will buy more imports. Consequently, with Canadian exports falling and imports rising, net export expenditures in Canada will diminish; this is a contractionary change, so Canada's expansionary fiscal policy will be partially cancelled.[1]

CONSIDER THIS | Financial Crisis in the U.S. Spills Over into Canada

Canadian economic growth was at best anemic from the beginning of 2008 up to September of that year, when it suddenly took a nosedive as a result of the turmoil in the U.S. housing and financial markets. Between October 1, 2008 and May 31, 2009 GDP fell over 2 percent, unemployment climbed almost 2.3 percentage points, and exports to the U.S. took their steepest drop in at least a generation. Moreover, the Canadian dollar was almost at par with the U.S. dollar at the start of September 2008, but was below U.S. 80¢ by early March 2009. While economic conditions improved in both Canada and the U.S. later in 2009, the so-called global financial crisis that hit the Canadian economy in 2008–09 was a textbook case of shocks emanating from abroad—in this case from the U.S., Canada's largest trading partner.

---

[1] The appreciation of the dollar will also reduce the dollar price of foreign resources imported to Canada. As a result, aggregate supply will increase and part of the contractionary net export effect described here may be offset.

TABLE 11-2	**Fiscal Policy and the Net Export Effect**

(1) **Expansionary fiscal policy**	(2) **Contractionary fiscal policy**
Problem: recession, slow growth	Problem: inflation
↓	↓
Expansionary fiscal policy	Contractionary fiscal policy
↓	↓
Higher domestic interest rate	Lower domestic interest rate
↓	↓
Increased foreign demand for dollars	Decreased foreign demand for dollars
↓	↓
Dollar appreciates	Dollar depreciates
↓	↓
Net exports decline (aggregate demand decreases, partially offsetting the expansionary fiscal policy)	Net exports increase (aggregate demand increases, partially offsetting the contractionary fiscal policy)

A return to our aggregate demand and supply analysis in Figure 11-5 will clarify this point. An expansionary fiscal policy aimed at increasing aggregate demand from AD_0 to AD_1 may hike the domestic interest rate and ultimately reduce net exports through the process just described. The decline in the net export component of aggregate demand will partially offset the expansionary fiscal policy. The aggregate demand curve will shift rightward from AD_0 to AD'_1, *not* to AD_1, and equilibrium GDP will not increase as much. Moreover, the price level in the economy will rise due to the ratchet effect. Thus, the net export effect of fiscal policy joins the problems of timing, politics, and crowding out in complicating the "management" of aggregate demand.

Table 11-2 summarizes the net export effect resulting from fiscal policy. Column 1 reviews the analysis just discussed. But note that the net export effect works in both directions. By reducing the domestic interest rate, a *contractionary* fiscal policy *increases* net exports. In this regard, you should follow through the analysis in column 2 in Table 11-2 and relate it to the aggregate demand–aggregate supply model.

Current Thinking on Fiscal Policy

Where do these complications leave us as to the advisability and effectiveness of discretionary fiscal policy? In view of the complications and uncertain outcomes of fiscal policy, some economists argue that it is better not to engage in it at all. Those holding that view point to the superiority of monetary policy (changes in interest rates engineered by the Bank of Canada) as a stabilizing device or believe that most economic fluctuations tend to be mild and self-correcting.

But most economists believe that fiscal policy remains an important, useful policy lever in the government's macroeconomic toolkit. The current popular view is that fiscal policy can help push the economy in a particular direction but cannot fine-tune it to a precise macroeconomic outcome. Mainstream economists generally agree that monetary policy is the best month-to-month stabilization tool for the Canadian economy. If monetary policy is doing its job, the government should maintain a relatively neutral fiscal policy, with a cyclically adjusted budget deficit or surplus of no more than 2 percent of potential GDP. It should hold major discretionary fiscal policy in reserve to help counter situations where recession threatens to be deep and long-lasting or where a substantial reduction in aggregate demand might help to eliminate a large inflationary gap and aid the Bank of Canada in its efforts to quell the major bout of inflation caused by that large inflationary gap. Finally, economists agree that proposed fiscal policy should be evaluated for its potential positive and negative impacts on long-run productivity growth. The short-run policy tools used for conducting active fiscal policy often have long-run impacts. Countercyclical fiscal policy should be shaped to strengthen, or at least not impede, the growth of long-run aggregate supply (shown as a rightward shift of the long-run aggregate supply curve in Figure 11-5). *(Key Question 8)*

QUICK REVIEW

▸ Time lags and political problems complicate fiscal policy.

▸ The crowding-out effect indicates that an expansionary fiscal policy may increase the interest rate and reduce investment spending.

▸ Fiscal policy may be weakened by the net export effect, which works through changes in (a) the interest rate, (b) exchange rates, and (c) exports and imports.

11.4 | Deficits, Surpluses, and the Federal Debt

A *budget deficit* is the amount by which a government's expenditures exceed its revenues during a particular year. For example, during 1995–96 the federal government spent $161 billion and its receipts were only $131 billion, resulting in a $30 billion deficit. In contrast, a *budget surplus* is the amount by which government revenues exceed government expenditures in a given year. For example, federal government revenues of $251 billion in 2008 exceeded expenditures of $237 billion, resulting in a $14 billion budget surplus.

public debt
The total amount owed by the federal government to the owners of government securities.

The national or **public debt** is the total accumulation of the federal government's total deficits and surpluses that have occurred through time. It represents the total amount of money owed by the federal government to holders of *Canadian government securities*. In 2008 the gross federal debt was $594 billion, or approximately 37 percent of GDP. These deficits have emerged mainly because of war financing, recessions, and fiscal policy.

- *Debt and GDP* A simple statement of the absolute size of the debt ignores the fact that the wealth and productive ability of our economy have also increased tremendously. A wealthy, highly productive nation can more easily incur and carry a large public debt than can a poor nation. It is more meaningful to measure changes in the public debt in relation to the economy's GDP. Figure 11-6 shows the size of the gross federal government public debt in relation to Canada's GDP. Notice this percentage reached almost 150 percent right after World War II, to reach a low of just over 30 percent in the mid-1970s, and rose back up to 75 percent by the mid-1990s. The gross federal government public debt as a percentage of GDP took a fairly precipitous drop in the last decade to about 37 percent.

- *International Comparisons* As shown in Global Perspective 11.2, Canada's public debt is one of the lowest as a percentage of GDP among the industrialized nations of the world.

- *Interest Charges* Many economists conclude that the primary burden of the debt is the annual interest charge accruing as a result. Interest payments increased significantly as a proportion of GDP beginning in the early 1980s, but have recently started to decline. This ratio reflects the level of taxation (the average tax rate) required to service the public debt. In 2008 government had to collect taxes equal to under 2 percent of GDP to pay interest on its debt.

CONSIDER THIS | The Federal Deficit Fallout from the Global Financial Crisis

The recession of 2008–09 took a heavy toll on the federal government's finances, after more than 10 years of budget surpluses. The combination of lower tax revenues and increased spending to stimulate the ailing Canadian economy was projected to result in a $50 billion deficit for fiscal year 2009–10. The finance department also projected a deficit of $30 billion in fiscal year 2010–11, and it did not expect the federal government to have a balanced budget or a small surplus until 2014.

| FIGURE 11-6 | The Gross Federal Debt as a Percentage of GDP |

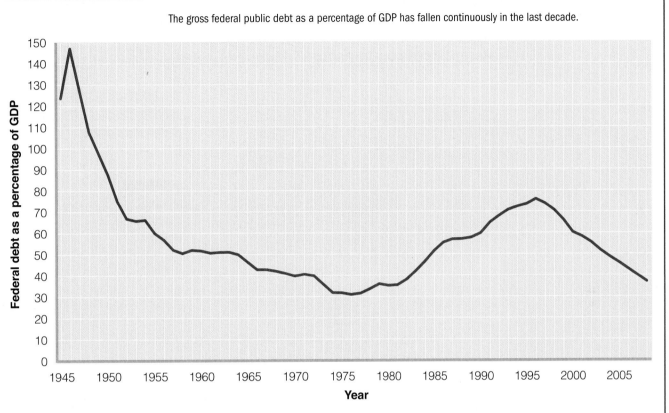

The gross federal public debt as a percentage of GDP has fallen continuously in the last decade.

SOURCE: Statistics Canada, CANSIM 380-0039, 380-0016, 385-0010. Accessed September 2009.

- *Ownership*   Figure 11-7 shows that about 9 percent of the total public debt is held by the Bank of Canada, and 76 percent by private individuals, chartered banks, insurance companies, and corporations in Canada. About 12 percent of the total debt is held by foreigners. The vast majority of the gross federal debt is thus held internally, not externally.

| FIGURE 11-7 | Ownership of Canada's Gross Public Debt in 2008 |

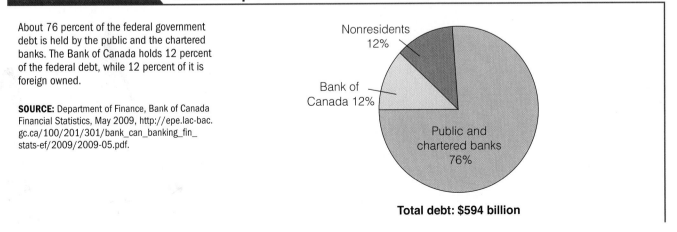

About 76 percent of the federal government debt is held by the public and the chartered banks. The Bank of Canada holds 12 percent of the federal debt, while 12 percent of it is foreign owned.

SOURCE: Department of Finance, Bank of Canada Financial Statistics, May 2009, http://epe.lac-bac. gc.ca/100/201/301/bank_can_banking_fin_ stats-ef/2009/2009-05.pdf.

Nonresidents 12%

Bank of Canada 12%

Public and chartered banks 76%

Total debt: $594 billion

11.2 | GLOBAL PERSPECTIVE

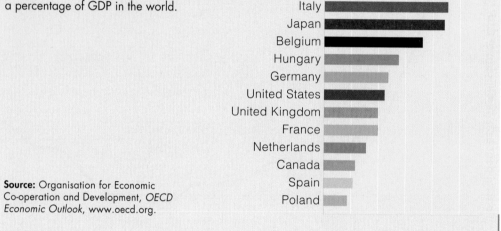

Publicly held debt: international comparisons

Canada has one of the lowest public debts as a percentage of GDP in the world.

Public sector debt as percentage of GDP, 2007

0   20   40   60   80   100

Italy
Japan
Belgium
Hungary
Germany
United States
United Kingdom
France
Netherlands
Canada
Spain
Poland

Source: Organisation for Economic Co-operation and Development, *OECD Economic Outlook*, www.oecd.org.

False Concerns

You may wonder whether a large public debt might bankrupt Canada or at least place a burden on our children and grandchildren. Fortunately, these are false concerns.

BANKRUPTCY

The public debt does not threaten to bankrupt the federal government, leaving it unable to meet its financial obligations, for two main reasons: refinancing and taxation.

- *Refinancing* The public debt is easily refinanced. As portions of the debt come due each month, the government in Ottawa does not cut expenditures or raise taxes to provide the funds required for its operation. Rather, the federal government refinances the debt by selling new bonds and using the proceeds to pay off holders of the maturing bonds. The new bonds are in strong demand because lenders (purchasers of government bonds) can obtain a relatively good interest return with little risk of default by the federal government.

- *Taxation* The federal government has the authority to levy and collect taxes. Parliament can impose a tax increase to pay interest and principal on the public debt. Financially distressed private households and corporations cannot resolve their financial difficulties by taxing the public. If their income or sales revenues fall short of their expenses, they can indeed go bankrupt. But the federal government has the option to impose new taxes or increase existing tax rates if necessary to finance its debt.

BURDENING FUTURE GENERATIONS

In 2008, public debt per capita was $14,970. Was each child born in 2008 handed a $14,970 bill from Ottawa? Not really! The public debt does not impose as much of a debt on future generations as generally thought.

Canada owes a substantial portion of the public debt to itself. Over 80 percent of Government of Canada bonds are held by citizens and institutions—banks, businesses, insurance companies,

CONSIDER THIS | Federal and Provincial per Capita Net Debt, 2008

Significant variance in per capita net debt exists among Canadian provinces. The federal government has a lower per capita debt than provincial governments, at about $14,970. Newfoundland and Labrador, at over $20,000, has the highest provincial per capita net debt among the provinces. Not far behind are Quebec and Nova Scotia. The provinces with the least per capita debt are to be found in Western Canada. British Columbia's per capita debt, at $5,435, is about a quarter that of Newfoundland and Labrador's. Alberta has the distinction of being the only province with a per capita credit of $9,683! This distinction is attributable to the revenues the Alberta government gets from its oil and gas sector, which also gives it the luxury of not having to have a provincial sales tax. Yukon and the Northwest Territories also have a per capita credit.

Canada	$14,970
Newfoundland and Labrador	20,266
Quebec	12,737
Nova Scotia	12,416
Ontario	11,868
P.E.I.	10,186
New Brunswick	9,688
Manitoba	7,785
Saskatchewan	6,329
British Columbia	5,435
Nunavut	1,965
Northwest Territories	− 2,512
Yukon	− 4,333
Alberta	− 9,683

Source: Calculated from population figures from Statistics Canada and net debt from the Department of Finance, *Fiscal Reference Tables*, 2008. Statistics Canada. At http://www40.statcan.ca/l01/cst01/demo31a-eng.htm. Accessed May 21, 2009.

government agencies, and pensions and trust funds—within Canada. While the public debt is a liability to Canadians (as taxpayers), part of the same debt is simultaneously an asset to Canadians (as bondholders).

To eliminate the Canadian-owned part of the public debt would require a gigantic transfer payment from Canadians to Canadians. Taxpayers would pay higher taxes and the government, in turn, would pay out those tax revenues to those same taxpaying individuals. Only the repayment of the approximately 12 percent of the public debt owned by foreigners would have a negative impact on Canadian purchasing power.

Substantive Issues

Although the above issues are of no real concern, there are a number of substantive issues relating to the public debt. Economists, however, attach varying degrees of importance to them.

INCOME DISTRIBUTION

The distribution of government securities ownership is uneven. Some people own much more than their $14,970-per-capita share of government securities; others own less or none at all. The ownership of the public debt is concentrated among wealthier groups. Because the federal tax system is only mildly progressive, payment of interest on the public debt probably increases income inequality. If greater income equality is one of our social goals, then this redistributive effect is undesirable.

INCENTIVES

The current federal public debt necessitates an annual interest payment of over $26 billion. This annual interest charge must be paid out of tax revenues. Higher taxes may dampen incentives to bear risk, to innovate, to invest, and to work. So, indirectly, the existence of a large debt may impair economic growth.

EXTERNAL DEBT

external public debt
Public debt owed to foreign citizens, firms, and institutions.

The 12 percent of Canada's debt held by citizens and institutions of foreign countries is an economic burden to Canadians. Because we do not owe that portion of the debt "to ourselves," the payment of interest and principal on this **external public debt** enables foreigners to buy some of our output. In return for the benefits derived from the borrowed funds, Canada transfers goods and services to foreign lenders. Of course, Canadians also own debt issued by foreign governments, so payment on principal and interest by these governments transfers some of their goods and services to Canadians. *(Key Question 10)*

CROWDING OUT REVISITED

There is a potentially more serious problem. The financing of the public debt can transfer a real economic burden to future generations by passing on a smaller stock of capital goods. This possibility involves the crowding-out effect: the idea that deficit financing will increase interest rates and thereby reduce private investment spending.

As we mentioned earlier, if public borrowing happened only during recessions, crowding out would not likely be much of a problem. Because private investment demand tends to be low during recessions, any increase in interest rates caused by public borrowing will at most cause a small reduction in investment spending. By contrast, a large public debt may cause crowding-out problems because the need to continuously refinance the debt will entail large amounts of borrowing not just during recessions but also during times when the economy is at full employment and investment demand tends to be very high. In such situations, any increase in interest rates caused by the borrowing necessary to refinance the debt may result in a substantial decline in investment spending. If the amount of current investment crowded out is extensive, future generations will inherit an economy with a smaller production capacity and, other things equal, a lower standard of living.

FIGURE 11-8 **The Investment Demand Curve and the Crowding-Out Effect**

If the investment demand curve (ID_1) is fixed, the increase in the interest rate from 6 percent to 10 percent caused by financing a large public debt will move the economy from *a* to *b* and crowd out $10 billion of private investment and decrease the size of the capital stock inherited by future generations. However, if the government spending enabled by the debt improves the profit expectations of businesses, the private investment demand curve will shift rightward, as from ID_1 to ID_2. That shift may offset the crowding-out effect wholly or in part. In this case, it moves the economy from *a* to *c*.

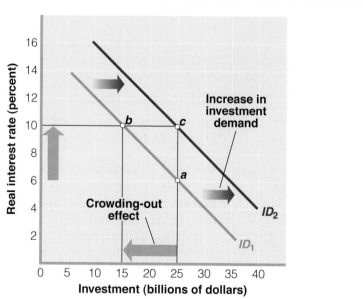

A Graphical Look at Crowding Out   We know from Chapter 10 there is an inverse relationship between the real interest rate and the amount of investment spending. When graphed, that relationship is shown as a downward-sloping investment demand curve, such as either ID_1 or ID_2 in Figure 11-8. Let's first consider curve ID_1 (ignore curve ID_2 for now). Suppose government borrowing increases the real interest rate from 6 to 10 percent. Investment spending will then fall from $25 billion to $15 billion, as shown by the economy's move from a to b. That is, the financing of the debt will compete with the financing of private investment projects and crowd out $10 billion of private investment. So the stock of private capital handed down to future generations will be $10 billion less than it would have been without the need to finance the public debt.

Public Investments and Public–Private Complementarities   But even with crowding out, two factors could partly or fully offset the net economic burden shifted to future generations. First, just as private expenditures may involve either consumption or investment, so it is with public goods. Part of the government spending enabled by the public debt is for public investment outlays (for example, highways, mass transit systems, and electric power facilities) and "human capital" (for example, investments in education, job training, and health). Like private expenditures on machinery and equipment, those **public investments** increase the economy's future production capacity. Because of the financing through debt, the stock of public capital passed on to future generations may be higher than otherwise. That greater stock of public capital may offset the diminished stock of private capital resulting from the crowding-out effect, leaving overall production capacity unimpaired.

So-called public–private complementarities are a second factor that could reduce the crowding-out effect. Some public and private investments are complementary. Thus, the public investment financed through the debt could spur some private-sector investment by increasing its expected rate of return. For example, a federal building in a city may encourage private investment in the form of nearby office buildings, shops, and restaurants. Through its complementary effect, the spending on public capital may shift the private investment demand curve to the right, as from ID_1 to ID_2 in Figure 11-8. Even though the government borrowing boosts the interest rate from 6 to 10 percent, total private investment need not fall. In the case shown as the move from *a* to *c* in Figure 11-8, it remains at $25 billion. *(Key Question 13)*

public investments
Government expenditures on public capital (such as roads and highways) and on human capital (such as education and health).

QUICK REVIEW

▶ The Canadian federal public debt is essentially the total accumulation of federal budget deficits minus surpluses over time; about 12 percent of the pubic debt is held by foreigners.

▶ As a percentage of GDP, the debt is lower today than it was in the mid-1990s and is in the low range of such debts among major industrial nations.

▶ There is no danger of the federal government going bankrupt because it need only refinance (not retire) the public debt and can raise revenues, if needed, through higher taxes.

▶ The borrowing and interest payments associated with the public debt may (a) increase income inequality, (b) require higher taxes, which may dampen incentives, and (c) impede the growth of the nation's stock of capital through crowding out of private investment.

The LAST WORD   The Leading Indicators

One of the several tools policymakers use to forecast the future direction of real GDP is a monthly index of a group of variables that in the past have provided advance notice of changes in GDP.

Statistics Canada's composite index of leading indicators historically has often (but not always) reached a peak or trough in advance of the corresponding turns in the business cycle. Thus, changes in the index of leading indicators provide a rough guide to the future direction of the economy, and such advance warning helps policymakers formulate appropriate macroeconomic policy.

Here is how each of the 10 components of the index would change if a decline in GDP were predicted, keeping in mind that the opposite changes forecast a rise in GDP.

1. **Retail trade furniture and appliance sales** A slump in these retail trade sales portends reduced future production—that is, a decline in GDP.

2. **Other durable goods sales** This part of retail trade is four times greater than the first. It includes sales of automobiles, which are more sensitive to interest rates than are purchases of other goods. A decline in sales here may be more a result of rising consumer loan rates than an impending downturn in the economy—though rising interest rates themselves often do precede a downturn.

3. **Housing index** This is a composite index of housing starts (units) and house sales. Decreases in the number of housing starts and in house sales forecast declines in investment and therefore the distinct possibility that GDP will decline or at least grow more slowly.

4. **New orders for durable goods** A decline in the number of orders received for durable goods indicates reduced future production—a reduction in aggregate demand, thus a decline in real GDP.

5. **Shipment-to-inventory ratio of finished products** A decline in the ratio—a decline in shipments and/or an increase in inventory—indicates that sales are declining and, probably, that undesired investment in inventories is occurring. In either case, a decline in production is probable.

6. **Average workweek (hours)** Decreases in the length of the average workweek in manufacturing foretell declines in future manufacturing output and a possible decline in GDP.

7. **Business and personal service employment** A decline in employment, especially in view of the continuing growth of our labour force of some 250,000 a year, indicates a serious slowdown in the economy and therefore GDP.

8. **United States composite leading index** Since about 75 percent

of our trade is with the United States —approximately 40 percent of our GDP—a slowdown in the United States is quickly transmitted to Canada. If the U.S. composite leading index is sharply down, Canada's GDP will almost certainly decline.

9. **S&P/TSX composite index** The Toronto Stock Exchange (TSX) is the country's largest, and the price movements of the 100 stocks that make up its index are a good indication of market sentiment in Canada. Declines in stock prices are often reflections of expected declines in corporate sales and profits. Also, lower stock prices diminish consumer wealth, leading to possible cutbacks in consumer spending. Lower stock prices also make it less attractive for firms to issue new shares of stock as a way of raising funds for investment. Thus, declines in stock prices can bring forth declines in aggregate demand and real GDP.

10. **Money supply** Decreases in the nation's money supply are associated with falling real GDP.

None of these factors alone consistently predicts the future course of the economy. It is not unusual in any month, for example, for one or two of the indicators to be decreasing while the other indicators are increasing. Rather, changes in the composite of the 10 components are what in the past have provided advance notice of a change in the direction of GDP. To the extent that the index has been successful, the rule of thumb is that three successive monthly declines or increases in the index indicate the economy will soon turn in that same direction.

But while that rule of thumb has correctly signalled business fluctuations on many occasions, it leaves a lot to be desired. At times the index has provided false warnings of recessions that never happened. In other instances, recessions have so closely followed the downturn in the index that policymakers have not had sufficient time to make use of the "early" warning. Moreover, changing structural features of the economy have, on occasion, rendered the existing index obsolete and necessitated its revision.

Given these caveats, the index of leading indicators can best be thought of as a helpful but rather unreliable signalling device that authorities must employ with considerable caution when formulating macroeconomic policy.

Question

What is the composite index of leading economic indicators and how does it relate to discretionary fiscal policy?

CHAPTER SUMMARY

11.1 ▶ FISCAL POLICY AND THE AD–AS MODEL

- Fiscal policy consists of deliberate changes in government spending, taxes, or some combination of both to promote full employment, price-level stability, and economic growth. Fiscal policy requires increases in government spending, decreases in taxes, or both—a budget deficit—to increase aggregate demand and push an economy from a recession. Decreases in government spending, increases in taxes, or both—a budget surplus—are appropriate fiscal policy for dealing with demand-pull inflation.

11.2 ▶ BUILT-IN STABILITY

- Built-in stability arises from net tax revenues, which vary directly with the level of GDP. During recession, the federal budget automatically moves toward a stabilizing deficit; during expansion, the budget automatically moves toward an anti-inflationary surplus. Built-in stability lessens, but does not fully correct, undesired changes in the real GDP.

- The cyclically adjusted budget, or full-employment budget, measures the federal budget deficit or surplus that would occur if the economy operated at full employment throughout the year. Cyclical deficits or surpluses are those that result from changes in the real GDP.

- Changes in the cyclically adjusted deficit or surplus provide meaningful information as to whether the government's fiscal policy is expansionary, neutral, or contractionary. Changes in the actual budget deficit or surplus do not, since such deficits or surpluses can include cyclical deficits or surplus.

11.3 ▶ PROBLEMS, CRITICISMS, AND COMPLICATIONS

- Certain problems complicate the enactment and implementation of fiscal policy. They include: (a) timing problems associated with recognition, administrative, and operational lags; (b) the potential for misuse of fiscal policy for political rather than economic purposes; (c) the tendency for provincial and municipal finances to be pro-cyclical; (d) potential ineffectiveness if households expect future policy reversals; (e) the possibility of fiscal policy crowding out private investment; and (f) complications relating to the effects of fiscal policy on exchange rates and net exports.

- Most economists believe that fiscal policy can help move the economy in a desired direction but cannot reliably be used to fine-tune the economy to a position of price stability and full employment. Nevertheless, fiscal policy is a valuable backup tool for aiding monetary policy in fighting significant recession or inflation.

11.4 ▶ DEFICITS, SURPLUSES, AND THE FEDERAL DEBT

- The public debt is the total accumulation of the government's deficits (minus surpluses) over time. Foreigners hold 12 percent of the Canadian portion of the federal debt. In 2008 interest payments as a percentage of GDP amounted to about 2 percent.

- The concern that a large public debt may bankrupt the government is a false worry because (a) the debt need only be refinanced rather than refunded and (b) the federal government has the power to increase taxes to make interest payments on the debt.

- In general, the public debt is not a vehicle for shifting economic burdens to future generations. Canadians inherit not only most of the public debt (a liability) but also most of the Canadian securities (an asset) that finance the debt.

- More substantive problems associated with public debt include the following: (a) payment of interest on the debt may increase income inequality, (b) interest payments on the debt require higher taxes, which may impair incentives, (c) paying interest or principal on the portion of the debt held by foreigners means a transfer of real output abroad,

and (d) government borrowing to refinance or pay interest on the debt may increase interest rates and crowd out private investment spending, leaving future generations with a smaller stock of capital than they would have otherwise.

- The increase in investment in public capital that may result from debt financing may partly or wholly offset the crowding-out effect of the public debt on private investment. Also, the added public investment may stimulate private investment, where the two are complements.

TERMS AND CONCEPTS

fiscal policy, p. 255
expansionary fiscal policy, p. 255
budget deficit, p. 255
contractionary fiscal policy, p. 256
budget surplus, p. 257
built-in stabilizer, p. 260

progressive tax, p. 261
proportional tax, p. 261
regressive tax, p. 261
cyclically adjusted budget, p. 261
cyclical deficit, p. 261
political business cycle, p. 266

crowding-out effect, p. 266
net export effect, p. 268
public debt, p. 270
external public debt, p. 274
public investments, p. 275

STUDY QUESTIONS

LO ▶ 11.1 1. **KEY QUESTION**   Assume that a hypothetical economy with an MPC of .8 is experiencing severe recession. By how much would government spending have to increase to shift the aggregate demand curve rightward by $25 billion? How large a tax cut would be needed to achieve the same increase in aggregate demand? Why the difference? Determine one possible combination of government spending increases and tax decreases that would accomplish the same goal.

LO ▶ 11.1 2. **KEY QUESTION**   What are the government's fiscal policy options for an inflationary gap caused by demand-pull inflation? Use the aggregate demand–aggregate supply model to show the impact of these policies on the price level. Which of these fiscal options do you think a person who wants to preserve the size of government might favour? A person who thinks the public sector is too large? How does the ratchet effect affect anti-inflationary fiscal policy?

LO ▶ 11.1 3. (For students assigned Chapter 9) Use the aggregate expenditures model to show how government fiscal policy could eliminate either a recessionary gap or an inflationary gap (Figure 9-7). Explain how equal increases in G and T could eliminate a recessionary gap and how equal decreases in G and T could eliminate an inflationary gap

LO ▶ 11.2 4. Explain how the built-in (or automatic) stabilizers work. What are the differences between a progressive, proportional, and regressive tax system as they relate to an economy's built-in stability?

5. **KEY QUESTION**   Define the cyclically adjusted budget, explain its significance, and state why it may differ from the actual budget. Suppose the full-employment, noninflationary level of real output is GDP_3 (not GDP_2) in the economy depicted in Figure 11-3. If the economy is operating at GDP_2 instead of GDP_3, what is the status of its cyclically adjusted budget? Of its current fiscal policy? What change in fiscal policy would you recommend? How would you accomplish that in terms of the G and T lines in the figure?   **LO ▶ 11.**

6. Some politicians have suggested Canada enact a constitutional amendment requiring the federal government to balance its budget annually. Explain why such an amendment, if strictly enforced, would force the government to follow a contractionary policy whenever the economy experienced a severe recession.   **LO ▶ 11.**

7. Complete the table below by stating whether the direction of discretionary fiscal policy was contractionary (C), expansionary (E), or neither (N), given the hypothetical budget data for an economy.   **LO ▶ 11.**

(1) Year	(2) Actual budget deficit (−) or surplus (+)	(3) Cyclically adjusted budget deficit (−) or surplus (+)	(4) Direction of fiscal policy
1	− 3.9%	− 2.1%	
2	− 4.5	− 2.6	_____
3	− 4.7	− 3.0	_____

(1) Year	(2) Actual budget deficit (–) or surplus (+)	(3) Cyclically adjusted budget deficit (–) or surplus (+)	(4) Direction of fiscal policy
4	– 3.9	– 2.6	_____
5	– 2.9	– 2.0	_____
6	– 2.2	– 1.9	_____

10▶11.3 8. **KEY QUESTION** Briefly state and evaluate the problems in enacting and applying fiscal policy. Explain the notion of a political business cycle. What is the crowding-out effect and why is it relevant to fiscal policy? In what respect is the net export effect similar to the crowding-out effect? In view of your answers, explain the following statement: "Although fiscal policy clearly is useful in combatting severe recession and demand-pull inflation, it is impossible to use fiscal policy to fine-tune the economy to the full-employment, noninflationary level of real GDP and keep the economy there indefinitely."

10▶11.2 9. **Advanced Analysis (for students assigned Chapter 9)** Assume that the consumption schedule, without taxes, for an economy is as shown below:

GDP (billions)	Consumption (billions)
$100	$120
200	200
300	280
400	360
500	440
600	520
700	600

a. Graph this consumption schedule and determine the size of the MPC.

b. Assume a lump-sum (regressive) tax is imposed such that the government collects $10 billion in taxes at all levels of GDP. Calculate the tax rate at each level of GDP.

Graph the resulting consumption schedule and compare the MPC and the multiplier with that of the pretax consumption schedule.

c. Now suppose a proportional tax with a 10 percent tax rate is imposed instead of the regressive tax. Calculate the new consumption schedule, graph it, and note the MPC and the multiplier.

d. Finally, impose a progressive tax such that the tax rate is zero percent when GDP is $100, 5 percent at $200, 10 percent at $300, 15 percent at $400, and so forth. Determine and graph the new consumption schedule, noting the effect of this tax on the MPC and the multiplier.

e. Explain why the proportional and progressive taxes contribute to greater economic stability, but the regressive tax does not. Demonstrate, using a graph similar to Figure 11-3.

10. **KEY QUESTION** How do economists distinguish between the absolute and relative sizes of the public debt? Why is the distinction important? Distinguish between refinancing the debt and retiring the debt. How does an internally held public debt differ from an externally held public debt? Contrast the effects of retiring an internally held debt and retiring an externally held debt. **LO▶11.4**

11. True or false? If false, explain why. **LO▶11.4**

a. The total public debt is more relevant to an economy than the public debt as percentage of GDP.

b. An internally held public debt is like a debt of the left hand owed to the right hand.

c. The Bank of Canada and federal government agencies hold more than three-fourths of the public debt.

12. Why might economists be quite concerned if the annual interest payments on the debt sharply increased as a percentage of GDP? **LO▶11.4**

13. **KEY QUESTION** Trace the cause-and-effect chain through which financing and refinancing of the public debt might affect real interest rates, private investment, the stock of capital, and economic growth. How might investment in public capital and complementarities between public capital and private capital alter the outcome of the cause–effect chain? **LO▶11.4**

INTERNET APPLICATION QUESTIONS @

1. **Leading Economic Indicators—How Goes the Economy?** Statistics Canada tracks the leading economic indicators. Check the summary of the index of leading indicators and its individual components for the latest month at the McConnell-Brue-Flynn-Barbiero Web site (Chapter 11). Is the index up or down? Which specific components are up, and which are down? What has been the trend of the composite index over the past three months?

2. **The Federal Budget Stance.** Go to the Department of Finance home page through the McConnell-Brue-Flynn-Barbiero Web site (Chapter 11) and click on the latest budget. Now, access the budget overview. What are the main targets of the federal government?

CHAPTER 12

Money, Banking, and Money Creation

Friedrich A. Hayek, recipient of a Nobel Prize in economics, makes the following observation about money:

> Money, the very "coin" of ordinary interaction, is … the object of the greatest unreasoning fantasy; and like sex it simultaneously fascinates, puzzles and repels. The literature treating it is probably greater than that devoted to any other single topic; and browsing through it inclines one to sympathise with the writer who long ago declared that no other subject, not even love, has driven more men to madness.[1]

In this chapter and the one that follows we want to unmask the critical role of money and the monetary system of the economy. When the monetary system is working properly, it provides the lifeblood of the circular flows of income and expenditure. A well-operating monetary system helps the economy achieve both full employment and the efficient use of resources. A malfunctioning monetary system creates severe fluctuations in the economy's levels of output, employment, and prices and distorts the allocation of resources.

In the first half of this chapter we will delve into the nature of money and its vital role in a modern economy. In the second half we investigate how money is created and how the Bank of Canada regulates the economy's money supply. We will see that Canada's central bank relies primarily on chartered banks to help expand the money supply to accommodate a growing economy.

---

[1] Hayek, F.A., *The Fatal Conceit* (Chicago: University of Chicago Press, 1988), pp. 101–102.

12.1 | The Definition and Functions of Money

money
Any item that is generally acceptable to sellers in exchange for goods and services.

Just what is **money**? There is an old saying that "money *is* what money *does*." In a general sense, anything that performs the functions of money *is* money. Here are those functions.

- *Medium of Exchange*   First and foremost, money is a **medium of exchange** that is used to buy and sell goods and services. A bakery worker in Montreal does not want to be paid 200 bagels per week. Nor does the bakery owner want to accept, say, halibut in exchange for bagels. Money, however, is readily acceptable as payment. As we saw in Chapter 2, money is a social invention with which resource suppliers and producers can be paid and that can be used to buy any of the full range of items available in the marketplace. As a medium of exchange, money allows society to escape the complications of **barter**. And, because it provides a convenient way of exchanging goods, money enables society to gain the advantages of geographic and human specialization.

medium of exchange
Items sellers generally accept and buyers generally use to pay for a good or service.

barter
The exchange of one good or service for another good or service.

unit of account
A standard unit in which prices can be stated and the value of goods and services can be compared.

- *Measure of Value*   Money is also a measure of value, or, more formally, a **unit of account.** A monetary unit—the dollar, in Canada—is a yardstick for measuring the relative worth of a wide variety of goods, services, and resources. Just as we measure distance in kilometres, we measure the value of goods and services in dollars.

    With money as an acceptable unit of account, the price of each item need be stated only in terms of the monetary unit. We need not state the price of cows in terms of corn, crayons, and computers. Money allows buyers and sellers to easily compare the prices of various goods, services, and resources. It also permits us to define debt obligations, determine taxes owed, and calculate the nation's GDP.

store of value
An asset set aside for future use.

- *Store of Value*   Money also serves as a **store of value** that makes it possible to acquire goods and services at a future date. People normally do not spend all their income on the day they receive it. To buy things later, they store (save) some of their wealth as money. The money you place in a safe or a chequing account will still be available to you a few weeks or months from now. When inflation is nonexistent or mild, holding money is a relatively risk-free way to preserve your wealth for later use.

People can, of course, choose to hold some or all of their wealth in a wide variety of assets besides money—real estate, stocks, bonds, precious metals such as gold, and even collectible items like fine art or comic books. But a key advantage that money has over all other assets is that it has the most *liquidity,* or spendability.

liquidity
The ease with which an asset can be converted quickly into cash with little or no loss of purchasing power.

An asset's **liquidity** is the ease with which it can be converted quickly into the most widely accepted and easily spent form of money, cash, with little or no loss of purchasing power. The more liquid an asset is, the more quickly it can be converted into cash and used either for purchases of goods and services or purchases of other assets.

Levels of liquidity vary radically. By definition, cash is perfectly liquid. By contrast, a house is highly illiquid for two reasons. First, it may take several months before a willing buyer can be found and a sale negotiated so that its value can be converted into cash. Second, there is a loss of purchasing power when the house is sold because numerous fees have to be paid to real estate agents and other individuals in order to complete the sale.

As we are about to discuss, our economy uses several different types of money including cash, coins, chequing account deposits, savings account deposits, and even more exotic things like deposits to money market mutual funds. As we describe the various forms of money in detail, take the time to compare their relative levels of liquidity—both with each other and as compared to other assets like stocks, bonds, and real estate. Cash is perfectly liquid. Other forms of money are highly liquid, but less liquid than cash.

Money is a medium of exchange that is used to buy and sell goods and services.

12.2 | The Components of the Money Supply

Money is a "stock" of some item or group of items (unlike income, for example, which is a "flow"). Societies have used many items as money, including whales' teeth, circular stones, elephant-tail bristles, gold coins, furs, cigarettes, playing cards, and pieces of paper. Anything that is widely accepted as a medium of exchange can serve as money. In Canada, currency is not the only form of money. As you will see, certain debts of government and financial institutions are also used as money.

Money Definition *M*1

M1
Currency (coins and paper money) and demand deposits in chartered banks.

The narrowest definition of the Canadian money supply is called **M1.** It consists of two items: (a) currency (coins and paper money) outside chartered banks, and (b) all **demand deposits,** meaning *chequing account deposits* in chartered banks.

Coins and paper money are issued by the Bank of Canada, and demand deposits—personal chequing accounts—are provided by chartered banks. When you deposit money in your chequing account, the chartered bank in which you deposited it "owes" you the amount of money you deposited. Your deposit is a chartered bank's debt.

demand deposit
A deposit in a chartered bank against which cheques may be written.

CURRENCY: COINS + PAPER MONEY

From copper pennies to "toonies," coins are the "small change" of our money supply. Coins, however, constitute a small portion of *M*1. All coins in circulation in Canada are **token money.** This means the *intrinsic value,* the value of the metal contained in the coin itself, is less than the face value of the coin. This is to prevent people from melting down the coins for sale as a commodity, in this case the metal. If our 25¢ pieces each contained 50¢ worth of silver bullion, it would be profitable to melt them and sell the metal. Although it is illegal to do so, 25¢ pieces would disappear from circulation. This happened with our *then* silver coins in the late 1960s and early 1970s; an 80-percent silver, pre-1967 quarter is now worth several dollars.

token money
Coins that have a face value greater than their intrinsic value.

Paper money and coins constitute about 24 percent of the economy's narrowly defined (*M*1) money supply. Paper currency is in the form of **Bank of Canada notes**—the paper notes you carry in your wallet—issued by our government-owned central bank. Every bill has "Bank of Canada" printed at the top of the face of the bill.

Figure 12-1 shows that together, coins and paper money amounted to $113 billion in December 2008, or about 24 percent of *M*1.

Bank of Canada notes
Paper money issued by Canada's government-owned central bank, the Bank of Canada.

DEMAND DEPOSITS

The safety and convenience of cheques and debit cards have made them the largest component of the M1 money supply. You would not think of stuffing $4896 in bills in an envelope and dropping it in a mailbox to pay a debt. But to write and mail a cheque or use a debit card for a large amount is commonplace. A cheque must be endorsed (signed on the reverse) by the person cashing it. Similarly, because a cheque requires endorsement, the theft or loss of a cheque is not nearly as unfortunate as losing an identical amount of currency. Finally, it is more convenient to write a cheque than to transport and count out a large sum of currency. For all these reasons, chequebook money, or demand deposits, is a large component of the stock of money. Almost 90 percent of M1 is in the form of demand deposits, on which cheques can be drawn.

It might seem strange that chequing account balances are regarded as part of the money supply. But the reason is clear: Cheques are nothing more than a way to transfer the ownership of deposits in chartered banks and are generally acceptable as a medium of exchange. Although cheques are less generally accepted than currency for small purchases, for major purchases most sellers willingly accept cheques as payment. Moreover, people can convert chequable deposits into paper money and coins on demand; cheques drawn on those deposits are thus the equivalent of currency.

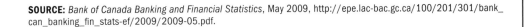

FIGURE 12-1   Components of Money Supply *M*1 and Money Supply *M*2+, in Canada

*M*1 is a narrow definition of the money supply that includes currency (in circulation) and demand deposits. *M*2+ is a broader definition that includes *M*1 along with several other account balances.

Currency
24%

Demand deposits
76%

**Money supply, *M*1
$469 billion**

Personal savings deposits and non-personal notice deposits
52%

*M*1
20%

Money market mutual funds and insurance annuities
9%

Deposits at non-chartered bank institutions
19%

**Money supply, *M*2+
$1217 billion**

SOURCE: *Bank of Canada Banking and Financial Statistics*, May 2009, http://epe.lac-bac.gc.ca/100/201/301/bank_can_banking_fin_stats-ef/2009/2009-05.pdf.

To summarize,

Money, *M*1 = currency in circulation + demand deposits

INSTITUTIONS THAT OFFER DEMAND DEPOSITS

In Canada, several types of financial institutions allow customers to write cheques on funds they have deposited. Chartered banks are the primary depository institutions. They accept the deposits of households and businesses, keep the money safe until it is demanded via cheques, and in the meantime use it to make available a wide variety of loans. Chartered bank loans provide short-term working capital to businesses, and finance consumer purchases of automobiles and other durable goods. There are six major chartered banks in Canada: the Royal Bank, the Canadian Imperial Bank of Commerce (CIBC), the Bank of Montreal, TD Canada Trust (TD), the Bank of Nova Scotia (Scotiabank), and the National Bank of Canada. Other institutions that offer chequing accounts in Canada are trust and mortgage loan companies, credit unions, and *caisses populaires*.

TWO QUALIFICATIONS

We must qualify our discussion in two important ways. First, currency held by the Bank of Canada and chartered banks is excluded from *M*1 and other measures of the money supply. A $5 bill in the wallet of, say, Emma Buck obviously constitutes just $5 of the money supply. But if we counted currency held by banks as part of the money supply, the same $5 would count for $10 of money supply when Emma deposited the currency into her chequing account in her bank. It would count for $5 of chequing deposit owned by Emma and also $5 of currency in the bank's cash drawer or vault. By excluding currency held by chartered banks when determining the total supply of money, we avoid this problem of double counting.

Also excluded from the money supply are any deposits of the federal government or the Bank of Canada that are held by chartered banks. This exclusion is designed to enable a better assessment of the amount of money available *to the private sector* for potential spending. The amount of money available to households and businesses is of keen interest to the Bank of Canada in conducting its monetary policy (a topic we cover in detail in Chapter 13).

Money Definition *M2*

near-monies
Financial assets, such as saving and term deposits in banks and savings institutions, that are not a medium of exchange but can be readily converted into money.

A second and broader definition of money includes *M*1 plus several near-monies. **Near-monies** are highly liquid financial assets that do not directly function as a medium of exchange but can be readily converted into currency or demand deposits. For example, you may withdraw currency from a *nonchequable savings account* at a chartered bank or trust and mortgage loan company, credit union, or *caisse populaire.* Or you may request that funds be transferred from a nonchequable savings account to a chequable account.

You cannot withdraw funds quickly from *term deposits*, which become available to a depositor only at maturity. The difference between a savings account and a term account is that there is a penalty if you withdraw money from your term account. For example, a 90-day or six-month term deposit is available when the designated period expires. Although term deposits are less liquid (spendable) than nonchequable savings accounts, they can be taken as currency or shifted into chequable accounts when they mature.

M2
A broad definition of money that includes M1 plus personal and business savings deposits that require notice before withdrawal.

If these "near-monies" are added to *M*1, we arrive at a broader definition of money. This is also set out in Table 12-1. Adding personal savings deposits and nonpersonal (business) notice deposits (requiring notice before withdrawal) to *M*1 gives us **M2,** also shown in Figure 12-1. At the end of 2008, *M*2 in Canada was about $879 billion.

Money Definition *M2+* and *M2++*

M2+
A broader definition of money that includes M2 plus deposits at credit unions, *caisses populaires*, trust companies, other nonbank deposit-taking institutions, and money market mutual funds.

An even broader monetary aggregate is **M2+**, which is *M*2 plus deposits at credit unions, *caisses populaires*, trust companies, other nonbank deposit-taking institutions, and money market mutual funds. *M*2+ totalled about $1217 billion in December 2008.

TABLE 12-1   Money in Canada,* December 2008

Money	Billions of dollars
Currency held outside banks	$ 113
+ Demand deposits at chartered banks held by individuals and businesses	416
= M1	529
+ Personal savings deposits and nonpersonal notice deposits at chartered banks	410
= M2	939
+ Deposits at trust and mortgage companies, credit unions, caisses populaires, and government savings institutions	226
+ Money market mutual funds and life insurance annuities	112
= M2+	$1277
+ Canada Saving Bonds and other retail instruments	13
+ Non–money market mutual funds	521
= M2++	$1811

* Seasonally adjusted average monthly data

Source: Bank of Canada, *Bank of Canada Banking and Financial Statistics*, May 2009.

Note the following about non-chartered banks and other financial institutions. Credit unions, *caisses populaires,* and trust companies gather the savings of households and businesses that are then used to finance housing mortgages and provide other loans. *Credit unions* accept deposits from, and lend to, "members"—usually a group of individuals who work for the same company or live in the same area. There are now some 533 credit unions of various sizes operating under the auspices of Credit Union Central of Canada. *Caisses populaires* can be found in Manitoba, Ontario, Quebec, and New Brunswick. The largest in Canada are those associated with the Caisses Desjardins. *Trust companies* are rapidly dwindling in number in Canada as they merge with chartered banks. For example, some years ago TD Bank merged with Canada Trust, to transform itself into TD Canada Trust.

Finally, the Bank of Canada's broadest monetary aggregate is *M2++*, which consists of *M2+* plus Canada Savings Bonds and non–money market mutual funds. At the end of 2008, *M2++* totalled more than $1.7 trillion, as shown in Table 12-1.

Which definition of money shall we use? The simple *M1* includes only items *directly* and *immediately* usable as a medium of exchange. For this reason it is an oft-cited statistic in discussions of the money supply. However, for some purposes economists prefer the broader *M2, M2+,* or *M2++* definition.

We will use the narrow *M1* definition of money in our discussion and analysis, unless stated otherwise. The important principles that apply to *M1* are also applicable to *M2, M2+,* and *M2++,* because *M1* is a base component in these broader measures. *(Key Question 3)*

M2++
The broadest definition of the Canadian money supply; consists of M2+ plus Canada Savings Bonds and non–money market mutual funds.

QUICK REVIEW

▶ Money serves as a medium of exchange, a unit of account, and a store of value.

▶ The narrow M1 definition of money includes currency held by the public and demand (chequable) deposits in chartered banks.

▶ The M2 definition of money includes M1 plus personal savings deposits and nonpersonal notice deposits at chartered banks.

▶ M2+ is made up of M2 plus deposits at credit unions, *caisses populaires,* trust companies, other nonbank deposit-taking institutions, and money market mutual funds.

▶ M2++ consists of M2+ plus Canada Savings Bonds and non–money market mutual funds.

12.3 | What Backs the Money Supply?

The money supply in Canada essentially is backed (guaranteed) by government's ability to keep the value of money relatively stable. Nothing more!

Money as Debt

The major components of the money supply—paper money and demand deposits—are debts, or promises to pay. In Canada, paper money is the circulating debt of the Bank of Canada. Demand deposits are the debts of chartered banks.

Paper currency and demand deposits have no intrinsic value. A $5 bill is just an inscribed piece of paper. A demand deposit is merely a bookkeeping entry. And coins, we know, have less intrinsic value than their face value. Nor will government redeem the paper money you hold for anything tangible, such as gold.

To many people, the fact that the government does not back the currency with anything tangible seems implausible and insecure. But the decision not to back the currency with anything tangible was made for a very good reason. If the government backed the currency with something tangible like gold, then the supply of money would vary with the amount of gold available. By not backing the currency, the government avoids this constraint and indeed receives a key freedom—the ability to provide as much or as little money as needed to maintain the value of money and to best suit the economic needs of the country. In effect, by choosing not to back the currency, the government has chosen to give itself the ability to freely manage the nation's money supply. Its monetary authorities attempt to provide the amount of money needed for the particular volume of business activity that will promote full employment, price-level stability, and economic growth.

Most economists agree that managing the money supply is certainly more sensible than linking it to gold or to some other commodity whose supply might change arbitrarily and capriciously. For instance, if we used gold to back the money supply so that gold was redeemable for money and vice versa, then a large increase in the nation's gold stock as the result of a new gold discovery might increase the money supply too rapidly and thereby trigger rapid inflation. Or a long-lasting decline in gold production might reduce the money supply to the point where recession and unemployment resulted.

In short, people cannot convert paper money into a fixed amount of gold or any other precious commodity. Money is exchangeable only for paper money. If you ask the Bank of Canada to redeem $5 of your paper money, it will swap one paper $5 bill for another bearing a different serial number. That is all you can get. Similarly, cheque money cannot be redeemed for gold but only for paper money—which, as we have just seen, the government will not redeem for anything tangible.

Value of Money

MONEY & INFLATION

So why are currency and demand deposits money, whereas, say, "money" from a Monopoly game is not? What gives a $20 bill or a $100 chequing account entry its value? The answer to these questions has three parts.

- *Acceptability* Currency and demand deposits are money because people accept them as money. By virtue of longstanding business practice, currency and demand deposits perform the basic function of money: they are acceptable as a medium of exchange. We accept paper money in exchange because we are confident it will be exchangeable for real goods, services, and resources when we spend it.

CONSIDER THIS | Are Credit Cards Money?

You may wonder if credit cards such as Visa and Master-Card are considered part of the money supply. After all, credit cards are a convenient way to make purchases. The answer is that a credit card is not really money but rather a means of obtaining a short-term loan from the chartered bank or other financial institution that issued the card.

What happens when you purchase an MP3 player with a credit card? The bank that issued the card will reimburse the store and later you will reimburse the bank. Credit cards are merely a means of deferring or postponing payment for a short period. You may have to pay an annual fee for the services provided, and, if you repay the bank in instalments, you will pay a sizable interest charge on the loan. Your chequing account balance that you use to pay your credit card bill is money: the credit card is *not* money.[*]

Although credit cards are not money, they allow individuals and businesses to economize in the use of money. Credit cards enable people to hold less currency in their billfolds and, prior to payment due dates, fewer chequable deposits in their bank accounts. Credit cards also help people coordinate the timing of their expenditures with their receipt of income.

---

[*] A bank debit card, however, is very similar to a cheque in your chequebook. Unlike a purchase with a credit card, a purchase with a debit card creates a direct "debit" (a subtraction) from your chequing account balance. That chequing account balance is money—it is part of the M1.

legal tender
Anything that government says must be accepted in payment of a debt.

- *Legal Tender*   Our confidence in the acceptability of paper money is strengthened because government has designated currency as **legal tender**. Specifically, each bill contains the statement "This note is legal tender." That means that paper currency must be accepted in payment of a debt. The paper money in our economy is fiat money; it is money because the government has declared it so, not because it can be redeemed for precious metal.

- *Relative Scarcity*   The value of money, like the economic value of anything else, depends on its supply and demand. Money derives its value from its scarcity relative to its utility (its want-satisfying power). The utility of money lies in its capacity to be exchanged for goods and services, now or in the future. The economy's demand for money thus depends on the total dollar-volume of transactions in any period plus the amount of money individuals and businesses want to hold for future transactions. With a reasonably constant demand for money, the supply of money provided by the monetary authorities will determine the value or "purchasing power" of the monetary unit (dollar, yen, peso, or whatever).

Money and Prices

The purchasing power of money is the amount of goods and services a unit of money will buy. When money rapidly loses its purchasing power, it loses its role as money.

THE PURCHASING POWER OF THE DOLLAR

The amount a unit of a currency, in our case a dollar, will buy varies inversely with the price level; that is, a reciprocal relationship exists between the general price level and the purchasing power of the dollar. When the Consumer Price Index (or "cost of living" index) goes up the purchasing power of the dollar goes down, and vice versa. Higher prices lower the purchasing power of the dollar, because more dollars are needed to buy a particular amount of goods, services, or resources. For example, if the price level doubles, the purchasing power of the dollar declines by one-half, or 50 percent.

Conversely, lower prices increase the purchasing power of the dollar, because fewer dollars are needed to obtain a specific quantity of goods and services. If the price level falls by, say, one-half, or 50 percent, the purchasing power of the dollar doubles.

In equation form, the relationship looks like this:

$$D = 1/P$$

To find the value of the dollar D, divide 1 by the price level P expressed as an index number (in hundredths). If the price level is 1.0, then the value of the dollar is 1. If the price level rises to, say, 1.20, D falls to 0.833; a 20 percent increase in the price level reduces the value of the dollar by 16.67 percent. Check your understanding of this reciprocal relationship by determining the value of D and its percentage rise when P falls by 20 percent to 0.80. (***Key Question 5***)

INFLATION AND ACCEPTABILITY

In Chapter 7 we noted situations in which a nation's currency became worthless and unacceptable in exchange. These instances of runaway inflation, or *hyperinflation,* happened when the government issued so many pieces of paper currency that the purchasing power of each of those units of money was almost totally undermined. The infamous post–World War I hyperinflation in Germany is an example. In December 1919 there were about 50 billion marks in circulation—four years later, there were 496,585,345,900 billion! The result? The German mark in 1923 was worth a very small fraction of its 1919 value.[2]

---

[2] Frank G. Graham, *Exchange, Prices and Production in Hyperinflation Germany, 1920–1923* (Princeton, N.J.: Princeton University Press, 1930), p. 13.

Runaway inflation will significantly depreciate the value of money between the time it is received and the time it is spent. Rapid declines in the value of a currency may cause it to cease being used as a medium of exchange. Businesses and households may refuse to accept paper money in exchange because they do not want to bear the loss in its value that will occur while it is in their possession. Without an acceptable domestic medium of exchange, the economy may revert to barter. Alternatively, a more stable currency, such as the European euro, may come into widespread use. At the extreme, the economy may adopt a foreign currency as its own official currency as a way to counter hyperinflation.

Similarly, people will use money as a store of value only as long as there is no sizable deterioration in the value of that money because of inflation. And an economy can effectively employ money as a unit of account only when its purchasing power is relatively stable. When the value of the dollar is declining rapidly, sellers do not know what to charge and buyers do not know what to pay.

STABILIZING THE PURCHASING POWER OF MONEY

Rapidly rising price levels (rapid inflation) and the consequent erosion of the purchasing power of money typically result from imprudent economic policies. Since the purchasing power of money and the price level vary inversely, stabilization of the purchasing power of a nation's money requires stabilization of the nation's price level. Such price-level stability (with 2 to 3 percent annual inflation) mainly necessitates prudent regulation of the nation's money supply and interest rates (*monetary policy*). It also requires appropriate *fiscal policy* supportive of the efforts of the nation's monetary authorities to hold down inflation. In Canada, a combination of legislation, government policy, and social practice inhibits imprudent expansion of the money supply that might jeopardize money's purchasing power. The critical role of the Canadian monetary authorities in maintaining the purchasing power of the dollar is the subject of Chapter 13. For now, simply note that the Bank of Canada makes available a particular quantity of money, such as $M1$ or $M2$ in Figure 12-1, and can change that amount through its policy tools.

QUICK REVIEW

▶ In Canada, all money consists essentially of the debts of government and chartered banks.

▶ These debts efficiently perform the functions of money so long as their value, or purchasing power, is relatively stable.

▶ The value of money is rooted not in specified quantities of precious metals but in the amount of goods, services, and resources that money will purchase.

▶ The value of the dollar (its domestic purchasing power) is inversely related to the price level.

▶ Government's responsibility in stabilizing the purchasing power of the monetary unit calls for (1) effective control over the supply of money by the monetary authorities, and (2) the application of appropriate fiscal policies by the federal government.

12.4 | The Canadian Financial System

The main component of the money supply—demand deposits—is created by and comes into circulation through the chartered banks. We now take a look at the framework of the Canadian banking system.

Money and banking are federal responsibilities. Under the Bank Act, each bank is incorporated under a separate Act of Parliament and granted a charter. This is why Canadian commercial banks are called **chartered banks.**

chartered bank
A multi-branched, privately owned, commercial financial intermediary that has received a charter by Act of Parliament.

At Confederation in 1867, there were 28 chartered banks; this number grew in the following years to 41, before failures and mergers brought the number to eight in the 1960s. The late 1960s and 1970s brought the formation of new banks, and after six more amalgamations and two failures there were 21 domestically owned banks by 2008. With the 1980 Bank Act revisions, foreign banks were allowed to establish Canadian subsidiaries. By 2008, there were 25 foreign bank subsidiaries, as well as 23 foreign bank branches in Canada. In total, the domestic and foreign banks had almost $3.0 trillion in assets at the end of 2008.

Canada's Chartered Banks

fractional reserve banking system
A banking system with a reserve ratio that is less than 100 percent of the deposit liabilities of a chartered bank.

Table 12-2 sets out the balance sheet of the Canadian chartered banks. Their cash reserves are only a small percentage of deposits. As we will discuss in the next chapter, our banking system is a **fractional reserve banking system**—chartered banks loan out most of their deposits, keeping only a small percentage to meet everyday cash withdrawals. If depositors in the chartered banks were to come all at once to withdraw their money, there would not be enough cash reserves to meet their requests. In such an unlikely event, chartered banks borrow from the Bank of Canada, the bankers' bank.

Making Loans

prime rate
The interest rate banks charge their most creditworthy borrowers.

Chartered banks are private companies owned by shareholders who seek a competitive return on their investments. Thus, the primary goal of chartered banks is to try to maximize profits. They loan out as much of their deposits as is prudently possible to increase profits. Those funds that cannot be safely loaned out are used to buy Government of Canada securities. The rate banks charge on loans to their best corporate customers is referred to as the **prime rate.** Banks earn a profit on the spread between deposit interest rates and loan interest rates.

Other Financial Intermediaries

financial intermediary
A chartered bank or other financial institution that uses the funds deposited with it to make loans.

Although the present analysis focuses on chartered banks, the banking system is supplemented by other **financial intermediaries.** These include trust companies, loan companies, credit unions, and *caisses populaires* that accept the funds of small savers and make them available to investors by extending mortgage loans or by purchasing marketable securities. Insurance companies accept

---

TABLE 12-2	The Balance Sheet of Canadian Chartered Banks, December 2008 (billions of dollars)

Assets		Liabilities	
Reserves (currency and chartered banks' deposits with Bank of Canada)	6	Demand deposits	257
Loans (determined in Canadian dollars)	615	Savings deposits	509
Government of Canada securities	193	Term deposits	350
Foreign-currency assets	1342	Foreign-currency liabilities	1334
		Government of Canada deposit	5
Other assets	1031	Other liabilities	727
Total	3182	Total	3182

Source: Bank of Canada, *Bank of Canada Banking and Financial Statistics,* May 2009.

12.1 │ GLOBAL PERSPECTIVE

The world's largest commercial banks and the four largest Canadian chartered banks in 2009

Assets (billions of U.S. dollars)

Bank	Assets
Barclays (U.K.)	$1,587
UBS (Switzerland)	1,519
Citigroup (U.S.)	1,494
ING Group (Netherlands)	1,370
Mizuho Financial (Japan)	1,325
Allianz Worldwide (Germany)	1,301
Bank of America (U.S.)	1,292
HSCB Group (U.K.)	1,274
BNP Paribas (France)	1,228
JPMorgan Chase (U.S.)	1,199
Royal Bank of Canada	398
TD Canada Trust	310
Scotiabank	265
Bank of Montreal	253

Source: Forbes Global 2000, www.forbes.com.

large volumes of savings in the form of premiums on insurance policies and annuities and use these funds to buy a variety of private, corporate, and government securities.

The Canadian financial system has been undergoing restructuring to permit more competition among the former "four pillars": the banking, insurance, trust, and securities industries.

Chartered banks and savings institutions have two basic functions: they hold the money deposits of businesses and households, and they make loans to the public in an effort to make profits. We will see in the next section that in doing so the intermediaries increase the economy's supply of money.

Cheque Clearing

A cheque is a written order that the drawer may use in making a purchase or paying a debt. A cheque is collected, or "cleared," when one or more banks or near-banks negotiates a transfer of part of the drawer's chequing account to the chequing account of the recipient. If Jones and Smith have chequing accounts in the same bank and Jones gives Smith a $10 cheque, Smith can collect this cheque by taking it to the bank, where his account will be increased by $10 and Jones's reduced by $10. In many cases, however, the drawer and the receiver will be located in different towns or provinces and therefore have their accounts in bank branches far from one another. Under federal law a *Canadian Payments Association* (CPA) was set up in 1982 to take over the inter-bank cheque clearing system, which had been run by the Canadian Bankers' Association. All the chartered banks are members of the CPA.

12.5 | Chartered Banks and the Creation of Money

Have you ever considered how money is created? You may believe that it is simply printed by the Bank of Canada. Although this is true, the creation of money is slightly more complex, and it is actually done with the help of Canada's chartered banks.

The Fractional Reserve System

Canada, like most other countries today, has a fractional reserve banking system in which only a portion (fraction) of the total money supply is held in reserve as currency. Our goal is to explain this system and show how chartered banks can create demand deposits by issuing loans. Our examples will involve chartered banks, but remember that credit unions, *caisses populaires*, and trust companies also provide deposits on which cheques can be written, though these institutions use the chartered banking system to clear the cheques written on their account.

Illustrating the Idea: the Goldsmiths

Because of the public's acceptance of the goldsmiths' receipts as paper money, the goldsmiths soon realized that owners rarely redeemed the gold they had in storage.

Here is the history behind the idea of the fractional reserve system. When early traders began to use gold in making transactions, they soon realized that it was both unsafe and inconvenient to carry gold and to have it weighed and assayed (judged for purity) every time they negotiated a transaction. So by the sixteenth century they had begun to deposit their gold with goldsmiths, who would store it in vaults for a fee. On receiving a gold deposit, the goldsmith would issue a receipt to the depositor. Soon people were paying for goods with goldsmiths' receipts, which served as one of the first types of paper money.

At this point the goldsmiths—budding bankers—used a 100 percent reserve system; they backed their circulating paper money receipts fully with the gold that they held "in reserve" in their vaults. But because of the public's acceptance of the goldsmiths' receipts as paper money, the goldsmiths soon realized that owners rarely redeemed the gold they had in storage. In fact, the goldsmiths observed that the amount of gold being deposited with them in any week or month was likely to exceed the amount that was being withdrawn.

Then some clever goldsmith hit on the idea that paper "receipts" could be issued in excess of the amount of gold held. Goldsmiths would put these receipts, which were redeemable in gold, into circulation by making interest-earning loans to merchants, producers, and consumers. A borrower might, for instance, borrow $10,000 worth of gold receipts today with the promise to repay $10,500 worth of gold receipts in one year (a 5 percent interest rate). Borrowers were willing to accept loans in the form of gold receipts because the receipts were accepted as a medium of exchange in the marketplace.

This was the beginning of the fractional reserve system of banking, in which reserves in bank vaults are a fraction of the total money supply. If, for example, the goldsmith issued $1 million in receipts for actual gold in storage and another $1 million in receipts as loans, then the total value of paper money in circulation would be $2 million—twice the value of the gold. Gold reserves would be a fraction (one-half) of outstanding paper money.

Significant Characteristics of Fractional Reserve Banking

The goldsmith story highlights two significant characteristics of fractional reserve banking. First, banks can create money through lending. In fact, goldsmiths created money when they made loans by giving borrowers paper money that was not fully backed by gold reserves. The quantity of such money goldsmiths could create depended on the amount of reserves they deemed prudent to have available. The smaller the amount of reserves thought necessary, the larger the amount of paper money the goldsmiths could create. Today, gold is no longer used as bank reserves. Instead, currency itself serves as bank reserves so that the creation of demand deposit money by banks (via their lending) is limited by the amount of *currency reserves* that the banks feel obligated to keep.

A second reality is that banks operating on the basis of fractional reserves are vulnerable to "panics" or "runs." A goldsmith who issued paper money equal to twice the value of his gold reserves would be unable to convert all that paper money into gold in the event that all the holders of that money appeared at his door at the same time demanding their gold. And, in fact, many European, U.S., and Canadian banks were once ruined by just this unfortunate circumstance. Rumours would spread that a bank was about to go bankrupt and that it had only a small amount of reserves left in its vaults—depositors would literally run to the bank trying to be one of the lucky few to withdraw their money while the bank had reserves left. The rumours were usually totally unfounded, but the bank would still go bankrupt even if it began the day with its normal amount of reserves. With so many customers withdrawing money simultaneously, the bank would run out of reserves and be forced to default on its obligations to its remaining depositors.

However, this kind of bank panic is highly unlikely if the banker's reserve and lending policies are prudent. Indeed, one reason why banking systems are highly regulated industries is to prevent bank runs. This is also why Canada has a system of deposit insurance. By guaranteeing deposits, deposit insurance helps to prevent the sort of bank runs that used to happen so often before deposit insurance was available. By guaranteeing that depositors will always get their money, deposit insurance removes the incentive to try to withdraw one's deposit before anyone else can. It thus stops most bank runs.

A Single Chartered Bank

balance sheet
A statement of the assets, liabilities, and net worth of a firm or individual at a certain time.

To illustrate the workings of the modern fractional reserve banking system, we need to examine a chartered bank's **balance sheet**—its statement of assets and claims on assets that summarizes the financial position of the bank at a certain time. Every balance sheet must balance; this means that the value of *assets* must equal the amount of claims against those assets. The claims shown on a balance sheet are divided into two groups: the claims of non-owners against the firm's assets, called *liabilities*, and the claims of the owners of the firm against the firm's assets, called *net worth*. A balance sheet is balanced because

Assets = liabilities + net worth.

For every $1 change in assets, there must be an offsetting $1 change in liabilities + net worth. For every $1 change in liabilities + net worth, there must be an offsetting $1 change in assets.

Now let's work through a series of bank transactions involving balance sheets to establish how individual banks can create money.

Formation of a Chartered Bank

To see how individual banks create money we must understand the items a bank carries on its balance sheet and how certain transactions affect the balance sheet. We begin with the organization of a local chartered bank.

TRANSACTION 1: CREATING A BANK

Suppose some citizens of Vancouver decide a new chartered bank is needed to provide banking services for their growing city. Once they get Parliament to pass an act granting a charter for their bank, they then sell, say, $250,000 worth of capital stock (equity shares) to buyers both in and out of the province. The Bank of Vancouver now exists. What does the bank's balance statement look like at this stage?

vault cash
The currency a bank has in its vault and cash drawers.

The owners of the new bank have sold $250,000 worth of shares of stock in the bank—some to themselves and some to other people. As a result, the bank now has $250,000 in cash on hand and $250,000 worth of capital stock outstanding. The cash is an asset to the bank. Cash held by a bank is sometimes called **vault cash** or "till money." The bank's balance sheet reads:

Creating a Bank

	Balance Sheet 1: Bank of Vancouver		
Assets		**Liabilities and net worth**	
Cash	$250,000	Capital stock	$250,000

Each item listed in a balance sheet such as this is called an *account.*

TRANSACTION 2: ACQUIRING PROPERTY AND EQUIPMENT

The first step for the new bank will be to acquire property and equipment. The bank purchases buildings for $220,000 and buys $20,000 worth of office equipment. This transaction changes the composition of the bank's assets. The bank now has $240,000 less in cash and $240,000 of new property assets. Using blue type to denote those accounts affected by each transaction, we find that the bank's balance sheet at the conclusion of Transaction 2 appears as follows:

Acquiring Property and Equipment

	Balance Sheet 2: Bank of Vancouver		
Assets		**Liabilities and net worth**	
Cash	$ 10,000	Capital stock	$250,000
Property	240,000		

Note that the balance sheet still balances, as it must.

TRANSACTION 3: ACCEPTING DEPOSITS

Chartered banks have two basic functions: to accept deposits of money and to make loans. Now that our bank is in operation, suppose the citizens and businesses of Vancouver decide to deposit $100,000 in the Bank of Vancouver. What happens to the bank's balance sheet?

The bank receives cash, an asset to the bank. Suppose this money is placed in the bank as demand deposits (chequing accounts), rather than savings accounts or term deposits. These newly created *demand deposits* are claims that depositors have against the assets of the Bank of Vancouver, thus creating a new liability account. The bank's balance sheet now looks like this:

Accepting Deposits

	Balance Sheet 3: Bank of Vancouver		
Assets		**Liabilities and net worth**	
Cash	$110,000	Demand deposits	$100,000
Property	240,000	Capital stock	250,000

There has been no change in the economy's total supply of money, but a change has occurred in the composition of the money supply as a result of Transaction 3. Demand deposits have *increased* by $100,000 and currency in circulation has *decreased* by $100,000. Note that currency held by a bank is *not* part of the economy's money supply.

A withdrawal of cash will reduce the bank's demand-deposit liabilities and its holdings of cash by the amount of the withdrawal. This, too, changes the composition, but not the total supply, of money in the economy.

Deposits in the Bank of Canada

desired reserves
The amount of vault cash each chartered bank chooses to keep on hand for daily transactions, plus its deposits at the Bank of Canada.

The Bank of Vancouver has to have sufficient *cash reserves* to serve the daily cash needs of the chartered bank's customers. Some of these cash reserves are held at the Bank of Canada (see Table 12-2). Cash reserves are also called **desired reserves.** Generally, banks keep a minimum percentage of their holdings in cash reserves. We refer to the "specified percentage" of deposit liabilities the chartered bank chooses to keep as vault cash as the **desired reserve ratio.** Up to the mid 1990s the Bank of Canada actually required chartered banks to hold a specified percentage of demand, savings, and term deposits, and referred to this as *required reserves* (we will say more about this in Chapter 13). The desired reserve ratio is calculated as follows:

desired reserve ratio
The specified percentage of deposit liabilities a chartered bank chooses to keep as vault cash.

$$\text{Desired reserve ratio} = \frac{\text{chartered bank's desired reserves}}{\text{chartered bank's demand} - \text{deposit liabilities}}$$

If the desired reserve ratio is 20 percent, our bank, having accepted $100,000 in deposits from the public, would keep $20,000 as reserves to meet its daily cash needs.

There are two things to note about reserves:

excess reserves
The amount by which a chartered bank's actual reserves exceed its desired reserves.

1. *Excess Reserves*   A bank's **excess reserves** are found by subtracting desired reserves from its **actual reserves.**

Excess reserves = actual reserves − desired reserves

In this case,

actual reserves
The funds that a bank has as vault cash plus any deposit it may have with the Bank of Canada.

Actual reserves	$110,000
Desired reserves	−20,000
Excess reserves	$ 90,000

The only reliable way of computing excess reserves is to multiply the bank's demand-deposit liabilities by the desired reserve ratio to obtain desired reserves ($100,000 × 20 percent = $20,000) and then to subtract desired reserves from the actual reserves listed on the asset side of the bank's balance sheet.

To test your understanding, compute the bank's excess reserves from balance sheet 3, assuming that the desired reserve ratio is (a) 5 percent, (b) 33.3 percent, and (c) 50 percent. We will soon demonstrate that the ability of a chartered bank to make loans depends on the existence of excess reserves. So, understanding this concept is crucial in seeing how the banking system creates money.

2. *Influence*   Excess reserves are a means by which the Bank of Canada can influence the lending ability of chartered banks. The next chapter will explain in detail how the Bank of Canada can implement certain policies that either increase or decrease chartered bank reserves and affect the ability of banks to make loans. To the degree that these policies are successful in influencing the volume of chartered bank credit, the Bank of Canada can help the economy smooth out business fluctuations. *(Key Question 9)*

TRANSACTION 4: CLEARING A CHEQUE DRAWN AGAINST THE BANK

Assume that Clem Bradshaw, a Vancouver lumberyard owner, deposited a substantial portion of the $100,000 in demand deposits that the Bank of Vancouver received in Transaction 3. Suppose Bradshaw buys $50,000 worth of lumber from the Ajax Forest Products Company of Chilliwack. Bradshaw pays for this lumber by writing a $50,000 cheque against his deposit in the Bank of

Vancouver. Ajax deposits the cheque in its account with the Bank of Manitoba, which has a branch in Chilliwack.

Note that the balance statements of the two banks will balance. The Bank of Vancouver will reduce both its assets and its liabilities by $50,000. The Bank of Manitoba will have $50,000 more in cash and in deposits. *Whenever a cheque is drawn against one bank and deposited in another bank, collection of that cheque will reduce both reserves and demand deposits by the bank on which the cheque is drawn.* In our example, the Bank of Vancouver loses $50,000 in both reserves and deposits to the Bank of Manitoba. But there is no loss of reserves or deposits for the banking system as a whole. What one bank loses, another bank gains.

If we bring all the other assets and liabilities back into the picture, the Bank of Vancouver's balance sheet looks like this at the end of Transaction 4:

Clearing a Cheque

Balance Sheet 4: Bank of Vancouver

Assets		Liabilities and net worth	
Reserves	$ 60,000	Demand deposits	$ 50,000
Property	240,000	Capital stock	250,000

Verify that with a 20 percent desired reserve ratio, the bank's excess reserves now stand at $50,000.

QUICK REVIEW

▶ When a bank accepts deposits of cash, the composition of the money supply is changed but the total supply of money is not directly altered.

▶ Chartered banks keep reserves (cash) equal to a desired percentage of their own deposit liabilities.

▶ The amount by which a bank's actual cash reserves exceeds its desired reserves is called excess reserves.

▶ A bank that has a cheque drawn and collected against it will lose to the recipient bank both cash and deposits equal to the value of the cheque.

Money-Creating Transactions of a Chartered Bank

The next two transactions are crucial because they explain (1) how a chartered bank can literally create money by making loans, and (2) how banks create money by purchasing government bonds from the public.

TRANSACTION 5: GRANTING A LOAN

Suppose the Grisley Meat Packing Company of Vancouver decides to expand. Suppose, too, that the company needs exactly $50,000—which just happens to be equal to the Bank of Vancouver's excess reserves—to finance this project.

Grisley requests a loan for this amount from the Bank of Vancouver. Convinced of Grisley's ability to repay, the bank grants the loan. Grisley hands a promissory note—a fancy IOU—to the bank. Grisley wants the convenience and safety of paying its obligations by cheque. So, instead of receiving cash from the bank, Grisley gets a $50,000 increase in its demand deposit account in the Bank of Vancouver.

The Bank of Vancouver has acquired an interest-earning asset (the promissory note) and has created a deposit (a liability) to pay for this asset. At the moment the loan is completed, the Bank of Vancouver's position is shown by balance sheet 5a:

When a Loan Is Negotiated

Balance Sheet 5a: Bank of Vancouver

Assets		Liabilities and net worth	
Reserves	$ 60,000	Demand deposits	$100,000
Loans	50,000	Capital stock	250,000
Property	240,000		

A close examination of the bank's balance statement will reveal a startling fact: *When a bank makes loans, it creates money.* The president of Grisley went to the bank with something that is not money—her IOU—and walked out with something that *is* money—a demand deposit.

When banks lend, they create demand deposits (chequing accounts) that *are* money. By extending credit, the Bank of Vancouver has "monetized" an IOU. Grisley and the bank have created and then swapped claims. The claim created by the bank and given to the Grisley Company is money; cheques drawn against a deposit are acceptable as a medium of exchange. It is through the extension of credit by chartered banks that the bulk of the money used in our economy is created.

Bank creation of money raises an interesting question: If banks create demand deposit money when they lend their excess reserves, is money destroyed when borrowers pay off their loans? The answer is yes. When loans are paid off the process just described works in reverse. Demand deposits decline by the amount of the loan repayment.

Assume that Grisley awards a $50,000 building contract to the Quickbuck Construction Company of Kamloops. Quickbuck completes the expansion job and is paid with a cheque for $50,000 drawn by Grisley against its demand deposit in the Bank of Vancouver. Quickbuck, with headquarters in Kamloops, does *not* deposit this cheque back in the Bank of Vancouver but instead deposits it in a Kamloops branch of the Bank of Manitoba. The Bank of Manitoba now has a $50,000 claim against the Bank of Vancouver. As a result, the Bank of Vancouver *loses* both reserves and deposits equal to the amount of the cheque; the Bank of Manitoba *acquires* $50,000 of reserves and deposits.

In summary, assuming a cheque is drawn by the borrower for the entire amount of the loan ($50,000) and given to a firm that deposits it in another bank, the Bank of Vancouver's balance sheet will read as follows after the cheque has been cleared against it:

After a Cheque Is Drawn on the Loan

Balance Sheet 5b: Bank of Vancouver

Assets		Liabilities and net worth	
Reserves	$ 10,000	Demand deposits	$ 50,000
Loans	50,000	Capital stock	250,000
Property	240,000		

WORKED PROBLEM 12.1
Single Bank Accounting

After the cheque has been collected, the Bank of Vancouver is just barely meeting its desired reserve ratio of 20 percent. The bank has no excess reserves; it is fully "loaned up." The money supply has not decreased due to the cheque drawn on the Bank of Vancouver; the money is simply showing up in the Bank of Manitoba. *(Key Questions 11 and 15)*

TRANSACTION 6: BUYING GOVERNMENT SECURITIES

When a chartered bank buys government bonds from the public, the effect is substantially the same as lending. New money is created.

Assume that the Bank of Vancouver's balance sheet initially stands as it did at the end of Transaction 4. Now suppose that instead of making a $50,000 loan, the bank buys $50,000 of government securities from a securities dealer. The bank receives the interest-bearing bonds, which appear on its balance statement as the asset "Securities" and give the security dealer an increase in its deposit account. The bank's balance sheet appears as follows:

Buying Government Securities

Balance Sheet 6: Bank of Vancouver			
Assets		**Liabilities and net worth**	
Reserves	$ 60,000	Demand deposits	$100,000
Securities	50,000	Capital stock	250,000
Property	240,000		

Demand deposits—that is, the supply of money—have increased by $50,000, as in Transaction 5a. *Bond purchases from the public by chartered banks increase the supply of money in the same way as does lending to the public.*

Finally, the selling of government bonds to the public (including securities dealers) by a chartered bank—like the repayment of a loan—reduces the supply of money. The securities buyer pays by cheque and both "Securities" and "Demand deposits" (the latter being money) decline by the amount of the sale.

Profits, Liquidity, and the Overnight Lending Rate

The asset items on a chartered bank's balance sheet reflect the banker's pursuit of two conflicting goals:

1. **Profit** One goal is profit. Chartered banks, like any other business, seek profits, which is why the bank makes loans and buys securities—the two major earning assets of chartered banks.

2. **Liquidity** The other goal is safety. For a bank, safety lies in liquidity, specifically such liquid assets as cash and excess reserves. A bank must be on guard for depositors who want to transform their demand deposits into cash. Bankers thus seek a balance between prudence and profit. The compromise is between assets that earn high returns and highly liquid assets.

An interesting way in which banks can partly reconcile the goals of profit and liquidity is to lend temporary excess reserves to other chartered banks. Normal day-to-day flows of funds to banks rarely leave all banks with their exact levels of desired reserves. Banks therefore lend these excess reserves to other banks on an overnight basis as a way to earn additional interest without sacrificing long-term liquidity. Banks that borrow in this market do so because they are temporarily short of the level of reserves they wish to hold. The interest rate paid on these overnight loans is called the **overnight lending rate.**

overnight lending rate
The interest rate banks charge to borrow and lend one-day funds to each other.

QUICK REVIEW

▸ Banks create money when they make loans; money vanishes when bank loans are repaid.

▸ New money is created when banks buy government bonds from the public; money disappears when banks sell government bonds to the public.

▸ Banks balance profitability and safety in determining their mix of earning assets and highly liquid assets.

12.6 | The Banking System: Multiple-Deposit Expansion

Thus far we have seen that a single bank in a banking system can lend one dollar for each dollar of its excess reserves. The situation is different for all chartered banks as a group. We will find that the chartered banking system can lend—that is, can create money—by a multiple of its excess reserves. This multiple lending is accomplished even though each bank in the system can lend only "dollar for dollar" with its excess reserves.

How do these seemingly paradoxical results come about? To answer this question succinctly, we will make three simplifying assumptions:

- The desired reserve ratio for all chartered banks is 20 percent.
- Initially all banks are meeting this 20 percent desired reserve ratio. No excess reserves exist; or, in the parlance of banking, they are "loaned up" (or "loaned out").
- If any bank can increase its loans as a result of acquiring excess reserves, an amount equal to those excess reserves will be lent to one borrower, who will write a cheque for the entire amount of the loan and give it to someone else, who will deposit the cheque in another bank. This third assumption means that the worst thing possible happens to every lending bank—a cheque for the entire amount of the loan is drawn and cleared against it in favour of another bank.

The Banking System's Lending Potential

Suppose a junkyard owner in Moncton finds a $100 bill while dismantling a car that has been on the lot for years. He deposits the $100 in bank A, which adds the $100 to its reserves. We will record only changes in the balance sheets of the various chartered banks. The deposit changes bank A's balance sheet as shown by entries (a_1):

Multiple-Deposit Expansion Process

Balance Sheet: Chartered Bank A			
Assets		**Liabilities and net worth**	
Reserves	$+100 (a_1)	Demand deposits	$+100 (a_1)
	− 80 (a_3)		+ 80 (a_2)
Loans	+ 80 (a_2)		− 80 (a_3)

Recall from Transaction 3 that this $100 deposit of currency does not alter the money supply. Although $100 of demand-deposit money comes into being, it is offset by the $100 of currency no longer in the hands of the public (the junkyard owner). What has happened is that bank A has acquired excess reserves of $80. Of the newly acquired $100 in reserves, 20 percent, or $20, is earmarked for the desired reserves on the new $100 deposit, and the remaining $80 becomes excess reserves. Since a single chartered bank can lend only an amount equal to its excess reserves, we conclude that bank A can lend a maximum of $80. When a loan for this amount is made, bank A's loans increase by $80 and the borrower gets an $80 demand deposit. We add these figures—entries (a_2)—to bank A's balance sheet.

But now we make our third assumption: The borrower draws a cheque ($80) for the entire amount of the loan, and gives it to someone who deposits it in bank B, a different bank. As we saw in Transaction 6, bank A loses both reserves and deposits equal to the amount of the loan, as indicated in entries (a_3). The net result of these transactions is that bank A's reserves now stand at +$20 (= $100 − $80), loans at +$80, and demand deposits at +$100 (= $100 + $80 − $80). When the dust has settled, bank A is just meeting the 20 percent reserve ratio.

Recalling our previous discussion, we know that bank B acquires both the reserves and the deposits that bank A has lost. Bank B's balance sheet is changed as in entries (b_1):

Multiple-Deposit Expansion Process

Balance Sheet: Chartered Bank B

Assets		Liabilities and net worth	
Reserves	$+80 ($b_1$)	Demand deposits	$+80 ($b_1$)
	−64 (b_3)		+64 (b_2)
Loans	+64 (b_2)		−64 (b_3)

When the borrower's cheque is drawn and cleared, bank A loses $80 in reserves and deposits and bank B gains $80 in reserves and deposits. But 20 percent, or $16, of bank B's new reserves are kept against the new $80 in demand deposits. This means that bank B has $64 (= $80 − $16) in excess reserves. It can therefore lend $64 [entries ($b_2$)]. When the new borrower draws a cheque for the entire amount and deposits it in bank C, the reserves and deposits of bank B both fall by $64 [entries ($b_3$)]. As a result of these transactions, bank B's reserves now stand at +$16 (= $80 − $64), loans at +$64, and demand deposits at +$80 (= $80 + $64 − $64). After all this, bank B is just meeting the 20 percent desired reserve ratio.

We are off and running again. Bank C acquires the $64 in reserves and deposits lost by bank B. Its balance sheet changes as in entries (c_1):

Multiple-Deposit Expansion Process

Balance Sheet: Chartered Bank C

Assets		Liabilities and net worth	
Reserves	$+64.00 ($c_1$)	Demand deposits	$+64.00 ($c_1$)
	−51.20 (c_3)		+51.20 (c_2)
Loans	+51.20 (c_2)		−51.20 (c_3)

Exactly 20 percent, or $12.80, of these new reserves will be kept as reserves, the remaining $51.20 are excess reserves. Hence, bank C can safely lend a maximum of $51.20. Suppose it does [entries (c_2)]. And suppose the borrower draws a cheque for the entire amount and gives it to someone who deposits it in another bank [entries (c_3)].

We could go ahead with this procedure by bringing banks D, E, F, G, … J and so on into the picture. In fact, the process will go on almost indefinitely, just as long as banks farther down the line receive at least one penny in new reserves that they can use to back another round of lending and money creation. But we suggest that you work through the computations for banks D, E, F, and G to be sure you understand the procedure.

The entire analysis is summarized in Table 12-3. Data for banks D through J are supplied on their own rows so that you may check your computations. The last row of the table consolidates into one row everything that happens for all banks down the line after bank J. Our conclusion is startling: On the basis of only $80 in excess reserves (acquired by the banking system when someone deposited $100 of currency in bank A), the entire chartered banking system is able to lend $400, the sum of the amounts in column 4. The banking system can lend excess reserves by a multiple of 5 (= $400/$80) when the reserve ratio is 20 percent. Yet each single bank in the banking system is lending only an amount equal to its own excess reserves. How do we explain this? How can the

TABLE 12·3	Expansion of the Money Supply by the Chartered Banking System			
Bank	**(1)** **Acquired reserves** **and deposits**	**(2)** **Desired reserves** **(reserve ratio = 0.2)**	**(3)** **Excess reserves,** **(1) – (2)**	**(4)** **Amount bank can** **lend; new money** **created = (3)**
Bank A	$100.00 (a_1)	$20.00	***$80.00***	$ 80.00 (a_2)
Bank B	80.00 (a_3, b_1)	16.00	64.00	64.00 (b_2)
Bank C	64.00 (b_3, c_1)	12.80	51.20	51.20 (c_2)
Bank D	51.20	10.24	40.96	40.96
Bank E	40.96	8.19	32.77	32.77
Bank F	32.77	6.55	26.21	26.21
Bank G	26.22	5.24	20.97	20.97
Bank H	20.98	4.20	16.78	16.78
Bank I	16.78	3.36	13.42	13.42
Bank J	13.42	2.68	10.74	10.74
Other banks	53.68	10.73	42.95	42.95
Total amount of money created (sum of the amounts in column 4)				***$400.00***

banking system as a whole lend by a multiple of its excess reserves, when each individual bank can lend only "dollar for dollar" with its excess reserves?

The answer is that reserves lost by a single bank are not lost to the banking system as a whole. The reserves lost by bank A are acquired by bank B. Those lost by B are gained by C; C loses to D, D to E, E to F, and so forth. Although reserves can be, and are, lost by individual banks in the banking system, there is no loss of reserves for the banking system as a whole.

An individual bank can safely lend only an amount equal to its excess reserves, *but the chartered banking system can lend by a multiple of its collective excess reserves.* This contrast, incidentally, is an illustration of why it is imperative that we keep the fallacy of composition (The Last Word, Chapter 1) firmly in mind. Chartered banks as a group can create money by lending in a manner much different from that of the individual banks in that group.

12.7 | The Monetary Multiplier

monetary multiplier
The multiple of excess reserves by which the banking system can expand demand deposits and thus the money supply by making new loans.

The banking system magnifies any original excess reserves into a larger amount of newly created demand-deposit money. The *demand-deposit multiplier,* or **monetary multiplier,** exists because the reserves and deposits lost by one bank are received by another bank. It magnifies excess reserves into a larger creation of demand-deposit money. The monetary multiplier m is the reciprocal of the desired reserve ratio R (the leakage into cash reserves that occurs at each step in the lending process). In short,

Monetary multiplier = 1/desired reserve ratio

or, in symbols,

$$m = 1/R$$

In this formula, m represents the maximum amount of new demand deposits that can be created by a single dollar of excess reserves, given the value of R. By multiplying the excess reserves E by m, we can find the maximum amount of new demand-deposit money, D, that can be created by the banking system. That is,

MATH 12.1
The Monetary
Multiplier

Maximum demand-deposit creation = excess reserves × monetary multiplier

or, more simply,

$$D = E \times m$$

In our example in Table 12-3, R is 0.20 so m is 5 (= 1/0.20). Then

$$D = \$80 \times 5 = \$400$$

**WORKED
PROBLEM 12.2**
Money Creation

Figure 12-2 depicts the final outcome of our example of a multiple-deposit expansion of the money supply. The initial deposit of $100 of currency into the bank (lower right-hand box) creates new reserves of an equal amount (upper box). With a 20 percent desired reserve ratio, however, only $20 of currency reserves is needed to "back up" this $100 chequable (demand) deposit. The excess reserves of $80 permit the creation of $400 of new demand deposits via the making of loans, confirming a monetary multiplier of 5. The $100 of new reserves supports a total supply of money of $500, consisting of the $100 initial demand deposit plus $400 of demand deposits created through lending.

Higher desired reserve ratios mean lower monetary multipliers and therefore less creation of new demand-deposit money via loans; smaller desired reserve ratios mean higher monetary multipliers and thus more creation of new demand-deposit money via loans. With a high desired reserve ratio, say 50 percent, the monetary multiplier would be 2 (= 1/0.5), and in our example the banking system could create only $100 (= $50 of excess reserves × 2) of new demand deposits. With a low desired reserve ratio, say 5 percent, the monetary multiplier would be 20 (= 1/0.05), and the banking system could create $1900 (= $95 of excess reserves × 20) of new demand deposits.

FIGURE 12-2   **The Outcome of the Money Expansion Process, New Reserves**

A deposit of $100 of currency into a chequing account creates an initial demand deposit of $100. If the desired reserve ratio is 20 percent, only $20 of reserves is required to support the $100 demand deposit. The $80 of excess reserves allows the banking system to create $400 of demand deposits through making loans. The $100 of reserves supports a total of $500 of money ($100 + $400).

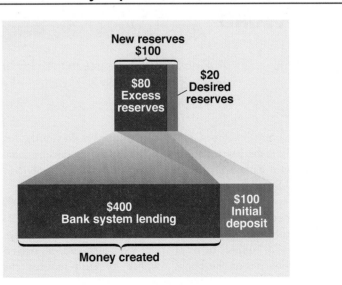

Experiment with the following two brainteasers to test your understanding of multiple credit expansion by the banking system:

- Re-work the analysis in Table 12-3 (at least three or four steps of it) assuming the desired reserve ratio is 10 percent. What is the maximum amount of money the banking system can create upon acquiring $100 in new reserves and deposits? (The answer is not $800!)

- Suppose the banking system is loaned up and has a 20 percent desired reserve ratio. Explain how it might have to reduce its outstanding loans by $400 when a $100 cash withdrawal from a demand-deposit account forces one bank to draw down its reserves by $100. *(Key Question 20)*

Reversibility: The Multiple Destruction of Money

The process we have described is reversible. Just as demand deposit money is created when banks make loans, demand deposit money is destroyed when loans are paid off. Loan repayment, in effect, sets off a process of multiple destruction of money the opposite of the multiple creation process. Because loans are both made and paid off in any period, the direction of the loans, demand deposits, and money supply in a given period will depend on the net effect of the two processes. If the dollar amount of loans made in some period exceeds the dollar amount of loans paid off, demand deposits will expand and the money supply will increase. But if the dollar amount of loans is less than the dollar amount of loans paid off, demand deposits will contract and the money supply will decline.

QUICK REVIEW

▶ A single bank in a multibank system can safely lend (create money) by an amount equal to its excess reserves; the banking system can lend (create money) by a multiple of its excess reserves.

▶ The monetary multiplier is the reciprocal of the desired reserve ratio; it is the multiple by which the banking system can expand the money supply for each dollar of excess reserves.

▶ The monetary multiplier works in both directions; it applies to money destruction from the payback of loans as well as the money creation from the making of loans.

The LAST WORD   The U.S. Bank Panics of 1930 to 1933

A series of bank panics in the U.S. in the early 1930s resulted in a multiple contraction of the money supply.

In the early months of the Great Depression—before there was deposit insurance—several financially weak banks in the U.S. went out of business. As word spread that customers of those banks had lost their deposits, a general concern arose that something similar could happen at other banks. The sudden run on the banks caused many previously financially sound banks to declare bankruptcy. More than 9000 American banks failed within three years.

The massive conversion of chequable deposits to currency during 1930–33 reduced the nation's money supply. This might seem strange, since a cheque written for cash reduces chequable-deposit money and increases currency in the hands of the public by the same amount. So how does the money supply decline? Our discussion of the money-creation process provides the answer, but now the story becomes one of money destruction.

Suppose that people collectively cash out $10 billion from their chequing accounts. As an immediate result, chequable deposit money declines by $10 billion, while currency held by the public increases by $10 billion. But here is the catch: Assuming a desired reserve ratio of 20 percent, the $10 billion of currency in the banks had been supporting $50 billion of deposit money, the $10 billion of deposits plus $40 billion created through loans. The $10 billion withdrawal of currency forces banks to reduce loans (and thus chequable-deposit money) by $40 billion to continue to meet their desired reserves. In short, a $40 billion destruction of deposit money occurs. This is the scenario that occurred in the early years of the 1930s in the U.S.

Accompanying this multiple contraction of chequable deposits was the banks' "scramble for liquidity" to try to meet further withdrawals of currency. To obtain more currency, they sold many of their holdings of government securities to the public. You know from this chapter that a bank's sale of government securities to the public, like a reduction in loans, reduces the money supply. People write cheques for the securities, reducing their chequable deposits, and the bank uses the currency it obtains to meet the ongoing bank run. In short, the loss of reserves from the banking system, in conjunction with the scramble for security, reduced the amount of chequable deposit money by far more than the increase in currency in the hands of the public. Thus, the money supply collapsed.

In 1933, President Franklin Roosevelt ended the bank panic by declaring a "national bank holiday." This closed all national banks for one week so that government inspectors could have time to go over each bank's accounting records. Only healthy banks with plenty of reserves were allowed to re-open. This meant that when the holiday was over, people could trust in any bank that had been allowed to reopen. This policy, along with the initiation of a federal deposit insurance program, reassured depositors and ended the bank panics. But before these policies could begin to turn things around, the money supply in the U.S. had plummeted by 25 to 33 percent (depending on how narrowly or broadly the money supply is defined). This was the largest drop in the money supply in U.S. history. The decline contributed substantially to the nation's deepest and longest depression. Simply put, less money meant less spending on goods and services as well as fewer loans for businesses. Both effects exacerbated the Great Depression. Today, a multiple contraction of the money supply of the 1930–33 magnitude is unthinkable. Insurance provided by the Federal Deposit Insurance Corporation (FDIC) has kept individual bank failures from becoming general panics. Also, while the American central bank ("the Fed") stood idly by during the bank panics of 1930–33, today it would take immediate and dramatic action to maintain the bank-

ing system's reserves and the nation's money supply.

Unlike the 1930s, the financial crisis of 2008–09 did not include major runs on American commercial bank deposits. To help prevent runs, in October 2008 the FDIC increased its insurance coverage for commercial bank accounts from $100,000 per account to $250,000 per account. At the same time, the Fed took lender-of-last-resort actions to make sure banks had adequate reserves. In fact, bank reserves were increased so much that in February 2009 the U.S. fractional reserve system had more reserves than chequable deposits! There was no multiple destruction of the nation's money supply as had occurred in the 1930s. The problem was simply unwillingness by banks to increase lending in an economic climate in which nearly all loans were perceived as being quite risky.

No bank failures occurred in Canada during the Great Depression, thanks to a stable banking sector that was well capitalized and took few risks. That same stability and conservative lending policies helped the Canadian chartered banks ride out the global financial crisis in 2008–09 relatively unscathed. The conservative lending policies of the Canadian chartered banks were held up as a model for all other banking systems to emulate during the global financial crisis, when which many major banks around the globe—in the U.S. and the U.K. in particular—found themselves needing to raise capital to stay afloat.

Question

Explain how the U.S. bank panics of 1930–33 produced a decline in the nation's money supply. Why are such panics highly unlikely today?

CHAPTER SUMMARY

12.1 ▶ THE DEFINITION AND FUNCTIONS OF MONEY

- Anything that is accepted as (a) a medium of exchange, (b) a unit of monetary account, and (c) a store of value can be used as money.

12.2 ▶ THE COMPONENTS OF THE MONEY SUPPLY

- Money is generally defined as demand deposits plus currency (coins and paper money) in circulation (M1). Demand deposits, the largest component of the money supply, are money because they can be spent by writing cheques against them. Savings, term, and notice deposits—some chequable and some not—are also money and are added to more broadly defined monetary aggregates (M2, M2+, and M2++). In our analysis we concentrate on M1 since its components are immediately spendable.

12.3 ▶ WHAT BACKS THE MONEY SUPPLY?

- Money is the debts of government and depository institutions (chartered banks, trust companies, and credit unions) and has value because of goods, services, and resources it will command in the market. Maintaining the purchasing power of money depends largely on the government's effectiveness in managing the money supply.

12.4 ▶ THE CANADIAN FINANCIAL SYSTEM

- The Canadian banking system is composed of (a) the Bank of Canada and (b) 20 Canadian-owned and 27 foreign-owned chartered banks. The chartered banks of the economy accept money deposits and make loans. The Canadian banking system is concentrated compared to other nations, particularly the United States.

12.5 ▶ CHARTERED BANKS AND THE CREATION OF MONEY

- Modern banking systems are fractional reserve systems: only a fraction of deposits are backed by currency.

- The operation of a chartered bank can be understood through its balance sheet, where assets equal liabilities plus net worth.

- Chartered banks keep reserves as vault cash and a small amount in the Bank of Canada for cheque-clearing purposes. This reserve is equal to a desired percentage of the chartered bank's deposit liabilities. Excess reserves are equal to actual reserves minus desired reserves.

- Banks lose both reserves and deposits when cheques are drawn against them.

- Chartered banks create money—create demand deposits, or deposit money—when they make loans. The creation of demand deposits by bank lending is the most important source of money in the Canadian economy. Money is destroyed when bank loans are repaid.

- The ability of a single chartered bank to create money by lending depends on the size of its excess reserves. Generally speaking, a chartered bank lends only an amount equal to the amount of its excess reserves.

- Rather than making loans, chartered banks may decide to use excess reserves to buy bonds from the public. In doing so, banks merely credit the demand-deposit accounts of the bond sellers, thus creating demand-deposit money. Money vanishes when banks sell bonds to the public because bond buyers must draw down their demand-deposit balances to pay for the bonds.

- Banks earn interest by making loans and by purchasing bonds; they maintain liquidity by holding cash and excess reserves. Banks with temporary excess reserves often lend them overnight to banks that are short of desired cash reserves. The interest rate paid on loans in this market is called the overnight lending rate.

12.6 ▶ THE BANKING SYSTEM: MULTIPLE-DEPOSIT EXPANSION

- The chartered banking system as a whole can lend by a multiple of its excess reserves because the banking system cannot lose reserves, although individual banks can lose reserves to other banks in the system.

12.7 ▶ THE MONETARY MULTIPLIER

- The multiple by which the banking system could lend on the basis of each dollar of excess reserves is the reciprocal of the desired reserve ratio. This multiple credit expansion process is reversible.

TERMS AND CONCEPTS

money, p. 281
medium of exchange, p. 281
barter, p. 281
unit of account, p. 281
store of value, p. 281
liquidity, p. 281
M1, p. 282
demand deposit, p. 282
token money, p. 282

Bank of Canada notes, p. 282
near-monies, p. 284
M2, p. 284
M2+, p. 284
M2++, p. 285
legal tender, p. 287
chartered bank, p. 288
fractional reserve banking system, p. 289
prime rate, p. 289

financial intermediary, p. 289
balance sheet, p. 292
vault cash, p. 292
desired reserves, p. 294
desired reserve ratio, p. 294
excess reserves, p. 294
actual reserves, p. 294
overnight lending rate, p. 297
monetary multiplier, p. 300

STUDY QUESTIONS

LO 12.1 1. What are the three functions of money? Describe how rapid inflation can undermine money's ability to perform each of its three functions.

LO 12.1 2. Explain and evaluate the following statements:

 a. The invention of money is one of the great achievements of humankind, for without it the enrichment that comes from broadening trade would have been impossible.

 b. Money is whatever society says it is.

 c. In most economies of the world, the debts of government and chartered banks are used as money.

 d. People often say they would like to have more money, but what they usually mean is that they would like to have more goods and services.

 e. When the prices of everything go up, it is not because everything is worth more but because the currency is worth less.

 f. Any central bank can create money; the trick is to create enough of it, but not too much of it.

LO 12.2 3. **KEY QUESTION** What are the components of the M1 money supply? What is the largest component? Which of the components of M1 is legal tender? Why is the face value of a coin greater than its intrinsic value? Distinguish between M2, M2+, and M2++. What are near-monies?

LO 12.3 4. What backs the money supply in Canada? What determines the value (domestic purchasing power) of money? How does the value of money relate to the price level? Who is responsible for maintaining the value of money?

LO 12.3 5. **KEY QUESTION** Suppose the price level and the value of the dollar in year 1 are 1.0 and $1.00, respectively. If the price level rises to 1.25 in year 2, what is the new value of the dollar? If instead the price level had fallen to 0.50, what would have been the value of the dollar? What generalization can you draw from your answers?

6. Complete the following table showing the relationship **LO 2.3** between a percentage change in the price level and the percentage change in the value of money. Calculate the percentage change in the value of money to one decimal place.

Change in price level	Change in value of money
a. rise by:	
8%	_____._____ %
16%	_____._____ %
24%	_____._____ %
b. fall by:	
8%	_____._____ %
16%	_____._____ %
24%	_____._____ %

7. What are the two basic functions of our chartered banks? **LO 2.4** How do chartered banks differ from other financial intermediaries?

8. Why must a balance sheet always balance? What are the **LO 12.4** major assets and claims on a chartered bank's balance sheet?

9. **KEY QUESTION** Why do chartered banks hold reserves? **LO 12.5** Explain why reserves are an asset to chartered banks but a liability to the Bank of Canada. What are excess reserves? How do you calculate the amount of excess reserves held by a bank? What is the significance of excess reserves?

10. "Whenever currency is deposited in a chartered bank, cash **LO 12.5** goes out of circulation and, as a result, the supply of money is reduced." Do you agree? Explain why or why not.

LO ▶ 12.5 11. **KEY QUESTION** "When a chartered bank makes loans, it creates money; when loans are repaid, money is destroyed." Explain.

LO ▶ 12.6 12. Explain why a single chartered bank could lend an amount equal only to its excess reserves, but the chartered banking system could lend by a multiple of its excess reserves. What is the monetary multiplier and how does it relate to the desired reserve ratio?

LO ▶ 12.6 13. Assume that Jones deposits $500 in currency in the Bank of Vancouver. A half-hour later, Smith obtains a loan for $750 at this bank. By how much and in what direction has the money supply changed? Explain.

LO ▶ 12.6 14. Suppose the Bank of Newfoundland has excess reserves of $8000 and outstanding deposits of $150,000. If the desired reserve ratio is 10 percent, what is the size of the bank's actual reserves?

LO ▶ 12.6 15. **KEY QUESTION** Suppose Yukon Bank has the following simplified balance sheet and that the desired reserve ratio is 20 percent.

Assets

		(1)	(2)
Reserves	$22,000	___	___
Securities	38,000	___	___
Loans	40,000	___	___

Liabilities and net worth

		(1)	(2)
Deposits	$100,000	___	___

a. What is the maximum amount of new loans this bank can make? Show in column 1 how the bank's balance sheet will appear after the bank has loaned this additional amount.

b. By how much has the supply of money changed? Explain.

c. How will the bank's balance sheet appear after cheques drawn for the entire amount of the new loans have been cleared against this bank? Show this new balance sheet in column 2.

d. Answer questions a, b, and c on the assumption that the desired reserve ratio is 15 percent.

LO ▶ 12.6 16. The Bank of Manitoba has reserves of $20,000 and deposits of $100,000. The desired reserve ratio is 20 percent. Households deposit $5,000 in currency in the bank, which is added to reserves. How much in excess reserves does the bank now have?

17. Suppose again that the Bank of Manitoba has reserves of **LO ▶ 12** $20,000 and deposits of $100,000. The desired reserve ratio is 20 percent. The bank now sells $5000 in securities to the Bank of Canada, receiving a $5000 increase in its deposit there in return. How much in excess reserves does the bank now have? Why does your answer differ (yes, it does!) from the answer to question 16?

18. Suppose a chartered bank discovers its reserves will tem- **LO ▶ 12** porarily fall slightly short of those it desires to hold. How might it remedy this situation? Now, assume the bank finds that its reserves will be substantially and permanently deficient. What remedy is available to this bank? (*Hint:* Recall your answer to question 11.)

19. Suppose Bob withdraws $100 of cash from his chequing **LO ▶ 12** account at Calgary Chartered Bank and uses it to buy a camera from Joe, who deposits the $100 in his chequing account in Annapolis Valley Chartered Bank. Assuming a desired reserve ratio of 10 percent and no initial excess reserves, determine the extent to which (a) Calgary Chartered Bank must reduce its loans and demand deposits because of the cash withdrawal, (b) Annapolis Valley Chartered Bank can safely increase its loans and demand deposits because of the cash deposit, and (c) the entire banking system, including Annapolis Valley, can increase loans and demand deposits because of the cash deposit. Have the cash withdrawal and deposit changed the total money supply?

20. **KEY QUESTION** Suppose the simplified consolidated **LO ▶ 12** balance sheet shown below is for the entire chartered banking system. All figures are in billions. The desired reserve ratio is 25 percent.

Assets

		(1)	(2)
Reserves	$ 52	___	___
Securities	48	___	___
Loans	100	___	___

Liabilities and net worth

		(1)	(2)
Deposits	$200	___	___

a. How much in excess reserves does the chartered banking system have? What is the maximum amount the banking system might lend? Show in column 1 how the consolidated balance sheet would look after this amount has been lent. What is the monetary multiplier?

b. Answer the questions in (a) assuming that the desired reserve ratio is 20 percent. Explain the resulting difference in the lending ability of the chartered banking system.

12.7 21. Answer the next questions based on the following consolidated balance sheet for the entire chartered banking system. Assume the desired reserve ratio is 25 percent. All figures are in billions of dollars.

Assets		Liabilities + Net Worth	
Reserves	$100	Demand deposits	$300
Securities	200	Stock shares	700
Loans	100		
Property	600		

a. What is the amount of excess reserves in the entire banking system?

b. What is the maximum amount that the money supply can be expanded?

c. If the desired reserve ratio fell to 10 percent, what is now the maximum amount that the money supply can be expanded?

INTERNET APPLICATION QUESTIONS @

1. **Monetary Aggregates.** Visit the Bank of Canada through the McConnell-Brue-Flynn-Barbiero Web site (Chapter 12) and click on "Rates and Statistics," then click on "Weekly Financial Statistics." Find the seasonally adjusted data for M1, M2, M2+, and M2++ for the most recent month. Have they increased or decreased from the previous year?

2. **How to Spot a Counterfeit Bank Note.** Counterfeit bank notes have always been a concern for the Bank of Canada. Visit the Bank of Canada through the McConnell-Brue-Flynn-Barbiero Web site (Chapter 12) to find out how to detect counterfeit Canadian bank notes.

3. **The Balance Sheet of Canadian Chartered Banks.** Statistics Canada provides the balance sheet of chartered banks. Access its Web site through the McConnell-Brue-Flynn-Barbiero Web site (Chapter 12). What has been the trend in the last five years for bank assets and liabilities?

CHAPTER 13

Interest Rates and Monetary Policy

In the previous two chapters you have become acquainted with the function of money in a market economy and how money is created (and destroyed). But what is the connection between the total money supply and the output performance and price level in an economy?

Recall from Chapter 7 that market economies are subject to fluctuations, often experiencing substantial unemployment and sometimes inflationary pressures. In this chapter you will learn that a change in money supply affects interest rates, which influence the level of investment and real GDP. Thus the Bank of Canada, within limits, can help smooth out the fluctuations in the Canadian economy by influencing interest rates through its control of the money supply. The main goal of the Bank of Canada policies is to achieve and maintain price stability, but it would also like to see the economy achieve full employment. Price stability facilitates the ultimate aim of ensuring a nation is employing all its resources—particularly its labour force—to their fullest extent.

13.1 | The Market for Money and the Determination of Interest Rates

The Bank of Canada's primary influence is on the money supply and interest rates. Interest rates can be thought of in several ways. Most basically, **interest** is the price paid for the use of money. And it is the price that borrowers need to pay lenders for transferring purchasing power to the future. It can be thought of as the amount of money that must be paid for the use of $1 for one year. Although there is a full cluster of Canadian interest rates that vary by purpose, size, risk, maturity, and taxability, we will simply speak of "*the* interest rate" unless stated otherwise.

Let's see how the interest rate is determined. Because it is a "price," we again turn to demand and supply analysis for the answer.

The Demand for Money

Why does the public want to hold some of its wealth as *money*? There are two main reasons: to make purchases with it and to hold it as an asset.

TRANSACTIONS DEMAND, D_t

People hold money because it is convenient for purchasing goods and services. Households usually are paid once a week, every two weeks, or monthly, whereas their expenditures are less predictable and typically more frequent. So households must have enough money on hand to buy groceries and pay mortgage and utility bills. Nor are business revenues and expenditures simultaneous. Businesses need to have money available to pay for labour, materials, power, and other inputs. The demand for money as a medium of exchange is called the **transactions demand for money.**

The level of nominal GDP is the main determinant of the amount of money demanded for transactions. The larger the total money value of all goods and services exchanged in the economy, the larger the amount of money demanded for transactions. The transactions demand for money varies directly with nominal GDP. We specify *nominal* GDP because households and firms will want more money for transactions if prices rise or if real output increases. In both instances there will be a need for a larger dollar volume to accomplish the desired transactions.

In **Figure 13-1a (Key Graph)** we graph the quantity of money demanded for transactions against the interest rate. For simplicity, let's assume that the amount demanded depends exclusively on the level of nominal GDP and is independent of the interest rate. (In reality, higher interest rates are associated with slightly lower volumes of money demanded for transactions.) Our simplifying assumption allows us to graph the transactions demand, D_t, as a vertical line. This demand curve is positioned at $100 billion, on the assumption that each dollar held for transactions purposes is used in transactions on an average of three times per year and that nominal GDP is $300 billion. Thus the public needs $100 billion (= $300 billion/3) to purchase that GDP.

ASSET DEMAND, D_a

The second reason for holding money derives from money's function as a store of value. People may hold their financial assets in many forms, including corporate stocks, corporate or government bonds, or money. To the extent they want to hold money as an asset, there is an **asset demand for money.**

People like to hold some of their financial assets as money (apart from using it to buy goods and services) because money is the most liquid of all financial assets: it is immediately usable for purchasing other assets when opportunities arise. Money is also an attractive asset to hold when the prices of other assets such as bonds are expected to decline. For example, when the price of a bond falls, the bondholder who sells the bond prior to the payback date of the full principal will suffer a loss (called a *capital loss*). That loss will partially or fully offset the interest received on the bond. There is no such risk of capital loss in holding money.

The disadvantage of holding money as an asset is that it earns no or very little interest. Chequable deposits pay either no interest or lower interest rates than bonds. Currency itself earns no interest at all.

Knowing these advantages and disadvantages, the public must decide how much of its financial assets to hold as money, rather than other assets such as bonds. The answer depends primarily on the rate of interest. A household or a business incurs an opportunity cost when it holds money; in both cases, interest income is forgone or sacrificed. If a bond pays 6 percent interest, for example, holding $100 as cash or in a non-interest chequable account costs $6 per year of forgone income.

The amount of money demanded as an asset therefore varies inversely with the rate of interest (which is the opportunity cost of holding money as an asset). When the interest rate rises, being liquid and avoiding capital losses becomes more costly. The public reacts by reducing its holdings of money as an asset. When the interest rate falls, the cost of being liquid and avoiding capital losses also declines. The public therefore increases the amount of financial assets that it wants to hold as money. This inverse relationship just described is shown by D_a in Figure 13-1b.

---

interest
The payment made for the use of money.

transactions demand for money
The amount of money people want to hold for use as a medium of exchange, and which varies directly with the nominal GDP.

asset demand for money
The amount of money people want to hold as a store of value; varies inversely with the rate of interest.

ORIGINS 13.1
Liquidity Preference

KEY GRAPH @

FIGURE 13-1 The Demand for Money, the Supply of Money, and the Equilibrium Interest Rate

The total demand for money D_m is determined by horizontally adding the asset demand for money D_a to the transactions demand D_t. The transactions demand is vertical because it is assumed to depend on nominal GDP rather than on the interest rate. The asset demand varies inversely with the interest rate because of the opportunity cost involved in holding currency and chequable deposits that pay no interest or very low interest. Combining the money supply (stock) S_m with total money demand D_m portrays the money market and determines the equilibrium interest rate i_e.

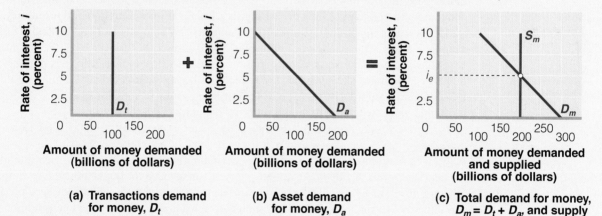

(a) Transactions demand for money, D_t

(b) Asset demand for money, D_a

(c) Total demand for money, $D_m = D_t + D_a$, and supply

Quick Quiz

1. In this graph, at the interest rate i_e:
   a. the amount of money demanded as an asset is $50 billion.
   b. the amount of money demanded for transactions is $200 billion.
   c. bond prices will decline.
   d. $100 billion is demanded for transactions, $100 billion is demanded as an asset, and the money supply is $200 billion.

2. In this graph, at an interest rate of 10 percent:
   a. no money will be demanded as an asset.
   b. total money demanded will be $200 billion.
   c. the Bank of Canada will supply $100 billion of money.
   d. there will be a $100 billion shortage of money.

3. Curve D_a slopes downward because:
   a. lower interest rates increase the opportunity cost of holding money.
   b. lower interest rates reduce the opportunity cost of holding money.
   c. the asset demand for money varies directly (positively) with the interest rate.
   d. the transactions-demand-for-money curve is perfectly vertical.

4. Suppose the supply of money declines to $100 billion. The equilibrium interest rate would:
   a. fall, the amount of money demanded for transactions would rise, and the amount of money demanded as an asset would decline.
   b. rise, and the amounts of money demanded both for transactions and as an asset would fall.
   c. fall, and the amounts of money demanded both for transactions and as an asset would increase.
   d. rise, the amount of money demanded for transactions would be unchanged, and the amount of money demanded as an asset would decline.

Answers: 1.d; 2.a; 3.b; 4.d

TOTAL MONEY DEMAND, D_m

As shown in Figure 13-1c, we find the **total demand for money** D_m by horizontally adding the asset demand to the transactions demand. The resulting downward-sloping line in Figure 13-1c represents the total amount of money the public wants to hold, both for transactions and as an asset, at each possible interest rate.

Recall that the transactions demand for money depends on the nominal GDP. A change in the nominal GDP—working through the transactions demand for money—will shift the total money demand curve. Specifically, an increase in nominal GDP means that the public wants to hold a larger amount of money for transactions, and that extra demand will shift the total money demand curve to the right. In contrast, a decline in the nominal GDP will shift the total money demand curve to the left. As an example, suppose nominal GDP increases from $300 billion to $450 billion and the average dollar held for transactions is still spent three times per year. Then the transactions demand curve will shift from $100 billion (= $300 billion/3) to $150 billion (= $450 billion/3). The total money demand curve will then be $50 billion farther to the right at each possible interest rate.

WORKED PROBLEM 13.1
Demand for Money

The Equilibrium Interest Rate

We combine the demand for money with the supply of money to determine the equilibrium rate of interest. In Figure 13-1c the vertical line, S_m, represents the money supply. It is a vertical line because the monetary authorities and financial institutions provide the economy with some particular stock of money. Here, it is $200 billion.

Just as in a product market or a factor market, the intersection of demand and supply determines the equilibrium price in the market for money. Here, the equilibrium "price" is the interest rate (i_e)—the price that is paid for the use of money over some time period.

Changes in the demand for money, the supply of money, or both can change the equilibrium interest rate. For reasons that will soon become apparent, we are most interested in changes in the supply of money. The important generalization is this: an increase in the supply of money will lower the equilibrium interest rate; a decrease in the supply of money will raise the equilibrium interest rate. *(Key Questions 1 and 2)*

Interest Rates and Bond Prices

Interest rates and bond prices are closely related. When the interest rate increases, bond prices fall; when the interest rate falls, bond prices rise. Why is this so? First understand that bonds are bought and sold in financial markets, and that the price of bonds is determined by bond demand and bond supply. Suppose that a bond with no expiration date (also called a *consol*) pays a fixed $50 annual interest and is selling for its face value of $1000. The interest yield on this bond is 5 percent:

$$\frac{\$50}{\$1000} = 5\% \text{ interest yield}$$

Now suppose the interest rate in the economy rises to 7.5 percent from 5 percent. Newly issued bonds will pay $75 per $1000 lent. Older bonds paying only $50 will not be saleable at their $1000 face value. To compete with the 7.5 percent bond, the price of this bond will need to fall to $667 to remain competitive. The $50 fixed annual interest payment will then yield 7.5 percent to whoever buys the bond:

$$\frac{\$50}{\$667} = 75\%$$

WORKED PROBLEM 13.2
Bond Prices and Interest Rates

Next suppose that the interest rate falls to 2.5 percent from the original 5 percent. Newly issued bonds will pay $25 on $1000 loaned. A bond paying $50 will be highly attractive. Bond buyers will bid up its price to $2000, at which price the yield will equal 2.5 percent.

$$\frac{\$50}{\$2000} = 2.5\%$$

The point is that bond prices fall when the interest rate rises and rise when the interest rate falls. There is an inverse relationship between the interest rate and bond prices. *(Key Question 3)*

QUICK REVIEW

▸ People demand money for transaction and asset purposes.

▸ The total demand for money is the sum of the transactions and asset demands; it is graphed as an inverse relationship (downward-sloping line) between the interest rate and the quantity of money demanded.

▸ The equilibrium interest rate is determined by money demand and supply; it occurs when people are willing to hold the exact amount of money being supplied by the monetary authorities.

▸ Interest rates and bond prices are inversely related.

13.2 | Functions of the Bank of Canada

The functions of the Bank of Canada, a Crown corporation, can be divided into five categories. We discuss the most important function last.

1. ***Acting as the "Bankers' Bank"*** You head for the nearest chartered bank if you want to deposit, withdraw, or borrow money; the chartered banks turn to the Bank of Canada as their "bank." As such, the Bank of Canada is sometimes referred to as "the lender of last resort." There are times when the chartered banks need to borrow from the central bank. Chartered banks also keep minimal reserves with the Bank of Canada to settle bilateral payment balances among themselves.

2. ***Issuing Currency*** The Bank of Canada supplies the economy with paper currency—Bank of Canada notes—and coins. This involves designing notes and coins; printing, stamping, and distributing new notes and coins; and replacing worn currency.

3. ***Acting as Fiscal Agent*** The Bank of Canada acts as the fiscal agent (provider of financial services, including banking) for the federal government. The federal government collects funds through taxation, spends these funds on a variety of goods and services, and sells and redeems bonds. The federal government uses the Bank of Canada's facilities to carry out these activities.

4. ***Supervising the Chartered Banks*** The Department of Finance and the Bank of Canada supervise the operations of chartered banks and other nonbank financial institutions. The Bank of Canada makes periodic assessments of the banks' profitability, to check that the chartered banks perform in accordance with the many regulations to which they are subject and to uncover questionable practices or fraud.

5. ***Regulating the Supply of Money*** Finally, and most important, the Bank of Canada has ultimate responsibility for regulating the supply of money, and this in turn enables it to influence interest rates. The major task of the central bank is to manage the money supply (and thus interest rates) according to the needs of the economy. This involves making available an amount of money consistent with high and steadily rising levels of output and employment and a relatively constant price level. While all of the other functions of the Bank of Canada are routine or of a service nature, managing the money supply requires making basic, but unique, policy decisions.

Bank of Canada Independence

Parliament purposely established the Bank of Canada as an independent agency of government. The objective was to protect the Bank of Canada from political pressures so that it could effectively control the money supply and maintain price stability. Political pressure may at times lead to inflationary fiscal policies, including tax cuts and special-interest spending. If the federal government also controlled the nation's monetary policy, citizens and lobbying groups undoubtedly would pressure elected officials to keep interest rates low even though at times high interest rates are necessary to reduce aggregate demand and thus control inflation. An independent monetary authority (the Bank of Canada) can take actions to increase interest rates when they are needed to reduce inflation. Studies show that countries with independent central banks like the Bank of Canada have lower rates of inflation, on average, than countries that have little or no central bank independence.

Consolidated Balance Sheet of the Bank of Canada

With this basic understanding of interest rates we can turn to monetary policy, which relies on changes in interest rates to be effective. The Bank of Canada balance sheet helps us consider how it conducts monetary policy. Table 13-1 consolidates the assets and liabilities of the Bank of Canada. You will see that some of the Bank of Canada's assets and liabilities differ from those found on the balance sheet of chartered banks.

Assets

The two main assets of the Bank of Canada are securities and (much smaller) advances to the chartered banks.

1. **Securities**　The securities shown in Table 13-1 are Government of Canada bonds (long-term securities) and Treasury bills (short-term securities) issued by the government of Canada to finance past and present budget deficits. These securities are part of the public debt—money borrowed by the federal government. Some were bought directly from the government, but most from the public (through investment dealers) and the chartered banks. Although they are an important source of interest income to the Bank of Canada, they are bought and sold primarily to influence the amount of chartered bank reserves, and therefore the banks' ability to create money by lending.

TABLE 13-1　**Bank of Canada Statement of Assets and Liabilities, December 31, 2008 (in millions)**

Assets		Liabilities	
Advances to chartered banks	$ 1,902	Notes in circulation	$53,731
Treasury bills of Canada	11,717	Government of Canada deposits	23,604
Other securities issued or guaranteed by Canada	29,266	Chartered bank deposits	26
		Other deposits	783
Securities purchased under resale agreement	35,327	Other liabilities	440
Other assets	372	Total	$78,584
Total	$78,584		

Source: Bank of Canada, Bank of Canada Banking and Financial Statistics, May 2009.

2. **Advances to Chartered Banks**   For reasons that will soon become clear, chartered banks occasionally borrow from the Bank of Canada. The promissory notes (IOUs) the chartered banks give to the Bank of Canada in negotiating advances are listed as advances to chartered banks. These IOUs are assets to the Bank of Canada because they are claims against the chartered banks. To the chartered banks, these IOUs are liabilities. Through borrowing, the chartered banks obtain increases in their reserves. Advances to the chartered banks are not large, usually making up less than 2 percent of its assets.

Liabilities

On the liability side of the Bank of Canada's consolidated balance sheet, there are three main items: chartered bank deposits, Government of Canada deposits, and notes in circulation.

1. **Chartered Bank Deposits**   These deposits are assets of the chartered banks but a liability to the Bank of Canada. Up to the early 1990s chartered banks were required by law to keep a specified percentage of their reserves with the Bank of Canada. Since the abolition of required reserves, these deposits have been considerably reduced because their only function is to permit cheque-clearing to settle payment balances among the chartered banks.

2. **Government of Canada Deposits**   The federal government keeps deposits at the Bank of Canada and draws cheques on them to pay its obligations. To the government, all such deposits are assets, while to the banks, including the central bank, they are liabilities.

3. **Notes in Circulation**   The supply of paper money in Canada consists of bank notes issued by the Bank of Canada. When this paper money is circulating outside the Bank of Canada, it is treated as claims against the assets of the Bank of Canada and is thus a liability.

13.3 | Goals and Tools of Monetary Policy

With this look at the Bank of Canada's consolidated balance sheet, we can now explore how the Bank of Canada can influence the money-creating abilities of the commercial banking system. The Bank of Canada is responsible for supervising and controlling the operation of the Canadian financial system. (For the names of central banks in various nations, see Global Perspective 13.1.)

monetary policy
A central bank's changing of the money supply to influence interest rates and assist the economy in achieving a full-employment, non-inflationary level of total output.

The objective of the Bank of Canada's **monetary policy** is to keep inflation low, stable, and predictable so as to help to moderate the business cycle and help the economy attain full employment and sustained economic growth. At the present time the Bank of Canada has an inflation target range of 1 to 3 percent annually. Monetary policy consists of altering the economy's money supply to influence interest rates, which indirectly affect the inflation rate, employment, and the level of economic activity in the Canadian economy. In a recession, or the anticipation of a slowdown, the Bank of Canada would increase the money supply, which decreases interest rates, to stimulate spending. If the Canadian economy were expanding too quickly and accompanied by inflation above 3 percent, the Bank of Canada would restrict the money supply to raise interest rates, which would help slow down the economy.

The Bank of Canada alters the amount of the nation's money supply by manipulating the amount of excess reserves held by chartered banks. Excess reserves, you will recall, are critical to the money-creating ability of the banking system. Once we see how the Bank of Canada controls excess reserves and the money supply, we will explain how changes in the stock of money affect interest rates, aggregate demand, and the economy.

Tools of Monetary Policy

The Bank of Canada implements monetary policy through its influence on short-term interest rates. We will see later in this chapter that monetary policy also affects the value of the Canadian

13.1 | GLOBAL PERSPECTIVE

Central banks, selected nations

The monetary policies of the central banks in the world's nations are often in the international news. Here are some of their official names, along with a few of their popular nicknames.

Australia: Reserve Bank of Australia ("RBA")
Canada: Bank of Canada
Euro Zone: European Central Bank ("ECB")
Japan: The Bank of Japan ("BOJ")
Mexico: Banco de Mexico ("Mex Bank")
Russia: Central Bank of Russia
Sweden: Sveriges Riksbank
United Kingdom: Bank of England
United States: Federal Reserve System (the "Fed") (12 regional Federal Reserve Banks)

ORIGINS 13.2
Tools of Monetary Policy

dollar on foreign exchange markets. The Bank of Canada keeps a watchful eye on the Canadian-dollar exchange rate, the output performance of the Canadian economy, and the behaviour of the Consumer Price Index (CPI), and implements monetary policy accordingly. Monetary policy is implemented primarily by influencing chartered bank reserves.

The Bank of Canada has one main instrument and one of lesser importance to influence and change chartered bank reserves: open-market operations and the bank rate.

Open-Market Operations

Bond markets are "open" to all buyers and sellers of corporate and government bonds (securities). The Bank of Canada is the largest single holder of Canadian government securities. The federal government, not the Bank of Canada, issues these Treasury bills and long-term bonds to finance past budget deficits. Over the decades, the Bank of Canada has purchased these securities from major financial institutions that buy and sell government and corporate securities for themselves or their customers.

open-market operations
The buying and selling of Canadian government bonds by the Bank of Canada to carry out monetary policy.

The Bank of Canada's **open-market operations** consist of the buying of government bonds from, or the selling of government bonds to, chartered banks and the general public. (The Bank of Canada actually buys and sells the government bonds to chartered banks and the public through a few large financial firms called "primary dealers.") Open-market operations are the Bank of Canada's most important instrument for influencing the money supply.

BUYING SECURITIES

Suppose the Bank of Canada decides to buy government bonds. It can purchase these bonds from chartered banks or the general public. In both cases, reserves of the chartered banks will increase.

From Chartered Banks   When the Bank of Canada buys government bonds from chartered banks,

(a)   The chartered banks give up a part of their holdings of securities (the government bonds) to the Bank of Canada.

(b)   The Bank of Canada, in paying for these securities, places newly created reserves in the accounts of the chartered banks at the Bank of Canada. (These reserves are created "out of thin air," so to speak!) The reserves of the chartered banks go up by the amount of the purchase of the securities.

We show these outcomes as (*a*) and (*b*) on the following consolidated balance sheet of the chartered banks and the Bank of Canada.

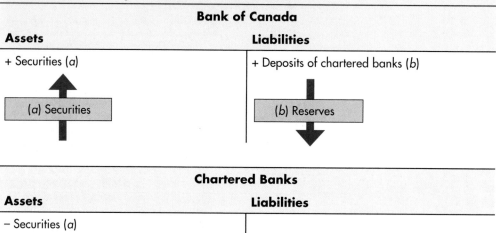

Bank of Canada Buys Bonds from Chartered Banks

Bank of Canada	
Assets	**Liabilities**
+ Securities (*a*)	+ Deposits of chartered banks (*b*)
(*a*) Securities	(*b*) Reserves

Chartered Banks	
Assets	**Liabilities**
− Securities (*a*)	
+ Reserves (*b*)	

The upward arrow shows that securities have moved from the chartered banks to the Bank of Canada. Therefore, we write "−Securities" (minus securities) in the asset column of the balance sheet of the chartered banks. For the same reason, we write "+Securities" in the asset column of the balance sheet of the Bank of Canada.

The downward arrow indicates that the Bank of Canada has provided reserves to the chartered banks. Therefore we write "+Reserves" in the asset column of the balance sheet of the chartered banks. The plus sign in the liability column of the balance sheet of the Bank of Canada indicates that chartered bank deposits have increased; they are a liability to the Bank of Canada because the reserves are owned by the chartered banks.

What is most important about this transaction is that when the Bank of Canada purchases securities from chartered banks, it increases the reserves in the banking system, which then increases the lending ability of the chartered banks.

From the Public   The effect on chartered bank reserves is much the same when the Bank of Canada purchases securities from the public (through investment dealers). Suppose Mariposa Investments Limited (a large Toronto dealer representing the public) has Government of Canada bonds that it sells in the open market to the Bank of Canada. The transaction has several elements:

(a)   Mariposa Investments gives up securities to the Bank of Canada and gets in payment a cheque drawn by the Bank of Canada on itself.

(b)   Mariposa Investments promptly deposits this cheque in its account with the Bank of York.

(c)   The Bank of York collects from the Bank of Canada and thus increases its reserves.

To keep things simple, we will dispense with showing the balance sheet changes resulting from the Bank of Canada's sale or purchase of bonds from the public. But two aspects of this transaction are particularly important. First, as with Bank of Canada purchases of securities directly from chartered banks, the purchase of securities increases the reserves and lending ability of the chartered banking system. Second, the supply of money is directly increased by the central bank's purchase of government bonds (aside from any expansion of the money supply that may occur from the increase in chartered bank reserves). This direct increase in the money supply has taken the form of an increased amount of chequing account money in the economy as a result of Mariposa's deposit.

There is a slight difference between the Bank of Canada's purchases of securities from the chartered banks and from the public. If we assume all chartered banks are "loaned up" initially, the Bank of Canada bond purchases *from chartered banks* increase actual reserves and excess reserves of chartered banks by the entire amount of the bond purchases. As shown in the left panel of Figure 13-2, a $1000 bond purchase from a chartered bank would increase both the actual and excess reserves of the chartered bank by $1000.

In contrast, Bank of Canada purchases of bonds *from the public* increase actual reserves but also increase demand deposits. Thus, a $1000 bond purchase from the public would increase demand deposits and hence actual reserves of the "loaned up" banking system by $1000. But with a 20 percent desired reserve ratio applied to demand deposits, the excess reserves of the banking system would be only $800.

@ **WORKED PROBLEM 13.3** Open Market Operations

However, in both transactions the end result is the same: *When the Bank of Canada buys securities (bonds) in the open market, chartered banks' reserves are increased.* When the chartered banks lend out an amount equal to their excess reserves, the nation's money supply will rise. Observe in Figure 13-2 that a $1000 purchase of bonds by the Bank of Canada results in a potential of $5000 of additional money, regardless of whether the purchase was made from the banks or the general public.

FIGURE 13-2   The Bank of Canada's Purchase of Bonds and the Expansion of the Money Supply

Assuming all chartered banks are "loaned up" initially, a Bank of Canada purchase of a $1000 bond from either a chartered bank or the public can increase the money supply by $5000 when the desired reserve ratio is 20 percent. In the left portion of the diagram, the purchase of a $1000 bond from a chartered bank creates $1000 of excess reserves that support an expansion of demand deposits of $5000 through making loans. In the right portion, the purchase of a $1000 bond from the public creates only $800 of excess reserves, because $100 of reserves are needed to "back up" the $1000 new demand deposit in the banking system. The chartered banks can therefore expand the money supply by $4000 by making loans. This $4000 of chequing account money plus the initial new demand deposit of $1000 together equal $5000 of new money.

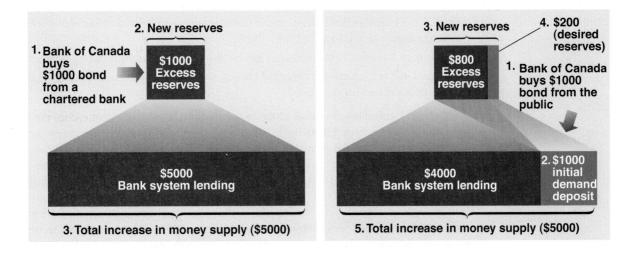

SELLING SECURITIES

As you may suspect, when the Bank of Canada sells government bonds chartered bank reserves are reduced. Let's see why.

To Chartered Banks   When the Bank of Canada sells government bonds in the open market to chartered banks:

(a) The Bank of Canada gives up securities that the chartered banks acquire.

(b) Chartered banks pay for those securities by drawing cheques against their deposits—that is, against their reserves—in the Bank of Canada. The Bank of Canada collects those cheques by reducing the chartered banks' reserves accordingly.

The balance sheet changes, again identified by (*a*) and (*b*), appear as follows:

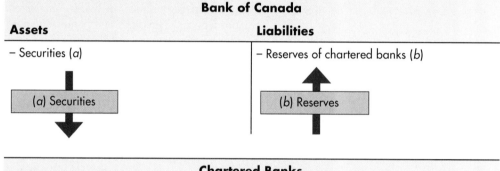

Bank of Canada Buys Bonds from Chartered Banks

Bank of Canada	
Assets	**Liabilities**
− Securities (*a*)	− Reserves of chartered banks (*b*)
(*a*) Securities	(*b*) Reserves

Chartered Banks	
Assets	**Liabilities**
− Reserves (*b*)	
+ Securities (*a*)	

The reduction in chartered bank deposits in the Bank of Canada is indicated by the minus signs before these entries.

To the Public   When the Bank of Canada sells securities to the public the outcome is much the same. Let's put Mariposa Investments Ltd. on the buying end of government bonds that the Bank of Canada is selling:

(a) The Bank of Canada sells Government of Canada bonds to Mariposa Investments, which pays a cheque drawn on the Bank of York.

(b) The Bank of Canada clears this cheque against the Bank of York by reducing York's reserves.

(c) The Bank of York returns the cancelled cheque to Mariposa Investments, reducing the company's demand deposit accordingly.

The Bank of Canada bond sales of $1000 to the chartered banking system reduce the system's actual and excess reserves by $1000. But a $1000 bond sale to the public reduces excess reserves by $800, because demand deposit money is also reduced by $1000 in the sale. Since the chartered banking system has reduced its outstanding deposits by $1000 it need only keep $200 less in reserves.

Whether the Bank of Canada sells securities to the public or to chartered banks, the conclusion is the same: *When the Bank of Canada sells securities in the open market, chartered bank reserves are reduced.*

If all excess reserves are already lent out, this decline in chartered bank reserves will translate into a decline in the nation's money supply. In our example, a $1000 sale of government securities will result in a $5000 decline in the money supply, whether the sale was made to chartered banks or the public. You can verify this by re-examining Figure 13-2 and tracing the effects of *a sale* of a $1000 bond by the Bank of Canada either to chartered banks or the public.

What makes chartered banks and the public willing to sell government securities to, or buy them from, the Bank of Canada? The answer lies in the price of bonds and their interest yields. We know that bond prices and interest rates are inversely related. When the Bank of Canada buys government bonds, the demand for them increases. Government bond prices rise and their interest yields decline. The higher bond prices and their lower yields prompt chartered banks, securities firms, and individual holders of government bonds to sell them to the Bank of Canada.

When the Bank of Canada sells government bonds, the additional supply of bonds in the bond market lowers bond prices and raises their yields, making government bonds attractive purchases for chartered banks and the public.

The Bank Rate and the Overnight Lending Rate

One of the functions of a central bank is to be a "lender of last resort," or, as we noted earlier, "the bankers' bank." Occasionally, chartered banks have unexpected and immediate needs for additional funds. In such cases, the Bank of Canada will make short-term loans to chartered banks.

When a chartered bank borrows, it gives the Bank of Canada a promissory note (IOU) drawn against itself and secured by acceptable collateral—typically, Canadian government securities. Just as chartered banks charge interest on their loans, so too the Bank of Canada charges interest on loans it grants to chartered banks. The interest rate it charges is called the **bank rate.** The bank rate influences other interest rates in the economy, and thereby indirectly the amount of lending by chartered banks.

In providing the loan, the Bank of Canada increases the reserves of the borrowing chartered bank. All new reserves acquired by borrowing from the Bank of Canada are excess reserves. *In short, borrowing from the Bank of Canada by chartered banks increases the reserves of the chartered banks and enhances their ability to extend credit.*

Since February 1996, the bank rate has been set at the upper end of the Bank of Canada's **operating band** for the **overnight lending rate,** the interest rate at which chartered banks, investment dealers, and other financial market participants borrow and lend funds for one day. The Bank of Canada has a publicized target on the overnight lending rate, and maintains it within a range of one-half of a percentage point (50 basis points) of the target range through its three main monetary policy tools. By lending and borrowing in the overnight market, the Bank of Canada affects the liquidity position of the chartered banks. *(Key Question 5)*

Relative Importance

Of the two policy instruments, buying and selling securities in the open market is by far the most important. We will see shortly that the Bank of Canada carries out open-market operations on the overnight loans market to achieve the desired interest rate. Open-market operations have the advantage of flexibility and the impact on chartered bank reserves is prompt. And compared to the other policy tools, open-market operations work subtly and less directly. Furthermore, the ability of the Bank of Canada to affect chartered bank reserves through the purchase and sale of securities is virtually unquestionable. A glance at the consolidated balance sheet for the Bank of Canada (Table 13-1) reveals very large holdings of Treasury bills and other government securities ($45.9 billion). The sale of those securities would reduce chartered bank reserves.

---

bank rate
The interest rate that the Bank of Canada charges on advances made to the chartered banks.

operating band
The Bank of Canada's 50-basis-point range (one-half of one percentage point) for the overnight lending rate.

overnight lending rate
The interest rate at which major participants in the money market borrow and lend one-day funds to each other.

QUICK REVIEW

▶ The main objective of monetary policy is to achieve price stability, and thereby help the economy achieve full employment.

▶ The Bank of Canada uses open-market operations to influence the overnight lend-ing rate and the amount of reserves in the banking system. The bank rate can also be used by the Bank of Canada to control reserves in the banking system, but is a more passive instrument.

13.4 | Targeting the Overnight Lending Rate

The Bank of Canada focuses monetary policy on the interest rate that it can best control: the overnight lending rate. This is the rate of interest that banks charge one another on overnight loans made from temporary excess reserves. Up to 1996, the bank rate was set one-quarter of a percentage point above the yield on the government three-month Treasury bill, set after a weekly auction. Since then the Bank of Canada has set the bank rate based on the upper limit of its operating band for the overnight lending rate. The Bank of Canada sets a target level for the overnight rate, often referred to as the *key policy rate* or *key interest rate*. The Bank of Canada uses predetermined dates, known as *fixed announcement dates*, to communicate the target for the overnight interest rate.

Recall from Chapter 12 that each chartered bank has a desired reserve ratio that it targets. At the end of any business day, some banks temporarily have excess reserves (more actual reserves than they feel comfortable holding) and other banks have reserve deficiencies (fewer reserves than they want). To earn some interest, chartered banks prefer to lend out their temporary excess reserves overnight to other banks that temporarily need them to meet their desired reserve ratio. An equilibrium interest rate arises in this overnight market for bank reserves.

The Bank of Canada uses its status as a supplier of reserves to target the specific overnight lending rate that it deems appropriate based on the expected future performance of the Canadian economy. We demonstrate how this works in Figure 13-3, where we initially assume the Bank of Canada desires a 4 percent overnight lending rate. The demand curve for reserves D_f slopes downward because lower interest rates give chartered banks with reserve deficiencies a greater incentive to borrow in the overnight market rather than reduce loans as a way to meet their desired reserve requirement. The supply curve for reserves, S_{f1}, is somewhat unusual. Specifically, it is horizontal at the targeted overnight rate, here 4 percent. (Disregard supply curves S_{f2} and S_{f3} for now.) It is horizontal because the Bank of Canada uses open-market operations to manipulate the supply of reserves so that the quantity supplied of reserves will exactly equal the quantity demanded of reserves at the targeted interest rate.

In this case, the Bank of Canada seeks to achieve an equilibrium overnight rate of 4 percent. In Figure 13-3 it is successful. Note that at the 4 percent overnight rate, the quantity of reserves supplied (Q_{f1}) equals the quantity of reserves demanded (also Q_{f1}). This 4 percent overnight rate will remain, as long as the supply curve of reserves is horizontal at 4 percent.

In recent years the overnight lending rate has been the primary vehicle through which the Bank of Canada has implemented monetary policy. It can enter the overnight loans market through a

---

FIGURE 13-3 | Targeting the Overnight Lending Rate

In implementing monetary policy, the Bank of Canada determines a desired overnight lending rate and then uses open-market operations (buying and selling of securities) to add or subtract chartered bank reserves to achieve and maintain that targeted rate. In an expansionary monetary policy, the Bank of Canada increases the supply of reserves, for example, from S_{f1} to S_{f2} in this case, to move the overnight lending rate from 4 percent to 3.5 percent. In a restrictive monetary policy, it decreases the supply of reserves, say, from S_{f1} to S_{f3}. Here, the overnight lending rate rises from 4 percent to 4.5 percent.

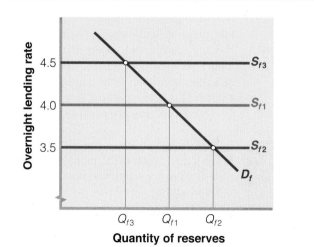

special purchase and resale agreement (SPRA), a transaction in which the Bank of Canada offers to purchase Government of Canada securities with an agreement to sell them back at a predetermined price the next business day. As you know by now, when the Bank of Canada buys bonds it puts downward pressure on short-term interest rates. Through SPRAs the Bank of Canada reinforces it target overnight rate.

Or, the Bank of Canada can enter a *sale and repurchase agreement* (SRA), in which it offers to sell Government of Canada securities to designated counterparties with an agreement to buy them back at a predetermined price the next business day. Selling securities puts upward pressure on interest rates; the Bank of Canada would enter into SRAs when it wants to see interest rates rise.

In Figure 13-3, if the demand for reserves increases (D_f shifts to the right along S_{f1}), the Bank of Canada will use its open-market operations to increase the availability of reserves through SPRAs (inject reserves) such that the 4 percent overnight rate is retained. If the demand for reserves in the overnight market declines (D_f shifts to the left along S_{f1}), the Bank of Canada will enter SRAs (withdrawn reserves) to keep the overnight rate at 4 percent.

Expansionary Monetary Policy

expansionary monetary policy
Bank of Canada actions that increase the money supply to lower interest rates and expand real GDP.

Suppose the economy faces recession and unemployment. How will the Bank of Canada respond? It will initiate an **expansionary monetary policy** (or *easy money policy*). This policy will lower interest rates to bolster borrowing and spending, which will increase aggregate demand and expand real output. The Bank of Canada's immediate step will be to announce a lower target for the overnight loans rate, say 3.5 percent instead of 4 percent. To achieve that lower rate the Bank of Canada will use open-market operations to buy bonds from banks and the public, which increases the reserves in the banking system.

The greater reserves in the banking system produce two critical results:

- The supply of reserves in the overnight market increases, lowering the overnight rate to the new targeted rate. We show this in Figure 13-3 as a downward shift to the horizontal supply curve from S_{f1} to S_{f2}. The equilibrium overnight rate falls to 3.5 percent, just as the Bank of Canada wanted. The equilibrium quantity of reserves in the overnight market for reserves rises from Q_{f1} to Q_{f2}.

- A multiple expansion of the nation's money supply occurs (as we demonstrated in Chapter 12). Given the demand for money, the larger money supply places a downward pressure on other interest rates.

prime interest rate
The interest rate banks charge their most creditworthy borrowers; the benchmark interest rate used by chartered banks as a reference point for a wide range of interest rates charged on loans to businesses and individuals.

One such rate is the **prime interest rate**—the benchmark interest rate used by chartered banks as a reference point for a wide range of interest rates charged on loans to businesses and individuals. The prime interest rate is higher than the overnight rate because the prime rate involves longer, more risky loans than overnight loans between chartered banks. But the overnight rate, the prime interest rate, and the bank rate closely track one another, as is evident in Figure 13-4.

CONSIDER THIS | The Bank of Canada as a Sponge

A good way to remember the role of the Bank of Canada in setting the overnight lending rate is to imagine a large bowl of water, with the amount of water in the bowl representing the stock of reserves in the banking system. Then think of the Bank of Canada as holding a large sponge, labelled "open-market operations." If the Bank of Canada wants to decrease the overnight lending rate, it uses the sponge—filled with reserves created by the Bank of Canada—to squeeze new reserves into the banking system's bowl. It continues this process until the greater supply of reserves reduces the overnight lending rate to the Bank of Canada's targeted level. If the Bank of Canada wants to increase the overnight rate, it uses the sponge to absorb reserves from the banking system. As the supply of reserves falls, the overnight rate rises to the Bank of Canada's targeted level.

| FIGURE 13-4 | The Prime Interest Rate, the Bank Rate, the Overnight Target Rate, and the Overnight Lending Rate in Canada, 1996–2008 |

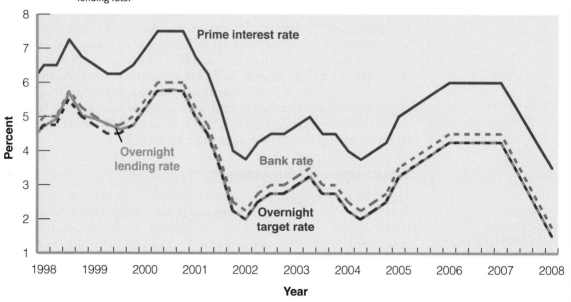

The prime interest rate rises and falls with changes in the bank rate, the overnight target rate, and the overnight lending rate.

SOURCE: Bank of Canada. Selected historical interest rates. At: http://www.bankofcanada.ca/en/rates/sel_hist.html.

Restrictive Monetary Policy

restrictive monetary policy
Bank of Canada actions that contract, or restrict, the growth of the nation's money supply for the purpose of reducing or eliminating inflation.

The opposite monetary policy is in order for periods of rising inflation. The Bank of Canada will then undertake a **restrictive monetary policy** (or *tight money policy*). This policy will increase the interest rate to reduce borrowing and spending, which will curtail the expansion of aggregate demand and hold down price-level increases. The Bank of Canada's immediate step will be to announce a higher target for the overnight rate, say 4.5 percent instead of 4 percent. Through open-market operations, the Bank of Canada will sell bonds to the chartered banks and the public and the sale of those bonds will absorb reserves in the banking system.

The smaller reserves in the banking system produce two results opposite those discussed for an expansionary monetary policy:

- The supply of overnight reserves decreases, raising the overnight lending rate to the new targeted rate. We show this in Figure 13-3 as an upward shift of the horizontal supply curve from S_A to S_B. The equilibrium overnight rate rises to 4.5 percent, just as the Bank of Canada wanted, and the equilibrium quantity of reserves in this market falls to Q_B.

- A multiple contraction of the nation's money supply occurs (as demonstrated in Chapter 12). Given the demand for money, the smaller money supply places an upward pressure on other interest rates. For example, the prime interest rate rises.

The Taylor Rule

Taylor rule
A modern monetary rule proposed by economist John Taylor that stipulates exactly how much a central bank should change interest rates in response to divergences of real GDP from potential GDP and divergences of actual rates of inflation from a target rate of inflation.

The proper overnight lending rate for a certain period is a matter of policy discretion by the Bank of Canada. It adheres to a strict inflationary target or monetary policy rule. And, as such, it appears to roughly follow a rule first established by economist John Taylor of Stanford University. The **Taylor rule** assumes that the central bank is willing to tolerate a 2 percent target rate of inflation, and that the central bank follows three rules when setting its target for the overnight funds rate:

- When real GDP is equal to potential GDP and inflation is equal to the target rate of 2 percent, the overnight lending rate should remain at about 4 percent, implying an overnight lending rate of 2 percent (= 4 percent nominal overnight rate – 2 percent inflation rate).

- For each 1 percent increase of real GDP above potential GDP, the central bank should raise the *real* overnight rate by one-half a percentage point.

- For each 1 percent increase in the inflation rate above its target of 2 percent, the central bank should raise the *real* overnight lending rate by one-half a percentage point. (Note, though, that in this case each one-half percentage point increase in the real rate will require a 1.5-percentage-point increase in the nominal rate to account for the underlying 1 percent increase in the inflation rate.)

The last two rules are applied independently of each other, so that if real GDP is above potential output and at the same time inflation is above the 2 percent target rate the Bank of Canada will apply both rules and raise real interest rates in response to both factors. For instance, if real GDP is 1 percent above potential output and inflation is simultaneously 1 percent above the 2 percent target rate, then the Bank of Canada will raise the *real* overnight lending rate by 1 percentage point (= one-half percentage point for the excessive GDP + one-half percentage point for the excessive inflation).

Also notice that the last two rules are reversed for situations in which real GDP falls below potential GDP or inflation falls below 2 percent. Each 1 percent decline in real GDP below potential GDP or fall in inflation below 2 percent calls for a decline of the *real* overnight lending rate by one-half percentage point.

 WORKED PROBLEM 13.4
The Taylor Rule

We reemphasize that the Bank of Canada has no official allegiance to the Taylor rule. It changes the overnight lending rate to any level that it deems appropriate.

QUICK REVIEW

▶ The Bank of Canada conducts its monetary policy by establishing a targeted overnight lending rate—the rate that chartered banks charge one another for overnight loans of reserves.

▶ An expansionary monetary policy (easy money policy) lowers the overnight rate, increases the money supply, and lowers other interest rates.

▶ A restrictive monetary policy (tight money policy) increases the overnight lending rate, reduces the money supply, and increases other interest rates.

▶ The Bank of Canada uses its discretion in setting the overnight lending rate, but its decisions regarding monetary policy and the target rate appear to be broadly consistent with the Taylor rule.

13.5 Monetary Policy, Real GDP, and Price Level

We have identified and explained the tools of expansionary and contractionary monetary policy. We now want to emphasize how monetary policy affects the economy's levels of investment, aggregate demand, real GDP, and prices.

Cause–Effect Chain: the Transmission Mechanism

The four diagrams in **Figure 13-5 (Key Graph)** will help you understand how monetary policy works toward the goal of achieving price stability, and, indirectly, full employment.

MARKET FOR MONEY

Figure 13-5a represents the market for money, in which the demand curve for money and the supply curve for money are brought together. Recall that the total demand for money is made up of transactions demand and asset demand.

KEY GRAPH @

FIGURE 13-5 Monetary Policy and Equilibrium GDP

An expansionary monetary policy that shifts the money supply curve rightward from S_{m1} to S_{m2} in (a) lowers the interest rate from 10 to 8 percent in (b). As a result, investment spending increases from $15 billion to $20 billion, shifting the aggregate demand curve rightward from AD_1 to AD_2 in (c) so that real output rises from the recessionary level of GDP_1 to the full employment at GDP_f along the horizontal dashed segment of aggregate supply. In figure (d), the economy at point *a* has an inflationary gap, thus GDP is above potential output. A restrictive monetary policy that shifts the money supply curve leftward from S_{m3} = $175 billion to just $162.5 billion in (a) will increases the interest rate from 6 to 7 percent. Investment spending thus falls from $25 billion to $22.5 billion in (b). The aggregate demand curve shifts leftward in (d) from AD_3 to AD_4, moving the economy along the horizontal dashed segment of aggregate supply to equilibrium *b*. This returns the economy to full employment and eliminates the inflationary gap.

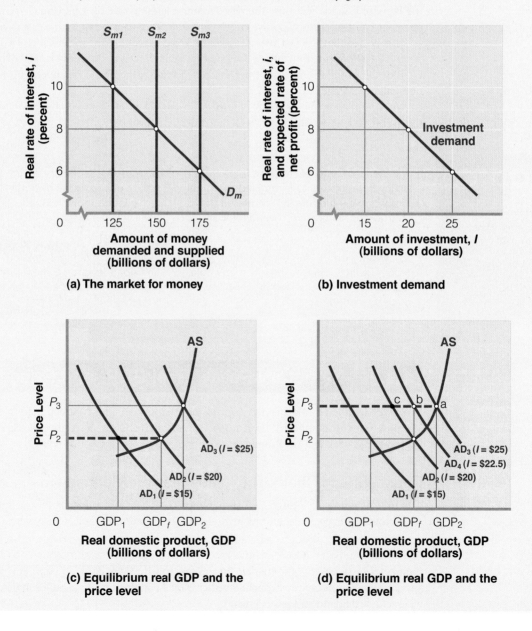

(a) The market for money

(b) Investment demand

(c) Equilibrium real GDP and the price level

(d) Equilibrium real GDP and the price level

Quick Quiz

1. **The ultimate objective of an expansionary money policy is depicted by**
   a. a decrease in the money supply from S_{m3} to S_{m2}.
   b. a reduction of the interest rate from 8 percent to 6 percent.
   c. an increase in investment from $20 billion to $25 billion.
   d. an increase in real GDP from GDP_1 to GDP_f.

2. **A successful restrictive policy is shown as a shift in the money supply curve from**
   a. S_{m3} to a halfway point between S_{m2} and S_{m3}, a decrease in investment from $25 billion to $22.5 billion, and a decline in aggregate demand from AD_3 to AD_4.
   b. S_{m1} to S_{m2}, an increase in investment from $20 billion to $25 billion, and an increase in real GDP from GDP_1 to GDP_f.
   c. S_{m3} to S_{m2}, a decrease in investment from $25 billion to $20 billion, and a decline in the price level from P_3 to P_2.
   d. S_{m3} to S_{m2}, a decrease in investment from $25 billion to $20 billion, and an increase in aggregate demand from AD_2 to AD_3.

3. **The Bank of Canada could increase the money supply from S_{m1} to S_{m2} by**
   a. increasing the bank rate.
   b. reducing taxes.
   c. buying government securities in the open market.
   d. selling government securities in the open market.

4. **If the spending–income multiplier is 4 in the economy depicted, an increase in the money supply from $125 billion to $150 billion will**
   a. shift the aggregate demand curve rightward by $20 billion.
   b. increase real GDP by $25 billion.
   c. increase real GDP by $100 billion.
   d. shift the aggregate demand curve leftward by $5 billion.

Answers: 1. d; 2. c; 3. c; 4. a

This figure also shows three potential money supply curves, S_{m1}, S_{m2}, and S_{m3}. In each case the money supply is shown as a vertical line representing some fixed amount of money determined by the Bank of Canada.

The equilibrium interest rate is the interest rate at which the amount of money demanded and the amount supplied are equal. With money demand D_m in Figure 13-5a, if the supply of money is $125 billion ($S_{m1}$), the equilibrium interest rate is 10 percent. With a money supply of $150 billion ($S_{m2}$), the interest rate is 8 percent; with a money supply of $175 billion ($S_{m3}$), it is 6 percent.

You know that the real, not the nominal, rate of interest is critical for investment decisions. So here we assume Figure 13-5a portrays real interest rates.

INVESTMENT

These 10 percent, 8 percent, and 6 percent real interest rates are carried rightward to the investment demand curve of Figure 13-5b. This curve shows the inverse relationship between the interest rate—the cost of borrowing to invest—and the amount of investment spending. At the 10 percent interest rate it will be profitable for the nation's businesses to invest $15 billion; at 8 percent, $20 billion; at 6 percent, $25 billion.

Changes in the interest rate mainly affect the investment component of total spending.

Changes in the interest rate mainly affect the investment component of total spending, although they also affect spending on durable consumer goods (such as autos and furniture) that are purchased on credit. The impact of changing interest rates on investment spending is great because of the large cost and long-term nature of capital purchases. Capital equipment, factory buildings, and warehouses are tremendously expensive. In absolute terms, interest charges on funds borrowed for these purchases are considerable. Similarly, the interest cost on a house purchased on a long-term contract is very large: A one-half percentage point change in the interest rate could amount to a difference of thousands of dollars in the total cost of buying a home.

In brief, the impact of changing interest rates is mainly on investment (and, through that, on aggregate demand, output, employment, and price level). Moreover, as Figure 13-5b shows, investment spending varies inversely with the interest rate.

EQUILIBRIUM GDP

Figure 13-5c shows the impact of our three interest rates and corresponding levels of investment spending on aggregate demand (ignore Figure 13-5d for the time being; we will return to it shortly). As noted, aggregate demand curve AD_1 is associated with the $15 billion level of investment, AD_2 with investment of $20 billion, and AD_3 with investment of $25 billion. That is, investment spending is one of the determinants of aggregate demand. Other things equal, the greater this investment spending, the farther to the right lies the aggregate demand curve.

Suppose the money supply in Figure 13-5a is $150 billion ($S_{m2}$), producing an equilibrium interest rate of 8 percent. In Figure 13-5b we see this 8 percent interest rate will bring forth $20 billion of investment spending. This $20 billion of investment spending joins with consumption spending, net exports, and government spending to yield aggregate demand curve AD_2 in Figure 13-5c. The equilibrium levels of real output and prices are GDP_f and P_2, as determined by the intersection of AD_2 and the aggregate supply curve AS.

To test your understanding of these relationships, explain why each of the other two levels of money supply in Figure 13-5a results in a different interest rate, level of investment, aggregate demand curve, and equilibrium real output and price level.

Effects of an Expansionary Monetary Policy

Recall that the inflationary ratchet effect discussed in Chapter 10 describes the fact that real-world price levels tend to be downwardly inflexible. Thus, with our economy starting from the initial equilibrium where AD_2 intersects AS, the price level will be downwardly inflexible at P_2 so that aggregate supply will be horizontal to the left of GDP_f. This means that if aggregate demand decreases, the economy's equilibrium will move leftward along the dashed horizontal line shown in Figure 13-5c.

Just such a decline would happen if the money supply fell to $125 billion ($S_{m1}$), shifting the aggregate demand curve leftward to AD_1 in Figure 13-5c. This results in a real output of GDP_1, less than the economy's full-employment GDP level. The economy will be experiencing recession, a negative GDP gap, and substantial unemployment. The Bank of Canada therefore should institute an expansionary monetary policy.

To increase the money supply the Bank of Canada will buy government securities from chartered banks and the public in the open market, while at the same time decreasing the bank rate. The intended outcome will be an increase in excess reserves in the chartered banking system and a decline in the overnight rate. Because excess reserves are the basis on which chartered banks can earn profit by lending and thereby expand the money supply, the nation's money supply likely will rise. An increase in the money supply will lower the interest rate, increasing investment, aggregate demand, and equilibrium GDP.

For example, an increase in the money supply from $125 to $150 billion ($S_{m1}$ to S_{m2}) will reduce the interest rate from 10 percent to 8 percent, as indicated in Figure 13-5a, and increase investment from $15 billion to $20 billion, as shown in Figure 13-5b. This $5 billion increase in investment spending will shift the aggregate demand curve rightward from AD_1 to AD_2, as shown in Figure 13-5c.

This rightward shift in the aggregate demand curve along the dashed horizontal part of the aggregate supply curve will increase from GDP_1 to the desired full-employment output at GDP_f, thereby closing the negative GDP gap.[1]

Column 1 of Table 13-2 summarizes the chain of events associated with an expansionary monetary policy.

Effects of a Restrictive Monetary Policy

To prevent Figure 13-5c from getting too crowded as we consider restrictive monetary policy, we will combine the money market in Figure 13-5a and the investment demand curve of Figure 13-5b that we have already been using with the aggregate demand and aggregate supply curves shown in Figure 13-5d. Figure 13-5d represents exactly the same economy as Figure 13-5c, but adds some extra curves that relate only to our explanation of restrictive monetary policy.

To see how restrictive monetary policy works, let us first consider a situation in which the economy moves from a full-employment equilibrium to operating at more than full employment so that inflation is a problem and restrictive monetary policy would be appropriate. Assume the economy begins at the full-employment equilibrium where AD_2 and AS intersect. At equilibrium GDP_f the price level is P_2. Next, assume that the money supply grows to $175 billion ($S_{m3}$) in Figure 13-5a. This results in an interest rate of 6 percent, investment spending of $25 billion, and aggregate demand AD_3. As the AD curve shifts to the right from AD_2 to AD_3 in Figure 13-5d, the economy will move along the upward-sloping AS curve until it comes to an equilibrium at point a, where AD_3 intersects AS. At the new equilibrium, the price level has risen to P_3 and the equilibrium level of real GDP at GDP_1, indicating an inflationary GDP gap. Aggregate demand AD_3 is excessive relative to the economy's full-employment level of real output GDP_f. To rein in spending, the Bank of Canada will institute a restrictive monetary policy. The Bank of Canada will undertake to sell government bonds to chartered banks and to the public in the open market, while at the same time increasing the bank rate. Banks then will discover their reserves are too low to meet possible cash withdrawals and therefore will need to reduce their demand deposits by refraining from issuing new loans as old loans are paid back. This will shrink the money supply and increase the interest rate. The higher interest rate will discourage investment, decreasing aggregate demand and restraining demand-pull inflation.

But the Bank of Canada must be careful about just how much to decrease the money supply. The problem is that the inflation ratchet will take effect at the new equilibrium point a, such that prices will be inflexible at price level P_3. As a result, aggregate supply to the left of point a will be the horizontal dashed line shown in Figure 13-5d. This means that the Bank of Canada cannot simply lower the money supply to S_{m2} in Figure 13-5a. If it were to do that, investment demand would fall to $20 billion in Figure 13-5b, and the AD curve would shift to the left from AD_3 back to AD_2. But because of inflexible prices, the economy's equilibrium would move to point c, where AD_2 intersects the horizontal dashed line that represents aggregate supply to the left of point a. This would put the economy into a recession, with equilibrium output below the full-employment output level of GDP_f. What the Bank of Canada needs to do to achieve full employment is to move the AD curve back only from AD_3 to AD_4, so that the economy will come to equilibrium at point b. This will require a decrease in aggregate demand, so that equilibrium output falls from GDP_2 at point a to GDP_f at point b. The Bank of Canada can achieve this shift by setting the supply of money in Figure 13-5a at $162.5 billion. To see how this works, draw in a vertical money supply curve in Figure 13-5a at $162.5 billion and label it as S_{m4}. It will be exactly halfway between money supply curves S_{m2} and S_{m3}. Notice that the intersection of S_{m4} with the money demand curve D_m will result in an interest rate of 7 percent. In Figure 13-5b, this interest rate of 7 percent will result in investment spending of $22.5 billion (halfway between $20 billion and $25 billion). Thus, by setting money supply at $162.5 billion, the Bank of Canada can reduce investment, lowering it to a level associated

---

[1] To keep things simple, we assume that the increase in real GDP does not increase the demand for money. In reality, the transactions demand for money would rise, slightly dampening the decline in the interest rate shown in Figure 13-5a.

TABLE 13-2	**Monetary Policy: The Transmission Mechanism**

(1) Expansionary monetary policy	**(2) Restrictive monetary policy**
Problem: unemployment and recession	Problem: Inflation
↓	↓
Bank of Canada buys bonds and lowers the bank rate	Bank of Canada sells bonds and raises the bank rate
↓	↓
Excess reserves increase	Excess reserves decrease
↓	↓
Overnight rate falls	Overnight rate rises
↓	↓
Money supply rises	Money supply falls
↓	↓
Interest rate falls	Interest rate rises
↓	↓
Investment spending increases	Investment spending decreases
↓	↓
Aggregate demand increases	Aggregate demand decreases
↓	↓
Real GDP rises	Inflation declines

with AD_4. This shift will move the economy to equilibrium b, returning output to the full employment level and eliminating the inflationary GDP gap.[2]

Column 2 of Table 13-2 summarizes the cause–effect chain of a restrictive money policy.

Monetary Policy: Evaluation and Issues

Monetary policy has become the dominant component of Canadian national stabilization policy. It has two key advantages over fiscal policy: speed and flexibility, and isolation from political pressure.

Compared with fiscal policy, monetary policy can be quickly altered. Recall that government deliberations can delay the application of fiscal policy. In contrast, the Bank of Canada can buy or sell securities from day to day and thus affect the money supply and interest rates almost immediately.

Also, because the Governor of the Bank of Canada is appointed and serves a seven-year term, the Bank of Canada is relatively isolated from lobbying and need not worry about being popular with voters. Thus, the Bank of Canada, more readily than the federal government, can engage in politically unpopular policies (higher interest rates) that may be necessary for the long-term health of the economy. Moreover, monetary policy is a subtler and more politically conservative measure than fiscal policy. Changes in government spending directly affect the allocation of resources, and changes in taxes can have extensive political ramifications. Because monetary policy works more subtly, it is more politically palatable.

Recent Monetary Policy in Canada

In the early 1990s, the restrictive monetary policy made the economic recovery after the recession of 1991–92 relatively slow. But the continued easing by the Bank of Canada after 1995 helped the Canadian economy grow at a healthy clip in the second half of the 1990s. By 2000 the Canadian unemployment rate had declined to 6.8 percent—the lowest rate in 25 years. To counter potential inflation during that strong expansion, the Bank of Canada began to reduce reserves in the banking system to raise the interest rate to keep inflation under control. The overnight rate was raised from a low of 3.0 percent in early 1997 to 5.75 percent in September 1998. The financial crisis in the Pacific Rim pressured the Bank of Canada to ease monetary policy late in 1998 and into mid-1999. But the vigorous Canadian economy and a stock market bubble in the making led the Bank of Canada to raise the overnight rate from 4.60 percent in May 1999 to 5.75 percent by the end of 2000 to slow down the economy and ward off potential inflationary pressures.

---

[2] Again, we assume for simplicity that the decrease in nominal GDP does not feed back to reduce the demand for money and thus the interest rate. In reality, this would occur, slightly dampening the increase in the interest rate shown in Figure 13-5a.

CONSIDER THIS | Monetary Policy during Financial Crises

During the depth of the financial crisis in early March of 2009, the Bank of Canada announced that it was lowering the overnight rate to a historic low of .25 percent. In its accompanying statement to the announcement, the Bank of Canada noted that "Given the low level of the target for the overnight rate, the bank is refining the approach it would take to provide additional monetary stimulus, if required, through credit and quantitative easing." While the Bank of Canada did not specify what it meant by "credit and quantitative easing," most observers understood that it would probably purchase any government bonds, asset-backed commercial paper, or corporate bonds. In other words, it was prepared to undertake extraordinary measures to support a floundering economy during a financial crisis that had spread, like a virus, to most economies around the world.

Although inflation remained low in the late 1990s, in the last quarter of 2000 the economy began to slow. The Bank of Canada responded by cutting interest rates early in 2001. As it became evident that investment spending was dropping sharply, the Bank of Canada began cutting rates aggressively. The terrorist attacks on September 11, 2001 in the United States gave the Bank of Canada more reason to continue reducing interest rates. The overnight rate went from 5.75 percent in January 2001 to 2.0 percent by early 2002.

In 2002 the Canadian economy began to expand again, and the Bank of Canada responded by increasing the overnight rate to 2.75 percent by the end of the year. Despite the increase in interest rates in 2002 the Canadian economy did very well, adding more than 500,000 jobs, and with GDP expanding at an annual rate of 3.1 percent.

Economists credit the Bank of Canada's adroit use of monetary policy as one of a number of factors that helped the Canadian economy achieve and maintain the rare combination of price stability and strong economic growth that occurred between 1996 and 2000. The Bank of Canada also deserves high marks for helping to keep the slowdown of 2001 relatively mild, particularly in view of the adverse economic impacts of September 11, 2001 in the United States, our largest trading partner, and the steep stock market drop in 2001–02.

In 2003 the Bank of Canada left the overnight rate at 2.75 as the economy continued to expand at an unremarkable annual rate 2 percent. In 2004 the Bank of Canada reduced the overnight rate to as low as 2 percent in an effort to stimulate the economy, and then began to raise the overnight rate toward the end of 2004. Indeed, in 2004 GDP rose just under 3 percent. But as the economy began to expand robustly in 2005, the Bank of Canada began a series of interest-rate hikes that saw the target overnight rate rise to 3.25 percent by the end of 2005. The purpose of the rate hikes was to boost the prime interest rate (5.00 percent at the end of 2005) and other interest rates to make sure that aggregate demand continued to grow at a pace consistent with low inflation. In that regard, the Bank of Canada was successful.

The Bank of Canada continued to hike the overnight lending rate throughout 2006 and 2007 as the economy continued to expand and as the threat of inflation increased because of rising oil prices. But by early 2008 it became evident that the Canadian economy was slowing along with the U.S., where a housing bubble was unwinding and had created a financial crisis that spread across the globe. The overnight rate dropped to 1.5 percent by the end of 2008. In the first quarter of 2009 the global financial crisis that had engulfed most of the major economies of the world forced the Bank of Canada to drop the target rate on the overnight lending rate to a historic low of 0.25 percent, as it became evident that the Canadian economy was in recession. The Bank of Canada felt the global economic slowdown merited keeping interest rates at these historic lows until the middle of 2010, by which time it expected the Canadian economy to be expanding once again.

13.6 | Problems and Complications

Despite its recent successes in Canada, monetary policy has certain limitations and faces real-world complications.

Lags

Recall that fiscal policy is hindered by three delays, or lags—a recognition lag, an administrative lag, and an operational lag. Monetary policy also faces a recognition lag and an operational lag, but because the Bank of Canada can decide and implement policy changes within days, it avoids the long administrative lag that hinders fiscal policy. A recognition lag affects monetary policy because normal monthly variations in economic activity and the price level mean that the Bank of Canada may not be able to quickly recognize when the economy is truly starting to recede or when inflation is really starting to rise. Once the Bank of Canada acts, an operation lag of three to six months affects monetary policy because that much time is typically required for interest-rate changes to have their full impacts on investment, aggregate demand, real GDP, and the price level. These two lags complicate the timing of monetary policy.

Cyclical Asymmetry

cyclical asymmetry
The idea that monetary policy may be more successful in slowing expansions and controlling inflation than in extracting the economy from severe recession.

Monetary policy may be highly effective in slowing expansions and controlling inflation but less reliable in pushing the economy from a severe recession. Economists say that monetary policy may suffer from **cyclical asymmetry.**

If pursued vigorously, a restrictive monetary policy could deplete chartered banking reserves to the point where banks would be forced to reduce the volume of loans. That would mean a contraction of the money supply, higher interest rates, and reduced aggregate demand. The Bank of Canada can absorb reserves and eventually achieve its goal.

But it cannot be certain of achieving its goal when it adds reserves to the banking system. An expansionary monetary policy suffers from a "You can lead a horse to water, but you cannot make it drink" problem. The Bank of Canada can create excess reserves, but it cannot guarantee that the banks will actually make the added loans and thus increase the supply of money. If chartered banks seek liquidity and are unwilling to lend, the efforts of the Bank of Canada will be of little avail. Similarly, businesses can frustrate the intentions of the Bank of Canada by not borrowing excess reserves. And the public may use money paid to them through Bank of Canada sales of Canadian securities to pay off existing bank loans, rather than increasing their spending on goods and services.

Furthermore, a severe recession may so undermine business confidence that the investment demand curve shifts to the left and frustrates an expansionary monetary. That is what happened in Japan in the 1990s and early 2000s. Although Japan's central bank drove the real interest rate to 0 percent, investment spending remained low and the Japanese economy stayed mired in recession. In fact, **deflation**—a fall in the price level—occurred. The Japanese experience reminds us that monetary policy is not an assured cure for the business cycle.

deflation
A decline in the economy's price level.

Inflation Targeting

inflation targeting
A Bank of Canada policy of maintaining the inflation rate within a specific range, currently 1 to 3 percent.

Some economists claim that the Bank of Canada's adoption of **inflation targeting**—the annual statement of a target range of inflation, currently 1 to 3 percent—for the economy is to be credited for its recent successes. The Bank of Canada now explains to the public how each monetary action fits within its overall strategy. If the Bank of Canada misses its target, it explains what went wrong. So inflation targeting has increased the "transparency" (openness) of monetary policy and increased the Bank of Canada's accountability. Proponents of inflation targeting say that, along with increasing transparency and accountability, it has focused Canada's central bank on what should be its main mission: controlling inflation. They say that an explicit commitment to price-level stability has created more certainty for households and firms about future product and input prices and

CONSIDER THIS | "Pushing on a String" during Severe Recession

In the late 1990s and early 2000s, the central bank of Japan used an easy money policy to reduce real interest rates to zero. Even with interest-free loans available, most consumers and businesses did not borrow and spend more. Japan's economy continued to sputter in and out of recession. The Japanese circumstance illustrates the possible *asymmetry* of monetary policy, which economists have likened to "pulling versus pushing on a string." A string may be effective at pulling something back to a desirable spot, but it is ineffective at pushing it toward a desired location.

So it is with monetary policy, say some economists. Monetary policy can readily *pull* the aggregate demand curve to the left, reducing demand-pull inflation. There is no limit on how much a central bank can restrict a nation's money supply and hike interest rates. Eventually, a sufficiently tight money policy will reduce aggregate demand and inflation.

But during severe recession, participants in the economy may be highly pessimistic about the future. If so, an easy money policy may not be able to push the aggregate demand curve to the right, increasing real GDP. The central bank can produce excess reserves in the banking system by purchasing government securities and lowering the bank rate. But chartered banks may not be able to find willing borrowers for those excess reserves, no matter how low interest rates fall. Instead of borrowing and spending, consumers and businesses may be more intent on reducing debt and increasing saving in preparation for expected worse times ahead. If so, monetary policy will be ineffective. Using it under those circumstances will be much like pushing on a string.

During the global financial crisis of 2008–09 central banks around the world lowered short-term interest rates in an attempt to fight a global recession of a severity not seen since the Great Depression. Banks were reluctant to lend because of the fear of not being able to recover those loans in a very bad economy. Consumers and businesses were reluctant to borrow because of the fear of a protracted recession that some had even dubbed a depression. While the severity of the slowdown was less pronounced in Canada, the Bank of Canada lowered short-term interest rates to historic lows. By the middle of 2009 the worst of the financial crisis appeared to be over; the Bank of Canada expected the economy to begin to expand by the end of the year on the assumption that the expectation of businesses and consumers improved and lending and borrowing would return to normal levels.

created greater output stability. The setting and meeting of an inflation target has also achieved its important subsidiary goals of full employment and economic growth. Several other countries have adopted inflation targeting, including New Zealand, Sweden, and the United Kingdom.

QUICK REVIEW

▶ The Bank of Canada is engaging in an expansionary monetary policy when it increases the money supply to reduce interest rates and increase investment spending and real GDP; it is engaging in a restrictive monetary policy when it reduces the money supply to increase interest rates and reduce investment spending and inflation.

▶ The main strengths of monetary policy are (a) speed and flexibility and (b) political acceptability; its main weaknesses are (a) time lags and (b) potential reduced effectiveness during recession.

▶ In the past two decades, the Bank of Canada has quite successfully used alternate restrictive and expansionary policies to stabilize the economy.

13.7 | Monetary Policy and the International Economy

In Chapter 9 we noted that linkages among the economies of the world complicate domestic fiscal policy. These linkages extend to monetary policy as well.

TABLE 13·3	Monetary Policy: and the Net Export Effect

(1) **Expansionary monetary policy**	(2) **Restrictive monetary policy**
Problem: recession, slow growth	Problem: inflation
↓	↓
Expansionary monetary policy (lower interest rate)	Restrictive monetary policy (higher interest rate)
↓	↓
Decreased foreign demand for dollars	Increased foreign demand for dollars
↓	↓
Dollar depreciates	Dollar appreciates
↓	↓
Net exports increase (aggregate demand increases, strengthening the expansionary monetary policy)	Net exports decrease (aggregate demand decreases, strengthening the restrictive monetary policy)

Net Export Effect

As we saw in Chapter 11, an expansionary fiscal policy (financed by government borrowing) may increase the domestic interest rate because the government competes with the private sector in obtaining loans. The higher interest rate causes the Canadian dollar to appreciate in the foreign exchange market. So imports rise and exports fall and the resulting decline in net exports weakens the stimulus of the expansionary fiscal policy. This is the so-called *net export effect* of fiscal policy.

Will an expansionary monetary policy have a similar effect? The answer is no. As outlined in column 1, Table 13-3, an expansionary monetary policy does indeed produce a net export effect, but its direction is opposite that of an expansionary fiscal policy. An expansionary monetary policy in, say, Canada reduces the domestic interest rate. The lower interest rate discourages the inflow of financial capital to Canada. The demand for dollars in foreign exchange markets falls, causing the Canadian dollar to depreciate in value. It takes more dollars to buy, say, a Japanese yen or a euro. All foreign goods become more expensive to Canadian residents, and Canadian goods become cheaper to foreigners. Canadian imports thus fall, and Canadian exports rise; so, Canada's net exports increase. As a result, aggregate expenditures and equilibrium GDP expand in Canada.

Conclusion: In contrast to an expansionary fiscal policy that reduces net exports, an expansionary monetary policy *increases* net exports and thus strengthens monetary policy. The depreciation of the Canadian dollar that results from the lower interest rate means that Canadian net exports rise along with domestic investment. Similarly, the net export effect strengthens a restrictive monetary policy. To see how this happens, follow through the analysis in column 2, Table 13-3.

Macroeconomic Stability and the Trade Balance

Assume that, in addition to domestic macroeconomic stability, a widely held economic goal is that Canada should balance its exports and imports on goods and services. That is, Canadian net exports should be zero. In simple terms, Canada wants to "pay its own way" in international trade by earning from its exports an amount of money sufficient to finance its imports.

Consider column 1 in Table 13-3 once again, but now suppose Canada initially has a very large balance-of-international-trade *deficit*, which means its imports exceed its exports and so it is *not* paying its way in world trade. By following through the cause–effect chain in column 1, we find that an expansionary monetary policy lowers the international value of the dollar so that Canadian exports increase and Canadian imports decline. This increase in net exports works to correct the initial balance-of-trade deficit.

Conclusion: *The expansionary monetary policy that is appropriate for the alleviation of unemployment and sluggish growth is compatible with the goal of correcting a balance-of-trade deficit.* Similarly, if the initial problem was a Canadian trade surplus, a restrictive monetary policy would tend to resolve that surplus.

Now consider column 2 in Table 13-3 and assume again that Canada has a large balance-of-trade deficit. In using a restrictive monetary policy to restrain inflation, the Bank of Canada would cause net exports to decrease—Canadian exports would fall and imports would rise. That would mean a larger trade deficit.

Conclusion: *A restrictive monetary policy is used to alleviate inflation conflicts with the goal of correcting a balance-of-trade deficit.* However, if the initial problem were a trade surplus, a restrictive monetary policy would help to resolve it.

Overall we find that an expansionary monetary policy alleviates a trade deficit and aggravates a trade surplus; a restrictive monetary policy alleviates a trade surplus and aggravates a trade deficit. The point is that certain combinations of circumstances create conflicts or tradeoffs between the use of monetary policy to achieve domestic stability and the realization of a balance in the nation's international trade. *(Key Question 8)*

The LAST WORD   The Mortgage Debt Crisis: the Fed Responds

In 2007, massive defaults on home mortgages threatened to bring the credit markets to a halt. The Fed acted quickly to restore confidence and keep loans flowing.

In 2007, a major wave of defaults on home mortgages threatened the health of any financial institution that had invested in home mortgages either directly or indirectly. A majority of these mortgage defaults were on *subprime mortgage loans*—high-interest-rate loans to home buyers with higher-than-average credit risk. Crucially, several of the biggest indirect investors in these subprime loans had been banks. The banks had lent money to investment companies that had invested in mortgages. When the mortgages started to go bad, many investment funds "blew up" and couldn't repay the loans they had taken out from the banks. The banks had to *write off* (declare unrecoverable) the loans they had made to the investment funds. Doing so meant reducing the banks' reserves, which in turn limited their ability to generate new loans. This was a major threat to the economy since both consumers and businesses rely on loans to finance consumption and investment expenditures.

In the second half of 2007 and into early 2008, the Federal Reserve took several important steps to increase bank reserves and avert a financial crisis. In August 2007, it fulfilled its important (but thankfully rarely needed) role as a "lender of last resort" by

lowering the discount rate and encouraging banks to borrow reserves directly from the Fed. When many banks proved reluctant to borrow reserves at the discount rate (because they thought that doing so might make them appear to be in bad financial condition and in need of a quick loan from the Fed), the Fed introduced the anonymous term auction facility in December as an innovative new way of encouraging banks to borrow reserves and thereby preserve their ability to keep extending loans. Most importantly, the Federal Open Market Committee (FOMC) lowered the target for the Federal funds rate—first from 5.25 percent to 4.75 percent in September, then to 4.50 percent in October, down to 4.25 percent in December, and then down to 2.00 percent in April 2008. To accomplish these rate cuts, it bought bonds in the open market and auctioned off reserves. The greater reserves expanded bank lending.

The lower Federal funds rate also resulted in lower interest rates in general, thereby bolstering aggregate demand. Many observers had been worried that the mortgage debt crisis might lead nervous consumers and businesses to cut back on spending out of fear that the crisis might increase the

likelihood of a recession. By increasing aggregate demand, the Fed decreased this possibility and reassured both consumers and businesses about the economy's prospects going forward. A strange thing about the crisis was that before it happened, banks had mistakenly believed that an innovation known as the "mortgage-backed security" had eliminated their exposure to mortgage defaults. Mortgage-backed securities are a type of bond backed by mortgage payments. To create them, banks and other mortgage lenders would first make mortgage loans. But then instead of holding those loans as assets on their balance sheets and collecting the monthly mortgage payments, the banks and other mortgage lenders would bundle hundreds or thousands of them together and sell them off as a bond—in essence selling the right to collect all of the future mortgage payments. The banks would get a cash payment for the bond and the bond buyer would start to collect the mortgage payments. From the banks' perspective, this seemed like a smart business decision because it transferred any future default risk on those mortgages to the buyer of the bond. The banks thought that they were off the hook. Unfortunately for them, however, they lent a substantial portion of the money they got selling the bonds to investment funds that invested in mortgage-backed bonds. So while the banks were no longer directly exposed to mortgage default risk, they were still indirectly exposed to it. And so when many homebuyers started to default on their mortgages, the banks still lost money. But what had caused the skyrocketing mortgage default rates in the first place? There were many causes, including declining real-estate values. But an important factor was the bad incentives provided by the bonds. Since the banks and other mortgage lenders thought that they were no longer exposed to mortgage default risk, they became very sloppy in their lending practices—so much so that people were granted subprime mortgage loans that they were very unlikely to be able to repay. Some mortgage companies were so eager to sign up new homebuyers (in order to bundle their loans together to sell bonds) that they stopped running credit checks and even

allowed applicants to claim higher incomes than they were actually earning in order to qualify for big loans. The natural result was that many of these people took on "too much mortgage" and were soon failing to make their monthly payments. Politicians and financial regulators are now examining whether tighter lending rules would help to offset the "pass the buck" incentives created by mortgage-backed securities and prevent loans from being issued to people who are very unlikely to be able to make the required monthly payments. They also are considering ways to help homeowners who took on too much debt to remain in their homes since defaults on these loans would increase the supply of homes for sale in the real estate market and reduce house prices, which in turn could produce further defaults and reduce confidence in the overall economy.

Unlike the 1930s, the current financial crisis has not included major runs on commercial bank deposits. To help prevent runs, the FDIC in October

2008 increased its insurance coverage for commercial bank accounts from $100,000 per account to $250,000 per account. At the same time, the Fed took lender-of-last-resort actions to make sure banks had adequate reserves. In fact, bank reserves were increased so much that in February 2009 the U.S. fractional reserve system had more reserves than chequable deposits! There was no multiple destruction of the nation's money supply as had occurred in the 1930s. The problem was simply unwillingness by banks to increase lending in an economic climate in which nearly all loans were perceived as being quite risky.

Luckily, the Canadian economy did not experience defaults on home mortgages anywhere to the same extent as in the U.S. and as a consequence the economic slowdown was less severe. Still, the severe slowdown for our major trading partner tipped the Canadian economy into recession beginning in the last quarter of 2008.

Question

How do mortgage-backed securities work? Why did banks think that selling mortgage-backed securities would relieve them of the risks involved with mortgage lending? How did the banks indirectly come to once again be exposed to mortgage lending risks? What happened to bank reserves during the mortgage debt crisis? How did the Fed respond?

CHAPTER SUMMARY

13.1 ▶ THE MARKET FOR MONEY AND THE DETERMINATION OF INTEREST RATES

- The total demand for money consists of the transactions demand and the asset demand for money. The amount of money demanded for transactions varies directly with the nominal GDP; the amount of money demanded as an asset varies directly with the interest rate. The market for money combines the total demand for money with the money supply to determine equilibrium interest rates.

- Interest rates and bond prices are inversely related.

13.2 ▶ FUNCTIONS OF THE BANK OF CANADA

- The major functions of the Bank of Canada are to (a) be a lender of last resort (bankers' bank) to the chartered banks, (b) supply the economy with paper currency, (c) act as fiscal agent for the federal government, (d) supervise the operations of chartered banks (together with the Department of Finance), and (e) regulate the supply of money.

- The Bank of Canada's major asset is Government of Canada securities. Its three major liabilities are chartered bank reserves, government of Canada deposits, and notes in circulation.

13.3 ▶ GOALS AND TOOLS OF MONETARY POLICY

- The goal of monetary policy is price stability. Full employment and economic growth are secondary objectives that follow directly from price stability.

- In regard to monetary policy, the most important assets of the Bank of Canada are Government of Canada bonds and Treasury bills.

- The two instruments of monetary policy are (a) open-market operations, and (b) the bank rate. The instrument used most often is open-market operations.

13.4 ▶ TARGETING THE OVERNIGHT LENDING RATE

- The overnight lending rate is the interest rate that banks charge one another for overnight loans of reserves. The prime interest rate is the benchmark rate that banks use as a reference rate for a wide range of interest rates on short-term loans to businesses and individuals.

- The Bank of Canada adjusts the overnight rate to a level appropriate for economic conditions. In an expansionary monetary policy, it purchases securities from chartered banks and the general public to inject reserves into the banking system. This lowers the overnight rate to the targeted level and also reduces other interest rates (such as the prime rate). In a restrictive monetary policy, the Bank of Canada sells securities to chartered banks and the general public via open-market operations. Consequently, reserves are removed from the banking system, and the overnight rate and other interest rates rise.

13.5 ▶ MONETARY POLICY, REAL GDP, AND PRICE LEVEL

- Monetary policy operates through a complex cause–effect chain: (a) policy decisions affect chartered bank reserves; (b) changes in reserves affect the supply of money; (c) changes in the money supply alter the interest rate; (d) changes in the interest rate affect investment; (e) changes in investment affect aggregate demand; (f) changes in aggregate demand affect equilibrium real GDP and the price level. Table 13-2 draws together all the basic notions relevant to the use of monetary policy.

- The advantages of monetary policy include its flexibility and political acceptability.

- Today nearly all economists view monetary policy as a significant policy tool.

- In the recent past, the Bank of Canada has adroitly used monetary policy to hold inflation in check as the economy boomed, avoided recession in the economic slowdown of 2001, and hastened economic recovery. The Bank of Canada's policy of *inflation* targeting appears to have been successful, although some critics believe it unnecessarily restricts the central bank's options in smoothing out economic fluctuations.

13.6 ▶ PROBLEMS AND COMPLICATIONS

- Monetary policy has two limitations and potential problems: (a) recognition and operation lags complicate the timing of monetary policy; and (b) in a severe recession, the reluctance by firms to borrow and spend on capital goods may limit the effectiveness of an expansionary monetary policy.

13.7 ▶ MONETARY POLICY AND THE INTERNATIONAL ECONOMY

- The effect of an expansionary monetary policy on domestic GDP is strengthened by the increase in net exports that results from a lower domestic interest rate. Likewise, a tight money policy is strengthened by a decline in net exports. Depending on the situation, there may be a conflict or complementarity between the effect of monetary policy on domestic and international policy goals.

TERMS AND CONCEPTS

STUDY QUESTIONS

LO ▶ 13.1 1. **KEY QUESTION** What is the basic determinant of (a) the transactions demand and (b) the asset demand for money? Explain how these two demands can be combined graphically to determine total money demand. How is the equilibrium interest rate in the money market determined? Use a graph to show the impact of an increase in the total demand for money on the equilibrium interest rate (no change in money supply). Use your general knowledge of equilibrium prices to explain why the previous interest rate is no longer sustainable.

LO ▶ 13.1 2. **KEY QUESTION** Assume that the following data characterize a hypothetical economy: money supply = $200 billion; quantity of money demanded for transactions = $150 billion; quantity of money demanded as an asset = $10 billion at 12 percent interest, increasing by $10 billion for each 2-percentage-point fall in the interest rate.

   a. What is the equilibrium interest rate? Explain.

   b. At the equilibrium interest rate, what are the quantity of money supplied, the total quantity of money demanded, the amount of money demanded for transactions, and the amount of money demanded as an asset?

LO ▶ 13.1 3. **KEY QUESTION** Suppose a bond with no expiration date has a face value of $10,000 and annually pays a fixed amount of interest of $800. (a) Compute and enter in the spaces provided in the table below either the interest rate that the bond would yield to a bond buyer at each of the bond prices listed or the bond price at each of the interest yields shown. (b) What generalization can be drawn from the completed table?

Bond price	Interest rate(s)
$ 8,000	_____
_____	8.9
$10,000	_____
$11,000	_____
_____	6.2

LO ▶ 13.2 4. Use chartered bank and Bank of Canada balance sheets to demonstrate the impact of the following transactions on chartered bank reserves: (a) The Bank of Canada purchases securities from dealers. (b) The Bank of Canada makes an advance to a chartered bank.

LO ▶ 13.3 5. **KEY QUESTION** In the table below you will find simplified consolidated balance sheets for the chartered banking system and the Bank of Canada. Use columns 1 through 3 to indicate how the balance sheets would read after each

transaction in (a) to (c) is completed. Do not accumulate your answers; analyze each transaction separately, starting in each case from the figures provided. All accounts are in billions of dollars.

**Consolidated Balance Sheet:
All chartered banks
(billions of dollars)**

Assets:		(1)	(2)	(3)
Reserves $33		___	___	___
Securities. 60		___	___	___
Loans 60		___	___	___

Liabilities:		(1)	(2)	(3)
Demand deposits $150		___	___	___
Advances from Bank of Canada 3		___	___	___

**Balance Sheet:
Bank of Canada
(billions of dollars)**

Assets:		(1)	(2)	(3)
Securities. $60		___	___	___
Advances to chartered banks. . .3		___	___	___

Liabilities:		(1)	(2)	(3)
Reserves of chartered banks . .$33		___	___	___
Government of Canada deposits. .3		___	___	___
Notes in circulation. 27		___	___	___

   a. A decline in the bank rate prompts chartered banks to borrow an additional $1 billion from the Bank of Canada. Show the new balance-sheet figures in column 1 of each table.

   b. The Bank of Canada sells $3 billion in securities to the public, who pay for the bonds with cheques. Show the new balance sheet figures in column 2 of each table.

   c. The Bank of Canada buys $2 billion in securities from chartered banks. Show the new balance sheet figures in column 3 of each table.

   d. Now review all of these transactions, asking yourself these three questions: (1) What change, if any, took place in the money supply as a direct and immediate result of each transaction? (2) What increase or decrease in chartered banks' reserves took place in each transaction? (3) Assuming a desired reserve ratio of 20 percent, what change in the money-creating potential of the chartered banking system occurred as a result of each transaction?

13.3 6. (a) What is the basic objective of monetary policy? (b) What are the major strengths of monetary policy? (c) Why is monetary policy easier to conduct than fiscal policy in a highly divided national political environment?

13.4 7. (a) Distinguish between the overnight lending rate and the prime interest rate. (b) Why is one higher than the other? (c) Why do changes in the two rates closely track one another?

13.4 8. **KEY QUESTION**   Suppose you are the governor of the Bank of Canada. The economy is experiencing a sharp and prolonged inflationary trend. What changes in (a) open-market operations and (b) the bank rate would you consider? Explain in each case how the change you advocate would affect chartered bank cash reserves and influence the money supply.

9. Suppose that the inflation rate is 2 percent, the overnight lending rate is 4 percent, and real GDP falls 2 percent below potential GDP. According to the Taylor rule, in what direction and by how much should the Bank of Canada change the real overnight lending rate?   **LO 13.4**

10. Explain the links between changes in the nation's money supply, the interest rate, investment spending, aggregate demand, and real GDP (and the price level).   **LO 13.5**

11. (a) What do economists mean when they say that monetary policy can exhibit cyclical asymmetry? (b) Why is this possibility significant to policymakers?   **LO 13.6**

12. (a) What is inflation targeting? (b) What are the main benefits of inflation targeting, according to its supporters? (c) Why do some economists feel it is not needed, or even oppose it?   **LO 13.6**

13. Suppose the Bank of Canada decides to engage in a restrictive monetary policy as a way to close an inflationary gap. (a) Use the aggregate demand–aggregate supply model to show what this policy is intended to accomplish in a closed economy. (b) Now introduce the open economy and explain how changes in the international value of the dollar might affect the location of the aggregate demand curve.   **LO 13.7**

INTERNET APPLICATION QUESTIONS @

1. **Monetary Policy Transmission Mechanism.** Go to the McConnell-Brue-Flynn-Barbiero Web site (Chapter 12) and access the Bank of Canada site, which shows how monetary policy affects the economy. What factors affect the transmission mechanism?

2. **The Bank of Canada's Monetary Policy Report.** Go to the McConnell-Brue-Flynn-Barbiero Web site (Chapter 13) and access the Bank of Canada's Monetary Policy Report. It provides an overview of the performance of the Canadian economy, and the Bank of Canada's monetary policy goals given the economy's performance. What is (are) the current monetary policy goal(s)?

www.mcgrawhillconnect.ca

CHAPTER 14

Financial Economics

Financial economics studies investor preferences and how they affect the trading and pricing of financial assets like stocks, bonds, and real estate. The two most important investor preferences are a desire for high rates of return and a dislike of risk and uncertainty. This chapter will explain how these preferences interact to produce a strong positive relationship between risk and return: the riskier an investment, the higher its rate of return. This positive relationship compensates investors for bearing risk, and is enforced by a powerful set of buying and selling pressures, known as arbitrage, that ensure consistency across investments so that assets with identical levels of risk generate identical rates of return. As we will demonstrate, this consistency makes it extremely difficult for anyone to "beat the market" by finding a set of investments that can generate high rates of return at low levels of risk. Instead, investors are stuck with having to make a tradeoff: If they want higher rates of return, they must accept higher levels of risk. On average, the greater risk results in higher returns—but it can also result in large losses, as it did for investors during the global financial crisis of late 2008 and early 2009.

14.1 | Financial Investment

Financial economics focuses on the investments that individuals and firms make in the wide variety of assets available to them in our modern economy. But before proceeding, it is important to remind you about the difference between economic investment and financial investment.

Economic investment refers either to paying for *new* additions to capital stock, or *new* replacements for capital stock that has worn out. Thus *new* factories, houses, retail stores, construction equipment, and wireless networks are all good examples of economic investments. And so are purchases of office computers to replace computers that have become obsolete as well as purchases of new commercial airplanes to replace planes that have served their useful lives.

In contrast, financial investment is a far broader, much more inclusive concept. It includes economic investment and a whole lot more. **Financial investment** refers to

economic investment
Paying for new additions to the nation's capital stock, or new replacements for capital stock that has worn out.

either buying or building an asset in the expectation of financial gain. It does not distinguish between new assets or old assets. Purchasing an old house or an old factory is just as much a financial investment as purchasing a new house or a new factory. For financial investment, it does not matter if the purchase of an asset adds to the capital stock, replaces the capital stock, or does neither. Investing in old comic books is just as much a financial investment as building a new refinery. Finally, unlike economic investment, financial investment can involve either *financial assets* (such as stocks, bonds, and futures contacts) or *real assets* (such as land, factories, and retail stores).

financial investment
Either buying or building an asset in the expectation that doing so will generate a financial gain.

When bankers, entrepreneurs, corporate executives, retirement planners, and ordinary people use the word "investment," they almost always mean financial investment. In fact, the ordinary meaning of the word investment *is* financial investment. So for this chapter, we will use the word investment in its ordinary sense of "financial investment" rather than in the sense of "economic investment" that is used throughout the rest of this book.

Present Value

present value
The present-day value, or worth, of returns or costs that are expected to arrive in the future.

One of the fundamental ideas in financial economics is **present value**—the present-day value, or worth, of returns or costs that are expected to arrive in the future. The ability to calculate present value is especially useful when investors wish to determine the proper current price to pay for an asset. In fact, the proper current price for any risk-free investment *is* the present value of its expected future returns. And while some adjustments have to be made when determining the proper price of a risky investment, the process is entirely based upon the logic of present value. So we begin our study of finance by explaining present value and how it can be used to price risk-free assets. Then we will turn our attention to risk and how the financial markets determine the prices of risky assets by taking into account investor preferences regarding the tradeoff between potential returns and potential risks.

COMPOUND INTEREST

The best way to understand present value is by first understanding compound interest. *Compound interest* describes how quickly an investment increases in value when interest is paid, or compounded, not only on the original amount invested but also on all interest payments that have been previously made.

To illustrate compound interest in action, Table 14-1 shows the amount of money that $100 invested today becomes if it increases—or compounds—at an 8 percent annual interest rate, i, for various numbers of years. To make things simple, let's express the 8 percent annual interest rate as a decimal: $i = 0.08$. The key to understanding compound interest is to realize that one year's worth of growth at interest rate i will always result in $(1 + i)$ times the amount of money at the end of a year as there was at the beginning of the year. In this case, if the first year begins with $100 and if $i = 0.08$, then $(1 + 0.08)$ or 1.08 times as much money—namely, $108—will be available at the end of the year. Column 2 of Table 14-1 shows the computation for the first year, and column 3 shows the $108 outcome. The same logic applies with other initial amounts. If a year begins with $500, there will be 1.08 times more money after one year, or $540. Algebraically, for any given number of dollars X at the beginning of a particular year, there will be $(1 + i)X$ dollars, or alternatively, $X(1 + i)$ dollars, after one year of growth.

We can use this formula to consider what happens if the initial investment of $100 that grew into $108 after one year continues to grow at 8 percent interest for a second year. The $108 available at the beginning of the second year will grow into an amount of money that is 1.08 times

TABLE 14-1	Compounding: $100 at 8 Percent Interest	
(1) Years of compounding	**(2) Compounding computation**	**(3) Value at year's end**
1	$100 (1.08)	$108.00
2	$100 (1.08)2	116.64
3	$100 (1.08)3	125.97
4	$100 (1.08)4	136.05
5	$100 (1.08)5	146.93
17	$100 (1.08)17	370.00

larger by the end of the second year. That amount, as shown in Table 14-1, is $116.64. Notice that the computation in the table is made by multiplying the initial $100 by $(1.08)^2$. That is because the original $100 is compounded by 1.08 into $108 and then the $108 is again compounded by 1.08. More generally, since the second year begins with $(1 + i)X$ dollars, it will grow to $(1 + i)(1 + i)X = (1 + i)^2X$ dollars by the end of the second year.

Similar reasoning shows that the amount of money at the end of three years has to be $(1 + i)^3X$, since the amount at the beginning of the third year, $(1 + i)^2X$, gets multiplied by $(1 + i)$ to convert it into the amount of money at the end of the third year. In terms of Table 14-1, that amount is $125.97, which is $(1.08)^3$$100.

As you can see, we now have a fixed pattern. The $100 that is invested at the beginning of the first year becomes $(1 + i)$$100 after 1 year, $(1 + i)^2$$100 after 2 years, $(1 + i)^3$$100 after 3 years, and so on. It therefore is clear that the amount of money after t years will be $(1 + i)^t$$100. This pattern always holds true, regardless of the size of the initial investment. So, investors know that if X dollars is invested today and earns compound interest at the rate i, it will grow into exactly $(1 + i)^tX$ dollars after t years. Economists express this fact by writing,

$$X \text{ dollars today} = (1 + i)^tX \text{ dollars in } t \text{ years.} \tag{1}$$

Equation (1) captures the idea that if investors have the opportunity to invest X dollars today at interest rate i, then they have the ability to transform X dollars today into $(1 + i)^tX$ dollars in t years.

But notice that the logic of the equality also works in reverse, so it can also be thought of as showing that $(1 + i)^tX$ dollars in t years can be transformed into X dollars today. That may seem very odd, but it is exactly what happens when people take out loans. For instance, consider a situation where an investor named Roberto takes out a loan for $100 today; the loan will accumulate interest at 8 percent per year for 5 years. Under such an arrangement, the amount Roberto owes will grow with compound interest into $(1.08)^5$$100 = $146.93 in 5 years. This means that Roberto can convert $146.93 in 5 years (the amount required to pay off the loan) into $100 today (the amount he borrows).

Consequently, the compound interest formula given in equation (1) defines not only the rate at which present amounts of money can be converted to future amounts of money. It also allows us to measure the so-called *time value of money*. In the model that follows, we exploit the ability of equation (1) to convert future dollars into present dollars.

THE PRESENT VALUE MODEL

The present value model simply rearranges equation (1) to make it easier to transform future amounts of money into present amounts of money. To derive the formula used to calculate the present value of a future amount of money, we divide both sides of equation (1) by $(1 + i)^t$ to obtain,

$$\frac{X}{(1 + i)^t} \text{ dollars today} = X \text{ dollars in } t \text{ years.} \tag{2}$$

WORKED PROBLEM 14.1
Present Value

The logic of equation (2) is identical to that of equation (1). Both allow investors to convert present amounts of money into future amounts of money, and vice versa. However, equation (2) makes it much more intuitive to convert a given number of dollars in the future into their present-day equivalent. It fact, it says that X dollars in t years converts into exactly $X/(1 + i)^t$ dollars today. This may not seem important, but it is actually very powerful because it allows investors to easily calculate how much they should pay for any given asset.

To see why this is true, understand that an asset's owner obtains the right to receive one or more future payments. If an investor is considering buying an asset, her problem is to try to determine how much she should pay today in order to buy the asset and receive those future payments. Equation (2) makes this task very easy. If she knows how large any given payment will be (X dollars), when it will arrive (in t years), and what the interest rate is (i), then she can apply equation (2) to determine the payment's present value: its value in present-day dollars. If she does this for each future payment the asset in question is expected to make, she will be able to calculate the overall present value of all the asset's future payments by simply summing together the present values of each of the individual payments. This will allow her to determine the price she should pay for the asset. In particular, *the asset's price should exactly equal the total present value of all the asset's future payments.*

As a simple example, suppose Cecilia has the chance to buy an asset that is guaranteed to return a single payment of exactly $370.00 in 17 years. Again let's assume the interest rate is 8 percent per year. Then the present value of that future payment can be determined using equation (2) to equal precisely $370.00/$(1 + 0.08)^{17}$ = $370.00/(1.08)^{17}$ = $100 today. This is confirmed in the row for year 17 in Table 14-1.

To see why Cecilia should be willing to pay a price that is *exactly* equal to the $100 present value of the asset's single future payment of $370.00 in 17 years, consider the following thought experiment. What would happen if she were to invest $100 today in an alternative investment guaranteed to compound her money for 17 years at 8 percent per year? How large would her investment in this alternative become? Equation (1) and Table 14-1 tell us that the answer is exactly $370.00 in 17 years. This is very important because it shows that Cecilia and other investors have two different possible ways of purchasing the right to receive $370.00 in 17 years. They can either purchase the asset, or invest $100 in the alternative.

Because either investment will deliver the same future benefit, the investments are in fact identical. Consequently, they should have identical prices—meaning that each will cost precisely $100 today. A good way to see why this must be the case is by considering how the presence of the alternative investment affects the behaviour of both the potential buyers and the potential sellers of the asset. First, notice that Cecilia and other potential buyers would never pay more than $100 for the asset because they know they could get the same future return of $370.00 in 17 years by investing $100 in the alternative investment. At the same time, people selling the asset would not sell it to Cecilia or other potential buyers for less than $100 since they know that the only other way for Cecilia and other potential buyers to get a future return of $370.00 in 17 years is by paying $100 for the alternative investment. Since Cecilia and the other potential buyers will not pay more than $100 for the asset and its sellers will not accept less than $100, the result will be that the asset and the alternative investment will have the exact same price of $100 today.

QUICK REVIEW

▶ Financial investment refers to buying an asset with the hope of financial gain.

▶ Compound interest is the payment of interest not only on the original amount invested but also on any interest payments previously made; X dollars today growing at interest rate i will become $(1 + i)^t X$ dollars in t years.

▶ The present value formula makes it easy to transform future amounts of money into present-day amounts; X dollars in t years converts into exactly $X/(1 + i)^t$ dollars today.

▶ An investment's proper current price is equal to the sum of the present values of all the future payments it is expected to make.

14.2 | Some Popular Investments

The number and types of financial "instruments" in which one can invest are very numerous, amazingly creative, and highly varied. Most are much more complicated than the investments we used to explain compounding and present value. But, fortunately, all investments share three common features:

• They require that investors pay some price determined in the market to acquire them.

• They give their owners the chance to receive future payments.

• The future payments are typically risky.

These features allow us to treat all assets in a unified way. Three of the more popular investments are stocks, bonds, and mutual funds.

Stocks

stocks
Ownership shares in a corporation.

Recall that **stocks** are ownership shares in a corporation. If an investor owns 1 percent of a corporation's shares, she gets 1 percent of the votes at the shareholder meetings that select the company's managers and she is also entitled to 1 percent of any future profit distributions.

There is no guarantee, however, that a company will be profitable. Firms often lose money and sometimes even go **bankrupt,** meaning that they are unable to make timely payments on their debts. In the event of a bankruptcy, control of a corporation's assets is given to a bankruptcy judge, whose job is to enforce the legal rights of the people who lent the company money by doing what he can to see that they are repaid. Typically, this involves selling off the corporation's assets (factories, real estate holdings, patents, etc.) in order to raise the money necessary to pay off the company's debts. The money raised by selling the assets may be greater than or less than what is needed to fully pay off the firm's debts. If it is more than what is necessary, any remaining money is divided equally among shareholders. If it is less than what is necessary, then the lenders do not get repaid in full and have to suffer a loss.

bankrupt
The situation when individuals or firms are unable to make timely payments on their debts.

A key point, however, is that the maximum amount of money shareholders can lose is what they paid for their shares. If the company goes bankrupt owing more than the value of the firm's assets, shareholders do not have to make up the difference. This **limited liability rule** limits the risks involved in investing in corporations and encourages investors to invest in stocks by capping their potential losses at the amount they paid for their shares.

limited liability rule
Rules that limit the risks involved in investing in corporations by capping their potential losses at the amount they paid for their shares.

When firms are profitable, however, investors can look forward to gaining financially in either or both of two possible ways. The first is through **capital gains,** meaning that they sell their shares in the corporation for more money than they paid for them. The second is by receiving **dividends,** which are equal shares of the corporation's profits. As we will soon explain, a corporation's current share price is determined by the size of the capital gains and dividends that investors expect the corporation to generate in the future.

capital gains
The result from selling shares in a corporation for more money than was paid for them.

dividends
Shares of the corporation's profits.

Bonds

bonds
Debt contracts; most often issued by governments and corporations.

Bonds are debt contracts that are most often issued by governments and corporations. They typically work as follows: An initial investor lends the government or corporation a certain amount of money, say $1000, for a certain period of time, say 10 years. In exchange, the government or corporation promises to make a series of semi-annual payments in addition to returning the $1000 at the end of the 10 years. The semi-annual payments constitute interest on the loan. For instance, the bond agreement may specify that the borrower will pay $30 every six months. This means that the bond will pay $60 per year in payments, which is equivalent to a 6 percent rate of interest on the initial $1000 loan.

The initial investor is free, however, to sell the bond at any time to another investor who then gains the right to receive the remaining semi-annual payments as well as the final $1000 payment when the bond expires after 10 years. As we will soon demonstrate, the price at which the bond will sell to another investor will depend on the current rates of return available on other investments offering a similar stream of future payments and facing a similar level of risk.

default
A failure to make a bond's promised payments.

The primary risk a bondholder faces is the possibility that the corporation or government that issued the bond will **default** on (fail to make) the bond's promised payments. This risk is much greater for corporations, but it also faces municipal and provincial governments in situations where they cannot raise enough tax revenue to make their bond payments, or where it is politically easier to default on bond payments than to reduce spending on other items. The federal government, however, has never defaulted on its bond payments and is very unlikely to ever default for the simple reason that it has the right to print money and can therefore just print whatever money it needs to make its bond payments on time.

Mutual Funds

mutual fund
A company that maintains a professionally managed portfolio, or collection, of stocks or bonds.

portfolio
A collection of investments.

index funds
Mutual funds that choose their portfolios to exactly match a stock or bond index.

actively managed funds
Mutual funds that constantly buy and sell assets in an attempt to generate high returns.

passively managed funds
Mutual funds that exactly match the assets contained in their respective underlying indexes.

percentage rate of return
The percentage gain or loss (relative to the buying price) on stocks or bonds over a given time period, typically a year.

A **mutual fund** is a company that maintains a professionally managed **portfolio,** or collection, of stocks or bonds. The portfolio is purchased by pooling money from many investors. Since these investors provide the money to purchase the portfolio, they own it and any gains or losses generated by the portfolio flow directly to them. Table 14-2 lists the 10 largest Canadian mutual fund companies based on their assets.

Most of the mutual funds currently operating in Canada choose to maintain portfolios that invest in rather specific categories of stocks or bonds. For instance, some fill their portfolios exclusively with the stocks of small tech companies, while others buy only bonds issued by government. In addition there are **index funds,** which choose their portfolios to exactly match a stock or bond index. Indexes follow the performance of a particular group of stocks or bonds in order to gauge how well a particular category of investments is doing. For instance, the S&P/TSX 60 Index contains the 60 largest stocks trading in Canada.

An important distinction must be drawn between actively managed and passively managed mutual funds. **Actively managed funds** have portfolio managers who constantly buy and sell assets in an attempt to generate high returns. By contrast, index funds are **passively managed funds** because the assets in their portfolios are chosen to exactly match whatever stocks or bonds are contained in their respective underlying indexes. In this chapter's Last Word we will discuss the relative merits of actively managed funds and index funds, but for now it should be pointed out that both types are very popular and that, overall, investors had placed $507 billion into mutual funds by the end of 2008. By way of comparison, Canadian GDP in 2008 was about $1.6 trillion.

Calculating Investment Returns

Investors buy assets in order to obtain future payments. The simplest case is purchasing an asset for resale. For instance, an investor may buy a house for $300,000 with the hope of selling it for $360,000 in one year. On the other hand, he could also rent out the house for $3,000 per month and thereby receive a stream of future payments. And he could of course do a little of both, paying $300,000 for the house now in order to rent it out for five years and then sell it. In that case, he is expecting a stream of smaller payments followed by a large one.

Economists have developed a common framework for evaluating the gains or losses of assets that make only one future payment as well as those that make many future payments. This is to state the gain or loss as a **percentage rate of return,** by which they mean the percentage gain or loss (relative to the buying price) over a given period of time, typically a year. For instance, if a person buys a comic book today for $100 and sells it in one year for $125, then she is said to make a 25 percent per year rate of return because she would divide the gain of $25 by the purchase price of $100. By contrast, if she were only able to sell it for $92, then she would be said to have made a loss of 8 percent per year since she would divide the $8 loss by the purchase price of $100.

A similar calculation is made for assets that deliver a series of payments. For instance, an investor who buys a house for $300,000 and expects to rent it out for $3,000 per month would be expecting to make a 12 percent per year rate of return because he would divide his $36,000 per year in rent by the $300,000 purchase price of the house.

The Ten Largest Mutual Fund Companies in Canada, December 2008

TABLE 14-2

Fund company	Assets under management, billions of dollars
RBC Asset Management Inc.	92.5
IGM Financial Inc.	84.2
T.D. Asset Management	47.1
CIBC Asset Management	41.9
Fidelity Investment of Canada Ltd.	32.0
BMO Investment Inc.	29.6
Invesco Trimark Ltd.	28.4
AGF Funds	19.6
Scotia Securities	18.6
Franklin Templeton	17.6

Source: The Investment Funds Institute of Canada, www.ific.ca/

Asset Prices and Rates of Return

A fundamental concept in financial economics is that *an investment's rate of return is inversely related to its price.* That is, the higher the price, the lower the rate of return. To see why this is true, consider a house that is rented out for $2000 per month. If an investor pays $100,000 for the house, he will earn a 24 percent per year rate of return since the $24,000 in annual rent payments will be divided by the $100,000 purchase price of the house. But suppose the purchase price of the house rises to $200,000. In that case, he would earn only a 12 percent per year rate of return since the $24,000 in annual rent payments would be divided by the much larger purchase price of $200,000. Consequently, as the price of the house goes up, the rate of return from renting it out goes down.

The underlying cause of this inverse relationship is the fact that the rent payments are fixed in value, so there is an upper limit to the financial rewards of owning the house. As a result, the more an investor pays for the house, the lower his rate of return will be.

Arbitrage

arbitrage
Occurs when investors try to profit from situations where two identical or nearly identical assets have different rates of return.

Arbitrage happens when investors try to profit from situations where two identical or nearly identical assets have different rates of return. They do so by simultaneously selling the asset with the lower rate of return and buying the asset with the higher rate of return. For instance, consider what would happen in a case where two very similar T-shirt companies start with different rates of return despite the fact that they are equally profitable and have equally good future prospects. For example, suppose a company called T4me starts out with a rate of return of 10 percent per year, while TSTG (T-Shirts to Go) starts out with a rate of return of 15 percent per year.

Since the companies are basically identical and have equally good prospects, investors in T4me will want to shift over to TSTG since it offers higher rates of return for the same amount of risk. As they begin to shift over, however, the prices of the two companies will change—and with them, the rates of return on the two companies. In particular, since so many investors will be selling the shares of the lower-return company, T4me, the supply of its shares trading on the stock market will rise so that its share price will fall. But since asset prices and rates of return are inversely related, this will cause its rate of return to rise.

At the same time, however, the rate of return on the higher-return company, TSTG, will begin to fall. This has to be the case because as investors switch from T4me to TSTG, the increased demand for TSTG's shares will drive up their price. And as the price of TSTG goes up, its rate of return must fall.

The interesting thing is that this arbitrage process will continue—with the rate of return on the higher-return company falling and the rate of return on the lower-return company rising—until both companies have the same rate of return. This convergence must happen because as long as the rates of return on the two companies are not identical, there will always be some investors who want to sell the shares of the lower-return company in order to buy the shares of the higher-return company. As a result, arbitrage will continue until the rates of return are equal.

QUICK REVIEW

▶ Three popular forms of financial investments are stocks (ownership shares in corporations that give their owners a share in any future profits), bonds (debt contracts that promise to pay a fixed series of payments in the future), and mutual funds (pools of investor money used to buy a portfolio of stocks or bonds).

▶ Investment gains or losses are typically expressed as a percentage rate of return: the percentage gain or loss (relative to the investment's purchase price) over a given period of time, typically a year.

▶ Asset prices and percentage rates of return are inversely related.

▶ Arbitrage refers to the buying and selling that takes place to equalize the rates of return on identical or nearly identical assets.

14.3 | Risk and Financial Investments

risk
Refers to the fact that investors never know with certainty what future payments on an asset will be.

Investors purchase assets in order to obtain one or more future payments. As used by financial economists, the word **risk** refers to the fact that investors never know with total certainty what those future payments will turn out to be.

The underlying problem is that the future is uncertain. Many factors affect an investment's future payments and each of these may turn out better or worse than expected. As a simple example, consider buying a farm. Suppose that in an average year the farm will generate a profit of $100,000. But if a freak hail storm damages the crops, the profit will fall to only $60,000. On the other hand, if weather conditions turn out to be perfect, the profit will rise to $120,000. Since there is no way to tell in advance what will happen, investing in the farm is risky.

Risk and Portfolio Diversification

diversification
The strategy of investing in a large number of investments in order to reduce the overall risk to the entire portfolio.

Investors have many options regarding their portfolios. Among other things, they can choose to concentrate their wealth in just one or two investments, or spread it out over a larger number. **Diversification** is the name given to the strategy of investing in a large number of investments in order to reduce the overall risk to the entire portfolio.

The underlying reason why diversification generally succeeds in reducing risk is best summarized by the old saying, "Don't put all your eggs in one basket." If an investor's portfolio consists of only one investment, say one stock, then if anything awful happens to that stock the investor's entire portfolio will suffer greatly. By contrast, if the investor spreads his wealth over many stocks, then a bad outcome for any particular stock will cause only a small amount of damage to the overall portfolio. In addition, it will typically be the case that if something bad is happening to one part of the portfolio, something good will be happening to another part of the portfolio and the two effects will tend to offset each other. Thus, the risk to the overall portfolio is reduced by diversification.

 ORIGIN 14.1
Portfolio
Diversification

It must be stressed, however, that while diversification can reduce a portfolio's risks, it cannot eliminate them entirely. The problem is that even if an investor has placed each of his eggs into a different basket, all of the eggs may still end up broken if all the different baskets somehow happen to get dropped simultaneously. That is, even if an investor has created a well-diversified portfolio, a chance still exists that all the investments may do badly simultaneously. As an example, consider recession: with economic activity declining and consumer spending falling, nearly all companies face reduced sales and lowered profits, a fact that will cause their stock prices to decline simultaneously. Consequently, even if an investor has diversified his portfolio across many different stocks, his overall wealth is likely to decline because nearly all of his many investments will do badly simultaneously.

diversifiable risk
The risk specific to a given investment; can be eliminated by diversification.

Financial economists build on the intuition behind the benefits and limits to diversification to divide an individual investment's overall risk into two components: diversifiable risk and non-diversifiable risk. **Diversifiable risk** (or "idiosyncratic risk") is the risk that is specific to a given investment and that can be eliminated by diversification. For instance, a cola maker faces the risk that the demand for its product may suddenly decline because people will want to drink mineral water instead of cola. But this risk does not matter if an investor has a diversified portfolio that contains stock in both the cola maker as well as stock in a mineral water maker. This is true because when the stock price of the cola maker falls due to the change in consumer preferences, the stock price of the mineral water maker will go up—so that, as far as the overall portfolio is concerned, the two effects will offset each other.

non-diversifiable risk
Risk that pushes all investments in the same direction at the same time; eliminates the possibility of using good effects to offset bad effects.

By contrast, **non-diversifiable risk** (or "systemic risk") pushes all investments in the same direction at the same time so that there is no possibility of using good effects to offset bad effects. The best example of a non-diversifiable risk is the business cycle. If the economy does well, then corporate profits rise and nearly every stock does well. But if the economy does badly, then corporate profits fall and nearly every stock does badly. As a result, even if one were to build a well-diversified portfolio, it would still be affected by the business cycle because nearly every asset contained in the portfolio would move in the same direction at the same time whenever the economy improved or worsened.

The next section shows how investors can measure each asset's level of non-diversifiable risk as well as its potential returns in order to facilitate such comparisons.

Comparing Risky Investments

Economists believe that the two most important factors affecting investment decisions are returns and risk—specifically non-diversifiable risk. But in order for investors to properly compare different investments on the basis of returns and risk, they need ways to measure returns and risk. The two standard measures are, respectively, the average expected rate of return and the beta statistic.

AVERAGE EXPECTED RATE OF RETURN

average expected rate of return
The probability weighted average of an investment's possible future rates of return.

Each investment's **average expected rate of return** is the probability weighted average of the investment's possible future rates of return. The term *probability weighted average* simply means that each of the possible future rates of return is multiplied by its probability expressed as a decimal (so that a 50 percent probability is 0.5 and a 23 percent probability is 0.23) before being added together to obtain the average. For instance, if an investment has a 75 percent probability of generating 11 percent per year and a 25 percent probability of generating 15 percent per year, then its average expected rate of return will be 12 percent = (.75 × 11 percent) + (.25 × 15 percent). By weighting each possible outcome by its probability, this process ensures that the resulting average gives more weight to those outcomes that are more likely to happen (unlike the normal averaging process, which would treat every outcome the same).

Once investors have calculated the average expected rates of return for all the assets they are interested in, there will naturally be some impulse to simply invest in those assets having the highest average expected rates of return. But while this might satisfy investor cravings for higher rates of return, it would not take proper account of the fact that investors dislike risk and uncertainty. To quantify their dislike, investors require a statistic that can measure each investment's risk level.

BETA

beta
A relative measure of non-diversifiable risk; measures the non-diversifiable risk of a given asset or portfolio.

market portfolio
Contains every asset available in a financial market.

One popular statistic that serves this purpose is called beta. **Beta** is a *relative* measure of non-diversifiable risk. It measures how the non-diversifiable risk of a given asset or portfolio of assets compares with that of the **market portfolio,** which is the name given to a portfolio that contains every asset available in the financial markets. The market portfolio is a useful standard of comparison because it is as diversified as possible. In fact, since it contains every possible asset, every possible diversifiable risk will be diversified away—meaning that it will *only* be exposed to non-diversifiable risk. Consequently, it can serve as a useful benchmark against which to measure the levels of non-diversifiable risk to which individual assets are exposed.

Such comparisons are very simple because the beta statistic is standardized such that the market portfolio's level of non-diversifiable risk is set equal to 1.0. Consequently, an asset with *beta = 0.5* has a level of non-diversifiable risk that is one half of that possessed by the market portfolio, while an asset with *beta = 2.0* has twice as much non-diversifiable risk as the market portfolio. In addition, the beta numbers of various assets can also be used to compare them with each other. For instance, an asset with *beta = 2.0* has four times as much exposure to non-diversifiable risk than an asset with *beta = 0.5.*

Another useful feature of beta is that it can be calculated not only for individual assets but also for portfolios. Indeed, it can be calculated for portfolios no matter how many or few assets they contain and no matter what those assets happen to be. This fact is very convenient for mutual fund investors because it means they can use beta to quickly see how the non-diversifiable risk of any given fund's portfolio compares with that of other potential investments they may be considering.

Relationship of Risk and Average Expected Rates

The fact that investors dislike risk has a profound effect on asset prices and average expected rates of return. In particular, their dislike of risk and uncertainty causes investors to pay higher prices for less risky assets and lower prices for more risky assets. But since asset prices and average expected rates of return are inversely related, this implies that less risky assets will have lower average expected rates of return than more risky assets.

Stated differently, risk levels and average expected rates of return are positively related. The more risky an investment is, the higher its average expected rate of return will be. A great way to understand this relationship is to think of higher average expected rates of return as being a form of compensation. Since investors dislike risk, they demand higher levels of compensation the more risky an asset is. The higher levels of compensation come in the form of higher average expected rates of return.

Be sure to note that this phenomenon affects all assets. Regardless of whether the assets are stocks or bonds or real estate or anything else, assets with higher levels of risk always end up with higher average expected rates of return to compensate investors for the higher levels of risk involved.

THE RISK-FREE RATE OF RETURN

We have just shown that there is a positive relationship between risk and returns, with higher returns serving to compensate investors for higher levels of risk. There is, however, one investment that is considered to be risk free for all intents and purposes. That investment is short-term Canadian government bonds.

These bonds are short-term loans to the federal government, with the duration of the loans ranging from three months to one year. They are considered to be essentially risk free because there is almost no chance that the Canadian government will not be able to repay these loans on time and in full. While it is true that the federal government may eventually be destroyed or disabled to such an extent that it will not be able to repay some of its loans, the chances of such a calamity happening within one year are essentially zero. Consequently, because it is a near certainty that the bonds will be repaid in full and on time, they are considered by investors to be risk free.

Since higher levels of risk lead to higher rates of return, a person might be tempted to assume—incorrectly—that since government bonds are risk free, they should earn a zero percent rate of return. The problem with this line of thinking is that it mistakenly assumes that risk is the *only* thing that rates of return compensate for. The truth is that rates of return compensate not only for risk but also for something that economists call time preference.

time preference
The fact that people typically prefer to consume things in the present rather than in the future.

Time preference refers to the fact that because people tend to be impatient, they typically prefer to consume things in the present rather than in the future. Stated more concretely, most people, if given the choice between a piece of their favourite dessert immediately or a piece of their favourite dessert in five years, will choose to consume a piece of their favourite dessert immediately.

This time preference for consuming sooner rather than later affects the financial markets because people want to be compensated for delayed consumption. In particular, if Dave asks Sally to lend him $1 million for one year, he is implicitly asking Sally to delay consumption for a year because if she lends Dave the $1 million, she will not be able to spend that money herself for at least a year. If Sally is like most people and has a preference for spending her $1 million sooner rather than later, the only way Dave will be able to convince Sally to let him borrow $1 million is to offer her some form of compensation. The compensation comes in the form of an interest payment that will allow Sally to consume more in the future than she can now. For instance, Dave can offer to pay Sally $1.1 million in one year in exchange for $1 million today. That is, Sally will get back the $1 million she lends to Dave today as well as an extra $100,000 to compensate her for being patient.

Notice the very important fact that this type of interest payment has nothing to do with risk. It is purely compensation for being patient and must be paid even if there is no risk involved and 100 percent certainty that Dave will fulfill his promise to repay.

14.1 | GLOBAL PERSPECTIVE

Investment risks vary across different countries

The International Country Risk Guide is a monthly publication that attempts to distill the political, economic, and financial risks facing 140 countries into a single "composite risk rating" number for each country, with higher numbers indicating less risk and more safety. The table below presents the January 2008 ranks and rating numbers for 15 countries including the three least risky (ranked 1 through 3) and the three most risky (ranked 138 through 140). Ratings numbers above 80 are considered *very low risk*; 70–80 are considered *low risk*; 60–70 *moderate risk*; 50–60 *high risk*; and below 50 *very high risk*.

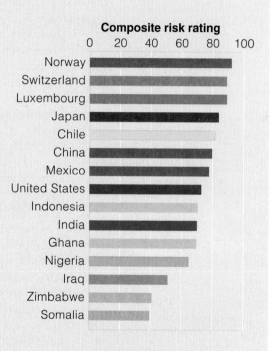

Source: The International Country Risk Guide, January 2008. Published by the PRS (Political Risk Survey) Group, Inc. www.prsgroup.com/icrg/icrg.html. Used with permission of the PRS Group, Inc.

---

risk-free interest rate
A rate of return that does not compensate for risk.

Since short-term federal government bonds are for all intents and purposes completely risk free and 100 percent likely to repay as promised, their rates of return are *purely* compensation for time preference and the fact that people must be compensated for delaying their own consumption opportunities when they lend money to the government. One consequence of this fact is that the rate of return earned by short-term federal government bonds is often referred to as the **risk-free interest rate**, or i^f, to make it clear that the rate of return they generate is not in any way a compensation for risk.

Keep in mind, however, that the Bank of Canada has the power to change the risk-free interest rate generated by short-term federal government bonds. As discussed in Chapter 13, the Bank of Canada can raise or lower the interest rate earned by government bonds by making large purchases or sales of bonds in the bond markets—an activity referred to as open market operations. This means that the Bank of Canada determines the risk-free interest rate and, consequently, the compensation that investors receive for being patient. As we will soon demonstrate, this fact is very important because by manipulating the reward for being patient, the Bank of Canada can affect the rate of return and prices of not only government bonds but all assets.

14.4 | Financial Assets and Non-Diversifiable Risk

Security Market Line
The relationship between average expected rates of return and risk levels that must hold for every asset or portfolio trading in a financial market.

Investors must be compensated both for time preference and for the amount of non-diversifiable risk that an investment carries with it. This section introduces a simple model called the **Security Market Line** that indicates how this compensation is determined for all assets no matter what their respective risk levels happen to be.

The underlying logic of the model is this: any investment's average expected rate of return has to be the sum of two parts—one that compensates for time preference and another that compensates for risk. That is,

Average expected rate of return = rate that compensates for time preference
+ rate that compensates for risk

As we explained above, the compensation for time preference is equal to the risk-free interest rate, i^f, that is paid on government bonds. So, this equation can be simplified as

Average expected rate of return = i^f + Rate that compensates for risk

risk premium
The rate of interest that compensates for risk; depends on the size of the investment's beta.

Finally, because economists typically refer to the rate that compensates for risk as the **risk premium,** this equation can be simplified even further, as

Average expected rate of return = i^f + risk premium

Naturally, the size of the risk premium that compensates for risk will vary depending on how risky an investment happens to be. In particular, it will depend on how big or small the investment's beta is. Investments with large betas and lots of non-diversifiable risk will obviously require larger risk premiums than investments that have small betas and low levels of non-diversifiable risk. And, in the most extreme case, risk-free assets that have betas equal to zero will require no compensation for risk at all since they obviously have no risk to compensate for.

This logic is translated into the graph presented in Figure 14-1. The horizontal axis of Figure 14-1 measures risk levels using beta while the vertical axis measures average expected rates of return. As a result, any investment can be plotted on Figure 14-1 just as long as we know its beta and its average expected rate of return.

We have plotted two investments in Figure 14-1. The first is a risk-free, short-term federal government bond, indicated by the blue dot. The second is the market portfolio, indicated by the red dot. The blue dot marking the position of the risk-free bond is located where it is because it is a risk-free asset having a *beta* = 0 and because its average expected rate of return is given by i^f. These values place the blue dot i^f percentage points up the vertical axis, as shown in Figure 14-1. Note that this

FIGURE 14-1 | The Security Market Line

The SML shows the relationship between average expected rates of return and risk levels that must hold for every asset or portfolio trading in the financial markets. Each investment's average expected rate of return is the sum of the risk-free interest rate that compensates for time preference as well as a risk premium that compensates for the investment's level of risk. The SML's upward slope reflects the fact that investors must be compensated for higher levels of risk with higher average expected rates of return.

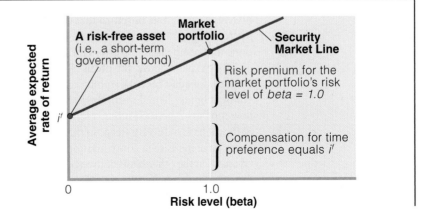

CONSIDER THIS | The Global Financial Crisis and the Stock Market

The special circumstances of the financial markets during the global financial crisis of 2008–09 provide an excellent illustration of both the impact of Bank of Canada actions and the idea of *time-varying risk premium*. The latter is the reality that the premium demanded by investors to take on risk may vary from one period (and one set of economic circumstances) to another period (and a different set of economic circumstances).

The Bank of Canada used expansionary monetary policy during this period to lower interest rates, including rates on short-term government bonds. Because the risk-free interest rate earned by these securities locates the vertical intercept of the Security Market Line (SML), the actual SML for the economy shifted downward from that shown in Figure 14-1. This decline is opposite the upward shift that we illustrate later in the chapter, in Figure 14-4.

But wouldn't we expect stock market prices to rise when the risk-free rate of return falls? That certainly did *not* happen in 2008 and early 2009. Yes, normally stock market prices rise when the risk-free interest rate falls. But during

this unusual period, investors became very fearful about losses from investments in general and began to look for any place of safety. As their appetite for risk decreased, they demanded a much higher rate of compensation for taking on any particular level of risk. In terms of Figure 14-4, the slope of the SML line greatly increased. Thus, between the Bank of Canada's deliberate reduction of the risk-free rate and investors' diminished appetite for risk, two things happened at once to the SML: (1) its intercept (the risk-free rate) dramatically fell, and (2) the SLM line became much steeper. In Figure 14-1, this would be shown by much steeper SLM line emanating from a much lower point on the vertical axis.

The increase in the slope of the SML line, however, overwhelmed the decline in the intercept. Investors sold off stocks, which greatly reduced stock prices, even though the risk-free interest rate fell. By mid-2009, the stock market had recovered most of its losses for the year. It remains to be seen whether we get another bout of selling if the global recession continues.

---

location conveys the logic that because this asset has no risk, its average expected rate of return only has to compensate investors for time preference—which is why its average expected rate of return is equal to precisely i^f and no more.

The market portfolio, by contrast, is risky so that its average expected rate of return must compensate investors not only for time preference but also for the level of risk to which the market portfolio is exposed, which by definition is *beta* = 1.0. This implies that the vertical distance from the horizontal axis to the red dot is equal to the sum of i^f and the market portfolio's risk premium.

The straight line connecting the risk-free asset's blue dot and the market portfolio's red dot is called the Security Market Line, or SML. The SML is extremely important because it defines the relationship between average expected rates of return and risk levels that must hold for all assets and all portfolios trading in the financial, or securities, markets. The SML illustrates the idea that every asset's average expected rate of return is the sum of a rate of return that compensates for time preference and a rate of return that compensates for risk. More specifically, the SML has a vertical intercept equal to the rate of interest earned by short-term federal government bonds and a positive slope that compensates investors for risk.

As we explain above, the precise location of the intercept at any given time is determined by the Bank of Canada's monetary policy and how it affects the rate of return on short-term federal government bonds. The slope of the SML, however, is determined by investor feelings about risk and how much compensation they require for dealing with it. If investors greatly dislike risk, then the SML will have to be very steep, so that any given increase in risk on the horizontal axis will result in a very large increase in compensation as measured by average expected rates of return on the vertical axis. On the other hand, if investors only moderately dislike risk, then the SML will be relatively flat since any given increase in risk on the horizontal axis would require only a moderate increase in compensation as measured by average expected rates of return on the vertical axis.

FIGURE 14-2   Risk Levels Determine Average Expected Rates of Return

The SML can be used to determine an investment's average expected rate of return based on its risk level. In this figure, investments having a risk level of beta = X will have an average expected rate of return of Y percent per year. This average expected rate of return will compensate investors for time preference in addition to providing them exactly the right sized risk premium to compensate them for dealing with a risk level of beta = X.

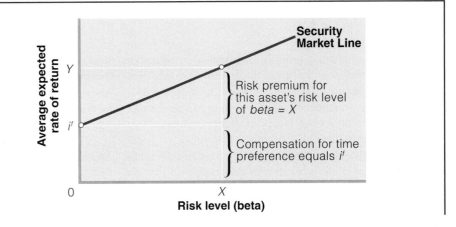

It is important to realize that once investor preferences about risk have determined the slope of the SML and monetary policy has determined its vertical intercept, the SML plots out the precise relationship between risk levels and average expected rates of return *that should hold for every asset.* For instance, consider Figure 14-2, where there is an asset whose risk level on the horizontal axis is beta = X. The SML tells us that every asset with that risk level should have an average expected rate of return equal to Y on the vertical axis. This average expected rate of return exactly compensates for both time preference and the fact that the asset in question is exposed to a risk level of beta = X.

Finally, it should be pointed out that arbitrage will ensure all investments having an identical level of risk will also have an identical rate of return—the return given by the SML. This is illustrated in Figure 14-3, where the three assets A, B, and C all share the same risk level of beta = X, but initially have three different average expected rates of return. Since asset B lies on the SML, it has the average expected rate of return Y that precisely compensates investors for time preference and risk level X. Asset A, however, has a higher average expected rate of return that overcompensates investors while asset B has a lower average expected rate of return that undercompensates investors.

FIGURE 14-3   Arbitrage and the Security Market Line

Arbitrage pressures will tend to move any asset or portfolio that lies off the SML back onto the line. For instance, asset A has an average expected rate of return that exceeds the average expected rate of return, Y, that the SML tells us is necessary to compensate investors for time preference and for dealing with risk level beta = X. As a result, asset A will become very popular and many investors will rush to buy it. This will drive its price up and (because prices and average expected rates of return are inversely related) drive its average expected rate of return down. Arbitrage will continue to happen until point A moves vertically down onto the SML. Arbitrage will also cause asset C, whose average expected rate of return is too low, to move up vertically onto the SML because as investors begin to sell asset C (because its average expected rate of return is too low) its price will fall, thereby raising its average expected rate of return.

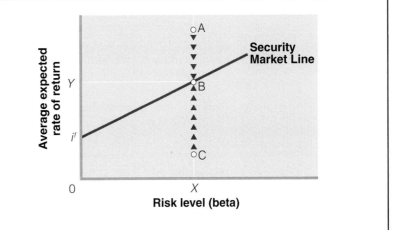

CONSIDER THIS | Does Ethical Investing Increase Returns?

In the last 10 years, ethical investment funds—which invest only in companies and projects consistent with the social and moral preferences of their investors—have become very popular. For instance, some avoid investing in tobacco or oil companies, while others seek to invest in companies that are developing alternative energy sources or companies that promise not to employ child labour in their factories. Some ethical investment funds deliver average rates of return that are better than those generated by ordinary funds that do not select investments based on ethical or moral criteria. This has led some people to conclude that "doing good leads to doing well."

However, this analysis fails to take into account the fact that riskier investments generate higher rates of return.

Indeed, a closer analysis shows that the higher returns generated by many ethical funds appear to be the result of their investing in riskier companies. So while there may be excellent moral reasons for investing in ethical funds, it appears to be the case that ethical investing, by itself, does not generate higher returns.

In fact, it is even possible to imagine a situation in which ethical investing could generate *lower* rates of return. Because of the inverse relationship between asset prices and average expected rates of return, if investors preferred ethical companies they would drive up their prices and thereby lower their rates of return relative to other companies. If that were to happen, then ethical investors might just have to seek solace in the adage "doing good is its own reward."

An Increase in the Risk-Free Rate

We have just explained how the position of the Security Market Line is fixed by two factors. The vertical intercept is set by the risk-free interest rate while the slope is determined by the amount of compensation investors demand for bearing non-diversifiable risk. As a result, changes in either one of these factors can shift the SML and thereby cause large changes in both average expected rates of return and asset prices.

As an example, consider what happens to the SML if the Bank of Canada changes policy and uses open-market operations (described in Chapter 13) to raise the interest rates of short-term government bonds. Since the risk-free interest rate earned by these bonds is also the SML's vertical intercept, an increase in their interest rate will cause the SML's vertical intercept to shift upward, as illustrated in Figure 14-4. This, in turn, causes a parallel upward shift of the SML from SML_1 to SML_2. (The shift is parallel because nothing has happened that would affect the SML's slope, which is determined by the amount of compensation that investors demand for bearing risk.)

Notice what this upward shift implies. Not only does the rate of return on short-term federal government bonds increase when the Bank of Canada changes policy, but the rate of return on risky assets increases as well. For instance, consider asset A that originally has rate of return Y_1. After the SML shifts upward, asset A ends up with the higher rate of return Y_2. There is a simple intuition behind this increase. Risky assets must compete with risk-free assets for investor money. When the Bank of Canada increases the rate of return on risk-free short-term federal government bonds, they become more attractive to investors. But to get the money to buy more risk-free bonds, investors have to sell risky assets. This drives down their prices and—because prices and average expected rates of return are inversely related—causes their average expected rates of return to increase. The result is that asset A moves up vertically in Figure 14-4, its average expected rate of return increasing from Y_1 to Y_2 as investors reallocate their wealth from risky assets like asset A to risk-free bonds.

FIGURE 14·4

An Increase in Risk-Free Interest Rates Causes the SML to Shift Up Vertically

The risk-free interest rate set by the Bank of Canada is the SML's vertical intercept. Consequently, if the Bank of Canada increases the risk-free interest rate, the SML's vertical intercept will shift up. This will cause a parallel upward shift of the SML from SML_1 to SML_2. As a result, the average expected rate of return on all assets will increase. Here, asset A with risk level *beta* = X sees its average expected rate of return rise from Y_1 to Y_2.

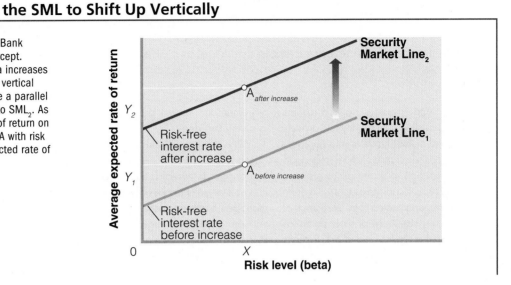

This process explains why investors are so sensitive to Bank of Canada policies. Any increase in the risk-free interest rate leads to a decrease in asset prices that directly reduces investors' wealth. This reduction obviously hurts investors personally but it may also have broader implications. As was pointed out in Chapter 8, the reduction of wealth caused by falling asset prices may lead to a reverse wealth effect, the result of which could be less spending by consumers. Thus, increases in interest rates matter greatly for the economy as a whole. They not only tend to cause direct reductions in investment spending and interest-sensitive consumption spending (the main intent of restrictive monetary policy), but also may reduce aggregate demand indirectly through their impact on asset prices.

The underlying reason why the Bank of Canada has so much power to manipulate asset prices by shifting the SML is because the SML defines all of the investment options available in the financial markets.

The **LAST WORD**   Why Do Index Funds Beat Actively Managed Funds?

Active trading by fund managers in the hope of higher returns rarely succeeds, and often backfires.

Mutual fund investors have a choice between putting their money into actively managed mutual funds or into passively managed index funds. Actively managed funds constantly buy and sell assets in an attempt to build portfolios that will generate average expected rates of return that are higher than those of other portfolios possessing a similar level of risk. In terms of Figure 14-3, they try to construct portfolios similar to point A, which has the same level of risk as portfolio B, but a much higher average expected rate of return. By contrast, the portfolios of index funds simply mimic the assets that are included in their underlying indexes and make no attempt whatsoever to generate higher returns than other portfolios having similar levels of risk.

As a result, it would only seem natural to expect actively managed funds to generate higher rates of return than index funds. Surprisingly, however, the exact opposite actually holds true. Once costs are taken into account, the average returns generated by index funds trounce those generated by actively managed funds by well over 1 percent per year. Now, 1 percent per year may not sound like a lot, but the compound interest formula of equation (1) shows that $10,000 growing for 30 years at 10 percent per year becomes $170,449.40, whereas that same amount of money growing at 11 percent for 30 years becomes $220,892.30. For anyone saving for

retirement, an extra 1 percent per year is a very big deal.

Why do actively managed funds do so much worse than index funds? The answer is twofold. First, arbitrage makes it virtually impossible for actively managed funds to select portfolios that will do any better than index funds that have similar levels of risk. As a result, *before taking costs into account*, actively managed funds and index funds produce very similar returns. Second, actively managed funds charge their investors much higher fees than do passively managed funds, so that, *after taking costs into account*, actively managed funds do worse by about 1 percent per year.

Let us discuss each of these factors in more detail. The reason why actively managed funds cannot do better than index funds before taking costs into account has to do with the power of arbitrage to ensure that investments having equal levels of risk also have equal average expected rates of return. As we explain above with respect to Figure 14-3, assets and portfolios that deviate from the SML are very quickly forced back onto the SML by arbitrage, so that assets and portfolios with equal levels of risk have equal average expected rates of return. This implies that index funds and actively managed funds with equal levels of risk will end up with identical average expected rates of return despite the best efforts

of actively managed funds to produce superior returns.

The reason why actively managed funds charge much higher fees than index funds is because they run up much higher costs while trying to produce superior returns. They not only have to pay large salaries to professional fund managers, but also have to pay for the massive amounts of trading that those managers engage in as they buy and sell assets in their quest to produce superior returns. The costs of running an index fund are, by contrast, very small since changes are made to an index fund's portfolio only on the rare occasions when the fund's underlying index changes. As a result, trading costs are low and there is no need to pay for a professional manager. The overall result is that while the largest and most popular index fund currently charges its investors only 0.18 percent per year for its services, the typical actively managed fund charges over 1.5 percent per year.

So why are actively managed funds still in business? The answer may well be that index funds are boring. Because they are set up to mimic indexes that are in turn designed to show what average performances levels are, index funds are by definition stuck with average rates of return and absolutely no chance to exceed average rates of return. For investors who want to try to beat the average, actively managed funds are the only way to go.

Question

Why is it so hard for actively managed funds to generate higher rates of return than passively managed index funds having similar levels of risk? Is there a simple way for an actively managed fund to increase its average expected rate of return?

CHAPTER SUMMARY

14.1 ▶ FINANCIAL INVESTMENT

- The compound interest formula shows how quickly a given amount of money will grow if interest is paid not only on the amount initially invested but also on any interest payments previously paid. It states that if X dollars is invested today at interest rate i and allowed to grow for t years, it will become $(1 + i)^t X$ dollars in t years.

- The present value model rearranges the compound interest formula to make it easy to determine the present value (number of current dollars) you would have to invest today in order to receive X dollars in t years. The present value formula says that you would have to invest $X/(1 + i)^t$ dollars today at interest rate i in order for it to grow into X dollars in t years.

- A wide variety of financial assets are available to investors, but it is possible to study them under a unified framework because they all share a common characteristic: in exchange for a certain price today, they promise to make one or more payments in the future. A risk-free investment's proper current price is simply equal to the sum of the present values of each of the investment's expected future payments.

14.2 ▶ SOME POPULAR INVESTMENTS

- The three most common and popular investments are stocks, bonds, and mutual funds. Stocks are ownership shares in corporations that give shareholders the right to future profits the corporations may generate. Their primary risk is that future profits are unpredictable and that companies may possibly go bankrupt.

- Bonds are a type of loan contract that give bondholders the right to receive a fixed stream of future payments that serve to repay the loan. They are risky because of the possibility that the corporations or government bodies that issued the bonds may default on them.

- Mutual funds are investment companies that pool the money of many investors in order to buy a portfolio of assets; any returns generated belong to fund investors. Their risks reflect the risks of the stocks and bonds that they hold in their portfolios. Some funds are actively managed, with portfolio managers constantly trying to buy and sell stocks to maximize returns while others are passively managed.

- Investors evaluate the possible future returns to risky projects using average expected rates of return, which give higher weight to outcomes that are more likely to happen.

- Average expected rates of return are inversely related to an asset's current price. When the price goes up, the average expected rate of return goes down.

- Arbitrage is the process whereby investors equalize the average expected rates of return generated by identical or nearly identical assets.

14.3 ▶ RISK AND FINANCIAL INVESTMENTS

- In finance, an asset is risky if its future payments are uncertain. Under this definition of risk, it does not matter whether the payments are big or small, positive or negative, good or bad—only that they are not guaranteed ahead of time.

- Diversification is an investment strategy that seeks to reduce the overall risk facing an investment portfolio by selecting a group of assets whose risks offset—so that when bad things are happening to some of the assets, good things are happening to others. Risks that can be cancelled out by diversification are called diversifiable risks. Risks that cannot be cancelled out by diversification are called non-diversifiable risks. Non-diversifiable risks include things like recessions that affect all investments in the same direction simultaneously so that it is not possible to select assets that offset each other.

- Beta is a statistic that measures the non-diversifiable risk of an asset or portfolio relative to the amount of non-diversifiable risk facing the market portfolio. By definition, the market portfolio has a beta of 1.0, so that if an asset has a beta of 0.5, it has half as much non-diversifiable risk as the market portfolio. Since the market portfolio is the portfolio that contains every asset trading in the financial markets, it is as diversified as possible and consequently has eliminated all of its diversifiable risk—meaning that the only risk to which it is exposed is non-diversifiable risk. Consequently, it is the perfect standard against which to measure levels of non-diversifiable risk.

- Because investors dislike risk, they demand compensation for bearing risk. The compensation comes in the form of higher average expected rates of return. The riskier the asset, the higher its average expected rate of return will be.

- Average expected rates of return must also compensate for time preference and the fact that, other things equal, most people prefer to consume sooner rather than later. The rate of return that compensates for time preference is assumed to be equal to the rate of interest generated by short-term federal government bonds.

14.4 ▶ FINANCIAL ASSETS AND NON-DIVERSIFIABLE RISK

- The Security Market Line (SML) is a straight line that plots how the average expected rates of return on assets and portfolios in the economy must vary with their respective levels of non-diversifiable risk as measured by beta. Arbitrage ensures that every asset in the economy should plot onto the SML. The slope of the SML indicates how much investors dislike risk. If investors greatly dislike risk, then the SML will be very steep, indicating that investors demand a great amount of compensation in terms of higher average expected rates of return for bearing increasingly large amounts of non-diversifiable risk. If investors are more comfortable with risk, then the SML will be flatter, indicating that that they require only moderately higher average expected rates of return to compensate them for higher levels of non-diversifiable risk.

- The SML also takes account of time preference and the fact that investors must be compensated for delaying consumption. Since the compensation for time preference is the risk-free interest rate on short-term federal government bonds that is controlled by the Bank of Canada, the Bank of Canada can shift the entire SML by changing risk-free interest rates and the compensation for time preference that must be paid to investors in all assets regardless of their risk level.

TERMS AND CONCEPTS

economic investment, p. 339
financial investment, p. 339
present value, p. 339
stocks, p. 342
bankrupt, p. 342
limited liability rule, p. 342
capital gains, p. 342
dividends, p. 342
bonds, p. 342
default, p. 342

mutual fund, p. 343
portfolio, p. 343
index funds, p. 343
actively managed funds, p. 343
passively managed funds, p. 343
percentage rate of return, p. 343
arbitrage, p. 344
risk, p. 345
diversification, p. 345

diversifiable risk, p. 345
non-diversifiable risk, p. 345
average expected rate of return, p. 346
beta, p. 346
market portfolio, p. 346
time preference, p. 347
risk-free interest rate, p. 348
Security Market Line, p. 349
risk premium, p. 349

STUDY QUESTIONS

LO 14.1 1. Suppose the province of British Columbia issues bonds to raise money to pay for a new tunnel linking Vancouver and Vancouver Island. Susan buys one of the bonds on the same day that British Columbia pays a contractor for completing the first stage of construction. Is Susan making an economic or a financial investment? What about the province of British Columbia?

LO 14.1 2. Suppose a risk-free investment will make three future payments of $100 in one year, $100 in two years, and $100 in three years. If the Bank of Canada has set the risk-free interest rate at 8 percent, what is the proper current price of this investment? What if the Bank of Canada raises the risk-free interest rate to 10 percent?

LO 14.2 3. How do stocks and bonds differ in terms of the future payments that they are expected to make? Which type of investment (stocks or bonds) is considered to be more risky? Given what you know, which investment (stocks or bonds) do you think commonly goes by the nickname "fixed income"?

LO 14.2 4. Mutual funds are very popular. What do they do? What sorts of different types of mutual funds are there? And why do you think they are so popular with investors?

LO 14.3 5. Consider an asset that costs $120 today. You are going to hold it for one year and then sell it. Suppose there is a 25 percent chance it will be worth $100 in a year, a 25 percent chance it will be worth $115 in a year, and a 50

percent chance it will be worth $140 in a year. What is its average expected rate of return? Next, figure out what the investment's average expected rate of return would be if its current price were $130 today. Does the increase in the current price increase or decrease the asset's average expected rate of return?

6. **KEY QUESTION**   Corporations often distribute profits to their shareholders in the form of dividends, which are simply cheques mailed out to shareholders. Suppose you have the chance to buy a share in a fashion company called Rogue Designs for $35 and that the company will pay dividends of $2 per year on that share every year. What is the annual percentage rate of return? Next, suppose that you and other investors could get a 12 percent per year rate of return by owning the stocks of other very similar fashion companies. If investors only care about rates of return, what should happen to the share price of Rogue Designs? (*Hint:* This is an arbitrage situation.) **LO 14**

7. This question compares two different arbitrage situations. Recall that arbitrage should equalize rates of return; we want to explore what this implies about equalizing prices. In the first situation, there are two assets, A and B, that will both make a single guaranteed payment of $100 in one year. But asset A has a current price of $80, while asset B has a current price of $90. **LO 14.**

a. Which asset has the higher expected rate of return at current prices? Given their rates of return, which asset should investors be buying and which asset should they be selling?

b. Assume that arbitrage continues until A and B have the same expected rate of return. When arbitrage ceases, will A and B have the same price?

Next, consider another pair of assets, C and D. Asset C will make a single payment of $150 in one year, while D will make a single payment of $200 in one year. Assume the current price of C is $120 and the current price of D is $180.

c. Which asset has the higher expected rate of return at current prices? Given their rates of return, which asset should investors be buying and which asset should they be selling?

d. Assume that arbitrage continues until C and D have the same expected rate of return. When arbitrage ceases, will C and D have the same price?

Compare your answers to questions *a* through *d* before answering question *e*.

e. We know that arbitrage will equalize rates of return. Does it also guarantee to equalize prices? In what situations will it also equalize prices?

[LO 14.4] 8. **KEY QUESTION**   Why is it reasonable to ignore diversifiable risk and care only about non-diversifiable risk? What about an investor who puts all of his money into only a single risky stock; can he properly ignore diversifiable risk?

9. **KEY QUESTION**   If we compare the betas of various investment opportunities, why do the assets that have higher betas also have higher average expected rates of return? **[LO 4.4]**

10. Above, we discuss short-term federal government bonds. But the federal government also issues longer-term bonds with horizons of up to 30 years. Why do 20-year bonds issued by the federal government have lower rates of return than 20-year bonds issued by corporations? And which would you consider more likely, that longer-term federal government bonds have a higher interest rate than short-term federal government bonds, or vice versa? Explain. **[LO 14.4]**

11. **KEY QUESTION**   Consider the Security Market Line (SML). What determines its vertical intercept? What determines its slope? And what will happen to an asset's price if it initially plots onto a point above the SML? **[LO 14.3]**

12. Suppose the Bank of Canada wants to increase stock prices. What should it do to interest rates? **[LO 14.3]**

13. Consider another situation involving the SML. Suppose the risk-free interest rate stays the same, but that investors' dislike of risk grows more intense. This will leave the vertical intercept of the SML fixed, but increase the slope of the SML. Given this change, will average expected rates of return rise or fall? Next, compare what will happen to the rates of return on low-risk and high-risk investments. Which will have a larger increase in average expected rates of return, investments with high betas or investments with low betas? And will high-beta or low-beta investments show larger percentage changes in their prices? **[LO 4.4]**

INTERNET APPLICATION QUESTIONS @

1. **Calculating Present Values Using Current Interest Rates.** To see the current interest rates ("yields") on bonds issued by the federal government, go to the McConnell-Brue-Flynn-Barbiero Web site (Chapter 14) to access the Bank of Canada website. What are the current yields on Government of Canada benchmark 2-year bonds and 10-year bonds? Use the current yield for the 2-year note to calculate the present value of an investment that will make a single payment of $95,000 in two years. Use the current yield on the 10-year bond to calculate the present value of an investment that will make a single payment of $95,000 in 30 years. To assist your computations, use the present value calculator located under Investment Calculators at www.timevalue.com/tools.html. Why the difference in present values in the two situations?

2. **Evaluating the Risk Levels of Top Mutual Funds.** The Security Market Line tells us that assets and portfolios that deliver high average expected rates of return should also have high levels of risk as measured by beta. Let us see if this appears to hold true for mutual fund portfolios. To access the Mutual Fund Center at Yahoo Finance, go to the McConnell-Brue-Flynn-Barbiero Web site (Chapter 14), click on Top Performers, and then click on Overall Top Performers. This will give you lists of funds with the 10 best rates of return over various time periods. Click on each of the 10 funds listed under "Top Performers—1 Year" and find each fund's beta listed in the section called Performance and Risk. Do any of the funds have a beta less than 1.0? Do these results make sense given what you have learned? Should you be impressed that funds with risky portfolios generate high returns?

PART 5

The Long Run and Current Issues in Macro Theory and Policy

IN THIS CHAPTER YOU WILL LEARN:

15.1 How the economy arrives at its long-run equilibrium

15.2 How to apply the long-run AD–AS model to explain inflation, recessions, and growth

15.3 About the short-run tradeoff between inflation and unemployment (the Phillips Curve)

15.4 Why there is no long-run tradeoff between inflation and unemployment

15.5 The relationship among tax rates, tax revenues, and aggregate supply

CHAPTER 15

Long-Run Macroeconomic Adjustments

During the early years of the Great Depression, many economists suggested that the economy would correct itself *in the long run* without government intervention. To this line of thinking, economist John Maynard Keynes remarked, "In the long run we are all dead!"

For several decades following the Great Depression, macroeconomists understandably focused on refining fiscal policy and monetary policy to smooth business cycles and address the problems of unemployment and inflation. The main emphasis was on short-run problems and policies associated with the business cycle. But over people's lifetimes, and from generation to generation, the long run is tremendously important for economic well-being. For that reason, macroeconomists have refocused attention on long-run macroeconomic adjustments, processes, and outcomes. The renewed emphasis on the long run has produced significant insights about aggregate supply, economic growth, and economic development. We will also see that it has renewed historical debates over the causes of macroeconomic instability and the effectiveness of stabilization policy.

Our goals in this chapter are to apply the long-run AD–AS model to analyze inflation and recession, examine the inflation–unemployment relationship, and assess the effect of taxes on aggregate supply. The latter is a key concern of so-called *supply-side economics*.

15.1 | From the Short Run to the Long Run

In Chapter 9, we noted that in macroeconomics the difference between the *short run* and the *long run* has to do with the flexibility of input prices. Input prices are inflexible or even totally fixed in the short run but fully flexible in the long run. (By contrast, output prices are assumed under these definitions to be fully flexible in both the short run *and* the long run.) The assumption that input prices are flexible only in the long run leads to large differences in the shape and position of the short-run aggregate supply curve and the long-run aggregate supply curve. As explained in Chapter 9, the short-run aggregate supply curve is an upward-sloping line, whereas the long-run aggregate supply curve is a vertical line situated directly above the economy's full-employment output level, GDP_f.

We will begin this chapter by studying how aggregate supply transitions *from* the short run *to* the long run. Once that is done, we will combine the short-run and long-run aggregate supply curves with the aggregate demand curve to form a single model that gives insight into how the economy adjusts to both economic shocks and changes in monetary and fiscal policy in the short run and the long run. That in turn will lead us to discuss how long-run aggregate supply is affected by economic growth, as well as how inflation and aggregate supply are related in both the short run and the long run. We will conclude with a discussion of economic policies that may help to increase aggregate supply in both the short run and the long run.

Short-Run Aggregate Supply

Our immediate objective is to demonstrate the relationship between short-run aggregate supply and long-run aggregate supply. We begin by briefly reviewing short-run aggregate supply.

Consider the short-run aggregate supply curve AS_1 in Figure 15-1a. This curve AS_1 is based on three assumptions: (1) the initial price level is P_1, (2) nominal wages have been established on the expectation that this price level will persist, and (3) the price level is flexible both upward and downward. Observe from point a_1 that at price level P_1 the economy is operating at its full-employment output GDP_f. This output is the real production forthcoming when the economy is operating at its natural rate of unemployment (or potential output).

Now let's review the short-run effects of changes in the price level, say from P_1 to P_2 in Figure 15-1a. The higher prices associated with P_2 increase revenues to firms, and because the nominal wages the firms are paying their workers and other input prices remain unchanged, profits rise. Responding to the higher profits, firms collectively increase their output from GDP_f to GDP_2; the economy moves from a_1 to a_2 on curve AS_1. At GDP_2 the economy is operating beyond its full-employment output.

FIGURE 15-1   Short-Run and Long-Run Aggregate Supply

Panel (a): In the short run, nominal wages and other input prices do not respond to price-level changes because of the expectation that price level P_1 will continue. An increase in the price level from P_1 to P_2 increases profits and output, moving the economy from a_1 to a_2; a decrease in the price level from P_1 to P_3 reduces profits and real output, moving the economy from a_1 to a_3. The short-run aggregate supply curve therefore slopes upward. Panel (b): In the long run, a price-level rise increases nominal wages and other input prices and thus shifts the short-run aggregate supply curve leftward. Conversely, a decrease in the price level reduces nominal wages and shifts the short-run aggregate supply curve rightward. After such adjustments, the economy reaches equilibrium at points such as b_1 and c_1. Thus, the long-run aggregate supply curve is vertical.

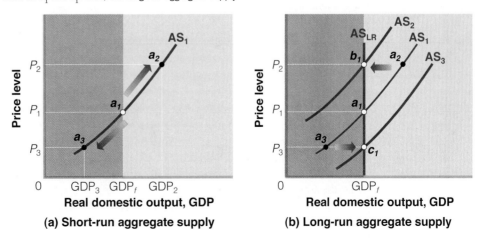

(a) Short-run aggregate supply

(b) Long-run aggregate supply

Firms make this possible by extending the hours of part-time and full-time workers, enticing new workers such as homemakers and retirees into the labour force, and hiring and training the structurally unemployed. Thus, the nation's unemployment rate declines below its natural rate.

How will firms respond when the price level *falls,* say from P_1 to P_3 in Figure 15-1a? Because the prices they receive for their products are lower while the nominal wages they pay workers remain unchanged, firms discover that their revenues and profits have diminished or disappeared. Under these circumstances, firms reduce their employment and production, and, as shown by the movement from a_1 to a_3, real output falls to GDP_3. The decline in real output is accompanied by increased unemployment; at output GDP_3 the unemployment rate is greater than the full employment associated with output GDP_f.

Long-Run Aggregate Supply

The outcomes are different in the long run. To see why, we need to extend the analysis of aggregate supply to account for changes in nominal wages that occur in response to changes in the price level. That will enable us to derive the economy's long-run aggregate supply curve. We illustrate the implications for the aggregate supply curve in Figure 15-1b. Again suppose the economy is initially at point a_1 (P_1 and GDP_f). As we just demonstrated, an increase in the price level from P_1 to P_2 will move the economy from point a_1 to a_2 along the short-run aggregate supply curve AS_1. At a_2, the economy is producing at more than its potential output. This implies very high demand for productive inputs, so that input prices will begin to rise. In particular, the high demand for labour will drive up nominal wages. Because nominal wages are one of the determinants of aggregate supply (refer to Figure 9-6), the short-run supply curve then shifts leftward from AS_1 to AS_2, which now reflects the higher price level P_2 and the new expectation that P_2, not P_1, will continue. The leftward shift in the short-run aggregate supply curve to AS_2 moves the economy from a_2 to b_1. Real output returns to its full-employment level GDP_f, and the unemployment rate returns to its natural rate.

What is the long-run outcome of a *decrease* in the price level? Assuming downward wage flexibility, a decline in the price level from P_1 to P_3 in Figure 15-1b works in the opposite way from a price-level increase. At first the economy moves from point a_1 to a_3 on AS_1. Profits are squeezed or eliminated because prices have fallen and nominal wages have not. But this movement along AS_1 is the short-run response that results only while input prices remain constant. As time passes, input prices will begin to fall because the economy is producing at below its full-employment output level. With so little output being produced, the demand for inputs will be low and their prices will begin to decline. In particular, the low demand for labour will drive down nominal wages. Lower nominal wages shift the short-run aggregate supply curve rightward from AS_1 to AS_3. Real output returns to its full-employment level of GDP_f at point c_1.

By tracing a line between the long-run equilibrium points b_1, a_1, and c_1, we obtain a long-run aggregate supply curve. Observe that it is vertical at the full-employment level of real GDP. After long-run adjustments in nominal wages, real output is GDP_f, regardless of the specific price level. (*Key Question 3*)

Long-Run Equilibrium in the AD–AS Model

Figure 15-2 helps us understand the long-run equilibrium in the AD–AS model, now extended to include the distinction between short-run and long-run aggregate supply. In the short run, equilibrium occurs wherever the downsloping aggregate demand curve and upsloping short-run aggregate supply curve intersect. This can be at any level of output, not simply the full-employment level. Either a negative GDP or a positive GDP gap is possible in the short run.

But in the long run, the short-run aggregate supply curve adjusts as we have just described. After those adjustments, long-run equilibrium occurs where the aggregate demand curve, vertical long-run aggregate supply curve, and short-run aggregate supply curve all intersect. Figure 15-2 shows the long-run outcome. Equilibrium occurs at point a, where AD_1 intersects both AS_{LR} and AS_1, and the economy achieves its full-employment (or potential) output, GDP_f. At long-run equilibrium price level P_1 and output level GDP_f, there is neither a negative GDP gap nor a positive GDP gap.

FIGURE 15·2      **Equilibrium in the Long-Run AD–AS Model**

The long-run equilibrium price level P_1 and level of real output GDP$_f$ occur at the intersection of the aggregate demand curve AD$_1$, the long-run aggregate supply curve AS$_{LR}$ (potential GDP), and the short-run aggregate supply curve AS$_1$.

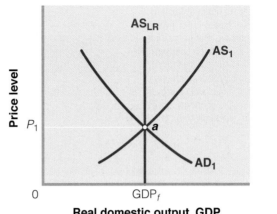

QUICK REVIEW

▶ The short-run aggregate supply curve has a positive slope, because nominal wages and other input prices are fixed while other output prices change.

▶ The long-run aggregate supply curve is vertical, because input prices eventually rise in response to changes in output prices.

▶ The long-run equilibrium GDP and price level occur at the intersection of the aggregate demand curve, the long-run aggregate supply curve, and the short-run aggregate supply curve.

15.2 | Applying the Long-Run AD–AS Model

The long-run AD–AS model helps clarify the long-run aspects of demand-pull inflation, cost-push inflation, and recession.

Demand-Pull Inflation in the Long-Run AD–AS Model

Recall that *demand-pull inflation* occurs when an increase in aggregate demand pulls up the price level. With a long-run aggregate supply, however, an increase in the price level will eventually produce an increase in nominal wages and thus a leftward shift of the short-run aggregate supply curve. This is shown in Figure 15-3, where we initially suppose the price level is P_1 at the intersection of aggregate demand curve AD$_1$, short-run supply curve AS$_1$, and long-run aggregate supply curve AS$_{LR}$. Observe that the economy is achieving its full-employment real output GDP$_f$ at point *a*.

Now consider the effects of an increase in aggregate demand as represented by the rightward shift from AD$_1$ to AD$_2$. This shift can result from any one of a number of factors, including an increase in investment spending or a rise in net exports. Whatever its cause, the increase in aggregate demand boosts the price level from P_1 to P_2 and expands real output from GDP$_f$ to GDP$_2$ at point *b*.

So far, none of this is new to you. But now we want to emphasize the distinction between short-run and long-run aggregate supply. With the economy producing above potential output, inputs will be in high demand. Input prices including nominal wages will rise. As they do, the short-run aggregate supply curve will eventually shift leftward until it intersects long-run aggregate supply at point *c*.[1] There, the economy has re-established long-run equilibrium, with the

| FIGURE 15-3 | Demand-Pull Inflation in the Long-Run AD–AS Model |

An increase in aggregate demand from AD$_1$ to AD$_2$ drives up the price level and increases real output in the short run. But in the long run, nominal wages rise and the short-run aggregate supply curve shifts leftward, as from AS$_1$ to AS$_2$. Real output then returns to its prior level, and the price level rises even more. In this scenario, the economy moves from a to b and then eventually to c.

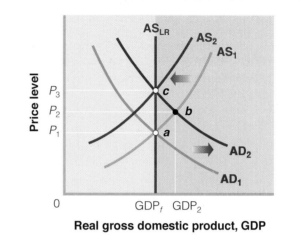

Real gross domestic product, GDP

price level and real output now P_3 and GDP$_0$ respectively. Only at point c does the new aggregate demand curve AD$_2$ intersect both the short-run aggregate supply curve AS$_2$ and the long-run aggregate supply curve AS$_{LR}$.

In the short run, demand-pull inflation drives up the price level and increases real output; in the long run, only the price level rises. In the long run, the initial increase in aggregate demand has moved the economy *along* its vertical aggregate supply curve AS$_{LR}$. For a while, an economy can operate beyond its full-employment level of output. But the demand-pull inflation eventually causes adjustments of nominal wages that move the economy back to its full-employment output GDP$_f$.

Cost-Push Inflation in the Long-Run AD–AS Model

Cost-push inflation arises from factors that increase the cost of production at each price level—that is, factors that shift the aggregate supply curve leftward—and therefore increase the price level. But in our previous analysis we considered only short-run aggregate supply. We now want to examine cost-push inflation in its long-run context.

ANALYSIS

Look at Figure 15-4, in which we again assume the economy is initially operating at price level P_1 and output level GDP$_f$ (point a). Suppose that international oil producers get together and boost the price of oil by, say, 100 percent. As a result, the per-unit production cost of producing and transporting goods and services rises substantially in the economy represented by Figure 15-4. The increase in per-unit production cost shifts the short-run aggregate supply curve to the left, as from AS$_1$ to AS$_2$, and the price level rises from P_1 to P_2 (as seen by comparing points a and b). In this case, the leftward shift of the aggregate supply curve is not a *response* to a price-level increase, as it was in our previous discussions of demand-pull inflation; it is the initiating *cause* of the price-level increase.

---

[1] We say "eventually" because the initial leftward shift in short-run aggregate supply will intersect the long-run aggregate supply curve AS$_{LR}$ at price level P_2 (review Figure 15-1). But the intersection of AD$_2$ and this new short-run aggregate supply curve (that is not shown in Figure 15-3) will produce a price level above P_2. (You may want to pencil this in to make sure you understand this point.) Again nominal wages will rise, shifting the short-run aggregate supply curve farther leftward. The process will continue until the economy moves to point c, where the short-run aggregate supply curve is AS$_2$, the price level is P_3, and real output is GDP$_f$.

| **FIGURE 15-4** | **Cost-Push Inflation in the Long-Run AD–AS Model** |

Cost-push inflation occurs when the short-run aggregate supply curve shifts leftward, as from AS_1 to AS_2. If government counters the decline in real output by increasing aggregate demand to the broken line, the price level rises even more. That is, the economy moves in steps from *a* to *b* to *c*. In contrast, if government allows a recession to occur, nominal wages eventually fall and the aggregate supply curve shifts back rightward to its original location. The economy moves from *a* to *b* and then eventually back to *a*.

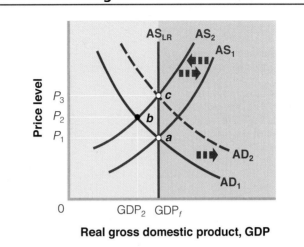

Real gross domestic product, GDP

By far the most controversial application of the long-run AD-AS model is to recession.

POLICY DILEMMA

Cost-push inflation creates a dilemma for policymakers. Without expansionary stabilization policy, aggregate demand in Figure 15-4 remains at AD_1—the curve does not shift—and real output declines from GDP_f to GDP_2. Government can counter this recession and the attendant rise in unemployment by using fiscal policy and/or monetary policy to increase aggregate demand to AD_2. But there is a potential policy trap here: An increase in aggregate demand to AD_2 will further increase inflation by increasing the price level from P_2 to P_3 (a move from point *b* to point *c*).

Suppose government recognizes this policy trap and decides *not* to increase aggregate demand from AD_1 to AD_2 (so you can now disregard the dashed AD_2 curve). Instead, it implicitly decides to allow a cost-push-created recession to run its course. How will that happen? Widespread layoffs, plant shutdowns, and business failures eventually occur. At some point the demands for oil, labour, and other inputs fall such that oil prices and nominal wages decline. When that happens, the initial leftward shift of the short-run aggregate supply curve is undone. In time the recession will shift the short-run aggregate supply curve rightward from AS_2 to AS_1. The price level will return to P_1, and the full-employment level of output will be restored at GDP_f (point *a* on the long-run aggregate supply curve AS_{LR}).

This analysis yields two generalizations:

- If government attempts to maintain full employment when there is cost-push inflation, even more inflation will occur.

- If government takes a hands-off approach to cost-push inflation, the recession will linger. Although falling input prices will eventually undo the initial rise in per-unit production costs, the economy in the meantime will experience high unemployment and a loss of real output.

Recession and the Long-Run AD–AS Model

By far the most controversial application of the long-run AD–AS model is to recession. We look at this controversy in detail in Internet Chapter 15W; here we simply want to present the model and identify the key point of contention.

Suppose in Figure 15-5 that aggregate demand initially is AD_1 and that short-run and long-run aggregate supply curves are AS_1 and AS_{LR}, respectively. Therefore, as shown by point *a*, the price level is P_1 and output is GDP_f. Now suppose that investment spending dramatically declines, reducing aggregate demand to AD_2. Real output declines from GDP_f to GDP_1, indicating a recession has

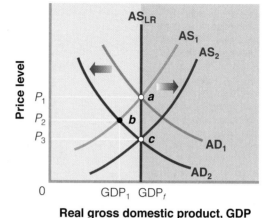

FIGURE 15-5   **Recession in the Long-Run AD–AS Model**

A recession occurs when aggregate demand shifts leftward, as from AD_1 to AD_2. If prices and wages are downwardly flexible, the price level falls from P_1 to P_2. This decline in the price level eventually reduces nominal wages, which in turn shift the aggregate supply curve from AS_1 to AS_2. The price level declines to P_3, and output increases back to GDP_f. The economy moves from a to b and then eventually to c.

occurred. But if we make the assumption that prices and wages are flexible downward, the price level falls from P_1 to P_2. With the economy producing below potential output at point b, demand for inputs will be low. Eventually, nominal wages themselves fall to restore the previous real wage; when this happens, the short-run aggregate supply curve shifts rightward from AS_1 to AS_2. The negative GDP gap evaporates without expansionary fiscal or monetary policy, since real output expands from GDP_1 (point b) back to GDP_f (point c). The economy is again located on its long-run aggregate supply curve AS_{LR}, but now at lower price level P_3.

There is disagreement among economists about this hypothetical scenario. The key point of dispute revolves around the degree to which both input and output prices may be downwardly inflexible and how long it would take in the real world for the necessary price and wage adjustments to occur to regain the full-employment level of output. Most economists believe that such adjustments are forthcoming, but will occur only after the economy has experienced a relatively long-lasting recession with its accompanying rise in unemployment and a loss of output. Therefore, economists recommend active monetary policy, and perhaps fiscal policy, to counteract recessions. (*Key Question 4*)

CONSIDER THIS | Deep Recession and Policy Intervention

In early 2009 it appeared the Canadian economy was entering a possible deep recession. A long-lasting and deep recession places downward pressure on wages and other input prices. Eventually these declines will shift the short-run aggregate supply curve to the right, as from AS_1 to AS_2 in Figure 15-5. In theory, the price level therefore will fall (deflation will occur) as the economy moves along AD_2 from a recessionary point like b to a point like c. At the lower price level more real output will be demanded, which means real GDP will "self-correct" back to potential output and full employment. But, most economists believe this process will

be excruciatingly slow and extremely costly in terms of lost output. Also, uncertain "wait-it-out" solutions to serious economic problems are often not politically viable. Most economists therefore support active monetary and fiscal policy to try to restore full-employment output via rightward shifts of the aggregate demand curve. In accordance with this generally held stance, the Bank of Canada reduced the target overnight lending rate 4¼ percent between December 2007 and April 2009 in an effort to stimulate aggregate demand. The federal government also committed itself to an expansionary fiscal policy to the same end.

Ongoing Inflation in the Long-Run AD–AS Model

In our analysis so far, we have seen how demand and supply shocks can cause, respectively, demand-pull inflation and cost-push inflation. But in all the cases we have analyzed, the extent of the inflation was *finite* because the size of the initial movement in either the AD curve or the AS curve was *limited*. For instance, in Figure 15-3 the aggregate demand curve shifts right by a limited amount, from AD_1 to AD_2. As the economy's equilibrium moves from *a* to *b* to *c*, the price level rises from P_1 to P_3. During this transition, inflation obviously occurs since the price level is rising. But once the economy reaches its new equilibrium at point *c*, the price level remains constant at P_3 and there is no further inflation. That is, the limited initial movement in aggregate demand has caused a limited amount of inflation that will come to a stop.

This fact is crucial to understanding why modern economies tend to experience positive rates of inflation. Simply put, there must be ongoing shifts in either the aggregate demand or aggregate supply curves since any single, finite shift in either curve will cause an inflation of only limited duration. In this section we explore this idea, pointing out two facts. First, ongoing economic growth causes continuous rightward shifts of the aggregate supply curve which, by themselves, would tend to cause an ongoing deflation. Second, at the same time central banks engineer ongoing increases in the money supply in order to cause slightly faster continuous rightward shifts of the aggregate demand curve. Taken alone, these rightward shifts in aggregate demand are inflationary. And because the central banks cause the inflationary rightward shifts of the aggregate demand curve to proceed just a little faster than the deflationary rightward shifts of the aggregate supply curve that are caused by economic growth, the net effect is (usually) a small positive rate of inflation. (We say "usually" because unexpected shocks to either aggregate demand or aggregate supply may cause inflation to be either a bit higher or a bit lower than the small positive rate that the central bank is attempting to engineer.)

ECONOMIC GROWTH AND AGGREGATE SUPPLY

As discussed in Chapter 6, economic growth is driven by supply factors such as improved technologies and access to more or better resources. Economic growth can be illustrated either as an outward shift of an economy's production possibilities curve or as a rightward shift of its long-run aggregate supply curve. As shown in Figure 15-6, the outward shift of the production possibilities curve from

---

FIGURE 15-6 **Production Possibilities and Long-Run Aggregate Supply**

Panel (a): Economic growth driven by supply factors (such as improved technologies or the use of more or better resources) shift an economy's production possibilities curve outward, as from *AB* to *CD*. Panel (b): Those same factors shift the economy's long-run aggregate supply curve to the right, as from AS_{LR1} to AS_{LR2}.

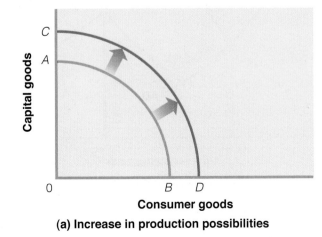

(a) Increase in production possibilities

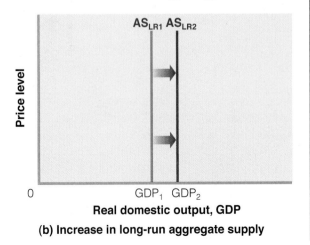

(b) Increase in long-run aggregate supply

AB to *CD* in graph (a) is equivalent to the rightward shift of the economy's long-run aggregate supply curve from AS_{LR1} to AS_{LR2} in Figure 15-6b.

LONG-RUN AD–AS MODEL

In Figure 15-7 we use the long-run AD–AS model to depict economic growth in Canada. Suppose the economy's aggregate demand curve, long-run aggregate supply curve, and short-run aggregate supply curve initially are AD_1, AS_{LR1}, and AS_1, as shown. The equilibrium price level and level of real output are P_1 and GDP_1. Now let's assume that economic growth driven by changes in the supply factors (quantity and quality of resources and technology) shift the long-run aggregate supply curve rightward from AS_{LR1} to AS_{LR2}. The economy's potential output has increased, as reflected by the expansion of available real output from GDP_1 to GDP_2.

With no change in aggregate demand, the increase in long-run aggregate supply from AS_{LR1} to AS_{LR2} in Figure 15-7 would expand real GDP and lower the price level. Put plainly, economic growth is deflationary, other things equal. But declines in the price level are not part of Canada's growth experience. The reason? The Bank of Canada has expanded the nation's money supply over the years such that increases in aggregate demand have more than matched increases in aggregate supply. We show this as the shift from AD_1 to AD_2.

The increases of aggregate supply and aggregate demand in Figure 15-7 have increased real output from GDP_1 to GDP_2 and have boosted the price level from P_1 to P_2. At the higher price level P_2, the economy confronts a new short-run aggregate supply curve AS_2. The changes described in Figure 15-7 describe the actual experience in Canada: economic growth, accompanied by mild inflation.

In brief, economic growth causes increases in long-run aggregate supply. Whether deflation, zero inflation, mild inflation, or rapid inflation accompanies growth depends on the extent to which aggregate demand increases relative to aggregate supply. Any inflation that occurs is the result of the growth of aggregate demand. It is not the result of the growth of real GDP. *(Key Question 5)*

FIGURE 15-7 **Depicting Canadian Growth in the Long-Run AD–AS Model**

Long-run and short-run aggregate supply have increased over time, as from AS_{LR1} to AS_{LR2} and AS_1 to AS_2. Simultaneously, aggregate demand has shifted rightward, as from AD_1 to AD_2. The actual outcome of these combined shifts has been economic growth, shown as the increase in real output from GDP_1 to GDP_2, accompanied by inflation, shown as the rise in the price level from P_1 to P_2.

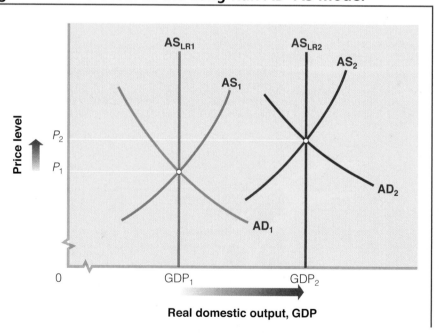

15.3 | The Inflation–Unemployment Relationship

INFLATION–UNEMPLOYMENT TRADEOFF

We have just seen that the Bank of Canada can determine how much inflation occurs in the economy by how much it causes aggregate demand to shift relative to aggregate supply. Given that low inflation and low unemployment rates are the Bank of Canada's major economic goals, its ability to control inflation brings up at least two interesting policy questions. Are low unemployment and low inflation compatible goals or conflicting goals? What explains situations in which high unemployment and high inflation coexist?

The long-run AD–AS model supports three significant generalizations relating to these questions:

- Under normal circumstances, there is a short-run tradeoff between the rate of inflation and the rate of unemployment.

- Aggregate supply shocks can cause both higher rates of inflation and higher rates of unemployment.

- There is no significant tradeoff between inflation and unemployment over long periods of time.

The first two generalizations are taken up in this section, and the third generalization is discussed in the next section.

ORIGIN 15.1
Phillips Curve

Phillips Curve
A curve showing the relationship between the unemployment rate and the annual rate of increase in the price level.

Short-Run Tradeoff

We can demonstrate the short-run tradeoff between the rate of inflation and the rate of unemployment through the **Phillips Curve,** named after A. W. Phillips, who developed the idea in Great Britain. This curve, generalized later in Figure 15-8a, suggests an inverse relationship between the rate of inflation and the rate of unemployment. Lower unemployment rates (measured as leftward movements on the horizontal axis) are associated with higher rates of inflation (measured as upward movements on the vertical axis).

The underlying rationale of the Phillips Curve becomes apparent when we view the short-run aggregate supply curve in Figure 15-9 and perform a simple mental experiment. Suppose that in some short-run period aggregate demand expands from AD_0 to AD_2, either because firms decided to buy more capital goods or the government decided to increase its expenditures. Whatever the cause, in the short run the economy experiences inflationary pressures. The price level thus rises from P_0 to P_2 and real output rises from GDP_0 to GDP_2. As real output rises, the unemployment rate falls.

Now let's compare what would have happened if the increase in aggregate demand had been larger, say from AD_0 to AD_3. The new equilibrium tells us that the price level and the growth of real output would both have been greater (and that the unemployment rate would have been lower).

FIGURE 15-8 — The Phillips Curve: Concept and Canadian Empirical Data

Panel (a): The Phillips Curve relates annual rates of inflation and annual rates of unemployment for a series of years. Because this is an inverse relationship, there presumably is a tradeoff between unemployment and inflation. Panel (b): Data points for the 1960s seemed to confirm the Phillips Curve concept.

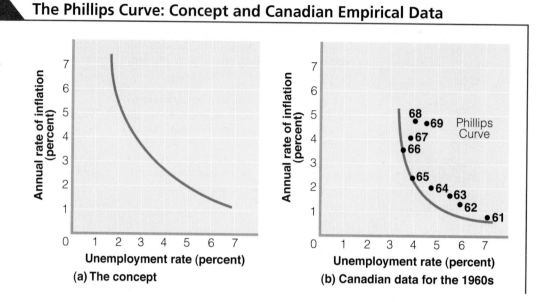

(a) The concept

(b) Canadian data for the 1960s

Similarly, suppose aggregate demand during the year had increased only modestly, from AD_0 to AD_1. Compared with our shift from AD_0 to AD_2, the amount of inflation and the growth of real output would have been smaller (and the unemployment rate higher).

The generalization we draw from this mental experiment is this: *Assuming a constant short-run aggregate supply curve,* high rates of inflation are accompanied by low rates of unemployment, and low rates of inflation are accompanied by high rates of unemployment. Other things equal, the expected relationship should look something like Figure 15-8a.

Figure 15-8b reveals that for Canada the facts for the 1960s nicely fit the theory. On the basis of that evidence and evidence from other countries, most economists working at the end of 1960s concluded there was a stable, predictable tradeoff between unemployment and inflation. Moreover, Canadian economic policy was built on that supposed tradeoff. According to this thinking, it was impossible to achieve "full employment without inflation": Manipulation of aggregate demand through fiscal and monetary measures would simply move the economy along the Phillips Curve. An expansionary fiscal and monetary policy that boosted aggregate demand and lowered the unemployment rate

FIGURE 15-9 — The Short-Run Effect of Changes in Aggregate Demand on Real Output and the Price Level

Comparing the effects of various possible increases in aggregate demand leads to the conclusion that the larger the increase in aggregate demand, the higher the rate of inflation and the greater the increase in real output. Because real output and the unemployment rate move in opposite directions, we can generalize that, given short-run aggregate supply, high rates of inflation should be accompanied by low rates of unemployment.

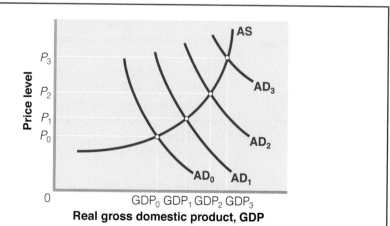

would simultaneously increase inflation. Society had to choose between the incompatible goals of price stability and full employment; it had to decide where to locate on its Phillips Curve.

For reasons we will soon see, many of today's economists reject the idea of a stable, predictable Phillips Curve. Nevertheless, they agree there is a short-run tradeoff between unemployment and inflation. *Given short-run aggregate supply,* increases in aggregate demand boost real output and reduce the unemployment rate. As the unemployment rate falls and dips below the natural rate, the excessive spending produces demand-pull inflation. Conversely, when recessions set in and the unemployment rate increases, the weak aggregate demand that caused the recession also leads to lower inflation rates. For example, from April 2008 to May 2009 the unemployment rate increased from 6 percent to 8.4 percent, but over the same time period the Consumer Price Index increased only 0.4 percent, compared to over 2 percent previously.

Aggregate Supply Shocks and the Phillips Curve

The unemployment–inflation experience of the 1970s and early 1980s demolished the idea of an always-stable Phillips Curve. In Figure 15-10 we show the Phillips Curve for the 1960s in green and then add the data points for 1970 through 2008. Observe that in most of the years of the 1970s and early 1980s the economy experienced both higher inflation rates and higher unemployment rates than in the 1960s. In fact, inflation and unemployment rose simultaneously in some of those years. This latter condition is called **stagflation**—a term that combines the words "stagnation" and "inflation." If a Phillips Curve existed it had clearly shifted outward, perhaps as shown.

ADVERSE AGGREGATE SUPPLY SHOCKS

The Phillips data points for the 1970s and early 1980s support our second generalization: *Aggregate supply shocks can cause both higher rates of inflation and higher rates of unemployment.* A series of

stagflation
Simultaneous increases in the price level and the unemployment rate.

FIGURE 15-10   **Inflation Rates and Unemployment Rates in Canada, 1961–2008**

A series of aggregate supply shocks in the 1970s resulted in higher rates of inflation and higher rates of unemployment. So, data points for the 1970s and 1980s tended to be above and to the right of the Phillips Curve for the 1960s. In the 1990s the inflation-unemployment data points slowly moved back toward the original Phillips Curve. Points for the late 1990s and 2000s are closer to those from the earlier era. (*Note:* Inflation rates are on a December-to-December basis.)

SOURCE: Statistics Canada. For inflation see: http//www40.statcan.ca/l01/cst01/econ163a-eng.htm. For unemployment see: http://www.40.statcan.ca/l01/cst01/econ10-eng.htm. Accessed May 21, 2009.

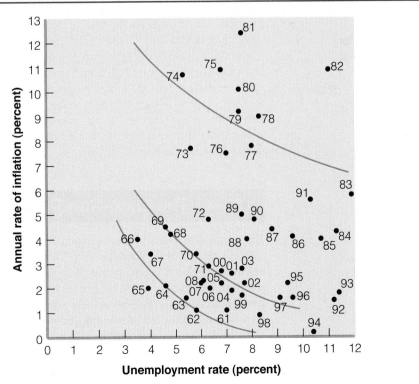

aggregate supply shocks
Sudden, large changes in resource costs that shift an economy's aggregate supply curve.

adverse **aggregate supply shocks**—sudden, large increases in resource costs that jolt an economy's short-run aggregate supply curve leftward—hit the economy in the 1970s and early 1980s. The most significant of these shocks was a quadrupling of oil prices by the Organization of the Petroleum Exporting Countries (OPEC). Consequently, the cost of producing and distributing virtually every product and service rose rapidly.

These shocks shifted the aggregate supply curve to the left and distorted the usual inflation–unemployment relationship. Recall that we derived the inverse relationship between the rate of inflation and the unemployment rate shown in Figure 15-8a by shifting the aggregate demand curve along a stable short-run aggregate supply curve (Figure 15-9). But the cost-push inflation model shown in Figure 15-4 tells us that a *leftward shift* of the short-run aggregate supply curve increases the price level and reduces real output (and increases the unemployment rate). This, say most economists, is what happened in two periods in the 1970s. The unemployment rate shot up from 5.6 percent in 1973 to 8.0 percent in 1977, contributing to a significant decline in real GDP. In the same period, the price level rose by over 40 percent. The stagflation scenario recurred in 1978, when OPEC increased oil prices by more than 100 percent. The Canadian price level rose by 50 percent over the 1978–82 period, while unemployment increased from 8.3 to 11.0 percent.

STAGFLATION'S DEMISE

Another look at Figure 15-10 reveals a generally inward movement of the inflation–unemployment points between 1983 and 1989. By 1989 the lingering effects of the earlier period had subsided. One precursor to this favourable trend was the deep recession of 1981–82, largely caused by a restrictive money policy aimed at reducing inflation. The recession increased the unemployment rate to 11.9 percent in 1983. With so many workers unemployed, those who were working accepted smaller increases in their nominal wages—or in some cases wage reductions—to preserve their jobs. Firms in turn restrained their price increases to try to retain their relative shares of a diminished market.

Other factors were at work. Foreign competition throughout this period held down wage and price hikes in several basic industries such as automobiles and steel. Deregulation of the airline and trucking industries also resulted in wage reductions or so-called "wage givebacks." A significant decline in OPEC's monopoly power and a greatly reduced reliance on oil in the production process produced a stunning fall in the price of oil and its derivative products, such as gasoline.

All these factors combined to reduce per-unit production costs and to shift the short-run aggregate supply curve rightward (as from AS_2 to AS_1 in Figure 15-4). Employment and output expanded and the unemployment rate fell from 11 percent in 1983 to 7.6 percent in 1989. Figure 15-10 reveals that the inflation–unemployment points for recent years are closer to the points associated with the Phillips Curve of the 1960s than to the points in the late 1970s and early 1980s. The points for 1999–2008, in fact, are close to points on the 1960s curve. (The low inflation and relatively low unemployment rates in this later period produced a lower value of the so-called *misery index,* as shown in Global Perspective 15.1.)

15.4 | The Long-Run Phillips Curve

The overall set of data points in Figure 15-10 points to our third generalization relating to the inflation–unemployment relationship: There is no apparent *long-run* tradeoff between inflation and unemployment. When decades as opposed to a few years are considered, any rate of inflation is consistent with the natural rate of unemployment prevailing at that time. We know from Chapter 6 that the natural rate of unemployment is the rate of unemployment that occurs when cyclical unemployment is zero; it is the rate of unemployment when the economy achieves its potential output.

How can there be a short-run inflation–unemployment tradeoff but not a long-run tradeoff? Figure 15-11 provides the answer.

15.1 | GLOBAL PERSPECTIVE

The misery index, selected nations, 1997–2007

The misery index adds together a nation's unemployment rate and its inflation rate to get a measure of national economic discomfort. For example, a nation with a 5 percent rate of unemployment and a 5 percent inflation rate would have a misery index number of 10, as would a nation with an 8 percent unemployment rate and a 2 percent inflation rate.

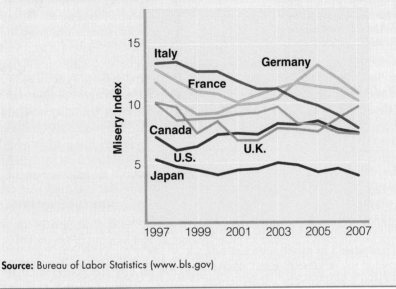

Source: Bureau of Labor Statistics (www.bls.gov)

The Short-Run Phillips Curve

Consider Phillips Curve PC_1 in Figure 15-11. Suppose the economy initially is experiencing a 3 percent rate of inflation and a 5 percent natural rate of unemployment. Such short-term curves as PC_1, PC_2, and PC_3 (drawn as straight lines for simplicity) exist because the actual rate of inflation is not always the same as the expected rate.

Establishing an additional point on Phillips Curve PC_1 will clarify this. We begin at a_1, where nominal wages are set on the assumption that the 3 percent rate of inflation will continue. That is, because workers expect output prices to rise by 3 percent per year, they negotiate wage contracts that feature 3 percent per year increases in nominal wages so that these increases will exactly offset the expected rise in prices and thereby keep real wages the same.

But suppose the rate of inflation rises to 6 percent, perhaps because the Bank of Canada has decided to move the AD curve to the right even faster than it had been before. With a nominal wage rate set on the expectation that the 3 percent rate of inflation will continue, the higher product prices raise business profits. Firms respond to the higher profits by hiring more workers and increasing output. In the short run, the economy moves to b_1, which, in contrast to a_1, is at a lower rate of unemployment (4 percent) and a higher rate of inflation (6 percent). The movement from a_1 to b_1 is consistent with both an upward-sloping aggregate supply curve and the inflation–unemployment tradeoff implied by the Phillips Curve analysis. But this short-run Phillips Curve simply is a manifestation of the following principle: *When the actual rate of inflation is higher than expected, profits temporarily rise and the unemployment rate temporarily falls.*

FIGURE 15·11   The Long-Run Vertical Phillips Curve

Increases in aggregate demand beyond those consistent with full-employment output may temporarily boost profits, output, and employment (as from a_1 to b_1). But nominal wages eventually will catch up so as to sustain real wages. When they do, profits will fall, negating the previous short-run stimulus to production and employment (the economy now moves from b_1 to a_2). Consequently, there is no tradeoff between the rates of inflation and unemployment in the long run; that is, the long-run Phillips Curve is roughly a vertical line at the economy's natural rate of unemployment.

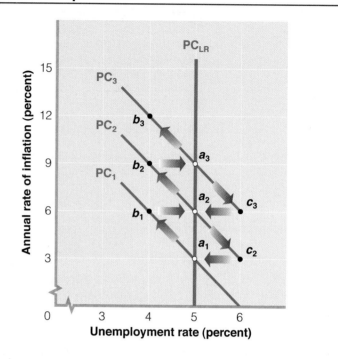

Expectation and the Long-Run Vertical Phillips Curve

But point b_1 is not a stable equilibrium. Workers will recognize that their nominal wages have not increased as fast as inflation and will therefore renegotiate their labour contracts so that they feature faster increases in nominal wages. These faster increases in nominal wages make up for the higher rate of inflation and restore the workers' lost purchasing power. As these new labour contracts kick in, business profits will fall to their prior level. The reduction in profits means that the original motivation to employ more workers and increase output has disappeared.

Unemployment then returns to its natural level at point a_2. Note, however, that the economy now faces a higher actual and expected rate of inflation—6 percent rather than 3 percent. This happens because the new labour contracts feature 6 percent per year increases in wages to make up for the 6 percent per year inflation rate. Because wages are a production cost, this faster increase in wage rates will imply faster future increases in output prices as firms are forced to raise prices more rapidly to make up for the faster future rate of wage growth. Stated a bit differently, the initial increase in inflation will become *persistent* because it leads to renegotiated labour contracts that will perpetuate the higher rate of inflation. In addition, because the new labour contracts are public, it will also be the case that the higher rates of inflation they will cause will be *expected* by everyone rather than being a surprise. In view of the higher 6 percent expected rate of inflation, the short-run Phillips Curve shifts upward from PC_1 to PC_2 in Figure 15-11. An "along-the-Phillips-curve" kind of movement from a_1 to b_1 on PC_1 is merely a short-run occurrence. As expectation of inflation adjusts in the long run, nominal wage contracts catch up with increases in the inflation rate, unemployment returns to its natural rate at a_2, and there is a new short-run Phillips Curve PC_2 at the higher expected rate of inflation.

The scenario repeats if aggregate demand continues to increase. Prices rise momentarily ahead of nominal wages, profits expand, and employment and output increase (as implied by the move from a_2 to b_2). But, in time, the expected rate of inflation changes, and nominal wages increase so as to restore real wages. Profits then fall to their original level, pushing employment back to the normal

ORIGIN 15.2
Long-Run Vertical
Phillips Curve

**long-run vertical
Phillips Curve**
A Phillips Curve that shows
that in the long run there
is no tradeoff between the
unemployment rate and
the annual rate of increase
in the price level.

disinflation
A reduction in the
rate of inflation.

rate at a_3. The economy's "reward" for lowering the unemployment rate below the natural rate is a still higher (9 percent) rate of inflation.

Movements along the short-run Phillips Curve (a_1 to b_1 on PC_1) cause the curve to shift to a less favourable position (PC_2, then PC_3, and so on). A stable Phillips Curve with the dependable series of unemployment rate–inflation rate tradeoffs simply does not exist in the long run. The economy is characterized by a **long-run vertical Phillips Curve.**

The vertical line through a_1, a_2, and a_3 shows the long-run relationship between unemployment and inflation. Any rate of inflation is consistent with the 5 percent natural rate of unemployment.

Disinflation

The distinction between the short-run and long-run Phillips Curve also helps explain **disinflation**—reductions in the inflation rate from year to year. Suppose that in Figure 15-11 the economy is at a_3, where the inflation rate is 9 percent. And suppose that a decline in the rate at which aggregate demand shifts to the right faster than aggregate supply (as happened during the 2008–09 recession) reduces inflation below the 9 percent expected rate to, say, 6 percent. Business profits fall, because prices are rising less rapidly than wages. The nominal wage increases, remember, were set on the assumption that the 9 percent rate of inflation would continue. In response to the decline in profits, firms reduce their employment and consequently the unemployment rate rises. The economy temporarily slides downward from point a_3 to c_3 along the short-run Phillips Curve PC_3. *When the actual rate of inflation is lower than the expected rate, profits temporarily fall and the unemployment rate temporarily rises.*

Firms and workers eventually adjust their expectations to the new 6 percent rate of inflation, and thus newly negotiated wage increases decline. Profits are restored, employment rises, and the unemployment rate falls back to its natural rate of 5 percent at a_2. Because the expected rate of inflation is now 6 percent, the short-run Phillips Curve PC_3 shifts leftward to PC_2.

If the rate at which aggregate demand shifts to the right faster than aggregate supply declines even more, the scenario will continue. Inflation declines from 6 percent to, say, 3 percent, moving the economy from a_2 to c_2 along PC_2. The lower-than-expected rate of inflation (lower prices) squeezes profits and reduces employment. But in the long run firms respond to the lower profits by reducing their nominal wage increases. Profits are restored and unemployment returns to its natural rate at a_1 as the short-run Phillips Curve moves from PC_2 to PC_1. Once again, the long-run Phillips Curve is vertical at the 5 percent natural rate of unemployment. *(Key Question 7)*

QUICK REVIEW

▶ As implied by the upward-sloping short-run aggregate supply curve, there may be a short-run tradeoff between the rate of inflation and the rate of unemployment. This tradeoff is reflected in the Phillips Curve, which shows that lower rates of inflation are associated with higher rates of unemployment.

▶ Aggregate supply shocks that produce severe cost-push inflation can cause stagflation—simultaneous increases in the inflation rate and the unemployment rate. Such stagflation occurred from 1973 to 1975 and recurred from 1978 to 1982, producing Phillips Curve data points above and to the right of the Phillips Curve for the 1960s.

▶ After all nominal wage adjustments to increases and decreases in the rate of inflation have occurred, the economy ends up back at its full-employment level of output and its natural rate of unemployment. The long-run Phillips Curve therefore is vertical at the natural rate of unemployment.

15.5 | Taxation and Aggregate Supply

supply-side economics
A view of macroeconomics that emphasizes the role of costs and aggregate supply in explaining inflation, unemployment, and economic growth.

A final topic in our discussion of aggregate supply is taxation. Government policies can either impede or promote rightward shifts of the short-run and long-run aggregate supply curve. One such policy is taxation. The effects of taxation on the supply curve is a key concern of **supply-side economics.** Supply-side economists (or "supply-siders") stress that changes in aggregate supply are an active force in determining the levels of inflation, unemployment, and economic growth. Government policies can either impede or promote rightward shifts of the short-run and long-run aggregate supply curves shown in Figure 15-1. One such policy is taxation.

These economists say that the enlargement of a nation's tax system influences the incentive to work, save, and invest. High tax rates impede productivity growth and hence the pace of expansion of long-run aggregate supply. By reducing the after-tax rewards of workers and producers, high tax rates reduce the financial attractiveness of work, saving, and investing. Particularly important are the *marginal tax rates*—the rates on extra dollars of income—because those rates affect the benefits from working, saving, and investing more.

Taxes and Incentives to Work

How long and how hard people work depends on the amount of additional after-tax earnings they derive from their efforts. Reductions in marginal tax rates on earned incomes induce more work, and therefore increase aggregate inputs of labour. Lower marginal tax rates make leisure relatively more expensive and thus work more attractive. The higher opportunity cost of leisure encourages people to substitute work for leisure. This increase in productive effort could be achieved in many ways: by increasing the number of hours worked per day or week, by encouraging workers to postpone retirement, by inducing more people to enter the labour force, by motivating people to work harder and giving people the incentive to avoid long periods of unemployment.

Incentives to Save and Invest

The rewards for saving and investing have also been reduced by high marginal tax rates. For example, suppose that Tom saves $10,000 at 8 percent, bringing him $800 of interest per year. If his marginal tax rate is 40 percent, his after-tax interest earnings will be $480, not $800, and his after-tax interest rate will fall to 4.8 percent. Although Tom might be willing to save (forgo current consumption) for an 8 percent return on his saving, he might prefer to consume when the return is only 4.8 percent.

Saving, remember, is the prerequisite of investment. Thus supply-side economists recommend lower marginal tax rates on interest earned from saving. They also call for lower taxes on income from capital to ensure that there are ready investment outlets for the economy's enhanced pool of saving. A critical determinant of investment spending is the expected after-tax return on that spending.

The Laffer Curve

In the supply-side view, reductions in marginal tax rates increase the nation's aggregate supply and can leave the nation's tax revenues unchanged, or even enlarge them. Thus, supply-side tax cuts need not result in federal budget deficits.

Laffer Curve
A curve relating government tax rates and tax revenues.

This idea is based on the **Laffer Curve,** named after Arthur Laffer, who popularized it. As Figure 15-12 shows, the Laffer Curve depicts the relationship between tax rates and tax revenues. As tax rates increase from zero to 100 percent, tax revenues increase from zero to some maximum level (at *m*) and then fall to zero. Tax revenues decline beyond some point because higher tax rates discourage economic activity, thereby shrinking the tax base. This is easiest to see at the extreme, where the tax rate is 100 percent. Tax revenues here are, in theory, reduced to zero because the 100 percent tax rate has halted production. A 100 percent tax rate applied to a tax base of zero yields no revenue.

In the early 1980s, Laffer suggested that at a point (such as *n* on the curve in Figure 15-12) tax rates are so high that production is discouraged to the extent that tax revenues are below the

FIGURE 15·12   The Laffer Curve

The Laffer Curve suggests that up to point *m* higher tax rates will result in larger tax revenues. But higher tax rates will adversely affect incentives to work and produce, reducing the size of the base (output and income) to the extent that tax revenues will decline. It follows that if tax rates are above *m*, reductions in tax rates will produce increases in tax revenues.

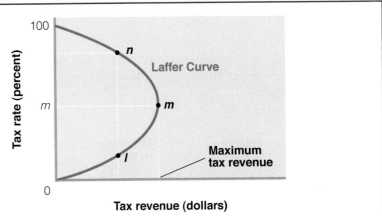

maximum (at *m*). If the economy is at *n*, then lower tax rates can either increase tax revenues or leave them unchanged. For example, lowering the tax rate point *n* to point *l* would bolster the economy such that the government would bring in the same total amount of tax revenue as before.

Laffer's reasoning was that lower tax rates stimulate incentives to work, to save and invest, to innovate, and to take business risks, thus triggering an expansion of real output and income. That enlarged tax base sustains tax revenues even though tax rates are lowered. Indeed, between *n* and *m* lower tax rates result in *increased* tax revenue.

Also, when tax rates are lowered, tax avoidance (which is legal) and tax evasion (which is not) decline. High marginal tax rates prompt taxpayers to avoid taxes through various tax shelters. Lower tax rates reduce the inclination to engage in either tax avoidance or tax evasion. *(Key Question 9)*

Criticisms of the Laffer Curve

The Laffer Curve and its supply-side implications have been subject to severe criticism.

TAXES, INCENTIVES, AND TIME

A fundamental criticism relates to the degree to which economic incentives are sensitive to changes in tax rates. Skeptics say that ample empirical evidence shows the impact of a tax cut on incentives is small, of uncertain direction, and relatively slow to emerge.

INFLATION

Most economists think that the demand-side effects of a tax cut are more immediate and certain than longer-term supply-side effects. Thus, tax cuts undertaken when the economy is at or near its full-employment level of output may produce increases in aggregate demand that overwhelm any increase in aggregate supply. Demand-pull inflation is the likely result. If so, the real interest rates will rise and investment will decline. That will defeat the purpose of the supply-side tax cut.

POSITION ON THE CURVE

Skeptics say the Laffer Curve is merely a logical proposition, and assert that there must be some level of tax rates between zero and 100 percent at which tax revenues will be at their maximum. Economists of all persuasions can agree with this. But the issue of where a particular economy is located on its Laffer Curve is an empirical question. If we assume that we are at point *n* in Figure 15-12, then tax cuts will increase tax revenues. But critics say that the economy's location on the Laffer Curve is undocumented and unknown. If the economy is at any point below *m* on the curve, then tax reductions will reduce tax revenues.

The LAST WORD   Do Tax Increases Reduce Real GDP?*

Determining the relationship between changes in taxes and permanent changes in real GDP is fraught with complexities and difficulties. University of California–Berkeley economists Christina Romer and David Romer have recently devised a novel new way to approach the topic. Their findings suggest that tax increases reduce real GDP.**

How do changes in the level of taxation affect the level of economic activity? The simple correlation between taxation and economic activity shows that, on average, when economic activity rises more rapidly, tax revenues also are rising more rapidly. But this correlation almost surely does not reflect a positive effect of tax increases on output. Rather, under our tax system, any positive shock to output raises tax revenues by increasing income. In "The Macroeconomic Effects of Tax Changes: Estimates Based on a New Measure of Fiscal Shocks," authors Christina Romer and David Romer observe that this difficulty is just one of many manifestations of a more general problem. Changes in taxes occur for many reasons. And, because the factors that give rise to tax changes often are correlated with other developments in the economy, disentangling the effects of the tax changes from the other effects of these underlying factors is inherently difficult. To address this problem, Romer and Romer use the narrative record—Presidential speeches, executive branch documents, Congressional reports, and so on—to identify the size, timing, and principal motivation for all major tax policy actions in the post–World War II United States. This narrative analysis allows them to separate revenue changes resulting from legislation from changes occurring for other reasons. It also allows them to classify legislated changes according to their primary motivation. Romer and Romer find that despite the complexity of the legislative process, most significant tax changes have been motivated by one of four factors: counteracting other influences in the economy; paying for increases in government spending (or lowering taxes in conjunction with reductions in spending); addressing an inherited budget deficit; and promoting long-run growth. They observe that legislated tax changes taken to counteract other influences on the economy, or to pay for increases in government spending, are very likely to be correlated with other factors affecting the economy. As a result these observations are likely to lead to unreliable estimates of the effect of tax changes. Tax changes that are made to promote long-run growth, or to reduce an inherited budget deficit, in contrast, are undertaken for reasons essentially unrelated to other factors influencing output. Thus, examining the behaviour of output following these tax changes is likely to provide more reliable estimates of the output effects of tax changes. *The results of this more reliable test indicate that tax changes have very large effects: a tax increase of 1 percent of GDP lowers real GDP by roughly 2 to 3 percent.* These output effects are highly persistent. The behaviour of inflation and unemployment suggests that this persistence reflects long-lasting departures of output from previous levels. Romer and Romer also find that output effects of tax changes are much more closely tied to the actual changes in taxes than news about future changes, and that investment falls sharply in response to tax changes. Indeed, the strong response of investment helps to explain why the output consequences of tax increases are so large. Romer and Romer find suggestive evidence that tax increases to reduce an inherited budget deficit have much smaller output costs than other tax increases. This is consistent with the idea that deficit-driven tax increases may have important expansionary effects through [improved] expectations and [lower] long-term interest rates, or through [enhanced] confidence. There is good reason to believe that these general results may also apply to the Canadian economy.

---

*Abridged from Les Picker, "Tax Increases Reduce GDP," *The NBER Digest*, February/March 2008. The *Digest* provides synopses of research papers in progress by economists affiliated with the National Bureau of Economic Research (NBER).

**Christina Romer and David Romer, "The Macroeconomic Effects of Tax Changes: Estimates Based on a New Measure of Fiscal Shocks," National Bureau of Economic Research Working Paper No. 13264, 2007.

Question

On average, does an increase in taxes raise or lower real GDP? If taxes as a percentage of GDP go up 1 percent, by how much does real GDP change? Are the decreases in real GDP caused by tax increases temporary or permanent? Does the intention of a tax increase matter?

CHAPTER SUMMARY

15.1 ▶ FROM THE SHORT RUN TO THE LONG RUN

- In macroeconomics, the short run is a period in which nominal wages do not respond to changes in the price level. In contrast, the long run is a period in which nominal wages fully respond to changes in the price level.

- The short-run aggregate supply curve is upward-sloping. Because nominal wages are fixed, increases in the price level (prices received by firms) increase profits and real output. Conversely, decreases in the price level reduce profits and real output. However, the long-run aggregate supply curve is vertical. With sufficient time for adjustment, nominal wages rise and fall with the price level, moving the economy along a vertical aggregate supply curve at the economy's full-employment output.

15.2 ▶ APPLYING THE LONG-RUN AD–AS MODEL

- In the short run, demand-pull inflation raises the price level and real output. Once nominal wages have increased, the temporary increase in real output is reversed.

- In the short run, cost-push inflation raises the price level and lowers real output. Unless the government expands aggregate demand, nominal wages eventually will decline under conditions of recession and the short-run aggregate supply curve will shift back to its initial location. Prices and real output will eventually return to their original levels.

- If prices and wages are flexible downward, a decline in aggregate demand will lower output and the price level. The decline in the price level will eventually lower nominal wages and shift the short-run aggregate supply curve rightward. Full-employment output will thus be restored.

- One-time shifts in the AD and AS curves can cause only limited bouts of inflation. Ongoing inflation is caused by the Bank of Canada constantly shifting AD to the right faster than the AS curve shifts to the right (due to economic growth).

15.3 ▶ THE INFLATION–UNEMPLOYMENT RELATIONSHIP

- Assuming a stable upward-sloping short-run aggregate supply curve, rightward shifts of the aggregate demand curve of various sizes yield the generalization that high rates of inflation are associated with low rates of unemployment, and vice versa. This inverse relationship is known as the Phillips Curve, and empirical data for the 1960s seem to be consistent with it.

- In the 1970s and early 1980s, the Phillips Curve apparently shifted rightward, reflecting stagflation—simultaneously rising inflation rates and unemployment rates. The standard interpretation is that the stagflation mainly resulted from huge oil price increases that caused large leftward shifts in the short-run aggregate supply curve (so-called supply shocks). The Phillips Curve shifted inward toward its original position in the 1980s. By 1989 stagflation had subsided.

15.4 ▶ THE LONG-RUN PHILLIPS CURVE

- Although there is a short-run tradeoff between inflation and unemployment, there is no such long-run tradeoff. Workers will adapt their expectations to new inflation realities, and when they do, and nominal wages adjust proportionately with the price level, the unemployment rate will return to the natural rate. The long-run Phillips Curve is therefore vertical at the natural rate, meaning that higher rates of inflation do not "buy" the economy less unemployment.

15.5 ▶ TAXATION AND AGGREGATE SUPPLY

- Supply-side economists focus on government policies, such as high taxation, that impede the expansion of aggregate supply. The Laffer Curve relates tax rates to levels of tax revenue and suggests that, under some circumstances, cuts in tax rates can expand the tax base (output and income) and increase tax revenues. Most economists, however, believe that Canada is operating in the range of the Laffer Curve where tax rates and tax revenues move in the same, not the opposite, direction.

- Today's economists recognize the importance of considering supply-side effects in designing optimal fiscal policy.

TERMS AND CONCEPTS

Phillips Curve, p. 367
stagflation, p. 369
aggregate supply shocks, p. 370

long-run vertical Phillips Curve, p. 373
disinflation, p. 373

supply-side economics, p. 374
Laffer Curve, p. 374

STUDY QUESTIONS

LO ▶ 15.1 1. Distinguish between the short run and the long run as they relate to macroeconomics. Why is the distinction important?

LO ▶ 15.1 2. Which of the following statements are true? Which are false? Explain why the false statements are untrue.

   a. Short-run aggregate supply curves reflect an inverse relationship between the price level and the level of real output.

   b. The long-run aggregate supply curve assumes that nominal wages are fixed.

   c. In the long run, an increase in the price level will result in an increase in nominal wages.

LO ▶ 15.1 3. **KEY QUESTION**   Suppose the full-employment level of real output (Q) for a hypothetical economy is $250 and the price level (P) initially is 100. Use the short-run aggregate supply schedules below to answer the questions that follow:

AS (P100)		AS (P125)		AS (P75)	
P	**Q**	**P**	**Q**	**P**	**Q**
125	280	125	250	125	310
100	250	100	220	100	280
75	220	75	190	75	250

   a. What will be the level of real output in the short run if the price level unexpectedly rises from 100 to 125 because of an increase in aggregate demand? What if the price level falls unexpectedly from 100 to 75 because of a decrease in aggregate demand? Explain each situation, using numbers from the table.

   b. What will be the level of real output in the long run when the price level rises from 100 to 125? When it falls from 100 to 75? Explain each situation.

   c. Show the circumstances described in parts (a) and (b) on graph paper, and derive the long-run aggregate supply curve.

LO ▶ 15.2 4. **KEY QUESTION**   Use graphical analysis to show how each of the following would affect the economy first in the short run and then in the long run. Assume that Canada is initially operating at its full-employment level of output, that prices and wages are eventually flexible both upward

and downward, and that there is no counteracting fiscal or monetary policy.

   a. Because of a war abroad, the oil supply to Canada is disrupted, sending oil prices rocketing upward.

   b. Construction spending on new homes rises dramatically, greatly increasing total Canadian investment spending.

   c. Economic recession occurs abroad, significantly reducing foreign purchases of Canadian exports.

5. **KEY QUESTION**   Between 1990 and 2008, the Canadian price level rose by about 46 percent while real output increased by about 61 percent. Use the AD–AS model to illustrate these outcomes graphically.   **LO ▶ 15**

6. Assume that a particular short-run aggregate supply curve exists for an economy and that the curve is relevant for several years. (a) Use the AD–AS analysis to show graphically why higher rates of inflation over this period would be associated with lower rates of unemployment, and vice versa. (b) What is this inverse relationship called?   **LO ▶ 15**

7. **KEY QUESTION**   Suppose the government judges the natural rate of unemployment to be much lower than it actually is, and thus undertakes expansionary fiscal and monetary policy to try to achieve the lower rate. (a) Use the concept of the short-run Phillips Curve to explain why these policies might at first succeed. (b) Use the concept of the long-run Phillips Curve to explain the long-run outcome of these policies.   **LO ▶ 15.**

8. What do the distinctions between short-run and long-run aggregate supply have in common with the distinction between the short-run and long-run Phillips Curve? Explain.   **LO ▶ 15.**

9. **KEY QUESTION**   What is the Laffer Curve and how does it relate to supply-side economics? Why is determining the location of the economy on the curve so important in assessing tax policy?   **LO ▶ 15.**

10. Why might one person work more, earn more, and pay more income tax when his or her tax rate is cut, while another person will work less, earn less, and pay less income tax under the same circumstance?   **LO ▶ 15.**

INTERNET APPLICATION QUESTIONS @

1. **The Phillips Curve—Do Real Data Confirm?** The Phillips Curve purports to show a stable relationship between the rate of inflation and the unemployment rate. Plot the data points between inflation and unemployment over the past five years. For inflation data, use the Consumer Price Index (all items). Both the CPI and unemployment data for the latest period can be retrieved from the McConnell-Brue-Flynn-Barbiero Web site (Chapter 15). Do any of your data point plots confirm the Phillips Curve concept?

2. **Dynamic Tax Scoring—What Is It and Who Wants It?** Go to the McConnell-Brue-Flynn-Barbiero Web site (Chapter 15) and search for information on "dynamic tax scoring." What is it? How does it relate to supply-side economics? Which political groups support this approach and why? Which groups oppose it and why?

International Economics

PART 6

CHAPTER 16

International Trade

Backpackers in the wilderness like to think they are leaving the world behind, but, like Atlas, they carry the world on their shoulders. Much of their equipment is imported—knives from Switzerland, rain gear from South Korea, cameras from Japan, aluminum pots from England, sleeping bags from China, hiking boots from Italy, and compasses from Finland. Moreover, they may have driven to the trailheads in Japanese-made Toyotas or German-made BMWs, sipping coffee from Colombia and snacking on bananas from Honduras.

International trade and the global economy affect all of us daily, whether we are hiking in the wilderness, driving our cars, listening to music, or working at our jobs. We cannot leave the world behind. We are enmeshed in a global web of economic relationships—trading of goods and services, multinational corporations, cooperative ventures among the world's firms, and ties among the world's financial markets.

In this chapter we provide an analysis of the benefits of international trade and an appraisal of the arguments for protectionism. Then in Chapter 17 we examine exchange rates and the balance of payments.

16.1 | Canada and International Linkages

As identified in Figure 16-1, four economic flows link the Canadian economy and the economies of other nations:

- **Goods and Services Flows (Trade Flows)** Canada exports goods and services to other nations and imports goods and services from them.
- **Capital and Labour Flows (Resource Flows)** Canadian firms establish production facilities—new capital—in foreign countries and foreign firms establish production facilities in Canada. Labour also moves between nations. Each year many foreigners immigrate to Canada and some Canadians move to other nations.

IN THIS CHAPTER YOU WILL LEARN:

16.1 Some key facts about Canada's international trade

16.2 About specialization, comparative advantage, and international trade

16.3 About supply and demand analysis of exports and imports

16.4 About trade barriers and their negative effects on nations' economic well-being

16.5 The usual arguments against free trade

16.6 The role played by free-trade zones and the World Trade Organization (WTO) in promoting international trade

FIGURE 16-1	International Linkages

The Canadian economy is intertwined with other national economies through goods and service flows (trade flows), capital and labour flows (resource flows), information and technology flows, and financial flows.

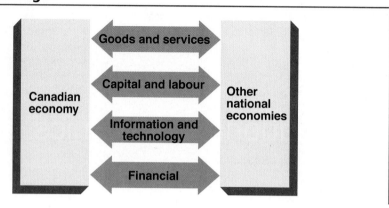

- *Information and Technology Flows*   Canada transmits information to other nations about Canadian products, price, interest rates, and investment opportunities and receives such information from abroad. Firms in other countries use technology created in Canada and Canadian businesses incorporate technology developed abroad.

- *Financial Flows*   Money is transferred between Canada and other countries for several purposes: paying for imports, buying foreign assets, paying interest on debt, purchasing foreign currencies, and providing foreign aid.

Canada and World Trade

What is the extent and pattern of international trade, and how much has that trade grown? Who are the major participants? Global Perspective 16.1 suggests the importance of world trade for selected countries. Canada, with a limited domestic market, cannot efficiently produce the variety of goods its citizens want. So we must import goods from other nations. That, in turn, means that we must export, or sell abroad, some of our own products. For Canada, exports make up about 35 percent of gross domestic product (GDP)—the market value of all goods and services produced in an economy. Other countries—the United States, for example—have a large internal market. Although the total volume of trade is huge in the United States, it constitutes 12 percent of its GDP, a much smaller percentage than in a number of other nations.

VOLUME

For Canada and for the world as a whole, the volume of international trade has been increasing both absolutely and relative to their GDP. A comparison of the boxed data in Figure 16-2 reveals substantial growth in the dollar amount of Canadian exports and imports over the past several decades. The graph shows the growth of Canadian exports and imports of goods and services as percentages of GDP. Canadian exports and imports currently are approximately 35 and 33 percent of GDP, respectively—substantially higher than in 1971.

DEPENDENCE

Canada is almost entirely dependent on other countries for bananas, cocoa, coffee, spices, tea, raw silk, tin, and natural rubber. Imported goods compete with Canadian goods in many of our domestic markets: Japanese cars, French and American wines, and Swiss and Austrian snow skis are a few examples.

16.1 | GLOBAL PERSPECTIVE

Shares of world exports, selected nations

Germany has the largest share of world exports, followed by the United States and China. The eight largest export nations account for nearly 50 percent of world exports.

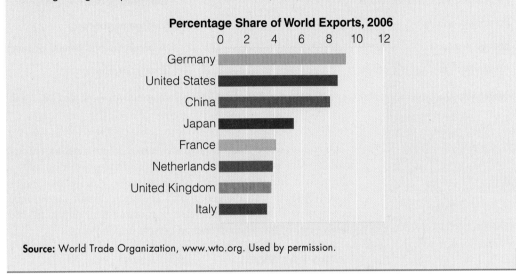

Percentage Share of World Exports, 2006

Germany
United States
China
Japan
France
Netherlands
United Kingdom
Italy

Source: World Trade Organization, www.wto.org. Used by permission.

FIGURE 16-2   **Canadian Trade as Percentage of GDP**

Canadian imports and exports of goods and services have increased both in volume and as a percentage of GDP since 1971.

SOURCE: Statistics Canada, CANSIM, http://www40.statcan.ca/l01/cst01/econ01a-eng.htm and http://www40.statcan.l01/cst01/econ04-eng.htm. Accessed May 19, 2009

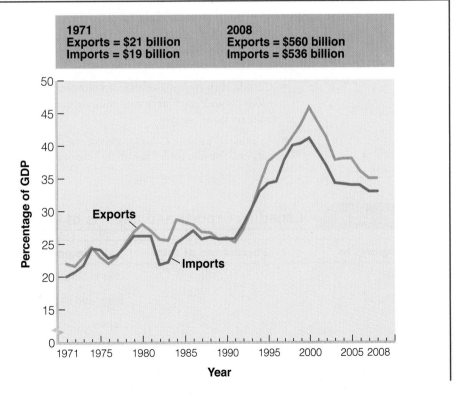

1971	2008
Exports = $21 billion	Exports = $560 billion
Imports = $19 billion	Imports = $536 billion

Exports

Imports

Percentage of GDP

Year

| TABLE 16-1 | Principal Canadian Exports and Imports of Goods, 2008 |

Exports	% of total	Imports	% of total
Machinery and equipment	19	Machinery and equipment	28
Automotive products	12	Automotive products	16
Industrial goods and materials	23	Industrial goods and materials	19
Forestry products	5	Consumer goods	10
Energy products	26	Agricultural and fishing products	7
Agricultural and fishing products	8	Energy products	12

Source: Statistics Canada. At: http://www40.statcan.ca/l01/cst01/gblec02a-eng.htm. Accessed May 18, 2009.

Of course, world trade is a two-way street. Many Canadian industries rely on exports to foreign markets. Almost all segments of Canadian agriculture rely on sales abroad; for example, exports of wheat, corn, and soybeans vary from one-tenth to more than three-quarters of the total output of those crops. The Canadian computer, chemical, aircraft, automobile, and machine tool industries, among many others, sell significant portions of their output in international markets. Table 16-1 shows some of the major Canadian exports and imports.

TRADE PATTERNS

The following facts will give you an overview of international trade:

- A *trade surplus* occurs when exports exceed imports. Canada had a trade surplus in goods in 2008: Canadian exports of goods exceeded Canadian imports of goods by $47 billion.

- A *trade deficit* occurs when imports exceed exports. Canada had a trade deficit in services (such as accounting services and financial services) in 2008. Canadian firms and citizens collectively supply (export) less transportation, banking, legal, and other services abroad than they purchase (import) from foreign firms and citizens. Canadian imports of services exceeded exports of services by $22 billion.

- Canada imports some of the same categories of goods that it exports, specifically automotive products and machinery and equipment (see Table 16-1). This type of trade is called intra-industry trade.

- As Table 16-2 shows, Canada's export and import trade is mainly with other industrially advanced nations. The remainder is with developing countries.

| TABLE 16-2 | Canadian Exports and Imports of Goods by Area, 2008 |

Exports to	Percentage of total	Imports from	Percentage of total
United States	76	United States	65
European Union	8	European Union	14
Japan	2	Japan	3
Other countries	14	Other countries	18

Source: Statistics Canada. http://www40.statcan.ca/l01/cst01/gblec04-eng.htm. Accessed May 19, 2009.

- The United States is Canada's most important trading partner quantitatively. In 2008, 76 percent of Canadian exported goods were sold to Americans, who in turn provided 63 percent of Canada's imports of goods (see Table 16-2).

Rapid Trade Growth

Several factors have propelled the rapid growth of international trade since World War II.

TRANSPORTATION TECHNOLOGY

High transportation costs are a barrier to any type of trade. But improvements in transportation have shrunk the globe and have fostered world trade. Container ships deliver self-contained boxcars of goods to ports, which offload them to waiting trucks and trains. We now routinely transport oil in massive tankers, significantly lowering the cost of transportation per barrel. Grain is loaded onto ocean-going ships at modern, efficient grain silos at Great Lakes and coastal ports. Natural gas flows through large-diameter pipelines from exporting to importing countries—for instance, from Russia to Germany and from Canada to the United States.

COMMUNICATIONS TECHNOLOGY

Dramatic improvements in communications technology have also advanced world trade. Computers, the Internet, telephones, and fax machines now directly link traders around the world, enabling exporters to assess overseas markets and to carry out trade deals. A distributor in Vancouver can get a price quotation on 1000 woven baskets in Thailand as quickly as a quotation on 1000 notebook computers in Ontario. Money moves around the world in the blink of an eye. Exchange rates, stock prices, and interest rates flash onto computer screens nearly simultaneously in Toronto, London, and Lisbon.

GENERAL DECLINE IN TARIFFS

Tariffs are excise taxes (duties) on imported products. They have had their ups and downs over the years, but since 1940 they have generally fallen. A glance ahead to Figure 16-9 on page 405 shows that Canadian tariffs as a percentage of imports are now about 5 percent, down from over 20 percent in the mid-1930s. Many nations still maintain barriers to free trade, but on average tariffs have fallen significantly, thus increasing international trade.

 CONSIDER THIS | The Global Financial Crisis and the Contraction of International Trade

The global financial crisis of 2008–09 had a serious dampening effect on world trade on a scale the world had not seen since the Great Depression. For example, Canada's exports to the U.S. fell almost 25 percent between March 2008 and March 2009. Exports to the United Kingdom during the same 12-month period dropped almost 35 percent, and exports to Japan fell 18 percent. As was to be expected, imports to Canada during the same period also experienced a drop—although not as severe, partly because Canada's economy fared relatively better during the financial crisis. Imports from Japan fell 29 percent, from the United Kingdom 16 percent, and from the U.S. 10 percent. The category of imports and exports that suffered the worst drop was energy. Exports of energy products (which includes oil) dropped 42 percent, while imports of energy products were down a whopping 50 percent. These sharp declines in international trade imply fewer world gains from specialization based on comparative advantage.

16.2 | **GLOBAL PERSPECTIVE**

Comparative exports

Germany, the United States, and China are the world's largest exporters. Canada is the world's ninth largest.

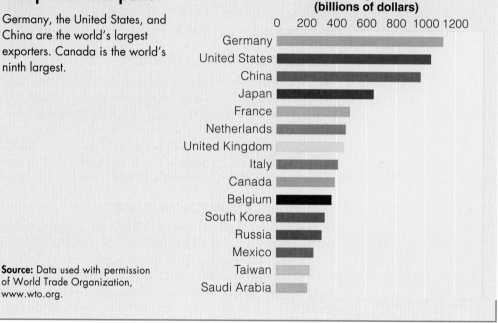

Exports of goods, 2006 (billions of dollars)

Source: Data used with permission of World Trade Organization, www.wto.org.

Participants in International Trade

All the nations of the world participate to some extent in international trade. Global Perspective 16.2 lists the top participants in world trade by total dollar volume (as opposed to percentage of GDP, as in Global Perspective 16.1). Observe that Germany, the United States, China, and Japan had combined exports of $3.6 trillion in 2006. Along with Germany, other western European nations such as France, Britain, and Italy are major exporters. Canada is a major exporter, ranking ninth in the world. So, too, are the Southeast Asian countries of South Korea, Taiwan, and Singapore, whose combined exports exceed those of France, Britain, or Italy. China, with its increased reliance on the market system and its reintegration of Hong Kong, has quickly emerged as a major international trader. In 1990 its exports were about $60 billion. In 2006 they were nearly $969 billion.

QUICK REVIEW

▶ Four main categories of economic flows link nations: goods and services flows, capital and labour flows, information and technology flows, and financial flows.

▶ Advances in transportation and communications technology and declines in tariffs have all helped expand world trade.

▶ World trade has increased globally and nationally. In terms of volume, Canada is the world's ninth largest exporter. With exports and imports of about 35 percent of GDP, Canada is more dependent on international trade than most other nations.

▶ Nearly all nations participate in world trade, but the United States, China, Japan, the Western European nations, and Canada dominate world trade by volume.

16.2 | The Economic Basis for Trade

SPECIALIZATION & TRADE

International trade enables nations to specialize their production, improve their resource productivity, and acquire more goods and services. Nations, like individuals and the regions of a nation, can gain by specializing in those products they can produce with greatest relative efficiency and trading them for those goods they cannot produce as efficiently. A more complete answer to the question "Why do nations trade?" hinges on three facts:

- The distribution of natural, human, and capital resources among nations is uneven; nations differ in their endowments of economic resources.

- Efficient production of various goods requires different technologies or combinations of resources.

- Products are differentiated as to quality and other nonprice attributes. Some people may prefer certain imported goods to similar goods made domestically.

To recognize the character and interaction of these three facts, think of different countries in the world. China, for example, has a large and well-educated labour force and therefore relatively inexpensive skilled labour. As a result, China can produce efficiently (at low cost) a variety of **labour-intensive goods** such as cameras, video game players, and video recorders, the design and production of which require much skilled labour. In contrast, Australia has vast amounts of land and can inexpensively produce such **land-intensive goods** as wheat, wool, and meat. Brazil has the soil, tropical climate, rainfall, and the ready supply of unskilled labour that are needed for the efficient, low-cost production of coffee. And industrially advanced economies with relatively large amounts of capital can inexpensively produce such **capital-intensive goods** as automobiles, agricultural equipment, machinery, and chemicals.

All nations, regardless of their labour, land, or capital intensity, can find special niches for individual products that are in demand worldwide because of their special qualities. Examples include fashions from Italy, luxury automobiles from Germany, software from the United States, watches from Switzerland, and ice wine from Canada.

The distribution of resources, technology, and product distinctiveness among nations, however, is not forever fixed. When that distribution changes, the relative efficiency and success with which nations produce and sell goods also changes. For example, in the past few decades South Korea has upgraded the quality of its labour force and has greatly expanded its stock of capital. Although South Korea was primarily an exporter of agricultural products and raw materials a half-century ago, it now exports large quantities of manufactured goods.

As national economies evolve, the size and quality of their labour forces may change, the volume and composition of their capital stocks may shift, new technologies may develop, and even the quality of land and the quantity of natural resources may be altered. As such changes occur, the relative efficiency with which a nation can produce specific goods will also change.

labour-intensive goods
Products that require a relatively large amount of labour to produce.

land-intensive goods
Products that require a relatively large amount of land to produce.

capital-intensive goods
Products that require a relatively large amount of capital to produce.

Specialization and Comparative Advantage

Let's now use the concept of comparative advantage to analyze the basis for international specialization and trade.

The Basic Principle

The central concept underlying comparative advantage can be illustrated by posing a problem. Suppose that Madison, a chartered accountant (CA), is a swifter painter than Mason, the professional painter she is thinking of hiring. Also assume that Madison can earn $50 per hour doing accounting and must pay Mason $15 per hour. And suppose that Madison would need 30 hours to paint her house but Mason would need 40 hours. Finally, assume Madison receives no special pleasure from painting.

All nations, regardless of their labour, land, or capital intensity, can find special niches for products that are in demand worldwide.

Should Madison take time off from accounting to paint her own house or should she hire the painter? Madison's opportunity cost of painting her house is $1500 (= 30 hours × $50 per hour of sacrificed income). The cost of hiring Mason is only $600 (= 40 hours × $15 per hour paid to the painter). Although Madison is better at both accounting and painting, she will get her house painted at lower cost by specializing in accounting and using some of the proceeds to hire a house painter.

Note that Madison has an **absolute advantage** in both accounting and painting: she can do accounting and paint more efficiently than our hypothetical house painter. Despite this, Madison should hire a house painter because of her "comparative advantage."

Similarly, Mason can reduce his cost of obtaining accounting services by specializing in painting and using some of his income to hire Madison to prepare his income tax forms. Suppose Mason would need 10 hours to prepare his income tax return, but Madison could handle this task in 2 hours. Mason would sacrifice $150 of income (= 10 hours × $15 per hour of sacrificed time) to get a task done that he could hire out for $100 (= 2 hours × $50 per CA hour). By using Madison to prepare his tax return, Mason *lowers his cost of getting the tax return prepared.*

What is true for our CA and house painter is also true for nations. Specializing enables nations to reduce the cost of obtaining goods and services they desire.

With this simple example in mind, let's turn to an international trade model to understand the gains from international specialization and trade.

Two Isolated Nations

Suppose the world economy has just two nations, Canada and Brazil. For simplicity, assume the labour forces in Canada and Brazil are of equal sizes. Each can produce both steel and soybeans, but at differing levels of economic efficiency. Suppose Canadian and Brazilian domestic production possibilities curves for soybeans and steel are as shown in Figures 16-3a and 16-3b. Note especially three characteristics of these production possibilities curves:

- *Constant Costs* The "curves" are drawn as straight lines, in contrast to the concave-from-the-origin production possibilities frontiers introduced in Chapter 1. This means the law of increasing costs has been replaced with the assumption of constant costs. This substitution simplifies our discussion but does not change our analysis and conclusions. Later we will consider the effect of the more realistic increasing opportunity costs.

- *Different Costs* The production possibilities curves of Canada and Brazil reflect different resource mixes and levels of technological progress. Specifically, the differing slopes of the two curves tell us that the opportunity costs of producing steel and soybeans differ between the two nations.

- *Canada Has Absolute Advantage in Both* In view of our assumption that the Canadian and Brazilian labour forces are of equal size, the two production possibilities curves show that Canada has an *absolute advantage* in producing both products. If Canada and Brazil use their entire (equal-size) labour forces to produce either steel or soybeans, Canada can produce more of either than Brazil. There are greater production possibilities in Canada using the same number of workers as in Brazil. So output per worker—labour productivity—in Canada exceeds that in Brazil in producing both products.

CANADA

In Figure 16-3a, with full employment, Canada will operate on its production possibilities curve. Canada can increase its output of steel from 0 to 30 tonnes by forgoing an output of 30 tonnes of soybeans. This means the slope of the production possibilities curve is −1 (= −30 soybeans/+30 steel), implying that 1 tonne of steel can be obtained for every tonne of soybeans sacrificed. In Canada the domestic exchange ratio or **opportunity-cost ratio** for the two products is 1 tonne of steel for 1 tonne of soybeans, or

$$1S_t = 1S_{oy}$$

absolute advantage
When a region or nation can produce more of good Z and good Y with less resources compared to other regions or nations.

opportunity-cost ratio
An equality showing the number of units of two products that can be produced with the same resources.

FIGURE 16-3 Production Possibilities Curve

The two production possibilities lines show the amounts of soybeans and steel (a) Canada and (b) Brazil can produce domestically. The curves for both countries are straight lines because we are assuming constant costs. The different cost ratios, 1 steel = 1 soybean for Canada, and 1 steel = 2 soybeans for Brazil are reflected in the different slopes of the two lines.

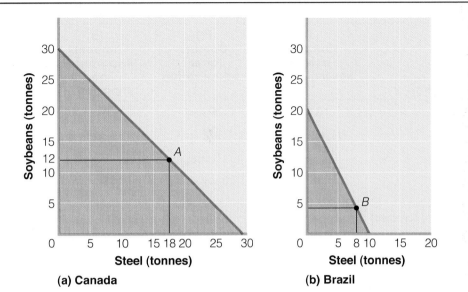

(a) Canada

(b) Brazil

Canada can internally "exchange" a tonne of steel for a tonne of soybeans. Our constant-cost assumption means this exchange or opportunity-cost equation prevails for all possible moves from one point to another along Canada's production possibilities curve.

BRAZIL

Brazil's production possibilities curve in Figure 16-3b represents a different opportunity-cost ratio. In Brazil 2 tonnes of soybeans must be given up to get 1 tonne of steel. The slope of the production possibilities curve is −2 (= −2 soybeans/+1 steel). This means that in Brazil the domestic cost ratio for the two goods is 1 tonne of steel for 2 tonnes of soybeans, or

$$1S_t = 2S_{oy}$$

SELF-SUFFICIENCY OUTPUT MIX

If Canada and Brazil are isolated and are to be self-sufficient, each must choose some output mix on its production possibilities curve. It will choose the mix that provides the greatest total utility, or satisfaction. Assume point A in Figure 16-3a is the optimal output mix in Canada. The choice of this combination of 18 tonnes of steel and 12 tonnes of soybeans equates the marginal benefit and marginal cost of both goods. Suppose Brazil's optimal product mix is 8 tonnes of steel and 4 tonnes of soybeans, indicated by point B in Figure 16-3b. These choices are reflected in column 1, Table 16-3.

Specialization Based on Comparative Advantage

Although Canada has an absolute advantage in producing both goods, gains from specialization and trade are possible. Specialization and trade are mutually beneficial or "profitable" to the two nations if the *comparative* opportunity costs of producing the two products within the two nations differ, as they do in this example. The **principle of comparative advantage** says that *total output will be greatest when each good is produced by that nation that has the lowest domestic opportunity cost for that good*. In our two-nation illustration, Canada's domestic opportunity cost is lower for steel. Canada need only forgo 1 tonne of soybeans to produce 1 tonne of steel, whereas Brazil

principle of comparative advantage
When a region or nation can produce a good at a lower domestic opportunity cost compared to a potential trading partner.

TABLE 16·3	International Specialization According to Comparative Advantage and the Gains from Trade (in tonnes)				
Country	(1) Outputs before specialization	(2) Outputs after specialization	(3) Amounts exported (−) and imported (+)	(4) Outputs available after trade	(5) Gains from specialization and trade (4) − (1)
Canada	18 steel	30 steel	−10 steel	20 steel	2 steel
	12 soybeans	0 soybeans	+15 soybeans	15 soybeans	3 soybeans
Brazil	8 steel	0 steel	+10 steel	10 steel	2 steel
	4 soybeans	20 soybeans	−15 soybeans	5 soybeans	1 soybeans
Total output (steel and soybeans)	42	50		50	8

must forgo 2 tonnes of soybeans for 1 tonne of steel. Canada has a comparative (cost) advantage in steel and should specialize in steel production. The "world" (that is, Canada and Brazil) is not economizing in the use of its resources if a high-cost producer (Brazil) produced a specific product (steel) when a low-cost producer (Canada) could have produced it. Having Brazil produce soybeans would mean that the world economy would have to give up more steel than is necessary to obtain a tonne of soybeans.

Brazil has the lower domestic opportunity cost for soybeans; it must sacrifice only 1/2 tonne of steel in producing 1 tonne of soybeans, whereas Canada must forgo 1 tonne of steel in producing 1 tonne of soybeans. Brazil has a comparative advantage in soybeans and should specialize in soybean production. Economizing requires that any particular good be produced by the nation with the lower domestic opportunity cost, or a comparative advantage. Canada should produce steel and Brazil soybeans. Note that this conclusion holds even though Canada has an absolute advantage in both steel and soybeans.

In column 2 of Table 16-3 we verify that specialization allows the world to get more output from fixed amounts of resources. By specializing completely in steel, Canada can produce 30 tonnes of steel and no soybeans; Brazil, by specializing completely in soybeans, produces 20 tonnes of soybeans and no steel. The world ends up with 4 more tonnes of steel (30 tonnes, compared with 26) *and* 4 more tonnes of soybeans (20 tonnes, compared with 16) than where there is self-sufficiency or unspecialized production.

Terms of Trade

But consumers of each nation want *both* steel and soybeans. They can have both if the two nations trade or exchange the two products. But what will be the **terms of trade**? At what exchange ratio will Canada and Brazil trade steel and soybeans?

Because $1S_t = 1S_{oy}$ in Canada, Canada must get *more than* 1 tonne of soybeans for each tonne of steel exported or it will not benefit Canada to export steel in exchange for Brazilian soybeans. Canada must get a better "price" (more soybeans) for its steel in the world market than it can get domestically, or there is no gain from trade and it will not occur.

Similarly, because $1S_t = 2S_{oy}$ in Brazil, Brazil must get 1 tonne of steel by exporting some amount *less than* 2 tonnes of soybeans. Brazil must pay a lower "price" for steel in the world market than it must pay domestically, or it will not want to trade. The international exchange ratio or terms of trade must lie somewhere between

$$1S_t = 1S_{oy} \text{ (Canada's cost conditions)}$$

@ **ORIGIN 16.1**
Comparative Advantage

terms of trade
The rate at which units of one product can be exchanged for units of another product.

and

$$1S_t = 2S_{oy} \text{ (Brazil's cost conditions)}$$

But where between these limits will the world exchange ratio fall? Canada will prefer a ratio close to $1S_t = 2S_{oy}$, say, $1S_t = 1\frac{3}{4}S_{oy}$. Canada wants to get the most soybeans possible for each tonne of steel it exports. Similarly, Brazil wants a rate near $1S_t = 1S_{oy}$, say $1S_t = 1\frac{1}{4}S_{oy}$. Brazil wants to export the least soybeans possible for each tonne of steel it receives in exchange.

The actual exchange ratio depends primarily on world supply and demand for the two products, but also the relative competitiveness of world markets for soybeans and steel. If overall world demand for soybeans is weak relative to its supply and the demand for steel is strong relative to its supply, the exchange ratio will settle nearer the $1S_t = 2S_{oy}$ figure Canada prefers. If overall world demand for soybeans is great relative to its supply and if the demand for steel is weak relative to its supply, the ratio will settle nearer the $1S_t = 1S_{oy}$ level favourable to Brazil. (We will take up the topic of equilibrium world prices later in this chapter.)

Gains from Specialization and Trade

Suppose the international exchange ratio or terms of trade is $1S_t = 1\frac{1}{2}S_{oy}$. The possibility of trading on these terms permits each nation to supplement its domestic production possibilities line with a **trading possibilities line.** This can be seen in **Figure 16-4 (Key Graph)**. Just as a production possibilities line shows the amount of these products a full-employment economy can obtain by shifting resources from one to the other, a trading possibilities line shows the amounts of two products a nation can obtain by specializing in one product and trading for another. The trading possibilities lines in Figure 16-4 reflect the assumption that both nations specialize based on comparative advantage: Canada specializes completely in steel (point *W* in Figure 16-4a) and Brazil completely in soybeans (at point *c* in Figure 16-4b).

IMPROVED OPTIONS

Now Canada is not constrained by its domestic production possibilities line, which requires it to give up 1 tonne of steel for every tonne of soybeans it wants as it moves up its domestic production possibilities line, say from point *W*. Instead, Canada, through trade with Brazil, can get 1½ tonnes of soybeans for every tonne of steel it exports to Brazil, so long as Brazil has soybeans to export. Trading possibility line *WC'* thus represents the $1S_t = 1\frac{1}{2}S_{oy}$ trading ratio.

Similarly, Brazil, starting at, say, point *c*, no longer has to move down its domestic production possibilities curve, giving up 2 tonnes of soybeans for each tonne of steel it wants. It can now export just 1½ tonnes of soybeans for each tonne of steel it wants by moving down its trading possibilities line *cw'*.

Specialization and trade create a new exchange ratio between steel and soybeans, reflected in a nation's trading possibilities line. This exchange ratio is superior for both nations to the self-sufficiency exchange ratio embodied in the production possibilities line of each. By specializing in steel and trading for Brazil's soybeans, Canada can obtain more than 1 tonne of soybeans for 1 tonne of steel. By specializing in soybeans and trading for Canada's steel, Brazil can get 1 tonne of steel for less than 2 tonnes of soybeans. In both cases, self-sufficiency is undesirable.

ADDED OUTPUT

By specializing according to comparative advantage and trading for those goods produced in other nations with greater domestic efficiency, Canada and Brazil can realize combinations of steel and soybeans beyond their production possibilities boundaries. Specialization according to comparative advantage results in a more efficient allocation of world resources, and larger outputs of both steel and soybeans are therefore available to both nations.

trading possibilities line Shows the different combinations of two products an economy is able to obtain when it specializes in the production of one product and exports it to obtain the other product.

Specialization according to comparative advantage results in more efficient allocation of world resources.

KEY GRAPH

FIGURE 16-4
Trading Possibilities Lines and the Gains from Trade

As a result of international specialization and trade, Canada and Brazil both can have levels of output higher than those attainable on their domestic production possibilities curves. Panel (a): Canada can move from point *A* on its domestic production possibilities curve to, say, *A'* on its trading possibilities line. Panel (b): Brazil can move from *B* to *B'*.

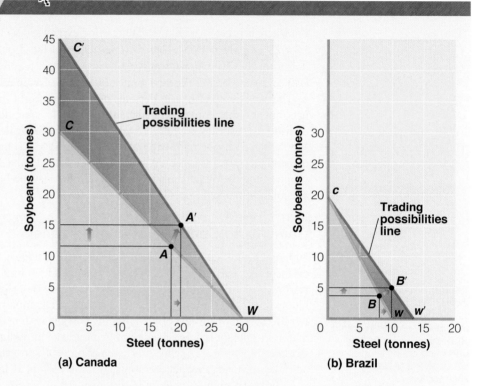

(a) Canada

(b) Brazil

Quick Quiz

1. **The production possibilities curves in graphs (a) and (b) imply:**
   a. increasing domestic opportunity costs.
   b. decreasing domestic opportunity costs.
   c. constant domestic opportunity costs.
   d. first decreasing, then increasing, domestic opportunity costs.

2. **Before specialization, the domestic opportunity cost of producing 1 unit of steel is:**
   a. 1 unit of soybeans in both Canada and Brazil.
   b. 1 unit of soybeans in Canada and 2 units of soybeans in Brazil.
   c. 2 units of soybeans in Canada and 1 unit of soybeans in Brazil.
   d. 1 unit of soybeans in Canada and 1/2 unit of soybeans in Brazil.

3. **After specialization and trade, the world output of steel and soybeans is:**
   a. 20 tonnes of steel and 20 tonnes of soybeans.
   b. 45 tonnes of steel and 15 tonnes of soybeans.
   c. 30 tonnes of steel and 20 tonnes of soybeans.
   d. 10 tonnes of steel and 30 tonnes of soybeans.

4. **After specialization and international trade:**
   a. Canada can obtain units of soybeans at less cost than before trade.
   b. Brazil can obtain more than 20 tonnes of soybeans, if it so chooses.
   c. Canada no longer has a comparative advantage in producing steel.
   d. Brazil can benefit by prohibiting soybean imports from Canada.

Answers: 1. c; 2. b; 3. c; 4. a

Suppose that at the $1S_t = 1\frac{1}{2}S_{oy}$ terms of trade, Canada exports 10 tonnes of steel to Brazil and in return Brazil exports 15 tonnes of soybeans to Canada. How do the new quantities of steel and soybeans available to the two nations compare with the optimal product mixes that existed before specialization and trade? Point A in Figure 16-4a reminds us that Canada chose 18 tonnes of steel and 12 tonnes of soybeans originally. But, by producing 30 tonnes of steel and no soybeans, and by trading 10 tonnes of steel for 15 tonnes of soybeans, Canada can obtain 20 tonnes of steel and 15 tonnes of soybeans. This new, superior combination of steel and soybeans is shown by point A' in Figure 16-4a. Compared with the non-trading figures of 18 tonnes of steel and 12 tonnes of soybeans, Canada's **gains from trade** are 2 tonnes of steel and 3 tonnes of soybeans.

gains from trade
The extra output that trading partners obtain through specialization of production and exchange of goods and services.

Similarly, recall that Brazil's optimal product mix was 4 tonnes of soybeans and 8 tonnes of steel (point B) before specialization and trade. Now, by specializing in soybeans and trading—producing 20 tonnes of soybeans and no steel and exporting 15 tonnes of its soybeans in exchange for 10 tonnes of Canadian steel—Brazil can have 5 tonnes of soybeans and 10 tonnes of steel. This new position is indicated by point B' in Figure 16-4b. Brazil's gains from trade are 1 tonne of soybeans and 2 tonnes of steel. *As a result of specialization and trade, both countries have more of both products.* Table 16-3, which summarizes the transaction and outcomes, merits careful study.

The fact that points A' and B' are positions superior to A and B is enormously important. We know that a nation can expand its production possibilities boundary by (1) expanding the quantity and improving the quality of its resources or (2) realizing technological progress. We have now established that international trade can enable a nation to get around the output constraint imposed by its production possibilities curve. The effects of international specialization and trade are the equivalent of having more and better resources or discovering improved production techniques.

**WORKED
PROBLEM 16.1**

Gains from Trade

Trade with Increasing Costs

To explain the basic principles underlying international trade, we simplified our analysis in several ways. For example, we limited discussion to two products and two nations. But multiproduct/multinational analysis yields the same conclusions. We also assumed constant opportunity costs (linear production possibilities curves), which is a more substantive simplification. Let's consider the effect of allowing increasing opportunity costs (concave-from-the-origin production possibilities curves) to enter the picture.

Suppose that Canada and Brazil are initially at positions on their concave production possibilities curves where their domestic cost ratios are $1S_t = 1S_{oy}$ and $1S_t = 2S_{oy}$, as they were in our constant-cost analysis. As before, comparative advantage indicates that Canada should specialize in steel and Brazil in soybeans. But now, as Canada begins to expand steel production, its $1S_t = 1S_{oy}$ cost ratio will *fall*; it will have to sacrifice *more than* 1 tonne of soybeans to get 1 additional tonne of steel. Resources are no longer perfectly shiftable between alternative uses, as the constant-cost assumption implied. Resources less and less suited to steel production must be allocated to the Canadian steel industry in expanding steel output, and this means increasing costs—the sacrifice of larger and larger amounts of soybeans for each additional tonne of steel.

Similarly, Brazil, starting from its $1S_t = 2S_{oy}$ cost ratio position, expands soybean production. But as it does, it will find that its $1S_t = 2S_{oy}$ cost ratio begins to *rise*. Sacrificing a tonne of steel will free resources that can be used to produce something less than 2 tonnes of soybeans, because these transferred resources are less suitable to soybean production.

As the Canadian cost ratio falls from $1S_t = 1S_{oy}$ and Brazil's rises from $1S_t = 2S_{oy}$, a point will be reached at which the cost ratios are equal in the two nations, perhaps at $1S_t = 1\frac{3}{4}S_{oy}$. At this point, the underlying basis for further specialization and trade—differing cost ratios—has disappeared. Most importantly, this point of equal cost ratios may be reached where Canada is still producing *some* soybeans along with its steel and Brazil is producing *some* steel along with its soybeans. *The primary effect of increasing costs is to make specialization less than complete.* For this reason we often find domestically produced products competing directly against identical or similar imported products within a particular economy. (**Key Question 7**)

The Case for Free Trade Restated

The case for free trade reduces to one compelling argument. Through free trade based on the principle of comparative advantage, the world economy can achieve a more efficient allocation of resources and a higher level of material well-being than without free trade.

Since the resource mixes and technological knowledge of each country are somewhat different, each nation can produce particular commodities at different real costs. Each nation should produce goods for which its domestic opportunity costs are lower than the domestic opportunity costs of other nations, and exchange these specialties for products for which its domestic opportunity costs are high relative to those of other nations. If each nation does this, the world can realize the advantages of specialization. The world and each free-trading nation can obtain a larger real income from the fixed supplies of resources available to it. One side benefit of free trade is that it promotes competition and deters monopoly. The increased competition from foreign firms forces domestic firms to adopt the lowest-cost production techniques. It also compels them to be innovative with respect to both product quality and production methods, thereby contributing to economic growth. And free trade provides consumers with a wider range of product choices. The reasons to favour free trade are the same reasons to endorse competition.

A second side-benefit of free trade is that it links national interest and breaks down national animosities. Confronted with political disagreements, trading partners tend to negotiate rather than make war.

QUICK REVIEW

▶ International trade has always been important to Canada, and it is becoming increasingly so.

▶ International trade enables nations to specialize, improve the productivity of their resources, and obtain a larger output.

▶ Comparative advantage means total world output will be greatest when each good is produced by that nation having the lowest domestic opportunity cost.

▶ Specialization is less than complete among nations because opportunity costs normally rise as any particular nation produces more of a particular good.

16.3 | Supply and Demand Analysis of Exports and Imports

Supply and demand analysis reveals how equilibrium prices and quantities of exports and imports are determined. The amount of a good or service that a nation will export or import depends on differences between equilibrium world and domestic prices. The interaction of *world* supply and demand determines **world price,** the price at which the quantities supplied and demanded are equal globally. *Domestic supply* and demand determine the equilibrium **domestic price**—the price that would prevail in a closed economy. It is a price at which domestic supply and demand are equal.

In the absence of trade, domestic prices in a closed economy may or may not equal world equilibrium prices. When economies are opened for international trade, differences between world and domestic prices motivate exports or imports. To see how, let's now look at the international effects of such price differences in a simple two-nation world consisting of Canada and the United States, which are both producing aluminum. We assume there are no trade barriers, such as tariffs and quotas, and no international transportation costs.

world price
The international market price of a good or service, determined by world demand and supply.

domestic price
The price of a good or service within a country, determined by domestic demand and supply.

FIGURE 16·5   Canadian Export Supply and Import Demand

In panel (a) world prices above the $1.25 domestic price create domestic surpluses of aluminum. As shown by the export supply curve in panel (b), these surpluses are exported. Domestic shortages occur when the world price is below $1.25 (a). These shortages are met by importing aluminum (b). The export supply curve shows the direct relationship between world prices and Canadian exports; the import supply curve portrays the inverse relationship between world prices and Canadian imports.

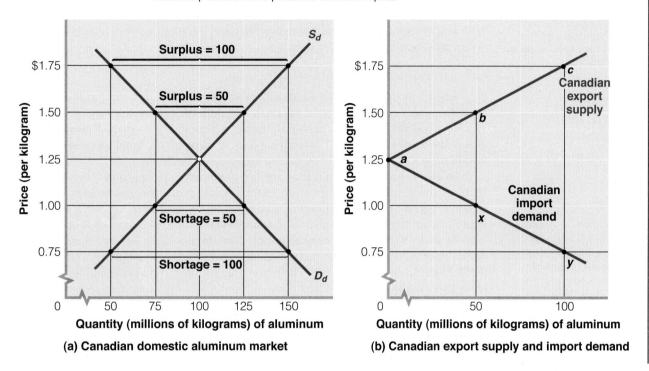

(a) Canadian domestic aluminum market

(b) Canadian export supply and import demand

Supply and Demand in Canada

Figure 16-5a shows the domestic supply curve S_d and domestic demand curve D_d for aluminum in Canada. The intersection of S_d and D_d determines the equilibrium domestic price of $1.25 per kilogram and the equilibrium domestic quantity is 100 million kilograms. Domestic suppliers produce 100 million kilograms and sell them at $1.25. So there are no domestic surpluses or shortages of aluminum.

But what if the Canadian economy is opened to world trade and the *world price* of aluminum is above or below this $1.25 domestic price?

CANADIAN EXPORT SUPPLY

If the world aluminum price exceeds $1.25, Canadian firms will produce more than 100 million kilograms and export the excess domestic output to the rest of the world (United States). First, consider a world price of $1.50. We see from the supply curve S_d that Canadian aluminum firms will produce 125 million kilograms of aluminum at that price. The demand curve D_d tells us that Canadians will purchase only 75 million kilograms at $1.50. The outcome is a domestic surplus of 50 million kilograms of aluminum. Canadian producers will export these 50 million kilograms at the $1.50 world price.

What if the world price is $1.75? The supply curve shows that Canadian firms will produce 150 million kilograms of aluminum, while the demand curve tells us that Canadian consumers will buy only 50 million kilograms. So Canadian producers will export the domestic surplus of 100 million kilograms.

In Figure 16-5b we assign the quantity of surplus or shortage to the horizontal scale. The domestic surpluses—the Canadian exports—occurring at world prices above the $1.25 domestic equilibrium price are plotted in red. When the world and domestic prices are equal (= $1.25), the quantity of exports supplied is zero (point *a*). There is no surplus of domestic output to export. But when the world price is $1.50, Canadian firms export 50 million kilograms of surplus aluminum (point *b*). At a $1.75 world price, the domestic surplus of 100 million kilograms is exported (point *c*).

The Canadian **export supply curve,** found by connecting points such as *a, b,* and *c,* shows the amount of aluminum that Canadian producers will export at each world price above $1.25. This curve *slopes upward*, revealing a direct or positive relationship between the world price and amount of Canadian exports. *As world prices increase relative to domestic prices, Canadian exports rise.*

CANADIAN IMPORT DEMAND

If the world price is below $1.25, Canada will end up importing aluminum. Consider a $1.00 world price. The supply curve in Figure 16-5a reveals that at that price Canadian firms will produce only 75 million kilograms of aluminum. But the demand curve shows that Canadians want to buy 125 million kilograms at that price. The result is a domestic shortage of 50 million kilograms. To satisfy that shortage, Canada will import 50 million kilograms of aluminum.

At an even lower $0.75 world price, Canadian producers will supply only 50 million kilograms. Because Canadian consumers want to buy 150 million kilograms, there is a domestic shortage of 100 million kilograms. Imports will flow to Canada to make up the difference. That is, at a $0.75 world price Canadian firms supply 50 million kilograms and 100 million kilograms will be imported.

In Figure 16-5b we plot the Canadian **import demand curve** from these data in blue. This *downward-sloping curve* shows the amounts of aluminum that will be imported at world prices below the $1.25 Canadian domestic price. The relationship between world prices and imports is inverse or negative. At a world price of $1.25, domestic output will satisfy Canadian demand; imports will be zero (point *a*). But at $1.00 Canadians will import 50 million kilograms of aluminum (point *x*); at $0.75, they will import 100 million kilograms (point *y*). Connecting points *a, x,* and *y* yields a *downward-sloping* Canadian import demand curve. *As world prices fall relative to domestic prices, Canadian imports increase.*

Supply and Demand in the United States

We repeat our analysis in Figure 16-6, this time for the United States. (We have converted U.S. dollar prices to Canadian dollar prices via an assumed exchange rate.) Note that the domestic supply curve S_d and demand curve D_d for aluminum in the United States yield a domestic price of $1.00, which is $0.25 lower than the $1.25 Canadian domestic price.

The analysis proceeds exactly as for Canada. If the world price is $1.00, Americans will neither export nor import aluminum (which gives us point *q* in Figure 16-6b). At world prices above $1.00, U.S. firms will produce more aluminum than U.S. consumers will buy. The surplus will be exported. At a $1.25 world price, Figure 16-6a tells us that the United States will export a domestic surplus of 50 million kilograms (yielding point *r*). At $1.50 it will export a domestic surplus of 100 million kilograms (point *s*). Connecting these points yields the red, upward-sloping U.S. export supply curve that reflects the domestic surpluses (and thus exports) occurring when the world price exceeds the $1.00 U.S. domestic price.

At world prices below $1.00 domestic shortages occur in the United States. At a $0.75 world price, Figure 16-6a shows that U.S. consumers want to buy 125 million kilograms of aluminum but U.S. firms will produce only 75 million kilograms. The shortage will bring 50 million kilograms of imports to the United States (point *t* in Figure 16-6b). The blue U.S. import demand curve in that figure shows U.S. imports at world aluminum prices below the $1.00 U.S. domestic price.

---

export supply curve
An upward-sloping curve that shows the amount of a product domestic firms will export at each world price that is above the domestic price.

import demand curve
A downward-sloping curve that shows the amount of a product an economy will import at each world price below the domestic price.

FIGURE 16-6   U.S. Export Supply and Import Demand

In panel (a) domestic production of aluminum in the United States exceeds domestic consumption at all world prices above the $1.00 domestic price. These domestic surpluses result in U.S. exports (b). When the domestic price falls below $1.00, domestic shortages occur (a) and imports flow to the United States (b). The U.S. export supply curve and import demand curve depict these relationships.

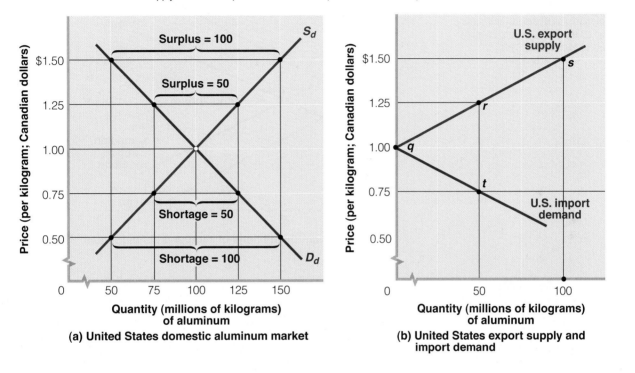

(a) United States domestic aluminum market

(b) United States export supply and import demand

Equilibrium World Price, Exports, and Imports

equilibrium world price
A price determined by the intersection of exporting nations' supply of a product and importing nations' demand for the same product.

We now have the tools to determine the **equilibrium world price** of aluminum and the equilibrium world levels of exports and imports. Figure 16-7 combines the Canadian export supply curve and import demand curve in Figure 16-5b and the U.S. export supply curve and import demand curve in Figure 16-6b. The two Canadian curves proceed rightward from the $1.25 domestic price; the two U.S. curves proceed rightward from the $1.00 U.S. domestic price.

International equilibrium occurs in this two-nation model where one nation's import demand curve intersects another nation's export supply curve. In this case Canada's import demand curve intersects America's export supply curve at *e*. There, the world price of aluminum is $1.125. The U.S. export supply curve indicates that the United States will export 25 million kilograms of aluminum at this price. Also at this price Canada will import 25 million kilograms from the United States, indicated by the Canadian import demand curve. The $1.125 world price equates the quantity of imports demanded and the quantity of exports supplied (= 25 million kilograms). Thus there will be world trade of 25 million kilograms of aluminum at $1.125 per kilogram.

Note that after trade, the single $1.125 world price will prevail in both Canada and the United States. Only one price for a standardized commodity can persist in a competitive market. With trade, all consumers can buy a kilogram of aluminum for $1.125 and all producers can sell it for that price.

Why would the United States willingly send 50 million kilograms of its aluminum output to Canada for consumption? After all, producing this output uses up scarce U.S. resources and drives up the price of aluminum for Americans. Americans are willing to export aluminum to Canada because they can gain the means—the earnings of Canadian dollars—to import other goods, say telecommunications equipment, from Canada.

 WORKED PROBLEM 16.2
Equilibrium World Price, Exports, and Imports

FIGURE 16-7   **Equilibrium World Price and Quantity of Exports and Imports**

In a two-nation world, the equilibrium world price (= $1.125) is determined at the intersection of one nation's export supply curve and another nation's import demand curve. This intersection also decides the equilibrium volume of exports and imports. Here, the United States exports 25 million kilograms of aluminum to Canada.

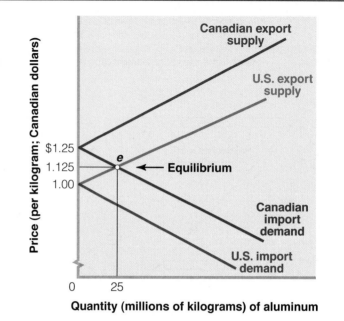

Quantity (millions of kilograms) of aluminum

QUICK REVIEW

▶ A nation will export a particular product if the world price exceeds the domestic price; it will import the product if the world price is less than the domestic price.

▶ In a two-country model, equilibrium world prices and equilibrium quantities of exports and imports occur when one nation's export supply curve intersects the other nation's import demand curve.

tariff
A tax imposed by a nation on an imported good.

revenue tariff
A tariff designed to produce income for the federal government.

protective tariff
A tariff designed to shield domestic producers of a good or service from the competition of foreign producers.

nontariff barrier
All restrictions other than tariffs that nations erect to impede international trade.

import quota
A limit imposed by a nation on the quantity (or total value) of a good that may be imported during some period of time.

16.4 | Trade Barriers

No matter how compelling the case for free trade, barriers to free trade *do* exist. Let's expand our discussion of trade barriers.

Excise taxes on imported goods are called **tariffs**; they may be imposed to raise government revenue or to protect domestic firms. A **revenue tariff** is usually applied to a product that is not being produced domestically—examples for Canada are tin, coffee, or bananas. Rates on revenue tariffs are modest; their purpose is to provide the federal government with revenues. A **protective tariff** is designed to shield domestic producers from foreign competition. Although protective tariffs are usually not high enough to stop the importation of foreign goods, they put foreign producers at a competitive disadvantage in selling in domestic markets.

A **nontariff barrier** refers either to a licensing requirement that specifies unreasonable standards pertaining to product quality and safety, or to unnecessary bureaucratic red tape that is used to restrict imports. Japan and the European countries frequently require their domestic importers of foreign goods to obtain licences. By restricting the issuance of licences, imports can be restricted. Great Britain used this barrier in the past to bar the importation of coal.

An **import quota** specifies the maximum amount of a commodity that may be imported in any period. Import quotas can slow down international commerce more effectively than tariffs. A product might be imported in large quantities despite high tariffs; low import quotas completely prohibit imports once quotas have been filled.

voluntary export restraint (VER)
Voluntary limitations by countries or firms of their exports to a particular foreign nation.

 ORIGIN 16.1
Mercantalism

A **voluntary export restraint (VER)** is a trade barrier by which foreign firms "voluntarily" limit the amount of their exports to a particular country. Exporters agree to VERs—which have the effect of import quotas—in the hope of avoiding more stringent trade barriers. In the late 1990s, for example, Canadian producers of softwood lumber (fir, spruce, cedar, pine) agreed to a VER on exports to the United States under the threat of a permanently higher U.S. tariff. In section 16.5 we consider the arguments protectionists make to justify trade barriers.

Economic Impact of Tariffs

Once again we use supply and demand analysis to examine the economic effects of protective tariffs. Curves D_d and S_d in **Figure 16-8 (Key Graph)** show domestic demand and supply for a product in which a nation, say Canada, has a comparative *dis*advantage—for example, DVD players. (Disregard $S_d + Q$ for now.) Without world trade, the domestic price and output would be P_d and q respectively.

Assume now that the domestic economy is opened to world trade and that the Chinese, who have a comparative advantage in DVD players, begin to sell them in Canada. We assume that with free trade the domestic price cannot differ from the world price, which here is P_w. At P_w domestic consumption is d and domestic production is a. The horizontal distance between the domestic supply and demand curves at P_w represents imports of ad. Thus far, our analysis is similar to the analysis of world prices in Figure 16-5.

DIRECT EFFECTS

Suppose now that Canada imposes a tariff on each imported DVD player. This will raise the domestic price from P_w to P_t and has four effects.

1. ***Decline in Consumption*** Consumption of DVD players in Canada declines from d to c as the higher price moves buyers up and to the left along their demand curve. The tariff prompts consumers to buy fewer DVD players and to reallocate a portion of their expenditures to less desired substitute products. Canadian consumers are injured by the tariff, since they pay $P_t - P_w$ more for each of the c units they now buy at price P_t.

2. ***Increased Domestic Production*** Canadian producers—who are not subject to the tariff—receive higher price P_t per unit. Because this new price is higher than the pre-tariff or world price of P_w, the domestic DVD player industry moves up and to the right along its supply curve S_d, increasing domestic output from a to b. Domestic producers thus enjoy both a higher price and expanded sales, which explains why domestic producers lobby for protective tariffs. But from a social point of view, the expanded domestic production of b instead of a means that the tariff permits domestic producers of DVD players to bid resources away from other, more efficient, Canadian industries.

3. ***Decline in Imports*** Chinese producers are hurt. Although the sale price of DVD players is higher by $P_t - P_w$, that amount accrues to the Canadian government, not to Chinese producers. The after-tariff world price, and thus the per-unit revenue to Chinese producers, remains at P_w, and the volume of Canadian imports (Chinese exports) falls from $d-a$ to $c-b$.

4. ***Tariff Revenue*** The shaded rectangle indicates the amount of revenue that the tariff yields. Total revenue from the tariff is determined by multiplying the tariff, $P_t - P_w$ per unit, by the number of imported DVD players, $c-b$. This tariff revenue is a transfer of income from consumers to government and does not represent any net change in the nation's economic well-being. The result is that government gains a portion of what consumers lose by paying more for DVD players.

KEY GRAPH

FIGURE 16-8 The Economic Effects of a Protective Tariff or an Import Quota

A tariff that increases the price of a good from P_w to P_t will reduce domestic consumption from d to c. Domestic producers will be able to sell more output (b rather than a) at a higher price (P_t rather than P_w). Foreign exporters are injured because they sell less output (bc rather than ad). The brown area indicates the amount of tariff paid by domestic consumers. An import quota of bc units has the same effect as the tariff, with one exception: The amount represented by the brown area will go to foreign producers rather than to the domestic government.

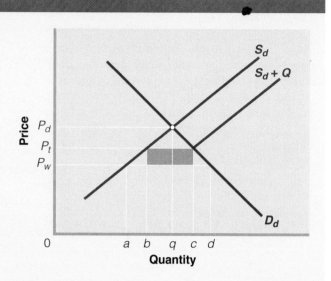

Quick Quiz

1. At world price P_w:
   a. domestic quantity demanded equals quantity supplied.
   b. domestic quantity demanded is less than quantity supplied.
   c. domestic quantity demanded is greater than quantity supplied.
   d. domestic quantity supplied is greater than quantity demanded.

2. At world prices above P_d Canada would:
   a. import.
   b. export.
   c. stop producing.
   d. none of the above.

3. A protective tariff:
   a. increases domestic production.
   b. decreases domestic production.
   c. does not affect domestic production.
   d. decreases government revenue.

4. A quota:
   a. decreases government revenue.
   b. increases government revenue.
   c. has no effect on government revenue.
   d. lowers domestic price.

INDIRECT EFFECTS

Tariffs have a subtle effect beyond what our supply and demand diagram can show. Because China sells fewer DVD players in Canada, China will earn fewer dollars with which to buy Canadian exports. Canadian export industries must then cut production and release resources. These are highly efficient industries, as evidenced by their comparative advantage and ability to sell goods in world markets.

Tariffs directly promote the expansion of inefficient industries that do not have a comparative advantage; they also indirectly cause contraction of relatively efficient industries that do have a comparative advantage. We know that specialization and world trade lead to more efficient use of world resources and greater world output. But protective tariffs reduce world trade. Therefore, tariffs also reduce efficiency and the world's real output.

Economic Impact of Quotas

The economic impact of quotas is similar to that of a tariff with one salient difference: Although tariffs generate revenue for the Canadian government, a quota transfers that revenue to foreign producers.

Suppose in Figure 16-8 that instead of imposing a tariff of P_wP_t per unit Canada prohibits any Chinese imports of DVD players in excess of bc units. In other words, an import quota of bc DVD players is imposed on China. We have deliberately chosen the size of this quota to be the same amount as imports would be under a P_wP_t tariff so we are comparing "equivalent" situations. As a consequence of the quota, the supply of DVD players is $S_d + Q$ in Canada. This consists of the domestic supply plus the constant amount, c-b ($= Q$), that importers will provide at each domestic price. The $S_d + Q$ supply curve does not exist below price P_w because Chinese producers would not export DVD players to Canada at any price *below* P_w; instead, they would sell them to other countries at the world market price of P_w.

Most of the economic results are the same as with a tariff. DVD player prices are higher (P_t instead of P_w) because imports have been reduced from d-a to c-b. Domestic consumption of DVD players is down from d-a to c-b. Canadian producers enjoy both a higher price (P_t rather than P_w) and increased sales (b rather than a).

The difference is that the price increase of P_wP_t paid by Canadian consumers on imports of c-b—the shaded area—no longer goes to the Canada Revenue Agency as tariff (tax) revenue, but flows to those Chinese firms that have acquired the quota rights to sell DVD players in Canada. The economic effects of a tariff are better for Canadian taxpayers than are those of a quota, other things being the same. A tariff generates government revenue, which can be used to cut other taxes or to finance public goods and services that benefit Canadian citizens. In contrast, the higher price created by quotas results in additional revenue for foreign producers.

Net Costs of Tariffs and Quotas

Figure 16-8 shows that tariffs and quotas impose costs on domestic consumers but provide gains to domestic producers and, in the case of tariffs, revenue to the federal government. The consumer costs of trade restrictions are calculated by determining the effect they have on consumer prices. Protection raises the price of a product in three ways: (1) the price of the imported product goes up, (2) the higher price of imports causes some consumers to shift their purchases to higher-priced domestically produced goods, and (3) the prices of domestically produced goods rise because import competition has declined.

Study after study finds that the costs to consumers substantially exceed gains to producers, workers and other suppliers of resources in the protected industry, and government. A sizable net cost or efficiency loss to society arises from trade protection. Furthermore, industries employ large amounts of economic resources to influence politicians to pass and retain protectionist laws. Because these rent-seeking efforts divert resources away from more socially desirable purposes, trade restrictions impose these additional costs on society as well.

16.5 | The Case for Protection: a Critical Review

Despite the compelling logic of specialization and trade, protectionists still exist in some union halls, corporate boardrooms, and the halls of Parliament. What arguments do protectionists make to justify trade barriers? How valid are these arguments?

Self-Sufficiency Argument

The argument here is not economic but political–military: Protective tariffs are needed to preserve or strengthen industries that produce the materials essential for national defence. In an uncertain world, the political–military objectives (self-sufficiency) sometimes must take precedence over economic goals (efficiency in the use of world resources).

Unfortunately, it is difficult to measure and compare the benefit of increased national security against the cost of economic inefficiency when protective tariffs are imposed. The economist can only point out that there are economic costs when a nation levies tariffs to increase military self-sufficiency.

The self-sufficiency argument is open to serious abuse. Nearly every industry can claim that it makes direct or indirect contributions to national security and hence deserves protection from imports.

Are there not better ways than tariffs to provide needed strength in strategic industries? When it is achieved through tariffs, this self-sufficiency increases the domestic prices of the products of the protected industry. Thus only those consumers who buy the industry's products shoulder the cost of greater military security. A direct subsidy to strategic industries, financed out of general tax revenues, would distribute these costs more equitably.

Diversification for Stability Argument

Highly specialized economies such as Saudi Arabia's (based on oil) and Cuba's (based on sugar) are very dependent on international markets for their incomes. In these economies, wars, international political developments, recessions abroad, and random fluctuations in world supply and

CONSIDER THIS | Shooting Yourself in the Foot

In the lore of the Wild West, a gunslinger on occasion would pull the trigger on his pistol while retrieving it from its holster, accidentally shooting himself in the foot. Since then, the phrase "shooting yourself in the foot" implies doing damage to yourself rather than the intended party. It's precisely how economist Paul Krugman sees a trade war:

> A trade war in which countries restrict each other's exports in pursuit of some illusory advantage is not much like a real war. On the one hand, nobody gets killed. On the other, unlike real wars, it is almost impossible for anyone to win, since the main losers when a country imposes barriers to trade are not foreign exporters but domestic residents. In effect, a trade war is a conflict in which each country uses most of its ammunition to shoot itself in the foot.*

The same analysis is applicable to trade boycotts between major trading partners. Such a boycott was encouraged by some American commentators against Canadian, French, and German imports because of these countries' opposition to the U.S.- and British-led war in Iraq. But the decline of exports to the United States would leave the Canadians, French, and Germans with fewer U.S. dollars to buy American exports. So the unintended effect would be a decline in U.S. exports to these countries and reduced employment in U.S. export industries. Moreover, such a trade boycott, if effective, might lead Canadian, French, and German consumers to retaliate against American imports. As with a "tariff war," a "boycott war" typically harms oneself as much as the other party.

* Paul Krugman, *Peddling Prosperity* (New York: Norton, 1994), p. 287.

demand for one or two particular goods can cause deep declines in export revenues and therefore in domestic income. Tariff and quota protection are allegedly needed in such nations to enable greater industrial diversification. That way, these economies will not be so dependent on exporting one or two products to obtain the other goods they need. Such goods will be available domestically, thereby providing greater domestic stability.

There is some truth in this diversification for stability argument. There are also two serious short-comings. First, the argument has little or no relevance to Canada and other advanced economies. Second, the economic costs of diversification may be great; for example, one-crop economies may be highly inefficient at manufacturing.

Infant-Industry Argument

The infant-industry argument says that protective tariffs are needed to allow new domestic industries to establish themselves. Temporarily shielding young domestic firms from the severe competition of more mature and more efficient foreign firms will give infant industries a chance to develop and become efficient producers.

This argument for protection rests on an alleged exception to the case for free trade. The exception is that young industries have not had—and, if they face mature foreign competition, will never have—the chance to make the long-run adjustments needed for larger scale and greater efficiency in production. In this view, tariff protection for such infant industries will correct a misallocation of world resources perpetuated by historically different levels of economic development between domestic and foreign industries.

COUNTER-ARGUMENTS

There are some logical problems with this infant-industry argument. In the developing nations it is difficult to determine which industries are the infants that are capable of achieving economic maturity and therefore deserving protection. Also, protective tariffs may persist even after industrial maturity has been realized.

Most economists believe that if infant industries are to be subsidized, there are better means than tariffs for doing it. Direct subsidies, for example, have the advantage of making explicit which industries are being aided and to what degree.

STRATEGIC TRADE POLICY

In recent years the infant-industry argument has taken a modified form in advanced economies. Now proponents contend that government should use trade barriers to reduce the risk of investing in product development by domestic firms, particularly where advanced technology is involved. Firms protected from foreign competition can grow more rapidly and achieve greater economies of scale than unprotected foreign competitors. The protected firms can eventually dominate world markets because of their lower costs. Supposedly, dominance of world markets will enable the domestic firms to return high profits to the home nation. These profits will exceed the domestic sacrifices caused by trade barriers. Also, advances in high-technology industries are considered to be beneficial because the advances achieved in one domestic industry often can be transferred to other domestic industries.

strategic trade policy
The use of trade barriers to reduce the risk inherent in product development by domestic firms, particularly that involving advanced technology.

Japan and South Korea, in particular, have been accused of using this form of **strategic trade policy.** These two countries, according to critics, protect what they consider to be key sectors from foreign competition. The problem with this strategy, and therefore this argument for tariffs, is that the nations put at a disadvantage by strategic trade policies tend to retaliate with tariffs of their own. The outcome may be higher tariffs worldwide, reductions of world trade, and the loss of potential gains from technological advances.

Protection against Dumping Argument

dumping
The sale in a foreign country of products below cost or below the prices charged at home.

The protection against dumping argument contends that tariffs are needed to protect domestic firms from "dumping" by foreign producers. **Dumping** is the sale of a product in a foreign country at prices either below cost or below the prices commonly charged at home. Economists cite two plausible reasons for this behaviour. First, with regard to below-cost dumping, firms in country A may dump goods at below cost into country B in an attempt to drive their competitors in country B out of business. If the firms in country A succeed in driving their competitors in country B out of business, they will enjoy monopoly power and monopoly prices and profits on the goods they subsequently sell in country B. Their hope is that the longer-term monopoly profits will more than offset the losses from below-cost sales that must take place while they are attempting to drive their competitors in country B out of business.

Second, dumping that involves selling abroad at a price below the price commonly charged in the home country (but still at or above production costs) may be a form of price discrimination, which is charging different prices to different customers. As an example, a foreign seller that has a monopoly in its home market may find that it can maximize its overall profit by charging a high price in its monopolized domestic market while charging a lower price in Canada, where it must compete with Canadian producers. Curiously, it may pursue this strategy even if it makes no profit at all from its sales in Canada, where it must charge the competitive price. So why bother selling in Canada? Because the increase in overall production that comes about by exporting to Canada may allow the firm to obtain the per-unit cost savings often associated with large-scale production. These cost savings imply even higher profits in the monopolized domestic market.

Because dumping is an "unfair trade practice," most nations prohibit it. For example, where dumping is shown to injure Canadian firms, the federal government imposes tariffs called *anti-dumping duties* on the goods in question. But relatively few documented cases of dumping occur each year, and specific instances of unfair trade do not justify widespread, permanent tariffs. Moreover, antidumping duties can be abused. Often, what appears to be dumping is simply comparative advantage at work.

Increased Domestic Employment Argument

Arguing for a tariff to "save Canadian jobs" becomes fashionable when the economy encounters a recession or experiences slow job growth during a recovery (as in the early 1990s in Canada). In an economy that engages in international trade, exports involve spending on domestic output and imports reflect spending to obtain part of another nation's output. So, in this argument, reducing imports will divert spending on another nation's output to spending on domestic output. Thus domestic output and employment will rise. But this argument has several shortcomings.

While imports may eliminate some Canadian jobs, they create others. Imports may have eliminated the jobs of some Canadian steel and textile workers in recent years, but other workers have gained jobs unloading ships, flying imported aircraft, and selling imported electronic equipment. Import restrictions alter the composition of employment, but they may have little or no effect on the volume of employment.

The *fallacy of composition*—the false idea that what is true for the part is necessarily true for the whole—is also present in this rationale for tariffs. All nations cannot simultaneously succeed in restricting imports while maintaining their exports; what is true for one nation is not true for all nations. The exports of one nation must be the imports of another nation. To the extent that one country is able to expand its economy through an excess of exports over imports, the resulting excess of imports over exports worsens another economy's unemployment problem. It is no wonder that tariffs and import quotas meant to achieve domestic full employment are called "beggar thy neighbour" policies: They achieve short-run domestic goals by making trading partners poorer.

Finally, forcing an excess of exports over imports cannot succeed in raising domestic employment over the long run. It is through Canadian imports that foreign nations earn dollars for buying Canadian exports. In the long run a nation must import in order to export. The long-run impact of tariffs is not an increase in domestic employment but, at best, a reallocation of workers away from export industries and to protected domestic industries. This shift implies a less efficient allocation of resources.

Cheap Foreign Labour Argument

The cheap foreign labour argument says that domestic firms and workers must be shielded from the ruinous competition of countries where wages are low. If protection is not provided, cheap imports will flood Canadian markets and the prices of Canadian goods—along with the wages of Canadian workers—will be pulled down. That is, the domestic living standards in Canada will be reduced.

This argument can be rebutted at several levels. The logic of the argument suggests that it is *not* mutually beneficial for rich and poor persons to trade with one another. However, that is not the case. A low-income farm worker may pick lettuce or tomatoes for a rich landowner, and both may benefit from the transaction. And both Canadian consumers and Chinese workers gain when they "trade" a pair of athletic shoes priced at $30 as opposed to Canadian consumers being restricted to buying a similar shoe made in Canada for $60.

Also, recall that gains from trade are based on comparative advantage, not on absolute advantage. Look back at Figure 16-3, where we supposed that Canada and Brazil had labour forces of exactly the same size. Noting the positions of the production possibilities curves, we observe that Canadian labour can produce more of *either* good. Thus, it is more productive; it has an absolute advantage in the production of both goods. Because of this greater productivity, we can expect wages and living standards to be higher for Canadian labour. Brazil's less productive labour will receive lower wages.

The cheap foreign labour argument suggests that, to maintain its standard of living, Canada should not trade with low-wage Brazil. What if it does not trade with Brazil? Will wages and living standards rise in Canada as a result? No. To obtain soybeans, Canada will have to reallocate a portion of its labour from its efficient steel industry to its less efficient soybean industry. As a result, the average productivity of Canadian labour will fall, as will real wages and living standards. The labour forces of *both* countries will have lower standards of living because without specialization and trade they will have less output available to them. Compare column 4 with column 1 in Table 16-2 or points *A'* and *B'* with *A* and *B* in Figure 16-3 to confirm this point.

Another problem with the cheap foreign labour argument is that its proponents incorrectly focus on labour costs per hour when what really matters is labour costs per unit. As an example, suppose a Canadian factory pays its workers $20 per hour while a factory in a developing country pays its workers $4 per hour. The proponents of the cheap foreign labour argument look at these numbers and conclude—incorrectly—that it is impossible for the Canadian factory to compete with the factory in the developing country. But this conclusion fails to take into account two crucial facts:

- What actually matters is labour costs per *unit*, not labour costs per *hour*.

- Differences in productivity typically mean that labour costs per unit are often nearly identical despite huge differences in labour costs per hour.

To see why these points matter so much, let's take into account how productive the two factories are. Because the Canadian factory uses much more sophisticated technology, better trained workers, and a lot more capital per worker, one worker in one hour can produce 20 units of output. Since the Canadian workers get paid $20 per hour, this means the Canadian factory's labour cost *per unit of output* is $1. The factory in the developing country is much less productive since it uses less efficient technology and its relatively untrained workers have a lot less machinery and equipment to work with. A worker there produces only 4 units per hour. Given the foreign wage of $4 per hour, this means that the labour cost per unit of output at the factory in the developing country is also $1. As you can see, the lower wage rate per hour at the factory in the developing country does not translate into lower labour costs per unit—meaning that it won't be able to undersell its Canadian competitor just because its workers get paid lower wages per hour.

Proponents of the cheap foreign labour argument tend to focus exclusively on the large international differences that exist in labour costs per hour. They typically fail to mention that these differences in labour costs per hour are mostly the result of tremendously large differences in productivity and that these large differences in productivity serve to equalize labour costs per unit of output. As a result, firms in developing countries only *sometimes* have an advantage in terms of labour costs per unit of output. Whether they do in any specific situation will vary by industry and firm and will depend upon differences in productivity as well as differences in labour costs per hour. For many goods, labour productivity in high-wage countries like Canada is so much higher than labour productivity in low-wage countries that it is actually cheaper *per unit of output* to manufacture those goods in high-wage countries. That is why, for instance, most automobiles are still produced in Canada, the United States, Japan, and Europe rather than in low-wage countries.

QUICK REVIEW

▶ A tariff on a product increases its price, reduces its consumption, increases its domestic production, reduces its imports, and generates tariff revenue for government; an import quota does the same, except a quota generates revenue for foreign producers rather than for the government imposing the quota.

▶ Most rationales for trade protections are special-interest requests that, if followed, would create gains for protected industries and their workers at the expense of greater losses for the economy.

16.6 | Multilateral Trade Agreements and Free-Trade Zones

When one nation enacts barriers against imports, the nations whose exports suffer may retaliate with trade barriers of their own. In such a *trade war*, escalating tariffs choke world trade and reduce everyone's economic well-being. Economic historians generally agree that high tariffs were a contributing cause of the Great Depression. Aware of that fact, nations have worked to lower tariffs worldwide. Their pursuit of free trade has been added by powerful domestic interest groups: Exporters of goods and services, importers of foreign components used in "domestic" products, and domestic sellers of imported products all strongly support lower tariffs.

Figure 16-9 makes clear that although Canada has been a high-tariff nation over much of its history, Canadian tariffs have declined substantially during the past half-century.

Reciprocal Trade Agreements

most-favoured-nation clause
An agreement by Canada to allow some other nation's exports into Canada at the lowest tariff levied by Canada.

The specific tariff reductions negotiated between Canada and any particular nation were generalized through **most-favoured-nation clauses,** which often accompany reciprocal trade agreements. These clauses stipulate that any subsequently reduced Canadian tariffs, resulting from negotiation with any other nation, would apply equally to any nation that signed the original agreement. So if Canada negotiates a reduction in tariffs on wristwatches with, say, France, the lower Canadian tariff on imported French watches also applies to the imports of the other nations having most-favoured-nation status, say, Japan and Switzerland. This way, the reduction in Canadian tariffs automatically applies to many nations. Today, most-favoured-nation status is so common that the Canadian government refers to it as *normal trade relations (NTR)* status.

| FIGURE 16·9 | **Canadian Tariff Rates, 1930–2008** |

Historically, Canadian tariff rates have fluctuated. But beginning with the mid-1930s, the trend has been downward.

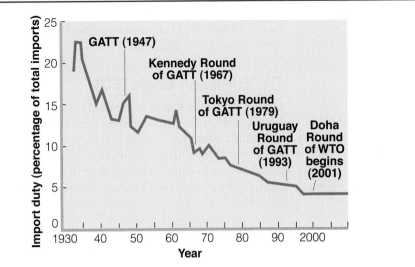

General Agreement on Tariffs and Trade (GATT)

General Agreement on Tariffs and Trade (GATT)
The international agreement reached in 1947 in which 23 nations agreed to give equal and non-discriminatory treatment to one another, to reduce tariff rates by multinational negotiations, and to eliminate export quotas.

In 1947, 23 nations, including Canada, signed the **General Agreement on Tariffs and Trade (GATT)**. GATT was based on three principles: (1) equal, non-discriminatory trade treatment for all member nations; (2) the reduction of tariffs by multilateral negotiation; and (3) the elimination of import quotas. Basically, GATT provided a forum for the negotiation of reduced trade barriers on a multilateral basis among nations.

Since World War II, member nations have completed eight "rounds" of GATT negotiations to reduce trade barriers. The eighth and last round of negotiations began in Uruguay in 1986. After seven years of complex discussions, in 1993 the 128 member nations reached a new agreement. The "Uruguay Round" agreement took effect on January 1, 1995, and its provisions were phased in through 2005. Under this agreement, tariffs on thousands of products were eliminated or reduced, with overall tariffs eventually dropping by 33 percent. The agreement also liberalized government rules that in the past impeded the global market for such services as advertising, legal services, tourist services, and financial services. Quotas on imported textiles and apparel were phased out and replaced with tariffs. Other provisions reduced agricultural subsidies paid to farmers and protected intellectual property (patents, trademarks, copyrights) against piracy.

World Trade Organization (WTO)

World Trade Organization (WTO)
An organization of 153 nations (as of 2008) that oversees the provisions of the current world trade agreement, resolves trade disputes stemming from it, and holds forums for further rounds of trade negotiations.

The Uruguay Round agreement established the **World Trade Organization (WTO)** as GATT's successor. In 2008, some 153 nations belonged to the WTO. The WTO oversees trade agreements reached by the member nations and rules on trade disputes among them. It also provides forums for further rounds of trade negotiations. The ninth and latest round of negotiations—the Doha Round—was launched in Doha, Qatar in late 2001. (The trade rounds occur over several years in various venues but are named after the city or country that hosts the first meeting.) The negotiations are aimed at further reducing tariffs and quotas, as well as agricultural subsidies that distort trade. As of mid-2009 the Doha Round of international trade negotiations is still stalled; periods of recession such as we experienced in 2008–09 are not at all conducive. One of this chapter's Internet Application Questions asks you to report on the progress of the Doha Round.

GATT and the WTO have been positive forces in the trend toward liberalized world trade. The trade rules agreed upon by the member nations provide a strong and necessary bulwark against the protectionism called for by special interest groups in various nations.

For that reason and others, the WTO is highly controversial. Critics are concerned that rules crafted to expand international trade and investment enable firms to circumvent national laws that protect workers and the environment. Proponents of the WTO respond that labour and environmental protections should be pursued directly in nations that have low standards and via international organizations other than the WTO.

The European Union (EU)

European Union (EU)
An association of European nations that have eliminated tariffs among themselves, established common tariffs for goods imported from outside the member nations, and allowed the free movement of labour and capital among themselves.

Countries have also sought to reduce tariffs by creating regional *free-trade zones*—also called *trade blocs*. The most dramatic example is the **European Union** (EU), formerly called the European Economic Community. Initiated in 1958 as the Common Market, in 2003 the EU comprised 15 European nations—France, Germany, United Kingdom, Italy, Belgium, the Netherlands, Luxembourg, Denmark, Ireland, Greece, Spain, Portugal, Austria, Finland, and Sweden. In 2004, the EU expanded by 10 additional European countries: Poland, Hungary, the Czech Republic, Slovakia, Lithuania, Latvia, Estonia, Slovenia, Malta, and Cyprus. In 2007, the addition of Bulgaria and Romania expanded the EU to 27 nations.

THE EU TRADE BLOC

trade bloc
A group of nations that lower or abolish trade barriers among members. Examples include the members of the European Union and the members of the North American Free Trade Agreement.

The EU has abolished tariffs and import quotas on nearly all products traded among the participating nations and established a common system of tariffs applicable to all goods received from nations outside the EU. It has also liberalized the movement of capital and labour within the EU and has created common policies in other economic matters of joint concern, such as agriculture, transportation, and business practices. The EU is now a strong **trade bloc:** a group of countries having common identity, economic interests, and trade rules.

EU integration has achieved for Europe increased regional specialization, greater productivity, greater output, and faster economic growth. The free flow of goods and services has created large markets for EU industries. The resulting economies of large-scale production have enabled them to achieve much lower costs than they could have achieved in their small, single-nation markets.

The effects of EU success on nonmember nations, such as Canada, have been mixed. A peaceful and increasingly prosperous EU makes its members better customers for Canadian exports. But Canadian firms and other nonmember nations' firms have been faced with tariffs and other barriers that make it difficult for them to compete against firms within the EU trade bloc. For example, autos produced in Germany and sold in Spain or France face no tariffs, whereas North American and Japanese autos sold in those EU countries do. This puts non-EU firms at a serious disadvantage. Similarly, EU trade restrictions hamper Eastern European exports of metals, textiles, and farm products, goods that the Eastern Europeans produce in abundance.

By giving preference to countries within their free-trade zone, trade blocs such as the EU tend to reduce their members' trade with non-bloc members. Thus, the world loses some of the benefits of a completely open global trading system. Eliminating that disadvantage has been one of the motivations for liberalizing global trade through the World Trade Organization.

THE EURO

euro
The common currency used by 15 European nations in the Euro Zone, which will eventually include all the member nations of the EU except Great Britain, Denmark, and Sweden.

One of the most significant accomplishments of the EU was the establishment of the so-called "Euro Zone" in the early 2000s. In 2008, 15 members of the EU used the **euro** as a common currency. Great Britain, Denmark, and Sweden have opted out of the common currency, at least for now. The other members of the EU are required to adopt the euro as their currency after they successfully meet certain economic criteria. Gone are French francs, German marks, Italian liras, and other national currencies within the Euro Zone.

Economists expect the adoption of the euro to raise the standard of living of the Euro Zone members over time. By ending the inconvenience and expense of exchanging currencies, the euro has enhanced the free flow of goods, services, and resources among the Euro Zone members. International trade among the member nations has increased by roughly 10 percent, with much of that increase happening because companies that previously sold products in only one or two European countries have now found it easier to market and sell their wares in all 15 Euro Zone countries. The euro has also allowed consumers and businesses to comparison shop for outputs and inputs, and this capability has increased competition, reduced prices, and lowered costs.

North American Free Trade Agreement (NAFTA)

North American Free Trade Agreement (NAFTA)
A 1993 agreement establishing a free trade zone composed of Canada, Mexico, and the United States.

In 1993, Canada, Mexico, and the United States formed a major trade bloc. **The North American Free Trade Agreement (NAFTA)** established a free-trade zone that has about the same combined output as the EU but encompasses a much larger geographical area. NAFTA has eliminated tariffs and other trade barriers among Canada, Mexico, and the United States for most goods and services.

Critics of NAFTA feared that it would cause a massive loss of Canadian jobs as firms moved to Mexico to take advantage of lower wages and weaker regulations on pollution and workplace safety. Also, there were concerns that Japan and South Korea would build plants in Mexico and transport goods tariff-free to Canada, further hurting Canadian firms and workers.

In retrospect, the critics were much too pessimistic. Since the passage of NAFTA in 1993, employment has increased in Canada by over 4 million workers and the unemployment rate fell from over 10 percent to under 7 percent in 2008. Increased trade among Canada, Mexico, and the United States has enhanced the standard of living in all three countries. *(Key Question 13)*

QUICK REVIEW

▶ Governments curtail imports and promote exports through protective tariffs, import quotas, nontariff barriers, and export subsidies.

▶ The General Agreement on Tariffs and Trade (GATT) established multinational reductions in tariffs and import quotas. The Uruguay Round of GATT (1993) reduced tariffs worldwide, liberalized international trade in services, strengthened protections for intellectual property, and reduced agricultural subsidies.

▶ The World Trade Organization (WTO)—GATT's successor—rules on trade disputes and provides forums for negotiations on further rounds of trade liberalization. The current round is called the Doha Round.

▶ The European Union (EU) and the North American Free Trade Agreement (NAFTA) have reduced internal trade barriers among their members by establishing large free-trade zones. Of the 27 EU members (as of 2008), 15 now have a common currency—the euro.

The LAST WORD   Fair-Trade Products

As a university or college student, you may be aware of fair-trade-certified products, such as those offered at Starbucks. On some campuses, proponents of fair-trade consumption are highly active in encouraging fellow students to purchase only fair-trade goods. What is fair trade all about? And how effective is it as an economic development strategy?

Imports of goods by high-income nations from low-income nations increase the demand for labour in low-income nations. Other things equal, increases in labour demand raise wages and incomes.

Some observers, however, conclude that the benefits low-income countries derive from increased production—especially increased exports of agricultural commodities—accrue mainly to large corpo-

rations in those countries, some of which are owned by shareholders from high-income nations. Because workers in many low-income countries are highly immobile, have few employment options, and are not unionized, the large dominant sellers can supposedly keep an undeservedly large portion of the proceeds from added exports for themselves (in the form of profits) while simultaneously denying a fair share to their workers (by keeping wages low).

To counter this purported problem, consumer organizations in some of the high-income countries have tried to bypass the usual distribution channels and buy imported goods directly from producers or producer cooperatives that agree to *fair-trade standards*. Such standards guarantee the producers higher-than-market prices if they agree to pay their workers higher-than-market wages and to abide by rules regarding working conditions and workplace safety. Producers and products that meet the fair-trade standards are certified as fair-trade employers and fair-trade products. Fair-trade advocates in the rich nations then strongly urge consumers to purchase products—for example, coffee, wine, bananas, tea, fresh fruit, and cocoa—only from certified fair-trade producers. When pressure is sufficient, some corporate buyers of these products conclude that it may be more profitable to provide fair-trade products to customers than to risk being labelled an exploiter of third-world labour. Because of the higher-than-market prices and wages, fair-trade goods usually are more expensive than noncertified products.

In economic terms, the purpose of the fair-trade movement is to redistribute more of the total gains from international trade directly to low-income producers and workers by increasing the demand for fair-trade imports relative to otherwise identical imports.

Do these efforts succeed? Economists agree that the efforts of fair-trade advocates do channel purchases away from otherwise identical substitutes and toward fair-trade goods—and that these increases in product demand do, in turn, increase the demand for the labour used to produce fair-trade goods. These increased demands and the increases in prices and wages that result suggests that the fair-trade strategy "works" insofar as it raises prices and wages for *some* sellers and *some* workers in low-wage countries—namely those involved with fair-trade programs.

Nevertheless, most economists question the overall effectiveness of the fair-trade approach as an economic development strategy. They say that price and wage setting by advocacy groups is based on highly subjective views of fairness that may be at odds with economic realities. Distortions of market prices and wages invite inefficiency and unintended consequences. (Recall our discussion of government price floors in Chapter 3.)

The consensus among economists is that fair-trade purchasing in the high-income nations simply shifts demand within low-wage countries (or among them). It does not increase the *average* pay of the workers within a particular low-wage nation. Sustainable increases in average pay require economy-wide gains in labour productivity—output per hour of work. Unlike increases in education, more and improved capital goods, and improved technology, fair-trade purchasing in high-income nations does little, if anything, to affect a nation's overall productivity and wage level.

Some economists say that other action by people in high-income nations might benefit the low-income nations more effectively than fair-trade purchasing. For example, pressing for the removal of agricultural subsidies in high-income areas such as Canada, the United States, and the European Union would reduce the overproduction of agricultural output that floods international markets and depresses international agricultural prices. Those low prices keep agricultural producers in low-income countries impoverished and unable to pay for the upgrades that would allow them to profitably diversify their agriculture into higher-profit food products. Instead, they tend to be stuck overproducing low-profit agricultural commodities such as coffee, bananas, and cocoa—keeping those prices artificially low. Ironically, those very low prices (and the low agricultural wages that result) are precisely what the fair-trade movement tries to increase.

Helping people in low-income nations improve their lot in life is certainly admirable. But figuring out the best way to achieve that goal is not always as easy as it may at first seem.

Question

How does a fair-trade product differ from an otherwise identical imported good? What is the purported benefit of fair-trade certification and purchases of goods such as chocolate, coffee, bananas, and tea? Do fair-trade goods improve average wage and level of income in low-income nations? Why or why not?

CHAPTER SUMMARY

16.1 ▶ CANADA AND INTERNATIONAL LINKAGES

- Goods and services flows, capital and labour flows, information and technology flows, and financial flows link Canada and other countries.

- International trade is growing in importance globally and for Canada. World trade is significant to Canada in two respects: (a) Canadian imports and exports as a percentage of domestic output are among the highest in the world; and (b) Canada is completely dependent on trade for certain commodities and materials that cannot be obtained domestically.

- Principal Canadian exports include automotive products, machinery and equipment, and grain; major Canadian imports are general machinery and equipment, automobiles, and industrial goods and machinery. Quantitatively, the United States is our most important trading partner.

- Global trade has been greatly facilitated by (a) improvements in transportation technology, (b) improvements in communications technology, and (c) general declines in tariffs. The world's major trading nations by volume of trade are Germany, the United States, China, and Japan. Other major traders include other western European nations (France, Netherlands, Italy, and the United Kingdom), along with Canada and the southeast Asian countries of South Korea, Taiwan, and Singapore.

16.2 ▶ THE ECONOMIC BASIS FOR TRADE

- World trade is based on three considerations: the uneven distribution of economic resources among nations, the fact that efficient production of various goods requires particular techniques or combinations of resources, and the differentiated products produced among nations.

- Mutually advantageous specialization and trade are possible between any two nations if they have different opportunity-cost ratios for any two products. By specializing based on comparative advantage, nations can obtain larger real incomes with fixed amounts of resources. The terms of trade determine how this increase in world output is shared by the trading nations. Increasing (rather than constant) costs limit specialization and trade.

16.3 ▶ SUPPLY AND DEMAND ANALYSIS OF EXPORTS AND IMPORTS

- A nation's export supply curve shows the quantity of product it will export at world prices that exceed the domestic price—the price in a closed, no-international-trade economy. Its import demand curve reveals the quantity of a product it will import at world prices below the domestic price.

- In a two-nation model, the equilibrium world price and the equilibrium quantities of exports and imports occur where one nation's import supply curve intersects the other nation's export demand curve.

16.4 ▶ TRADE BARRIERS

- Trade barriers take the form of protective tariffs, quotas, nontariff barriers, and "voluntary" export restraints. Supply and demand analysis reveals that protective tariffs and quotas increase the prices and reduce the quantities demanded of affected goods. Sales by foreign exporters diminish; domestic producers, however, enjoy higher prices and enlarged sales. Consumer losses from trade restrictions greatly exceed producer and government gains, creating an efficiency loss to society.

16.5 ▶ THE CASE FOR PROTECTION: A CRITICAL REVIEW

- The strongest arguments for protection are the infant industry and military self-sufficiency arguments. Most other arguments for protection are interest-group appeals or reasoning fallacies that emphasize producer interests over consumer interests or stress the immediate effects of trade barriers while ignoring long-run consequences. The cheap foreign labour argument for protection fails because it focuses on labour costs per hour rather than on what really matters, labour costs per unit of output. Due to higher productivity, firms in high-wage countries like Canada can have lower wage costs per unit of output than competitors in low-wage countries. Whether they do will depend on how their particular wage and productivity levels compare with those of their competitors in low-wage countries.

16.6 ▶ MULTILATERAL TRADE AGREEMENTS AND FREE-TRADE ZONES

- In 1947 the General Agreement on Tariffs and Trade (GATT) was formed to encourage nondiscriminatory treatment for all member nations, to reduce tariffs, and to eliminate import quotas. The Uruguay Round of GATT negotiations (1993) reduced tariffs and quotas, liberalized trade in services, reduced agricultural subsidies, reduced pirating of intellectual property, and phased out quotas on textiles.

- GATT's successor, the World Trade Organization (WTO), had 153 member nations in 2008. The WTO oversees trade agreements among its members, resolves disputes over the rules, and periodically meets to discuss and negotiate further trade liberalization. In 2001 the WTO initiated a new round of trade negotiations in Doha, Qatar. By mid-2009 the Doha Round was still in progress.

- Free-trade zones (trade blocs) liberalize trade within regions but may at the same time impede trade with non–bloc members. Two examples of free-trade agreements are the 27-member European Union (EU) and the North American Free Trade Agreement (NAFTA) comprising Canada, Mexico, and the United States. Fifteen of the EU nations have agreed to abandon their national currencies for a common currency called the euro.

TERMS AND CONCEPTS

labour-intensive goods, p. 385
land-intensive goods, p. 385
capital-intensive goods, p. 385
absolute advantage, p. 386
opportunity-cost ratio, p. 386
principle of comparative advantage,
  p. 387
terms of trade, p. 388
trading possibilities line, p. 389
gains from trade, p. 391
world price, p. 392

domestic price, p. 392
export supply curve, p. 394
import demand curve, p. 394
equilibrium world price, p. 395
tariff, p. 396
revenue tariff, p. 396
protective tariff, p. 396
nontariff barrier, p. 396
import quota, p. 396
voluntary export restraint (VER), p. 397
strategic trade policy, p. 401

dumping, p. 402
most-favoured-nation clause, p. 404
General Agreement on Tariffs and
  Trade (GATT), p. 405
World Trade Organization (WTO),
  p. 405
European Union (EU), p. 406
trade bloc, p. 406
euro, p. 406
North America Free Trade Agreement
  (NAFTA), p. 407

STUDY QUESTIONS

LO ▶ 16.1 1. Describe the three major economic flows that link Canada with other nations. Provide a specific example to illustrate each flow. Explain the relationships between the top and bottom flows in Figure 16-1.

LO ▶ 16.1 2. How important is international trade to the Canadian economy? Who is Canada's most important trade partner? How can persistent trade deficits be financed? "Trade deficits mean we get more merchandise from the rest of the world than we provide them in return. Therefore, trade deficits are economically desirable." Do you agree? Why or why not?

LO ▶ 16.1 3. What factors account for the rapid growth of world trade since World War II? Who are the major players in international trade today? Besides China and Japan, what other Asian nations play a significant role in international trade?

LO ▶ 16.1 4. Quantitatively, how important is international trade to Canada relative to other nations?

LO ▶ 16.2 5. Distinguish among land-, labour-, and capital-intensive commodities, citing an example of each. What role do these distinctions play in explaining international trade?

LO ▶ 16.2 6. Suppose nation A can produce 80 units of X by using all its resources to produce X and 60 units of Y by devoting all its resources to Y. Comparative figures for nation B are 60 of X and 60 of Y. Assuming constant costs, in which product should each nation specialize? Why? What are the limits of the terms of trade?

7. **KEY QUESTION** The following are hypothetical production possibilities tables for New Zealand and Spain.   **LO ▶ 16**

New Zealand's Production Possibilities Table (millions of bushels)

Product	Production alternatives			
	A	**B**	**C**	**D**
Apples	0	20	40	60
Plums	15	10	5	0

Spain's Production Possibilities Table (millions of bushels)

Product	Production alternatives			
	R	**S**	**T**	**U**
Apples	0	20	40	60
Plums	60	40	20	0

Plot the production possibilities data for each of the two countries separately. Referring to your graphs, determine:

a. Each country's cost ratio of producing plums and apples.

b. Which nation should specialize in which product.

c. The trading possibilities lines for each nation if the actual terms of trade are 1 plum for 2 apples. (Plot these lines on your graph.)

d. Suppose the optimum product mixes before specialization and trade were B in New Zealand and S in Spain. What are the gains from specialization and trade?

16.3 8. "Canada can produce product X more efficiently than can Great Britain. Yet we import X from Great Britain." Explain.

16.4 9. "The potentially valid arguments for tariff protection are also the most easily abused." (a) What are these particular arguments? (b) Why are they susceptible to abuse? (c) Evaluate the use of artificial trade barriers, such as tariffs and import quotas, as a means of achieving and maintaining full employment.

16.4 10. Evaluate the following statements:

a. "Protective tariffs limit both the imports and the exports of the nation levying tariffs."

b. "The extensive application of protective tariffs destroys the ability of the international market system to allocate resources efficiently."

c. "Unemployment can often be reduced through tariff protection, but by the same token inefficiency typically increases."

d. "Foreign firms that 'dump' their products onto the Canadian market are in effect presenting the Canadian people with gifts."

e. "In view of the rapidity with which technological advance is dispersed around the world, free trade will inevitably yield structural maladjustments, unemployment, and balance of payments problems for industrially advanced nations."

f. "Free trade can improve the composition and efficiency of domestic output. Only the Volkswagen forced Detroit to make a compact car, and only foreign success with the oxygen process forced Canadian steel firms to modernize."

g. "In the long run foreign trade is neutral with respect to total employment."

LO 6.4 11. Suppose Japan agreed to a voluntary export restraint that reduced Canadian imports of Japanese automobiles by about 10 percent. What would you expect the short-run effects to have been on the Canadian and Japanese automobile industries? If this restriction were permanent, what would be its long-run effects in the two nations on (a) the allocation of resources, (b) the volume of employment, (c) the price level, and (d) the standard of living?

LO 16.5 12. In 2005, manufacturing workers in Canada earned an average wage of $23.65 per hour. That same year, manufacturing workers in Mexico earned an average wage of $2.63 per hour. (a) How can Canadian manufacturers possibly compete? (b) Why isn't all manufacturing done in Mexico and other low-wage countries?

LO 16.6 13. **KEY QUESTION**   Identify and state the significance of each of the following: (a) WTO; (b) EU; (c) the euro; and (d) NAFTA. What commonality do they share?

LO 6.6 14. What is the WTO and how does it relate to international trade? How many nations belong to the WTO? (Update the number given in this book with data from www.wto. org.) What did the Uruguay Round (1994) of WTO accomplish? What is the name of the current WTO round of trade negotiations?

LO 16.6 15. Explain: "Free-trade zones such as the EU and NAFTA lead a double life: they can promote free trade among members, but they pose serious trade obstacles for nonmembers." (a) Do you think the net effects of trade blocs are good or bad for world trade? Why? (b) How do the efforts of the WTO relate to these trade blocs?

INTERNET APPLICATION QUESTIONS @

1. **Trade Liberalization—The WTO.** Access the World Trade Organization (WTO) Web site from the McConnell-Brue-Flynn-Barbiero Web site (Chapter 16) and retrieve the latest news from the WTO. List and summarize three recent news items relating to the WTO.

2. **Canada's Main Trading Partners.** Statistics Canada lists Canada's main trading partners. Go to the McConnell-Brue-Flynn-Barbiero Web site (Chapter 16). Which country is our largest trading partner? What is Canada's biggest export sector? What sector is a close second?

3. **The Doha Round—What Is the Current Status?** Determine and briefly summarize the current status of the Doha Round of trade negotiations by accessing the World Trade Organization site through the McConnell-Brue-Flynn-Barbiero Web site (Chapter 16). Is the round still in progress or has it been concluded with an agreement? If the former, when and where was the latest ministerial meeting? If the latter, what are the main features of the agreement?

CHAPTER 17

Exchange Rates and the Balance of Payments

If you take a Canadian dollar to the bank and ask to exchange it for Canadian currency, you will get a puzzled look. If you persist, you may get a dollar's worth of change: One Canadian dollar can buy exactly one Canadian dollar. But in May 2009, for example, one Canadian dollar could buy 6.1 Chinese renminbi, 1.14 Australian dollars, 0.56 British pounds, 0.90 American dollars, 0.64 European euro, 87 Japanese yen, or 42 Indian rupees. What explains this seemingly haphazard array of exchange rates?

In Chapter 16 we examined comparative advantage as the underlying economic basis of world trade and discussed the effects of barriers to free trade. Now we introduce the highly important monetary or financial aspects of international trade.

17.1 | Financing International Trade

This chapter focuses on international financial transactions, the vast majority of which fall into two broad categories: international trade and international asset transactions. International trade involves either purchasing or selling currently produced goods or services across an international border. Examples include an Egyptian firm exporting cotton to Canada and a Canadian company hiring an Indian call centre to answer its phones. International asset transactions involve the transfer of the property rights to either real or financial assets between the citizens of one country and the citizens of another country. It includes activities like buying foreign stocks or selling your house to a foreigner.

These two categories of international financial transactions reflect the fact that whether they are from different countries or the same country, individuals and firms can exchange only two things with each other: currently produced goods and services or pre-existing assets. With regard to assets, however, money is by far the most commonly exchanged asset. Only rarely would you ever find a barter situation in which people directly exchanged other assets—such as trading a car for 500 shares of Research In Motion stock, or a cow for 30 chickens and a tank of diesel fuel. As a result, there are two basic types of transactions: people trading either goods or services for money, or people trading assets for money. In either case, money flows from the buyers of the goods, services, or assets to the sellers of the goods, services, or assets.

When the people engaged in any such transactions are both from places that use the same currency, what type of money to use is not an issue. Canadians from Alberta and Newfoundland will use their common currency, the Canadian dollar. People from France and Germany will use their common currency, the euro. However, when the people involved in an exchange are from places that use different currencies, an intermediate asset transaction has to take place: the buyer must convert her type of money into the currency that the seller uses and accepts.

As an example, consider the case of a British software design company that wants to buy a supercomputer made by a Canadian company. The Canadian company sells these high-powered machines for $300,000. To pay for the machine, the British company has to convert some of the money it has (British pounds sterling) into the money that the Canadian company will accept (Canadian dollars). This process is not difficult. As we will soon explain in detail, there are many easy-to-use **foreign exchange markets** (or currency markets) in which those who wish to sell pounds and buy dollars can interact with others who wish to sell dollars and buy pounds. The demand and supply created by these two groups determines the equilibrium exchange rate, which in turn determines how many pounds our British company will have to convert in order to pay for the supercomputer. If, for instance, the exchange rate is $2 = £1, then the British company will have to convert £150,000 in order to obtain the $300,000 necessary to purchase the computer. *(Key Question 2)*

foreign exchange market
A market in which the money (currency) of one nation can be used to purchase (can be exchanged for) the money of another nation.

SPECIALIZATION & TRADE

17.2 | The Balance of International Payments

balance of payments
A summary of all the transactions that took place among the individuals, firms, and government units of one nation and those of all other nations during a year.

A nation's **balance of payments** (also referred to as the balance of international payments) is the sum of all the financial transactions that take place between its residents and the residents of foreign nations. The large majority of these transactions fall into the two main categories that we have just discussed: international trade and international asset transactions. As a result, the majority of the items included in the balance of payments are things like exports and imports of goods, exports and imports of services, and international purchases and sales of financial and real assets. But the balance of payments also includes international transactions that fall outside these main categories—things such as tourist expenditures, interest and dividends received or paid abroad, debt forgiveness, and remittances made by immigrants to their relatives back home.

Statistics Canada compiles a balance-of-payments statement each year. This statement summarizes all of the millions of payments that individuals and firms in Canada receive from foreigners as well as all of the millions of payments that individuals and firms in Canada make to foreigners. It shows "flows" of inpayments of money *to* Canada and outpayments of money *from* Canada. For convenience, all of these money payments are given in terms of dollars. This is true despite the fact that some of them actually may have been made using foreign currencies—as when, for instance, a Canadian company converts dollars into euros to buy something from an Italian company.

When including this outpayment of money from Canada, the accountants who compile the balance of payments statement use the number of dollars the Canadian company converted—rather than the number of euros that were actually used to make the purchase.

Table 17-1 is a simplified balance of payments statement for Canada in 2008. Because the vast majority of international financial transactions fall into only two categories—international trade and international asset exchanges—the balance of payments statement is organized into two broad categories. The *current account* given at the top of the table mostly deals with international trade. The *capital and financial account* at the bottom of the table mostly deals with international asset exchanges.

current account
The section in a nation's balance of payments that records its exports and imports of goods and services, its net investment income, and its net transfers.

TABLE 17·1	Canada's Balance of Payments, 2008 (in billions)		

Current Account

(1) Merchandise exports	$+490		
(2) Merchandise imports	−443		
(3) *Balance of trade*		+47	
(4) Exports of services	+68		
(5) Imports of services	−90		
(6) *Balance on goods and services* . .		+25	
(7) Net investment income	−14.0		
(8) Net transfers	−1		
(9) **Current account balance** . . .		**+10**	

Capital and financial account:

(10) Foreign purchases of assets in Canada (capital inflow)	+89	
(11) Canadian purchases of assets abroad (capital outflow)	−102	
(12) Statistical discrepancy		+5
(13) **Capital account balance** . . .		**−8**

Official settlement account:

(14) Official international reserves		−2
Balance of payments		**0**

Source: Statistics Canada. At: http://www40.statcan.ca/l01/cst01/econ01a-eng.htm. Accessed May 19, 2009.

balance on goods and services
The exports of goods and services of a nation less its imports of goods and services in a year.

trade surplus
The amount by which a nation's exports of goods (or goods and services) exceed its imports of goods (or goods and services).

trade deficit
The amount by which a nation's imports of goods (or goods and services) exceed its exports of goods (or goods and services).

Current Account

The top portion of Table 17-1 summarizes Canada's trade in currently produced goods and services and is called the **current account.** Items 1 and 2 show exports and imports of goods (merchandise) in 2008. Exports have a *plus* (+) sign because they are a credit; they generate flows of money into Canada. Canadian imports have a *minus* (−) sign because they are a debit; they cause flows of money out of Canada.

BALANCE ON GOODS

Items 1 and 2 in Table 17-1 reveal that in 2008 Canada's goods exports of $490 billion earned enough foreign currencies to more than finance Canada's goods imports of $443 billion. A country's *balance of trade on goods* is the difference between its exports and imports of goods. If exports exceed imports, the result is a trade surplus or "favourable balance of trade." If imports exceed exports, there is a trade deficit or "unfavourable balance of trade." We note in item 3 that in 2008 Canada had a trade surplus (of goods) of $47 billion. (Global Perspective 17.1 shows Canadian trade deficits and surpluses with selected nations or groups of nations.)

BALANCE ON SERVICES

Canada exports not only goods, such as airplanes and computer software, but also services, such as insurance, consulting, travel, and brokerage services, to residents of foreign nations. Item 4 in Table 17-1 shows that these service "exports" totalled $68 billion in 2008. Since they generate flows into Canada, they are a credit (thus the + sign). Item 5 indicates that Canadians "import" similar services from foreigners; these service imports were $90 billion in 2008 and are a debit (thus the − sign).

The **balance on goods and services,** shown as item 6, is the difference between Canadian exports of goods and services (items 1 and 4) and Canadian imports of goods and services (items 2 and 5). In 2008, Canadian exports of goods and services exceeded Canadian imports of goods and services by $25 billion. So, a **trade surplus** occurred. In contrast, a **trade deficit** occurs when imports of goods and services exceed exports of goods and services. (Global Perspectives 17.1 shows Canada's trade deficits and surpluses with selected nations.)

BALANCE ON CURRENT ACCOUNT

Items 7 and 8 do not have to do with international trade in goods and services. But they are listed as part of the current account (which is mostly about international trade in goods and services) because they can be thought of as dealing with international financial flows that in some sense compensate for things that can be conceptualized as being like international trade in either goods or services. For instance, item 7, net investment income, represents the difference between interest and dividend payments people abroad have paid Canadians for the services of exported Canadian capital ("exported" capital) and what Canadians paid in interest and dividends for the use of foreign capital ("imported" capital) invested in Canada. Observe that in 2008 Canadian net investment income was $−14.0 billion; we paid more in interest and dividends to people abroad than they paid us.

17.1 | GLOBAL PERSPECTIVE

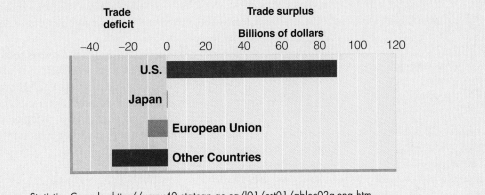

Canada's trade balance with selected nations, 2008

Canada has a net export surplus with the United States but a net export deficit with Japan, the European Union, and other countries.

Source: Statistics Canada. http://www40.statcan.gc.ca/l01/cst01/gblec02a-eng.htm.

Item 8 shows net transfers, both public and private, between Canada and the rest of the world. Included here is foreign aid, pensions paid to citizens living abroad, funds received from home by international students, and remittances by immigrants to relatives abroad. These $1 billion of transfers are net Canadian outpayments that decrease available supplies of foreign exchange. They are, in a sense, the exporting of goodwill and the importing of "thank-you notes."

By adding all transactions in the current account, we obtain the *current account balance* shown in item 9. In 2008 Canada had a current account surplus of $10 billion. This means that Canada's current account transactions (items 2, 5, and 8) created a greater inpayment of foreign currencies to Canada than an outpayment of foreign currencies from Canada.

Capital and Financial Account

capital and financial account
The section of a nation's international balance of payments statement that records the foreign purchases of assets in Canada and Canadian purchases of assets abroad.

The second account within the overall balance of payment account is the **capital and financial account,** which summarizes the flows of payments (money "capital") from the purchase or sale of real or financial assets. For example, a foreign firm may buy a *real* asset, say, an office tower in Canada, or a financial asset, for instance, a Canadian government bond. Both kinds of transactions involve the "export" of the ownership of Canadian assets from Canada in return for inpayments of foreign currency (money "capital" inflows). As indicated in line 10, these "exports" of ownership of assets are designated *foreign purchases of assets in Canada.* It has a *plus* sign, since like exports of Canadian goods and services, it represents an inpayment of foreign currencies.

Conversely, a Canadian firm may buy, say, a hotel chain (real asset) in a foreign country or common stock (financial asset) of a foreign firm. Both transactions involve "imports" of the ownership of real or financial assets to Canada and are paid for by outpayments of Canadian currency (money "capital" outflows). These "imports" are designated *Canadian purchases of assets abroad* and, as shown in line 11, has a minus sign; like Canadian imports of goods and services, it represents an outpayment of foreign currencies from Canada.

Before we can arrive at the *capital account balance* we need to include a *statistical discrepancy* (line 12), which is the unaccounted discrepancy between the balance on the current and capital accounts. Line 13 gives us the actual capital account balance, which amounted to $–8 billion in 2008. This capital account deficit depleted $8 billion of foreign currencies from Canada.

Official Settlement Account

official international reserves
Foreign currencies owned by the central bank of a nation.

The third account in the overall balance of payments is the official settlement account. The central banks of nations hold quantities of foreign currencies called **official international reserves.** These reserves can be drawn on to make up any net deficit in the combined current and capital accounts (much as you would draw on your savings to pay for a special purchase). In 2008 Canada had a $2 billion surplus in the combined current and capital accounts (line 9 plus line 13). Balance in the Canadian international payments led the Canadian government to increase its official international reserves of foreign currencies by $2 billion (item 14). The *negative* sign indicates that this increase of reserves is a debit—the inpayment to official international reserves needed to balance the overall balance of payments account.

In some years, the sum of the current and capital accounts balances may be negative, meaning that Canada earned less foreign currencies than it needed. The deficit would create an outpayment from the stock of official international reserves. As such, item 14 would have a positive sign since it is a credit.

The three components of the balance of payments—the current account, the capital and financial account, and the official settlement account—must together equal zero. Every unit of foreign exchange used (as reflected in a *minus* outpayment or debit transaction) must have a source (a *plus* inpayment or credit transaction).

Why the Balance of Payments Balances

The balance on the current account and the balance on the capital and financial account must always sum to zero because any deficit or surplus in the current account automatically creates an offsetting entry in the capital and financial account. This happens because, as we keep emphasizing, people can trade only one of two things with each other: currently produced goods and services or pre-existing assets. An important result of this fact is that if trading partners have an imbalance in their trade of currently produced goods and services, the only way to make up for that imbalance is with a net transfer of assets from one party to the other.

To see why this is true, let's use an example that involves trade between individuals rather than countries. Suppose John makes shoes and Henri makes watches, and they trade only with each other. In addition, each of them begins the year with assets worth $1000. To keep things simple, these assets are all in the form of money: each of them has $1000 in the bank at the beginning of the year. Next, suppose that this year John sells (exports) $300 worth of shoes to Henri while buying (importing) $500 worth of watches from Henri. The result is that John ends the year with a $200 trade deficit with Henri.

This trade deficit implies that there will be an *automatic and unavoidable* asset transfer from John to Henri. This happens because each goods transaction is paid for using an asset—money. When John exports shoes to Henri, Henri pays for them by transferring $300 of money to John. Shoes flow from John to Henri and $300 of money flows from Henri to John. Similarly, when John imports watches from Henri, John pays for them by transferring $500 of money to Henri. Watches flow from Henri to John and $500 of money flows from John to Henri.

Now consider what these transfers of assets do to their respective total asset holdings. In our simple example, each starts out the year with initial assets consisting of $1000 of money. But at the end of the year, John will have only $800 of money while Henri will have $1200 of money. In John's case, he started out with $1000, received an inflow of $300 for exporting shoes to Henri, and then made an outflow of $500 when importing watches from Henri. Adding these up shows that John ends the year with $800 (= $1000 + $300 − $500). A similar calculation shows that Henri ends up with $1200.

Thus, the $200 trade deficit that John has with Henri automatically causes $200 worth of John's initial asset holdings of $1000 to be transferred to Henri. This is unavoidable. Because John's exports generate an inflow of cash worth only $300, the only way for him to pay for his $500 worth of imports is to dip into his initial asset holdings. Put slightly differently, the $300 he makes from his exports pays for only the first $300 of his $500 worth of imports. The only way for him to pay for the remaining $200 worth of imports is for him to give up some of his initial asset holdings. Thus, $200 of John's initial asset holdings get transferred to Henri.

This automatic asset transfer is why the current account and the capital and financial account always sum to zero. Consider John's balance of payments statement. His $200 trade deficit would go into the current account at the top of the statement as a –$200 entry because the current account deals with flows of money related to currently produced goods and services and his trade deficit creates a $200 flow of money from John to his foreign trading partner (Henri). At the same time, that $200 flow of money is also recognized as an asset transfer from John to Henry in the capital and financial account at the bottom of the statement. The only confusing part is that it goes in as a +$200 entry under "foreign purchases of assets." Why there? Because we can think of what happened this year as Henri using $200 worth of currently produced goods to purchase $200 worth of John's initial holding of assets. John didn't give those assets to Henri for nothing. Henri had to purchase them by giving $200 worth of watches to John. The +$200 entry under "foreign purchases of assets" recognizes this fact.

Thus, the balance of payments always balances because any current account deficit or surplus in the top half of the statement automatically generates an offsetting international asset transfer that shows up in the capital and financial account in the bottom half of the statement. More specifically, current account deficits automatically generate transfers of assets *to* foreigners while current account surpluses automatically generate transfers of assets *from* foreigners.

The Bank of Canada held about $44 billion of official reserves in 2008. The typical annual depletion or addition of official reserves is not of major concern, particularly because withdrawals and deposits roughly balance overtime.

Payments Deficits and Surpluses

balance of payments deficit
The amount by which the sum of the balance on current account and the balance on the capital account is negative in a year.

balance of payments surplus
The amount by which the sum of the balance on current account and the balance on the capital account is positive in a year.

Although the balance of payments must always sum to zero, as in Table 17-1, economists and policymakers sometimes speak of **balance-of-payments deficits** and **surpluses.** The central banks of nations hold quantities of official international reserves, consisting of foreign currencies, reserves held in the International Monetary Fund, and stocks of gold. These reserves are drawn on—or replenished—to make up any net deficit or surplus that otherwise would occur in the balance of payments account. (This is much as you would draw on your savings or add to your savings as a way to balance your annual income and spending.) In some years, a nation must make an inpayment of official international reserves to its capital and financial account in order to balance it with the current account. In these years, a *balance-of-payments deficit* is said to occur. In other years, an outpayment of official international reserves from the capital and financial account must occur to balance that account with the current account. The outpayment adds to the stock of official international reserves. A *balance-of-payments surplus* is said to exist in these years.

Figure 17-1 shows the trend in Canada's current, capital, and official international reserves since 1985. What stands out is that for the period between 1985 and 1995 Canada's current account had a persistent deficit, while the capital account was in a surplus. The cause of the current account deficit during this period was the persistent deficit in services and investment income. The deficit in services and investment income still persists. But since 1995 the current account has actually swung to a surplus because of the large surplus in Canada's balance of trade, while the capital account surpluses of the 1985–95 period have turned into deficits.

A balance of payments deficit is not necessarily bad, nor is a balance of payments surplus necessarily good. Both simply are realities. However, any nation's official international reserves are limited. Persistent payments deficits, which must be financed by drawing down those reserves, would ultimately deplete the international reserves. That nation would have to make policies to correct its balance of payments. These policies might require painful macroeconomic adjustments, trade barriers and similar restrictions, or a major depreciation of its currency. For this reason, nations seek to achieve payments balance, at least over several-year periods. *(Key Question 3)*

WORKED PROBLEM 17.1
Balance of Payments

CONSIDER THIS | Global Recession and the Deterioration of Canada's Current Account

Canada's exports fell precipitously during the global recession of 2008–09: Merchandise exports fell 19 percent between March 2008 and March 2009, while merchandise imports fell 9 percent. Overall, our current account balance deteriorated 8 percent during this one-year period. Canada's exports were particularly affected because of the severity of the financial crisis in our main trading partner, the U.S. The severe global recession substantially reduced our export of oil, as demand for it dried up. The extend of the reduction in oil demand was reflected in the price of oil, which dropped to about US$40 in early 2009 from a high of more than $130 in 2008.

FIGURE 17·1 **The Balance of Payments: 1985–2008**

Over the last three decades the current and capital accounts changed from surpluses to deficits several times.

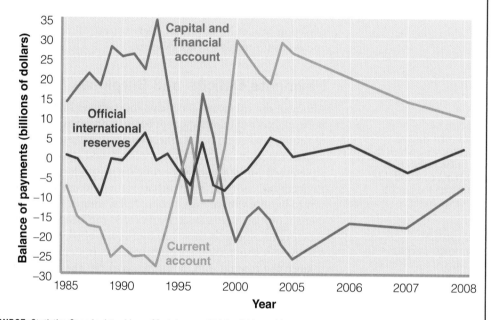

SOURCE: Statistics Canada, http://www40.statcan.ca/l01/cst01/econ01a-eng.htm; various years. Accessed May 19, 2009.

QUICK REVIEW

▶ A nation's balance of payments statement summarizes all the international financial transactions that take place between its residents and the residents of all foreign nations. It includes the current account balance and the capital and financial account balance.

▶ The current account balance is a nation's exports of goods and services less its imports of goods and services plus its net investment income and net transfers.

▶ The capital and financial account balance includes the net amount of the nation's debt forgiveness as well as the nation's sale of real and financial assets to people living abroad less its purchases of real and financial assets from foreigners.

▶ The current account balance and the capital and financial account balance always sum to zero because any current account imbalance automatically generates an offsetting international asset transfer.

| **17.3** | Foreign Exchange Markets: Flexible Exchange Rates |

We noted earlier that in a foreign exchange market, national currencies are exchanged for one another. The equilibrium prices in these markets are called **exchange rates**—the rate at which the currency of one nation is exchanged for the currency of another nation. (See Global Perspective 17.2.) Two points about the foreign exchange market are particularly noteworthy:

1. *A Competitive Market*   Real-world foreign exchange markets conform closely to the markets discussed in Chapter 3. They are competitive markets characterized by large numbers of buyers and sellers dealing in standardized products such as the Canadian dollar, the European euro, the British pound, the Swedish krona, and the Japanese yen.

2. *Linkages to All Domestic and Foreign Prices*   The market price or exchange rate of a nation's currency is an unusual price; it links all domestic (say, Canadian) prices with all foreign (say, Japanese or German) prices. Exchange rates enable consumers in one country to translate prices of foreign goods into units of their own currency: They need only multiply the foreign product price by the exchange rate. If the dollar–yen exchange rate is $0.01 (1 cent) per yen, a Sony television set priced at ¥20,000 will cost a Canadian $200 (= 20,000 × $0.01). If the exchange rate is $0.02 (2 cents) per yen, it will cost a Canadian $400 (= 20,000 × $0.02). Similarly, all other Japanese products would double in price to Canadian buyers. As you will see, a change in exchange rates has important implications for a nation's level of domestic production and employment.

Flexible Exchange Rates

Both the size and persistence of a nation's balance of payments deficits and surpluses and the adjustments it must make to correct these imbalances depend on the system of exchange rates being used. There are two "pure" types of exchange-rate systems:

- A **flexible** or **floating exchange-rate system** by which the rates that national currencies are exchanged for one another are determined by demand and supply. In such a system no government intervention occurs.

- A **fixed exchange-rate system** by which governments determine the rates at which currencies are exchanged and make necessary adjustments in their economies to ensure that these rates continue.

We begin by looking at flexible exchange rates. Let's examine the rate, or price, at which Canadian dollars might be exchanged for British pounds. **Figure 17-2 (Key Graph)** shows demand D_1 and supply S_1 of pounds in the currency market.

The *demand for pounds curve* is downward sloping because, if pounds become less expensive to Canadians, then all British goods and services will be cheaper to Canadians. That is, at lower dollar prices for pounds, Canadians can obtain more pounds and therefore more British goods and services per dollar. To buy these cheaper British goods, Canadian consumers will increase the quantity of pounds they demand.

The *supply of pounds curve* is upward sloping because, as the dollar price of pounds rises (that is, the pound price of dollars falls), the British will purchase more Canadian goods. When the British buy more Canadian goods, they supply a greater quantity of pounds to the foreign exchange market. In other words, they must exchange pounds for dollars to purchase Canadian goods. So, when the price of pounds rises, the quantity of pounds supplied goes up.

The intersection of the supply curve and demand curve will determine the dollar price of pounds. Here, that price (exchange rate) is $2 for £1.

exchange rate
The rate at which the currency of one nation is exchanged for the currency of another nation.

flexible (or floating) exchange rate system
A rate of exchange determined by the international demand for and supply of a nation's currency.

fixed exchange-rate system
A rate of exchange that is prevented from rising or falling with changes in currency supply and demand.

17.2 | GLOBAL PERSPECTIVE

Exchange rates: foreign currency per Canadian dollar

The amount of foreign currency that a dollar will buy varies greatly from nation to nation. These amounts are for May 2009 and fluctuate in response to supply and demand changes in the foreign exchange market.

$1 will buy

0.56 British pounds
0.90 U.S. dollars
11.8 Mexican pesos
0.64 Euros
87 Japanese yen
6.1 Chinese renminbi
42 Indian rupees

Source: Bank of Canada Banking and Financial Statistics, May 2009.

Depreciation and Appreciation

depreciation
A decrease in the value of the dollar relative to another currency, so a dollar buys a smaller amount of the foreign currency and therefore of foreign goods.

appreciation
An increase in the value of the dollar relative to another currency, so a dollar buys a larger amount of the foreign currency and therefore of foreign goods.

An exchange rate determined by market forces can, and often does, change daily, just as do stock and bond prices. When the dollar price of pounds rises, for example, from $2 = £1 to $3 = £1, we say a **depreciation** of the dollar relative to the pound has occurred. When a currency depreciates, more units of it (dollars) are needed to buy a single unit of some other foreign currency (a pound).

When the dollar price of pounds falls, for example from $2 = £1 to $1 = £1, an **appreciation** of the dollar relative to the pound has occurred. When a currency appreciates, fewer units of it (dollars) are needed to buy a single unit of some foreign currency (pounds).

In our Canada–Britain illustrations, depreciation of the dollar means an appreciation of the pound, and vice versa. When the dollar price of a pound jumps from $2 = £1 to $3 = £1 the pound has appreciated relative to the dollar because it takes more dollars to buy £1. But it now takes fewer pounds to buy $1. At $2 = £1, it took £1/2 to buy $1; at $3 = £1, it takes only £1/3 to buy $1.

Determinants of Exchange-Rate Changes

What factors would cause a nation's currency to appreciate or depreciate in the market for foreign exchange? Here are three generalizations:

- If the demand for a nation's currency increases (all else equal), that currency will appreciate; if the demand declines, that currency will depreciate.

- If the supply of a nation's currency increases, that currency will depreciate; if the supply decreases, that currency will appreciate.

- If a nation's currency appreciates, some foreign currency depreciates relative to it.

With these generalizations in mind, let's examine the determinants of exchange rates, the factors that shift the demand or supply curve for a certain currency. As we do so, keep in mind that the other-things-equal assumption is always in force. Also note that we are discussing factors *that change the exchange rate*, not things that change *as a result of* a change in the exchange rate.

CHANGES IN TASTES

Canadian exports create a foreign demand for dollars.

Any change in consumer tastes or preferences for the products of a foreign country may alter the demand for that nation's currency and change its exchange rate. If technological advances in lumber make it more attractive to British consumers and businesses, then the British will supply more pounds in the exchange market in order to purchase more Canadian lumber. The supply-of-pounds curve will shift rightward, the pound will depreciate, and the dollar will appreciate.

KEY GRAPH

FIGURE 17-2   The Market for Foreign Currency (Pounds)

The intersection of the demand for pounds D_1 and the supply of pounds S_1 determines the equilibrium dollar price of pounds, here, $2. That means that the exchange rate is $2 = £1. The upward green arrow is a reminder that a higher dollar price of pounds (say, $3 = £1) means that the dollar has depreciated (pound has appreciated). The downward green arrow tells us that a lower dollar price of pounds (say, $1 = £1) means that the dollar has appreciated (pound has depreciated). Such changes in equilibrium exchange rates would result from shifts of the supply and demand curves.

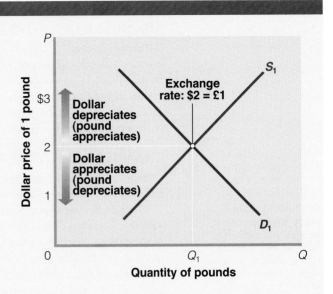

Quick Quiz

1. **Which of the following is a true statement?**
   a. The quantity of pounds demanded falls when the dollar appreciates.
   b. The quantity of pounds supplied declines as the dollar price of pounds rises.
   c. At the equilibrium exchange rate, the pound price of $1 is 1/2 pound.
   d. The dollar would appreciate if the demand for pounds increased.

2. **At the price of $2 for £1 in this figure**
   a. the dollar–pound exchange rate is unstable.
   b. the quantity of pounds supplied equals the quantity demanded.
   c. the dollar price of 1 pound equals the pound price of $1.
   d. Canadian merchandise exports to Britain must equal Canadian merchandise imports from Britain.

3. **All else equal, a leftward shift of the demand curve in this figure**
   a. would depreciate the dollar.
   b. creates a shortage of pounds at the previous price of $2 for £1.
   c. might be caused by a major recession in Canada.
   d. might be caused by a significant rise of real interest rates in Britain.

4. **All else equal, a rightward shift of the supply curve in this figure would**
   a. depreciate the dollar and might be caused by a significant rise of real interest rates in Britain.
   b. depreciate the dollar and might be caused by a significant fall of real interest rates in Britain.
   c. appreciate the dollar and might be caused by a significant rise of real interest rates in Canada.
   d. appreciate the dollar and might be caused by a significant fall of real interest rates in Canada.

Answers: 1. c; 2. b; 3. c; 4. c

In contrast, the demand curve for pounds will shift to the right if British woollen apparel becomes more fashionable in Canada. So the pound will appreciate and the Canadian dollar will depreciate.

CHANGES IN RELATIVE INCOME

A nation's currency is likely to depreciate if its growth of national income is more rapid than that of other countries. Here's why. A country's imports vary directly with its level of income. As total income rises in Canada, Canadians buy both more domestically produced goods and more foreign goods. If the Canadian economy is expanding rapidly and the British economy is stagnant, Canadian imports of British goods, and therefore Canadian demands for pounds, will increase. The dollar price of pounds will rise, so the Canadian dollar will depreciate.

CHANGES IN RELATIVE PRICE LEVEL

Changes in the relative price levels of two nations can change the demand and supply of currencies and alter the exchange rate between the two nations' currencies.

purchasing power parity theory
The idea that exchange rates between any two nations adjust to reflect the price level differences between the countries.

The **purchasing power parity theory** holds that exchange rates equate the purchasing power of various currencies. That is, the exchange rates among national currencies adjust to match the ratios of the nations' price levels: If a certain market basket of goods costs $10,000 in Canada and £5000 in Great Britain, according to this theory the exchange rate will be $2 = £1. That way a dollar spent in Canada will buy exactly as much output as it would if it were first converted to pounds (at the $2 = £1 exchange rate) and used to buy output in Great Britain.

In practice, however, exchange rates depart from purchasing power parity, even over long periods. Nevertheless, changes in relative price levels are a determinant of exchange rates. If, for example, the domestic price level rises rapidly in Canada and remains constant in Great Britain, Canadian consumers will seek out low-priced British goods, increasing the demand for pounds. The British will purchase fewer Canadian goods, reducing the supply of pounds. This combination of demand and supply changes will cause the pound to appreciate and the dollar to depreciate.

RELATIVE INTEREST RATES

Changes in relative interest rates between two countries may alter their exchange rate. Suppose that real interest rates rise in Canada but stay constant in Great Britain. British citizens will then find Canada a more attractive place in which to loan money directly or loan money indirectly by buying bonds. To make these loans, they will have to supply pounds in the foreign exchange market to obtain dollars. The increase in the supply of pounds results in depreciation of the pound and appreciation of the Canadian dollar.

CHANGES IN RELATIVE EXPECTED RETURNS ON STOCKS, REAL ESTATE, AND PRODUCTION FACILITIES

International investing extends beyond buying foreign bonds. It includes international investments in stocks and real estate as well as foreign purchases of factories and production facilities. Other things equal, the extent of this foreign investment depends on relative expected returns. To make the investments, investors in one country must sell their currencies to purchase the foreign currencies needed for the foreign investments.

For instance, suppose that investing in England suddenly becomes more popular due to a more positive outlook regarding expected returns on stocks, real estate, and production facilities there. Canadian investors therefore will sell Canadian assets to buy more assets in England. The Canadian assets will be sold for dollars, which will then be brought to the foreign exchange market and exchanged for pounds, which will in turn be used to purchase British assets. The increased supply of dollars that is brought to the foreign exchange market will cause the dollar to depreciate relative to the pound.

SPECULATION

Currency speculators buy and sell currencies with an eye to reselling or repurchasing them at a profit. Suppose speculators expect the Canadian economy to (1) grow more rapidly than the British economy and (2) experience a more rapid rise in its price level than Britain. These expectations translate to an anticipation that the pound will appreciate and the Canadian dollar will depreciate. Speculators who are holding dollars will therefore try to convert them into pounds. This effort will increase the demand for pounds and cause the dollar price of pounds to rise (that is, the dollar to depreciate). A self-fulfilling prophecy occurs: The pound appreciates and the dollar depreciates because speculators act on the belief that these changes will in fact take place. In this way, speculation can cause changes in exchange rates. (We deal with currency speculation in more detail in this chapter's Last Word.)

Table 17-2 has more illustrations of the determinants of exchange rates and is worth careful study.

Advantages of Flexible Rates

THE EFFECTIVENESS OF MARKETS

Proponents of flexible exchange rates say they have an important feature: They automatically adjust to eventually eliminate balance of payment deficits or surpluses. We can explain this concept with S_1 and D_1 in Figure 17-3, where they are the supply and demand curves for pounds from Figure 17-2.

The equilibrium exchange rate of $2 = £1 means there is no balance of payments deficit or surplus between Canada and Britain. At the $2 = £1 exchange rate, the quantity of pounds demanded by Canadian consumers to import British goods, buy British transportation and insurance services, and pay interest and dividends on British investments in Canada equals the number of pounds

TABLE 17-2

Determinants of Exchange-Rate Changes: Factors That Change the Demand or the Supply of a Particular Currency and Thus Alter the Exchange Rate

Determinant	Examples
Changes in tastes	Japanese electronic equipment declines in popularity in Canada (Japanese yen depreciates, Canadian dollar appreciates)
	European tourists reduce visits to Canada (Canadian dollar depreciates; European euro appreciates).
Changes in relative incomes	England encounters a recession, reducing its imports, while Canadian real output and real income surge, increasing Canadian imports (British pound appreciates, Canadian dollar depreciates).
Changes in relative prices	Switzerland experiences a 3 percent inflation rate compared to Canada's 10 percent rate (Swiss franc appreciates; Canadian dollar depreciates).
Changes in relative real interest rates	The Bank of Canada drives up interest rates in Canada while the Bank of England takes no such action (Canadian dollar appreciates; British pound depreciates).
Changes in relative expected returns on stocks, real estate, or production facilities	Corporate tax cuts in Canada raise expected after-tax investment returns in the Canada rise relative to those in Europe (Canadian dollar appreciates; the euro depreciates)
Speculation	Currency traders believe South Korea will have much greater inflation than Taiwan (South Korean won depreciates; Taiwanese dollar appreciates)
	Currency traders think Finland's interest rates will plummet relative to Denmark's rates (Finland's markka depreciates; Denmark's krone appreciates)

CONSIDER THIS | Purchasing Power Parity: The Case of Hamburgers

Since 1986, *The Economist* magazine has offered a light-hearted test of the purchasing power parity theory through its "Big Mac index." It uses the exchange rates of 100 countries to convert the domestic currency price of Big Macs into U.S.-dollar prices. If the converted U.S.-dollar price in, say, Britain exceeds the dollar price in Canada, *The Economist* concludes (with a wink) that the pound is overvalued relative to the Canadian dollar. On the other hand, if the adjusted dollar price of the Big Mac in Britain is less than the dollar price in Canada, then the pound is undervalued relative to the Canadian dollar. *The Economist* finds wide divergences in actual dollar prices across the globe and thus little support for the purchasing power parity theory. Yet it humorously trumpets any predictive success it can muster (or is that "mustard"?):

> Some readers find our Big Mac index hard to swallow. This year (1999), however, has been one to relish. When the euro was launched at the start of the year most forecasters expected it to rise. The Big Mac index, however, suggested the euro was overvalued against the U.S. dollar—and indeed it has fallen [13 percent] … Our

correspondents have once again been munching their way around the globe … [and] experience suggests that investors ignore burgernomics at their peril.[*]

Maybe so—bad puns and all. Economist Robert Cumby examined the Big Mac index for 14 countries for ten years.[**] Among his findings:

- A 10 percent undervaluation according to the Big Mac standard in one year is associated with a 3.5 percent appreciation of that currency over the following year.

- When the U.S. dollar price of Big Macs is high in a country, the relative local currency price of Big Macs in that country generally declines during the following year.

Hmm. Not bad.

[*] "Big Mac Currencies," *The Economist*, April 3, 1999; "Mcparity," *The Economist*, December 11, 1999.

[**] Robert Cumby, "Forecasting Exchange Rates and Relative Prices with the Hamburger Standard: Is What You Want What You Get with Mcparity?" National Bureau of Economic Research, January 1997

---

supplied by the British in buying Canadian exports, purchasing services from the Canadians, and making interest and dividend payments on Canadian investments in Britain. Canada would have no need to either draw down or build up its official international reserves to balance its payments.

Suppose tastes change and Canadians buy more British automobiles, the Canadian price level increases relative to Britain's, or interest rates fall in Canada compared to those in Britain. Any or all of these changes will cause the Canadian demand for British pounds to increase from D_1 to, say, D_2 in Figure 17-3.

If the exchange rate remains at the initial $2 = £1, a Canadian balance of payments deficit will be created in the amount of *ab*. That is, at the $2 = £1 rate, Canadians consumers will demand the quantity of pounds represented by point *b*, but Britain will supply the amount represented by *a*; there will be a shortage of pounds. But this shortage will not last, because this is a competitive market. Instead, the dollar price of pounds will rise (the Canadian dollar depreciates) until the balance of payment deficit is eliminated. That occurs at the new equilibrium exchange rate of $3 = £1, where the quantity of pounds demanded and supplied are equal again.

To explain why this occurred, we need to re-emphasize that the exchange rate links all domestic (Canadian) prices with all foreign (British) prices. The dollar price of a foreign good is found by multiplying the foreign price by the exchange rate (in dollars per unit of the foreign currency). At an exchange rate of $2 = £1, a British automobile priced at £15,000 will cost a Canadian consumer $30,000 (= 15,000 × $2).

A change in the exchange rate alters the prices of all British goods to Canadian consumers and all Canadian goods to British buyers. The shift in the exchange rate (here from $2 = £1 to $3 = £1) changes the relative attractiveness of Canadian imports and exports and restores equilibrium in the Canadian (and British) balance of payments. From the Canadian point of view, as the dollar price of pounds changes from $2 to $3, the British auto priced at £15,000, which formerly cost

FIGURE 17-3   **Adjustments under Flexible Exchange Rates**

Under flexible exchange rates, a shift in the demand for pounds from D_1 to D_2, other things equal, would cause a Canadian balance of payments deficit *ab*; it would be corrected by a change in the exchange rate from $2 = £1 to $3 = £1.

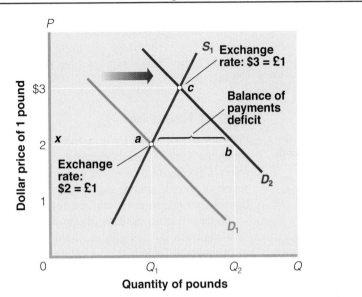

a Canadian consumer $30,000, now costs $45,000 (= 15,000 × $3). Other British goods will also cost Canadian consumers more, and Canadian imports of British goods will decline. A movement from point *b* toward point *c* in Figure 17-3 graphically illustrates this concept.

From Britain's standpoint, the exchange rate (the pound price of dollars) has fallen (from £1/2 to £1/3 for $1). The international value of the pound has appreciated. The British previously got only $2 for £1; now they get $3 for £1. Canadian goods are therefore cheaper to the British, and Canadian exports to Britain will rise. In Figure 17-3, this is shown by a movement from point *a* toward point *c*.

The two adjustments—a decrease in Canadian imports from Britain and an increase in Canadian exports to Britain—are just what are needed to correct the Canadian balance of payments deficit. These changes end when, at point *c*, the quantities of British pounds demanded and supplied are equal. *(Key Questions 7 and 10)*

Disadvantages of Flexible Exchange Rates

Even though flexible exchange rates automatically work to eliminate payment imbalances, they may cause several significant problems. These problems include (a) reduced trade because of the risks and uncertainties associated with constantly changing exchange rates; (b) worsening terms of trade if there is a sizable depreciation; and (c) the challenges to managing and designing domestic macro-economic policies, particularly those economies heavily dependent on trade.

17.4 | Fixed Exchange Rates

To avoid the disadvantages of flexible exchange rates, nations have at times fixed or "pegged" their exchange rates. For our analysis of fixed exchange rates, we assume Canada and Britain agree to maintain a $2 = £1 exchange rate. The problem is that such a governmental agreement cannot keep the demand for and supply of pounds from changing. With the rate fixed, a shift in demand or supply will put pressure on the exchange rate system, and government (through the central bank) must intervene if the exchange rate is to be maintained.

In Figure 17-4, suppose the Canadian demand for pounds increases from D_1 to D_2 because, again, Canadians buy more British automobiles. A Canadian payment deficit *ab* arises, and if the Canadian government is committed to an exchange rate ($2 = £1), the new equilibrium rate ($3 = £1) is below the targeted rate of $2 = £1. How can the Bank of Canada prevent the shortage of pounds from driving the exchange rate up to the new equilibrium level? The answer is to alter market demand and/or market supply so that they will intersect at the $2 = £1 rate of exchange. There are several ways to do this.

Use of Reserves

currency intervention
A government's buying and selling of its own currency or foreign currencies to alter international exchange rates.

One way to maintain a fixed exchange rate is to engage in **currency interventions,** situations in which the Bank of Canada manipulates an exchange rate through the use of official international reserves. For instance, by selling part of its reserves of pounds, the Bank of Canada can increase the supply of pounds, shifting supply curve S_1 right to S_2 so that it intersects D_2 at *b* in Figure 17-4 and thereby maintaining the exchange rate at $2 = £1.

Notice that when the Bank of Canada sells some of its reserves of pounds it is transferring assets to foreigners (since they gain ownership of the pounds). In terms of the balance of payments statement shown in Table 17-1, this transfer of assets enters positively on line (11), "Foreign purchases of assets in Canada." This positive entry is what offsets the balance of payments deficit caused by the fixed exchange rate and ensures that Canada's balance of payments does in fact balance.

How do official international reserves originate? Perhaps a balance of payments surplus occurred in the past. The Bank of Canada would have purchased that surplus. That is, at some earlier time, the Bank of Canada may have spent dollars to buy surplus pounds that were threatening to reduce the exchange rate to below the $2 = £1 fixed rate. Those purchases would have built up the Canadian official reserves of pounds.

Nations also have used gold as "international money" to obtain official international reserves. In our example, the Bank of Canada could sell some of the gold it owns to Britain to obtain pounds. It could then sell pounds for dollars. That would shift the supply of pounds to the right and the $2 = £1 exchange rate could be maintained.

FIGURE 17-4   Adjustments under Fixed Exchange Rates

Under fixed exchange rates, the Bank of Canada would cover the shortage of pounds *ab* by using international monetary reserves. The central bank can also restrict trade, implement exchange controls, or enact a contractionary stabilization policy so as to reduce the demand for pounds and increase the supply of pounds.

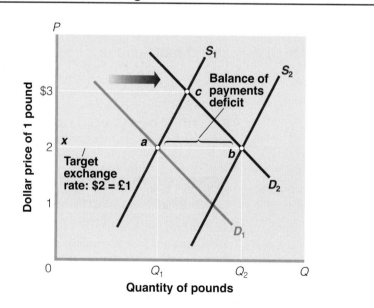

It is critical that the amount of international reserves and gold be enough to accomplish the required increase in the supply of pounds. This is not a problem if deficits and surpluses occur more or less randomly and are about the same size. Then, last year's balance of payments surplus with Britain will increase Canada's reserve of pounds, and that reserve can be used to "finance" this year's deficit. But if Canada encounters persistent and sizable balance of payments deficits for an extended period, its international reserves can become depleted, forcing it to abandon fixed exchange rates. Or, if a nation with inadequate international reserves wishes to maintain fixed exchange rates, it must use less appealing options to maintain exchange rates. Let's consider some of those options.

Trade Policies

To maintain fixed exchange rates, a nation can try to control the flow of trade and finance directly. Canada could try to maintain the $2 = £1 exchange rate in the face of a shortage of pounds by discouraging imports of automobiles (thereby reducing the demand for pounds back to D_1 in Figure 17-4) and encouraging exports (thus increasing the supply of pounds to S_2 in Figure 17-4). Imports could be reduced with new tariffs or import quotas on automobiles; special taxes could be levied on the interest and dividends Canadian financial investors receive from foreign investments. Also, the Canadian government could subsidize certain Canadian exports to increase the supply of pounds.

The fundamental problem is that these policies reduce the volume of world trade and change its makeup from what is economically desirable. When nations impose tariffs and quotas, they lose the economic benefits of a free flow of world trade. That loss should not be underestimated: Trade barriers by one nation lead to retaliatory responses from other nations, multiplying the loss.

Exchange Controls and Rationing

exchange control
The control a government may exercise over the quantity of foreign currency demanded by its citizens and firms and over the rates of exchange in order to limit its outpayments to its inpayments (to eliminate a payments deficit).

Another option is exchange controls and rationing. Under **exchange controls,** the Canadian government could handle the problem of a pound shortage by requiring that all pounds obtained by Canadian exporters be sold to the Bank of Canada. Then the government would allocate or ration this short supply of pounds (represented by *xa* in Figure 17-4) among various Canadian importers, who actually demand the quantity *xb*. The effect of this policy is to restrict the value of Canadian imports to the amount of foreign exchange earned by Canadian exports. Assuming balance in the capital account, there is then no balance of payments deficit. Canadian demand for British imports with the value *ab* would simply not be fulfilled. Major objections to exchange controls include:

- **Distorted Trade** Like tariffs, quotas, and export subsidies (trade controls), exchange controls distort the pattern of international trade away from that suggested by comparative advantage.

- **Favouritism** The process of rationing scarce foreign exchange can lead to government favouritism toward selected importers (big contributors to re-election campaigns, for example).

- **Restricted Choice** Controls limit freedom of consumer choice. The Canadian consumers who prefer foreign-produced Volkswagens may have to buy domestically produced Chevrolets. The business opportunities for some Canadian importers may be impaired because government limits imports.

- **Black Markets** There are likely to be enforcement problems. Canadian importers might want foreign exchange badly enough to pay more than the $2 = £1 official rate, setting the stage for black-market dealings between importers and illegal sellers of foreign exchange.

Domestic Macroeconomic Adjustments

A final way to maintain a fixed exchange rate is to use domestic stabilization policies (monetary policy and fiscal policy) to eliminate the shortage of foreign currency. Tax hikes, reductions in government spending, and a high-interest-rate policy would reduce total spending in the Canadian economy and thus domestic income. Because imports vary directly with domestic income, demand for British goods (automobiles, in our example), and therefore for pounds, would be restrained.

If these "contractionary" policies reduce the domestic price level relative to Britain's, Canadian buyers of consumer and capital goods would divert their demands from British goods to Canadian goods, also reducing the demand for pounds. In our example of automobiles, Canadians would increase their purchases of Canadian-made cars and reduce their demand of British-made cars. Moreover, the high-interest-rate policy would lift Canadian interest rates relative to those in Britain.

Lower prices on Canadian goods and higher Canadian interest rates would increase British imports of Canadian goods and increase British financial investment in Canada. Both developments would increase the supply of pounds. The combination of a decrease in the demand for and an increase in the supply of pounds would reduce or eliminate the original Canadian balance of payments deficit. In Figure 17-4 the new supply and demand curves would intersect at some new equilibrium point on line *ab*, where the exchange rate remains at $2 = £1.

Maintaining fixed exchange rates is hardly appealing. The "price" of exchange-rate stability for Canada would be falling output, employment, and price levels—in other words, a recession. Eliminating a balance of payments deficit and realizing domestic stability are both important national economic goals, but to sacrifice stability for payments balance is to let the tail wag the dog.

QUICK REVIEW

▶ In a system in which exchange rates are flexible (meaning that they are free to float), the rates are determined by the demand for and supply of individual national currencies in the foreign exchange market.

▶ Determinants of flexible exchange rates—factors that shift currency supply and demand curves—include changes in (a) tastes, (b) relative national incomes, (c) relative price levels, (d) relative interest rates,

(e) relative expected returns on stocks, real estate, and production facilities, and (f) speculation.

▶ Under a system of fixed exchange rates, nations set their exchange rates and then maintain them by buying or selling reserves of currencies, establishing trade barriers, employing exchange controls, or incurring inflation or recession.

17.5 | The Current Exchange-Rate System: the Managed Float

Over the past 150 years, the world's nations have used three different exchange-rate systems. From 1879 to 1934 most nations used a gold standard, which implicitly created fixed exchange rates. From 1944 to 1971, most countries participated in the Bretton Woods system, which was a fixed-exchange-rate system indirectly tied to gold. And since 1971, most have used managed floating exchange rates, which mix mostly flexible exchange rates with occasional currency interventions. Naturally, our focus here is on the current exchange-rate system. However, the history of the previous systems and why they broke down is highly fascinating. For that reason, we have included information about them at the book's Web site along with other Chapter 17 materials.

The current international exchange-rate system (1971–present) is an "almost" flexible system called **managed floating exchange rates.** Exchange rates among major currencies are free to float to their equilibrium market levels, but nations occasionally intervene in the foreign exchange market to smooth out fluctuations.

managed floating exchange rate
An exchange rate that is allowed to change (float) as a result of changes in currency supply and demand but at times is altered (managed) by governments via their buying and selling of particular currencies.

Normally, the major trading nations allow their exchange rates to float up or down to equilibrium levels based on supply and demand in the foreign exchange market. They recognize that changing economic conditions among nations require continuing changes in equilibrium exchange rates to avoid persistent payment deficits or surpluses. They rely on freely operating foreign exchange markets to accomplish the necessary adjustments. The result has been considerably more volatile exchange rates than during the Bretton Woods era.

But nations also recognize that some trends in the movement of equilibrium exchange rates may be at odds with national or international objectives. On occasion, nations therefore intervene in the foreign exchange market by buying or selling large amounts of specific currencies. This way, they can "manage" or stabilize exchange rates by influencing currency demand and supply.

The leaders of the G8 nations (Canada, France, Germany, Russia, Italy, Japan, United Kingdom, and the United States) meet regularly to discuss economic issues and try to coordinate economic policies. At times, they have collectively intervened to stabilize currencies. For example, in 2000 they sold dollars and bought euros in an effort to stabilize the falling value of the euro relative to the American dollar. In the previous year the euro (€) had depreciated from 1 = U.S.$1.17 to 1 = U.S.$0.87.

The current exchange-rate system is thus an "almost" flexible exchange-rate system. The "almost" mainly refers to the periodic currency interventions by central banks. It also refers to the fact that the actual system is more complicated than described. While the major currencies—dollars, pounds, yen, and the like—fluctuate in response to changing supply and demand, some of the European nations have unified their currency into one, the euro. Also, many developing nations peg their currencies to the U.S. dollar and allow their currencies to fluctuate with it against other currencies. Finally, some nations peg the value of their currencies to a "basket" or group of other currencies.

How well has the managed float worked? It has both proponents and critics. Proponents argue that the managed float has functioned far better than anticipated. But skeptics say the managed float is basically a "non-system": the guidelines of what a nation may or may not do are not specific enough to keep the system working in the long run. *(Key Question 13)*

So what are we to conclude? Flexible exchange rates have not worked perfectly, but neither have they failed miserably. On balance, most economists favour continuation of the present system of "almost" flexible exchange rates.

QUICK REVIEW

▶ The managed floating system of exchange rates (1971–present) relies on foreign exchange markets to establish equilibrium exchange rates.

▶ The system permits nations to buy and sell foreign currency to stabilize short-term changes in exchange rates or to correct exchange-rate imbalances that are negatively affecting the world economy.

▶ Proponents point out that international trade and investment have grown tremendously under the system. Critics say that it is a "non-system" and argue that the exchange rate volatility allowed under the managed float discourages international trade and investment. That is, trade and investment would be even larger if exchange rates were more stable.

The LAST WORD   Speculation in Currency Markets

Contrary to popular belief, speculators often play a positive role in currency markets.

Most people buy foreign currency to facilitate the purchase of goods or services produced in another country. A Canadian importer buys Japanese yen to purchase Japanese-made automobiles. A British investor purchases euros to buy shares in the German stock market. But there is another group of participants in the currency market—speculators—who buy foreign currencies solely to resell for profit.

1. ***Contributing to Exchange-Rate Fluctuations*** Speculators were much in the news in late 1997 and 1998 when they were widely accused of driving down the values of the South Korean won, Thailand baht, Malaysian ringgit, and Indonesian rupiah. The value of these currencies fell by as much as 50 percent within 1 month, and speculators undoubtedly contributed to the swiftness of those declines.

   The expectation of currency depreciation (or appreciation) can be self-fulfilling. If speculators, for example, expect the Indonesian rupiah to be devalued or to depreciate, they quickly sell rupiah and buy currencies that they think will increase in relative value. The sharp increase in the supply of rupiah indeed reduces its value; this reduction then may trigger further selling of rupiah in expectation of further declines in its value. But changed economic realities, not speculation, are normally the underlying causes of changes in currency values.

   That was largely the case with the southeast Asian countries in which actual and threatened bankruptcies in the financial and manufacturing sectors undermined confidence in the

strength of the currencies. Anticipating the eventual declines in currency values, speculators simply hastened those declines. That is, the declines in value probably would have occurred with or without speculators. Moreover, on a daily basis, speculation clearly has positive effects in foreign exchange markets.

Smoothing Out Short-Term Fluctuations in Currency Prices When temporarily weak demand or strong supply reduces a currency's value, speculators quickly buy the currency, adding to its demand and strengthening its value. When temporarily strong demand or weak supply increases a currency's value, speculators sell the currency. That selling increases the supply of the currency and reduces its value. In this way speculators smooth out supply and demand, and thus exchange rates, over short time periods. This day-to-day exchange-rate stabilization aids international trade.

2. ***Absorbing Risk*** Speculators aid international trade in another way: *They absorb risk that others do not want to bear.* International transactions are riskier than domestic transactions because of potential adverse changes in exchange rates. Suppose AnyTime, a hypothetical Canadian retailer, signs a contract with a German manufacturer to

buy 10,000 German clocks to be delivered in three months. The stipulated price is €75 per clock, which in Canadian dollars is $120 per clock at an exchange rate of $1 = 0.625. Any-Time's total bill will be $1,200,000 (= 750,000).

But if the euro were to appreciate, say to $1 = 0.5, the dollar price per clock would rise from $120 to $150 and AnyTime would owe $1,500,000 for the clocks (= 750,000). AnyTime may reduce the risk of such an unfavourable exchange-rate fluctuation by hedging in the futures market. Hedging is an action by a buyer or a seller to protect against a change in future prices. The futures market is a market where items are bought and sold at prices fixed now, for delivery at a specified date in the future.

AnyTime can arrange now to purchase the needed 750,000 at the current $1 = 0.625 exchange rate, but with delivery in three months when the German clocks are delivered. And here is where speculators arrive on the scene. For a price determined in the futures market, they agree to deliver the 750,000 to AnyTime in three months at the $1 = 0.625 exchange rate, regardless of the exchange rate then. The speculators need not own euros at the time the agreement is made. If the euro *depreciates* to, say, $1 = €1 in this period, the speculators make a profit. They can buy the €750,000 stipulated in the contract for $750,000, pocketing the difference between that amount and the $1,200,000 AnyTime has agreed to pay for the €750,000. If the euro *appreciates*, the speculators—but not AnyTime—suffer a loss.

The amount AnyTime will have to pay for this futures contract will depend on how the market views the likelihood of the euro depreciating, appreciating, or staying constant over the three-month period. As in all highly competitive markets, supply and demand determine the price of the futures contract.

The futures market thus eliminates much of the exchange-rate risk associated with buying foreign goods for future delivery. Without it AnyTime might have decided against importing German clocks. But the futures market and currency speculators greatly increase the likelihood the transaction will occur. Operating through the futures market, speculation promotes international trade.

Question

Suppose Sportif de l'Hiver—a hypothetical French retailer of snowboards—wants to order 5000 snowboards made in Canada. The price per board is $200, the present exchange rate is €1 = $1, and payment is due in dollars when the boards are delivered in three months. Use a numerical example to explain why exchange-rate risk might make the French retailer hesitant to place the order. How might speculators absorb some of Sportif de l'Hiver's risk?

CHAPTER SUMMARY

17.1 ▶ FINANCING INTERNATIONAL TRADE

- International financial transactions involve trade either in currently produced goods and services or in pre-existing assets. Exports of goods, services, and assets create inflows of money, while imports cause outflows of money. If buyers and sellers use different currencies, then foreign exchange transactions take place so that the exporter can be paid in his or her own currency.

17.2 ▶ THE BALANCE OF INTERNATIONAL PAYMENTS

- The balance of payments records all international trade and financial transactions taking place between a given nation and the rest of the world. The trade balance compares exports and imports of goods. The balance on goods and services compares exports and imports of both goods and services. The current account balance includes not only goods and services transactions but also net investment income and net transfers.

- The capital and financial account includes (a) the net amount of the nation's debt forgiveness and (b) the nation's sale of real and financial assets to people living abroad less its purchases of real and financial assets from foreigners.

- The current account and the capital and financial account always sum to zero. A deficit in the current account is always offset by a surplus in the capital and financial account. Conversely, a surplus in the current account is always offset by a deficit in the capital and financial account.

- A balance of payments deficit occurs when the sum of the current and capital accounts is negative. Such a deficit is financed with official international reserves. A balance of payments surplus occurs when the sum of the current and capital accounts is positive. A payments surplus results in an increase in official international reserves. The desirability of a balance of payments deficit or surplus depends on its size and its persistence.

17.3 ▶ FOREIGN EXCHANGE MARKETS: FLEXIBLE EXCHANGE RATES

- Flexible or floating exchange rates between international currencies are determined by the demand for and supply of those currencies. Under floating rates a currency will depreciate or appreciate as a result of changes in tastes, relative income changes, relative price changes, relative changes in real interest rates, and speculation.

17.4 ▶ FIXED EXCHANGE RATES

- The maintenance of fixed exchange rates requires adequate international reserves to accommodate periodic payments deficits. If reserves are inadequate, nations must invoke protectionist trade policies.

17.5 ▶ THE CURRENT EXCHANGE-RATE SYSTEM: THE MANAGED FLOAT

- Since 1971 the world's major nations have used a system of managed floating exchange rates. Rates are generally set by market forces, although governments intervene with varying frequency to alter their exchange rates.

www.mcgrawhillconnect.ca

TERMS AND CONCEPTS

foreign exchange market, p. 413
balance of payments, p. 413
current account, p. 413
balance on goods and services, p. 414
trade surplus, p. 414
trade deficit, p. 414
capital and financial account, p. 415

official international reserves, p. 416
balance of payments deficit, p. 417
balance of payments surplus, p. 417
exchange rate, p. 419
flexible or floating exchange-rate system, p. 419
fixed exchange-rate system, p. 419

depreciation, p. 420
appreciation, p. 420
purchasing power parity theory, p. 422
currency intervention, p. 426
exchange control, p. 427
managed floating exchange rates, p. 428

STUDY QUESTIONS

LO ▶ 17.1 1. Do all international financial transactions involve exchanging one currency for another? Could a nation that neither imports nor exports goods and services still engage in international financial transactions?

LO ▶ 17.1 2. **KEY QUESTION** Indicate whether each of the following creates a demand for, or a supply of, European euros in foreign exchange markets:

a. A Canadian importer purchases a shipload of Bordeaux wine.

b. An Italian automobile firm decides to build an assembly plant in Halifax.

c. A Canadian university student decides to spend a year studying at the Sorbonne.

d. A German manufacturer ships machinery from one French port to another on a Canadian freighter.

e. Spain incurs a balance of payments deficit in its transactions with France.

f. A Canadian government bond held by a French citizen matures and the loan amount is paid back to that person.

g. It is widely believed that the international value of the euro will fall in the near future.

LO ▶ 17.2 3. **KEY QUESTION** Alpha's balance of payments data for 2005 are shown below. All figures are in billions of dollars. What are (a) the balance of trade, (b) the balance on goods and services, (c) the balance on current account, and (d) the balance on capital account? Does Alpha have a balance of payments deficit or surplus? Explain.

Goods exports	+$40
Goods imports	–30
Service exports	+15
Service imports	–10
Net investment income	–5
Net transfers	+$10
Foreign investment in Canada	+10
Foreign investment abroad	–40
Official international reserves	+10

4. China had a $372 billion overall current account surplus **LO ▶ 17** in 2008. Assuming that China's debt forgiveness was zero in 2008 (its capital account balance was zero), what can you specifically conclude about the relationship of Chinese purchases of financial and real assets abroad versus foreign purchases of Chinese financial and real assets?

5. "A rise in the dollar price of yen necessarily means a **LO ▶ 17** fall in the yen price of dollars." Do you agree? Illustrate and elaborate: "The critical thing about exchange rates is that they provide a direct link between the prices of goods and services produced in all trading nations of the world." Explain the purchasing power parity theory of exchange rates.

6. Suppose that a Swiss watchmaker imports watch components from Sweden and exports watches to Canada. Also suppose the Canadian dollar depreciates, and the Swedish krona appreciates, relative to the Swiss franc. Speculate as to how each would hurt the Swiss watchmaker. **LO ▶ 17**

7. **KEY QUESTION** Explain why the Canadian demand **LO ▶ 17** for Mexican pesos is downward sloping and the supply of pesos to Canadians is upward sloping. Assuming a system of flexible exchange rates between Mexico and Canada, indicate whether each of the following would cause the Mexican peso to appreciate or depreciate:

a. Canada unilaterally reduces tariffs on Mexican products.

b. Mexico encounters severe inflation.

c. Deteriorating political relations reduce Canadian tourism in Mexico.

d. The Canadian economy moves into a severe recession.

e. Canada engages in a high-interest-rate monetary policy.

f. Mexican products become more fashionable to Canadians.

g. The Mexican government encourages Canadian firms to invest in Mexican oil fields.

h. The rate of productivity growth in Canada diminishes sharply.

17.3 8. Explain why you agree or disagree with the following statements:

a. "A country that grows faster than its major trading partners can expect the international value of its currency to depreciate."

b. "A nation with an interest rate that is rising more rapidly than in other nations can expect the international value of its currency to appreciate."

c. "A country's currency will appreciate if its inflation rate is less than that of the rest of the world."

17.2 9. "Exports pay for imports. Yet in 1993 the rest of the world exported about $3.2 billion more worth of goods and services to Canada than were imported from Canada." Resolve the apparent inconsistency of these two statements.

17.3 10. **KEY QUESTION** Diagram a market in which the equilibrium dollar price of one unit of fictitious currency Zee is $5 (the exchange rate is $5 = Z1). Then show on your diagram a decline in the demand for Zee.

a. Referring to your diagram, discuss the adjustment options Canada would have in maintaining the exchange rate at $5 = Z1 under a fixed exchange-rate system.

b. How would the Canadian balance of payments surplus that is created (by the decline in demand) get resolved under a system of flexible exchange rates?

17.3 11. In the table below are the supply and demand schedules
17.4 for euros.

Quantity of euros supplied	Price	Quantity of euros demanded
800	$1.20	200
700	1.15	400
600	1.10	600
500	1.05	800
400	0.95	1000
300	0.90	1200
200	0.85	1400

a. What will be the rate of exchange for the euro and for the Canadian dollar?

b. What would happen if Canada and European governments wanted to fix or "peg" the price of a euro at $0.95?

12. The table below shows four different currencies and how **LO** **7.3** much of each currency can be purchased with a Canadian dollar.

Currency per Canadian $			
Country	Currency	Year 1	Year 2
Britain	pound	0.50	0.60
Mexico	peso	6.00	6.50
Germany	euro	1.20	1.00
Japan	yen	110.00	125.00

Among which nations has the Canadian dollar appreciated (A) or depreciated (D) from year 1 to year 2? Explain the appreciation or depreciation using the nations and numbers in the table.

13. **KEY QUESTION** Suppose that a country follows a **LO** **7.5** managed-float policy but that its exchange rate is currently floating freely. In addition, suppose that it currently has a massive current account deficit. Does it also have a balance of payments deficit? If it decides to engage in a currency manipulation in order to reduce the size of its current account deficit, will it buy or sell its own currency? As it does so, what will happen to its official reserves of foreign currencies? Will they get larger or smaller? And, finally, will the country have a balance of payments deficit while it is manipulating the exchange rate?

INTERNET APPLICATION QUESTIONS @

1. **Canada's International Trade in Goods and Services.** Go to the McConnell-Brue-Flynn-Barbiero Web site (Chapter 17) to access data on Canada's merchandise trade balance for the last five years. Has Canada had a surplus or deficit on the merchandise trade balance in the last five years? With which country do we have a trade deficit? A trade surplus?

2. **Canada's Balance of International Payments.** Go to the McConnell-Brue-Flynn-Barbiero Web site (Chapter 17) to access the International Monetary Fund (IMF) data that set out Canada's balance of international payments for the latest quarter for which data are available. What did Canada hold in international reserves in the latest quarter? What is the exchange rate between the Canadian and U.S. dollar for the latest period? Has the Canadian dollar appreciated or depreciated against the U.S. dollar in the last year?

Credits

TEXT CREDITS

Chapter 1
Page 8, www.worldbank.org.

Chapter 2
Page 34, The Heritage Foundation (www. heritage.org) and *The Wall Street Journal.* Page 43, *CIA World Fact Book,* 2008, www. cia.gov. Page 46, Abridged from Donald J. Boudreaux "Mutual Accommodation" *Ideas on Liberty,* May 2000 pp. 4–5.

Chapter 4
Page 85, International Monetary Fund, www. imf.org; and *CIA World Factbook,* www.cia. gov. Page 91, Source: Mark Bils and Peter J. Klenow, "Some Evidence on the Importance of Sticky Prices," *Journal of Political Economy,* October 2004, pp. 947–985.

Chapter 5
Page 101, Statistics Canada Gross Domestic Product, expenditure-based. Updates at http://www40.statcan.ca/l01/cst01/econ04-eng.htm. Accessed May 1, 2009. Page 105, Statistics Canada Gross Domestic Product, expenditure-based. Updates at http://www40.statcan.ca/l01/cst01/econ03-eng.htm. Accessed May 1, 2009. Page 111, Statistics Canada. Gross GDP at: http://www40.statcan.ca/l01/cst01/econ03-eng.htm and Real GDP, expenditure-based at: http://www40.statcan.ca/l01/cst01/econ05-eng.htm. Accessed May 5, 2009. Page 113, Source: Friedrich Schneider and Dominik H. Enste, "Shadow Economies: Size, Causes, and Consequences," *Journal of Economic Literature* (March 2000), p. 104. The figure for Canada is from David E. A. Giles and Lindsay M. Tedds, *Taxes and the Canadian Underground Economy,* Toronto: Canadian Tax Foundation, 2002. Page 115, Source: Statistics Canada, *Gross Domestic Product by Industry: Sources and Methods,* 2002, p. 7, Catalogue No. at-547-XIE.

Chapter 6
Page 121, Statistics Canada. GDP, income-based at: http://www40.statcan.ca/l01/cst01/econ03-eng.htm; Real GDP, expenditure-based at: http://www40.statcan.ca/l01/cst01/econ05-eng.htm. Accessed May 6, 2009.

Page 124, Angus Maddison, *The World Economy: A Millennial Perspective* (Paris: OECD, 2001), p. 264. Page 125, Source: Penn World Table version 6.2, at: http://pwt.econ.upenn.edu/php_site/pwt62_form.php. Page 131, Statistics Canada, The Canadian Productivity Accounts, http://www.statcan.gc.ca/bsolc/olc-cel/olc-cel?lang=eng&catno=15-003-X. Page 137, Source: Compiled and directly quoted from W. Michael Cox and Richard Alm, "The New Paradigm." *Federal Reserve Bank of Dallas Annual Report,* May 2000, various pages. Amounts are in U.S. dollars. Page 138, World Economic Forum, www. weforum.org.

Chapter 7
Page 147, (top) Statistics Canada. Updates at: http://www40.statcan.ca/l01/cst01/media01-eng.htm. Accessed May 7, 2009; (bottom) Statistics Canada. Updates at: http://www.statcan.gc.ca/daily-quotidien/090427/dq090427a-eng.htm. Accessed May 11, 2009. Page 150, The Labour Force, Employment, and Unemployment, 2008. Updates at: http://www40.statcan.ca/l01/cst01/econ10-eng.htm. Accessed May 11, 2009. Page 154, Sources (a) Bank of Canada, *Monetary Policy Report,* October 2005 and the author's calculations (b) Statistics Canada. At: http://www40.statcan.ca/l01/cst01/econ10-eng.htm. Accessed May 15, 2009. Page 155, Statistics Canada. Table: Employment by age, sex, type of work, class of worker and province (monthly). Updates at: http://www40.statcan.ca/l01/cst01/labr66a-eng.htm. Accessed May 18, 2009. Page 156, (top) Statistics Canada. Updates at: http://www.statcan.gc.ca/daily-quotidien/090427/dq090427a-eng.htm. Accessed May 18, 2009; (bottom) Bureau of Labour Statistics, www.bls.gov. Page 158, Updates at: http://www40.statcan.ca/l01/cst01/econ163a-eng.htm. Accessed May 18, 2009. Page 159, U.S. Bureau of Labor Statistics, www.bls.gov.

Chapter 8
Page 171, Statistics Canada. *National Income and Expenditure Accounts,* various years. Page 172, Statistics Canada. At: http://www.40.statcan.ca/l01/cst01/econ04-eng.htm. Page 174, Source: *Statistical Abstract of the*

United States 2006, p. 875 and authors' calculations. Page 184, *International Financial Statistics,* International Monetary Fund, www.imf.org. Used with permission.

Chapter 9
Page 206, Source: World Trade Organization, WTO Publications, www.wto.org. Used with permission.

Chapter 11
Page 263, Source: Minister of Public Works and Government Services Canada, Department of Finance, *Fiscal Reference Tables.* http://www.fin.gc.ca/frt-trf/2008/frt08_8-eng.asp#46. Page 264, Organisation for Economic Co-operation and Development, *OECD Economic Outlook,* www.oecd.org. Page 271, (top) Statistics Canada, CANSIM 380-0039, 380-0016, 385-0010. Accessed September 2009; (bottom) Department of Finance, Bank of Canada Financial Statistics, May 2009, http://epe.lac-bac.gc.ca/100/201/301/bank_can_banking_fin_stats-ef/2009/2009-05.pdf. Page 272, Organisation for Economic Co-operation and Development, *OECD Economic Outlook,* www.oecd.org. Page 273, Calculated from population figures from Statistics Canada and net debt from the Department of Finance, *Fiscal Reference Tables,* 2008; Statistics Canada. At: http://www40.statcan.ca/l01/cst01/demo31a-eng.htm. Accessed May 21, 2009.

Chapter 12
Page 283, *Bank of Canada Banking and Financial Statistics,* May 2009. At: http://epe.lac-bac.gc.ca/100/201/301/bank_can_banking_fin_stats-ef/2009/2009-05.pdf. Page 284, *Bank of Canada Banking and Financial Statistics,* May 2009. Page 289, *Bank of Canada Banking and Financial Statistics,* May 2009. Page 290, Forbes Global 2000, www.forbes.com.

Chapter 13
Page 313, *Bank of Canada Banking and Financial Statistics,* May 2009. Updated to 2008. Page 322, Bank of Canada. Selected historical interest rates. At: http://www.bankofcanada.ca/en/rates/sel_hist.html. Updated to 2008.

Chapter 14

Page 343, The Investment Funds Institute of Canada, www.ific. Page 348, The International Country Risk Guide, January 2008. Published by the PRS (Political Risk Survey) Group, Inc. www.prsgroup.com/icrg/icrg.html. Used with permission of the PRS Group, Inc.

Chapter 15

Page 369, For inflation see http://www40.statcan.ca/l01/cst01/econ163a-eng.htm. For Unemployment see http://www40.statcan.ca/l01/cst01/econ10-eng.htm. Accessed May 21, 2009. Page 371, Bureau of Labor Statistics (www.bls.gov).

Chapter 16

Page 381, (top) Data used with permission of World Trade Organization. www.wto.org; (bottom) Statistics Canada: http://www40.statcan.ca/l01/cst01/econ01a-eng.htm and http://www40.statcan.ca/l01/cst01/econ04-eng.htm. Accessed May 19, 2009. Page 382, (top) Statistics Canada. At: http://www40.statcan.ca/l01/cst01/gblec02a-eng.htm. Accessed May 18, 2009; (bottom) Statistics Canada, http://www40.statcan.ca/l01/cst01/gblec04a-eng.htm. Accessed May 19, 2009. Page 384, Data used with permission of World Trade Organization. www.wto.org.

Chapter 17

Page 414, Statistics Canada. At: http://www40.statcan.ca/l01/cst01/econ01a-eng.htm. Accessed May 19, 2009. Page 415, Statistics Canada: http://www40.statcan.gc.ca/l01/cst01/gblec02a-eng. htm. Page 418, http://www40.statcan.ca/l01/cst01/econ01a-eng.htm, various years. Accessed May 19, 2009. Page 420, Bank of Canada Banking and Financial Statistics, May 2009.

PHOTOGRAPHS

Chapter 1

page 2, Arthur S. Aubry/Getty Images; page 20, © James Leynse/CORBIS;

Chapter 2

page 46, © Royalty Free/CORBIS

Chapter 3

page 50, Ryan McVay/Getty Images; page 66, Ryan McVay/Getty Images; page 68, Royalty-Free/CORBIS

Chapter 5

page 101, Jack Star/PhotoLink/Getty Images

Chapter 6

page 134, Ryan McVay/Getty Images; page 141, John Lawrence/Getty Images

Chapter 7

page 167, Ryan McVay/Getty Images;

Chapter 8

page 177, Ryan McVay/Getty Images; page 183, Royalty-Free/CORBIS; page 190, © Getty Images

Chapter 9

Page 218, From *The General Theory of Employment, Interest, and Money*, by John Maynard Keynes, cover image (1997). (Amherst, NY: Prometheus Books). Reprinted with permission of the publisher.

Chapter 10

page 234, John A. Rizzo/Getty Images; page 242, Royalty-Free/CORBIS; page 244, © Creatas/PunchStock; page 246, © Getty Images

Chapter 11

page 255, © image100/PunchStock; page 276, © Getty Images

Chapter 12

page 281, Digital Vision/Getty Images; page 291, PhotoLink/Getty Images

Chapter 13

page 326, Digital Vision/PunchStock;

Chapter 15

page 363, © Robert Lopshire/iStockphoto

Chapter 16

page 385, Getty Images/Steve Allen; page 389 © Creatas/PunchStock; page 408, © Getty Images

Chapter 17

page 420, Digital Vision/Getty Images; page 430, © PhotoLink/Getty Images

Glossary

A

Absolute advantage When a region or nation can produce more of good Z and good Y with fewer resources compared to other regions or nations.

Actively managed funds Mutual funds that constantly buy and sell assets in an attempt to generate high returns.

Actual investment The amount that firms do invest; equal to planned investment plus unplanned investment.

Actual reserves The funds that a bank has as vault cash plus any deposit it may have with the Bank of Canada.

Adjustable pegs The device used in the Bretton Woods system to alter exchange rates in an orderly way to eliminate persistent payments deficits and surpluses. Each nation defined its monetary unit in terms of (pegged it to) gold or the U.S. dollar, kept the rate of exchange for its money stable in the short run, and adjusted its rate in the long run when faced with international payments disequilibrium.

Aggregate A collection of specific economic units treated as if they were one unit.

Aggregate demand A schedule or curve that shows the total quantity of goods and services demanded (purchased) at different price levels.

Aggregate demand–aggregate supply (AD–AS) model The macroeconomic model that uses aggregate demand and aggregate supply to explain price level and real domestic output.

Aggregate expenditures The total amount spent for final goods and services in an economy.

Aggregate expenditures schedule A schedule or curve that shows the total amount spent for final goods and services at different levels of GDP.

Aggregate expenditures-domestic output approach Determination of the equilibrium gross domestic product by finding the real GDP at which aggregate expenditures equal domestic output.

Aggregate supply A schedule or curve that shows the total quantity of goods and services supplied (produced) at different price levels.

Aggregate supply shocks Sudden, large changes in resource costs that shift an economy's aggregate supply curve.

Aggregation Combining individual units or data into one unit or number. For example, all prices of individual goods and services are combined into a price level, or all units of output are aggregated into real gross domestic product.

Allocative efficiency The distribution of resources among firms and industries to produce the goods most wanted by society.

Anticipated inflation Increases in the price level that occur at the expected rate.

Applied economics (See Policy economics.)

Appreciation (of the dollar) An increase in the value of the dollar relative to the currency of another nation so that a dollar buys a larger amount of the foreign currency and thus of foreign goods.

Arbitrage Occurs when investors try to profit from situations where two identical or nearly identical assets have different rates of return.

Asset Anything of monetary value owned by a firm or individual.

Asset demand for money The amount of money people want to hold as a store of value; this amount varies inversely with the rate of interest.

Average expected rate of return The probability weighted average of an investment's possible future rates of return.

Average propensity to consume The fraction (or percentage) of disposable income that households plan to spend for consumer goods and services.

Average propensity to save The fraction (or percentage) of disposable income that households save.

Average tax rate Total tax paid divided by total (taxable) income, as a percentage.

B

Balanced-budget multiplier The extent to which an equal change in government spending and taxes changes equilibrium gross domestic product; always has a value of 1, since it is equal to the amount of the equal changes in G and T.

Balance of payments A summary of all the transactions that took place between the individuals, firms, and government units of one nation and those in all other nations during a year.

Balance of payments deficit The amount by which the sum of the balance on current account and the balance on the capital account is negative in a year.

Balance of payments surplus The amount by which the sum of the balance on current account and the balance on the capital account is positive in a year.

Balance on current account The exports of goods and services of a nation less its imports of goods and services plus its net investment income and net transfers in a year.

Balance on goods and services The exports of goods and services of a nation less its imports of goods and services in a year.

Balance on the capital and financial account The foreign purchases of assets in a nation less its purchases of assets abroad in a year.

Balance sheet A statement of the assets, liabilities, and net worth of a firm or individual at a certain time.

Bank deposits The deposits that individuals or firms have at financial institutions or that banks have at the central bank.

Bank of Canada notes Paper money issued by the Bank of Canada.

Bank rate The interest rate that the Bank of Canada charges on advances made to the chartered banks.

Bankrupt The situation when individuals or firms are unable to make timely payments on their debts.

Bankers' bank A bank that accepts the deposits of and makes loans to chartered banks; in Canada, the Bank of Canada.

Barter The exchange of one good or service for another good or service.

Base year The year with which other years are compared when an index is constructed; for example, the base year for a price index.

Beta A relative measure of non-diversifiable risk; measures the non-diversifiable risk of a given asset or portfolio.

Bond A financial device through which a borrower (a firm or government) is obligated to pay the principal and interest on a loan at a specific date in the future.

Break-even income The level of disposable income at which households plan to consume all their income and to save none of it.

Bretton Wood system The international monetary system developed after World War II in which adjustable pegs were employed, the International Monetary Fund helped to stabilize foreign exchange rates, and gold and the U.S. dollar were used as international monetary reserves.

Budget deficit The amount by which the expenditures of the federal government exceed its revenues in any year.

Budget line A schedule or curve that shows various combinations of two products a consumer can purchase with a specific money income.

Budget surplus The amount by which the revenues of the federal government exceed its expenditures in any year.

Built-in stabilizer A mechanism that increases government's budget deficit (or reduces its surplus) during a recession and increases government's budget surplus (or reduces its deficit) during inflation without any action by policymakers.

Business cycle Recurring increases and decreases in the level of economic activity over periods of years. Consists of peak, recession, trough, and expansion phases.

Business firm (See Firm.)

C

Capital Human-made resources (buildings, machinery, and equipment) used to produce goods and services.

Capital and financial account The section of a nation's international balance of payments statement that records the foreign purchases of assets in Canada and Canadian purchases of assets abroad.

Capital and financial account deficit A negative balance on the capital account.

Capital and financial account surplus A positive balance on the capital account.

Capital consumption allowance Estimate of the amount of capital worn out or used up (consumed) in producing the gross domestic product; depreciation.

Capital gain The gain realized when securities or properties are sold for a price greater than the price paid for them.

Capital goods Goods that do not directly satisfy human wants.

Capital-intensive goods Products that require a relatively large amount of capital to produce.

Capitalism An economic system in which property resources are privately owned and markets and prices are used to direct and coordinate economic activities.

Capital stock The total available capital in a nation.

Capital-using technology Technology that requires the use of a greater amount of capital to produce a specific quantity of a product.

Cartel A formal agreement among firms (or countries) in an industry to set the price of a product and establish the outputs of the individual firms (or countries) or to divide the market for the product geographically.

Central bank A bank whose chief function is the control of the nation's money supply; in Canada, the Bank of Canada.

Central economic planning Government determination of the objectives of the economy and how resources will be directed to attain those goals. Ceteris paribus assumption. (See Other-things-equal assumption.)

Change in demand A change in the quantity demanded of a good or service at every price.

Change in quantity demanded A movement from one point to another on a demand curve.

Change in quantity supplied A movement from one point to another on a fixed supply curve.

Change in supply A change in the quantity supplied of a good or service at every price; a shift of the supply curve to the left or right.

Chartered bank One of the multi-branched, privately owned, commercial, financial intermediaries that have received charters by Act of Parliament and that may call themselves "banks."

Chequable (demand) deposit Any deposit in a financial institution against which a cheque may be written and which deposit, if it is in a bank, is thus part of the M1 money supply.

Chequing account A demand deposit in a financial institution.

Circular flow diagram The flow of resources from households to firms and of products from firms to households. These flows are accompanied by reverse flows of money from firms to households and from households to firms.

Classical economics The macroeconomic generalizations accepted by most economists before the 1930s that led to the conclusion that a capitalistic economy was self-regulating and therefore would usually employ its resources fully.

Closed economy An economy that neither exports nor imports goods and services.

COLA (See Cost-of-living adjustment.)

Command system An economic system in which most property resources are owned by the government and economic decisions are made by a central government body.

Commercial bank (See Chartered bank.)

Communism (See Command system.)

Comparative advantage When a region or nation can produce a good at a lower domestic opportunity cost compared to a potential trading partner.

Competition The presence in a market of a large number of independent buyers and sellers competing with one another and the freedom of buyers and sellers to enter and leave the market.

Complementary goods Products and services that are used together.

Complex multiplier The multiplier that exists when changes in the gross domestic product change net taxes and imports, as well as saving.

Conglomerates Firms that produce goods and services in two or more separate industries.

Constant opportunity cost An opportunity cost that remains the same for each additional unit as a consumer (or society) shifts purchases (production) from one product to another along a straight-line budget line (production possibilities curve).

Consumer goods Products and services that satisfy human wants directly.

Consumer Price Index (CPI) An index that measures the prices of a fixed "market basket" of goods and services bought by a "typical" consumer.

Consumer sovereignty Determination by consumers of the types and quantities of goods and services that will be produced with the scarce resources of the economy.

Consumption of fixed capital Estimate of the amount of capital worn out or used up (consumed) in producing the gross domestic product; also called depreciation.

Consumption schedule A schedule showing the amounts households plan to spend for consumer goods at different levels of disposable income.

Contractionary fiscal policy A decrease in government spending, an increase in net taxes, or some combination of the two, for the purpose of decreasing aggregate demand and thus controlling inflation.

Coordination failure A situation in which people do not reach a mutually beneficial outcome because they lack some way to jointly coordinate their actions; a possible cause of macroeconomic instability.

Corporate income tax A tax levied on the net income (profit) of corporations.

Corporation A legal entity ("person") chartered by a province or the federal government that is distinct and separate from the individuals who own it.

Correlation A systematic and dependable association between two sets of data (two kinds of events); does not necessarily indicate causation.

Cost-of-living adjustment (COLA) An automatic increase in the incomes (wages) of workers when inflation occurs.

Cost-push inflation Increases in the price level resulting from an increase in resource costs and hence in per-unit production costs.

Creative destruction The hypothesis that the creation of new products and production methods simultaneously destroys the market power of firms that are wedded to existing products and older ways of doing business.

Credit An accounting item that increases the value of an asset (such as the foreign money owned by the residents of a nation).

Credit union An association of persons who have a common tie (such as being employees of the same firm or members of the same labour union) that sells shares to (accepts deposits from) its members and makes loans to them.

Crowding-out effect A rise in interest rates and a resulting decrease in planned investment caused by the federal government's increased borrowing in the money market.

Currency Coins and paper money.

Currency appreciation (See Exchange rate appreciation.)

Currency depreciation (See Exchange rate depreciation.)

Currency intervention A government's buying and selling of its own or of foreign currencies to alter international exchange rates.

Current account The section in a nation's international balance of payments that records its exports and imports of goods and services, its net investment income, and its net transfers.

Cyclical asymmetry The idea that monetary policy may be more successful in slowing expansions and controlling inflation than in extracting the economy from severe recession.

Cyclical deficit A federal budget deficit that is caused by a recession and the consequent decline in tax revenues.

Cyclically adjusted budget What the budget balance would be for the total government sector if the economy were operating at full employment.

Cyclically balanced budget The equality of government expenditures and net tax collections over the course of a business cycle.

Cyclical unemployment Unemployment caused by a decline in total spending (or by insufficient aggregate demand).

D

Debit An accounting item that decreases the value of an asset (such as the foreign money owned by the residents of a nation).

Default A failure to make a bond's promised payments.

Deflating Finding the real gross domestic product by decreasing the dollar value of the GDP for a year in which prices were higher than in the base year.

Deflation A decline in the economy's price level.

Demand A schedule or curve that shows the various amounts of a product that consumers are willing and able to purchase at each of a series of possible prices during a specified period of time.

Demand curve A curve illustrating the inverse (negative) relationship between the quantity demanded of a good or service and its price, other things equal.

Demand deposit A deposit in a chartered bank against which cheques may be written.

Demand-deposit multiplier (See Monetary multiplier.)

Demand factor (in growth) The increase in the level of aggregate demand that brings about the economic growth made possible by an increase in the production potential of the economy.

Demand management The use of fiscal policy and monetary policy to increase or decrease aggregate demand.

Demand-pull inflation Increases in the price level caused by an excess of total spending beyond the economy's capacity to produce.

Demand shocks Sudden, unexpected changes in demand.

Dependent variable A variable that changes as a consequence of a change in some other (independent) variable; the "effect" or outcome.

Depreciation (See Capital consumption allowance.)

Depreciation (of the dollar) A decrease in the value of the dollar relative to another currency so that a dollar buys a smaller amount of the foreign currency and therefore of foreign goods.

Derived demand The demand for a factor of production that depends on the demand for the products it can be used to produce.

Desired reserve ratio The specified percentage of deposit liabilities a chartered bank chooses to keep as vault cash.

Desired reserves The amount of vault cash each chartered bank chooses to keep on hand for daily transactions, plus its deposits at the Bank of Canada.

Determinants of aggregate demand Factors (such as consumption spending, investment, government spending, and net exports) that shift the aggregate demand curve.

Determinants of aggregate supply Factors (such as input prices, productivity, and the legal-institutional environment) that shift the aggregate supply curve.

Determinants of demand Factors other than its price that determine the quantities demanded of a good or service.

Determinants of supply Factors other than its price that determine the quantities supplied of a good or service.

Devaluation A decrease in the governmentally defined value of a currency.

Developing countries (DVCs) Many countries of Africa, Asia, and Latin America that are characterized by a lack of capital goods, use of nonadvanced technologies, low literacy rates, high unemployment, rapid population growth, and labour forces heavily committed to agriculture.

Diminishing marginal utility As a consumer increases the consumption of a good or service, the marginal utility obtained from each additional unit of the good or service decreases.

Direct relationship The relationship between two variables that change in the same direction, for example, product price and quantity supplied.

Discouraged workers People who have left the labour force because they have not been able to find employment.

Discretionary fiscal policy Deliberate changes in taxes (tax rates) and government spending by Parliament to promote full employment, price stability, and economic growth.

Discrimination According individuals or groups different treatment in hiring, occupational access, education and training, promotion, wage rates, or working conditions, even though they have the same abilities, education and skills, and work experience as other workers.

Disinflation A reduction in the rate of inflation.

Disposable income (DI) Personal income less personal taxes.

Dissaving Spending for consumer goods and services in excess of disposable income; the amount by which personal consumption expenditures exceed disposable income.

Diversifiable risk The risk specific to a given investment; can be eliminated by diversification.

Diversification The strategy of investing in a large number of investments in order to reduce the overall risk to the entire portfolio.

Dividends Payments by a corporation of all or part of its profit to its shareholders (the corporate owners).

Division of labour Dividing the work required to produce a product into a number of different tasks that are performed by different workers.

Doha Round The latest, uncompleted (as of Spring 2006) sequence of trade negotiations by members of the World Trade Organization; named after Doha, Qatar, where the set of negotiations began.

Dollar votes The "votes" that consumers and entrepreneurs cast for the production of consumer and capital goods, respectively, when they purchase them in product and resource markets.

Domestic capital formation Addition to a nation's stock of capital by saving and investing part of its own domestic output.

Domestic price The price of a good or service within a country, determined by domestic demand and supply.

Dumping The sale in a foreign country of products below the cost or below the prices charged at home.

Durable good A consumer good with an expected life (use) of three or more years.

E

Earnings The money income received by a worker; equal to the wage (rate) multiplied by the amount of time worked.

Economic cost A payment that must be made to obtain and retain the services of a resource; the income a firm must provide to a resource supplier to attract the resource away from an alternative use; equal to the quantity of other products that cannot be produced when resources are instead used to make a particular product.

Economic efficiency Obtaining the socially optimal amounts of goods and services using minimum necessary resources; entails both productive efficiency and allocative efficiency. (1) An outward shift in the production possibilities curve that results from an increase in factor supplies or quality or an improvement in technology; (2) an increase either in real output (gross domestic product) or in real output per capita.

Economic growth An increase either in real output (GDP) or in real output per capita.

Economic investment Paying for new additions to the nation's capital stock, or new replacements for capital stock that has worn out.

Economic law An economic principle that has been tested and retested and has stood the test of time.

Economic model A simplified picture of economic reality; an abstract generalization.

Economic perspective A viewpoint that envisions individuals and institutions making rational decisions by comparing the marginal benefits and marginal costs associated with their actions.

Economic policy A course of action intended to correct or avoid a problem.

Economic principle A statement about economic behaviour or the economy that enables prediction of the probable effects of certain actions.

Economic problem The need to make choices because society's material wants for goods and services are unlimited but the resources available to satisfy these wants are limited (scarce).

Economic profit The total revenue of a firm less its economic costs (which includes both explicit costs and implicit costs); also called "pure profit" and "above normal profit."

Economic resources The land, labour, capital, and entrepreneurial ability that are used in the production of goods and services.

Economics The social science concerned with how individuals, institutions, and society make optimal (best) choices under conditions of scarcity.

Economic system A particular set of institutional arrangements and a coordinating mechanism for producing goods and services.

Economic theory Deriving economic principles from relevant economic facts; an economic principle.

Economies of scale Reductions in the average total cost of producing a product as the firm expands the size of plant (its output) in the long run.

Efficiency factor (in growth) The capacity of an economy to combine resources effectively to achieve growth of real output that the supply factors make possible.

Efficiency loss Reductions in combined consumer and producer surplus caused by an underallocation or overallocation of resources to the production of a good or service. Also called deadweight loss.

Efficiency wages Wages that elicit maximum work effort and thus minimize labour cost per unit of output.

Efficient allocation of resources That allocation of an economy's resources among the production of different products that leads to the maximum satisfaction of consumers' wants; producing the socially optimal mix of output with society's scarce resources.

Employment rate The percentage of the civilian labour force employed at any time.

Entrepreneurial ability The human talents that combine the other resources to produce a product, make nonroutine decisions, innovate, and bear risks.

Equation of exchange $MV = PQ$, in which M is the supply of money, V is the velocity of money, P is the price level, and Q is the physical volume of final goods and services produced.

Equilibrium GDP The level at which the total quantity of goods produced (GDP) equals the total quantity of goods purchased.

Equilibrium price The price in a competitive market at which the quantity demanded and the quantity supplied are equal.

Equilibrium price level The price level at which the aggregate demand curve intersects the aggregate supply curve.

Equilibrium quantity The quantity demanded and supplied at the equilibrium price in a competitive market.

Equilibrium real domestic output The real domestic output at which the aggregate demand curve intersects the aggregate supply curve.

Equilibrium world price A price determined by the intersection of exporting nations' supply of a product and importing nations' demand for the same product.

Euro The common currency used by 15 European nations (as of 2008) in the Euro Zone, which consists of Austria, Belgium, Finland, France, Germany, Greece, Ireland, Italy, Luxembourg, the Netherlands, Portugal, and Spain, and will eventually include all member nations of the European Union except Great Britain, Denmark, and Sweden.

European Union (EU) An association of 27 nations (as of 2008) that has eliminated tariffs among themselves, established common tariffs for goods imported from outside the member nations, and allowed the free movement of labour and capital among themselves.

Excess reserves The amount by which a chartered bank's actual reserves exceed its desired reserves.

Exchange control (See Foreign exchange control.)

Exchange rate The rate at which the currency of one nation is exchanged for the currency of another nation.

Exchange rate appreciation An increase in the value of a nation's currency in foreign exchange markets; an increase in the rate of exchange for foreign currencies.

Exchange rate depreciation A decrease in the value of a nation's currency in foreign exchange markets; a decrease in the rate of exchange for foreign currencies.

Excise tax A tax levied on the production of a specific product or on the quantity of the product purchased.

Exclusion principle The ability to exclude those who do not pay for a product from receiving its benefits.

Expansion The phase of the business cycle during which output and employment rise toward full employment.

Expansionary fiscal policy An increase in government spending, a decrease in net taxes, or some combination of the two, for the purpose of increasing aggregate demand and expanding real output.

Expansionary monetary policy Bank of Canada actions to increase the money supply, lower interest rates, and expand real GDP; an easy money policy.

Expectations The anticipations of consumers, firms, and others about future economic conditions.

Expected rate of return The increase in profit a firm anticipates it will obtain by purchasing capital.

Expenditures approach The method that adds all expenditures made for final goods and services to measure the gross domestic product.

Exports Goods and services produced in a nation and sold to customers in other nations.

Export subsidies Government payments to domestic producers to enable them to reduce the price of a good or service to foreign buyers.

Export supply curve An upward-sloping curve that shows the amount of a product domestic firms will export at each world price above the domestic price.

External benefit (See Positive externality.)

External cost (See Negative externality.)

External debt Private or public debt owed to foreign citizens, firms, and institutions.

External public debt Public debt owed to foreign citizens, firms, and institutions.

Externality Benefits or costs from production or consumption accruing without compensation to nonbuyers and nonsellers of the product (see negative externality and positive externality).

F

Face value The dollar or cents value stamped on a coin.

Factor market A market in which households sell and firms buy factors of production.

Factors of production Economic resources: land, capital, labour, and entrepreneurial ability.

Fair-trade movement The efforts by groups in high-income nations to get growers of agricultural crops in low-income nations to adhere to certain wage and workplace standards in exchange for their goods being promoted as "fair-trade goods" to consumers; also efforts by these groups to convince consumers to buy these goods instead of otherwise close substitutes.

Fallacy of composition The false notion that what is true for the individual (or part) is necessarily true for the group (or whole).

Fiat money Anything that is money because government has decreed it to be money.

Final goods Goods and services that have been purchased for final use and not for resale or further processing or manufacturing.

Financial intermediary A chartered bank or other financial institution that uses the funds deposited with it to make loans.

Financial investment Either buying or building an asset in the expectation that doing so will generate a financial gain.

Firm An organization that employs resources to produce a good or service for profit.

Fiscal policy Changes in government spending and tax collections designed to achieve a full-employment and noninflationary domestic output.

Fixed cost Any cost which in total does not change when the firm changes its output; the cost of fixed resources.

Fixed exchange rate A rate of exchange that is prevented from rising or falling with changes in currency supply and demand.

Flexible exchange rate A rate of exchange determined by the international demand for and supply of a nation's currency.

Flexible prices Product prices that react within seconds to changes in supply and demand.

Floating exchange rate (See Flexible exchange rate.)

Follower countries As it relates to economic growth, countries that adopt advanced technologies that previously were developed and used by leader countries.

Foreign exchange control The control a government may exercise over the quantity of foreign currency demanded by its citizens and firms and over the rates of exchange in order to limit its outpayments to its inpayments (to eliminate a payments deficit).

Foreign exchange market A market in which the money (currency) of one nation can be used to purchase (can be exchanged for) the money of another nation.

Foreign exchange rate (See Rate of exchange.)

Foreign trade effect The inverse relationship between the net exports of an economy and its price level relative to price levels in the economies of trading partners.

45° (degree) line A reference line that bisects the 90° angle formed by the two axes, and along which consumption equals disposable income.

Fractional reserve banking system A banking system with a reserve ratio that is less than 100 percent of the deposit liabilities of a chartered bank.

Freedom of choice The freedom of owners of property resources to employ or dispose of them as they see fit, and of consumers to spend their incomes in a manner that they think is appropriate.

Freedom of enterprise The freedom of firms to obtain economic resources, to use these resources to produce products of the firm's own choosing, and to sell their products in markets of their choice.

Free-rider problem The inability of potential providers of an economically desirable but indivisible good or service to obtain payment from those who benefit.

Free trade The absence of artificial (government-imposed) barriers to trade among individuals and firms in different nations.

Frictional unemployment A type of unemployment caused by workers voluntarily changing jobs and by temporary layoffs; unemployed workers between jobs.

Full employment Use of all available resources to produce want-satisfying goods and services.

Full-employment unemployment rate The unemployment rate at which there is no cyclical unemployment of the labour force; equal to about 7.5 percent in Canada because some frictional and structural unemployment is unavoidable.

Full production Employment of available resources so that the maximum amount of goods and services is produced.

G

G-8 Nations A group of eight major industrial nations (the United States, Japan, Germany, United Kingdom, France, Italy, Russia, and Canada) whose leaders meet regularly to discuss common economic problems and try to coordinate economic policies.

Gains from trade The extra output that trading partners obtain through specialization of production and exchange of goods and services.

GDP (See Gross domestic product.)

GDP deflator An implicit price index calculated by dividing nominal GDP by real GDP and multiplying by 100.

GDP gap The amount by which actual gross domestic product falls below potential gross domestic product.

General Agreement on Tariffs and Trade (GATT) The international agreement reached in 1947 in which 23 nations agreed to give equal and nondiscriminatory treatment to the other nations, to reduce tariff rates by multinational negotiations, and to eliminate import quotas. It now includes most nations and has become the World Trade Organization.

Generalization Statement of the nature of the relation between two or more sets of facts.

Gold standard A historical system of fixed exchange rates in which nations defined their currency in terms of gold.

Government deposit switching Action of the Bank of Canada to increase (decrease) backing for money supply by switching government deposits from (to) itself to (from) the chartered banks.

Government purchases (G) The expenditures of all governments in the economy for final goods and services.

Government transfer payment The disbursement of money (or goods and services) by government for which government receives no currently produced good or service in return.

Gross domestic product (GDP) The total market value of all final goods and services produced annually within the boundaries of Canada.

Gross investment Expenditures for newly produced capital goods (such as machinery, equipment, tools, and buildings) and for additions to inventories.

Gross private domestic investment Expenditures for newly produced capital goods (such as machinery, equipment, tools, and buildings) and for additions to inventories.

Guiding function of prices The ability of price changes to bring about changes in the quantities of products and resources demanded and supplied.

H

Horizontal axis The "left–right" or "west–east" axis on a graph or grid.

Household An economic unit (of one or more persons) that provides the economy with resources and uses the income received to purchase goods and services that satisfy material wants.

Human capital The accumulation of prior investments in education, training, health, and other factors that increase productivity.

Human-capital investment Any expenditure undertaken to improve the education, skills, health, or mobility of workers, with an expectation of greater productivity and thus a positive return on the investment.

Hyperinflation A very rapid rise in the price level.

Hypothesis A tentative, untested economic principle.

I

IMF (See International Monetary Fund.)

Immediate-short-run aggregate supply curve (AS$_{ISR}$) An aggregate supply curve for which real output, but not the price level, changes when the aggregate demand curve shifts.

Import competition The competition that domestic firms encounter from the products and services of foreign producers.

Import demand curve A downward-sloping curve that shows the amount of a product that an economy will import at each world price below the domestic price.

Import quota A limit imposed by a nation on the quantity (or total value) of a good that may be imported during some period of time.

Imports Spending by individuals, firms, and governments for goods and services produced in foreign nations.

Income approach The method that adds all the income generated by the production of final goods and services to measure the gross domestic product.

Income effect A change in the price of a product changes a consumer's real income (purchasing power) and thus the quantity of the product purchased.

Increase in demand An increase in the quantity demanded of a good or service at every price; a shift of the demand curve to the right.

Increase in supply An increase in the quantity supplied of a good or service at every price; a shift in the supply curve to the right.

Increasing returns An increase in a firm's output by a larger percentage than the percentage increase in its inputs.

Independent goods Products or services for which there is no relationship between the price of one and the demand for the other; when the price of one rises or falls, the demand for the other remains constant.

Independent variable The variable causing a change in some other (dependent) variable.

Index funds Mutual funds that choose their portfolios to exactly match a stock or bond index.

Indirect taxes Such taxes as sales, business property taxes, and custom duties that firms treat as costs of producing a product.

Industrially advanced countries (IACs) High-income countries such as Canada, the United States, Japan, and the nations of Western Europe that have highly developed market economies based on large stocks of technologically advanced capital goods and skilled labour forces.

Industry A group of (one or more) firms that produce identical or similar products.

Inferior good A good or service whose consumption declines as income rises (and conversely), price remaining constant.

Inflating Determining real gross domestic product by increasing the dollar value of the nominal gross domestic product produced in a year in which prices are lower than in a base year.

Inflation A rise in the general level of prices in an economy.

Inflation premium The component of the nominal interest rate that reflects anticipated inflation.

Inflation targeting A Bank of Canada policy of maintaining the inflation rate within a specific range, currently 1–3 percent.

Inflationary expectations The belief of workers, firms, and consumers that substantial inflation will occur in the future.

Inflationary gap (inflationary expenditure gap) The amount by which the equilibrium GDP exceeds full-employment GDP.

Inflexible prices (sticky prices) Product prices that remain in place (at least for a while) even though supply or demand has changed; also called sticky prices.

Information technology New and more efficient methods of delivering and receiving information through use of computers, cellular phones, and the Internet.

Infrastructure The capital goods usually provided by the public sector for the use of its citizens and firms (for example, highways, bridges, transit systems, wastewater treatment facilities, municipal water systems, and airports).

Injection An addition of spending to the income-expenditure stream.

Innovation The first commercially successful introduction of a new product, the use of a new method of production, or the creation of a new form of business organization.

Inpayments The receipts of its own or foreign money that individuals, firms, and governments of one nation obtain from the sale of goods and services abroad, or as investment income, remittances, and capitals inflows from abroad.

Insider-outsider theory The hypothesis that nominal wages are inflexible downward because firms are aware that workers ("insiders") who retain employment during recession may refuse to work cooperatively with previously unemployed workers ("outsiders") who offer to work for less than the current wage.

Interest The payment made for the use of money (of borrowed funds).

Interest income Payments of income to those who supply the economy with capital.

Interest rate The annual rate at which interest is paid; a percentage of the borrowed amount.

Interest-rate effect The direct relationship between price level and the demand for money, which affects interest rates, and, as a result, total spending in the economy.

Intermediate goods Products that are purchased for resale or further processing or manufacturing.

Internally held public debt Public debt owed to citizens, firms, and institutions of the same nation issuing the debt.

International balance of payments (See Balance of payments.)

International balance of payments deficit (See Balance of payments deficit.)

International balance of payments surplus (See Balance of payments surplus.)

International gold standard (See Gold standard.)

International Monetary Fund (IMF) The international association of nations formed after World War II to make loans of foreign monies to nations with temporary payments deficits and, until the early 1970s, to administer the adjustable-peg system. It now makes loans to nations facing possible defaults on private or governmental bans.

International monetary reserves The foreign currencies and such assets as gold a nation may use to settle a payments deficit.

International value of the dollar The price that must be paid in foreign currency (money) to obtain one Canadian dollar.

Intrinsic value The market value of the metal within a coin.

Inventory Goods that have been produced but are still unsold.

Inverse relationship The relationship between two variables that change in opposite directions, for example, product price and quantity demanded.

Investment Spending for the production and accumulation of capital and additions to inventories.

Investment demand curve A curve that shows the amount of investment demanded by an economy at a series of real interest rates.

Investment goods (See Capital.)

Investment schedule A curve or schedule that shows the amounts firms plan to invest at various possible values of real gross domestic product.

Investment in human capital (See Human-capital investment.)

Invisible hand The tendency of firms and resource suppliers seeking to further their own self-interests in competitive markets to also promote the interest of society as a whole.

K

Keynesian economics The macroeconomic generalizations that lead to the conclusion that a capitalistic economy is characterized by macroeconomic instability and that fiscal policy and monetary policy can be used to promote full employment, price-level stability, and economic growth.

Keynesianism The philosophical, ideological, and analytical views pertaining to Keynesian economics.

L

Labour The physical and mental talents and efforts of people that are used to produce goods and services.

Labour force Persons 15 years of age and older who are not in institutions and who are employed or are unemployed and seeking work.

Labour-force participation rate The percentage of the working-age population that is actually in the labour force.

Labour-intensive goods Products that require a relatively large amount of labour to produce.

Labour productivity The average product of labour or output per worker per hour.

Labour union A group of workers organized to advance the interests of the group (to increase wages, shorten the hours worked, improve working conditions, and so on).

Laffer Curve A curve relating government tax rates and tax revenues.

Laissez-faire capitalism (See Capitalism.)

Land Natural resources ("free gifts of nature") used to produce goods and services.

Land-intensive goods Products that require a relatively large amount of land to produce.

Law of demand All else equal, as price falls, the quantity demanded rises, and vice versa.

Law of increasing opportunity costs As the production of a good increases, the opportunity cost of producing an additional unit rises.

Law of supply The principle that, other things equal, an increase in the price of a product will increase the quantity of it supplied; and conversely for a price decrease.

Leader countries As it relates to economic growth, countries that develop and use advanced technologies, which then become available to follower countries.

Leakage (1) A withdrawal of potential spending from the income-expenditures stream via saving, tax payments, or imports. (2) A withdrawal that reduces the lending potential of the banking system.

Learning-by-doing Achieving greater productivity and lower average total cost through gains in knowledge and skill that accompany repetition of a task; a source of economies of scale.

Legal tender Anything that government says must be accepted in payment of a debt.

Lending potential of an individual chartered bank The amount by which a single bank can safely increase the money supply by making new loans to (or buying securities from) the public; equal to the bank's excess reserves.

Lending potential of the banking system The amount by which the banking system can increase the money supply by making new loans to (or buying securities from) the public; equal to the excess reserves of the banking system multiplied by the monetary multiplier.

Liability A debt with a monetary value; an amount owed by a firm or an individual.

Limited liability Restriction of the maximum loss to a predetermined amount for the owners (stockholders) of a corporation, the maximum loss is the amount they paid for their shares of stock.

Limited liability rule Rules that limit the risks involved in investing in corporations by capping their potential losses at the amount they paid for their shares.

Limited-liability company An unincorporated business whose owners are protected by limited liability.

Liquidity The ease with which an asset can be converted into cash with little or no loss of purchasing power.

Long run (1) In microeconomics, a period of time long enough to enable producers of a product to change the quantities of all the resources they employ; period in which all resources and costs are variable and no resources or costs are fixed. (2) In macroeconomics, a period sufficiently long for nominal wages and other input prices to change in response to a change in the nation's price level.

Long-run aggregate supply curve The aggregate supply curve associated with a time period in which input prices (especially nominal wages) are fully responsive to changes in the price level.

Long-run vertical Phillips Curve A Phillips Curve that shows that in the long run there is no trade-off between the unemployment rate and the annual rate of increase in the price level.

Lump-sum tax A tax that yields the same amount of tax revenue at all levels of GDP.

M

M1 Currency (coins and paper money) and demand deposits in chartered banks.

M2 A broad definition of money that includes M1 plus personal and business savings deposits requiring notice before withdrawal.

M2+ A broader definition of money that includes M2 plus deposits at non-bank deposit-taking institutions, money market mutual funds, and individual annuities at life insurance companies.

M2++ The broadest definition of the Canadian money supply, which consists of M2+ plus Canada Savings Bonds and non-money market mutual funds.

Macroeconomics The part of economics concerned with the economy as a whole.

Managed floating exchange rate An exchange rate that is allowed to change (float) as a result of changes in currency supply and demand but at times is altered (managed) by governments via their buying and selling of particular currencies.

Marginal analysis The comparison of marginal ("extra" or "additional") benefits and marginal costs, usually for decision making.

Marginal benefit The extra (additional) benefit of consuming one more unit of some good or service; the change in total benefit when one more unit is consumed.

Marginal cost (MC) The extra (additional) cost of producing one more unit of output; equal to the change in total cost divided by the change in output (and in the short run to the change in total variable cost divided by the change in output).

Marginal propensity to consume (MPC) The fraction (or percentage) of any change in disposable income spent for consumer goods.

Marginal propensity to import (MPI) The fraction (or percentage) of any change in GDP spent for imported goods and services.

Marginal propensity to save (MPS) The fraction (or percentage) of any change in disposable income that households save.

Marginal tax rate The tax rate paid on each additional dollar of income.

Market Any institution or mechanism that brings together buyers and sellers of particular goods, services, or resources for the purpose of exchange.

Market demand (See Total demand.)

Market failure The inability of markets to bring about the allocation of resources that best satisfies the wants of society.

Market portfolio Contains every asset available in a financial market.

Market system An economic system in which property resources are privately owned and markets and prices are used to direct and coordinate economic activities.

Medium of exchange Items sellers generally accept and buyers generally use to pay for a good or service.

Menu costs Costs associated with changing the prices of goods and services.

Microeconomics The part of economics concerned with such individual units as industries, firms, and households.

Minimum wage The lowest wage employers may legally pay for an hour of work.

Modern economic growth The historically recent phenomenon in which nations for the first time have experienced sustained increases in real GDP per capita.

Monetarism The macroeconomic view that the main cause of changes in aggregate output and the price level are fluctuations in the money supply; advocates a monetary rule.

Monetary multiplier The multiple of its excess reserves by which the banking system can expand demand deposits and thus the money supply by making new loans.

Monetary policy A central bank's changing of the money supply to influence interest rates and assist the economy in achieving a full-employment, non-inflationary level of total output.

Monetary rule The rule suggested by monetarism; as traditionally formulated, the rule says that the money supply should be expanded each year at the same annual rate as the potential rate of growth of the real gross domestic product; the supply of money should be increased steadily between 3 to 5 percent per year. (Also see Taylor rule.)

Money Any item that is generally acceptable to sellers in exchange for goods and services.

Money capital Money available to purchase capital.

Money income (See Nominal income.)

Money market The market in which the demand for and the supply of money determine the interest rate in the economy.

Money supply Narrowly defined, M1; more broadly defined, M2, M2+, and M2++.

Monopoly A market structure in which the number of sellers is so small that each seller is able to influence the total supply and the price of the good or service.

Most-favoured-nation (MFN) clause An agreement by Canada to allow some other nation's exports into Canada at the lowest tariff level levied by Canada.

Multinational corporation A firm that owns production facilities in other countries and produces and sells its product abroad.

Multiple counting Wrongly including the value of intermediate goods in the gross domestic product; counting the same good or service more than once.

Multiplier The ratio of a change in the equilibrium GDP to the change in investment or in any other component of aggregate expenditures.

Multiplier effect The effect on equilibrium GDP of a change in aggregate expenditures or aggregate demand (caused by a change in the consumption schedule, investment, government expenditures, or net exports).

Mutual fund A professionally managed portfolio, or collection, of stocks or bonds.

N

National income Total income earned by resource suppliers for their contributions to gross national product; equal to the gross domestic product minus nonincome charges, minus net foreign factor income.

National income accounting The techniques used to measure the overall production of the economy and other related variables for the nation as a whole.

Natural monopoly An industry in which economies of scale are so great the product can be produced by one firm at a lower average total cost than if the product were produced by more than one firm.

Natural rate of unemployment (NRU) The unemployment rate that occurs when there is no cyclical unemployment and the economy is achieving its potential output.

Near-monies Financial assets, such as saving and term deposits in banks and savings institutions, that are not a medium of exchange but can be readily converted into money.

Negative externality A cost imposed without compensation on third parties by the production or consumption of sellers or buyers. Example: A manufacturer dumps toxic chemicals into a river, killing the fish sought by sport fishers. An external cost or a spillover cost.

Negative relationship (See Inverse relationship.)

Net domestic income All the income earned by Canadian-supplied resources.

Net domestic product (NDP) Gross national product less the part of the year's output needed to replace the capital goods worn out in producing the output.

Net export effect The idea that the impact of a change in monetary policy or fiscal policy will be strengthened or weakened by the consequent change in net exports.

Net exports Exports minus imports.

Net investment Gross investment less consumption of fixed capital.

Net investment income The interest and dividend income received by the residents of a nation from residents of other nations less the interest and dividend payments made by the residents of that nation to the residents of other nations.

Net National Income (NNI) Total income earned by resource suppliers for their contribution to GDP.

Net taxes The taxes collected by government less government transfer payments.

Net transfers The personal and government transfer payments made by one nation to residents of foreign nations, less the personal and government transfer payments received from residents of foreign nations.

Network effects Increases in the value of a product to each user, including existing users, as the total number of users rises.

Net worth The total assets less the total liabilities of a firm or an individual; the claims of the owners of a firm against its total assets.

New classical economics The theory that, although unanticipated price level changes may create macroeconomic instability in the short run, the economy is stable at the full-employment level of domestic output in the long run because prices and wages adjust automatically to correct movements away from the full-employment, non-inflationary output.

Nominal GDP (see nominal gross domestic product)

Nominal gross domestic product The GDP measured in terms of the price level at the time of measurement (unadjusted for inflation).

Nominal income The number of current dollars received as wages, rent, interest, or profits.

Nominal interest rate The interest rate expressed in terms of annual amounts currently charged for interest and not adjusted for inflation.

Nominal wage The amount of money received by a worker per unit of time (hour, day, etc.); money wage.

Nondiscretionary fiscal policy (See Built-in stabilizer.)

Non-diversifiable risk Risk that pushes all investments in the same direction at the same time; eliminates the possibility of using good effects to offset bad effects.

Nondurable good A consumer good with an expected life (use) of less than three years.

Non-exhaustive expenditure An expenditure by government that does not result directly in the employment of economic resources or the production of goods and service (see Government transfer payment).

Nonfinancial investment An investment that does not require households to save a part of their money incomes, but which uses surplus (unproductive) labour to build capital goods.

Non-income charges Consumption of fixed capital and indirect business taxes; amounts subtracted from GDP (along with net foreign factor income) in determining national income.

Non-income determinants of consumption and saving All influences on consumption and saving other than the level of GDP.

Non-interest determinants of investment All influences on the level of investment spending other than the interest rate.

Non-investment transaction An expenditure for stocks, bonds, or second-hand capital goods.

Nonmarket transactions The production of goods and services excluded in the measurement of the gross domestic product because they are not bought and sold.

Nonproduction transaction The purchase and sale of any item that is not a currently produced good or service.

Nontariff barrier All restrictions other than tariffs that nations erect to impede international trade.

Normal good A good or service whose consumption rises when income increases and falls when income decreases, price remaining constant.

Normal profit The payment made by a firm to obtain and retain entrepreneurial ability; the minimum income entrepreneurial ability must receive to induce it to perform entrepreneurial functions for a firm.

Normative economics The part of economics involving value judgments about what the economy should be like.

North American Free Trade Agreement (NAFTA) A 1993 agreement establishing, over a 15-year period, a free trade zone composed of Canada, Mexico, and the United States.

O

Official international reserves Foreign currencies owned by the central bank of a nation.

Offshoring The practice of shifting work previously done by Canadian workers to workers located abroad.

Okun's Law The generalization that any one percentage point rise in the unemployment rate above the natural rate of unemployment will increase the GDP gap by 2 percent of the potential output (GDP) of the economy.

Old Age Security Act The 1951 federal act, as subsequently amended, by which a pension is payable to every person aged 65 and older provided the person has resided in Canada for ten years immediately preceding the approval of an application for pension; in addition a Guaranteed Income Supplement may be paid; the pension is payable in addition to the Canada Pension.

OPEC (See Organization of Petroleum Exporting Countries.)

Open economy An economy that exports and imports goods and services.

Open-market operations The buying and selling of Canadian government bonds by the Bank of Canada to carry out monetary policy.

Operating band The Bank of Canada's 50-basis-point range (one half of one percentage point) for the overnight lending rate.

Opportunity cost The amount of other products that must be forgone or sacrificed to produce a unit of a product.

Opportunity-cost ratio An equality showing the number of units of two products that can be produced with the same resources; e.g., the cost 1 corn = 3 olives shows that the resources required to produce 3 units of olives must be shifted to corn production to produce 1 unit of corn.

Organization of Petroleum Exporting Nations (OPEC) A cartel of 11 oil-producing countries (Algeria, Indonesia, Iran, Iraq, Kuwait, Libya, Nigeria, Qatar, Saudi Arabia, Venezuela, and the UAE) that controls the price and quantity of crude oil exported by its members, and that accounts for 60 percent of the world's export of oil.

Other-things-equal assumption The assumption that factors other than those being considered are held constant.

Outpayments The expenditures of its own or foreign currency that the individuals, firms, and governments of one nation make to purchase goods and services, for remittances, as investment income, and capital outflows abroad.

Overnight lending rate The interest rate at which major participants in the money market borrow and lend one-day funds to each other.

P

Paper money Pieces of paper used as a medium of exchange; in Canada, Bank of Canada notes.

Passively managed funds Mutual funds that exactly match the assets contained in their respective underlying indexes.

Patent An exclusive right to inventors to produce and sell a new product or machine for a set period of time.

Payments deficit (See Balance of payments deficit.)

Payments surplus (See Balance of payments surplus.)

Peak A phase in the business cycle during which the economy is at full employment and the level of real output is at or very close to the economy's capacity.

Per-capita GDP Gross domestic product (GDP) per person; the average GDP of a population.

Per-capita income A nation's total income per person; the average income of a population.

Percentage rate of return The percentage gain or loss (relative to the buying price) on stocks or bonds over a given time period, typically a year.

Personal consumption expenditures (C) The expenditures of households for durable and nondurable consumer goods and services.

Personal income The earned and unearned income available to resource suppliers and others before the payment of personal income taxes.

Personal income tax A tax levied on the taxable income of individuals, households, and unincorporated firms.

Personal saving The personal income of households less personal taxes and personal consumption expenditures; disposable income not spent for consumer goods.

Per-unit production cost The average production cost of a particular level of output; total input cost divided by units of output.

Phillips Curve A curve showing the relationship between the unemployment rate and the annual rate of increase in the price level.

Planned investment The amount that firms plan or intend to invest.

Portfolio A collection of investments.

Policy economics The formulation of courses of action to bring about desired economic outcomes or to prevent undesired occurrences.

Political business cycle The alleged tendency of government to destabilize the economy by reducing taxes and increasing government expenditures before elections and to raise taxes and lower expenditures after elections.

Positive economics The analysis of facts or data to establish scientific generalizations about economic behaviour.

Positive externality A benefit obtained without compensation by third parties from the production or consumption of sellers or buyers. Example: A beekeeper benefits when a neighbouring farmer plants clover. An external benefit or spillover benefit.

Positive GDP gap A situation in which actual gross domestic product exceeds potential output.

Positive relationship Direct relationship between two variables.

***Post hoc, ergo propter hoc* fallacy** Incorrectly reasoning that when one event precedes another the first event must have caused the second event.

Potential GDP The real output (GDP) an economy can produce when it fully employs its available resources.

Present value The present-day value, or worth, of returns or costs that are expected to arrive in the future.

Price The amount of money needed to buy a particular good, service, or resource.

Price ceiling A legally established maximum price for a good or service.

Price floor A legally determined price above an equilibrium prices.

Price index An index number that shows how the weighted average price of a "market basket" of goods changes through time.

Price level The weighted average of the prices of all the final goods and services produced in an economy.

Price-level surprises Unanticipated changes in the price level.

Price-level stability A steadiness of the price-level from one period to the next; zero or low annual inflation; also called "price stability."

Price-wage flexibility Changes in the prices of products and in the wages paid to workers; the ability of prices and wages to rise or fall.

Price war Successive and continued decreases in the prices charged by the firms in an oligopolistic industry; each firm lowers its price below rivals' prices, hoping to increase it sales and revenues at its rivals' expense.

Prime (interest) rate The interest rate banks charge their most creditworthy borrowers. The benchmark interest rate used by chartered banks as a reference point for a wide range of interests rates charged on loans to businesses and individuals.

Principal–agent problem A conflict of interest that occurs when agents (workers or managers) pursue their own objectives to the detriment of the principals' (stockholders') goals.

Principle of comparative advantage (see comparative advantage)

Private good A good or service that is individually consumed and that can be profitably provided by privately owned firms because they can exclude non-payers from receiving the benefits.

Private property The right of private persons and firms to obtain, own, control, employ, dispose of, and bequeath land, capital, and other property.

Private sector The households and business firms of the economy.

Production possibilities curve A curve showing the different combinations of goods or services that can be produced in a full-employment, full-production economy where the available supplies of resources and technology are fixed.

Productive efficiency The production of a good in the least costly way.

Productivity A measure of average output or real output per unit of input.

Productivity growth The percentage change in productivity from one period to another.

Product market A market in which products are sold by firms and bought by households.

Profit The return to the resource entrepreneurial ability (see Normal profit); total revenue minus total cost (see Economic profit).

Progressive tax A tax with an average tax rate that increases as the taxpayer's income increases and decreases as the taxpayer's income decreases.

Property tax A tax on the value of property (capital, land, stocks and bonds, and other assets) owned by firms and households.

Proportional tax A tax with an average tax rate that remains constant as the taxpayer's income increases or decreases.

Protective tariff A tariff designed to shield domestic producers of a good or service from the competition of foreign producers.

Public debt The total amount owed by the federal government to the owners of government securities.

Public good A good or service that can be simultaneously consumed by everyone, and from which no one can be excluded, even if they don't pay for it.

Public investments Government expenditures on public capital (such as roads and highways) and on human capital (such as education and health).

Public sector The part of the economy that contains all government entities; government.

Purchasing power The amount of goods and services that a monetary unit of income can buy.

Purchasing power parity theory The idea that exchange rates between any two nations adjust to reflect the price level differences between the countries.

Pure rate of interest An essentially risk-free, long-term interest rate that is free of the influence of market imperfections.

Q

Quantity demanded The amount of a good or service buyers (or a buyer) desire to purchase at a particular price during some period.

Quantity supplied The amount of a good or service producers (or a producer) offer to sell at a particular price during some period.

Quasi-public good A good or service to which the exclusion principle could apply, but that has such a large spillover benefit that government sponsors its production to prevent an underallocation of resources.

R

R&D Research and development activities undertaken to bring about technological advance.

Rate of exchange The price paid in one's own money to acquire one unit of a foreign currency; the rate at which the money of one nation is exchanged for the money of another nation.

Rate of return The gain in net revenue divided by the cost of an investment or an R&D expenditure; expressed as a percentage.

Rational expectations theory The hypothesis that firms and households expect monetary and fiscal policies to have certain effects on the economy and (in pursuit of their own self-interests) take actions that make these policies ineffective.

Rationing function of prices The ability of the competitive forces of supply and demand to establish a price at which selling and buying decisions are consistent.

Real-balances effect The inverse relationship between the price level and the real value (or purchasing power) of financial assets with fixed money value.

Real-business-cycle theory The theory that business cycles result from changes in technology and resource availability, which affect productivity and thus increase or decrease long-run aggregate supply.

Real capital (See Capital.)

Real GDP per capita The real GDP per person, found by dividing real GDP by a country's population.

Real gross domestic product (GDP) Nominal gross domestic product adjusted for inflation.

Real GDP (See Real gross domestic product.)

Real income The amount of goods and services that nominal income can buy.

Real interest rate The interest rate expressed in dollars of constant value (adjusted for inflation).

Real wage The amount of goods and services a worker can purchase with his or her nominal wage; the purchasing power of the nominal wage.

Recession A period of declining real GDP, accompanied by lower real income and higher unemployment.

Recessionary gap (recessionary expenditure gap) The amount by which equilibrium GDP falls short of full-employment GDP.

Refinancing the public debt Paying owners of maturing government securities with money obtained by selling new securities or with new securities.

Regressive tax A tax with an average tax rate that decreases as the taxpayer's income increases and increases as the taxpayer's income decreases.

Restrictive monetary policy Bank of Canada actions to reduce the money supply, increase interest rates, and reduce inflation; a tight money policy.

Retiring the public debt Reducing the size of the public debt by paying money to owners of maturing Government of Canada securities.

Revenue tariff A tariff designed to produce income for the federal government.

Risk Refers to the fact that investors never know with certainty what future payments on an asset will be.

Risk-free interest rate A rate of return that does not compensate for risk.

Risk premium The rate of interest that compensates for risk; depends on the size of the investment's beta.

Roundabout production The construction and use of capital to aid in the production of consumer goods.

Rule of 70 A method for determining the number of years it will take for some measure to double, given its annual percentage increase by dividing that percentage increase into 70.

S

Sales tax A tax levied on the cost (at retail) of a broad group of products.

Saving Disposable income not spent for consumer goods; equal to disposable income minus personal consumption expenditures.

Savings deposit A deposit that is interest-bearing and that can normally be withdrawn by the depositor at any time.

Saving schedule A schedule that shows the amounts households plan to save at different levels of disposable income.

Say's law The largely discredited macroeconomic generalization that the production of goods and services (supply) creates an equal demand for these goods and service.

Scarce resources The limited quantities of land, capital, labour, and entrepreneurial ability that are never sufficient to satisfy the virtually unlimited material wants of humans.

Scientific method The systematic pursuit of knowledge through the formulation of a problem, collection of data, and the formulation and testing of hypotheses to obtain theories, principles, and laws.

Seasonal unemployment Unemployment caused by seasonal factors.

Seasonal variations Increases and decreases in the level of economic activity within a single year, caused by a change in the season.

Secular trend Long-term tendency; change in some variable over a very long period of years.

Security Market Line The relationship between average expected rates of return and risk levels that must hold for every asset or portfolio trading in a financial market.

Self-interest That which each firm, property owner, worker, and consumer believes is best for itself.

Service An (intangible) act or use for which a consumer, firm, or government is willing to pay.

Shirking Actions by workers to increase their utility or well-being by neglecting or evading work.

Shocks Situations in which one thing is expected to occur but in reality something different occurs.

Shortage The amount by which the quantity demanded of a product exceeds the quantity supplied at a particular (below-equilibrium) price.

Short run (1) In macroeconomics, a period in which nominal wages and other input prices do not change in response to a change in the price level. (2) In microeconomics, a period of time in which producers are able to change the quantity of some but not all of the resources they employ; a period in which some resources (usually plant) are fixed and some are variable.

Short-run aggregate supply A schedule or curve that shows the level of real domestic output that will be produced at each price level.

Simple multiplier The multiplier in an economy in which government collects no net taxes, there are no imports, and investment is independent of the level of income; equal to one divided by the marginal propensity to save.

Slope of a line The ratio of the vertical change (the rise or fall) to the horizontal change (the run) between any two points on a line. The slope of an upward sloping line is positive, reflecting a direct relationship between two variables; the slope of a downward sloping line is negative, reflecting an inverse relationship between two variables.

Sole proprietorship An unincorporated firm owned and operated by one person.

Specialization The use of the resources of an individual, a firm, a region, or a nation to produce one or a few goods and services.

Speculation The activity of buying or selling with the motive of later reselling or rebuying for profit.

Stagflation Simultaneous increases in the price level and the unemployment rate.

Start-up firm A new firm focused on creating and introducing a particular new product or employing a specific new production or distribution method.

Stock (corporate) An ownership share in a corporation.

Store of value An asset set aside for future use.

Strategic trade policy The use of trade barriers to reduce the risk inherent in product development by domestic firms, particularly that involving advanced technology.

Structural unemployment Unemployment of workers whose skills are not demanded by employers, who lack sufficient skill to obtain employment, or who cannot easily move to locations where jobs are available.

Subprime mortgage loans High-interest-rate loans to home buyers with above-average credit risk.

Subsidy A payment of funds (or goods and services) by a government, firm, or household for which it receives no good or service in return; when made by a government, it is a government transfer payment.

Substitute goods Products or services that can be used in place of each other.

Substitution effect (1) A change in the price of a consumer good changes the relative expensiveness of that good and hence changes the consumer's willingness to buy it rather than other goods. (2) The effect of a change in the price of a resource on the quantity of the resource employed by a firm, assuming no change in its output.

Supply A schedule or curve that shows the amounts of a product that producers are willing and able to make available for sale at each of a series of possible prices during a specific period.

Supply curve A curve illustrating the positive (direct) relationship between the quantity supplied of a good or service and its price, other things equal.

Supply factor (in growth) An increase in the availability of a resource, an improvement in its quality, or an expansion of technological knowledge that makes it possible for an economy to produce a greater output of goods and services.

Supply shocks Sudden, unexpected changes in aggregate supply.

Supply-side economics A view of macroeconomics that emphasizes the role of costs and aggregate supply in explaining inflation, unemployment, and economic growth.

Surplus The amount by which the quantity supplied of a product exceeds the quantity demanded at a specific (above-equilibrium) price.

T

Tariff A tax imposed by a nation on an imported good.

Taylor Rule A modern monetary rule proposed by economist John Taylor that stipulates exactly how much a central bank should change interest rates in response to divergences of real GDP from potential GDP and divergences of actual rates of inflation from a target rate of inflation.

Tax An involuntary payment of money (or goods and services) to a government by a household or firm for which the household or firm receives no good or service directly in return.

Tax incidence The person or group who ends up paying a tax.

Technology The body of knowledge and techniques that can be used to produce goods and services from economic resources.

Technological advance New and better goods and services and new and better ways of producing or distributing them.

Terms of trade The rate at which units of one product can be exchanged for units of another product.

Theoretical economics The process of deriving and applying economic theories and principles.

Till money (See Vault cash.)

Time preference The fact that people typically prefer to consume things in the present rather than in the future.

Token money Coins that have a face value greater than their intrinsic value.

Total cost The sum of fixed cost and variable cost.

Total demand The demand schedule or the demand curve of all buyers of a good or service; also called market demand.

Total demand for money The sum of the transactions demand for money and the asset demand for money.

Total spending The total amount buyers of goods and services spend or plan to spend; also called aggregate expenditures.

Total supply The supply schedule or the supply curve of all sellers of a good or service; also called market supply.

Trade balance The export of goods (or goods and services) of a nation less its imports of goods (or goods and services).

Trade bloc A group of nations that lower or abolish trade barriers among members. Examples include the European Union and the nations of the North American Free Trade Agreement.

Trade controls Tariffs, export subsidies, import quotas, and other means a nation may employ to reduce imports and expand exports.

Trade deficit The amount by which a nation's imports of goods (or goods and services) exceed its exports of goods (or goods and services).

Tradeoff The sacrifice of some or all of one economic goal, good, or service to achieve some other goal, good, or service.

Trade surplus The amount by which a nation's exports of goods (or goods and services) exceed its imports of goods (or goods and services).

Trading possibilities line A line that shows the different combinations of two products an economy is able to obtain when it specializes in the production of one product and exports it to obtain the other product.

Transactions demand for money The amount of money people want to hold for use as a medium of exchange, and which varies directly with the nominal GDP.

Transfer payment A payment of money (or goods and services) by a government to a household or firm for which the payer receives no good or service directly in return.

Trough A recession or depression, when output and employment reach their lowest levels.

U

Unanticipated inflation Increases in the price level that occur at a rate greater than expected.

Underemployment A situation in which workers are employed in positions requiring less than the amount of education and skill than they have.

Undistributed corporate profits After-tax corporate profits not distributed as dividends to shareholders; corporate or business saving; also called retained earnings.

Unemployment Failure to use all available economic resources to produce goods and services; failure of the economy to fully employ its labour force.

Unemployment rate The percentage of the labour force unemployed at any time.

Unit labour cost Labour costs per unit of output; total labour cost divided by total output; also equal to the nominal wage rate divided by the average product of labour.

Unit of account A standard unit in which prices can be stated and the value of goods and services can be compared.

Unlimited wants The insatiable desire of consumers for goods and services that will give them satisfaction or utility.

Unplanned changes in inventories Changes in inventories that firms did not anticipate.

Unplanned investment Actual investment less planned investment; increases or decreases in the inventories of firms resulting from production greater than sales.

Uruguay Round A 1995 trade agreement (that was fully implemented by 2005) that established the World Trade Organization (WTO), liberalized trade in goods and services, provided added protection to intellectual property (for example, patents and copyrights), and reduced farm subsidies.

Utility The satisfaction a person gets from consuming a good or service.

V

Value added The value of the product sold by a firm, less the value of the products purchased and used by the firm to produce the product.

Value judgment Opinion of what is desirable or undesirable; belief regarding what ought or ought not to be (regarding what is right or just and wrong or unjust).

Value of money The quantity of goods and services for which a unit of money (a dollar) can be exchanged; the purchasing power of a unit of money; the reciprocal of the price level.

Vault cash The currency a bank has in its vault and cash drawers.

Vertical axis The "up–down" or "north–south" axis on a graph or grid.

Vertical intercept The point at which a line meets the vertical axis of a graph.

Voluntary export restraint Voluntary limitations by countries or firms of their exports to a particular foreign nation.

W

Wage The price paid for the use or services of labour per unit of time (per hour, per day, and so on).

Wage rate (See Wage.)

Wealth effect A downward shift of the saving schedule and an upward shift of the consumption schedule due to higher asset wealth.

World Bank A bank that lends (and guarantees loans) to developing nations to assist them in increasing their capital stock and thus to achieve economic growth; formally, the International Bank for Reconstruction and Development.

World price The international market price of a good or service, determined by world demand and supply.

World Trade Organization (WTO) An organization established of 149 nations (as of summer 2006) that oversees the provisions of the current world trade agreement, resolves trade disputes stemming from it, and holds forums for further rounds of trade negotiations.

Index